Theirs Was the Kingdom

THEIRS WAS THE KINGDOM

Lila and DeWitt Wallace
and the Story of the
Reader's Digest

JOHN HEIDENRY

W. W. Norton & Company

New York   London

The text of this book is composed in 12/13.5 Monotype Garamond 156
with the display set in Garamond Bold 201 at 85% horizontal scale
Composition and Manufacturing by the Haddon Craftsmen, Inc.
Book design by Margaret M. Wagner

Library of Congress Cataloging-in-Publication Data
Heidenry, John.
Theirs was the kingdom : Lila and DeWitt Wallace and the story of the Reader's Digest /
John Heidenry.
    p.   cm.
Includes bibliographical references and index.
1. Reader's digest.   2. Wallace, DeWitt, 1889–1981.   3. Wallace
Lila Acheson, 1889–1984.   4. Publishers and publishing—United
States—Biography.   I. Title.
PN4900.R3H45   1993
051—dc20   93-12764

ISBN 0-393-03466-6

W. W. Norton & Company, Inc., 500 Fifth Avenue, New York, N.Y. 10110
W. W. Norton & Company Ltd., 10 Coptic Street, London WC1A 1PU

2   3   4   5   6   7   8   9   0

To my father
John J. Heidenry
passionate lover of words and the Word
whose lifelong encouragement and enthusiasm
made this book possible

Contents

Photographs appear following pages 224 and 480.

THEIRS WAS THE KINGDOM

Prologue

As Lila Lay Dying

WHEN the mountain would not come to Lila Acheson Wallace, she went to the mountain. Or rather, with all the good old American self-reliance and ingenuity that a million and a half Depression dollars could buy, she ordered her work crews to move thousands of tons of earth, shaping it into a small, condensed sort of mountain perfect as the site for the new headquarters of the *Reader's Digest*.

At the time, the *Digest* was still an adolescent among magazines, an upstart rich kid scarcely fifteen years old. But even before its second birthday it had toddled to a different drummer, moving out of the publishing capital of the United States and setting up shop forty miles north of Grand Central Station. In professional terms, Pleasantville, New York, in Westchester County, might just as well have been Peoria, Podunk, or Kalamazoo.

But the *Digest* was also a state of mind as broad as the country itself. When Mr. and Mrs. Middle America sat down on their front porch to read, in their small town far from the Madison Avenue crowd, the magazine that brought a smile to their faces was the *Reader's Digest*. Its mildly off-color humor went just far enough to titillate but did not offend their deeply conservative yet earthy sensibilities. They also enjoyed its easy-to-read, inspirational articles about turning tragedy into triumph, its God-fearing, flag-waving exaltation of the American way of life, its rough-and-tumble government bashing, and its disturbing insights into the strange and sometimes dangerous ways of foreigners. It made no difference where founders DeWitt and Lila Acheson Wallace located the *Digest*, because it took root in the hearts of its readers as no other magazine ever has or likely ever will again.

13

The *Digest* headquarters that Lila caused to go up was equally improbable—a long, low, three-story building made of red brick modeled on the governor's palace of Colonial Williamsburg. That charming neo-Georgian village had only recently been restored with Rockefeller money, and in due time the Wallaces themselves also became—albeit unwittingly, in one of the more curious chapters of modern American philanthropy—two of its primary benefactors.

In 1937 the Williamsburg look was not yet the architectural cliché of shopping malls in search of instant gentrification. Rather, it had for Lila and her husband, DeWitt, several important *Digest*-like ingredients: simplicity, individuality, and impeccable patriotic bona fides. But Lila also had an artistic side, and so the white cupola sprouted a distinctly uncolonial touch—four pale blue Disney-like replicas of Pegasus, the winged horse of Greek mythology, facing to the four winds.

To round out this corporate Eden—"What God would have done," said one wag at the time, "if He had the money"—Lila planted fullgrown oaks and beeches in front of the main entrance and along the driveway up to headquarters, installed a mature apple orchard, trimmed every walkway and courtyard with dogwoods and flowering shrubs, and decreed that the grounds were to bloom every spring and summer with tens of thousands of daffodils, hyacinths, and tulips.

When the *Digest* finally moved out of its fourteen locations scattered around Pleasantville in 1939 and into its new home in adjacent Chappaqua, it was like a small-scale reenactment of the seven days of creation. Only the ivy on the walls needed time to grow. Even so, DeWitt and Lila prudently decided to keep Pleasantville as the official address of the *Reader's Digest* because it sounded more, well, *Digest*-like.

Nearly a half century later, as Lila Acheson Wallace lay near death, not a whole lot had changed. By March 1984 the various additions and extensions, all connected by a maze of passageways, had blended in somehow—as though, like the magazine itself, the company's world headquarters could expand and grow and still look almost the same year after year. Similarly, the surrounding landscape had gone from a genteel wilderness to a prosperous exurb where most of the upperechelon *RD* editors and managers now lived.

Among the exclusive hearths of wealthy Westchester County, one of the most imposing was High Winds, the twenty-two-room Norman castle Lila and DeWitt had built shortly before the Chappaqua headquarters went up. Turreted and ornate, with a striking blue roof, the Wallaces' home was everything architecturally the editorial and administrative offices were not. What the twin temples of the *Digest* did share, though, was one of the finest private art collections in the world.

Now ninety-five and near death, Lila had lived all alone in her castle for the past three years—a wispy, white-haired woman, once the epitome of fashion, who wore only a simple housedress and stared sadly into space. Her mind was nearly gone, just as DeWitt's had been before he died in 1981, at the age of ninety-one. Despite her frailty and isolation, however, Lila had recently endowed the Metropolitan Museum of Art in New York with $11 million to build a new wing to house contemporary American art. That she was not aware of having done so, and that she in fact had always detested contemporary American art, was one more indication of how strange things were in Chappaqua in the last days of the Wallace era.

The latest story making the rounds in Pleasantville about Lila was told by a nurse hired to watch over her. On occasion the half-senile matriarch of the *Digest* clan was brought down to the Guest House to join executives for lunch. The nurse accompanying her one day cut up some food, then held a forkful in midair and waited patiently for the old woman to open her mouth. Finally in exasperation the nurse said, "You don't have to eat it if you don't want to."

Snapped Lila, proving she still enjoyed some moments of clarity, "It was ever so!"

It had been so, once upon a time, when Lila Acheson Wallace was among the greatest philanthropists of her age, the richest woman in the United States, the wife of the most successful editor and publisher of all time, and the friend of countless statesmen, artists, business barons, and not a few rogues and charlatans as well. But now the advent of spring found her too feeble to understand the ugly turmoil taking place behind the beautiful *Digest* façade. In the extreme winter of Lila's years, the empire of the Reader's Digest Association was, if not in its death throes, in a state of perilous collapse. Both at High Winds and at Chappaqua, cofounder and company alike lay nearly comatose.

Yet there was one man—one above all others—who had resolved that the *Digest* should be reborn. Former business manager Albert Leslie Cole had not worked for the company in a score of years and left Pleasantville only because he was summarily booted out by DeWitt Wallace himself on a memorable December 24 that in *Digest* lore was known as "the Christmas Eve massacre."

With the mule-headed determination for which he was justly famous, the eighty-four-year-old Cole mistakenly blamed most of the *Digest*'s troubles on the "liberal" editorial policies of editor in chief Ed Thompson—a myopic view passionately shared by the mostly conservative to right-wing editorial staff both in Pleasantville and especially in the magazine's viciously anti-Thompson Washington bureau.

Another powerful member of the *Digest* gerontocracy was seventy-four-year-old Laurance S. Rockefeller, conservationist, resort owner, and former chairman of the Rockefeller Brothers Fund, a philanthropic foundation. He and eighty-three-year-old Harold Helm, former chairman of Chemical Bank, were the company's two outside directors. The six members of the board of trustees, whose composition had never been publicly revealed, voted by proxy on the ten thousand shares of voting stock, all owned by Lila Acheson Wallace. The childless Wallaces had left no heirs.

Among the *Digest*'s old-timers, Al Cole—stocky, blunt-spoken, the consummate corporation man whose personal life was lived almost as an afterthought—was rightly regarded as primus inter pares. He had been the magazine's master business strategist, coming on board back in 1939 when he was president of *Popular Science*. It was Cole who persuaded DeWitt Wallace to put the *Digest* on the newsstands and stop worrying about his promise that the magazine was an exclusive service for subscribers, or his fear that his source magazines would find out how successful the *Digest* was and not allow it to excerpt from them in the future.

It was Cole who drew up the *Digest*'s blueprint for worldwide expansion, overseeing the opening of the first foreign office, in London, in 1938 and the first foreign-language edition, in Havana, two years later. When World War II broke out, it was Al Cole who secured federal approval for priority paper allotments and then arranged for the air force to distribute the magazine to every foxhole and canteen in Europe and the Pacific so that the troops could have a heartwarming monthly reminder of the American values they were fighting to preserve. That brilliant stroke had caused circulation to shoot up from under four million to more than nine million, preparing the way for the *Digest*'s own postwar conquest of the world.

And when the time came for the magazine to choose between raising its cover price and breaking its long-standing ban on advertising, it was Al Cole, the unapologetic pragmatist, who advised Wallace to execute the biggest turnabout in publishing history. An extremely resourceful behind-the-scenes figure, who had spent most of his forced retirement climbing back up the mountain, Cole was for all practical purposes DeWitt Wallace's stand-in, his living ghost.

The company's Scottish-born president, Jack O'Hara, did not belong to the *Digest*'s old guard and actually had a lot more in common with Ed Thompson than with anybody else. Both men, at age fifty-six, were in the prime of life. Each had also been named a coexecutor of DeWitt's and Lila's wills. As a result, both were members of the exclusive club of six trustees who voted on Lila's stock. For the last eight years, O'Hara and Thompson had shared responsibilities and power equally, dividing the administrative and editorial halves of the company between them.

Now the hyperintense, cigar-chomping O'Hara had joined forces with Rockefeller, Helm, and Cole to unseat his coequal. If all went well, he hoped to emerge as undisputed ruler over a $1.4 billion empire with magazine, book, marketing, and investment operations in 127 countries.

Unfortunately, in 1984 the RDA's finances were as much a source of scandal to the company's fiscal conservatives as the editorial product was to the magazine's outraged colonels in the Washington bureau. Advertising revenues had yet to recover from the 1982 recession, and circulation was stagnant. Moreover, as a result of what some saw as an erratic, almost hip-pocket expansion program, the company had lost tens of millions in assorted unprofitable ventures. One former executive had recently complained that the Reader's Digest Association had become a "reverse Midas. All the gold it touches turns to lead." After-tax profits had slumped to a pitiful $5 million.

In deciding to get rid of Thompson, O'Hara was stalling for time. By making enough fuss about the editorial mess, the RDA's president hoped to create a smoke screen that would give him an opportunity to improve its profit picture, especially now that DeWitt Wallace was dead. Up to the very end, the company's founder had all but declared unnecessary profit in poor corporate taste—another reason everything had been so topsy-turvy in Pleasantville in recent years.

But the labyrinth of intrigue was far more complicated than even O'Hara suspected. A much deeper game was being played by his lieutenants, who had decided that the only way to get rid of the RDA's president was first to eliminate the editor in chief. As the company's golden boy—blond, tall, and handsome—Thompson was immensely popular with the younger generation of Digesters, who welcomed his contempt for partisan Republican politics, his casual executive style, his willingness to experiment and learn. Thompson also had a reputation for loyalty—presumably, above all, to his friend O'Hara. Fortunately, all the editorial commotion could not have suited better the purposes of those plotting the double coup d'état—publisher George V. Grune, director of new business planning Richard F. McLoughlin, director of administration and finance William J. Cross, and, in the background, as ever, Rockefeller.

A further complication, and ultimately the main reason for all the haste, was a clause in Lila Acheson Wallace's will. She had decreed that, upon her death, her executors would control 50 percent of the voting stock. That meant Thompson and O'Hara, if they supported each other, were theoretically untouchable and the other trustees powerless to remove them.

Obviously, if O'Hara the out-of-control company president and Thompson the renegade editor were to be brought down, the board had to act quickly—before Lila died, which might be literally at any hour.

I

THE STABLE

[1922–1936]

1

A Man of Few Words

THOSE who knew DeWitt Wallace best, and were friends of his for a lifetime, all agreed that, in the end, he was an enigma. He once gave hundreds of thousands of dollars to the owner of his favorite local restaurant so that it could stay in business, yet liked to wander the halls of the *Reader's Digest* and turn off lights to save pennies. A lifelong animal lover, he beat two dogs to death with a chain. He could see through a person in an instant, yet was hoodwinked by any number of charlatans and phonies. He was a strident anti-Communist with a low opinion of Joe McCarthy; a man of the broadest conservative stripe who enthusiastically promoted one-worldism, divorce reform, birth control, and the legalization of abortion; a poker-playing connoisseur of dirty jokes who seldom went to church and even owned a rather tame collection of pornography. At the same time, he supported the nation's blue laws because he thought America ought to remain "a Christian country."

Another word frequently used to describe Wallace, though often with some misgiving, was "genius." He was a genius because he had created a magazine that made him one of the world's wealthiest men; because he had the most uncanny instinct for what the average American wanted to read; because he was better at finding articles for reprint, condensing them, and originating original articles than any other editor on the staff.

Yet there was always a lingering doubt about Wallace's genius—as though it were of a secondary kind of originality, dependent on somebody else's creation for its own existence. Further, the *Digest* had made its mark by going in a reverse direction—by finding the lowest common editorial denominators in order to appeal to as many readers as possible, instead of breaking new literary ground and earning the admiration of a discriminating elite.

DeWitt Wallace also never seemed to be especially impressed by his own wealth and power. Though he never shied away from using money or the pages of the magazine to accomplish his goals, sometimes astutely and at other times with an obstinacy verging on the foolish, both his failures and his successes were singularly lacking in ego. In that and other respects he bore little resemblance to two of his more widely known contemporaries, Henry R. Luce of *Time* and Harold Ross of the *New Yorker,* whose own magazines were begun around the same time as the *Digest.* Moreover, within the context of fabulous wealth and privilege, he and Lila lived a life that might almost be called unostentatious.

That is not to say DeWitt Wallace did not passionately believe that the *Reader's Digest* was the greatest magazine the world had ever seen. That was the simple and supreme credo of his existence. He lived for nothing else, and what most rankled him was having to share the credit with anyone—even with his wife of sixty years, as he was sometimes obliged to do when the *Digest* later attempted to refashion its origins into a *Digest*-like myth of noble idealism and inspirational triumph. In the end it *was* that—but with squalid and mean passages deleted, in tried-and-true *Digest* fashion, from gritty tales of the human spirit struggling against heavy odds.

———

THE central figure in DeWitt Wallace's life was his father, Dr. James T. Wallace. In 1876 Dr. Wallace, a twenty-seven-year-old professor of Greek and modern languages at Wooster College in Wooster, Ohio, fell in love with one of his first-year students, Janet Davis, ten years his junior. Like him, she was of Scotch–Northern Irish descent and devoutly religious.

Janet's father was Dr. Thomas K. Davis, an ordained minister who had studied at Yale University and Princeton Theological Seminary before becoming librarian at Wooster, a Presbyterian-affiliated institution. He was also one of James Wallace's closest friends, sharing with him a double bond—the academic life and the Presbyterian faith.

Unfortunately, Janet's own religious idealism exceeded that of her teacher and seemed symptomatic of an emotional disorder. She was unable to complete the academic year and in the following summer was sent to a sanitarium in Dansville, New York, accompanied by her sister Miriam, to rest and take the waters. While recuperating, Janet confided to her diary that she was resolved to become a missionary and a vegetarian.

Reenrolling as a freshman in the fall, she again signed up to study Greek with her favorite professor. The two became secretly engaged shortly before he left for a year of study in Greece and the Holy Land. Janet harbored a hidden desire to turn the trip into an extended honeymoon, but the professor preferred to pursue his studies without the distractions of a loving young wife.

When James Wallace returned from his year abroad, he and Janet were married at the Davis home on the college campus on September 2, 1878. Janet again dropped out of college, though she later memorized Sir Walter Scott's *The Lady of the Lake* in its entirety and recited it to her husband. For his part, James Wallace learned by heart the whole of the Gospel of Saint John as part of his religious studies, which he pursued as a complement to his private devotions.

From the beginning the marriage was not a happy one. James Wallace was a man of considerable energy and ambition, but there was little time left over for his family. In addition to teaching, he was busy writing a Greek grammar and, on the side, modestly speculating in real estate.

Despite his investments, the young family lived most of the time with the bride's family, and it was in the Davis home that the oldest child, Miriam, was born in 1880. Later Janet gave birth to another girl, Helen. In 1882 a son, Benjamin, was born—Janet's third child in as many years—and the family finally moved into its own home. Somewhat surprisingly, it was James who came down with a case of postpartum depression. At his wife's urging, the young scholar, father, and investor traveled up to a sanitarium in Clifton Springs, New York, for a stay lasting several weeks. Some time after his return, another son, Robert, was born.

Later, with two other professors, James invested in a newspaper, the Wayne County, Ohio, *Herald,* which vigorously supported the Republican candidate and Ohio native James Garfield in the 1880 election. Wallace and his colleagues also crusaded in behalf of the temperance movement and called for the establishment of a national prohibition party.

In 1887 Dr. Wallace accepted an appointment as professor of Greek and Old English at a small Presbyterian college in St. Paul, Minnesota. Macalester College was scarcely two years old and consisted of only one large brick building on the edge of a cornfield. The young couple's home at 1596 Summit Avenue was a large frame house on a corner of the campus, though Janet remained behind with her family in Wooster that first year while James went on ahead.

During their long separation the Wallaces' oldest child, Miriam, died of malaria and Dr. Wallace continued to suffer from bouts of depression. Janet also worried that the separation was not "consistent" with their marriage vows, while Dr. Wallace wrote in his loneliness, "Now if you were here to count my hairs, kiss me, and do all your conjugal duties toward me I could be in a very complacent frame of mind." Nevertheless, he successfully applied for a license to preach as a layman in the Presbyterian communion and was able to complete an annotated edition of Xenophon's *Anabasis*.

In the summer of 1888 Janet Wallace moved to St. Paul. Their fifth child, another boy, was born on November 12, 1889. Janet wanted to name her new baby James. The father favored John, "without any middle name or any other 19th Century varnish." But the parents could not agree, and Dr. Wallace wrote to a friend, "So I guess we'll call him Anonymous for a while." Later they compromised on Roy William DeWitt—the last layer of varnish in honor of a favorite cousin of James.

Janet Wallace later gave birth to a set of twins, both girls. Miriam survived, but Janet Macalester died of dysentery the day after she was born. The strain of seven deliveries, compounded by her husband's frequent absences, now began to take their toll on the young wife and mother, who had once complained of being, at the age of thirty, "an old, worn-out woman." Increasingly, she exhibited signs of mental disorder and hyperreligiosity.

During the depression of 1894, James Wallace assumed the presidency of Macalester College, whose financial troubles were to preoccupy him for the rest of his life. Often, while he was off canvassing for funds among wealthy congregations around the country, Janet and her children visited with her parents in Ohio, so that Roy—or "Dee," as she sometimes called her youngest son—shuttled between two households. The last such "visit" lasted for two years.

The long separation became so serious that James Wallace's own family decided to intervene. Janet felt humiliated and spent much of her time in tears and prayer. "Why should you forsake your own five bairns," his sister wrote him, "and good ones, too, for the sake of even a hundred others?" Chastened, Dr. Wallace brought his family back to the little-used house on Summit Avenue.

In St. Paul, Roy was enrolled in a private elementary school, the Ramsey School, where he proved to be such a good student that he was advanced two grades.

In 1900 Dr. Wallace used some of the money he inherited from his well-to-do farmer father to purchase a hundred acres on Wapogasset Lake, near Amery, Wisconsin. The property was easily reached by train from St. Paul. That year, their first summer at the lake, the boys helped put up a tent for the family to use until a permanent structure could be built. It lasted two summers. By the third year a house was built with leftover lumber from an abandoned planing mill down by the lake-shore. The summer home was affectionately known as Wappy, and for many years young Roy spent his vacations there with his family.

While Janet's health deteriorated, Dr. Wallace's career flourished. He had sacrificed his ambitions as a scholar and teacher in order to put the small, struggling college on a secure financial footing. Before the altar of Presbyterian higher education, he also sacrificed his marriage and the well-being of his family, for more than ever his duties required him to be away from home, preaching and fund-raising. In the strict atmosphere of the Wallace household, any protest from Janet would have seemed sinful and unworthy of her husband's noble cause. Her only recourse was to seek solace in her faith, but what she found instead was a maze from which she would never exit.

As soon as he reached high school age, Roy was enrolled in Macalester Academy, a preparatory school, though as a boarder—most likely in consideration of his mother's fragile health. His first literary effort, a handwritten "newspaper" called the *Parthenon Nonsensical Frivolatine,* "a paper devoted to the betterment of farm and student life," suggests why the high-spirited teenager may have been too much of a burden for Janet Wallace. Among the items was a story describing a raid orchestrated by the author on two women's dormitories.

Like many a hyperactive boy from a troubled household, Roy quickly found his true academic calling in playing pranks. His grades plummeted, and it was decided to send him to evangelist Dwight L. Moody's Mount Hermon Boys' School, in Northfield, Massachusetts.

In a moment of manful remorse, Roy prophetically declared in his letter of application, "Whatever my occupation may be, I intend to do as much good in the world as possible."

But that lay far in the future. Traveling by train to Northfield, where he had been accepted, he entered his senior year. At the same time, Janet and James Wallace were to endure another long separation. The latter had been asked to teach a course in hermeneutics, or scriptural interpretation, at the Biblical Seminary in New York, beginning in the fall. Janet traveled to East Northfield, Massachusetts, again accompanied by her sister Miriam, to live in the quiet of a small New England town and be near her youngest son.

With the family's domestic life in upheaval, Roy wasted no time trying to draw attention to himself. Within a few months he was caught taking part in another dormitory ruckus. Knowing he faced expulsion a second time, he and a friend hitchhiked first to Boston, then to New York, and finally to San Francisco, which was still in the midst of rebuilding itself after the recent devastating earthquake. Construction jobs were easy to come by, and the two young men progressed through a series of higher-paying jobs without losing a day's work. At the time Roy, a strapping six-footer with penetrating blue eyes and close-cropped blond hair, was only seventeen.

In early spring Janet and Miriam sailed to England, where the bookish Benjamin, Minnesota's first Rhodes scholar, was studying at Oxford. The trip abroad was designed to provide Janet with a change of scenery and a complete rest. The two women crossed the Atlantic in a cattle-carrying freighter, but after a brief stay they returned to the United States and were surprised to learn that James had now also decided to take a trip abroad. Despite Janet's failing health and Roy's uncertain academic future, Dr. Wallace wanted to revisit the Mediterranean. Once again he elected to go on the voyage alone.

While he was away, Miriam escorted her sister Janet to a sanitarium in Oak Bluff, Massachusetts, near Northfield. From there Janet wrote to her "Beloved Roy" in San Francisco, complaining about a recent letter from Dr. Wallace in which he spoke "of 'pacing the deck with exultant mien.' " She added, "So I rallied [teased] him over feeling so elated after putting hundreds of miles between himself and his family."

She also wrote to the board of Macalester College, without her husband's consent, and asked it to extend his leave of absence by another year. Upon his return James Wallace—surprised at having yet another sabbatical—chose to spend the upcoming academic year teaching again in New York at the Biblical Seminary. Janet, still unwell, was sent in the fall of 1907 to Battle Creek Sanitarium, in Battle Creek, Michigan. Later she moved back to Clifton Springs, where her husband had been treated for depression. Dr. Wallace now decided that her troubles stemmed from a "diabetic tendency."

That same fall, with a little help from the college president in absentia, Roy was accepted by Macalester College, from which his sister Helen had graduated five years earlier. In September he wrote to his mother, telling her he wanted to join a fraternity because it was more important "to make intimate friends among the fellows than it is among the girls."

Before long, though, the fun-loving freshman and a friend were in trouble for having made off with a ragman's horse and wagon. When the indignant victim went to the college to complain, he was ushered into a vacant classroom and presented to the "president of the college"—another student, dressed in black cap and gown. Later the mortarboard was passed around, and the ragman collected five dollars to replace a broken harness.

In January 1908 Janet wrote to her "Dearest Boy," telling him of her recent journey to Clifton Springs, but soon descending into impenetrable gibberish: "There was a letter to mail to Dear-love (I think), she needed stamps & she c'd see no ladies' waiting room! Instantly Little Bright Eyes No. 2 came up it seemed thro the floor." Her symptoms suggested she was by now suffering from acute schizophrenia.

Roy somehow managed to complete his freshman year without another mishap. That summer the family was reunited for the last time when James and Janet Wallace, her sister Miriam, Roy, and assorted brothers and sisters assembled at Wappy for a long vacation by the lake. Dr. Wallace also resigned the presidency of Macalester College and accepted an appointment as a professor of religious studies.

At the beginning of the school year, Roy returned to his dormitory and Dr. and Mrs. Wallace prepared to move back into their former home on Summit Avenue, only to discover that the college—which owned the property—wanted them to share it with another faculty family. Instead, the Wallaces rented a house elsewhere. Before long, however, Janet was back in Battle Creek. On November 11, 1908, she sent a lengthy rhymed birthday greeting full of religious symbolism to "My dear, dear Dee" that began, "Oh, Dee, my dear, now 'listen here'" to what I have to say. For, before very long, I'll join the *New Song,* & be far, *far* away."

How Roy and the rest of the family dealt with Mrs. Wallace's illness on a daily basis is not known, though her youngest son does not seem to have been outwardly affected—unless it was simply to throw himself even more energetically into a variety of activities. During his sophomore year at Macalester, Roy played quarterback on the school's football team and second base on the baseball team, which won its conference championship. He also joined the hockey team and was a member of the Parthenon Literary Society. Toward the end of the school year, he and some friends installed a horse in the third-floor chapel where his father had often preached. Roy was not expelled, probably in order to spare Dr. Wallace further embarrassment. But the young man's career at Macalester had come to an ignominious end.

Ever the enthusiast for exercise and manual work, Roy next applied for a job with the Oliver Iron Mining Company on the Mesabi Range in northern Minnesota, the state's last wilderness. He was told that no positions were open. But John Wallace, an uncle who helped run the Wallace Lumber Company in Monte Vista, Colorado, offered the college dropout a summer job. Although Dr. Wallace encouraged his son to take it, Roy chose to play baseball on a semipro circuit centered in Oregon and the Dakotas, flippantly explaining to his folks, "A boy's summer education is worth as much as a school year." Later, while on a road trip to North Dakota, he talked of one day taking a cross-country motorcycle trip and writing for magazines. More important, though, he was "fielding practically errorless ball."

At the end of summer Roy did travel to Monte Vista, taking a job as a bank teller with another uncle, Robert Wallace, who also lived in town. To occupy his spare time, Roy began to write down his thoughts in notebooks and on index cards and loose sheets of paper—not just occasionally, but passionately, voluminously, for hours at a time and long into the night. It was a habit that was to last well into middle age. Those long, earnest, youthful memorandums to himself—full of aphorisms and quotations, lists for self-improvement, ideas for making money—were the embryonic stirrings of what was to become the *Reader's Digest.* One of his proposals was for the bank to give away a tree worth ten dollars to anyone who opened a new account.

When he was not writing, Roy read magazines omnivorously and kept a card file of the salient points of articles he enjoyed. The great age of muckraking had only recently begun, with a series of articles by

Lincoln Steffens in *McClure's* magazine on municipal corruption. They were later collected and brought out as a book, *The Shame of the Cities.* Another reporter for *McClure's* was Ida Tarbell, whose series on corporate corruption was later published as *The History of the Standard Oil Company.*

Young Wallace was almost certainly familiar with both, and with another famous early-twentieth-century journalist—George Horace Lorimer, editor of the *Saturday Evening Post,* which was not part of the muckraking crowd, though it did run articles by the famous Kansas newspaperman William Allen White and backed the reformist programs of President Theodore Roosevelt.

In due course, Steffens, Tarbell, and White's son, William L. White, were all to write for the *Reader's Digest.* Lorimer would go to work for it as a consultant. And in 1938 Wallace, by then the successful editor, would drive over to the Roosevelt home in Oyster Bay, Long Island, for a game of softball with the president's son Theodore Roosevelt, Jr.

———

ANY notion of publishing a magazine still lay well in the future for young Roy DeWitt Wallace, the wandering nonscholar. At most he thought he might write a few articles for some of the popular magazines if he ever took that motorcycle trip.

Roy's sudden and inexplicable industriousness—his notes would in book form fill a substantial volume—was comparable to a religious experience insofar as it marked the onset of a completely different form of behavior and happened without warning. Yet it was a conversion without overt religious overtones and lacked any trace of fanatical excess. Roy still intended to have plenty of un-Calvinist fun. Already he had developed an appetite for girls, poker, smoking, gin martinis, travel, secondhand cars, and theater, and these were to remain the joyful obsessions of a lifetime.

But Roy did have a great deal to be very thoughtful about. By the age of twenty he had been expelled, virtually or in fact, from three schools. For an ex–boy of summer, currently working as a bank teller in a remote town in the Rockies, whose mother was seriously ill and whose father had little tolerance for his contrary behavior, that had to be a sobering set of circumstances.

Despite James Wallace's persistent complaints about his son's seemingly purposeless existence, which exhibited none of his father's or older brother Ben's scholarly interests and Presbyterian idealism, Roy

continued to show little curiosity about literature, history, or scholarship for its own sake.

Yet during his own self-imposed sabbatical, and as a result of his
quasi-religious awakening, Roy did develop a positive passion for practical knowledge and useful information that would help a person get
ahead in life. Toward religion itself he evinced a benign indifference
that later in life developed into benign approbation—not a whole lot
of difference between the two. The result was that Roy remained the
exact opposite of his father and yet became a faithful, perverse image
at the same time—both rebel and replica.

In the fall of 1910 Roy DeWitt Wallace returned to California,
where he tried to gain admittance into the School of Horticulture of
the University of California at Berkeley—most likely because of a
spontaneous enthusiasm inspired by his older brother Bob's enrollment in Yale University's renowned School of Forestry. After being
turned down, he enrolled as a freshman in the College of Liberal Arts
"because the first year is more fun," as he brashly explained to his
father. Unconsciously, he may also have been emulating his mother,
who had also enrolled twice as a freshman, never to graduate. Roy
added that his academic goal that year was to become "the Playboy of
the Western World." As a theater buff, he had no doubt read about the
riots attending the opening of John Millington Synge's controversial
play of the same name at the Abbey Theatre only three years before, in
1907. But it is unlikely his father picked up on the literary allusion. If
there was a subconscious message in Roy's boast, both men were
probably oblivious to it: Synge's play is about a man who murders his
father.

In pursuit of his playboy ambition, in which he was to succeed
beyond all doubt, Roy also joined a fraternity, Psi Upsilon. Increasingly, though, he began to sign his letters DeWitt—as his father called
him. Meanwhile, his mother's health continued to decline.

At Berkeley, DeWitt renewed his friendship with an old Macalester
schoolmate, Barclay Acheson, also the son of a Presbyterian minister.
Acheson was then studying for the ministry at San Francisco Presbyterian Seminary, but like DeWitt showed a streak of devilment. Over the
Christmas vacation of 1910, the two young men traveled to the Acheson family home in Tacoma, Washington. Pooling their cash to buy
steamship tickets, they sailed from San Francisco to Portland aboard
the SS *Watson.*

"Destiny held your hand," Barclay later told DeWitt, who was pleased to discover that Acheson had five sisters. The young visitor was smitten by the oldest, Bessie Jane, and somehow managed to raise enough money to ask her out. But he liked all of the Acheson girls, including the youngest, Eliza Bell, then twenty-two and engaged to be married. A petite, blue-eyed blonde standing five feet two inches, Eliza had recently exchanged the biblical name given to her by her parents for the more ladylike Lila. Bell was the name of her maternal grandparents.

The method of self-instruction that DeWitt had begun in Colorado seems to have had some good effect on his study habits. His report card for his first semester showed a grade of 1 (A) in industrial chemistry, military, and physical culture; a 2 in economics; and a passing grade of 3 in economic history, constitutional law, and principles of economics.

But DeWitt's father was far from satisfied. Particularly disturbing to the money-conscious Dr. Wallace were his son's spendthrift ways. After receiving an especially severe reprimand, DeWitt solemnly promised to reform: "My one purpose in life now is to become a man in whom my parents . . . may be proud indeed—a son pleasing in the sight of God and man." He also asked for a loan of $250. He was to keep the promise—more or less.

The next summer DeWitt decided to give up baseball to peddle maps door-to-door in rural Oregon. Not having a car, he was obliged to walk from farmhouse to farmhouse; one day he covered twenty-five miles. His job was to sell subscriptions to a wall-mounted Washington-Oregon survey map depicting, according to the sales brochure, "distances and electric as well as steam railroads and a complete list of towns with populations from the 1910 census with an index for locating them." The cost was $2.50—high by 1911 standards.

That experience changed his life, for it gave him an insight into people's need for practical information—as opposed to the academic knowledge so prized by his father, brother, and schoolmasters. But the most important lesson DeWitt learned that summer occurred after he stopped by a courtroom and watched the contest of wits between two attorneys. Later he walked two miles in the rain to the Medford Carnegie Library to obtain Francis Wellman's great legal classic, *The Art of Cross-Examination,* and then spent the next day reading it.

One of America's great nineteenth-century trial lawyers, Wellman explained and simplified the principles of questioning while providing generous excerpts from the transcripts of famous trials. He condemned the browbeating of witnesses as a tactic that succeeded only in causing confusion and eliciting jury sympathy for the individual being questioned; a "courteous and conciliatory" approach, by contrast, invited a witness to enter into a discussion during which a clever cross-examiner could easily discover the weak points in the testimony. In particular, Wellman championed a subtle line of inquiry focusing if possible on self-interest on the part of the witness, or on that often inevitable point in the testimony where even an honest witness was apt to have "recourse to . . . imagination."

The book made a profound impression on DeWitt, and later he informed his father that it was possible to apply the techniques of examining witnesses to every imaginable life situation. As he continued to walk across Oregon, the young Minnesotan sought out veteran salesmen in hotel lobbies and delighted in cross-examining them, trying to pick up their stratagems.

Another formative influence on twenty-one-year-old DeWitt Wallace was, of course, America itself—in 1911 a country of less than 100 million, more than half of whom still lived on farms. Though a city boy born and bred, DeWitt had spent a good part of his childhood and adolescence in the small towns of the Midwest, mountain states, and Northwest—Wooster, Ohio, where his mother once took him to live for two years; Amery, Wisconsin, where the family spent its summer vacations; Monte Verde, a lumber outpost in the Colorado Rockies; and finally the string of towns in Oregon, Washington, and the Dakotas where he played semipro ball and was now selling maps door-to-door. He had also hitchhiked from one end of the country to the other, gone to school on both coasts, and, thanks to his extensive magazine reading, probably become reasonably well informed on most major political and cultural issues of the day.

The America that DeWitt experienced, in the Indian summer of his youth, was also enjoying its last moments of innocence. Already the frontier was a thing of the past. Though railroads had spawned enormous westward development, technology had just recently leapt into the modern age when the Wright brothers became the first to fly an airplane, in Kitty Hawk, North Carolina, in 1903. Many homes were already equipped with electricity, and the transcontinental telephone and wireless radio—another medium of mass communication—were just around the corner. In particular, though, three developments of the late nineteenth century laid the groundwork for publishers to reach a heretofore unsuspected market numbering in the millions—a highly efficient, inexpensive postal system; the invention of the Linotype machine by Ottmar Mergenthaler; and the evolution of the web press and folding machinery, which made it possible to print up to 240,000 eight-page newspapers in an hour. Two magazines above all—*Reader's Digest* and *Time*—were eventually to take full advantage of that serendipitous set of circumstances.

The people, too, were changing, with immigrants flooding into Ellis Island at an unparalleled rate. In Washington, New York, and other industrial capitals, the major issues of the day centered on antitrust legislation, tariffs, women's suffrage, and child labor. The country's celebrities were its new breed of millionaires—Andrew Carnegie, J. P. Morgan, Cornelius Vanderbilt. Though William Taft was president, the country still pursued the imperialist course of his predecessor, Teddy Roosevelt. America's colonial influence now extended not only to Cuba but also to the Philippines, Puerto Rico, and Central America, where the United States had recently begun building the Panama Canal. Popular entertainment emphasized sensationalism and spectacle over subtlety—circuses, dime novels, silent movies that served up mostly bathos and slapstick. It is safe to say that young DeWitt Wallace unequivocally embraced this vision of a simple, innocent, all-powerful America. In time, the *Reader's Digest* reflected his lifelong effort to preserve and reinvent it.

———

DURING that summer of 1911, all mail to the peripatetic DeWitt was sent to him in care of the Achesons in Tacoma. Lila forwarded the mail—much of it from DeWitt's many girlfriends back home in St. Paul—and often attached clever little notes of her own on the outside of the envelopes. Lila's father was now vice-president of Whitworth College—like Macalester, a Presbyterian-affiliated school—in Sumner, just outside Tacoma. On July 15, 1911, she wrote to her brother's friend on college stationery, inviting him on Barclay's instructions "to come right along to Tacoma on the first train," adding, "He would welcome you with open arms—so say we all!"

That summer, the fun-loving but hardworking DeWitt signed up an impressive 233 customers in Jackson and Josephine counties, for a total gross of $582.50. With his earnings he bought himself a "flivver," or Model T, and in the fall returned to the University of California. The semester passed uneventfully. Again he spent his Christmas vacation with the Acheson family in Tacoma. On December 28, 1911, he wrote pensively to his mother:

> I think of you constantly, hoping you are growing stronger, enjoying life, not doing any work & not worrying about your children. . . . It almost takes my breath away tho when I think that the time is almost at hand when I settle down and enter the "arena of life" with probably the happiest days of my life behind. Altho I don't see why they should be exactly. . . . It is sometimes said of course too that matrimony has its compensating joys altho I was reading today that the minute after the ceremony and from then on the wife & husband become bores to each other, generally. . . . I think the oldest Acheson girl is about the classiest cutest prettiest little bunch of femininity I ever saw.

Back in the Midwest, by way of Tacoma, at the conclusion of the spring semester, DeWitt found work as an office clerk in Frederick, Wisconsin, but soon returned again to St. Paul and was hired to write promotion letters for the book department of the Webb Publishing Company. Dr. Edward Downing, DeWitt's former college professor at Macalester, was editor of the book division of Webb, which published farm magazines, textbooks, and pamphlets used in agricultural schools. Young Wallace's job was to field inquiries about the firm's agricultural publications.

For the next several years his life was to be divided between courting a considerable number of young women and familiarizing himself with the editorial operations of a small, specialized publishing company. By now DeWitt had decided not to return to Berkeley for his junior year. He soon forgot all about Bessie Jane Acheson and was no longer in touch with Barclay.

———

In 1914 Janet Wallace passed away. Few details of her death survive. Refusing medical treatment and trusting only in her vegetarian diet, she had lapsed into unconsciousness in January and was taken to a sanitarium, where she died two months later. In a book-length family history that he later composed, in which his wife made only a fleeting appearance, Dr. Wallace discreetly memorialized the moment: "The intense and sacrificial life she lived in the thirty-six years of her wifehood and exacting motherhood of seven children proved too much for a body never very robust and she left us a sweet memory March 27, 1914, age 56."

By 1915 DeWitt was growing restless again. Webb was an old-fashioned, conservative publishing house, deeply set in its ways. And St. Paul, a provincial backwater with a population of about 200,000, did not offer much opportunity for DeWitt to enjoy anything like the theater and freewheeling nightlife available to him in San Francisco. By reason of social standing and religion, the Wallaces were also isolated both geographically and culturally from other St. Paulitans. In recent decades the population of St. Paul—poorer and smaller than Minneapolis, across the Mississippi River—had nearly doubled. Most of the new arrivals were Catholic working-class Germans and Irish lured by the prospect of finding work related to the city's role as a hub of transportation.

But the Wallaces belonged to the Protestant minority, and their home adjoined the city's most affluent neighborhood, where railroad tycoon James Hill and others lived in mansions that were among the most ostentatious symbols of the Gilded Age. Though hardly entitled to call himself an aristocrat, DeWitt belonged to an elite that had virtually nothing in common with the masses who were to be his future audience. Moreover, particularly in its first decades, the *Digest* was to exhibit an almost rabid hostility toward immigrants and Catholics—as though to suggest that DeWitt was not only bored but horrified by his hometown's transformation into a Catholic, working-class city.

In February the Baker Land and Title Company of St. Croix Falls, Wisconsin, offered him a job as manager of the Burnett County Abstract Company, with the opportunity to earn up to $2,500 a year and the use of a car. Though the prospect of travel and escape from the office was appealing, DeWitt had by now decided that he wanted to stay in publishing. Also he had an idea.

At Webb he was struck by all the pointless information buried in the company's assorted publications, including one called *The Farmer,* a comprehensive annual catalog of the innumerable bulletins issued by state and federal agricultural departments. Though the bulletins were free, obtaining them cost time and money. DeWitt proposed to the supervisor of Webb's agricultural department that *The Farmer* distill only the most practical material for the use of farmers, pointing out that they had little time to read. In his enthusiasm he had also prepared a summary of what was wrong with several other Webb publications as well. The supervisor read the long, annotated list, then said, "This is an interesting document, DeWitt. I'm sorry it means you're fired. We don't believe in this sort of thing."

Though bewildered by the company's sensitivity to criticism, De-Witt obtained from his ex-employer a credit of $700 to proceed with his own farmer's digest. He was determined to prove to his former company and to himself that his idea was a sound one. Culling the best of the information contained in the hundreds of bulletins issued by the various agricultural departments, he created a 128-page, digest-sized booklet titled *Getting the Most Out of Farming,* subtitled *A Selected List of Publications, of Value to the Farmer and Farmer's Wife, Available for Free Distribution by the Government and State Experiment Stations.*

In small print at the bottom of the title page was the notice "Pre-pared by DeWitt Wallace." It was his first and last byline. The year of publication was given as 1916 to ensure that the booklet was still current a year later. The young publisher had enough confidence in his very first product, and enough credit from Webb, to print 100,000 copies.

In fundamental respects, *Farming* was both precursor and model for the *Digest*—full of practical information about crops, as well as mind-ful of such quality-of-life matters as women's clubs and community service. Each page was spiced with drawings and adages. One sketch showed a cockerel and a hen over the caption "The hen is not large, but many a flock has lifted the mortgage on a farm." In a dialogue between an editor and a farmer, the latter was encouraged to "wise up" and subscribe to farm magazines because knowledge meant profit.

The next step was a five-state selling tour. DeWitt decided to con-centrate on the farming area he knew best—Minnesota, North Da-kota, Montana, Oregon, and Washington—targeting primarily banks and seed stores. His plan, a variation of his idea for giving away trees, was to persuade commercial institutions to purchase the booklet in bulk as a premium for customers. Individual copies sold for thirty-five cents, at a time when most magazines sold for a nickel or a dime.

During the first leg of the tour, through Minnesota, DeWitt traveled by train since he no longer had a car. In three weeks he sold a respectable 4,100 copies, but train fare proved too expensive. Returning to St. Paul, he bought another Model T and persuaded his cousin Conrad Davis to join him and share expenses. Conrad's plan was to work the service stations, selling spark plugs. To save further on overhead, they put hinges on the port seat so that it could convert into a bed. Since they also intended the long trip west to be an adventure, the two friends planned to supplement their income by taking small jobs along the way.

Out west again, DeWitt found "merchants as good as the banks," as he wrote home, and in ten consecutive working days once made $210. Then he hit three days of "bum territory" and sold only a hundred books. On May 21, 1916, he wrote from Valley City, North Dakota, to his father, "I slept in the car every night while in Wahpeton—it was beastly cold weather, but I kept very snug and warm."

He was not discouraged, however, and even began to think about preparing a similar booklet, digesting the best of advertising and merchandising trade journals and selling the service to department stores.

Then he got an even better inspiration.

One summer night in Montana, DeWitt was lying awake at two in the morning in the bunkhouse of a sheep ranch where he and Conrad had found part-time work. The bunkhouse was set in the middle of a hayfield. Despite the late hour, the other ranch hands were being particularly rowdy. But DeWitt was transported onto another plane by the most incredible idea of his life—in fact, one of the best publishing ideas of the century. He wondered why, instead of digesting only the best of specialized information for farmers or trades people, he could not simply digest the best of all magazines and sell his product to everybody.

Afterward the two traveling salesmen made their way to Yellowstone National Park, where they remained two weeks, working in the kitchens of the Wylie camps to earn their keep. At the end of summer they returned to St. Paul. Though he made no profit, DeWitt had sold all 100,000 copies of *Getting the Most Out of Farming*. He was also able to pay off his loan from Webb and cover his expenses. Moreover, he had not simply learned how to edit, print, and distribute a publication. Once again he had obtained firsthand evidence that what the average hardworking American family most wanted in a publication was information.

Under pressure from his father, DeWitt next found employment as mail-order correspondence manager for Brown & Bigelow, a local calendar and greeting-card company. By comparison with his older brothers, Ben and Bob, who were pursuing careers in civil service and farming, respectively, he now seemed destined—after that experiment in publishing—for a life of mediocre achievement at best. Helen, his oldest sister, had married a Presbyterian minister. By contrast DeWitt was, at the age of twenty-six, a college dropout with a menial, anonymous job. Though he continued to write voluminous notes to himself about how he planned to get ahead in life, his main goal still seemed to be to win the hearts of as many young women as possible. He had not yet found any who had won his.

———

IN APRIL 1917 DeWitt was delivered from his torpor when the United States declared war on Germany. From the outbreak of hostilities between England and Germany, in July 1914, American public opinion had been favorable to the Allies. Most Americans were also outraged by the sinking of the *Lusitania* and considered Germany's aggressive U-boat policy a flagrant violation of international law and morality. Ultimately, President Woodrow Wilson became convinced the United States had to play a role in maintaining world peace. Earlier in 1917 he had announced a fourteen-point program that included freedom of the seas and the establishment of a League of Nations to enforce peace—a proposal heartily endorsed by DeWitt's father, Dr. James Wallace. (Wilson was also Presbyterian.) But the president's appeal fell on deaf ears. When the Germans resumed their unrestricted U-boat warfare, which they had suspended to placate U.S. public opinion, America entered the war.

DeWitt's boredom had been so great that he was among the first twenty-five men from the area to volunteer for the army. He and the others were sent to Fort Dodge, Iowa, where he was soon promoted to sergeant-instructor—another dull, dead-end job. When the year was up, he volunteered a second time—now as a private, in order to be sent overseas. Assigned to the Thirty-fifth Infantry Division, he got his wish and was posted to France.

Like millions of other young men, American and European, DeWitt went almost overnight from a world of domestic comfort into a nightmare zone of trenches, dugouts, barbed wire, and mud. After the first and second battles of the Marne, combat had degenerated into nearly nonstop exchanges of artillery fire and suicidal infantry assaults across the infamous no-man's-land separating the two armies—each onslaught preceded by a barrage of chlorine gas that often wafted back onto the advancing soldiers.

Yet Private Wallace made even war seem like jolly good fun, writing home on September 4, from an unidentified location in France, ". . . we were up in the wee hours listening to that most enrapturing of all rhapsodies—shells bursting in 6/8 time, all the bars and clefs in action and with full orchestral accompaniment. We couldn't see the leader of the Band, of course, but I imagine he was back there somewhere frantically waving his sword in one hand and a stein of beer in the other."

But one dark night, as shells burst overhead, DeWitt barely escaped being shot by his own fellow soldiers. Deciding to visit an army field hospital, he sloshed through the trenches to the command post, where two guards asked the gas-masked visitor for the password. Unable to understand his muffled reply, they panicked and opened fire at a distance of only six feet. "It was almost a miracle a man could shoot that close and not hit me," DeWitt later recounted.

A few days later he was not so fortunate. Toward the end of September, more than a million American soldiers were ordered to attack the entrenched German army that had retreated behind the fortified Siegfried line. Known as the Meuse-Argonne offensive, the campaign resulted in the highest casualty rate of the war—one out of every ten soldiers wounded or killed. By the fifth day, nearly half of the members of DeWitt's company were among the dead or disabled. On September 29, just as his company was about to be withdrawn, Private Wallace was hit by shrapnel and taken to a first-aid station. A doctor quickly located a flesh wound about the size of a hand below DeWitt's stomach and said, "Pretty lucky! A mighty dangerous place [to be hit]."

At the field hospital another doctor dressed a wound to his neck. "Pretty lucky!" the doctor observed. "It came within an ace of your jugular vein."

Some time later, yet another doctor told the wounded soldier, "Pretty lucky that it missed your larynx."

The adjutant general of the War Office later wrote to inform Dr. Wallace, "An examination of reports received by courier indicates that Sergeant Roy DeWitt Wallace, Infantry, was under treatment for slight gun shot wound in back, neck and shoulders, in Evacuation Hospital

#9, AEF, September 29, 1918." No mention was made of a wound to the abdomen, though that was perhaps an oversight. The thrice-fortunate private had also been promoted back to his old rank of sergeant.

On October 8 DeWitt was transferred to Base Hospital No. 44, a former casino, at Ponger-des-Eaux, where—like all other patients from the front—he was deloused. Later he was sent to an army hospital in Aix-les-Bains. On November 11 the armistice was declared.

DeWitt spent nearly six months in the army hospital, where he passed his twenty-ninth birthday. During this time he was preoccupied with the idea that had come to him years earlier in a Montana bunkhouse. To fill the long hours while he recuperated, he read through the plentiful supply of American magazines provided for the soldiers. But once again he was struck by the needless length of so many articles. He thought most could be cut to a quarter of their original size and still retain their essence.

Instead of doing crossword puzzles or playing chess, DeWitt relaxed by practicing condensation techniques on the *Saturday Evening Post, Vanity Fair,* and *Scribner's.* He made a point of reducing only practical articles "of lasting interest" that would appeal to as broad a readership as possible. His success in condensing articles while retaining both their style and their substance resolved him on a new course. He decided, on returning to the States, to publish another booklet—to be called the *Reader's Digest.*

When not reading and condensing, DeWitt took long walks in the countryside and also "leisurely rambles in the realm of thought," as he wrote home to a friend. He looked forward to receiving his first service stripe and to being sent home within six months. In April 1919 he returned by transport ship to the United States and was discharged from the army at the point of debarkation, in Norfolk, Virginia.

BACK in St. Paul, DeWitt spent the next six months in the Minneapolis Public Library, where his aunt Miriam was librarian, and worked feverishly to put together a sample issue of the *Reader's Digest.* The articles that he selected, some of them ten years old, were cut down to as little as 25 percent of their original length. At first he was careful to ask publishers for permission to reprint.

DeWitt also renewed his friendship with Barclay Acheson, who was by now an ordained minister serving as a field director for a Presbyterian relief organization headquartered in New York. During the war he had taught at an American college in Beirut and later worked with the YMCA in Portland, Oregon. DeWitt caught up on all the news about the Acheson family and learned that Lila Bell, the youngest daughter, had not married after all and was now a social worker for the YWCA in New York City, helping to improve the working conditions for women in industry.

On December 22, 1919, DeWitt sent Lila a holiday greeting card with a tongue-in-cheek message, inviting her to the Twin Cities, because working conditions for women were "awful," and adding, "It would take you some time to straighten things out—but you ought to come. Also . . . there is tobogganing."

By January 1920 DeWitt had prepared a sample issue of the *Reader's Digest.* The booklet, suitable for slipping into a coat pocket or purse, was sixty-four pages long, including its basic yellow and green cover. Though the 25-cent cover price was still relatively high, there were considerations that to DeWitt's mind made it a good investment. It contained no advertising, only information. Its thirty-one articles, one for each day of the month, were culled from leading magazines— "each article of enduring value and interest, in condensed and permanent form."

Among those represented were the *Literary Digest, Woman's Home Companion,* the *New Republic, Country Life, Vanity Fair,* the *National Geographic,* the *Atlantic Monthly, McClure's,* and the *Saturday Evening Post.* The articles ranged in subject matter from humor, sex, health, and human interest to art-of-living suggestions applicable to the life of the average person, such as "How to Regulate Your Weight." Two other departments were "The Spice of Life" and "Remarkable Remarks."

DeWitt's goal was a circulation of 5,000, which he thought might allow him to live comfortably in an uptown neighborhood. Five hundred copies were printed up by the Stearns Printing Company in St. Paul and paid for with $600 borrowed from his father, who had at first turned him down, and his brother Ben. But Stearns informed DeWitt that if he wanted to publish a second issue, the printing bill would be considerably higher. Headquarters of the Reader's Digest Association, as DeWitt named his company, were in the Globe Building in St. Paul, Minnesota.

The *Reader's Digest,* though, was not the first magazine to provide its readers with a sampling from other publications. As early as 1844

Littell's Living Age had reprinted articles from other periodicals. Others offering reprints included the *Eclectic,* a highbrow journal that flourished in Boston in the 1870s; *Comfort,* a rural magazine founded in 1888 that survived well into the twentieth century; and the short-lived *Scrap-Book,* which originated in Buffalo in 1889. But DeWitt was the first to hit upon condensation.

The idea of getting the most out of every minute was very much in the air in the twenties. More Americans than ever were buying their first automobile, joining the Rotary or other fashionable clubs, breaking out of the constrictive six-day workweek. Radio, motion pictures, and the Sunday drive in the family automobile now determined how Americans spent their leisure time, which reading and churchgoing had once monopolized.

By 1920, Americans were also tiring of long investigative pieces by muckrakers like Tarbell and Steffens, not to mention their relentlessly gloomy portrayals of U.S. business and society. Shorter articles and even news summaries were now in vogue. *Liberty* magazine had gone so far as to post, at the head of each article, the reading time: six minutes; eight minutes and twenty seconds; ten minutes, if it was a "long" article. *Collier's* had pioneered the brief article and was experimenting with the one-page short story. Soon almost every popular magazine, including the *Saturday Evening Post,* was beginning to shorten its once formidably long short stories and features.

Self-improvement, another obsession of the twenties, was a holdover of the country's nineteenth-century optimism. But eight-week Chautauqua summer courses and Dr. Eliot's "five-foot shelf"—named after Harvard's president, who advocated the study of classics—were giving way to weight-loss and body-building programs promising results in thirty days. Generic moral uplift designed to make its audience feel good was eroding the Puritan-Calvinist grip on America's collective conscience. Inspirational poetry, homilies, and ersatz Emersoniana were staples of almost every magazine and newspaper.

DeWitt's most original insight, based on his earlier experiences as a calendar salesman and publisher of a booklet for farmers, was to provide a magazine devoted primarily to fact. Almost every other commercial magazine of any consequence offered mainly fiction.

"Never fear, there is a strong undercurrent of desire for knowledge," DeWitt confidently wrote to himself. "Supply it and every dollar's worth of printed matter will come home to roost."

His next step was to circulate the proposal among publishers in New York, St. Paul, and elsewhere. At this point he was willing simply to give the *Reader's Digest* away to anyone who would pay him a salary to be its editor. To that end, he wrote to every major magazine publisher in the country, as well as to a number of lesser ones, sending them a sample copy of his proposed new publication. All turned him down flat. The only exception was William Randolph Hearst, who declined with the comment that the magazine could hope for only a 300,000 circulation—too small for him to bother with.

After being rebuffed by Hearst, DeWitt got more bad news. Horace Klein, a partner in the Webb Publishing Company, returned from a visit to New York, where he had met with Gertrude Battles Lane, editor of *Woman's Home Companion.* At DeWitt's request, Klein had asked for her opinion of the *Reader's Digest.* Lane did not rise to the bait but loftily observed that magazines carried articles only to attract advertisers. A magazine with no advertisements, no fiction, no illustrations, and no color seemed a contradiction in terms, a formula for failure.

In the face of such rejection, DeWitt fell into a long period of depression. To make ends meet, he took a job with the McMurray Company, a wholesale grocer. It was during this period, in the summer of 1920, that Dr. Wallace, then seventy-one years old, married his sister-in-law Miriam Davis. The two were wed at Wappy in an outdoor ceremony, which took place in a pergola overlooking the lake. The bride was fifty-eight. Dr. Wallace was now head of the Department of Religious Education at Macalester. He had paid off the college's $125,-000 debt and received from the College of Wooster an honorary doctor of laws degree. Later the trustees of Macalester were to confer on him an honorary doctorate in divinity. In everything he put his hand to, he seemed a success, while everything DeWitt touched seemingly turned to dust.

In the fall of 1920 DeWitt was rescued from the doldrums by a vivacious social worker who provided the one thing he lacked—encouragement. As if in answer to his facetious invitation of a year before to go tobogganing, Lila Bell Acheson was sent to St. Paul by the YWCA to look into conditions of women working in local canneries.

Their courtship was a model of condensation. On October 15, the first day of her arrival in the Twin Cities, DeWitt proposed marriage on a scenic bluff overlooking the St. Croix River. On the second, she accepted—and assured him that the idea for his new publication was "gorgeous." However, since neither had enough money even to get married, much less start up the *Digest,* Lila eventually returned to New York. Meanwhile, DeWitt's brother Ben arranged for him to get a job in Pittsburgh writing promotional copy for the Westinghouse Company. Lila planned to join him as soon as possible.

THE youngest daughter of the Reverend Thomas Davis Acheson and Mary Eliza Huston, Lila Bell Acheson was born on Christmas Day, 1888, while her mother was visiting her parents in the farming community of Virden, in Manitoba Province, Canada. An amateur painter, Mrs. Acheson was also a cousin of the Right Honorable Arthur Meighen, prime minister of Canada, who once visited the family home. But the family moved frequently, as Dr. Acheson accepted one pastorate after another—in North Dakota, Minnesota, and other points in the Midwest.

When the family settled in Lewiston, Illinois, Lila attended the Lewiston Community High School, from which she graduated. The rest of her education similarly reflected her father's itinerant existence—two years at Ward-Belmont, a two-year Presbyterian college in Nashville, Tennessee; followed by six months at the University of Oregon in Eugene, where she received her bachelor of arts degree. Like her father and brother, Lila then chose to pursue a life of service, entering the profession of social work under a program sponsored jointly by the U.S. Department of Labor and the YWCA.

During the war Lila was placed in charge of the Industrial Service Center at the DuPont munitions plant in Pompton Lakes, New Jersey, where she lived and worked among the women just beginning to enter the labor force. She found employee turnover high, community acceptance of women low, and working conditions deplorable. Under her direction a new social center was built. For the first time, hot meals were served to night-shift workers. She also introduced music and recreational facilities and helped to improve plant–community relations.

After the armistice the Labor Department sent Lila Bell to other industrial centers to perform similar activities. In New Orleans she helped establish such innovations as classes in music, languages, homemaking, and the arts for women industrial workers. Later, through public speeches and personal meetings, she persuaded factory owners in small canning towns to build schools and recreation centers for migrant workers. She was also borrowed by the Inter-Church World Movement to work among migrant families in Mississippi and New England.

Despite such herculean labors on behalf of women and the poor, Lila appears to have been motivated less by the high missionary ideals of Presbyterianism than by the simple dictates of making a living. In later life she was singularly lacking in feminist sympathies and showed no interest in organized religion. But the experience did make her sensitive to employee working conditions. Years later, when the preacher's daughter had more money than some churches, she made it her personal mission to create one of the most comfortable and caring work environments anywhere in the world.

—

ON DECEMBER 8, 1920, DeWitt wrote prophetically to Lila from Pittsburgh, "I am more & more convinced that I have in me the ability to make good in a very satisfying way ultimately—but we will love each other so devotedly that I'm sure you will be happy while I am climbing. I loved what you said once about your having a share in my success. You don't know what an immense inspiration you are to me to make good—and I know I will."

DeWitt also sang Lila's praises to his family, writing home, "She . . . is a fiend for reading & improving her mind, loves music, loves to take hikes, actually enjoys to keep house, has very good taste, is economical, never has been sick, is very easy to look at, is thotful, considerate & *affectionate,* is very jolly, all kinds of substantial character—so what more could a man want[?]"

Though Lila Bell's enthusiasm for the *Reader's Digest* considerably restored his confidence, DeWitt was still perplexed about how to sell his magazine if no major publishers were interested. Fortunately, at this critical juncture, he showed his sample issue to a co-worker at Westinghouse, who that night read it from cover to cover. The next day he convinced DeWitt that he could sell the *Digest* by direct mail. Despite that salutary insight, which completely altered DeWitt's approach to publishing, more bad news was to come. In 1921 the country was in the grip of a severe recession, and Westinghouse found it necessary to lay off personnel. Six months after DeWitt's arrival, he was laid off.

This time DeWitt was determined not to let any obstacle deter him.

Once again, though, he had to resort to asking his father and brother Ben for a loan—for $3,000. Instead, Dr. Wallace came up with $300 and Ben another $300. For the time being, that was enough, and DeWitt set about trying to sell enough subscriptions to justify printing the first issue of his magazine. For the next four months, working out of his Pittsburgh living quarters, he mailed hundreds of circulars and provisional *Digest* subscription orders, along with brief personalized typewritten notes, to carefully selected lists of prospective subscribers. A year's subscription cost $2.97—again a high price compared with that of other large-circulation magazines of the day, many of which cost half as much or less. And a single copy of the *Digest* still sold for a quarter.

DeWitt's first mailing was to the members of the Business and Professional Women's Club in Pittsburgh. He had decided that his new magazine would be of interest primarily to women and, to that end, even named Lila Bell Acheson and her cousin Hazel Cubberley as coeditors of his fledgling publication. Cubberley, who headed the women's physical education department at Columbia University, never had any actual connection with the magazine. The two cousins lived in a boardinghouse in a little town called Pleasantville, forty miles north of New York.

The response to the mailing encouraged him to send out circulars to more business and professional women. After receiving subscription orders by return mail, he forwarded them to Lila Bell and Hazel, who signed each subscription order as a personal pledge that the subscriber could demand her money back if not satisfied.

At the end of four months, DeWitt moved to New York. Until he and Lila found an apartment, he wanted to be near the New York Public Library's main branch, on Fifth Avenue at Forty-second Street. When not sending out more solicitations, he spent long hours in the periodicals room, searching through hundreds of publications for articles and remarkable remarks of lasting value that he could condense or preserve. On some evenings and on the weekends, he took a train up to Pleasantville to see his fiancée.

DeWitt wanted to live in Greenwich Village, birthplace of many other magazines and literary journals and the bohemian capital of America. True to form, he intended to have as much fun as possible as he struggled to bring his idea to fruition. Eventually, he and Lila found a small apartment at 76 MacDougal Street, where they planned to live after they were married. They also rented a tiny basement office under a speakeasy, to serve as headquarters of the Reader's Digest Association at 1 Minetta Lane, just around the corner. The officers of the new corporation were DeWitt Wallace, who owned 52 percent of the stock, and Lila Bell Acheson, who owned the remaining 48 percent. DeWitt had no intention of giving his father or brother, who had lent him seed money, any ownership in the company—a decision that later became a source of considerable family friction.

In 1921 Greenwich Village was approaching its zenith as a mecca for writers, artists, and actors. Among its residents were dancer Martha Graham and socialist editor Max Eastman, both of whom were later to figure in the world of the *Reader's Digest*. Living only blocks away from the Wallaces were Marianne Moore, Theodore Dreiser, E. B. White, Carl Van Doren, and James Thurber. Just a short walk up the street, at 133 MacDougal, was the Provincetown Playhouse, where Eugene O'Neill got his start.

But the *Reader's Digest* was a Village anomaly. Unlike the *Masses,* the *Little Review,* the *Seven Arts,* or other legendary publications born in the crooked lanes south of Fourteenth Street, the *Digest* drew its inspiration not from the speakeasies and jazz clubs, from the plight of the oppressed or the latest aesthetic theory, but from the rolling cornfields and quiet small towns of the faraway heartland. Lila loved to dance and DeWitt liked to drink and party, but they were two unknowns living on the margins of bohemia, putting together a magazine that Village radicals would have sneered at if they had ever seen a copy.

As their wedding day approached, DeWitt and Lila worked feverishly to send out thousands of additional subscription appeals. He also wrote Barclay, who had by now married into money, thanking him for a $100 check. The hard-pressed young entrepreneur proceeded to ask him for another loan, explaining he wanted to do another mailing of 10,000 to solicit subscribers. At the end he summed up, "We have a good thing and must push it diligently."

Acheson and his wife, Pat, lived in an apartment on West 176th Street, and Lila doted on their only child, Judy. One autumn afternoon Acheson took a photograph of DeWitt and Lila in a neighborhood "snuggery." On everyone's mind, as Acheson later wrote his brother-in-law, were "two exciting subjects"—the imminent launch of what became the most widely read publication on earth and a wedding that united "two compatible hearts and heads for life."

Barclay Acheson himself soon set off for the war-ravaged Middle East, to work with the Near East Relief Fund and help establish the American University in Beirut.

On October 15, 1921, DeWitt, then thirty-two, and Lila, thirty-three, were married in the small Presbyterian church of Pleasantville, with Barclay officiating.* The only member of DeWitt's family in attendance was his brother Ben, who served as best man; his father and favorite aunt, Miriam, now Mrs. James Wallace, were conspicuously absent. Though Lila was close to her sisters, maid of honor was Hazel Cubberley. Lila's family was also represented by Barclay, his wife, and daughter, as well as by another Cubberley.

Afterward the small wedding party went next door to Mrs. Cornell's boardinghouse, where Lila had been a lodger. The wedding feast was prepared by Mrs. Essie Clark, the Negro cook. Then the newlyweds set off for the Poconos for a two-week honeymoon.

Upon their return DeWitt and Lila discovered that their last direct-mail effort had produced an extremely poor return. In despair, DeWitt wanted to abandon the project. But Lila continued to encourage him until his black mood passed. More important, she arranged for exactly what the struggling enterprise needed—a lot more money—by prevailing on Barclay to lend them $5,000. Meanwhile, she herself continued to work full-time with the Presbyterian board. To save on money, DeWitt and Lila sublet one room of their small apartment to a New York University instructor and his wife, sharing with them the kitchen and bath.

After several more mailings, DeWitt decided he had collected enough subscriptions to begin publishing and made arrangements with a Pittsburgh printer to prepare 5,000 copies. However, as it was too late to launch the publication in January, volume 1, number 1, of the *Reader's Digest* made its debut in February 1922.

---

*Curiously, no record of the ceremony exists in the church where the marriage took place, nor was the marriage recorded on the civil rolls of New York State. Similarly, there is no record of any legal union between DeWitt Wallace and Lila Bell Acheson in the archives of New York City, St. Paul, and Pittsburgh or their surrounding counties, where a marriage license might have been obtained. Yet some sort of ceremony indisputably took place on October 15, 1921, at the Presbyterian church, though the marriage certificate only compounds the mystery. While the names of DeWitt and Lila, the officiating minister, and all the guests are duly entered, the space for where the ceremony took place is conspicuously blank. Possibly, given DeWitt's later extramarital behavior, which Lila apparently tolerated and even to some degree emulated, an agreement to enter into an unconventional marriage was reached between the two, and what took place on October 15, 1921, was not a legal union but a purely ecclesiastical exchange of vows on the anniversary of the day of their engagement.

Only slightly less austere than the sample that DeWitt had prepared two years previously, the premier issue numbered sixty-four pages, including the black-and-white wraparound cover. At a pocket- or purse-sized five and a half by seven and a half inches, it was also an inch shorter and half an inch narrower than the original dummy of 1920. Several articles condensed for the archetype were included—testifying to DeWitt's belief that he was publishing material of permanent value. A block of type midway down the cover boldly stated that credo:

THIRTY-ONE ARTICLES EACH MONTH FROM LEADING MAGAZINES
—EACH ARTICLE OF ENDURING VALUE AND INTEREST, IN CONDENSED AND COMPACT FORM

Over those words, probably at Lila's suggestion, was a small art nouveau drawing of a young woman sitting within a circle, her voluminous skirt spilling into the white space below. In one hand she held a scroll, while with the other she composed with a long quill unfurling over her shoulder.

From its very first issue, the *Reader's Digest* established an editorial formula that it more or less faithfully adhered to for the next three-quarters of a century: three pleasantly patronizing tributes to women, two to animals; an inspirational profile of one of DeWitt's heroes, Henry Ford; useful pointers on how to get ahead in life and work; and assurances that common sense and a grasp of facts were society's great equalizers. The low proportion of humor in the first years of the magazine reflected his conviction that reading should be primarily informative, not entertaining. Only after success seemed assured did DeWitt open the floodgates of anecdotal Americana, jokes and double entendres, one-liners, and all variety of wordplay.

More significant, the young publisher also packed his fledgling magazine with articles pandering to the most reactionary elements among his readers. The only consistent liberal exceptions were those concerning sexual relationships, birth control, divorce reform, and similar topics, though always with a strong emphasis on monogamous marriage as a bedrock of society. The dichotomy between conservative publisher and sexually liberal, even radical, individual can be understood only by examining the public and private personas of DeWitt Wallace himself—a thirty-three-year-old man who was equally the creature of conservative midwestern values and the Roaring Twenties, the son of a Presbyterian preacher who was also the self-appointed "playboy of the Western world." In Wallace those disparate forces combined to form an astute opportunist who used the digest format of his publication as both pulpit and fig leaf. In promoting one set of values while pursuing another, he also established a pattern not only for himself but for dozens of top-rank Digesters that was to endure in Pleasantville for three generations. Hypocrisy, too, was a factor in the *Digest*'s editorial mix from the very start.

In its premier issue, the magazine struck a racist chord it was to sound in countless subtle variations over subsequent decades—in this instance, a crude endorsement of eugenics in an article reprinted from *Physical Culture* magazine entitled "Can We Have a Beautiful Human Race?" In the article author Albert Edward Wiggam complained that shiploads of "ugly women" were arriving by the millions at Ellis Island every year. "These women are giving us nearly *three* babies where the beautiful women of old American stocks are giving us *one*," huffed Wiggam, with the result that "the beauty of the American woman will steadily decline." His solution was to study the breeding methods of farmers who raised prizewinning horses and hogs. Another article discussed the "typically equivocal oriental" attitudes of Filipinos, who wanted at once independence from and the protection of the United States. Both selections implied that Protestant women were fair and Catholic women homely and ungrateful.

Sex was also modestly omnipresent in the maiden issue, although the emancipation of women was another bête noire for conservatives of the twenties, thanks to the suffrage movement, labor-saving devices liberating mothers and daughters from stove and washtub, and even a growing sophistication in the practice of birth control. Clara Bow had became the "It" girl of the silver screen, and everybody knew that "it" was sex appeal. And another St. Paul native, F. Scott Fitzgerald— DeWitt's junior by only seven years—had caused a sensation in 1920 with a first novel, *This Side of Paradise,* which related the adventures of its promiscuous hero Amory Blaine. By 1922, when the dowdy *RD* first stepped out, the hemline on women's skirts was knee high, and burlesque houses and taxi dance halls were common urban haunts. Not surprisingly, many conservatives saw all this commotion in the erogenous zone as a crisis of morality and the family.

DeWitt poked fun at those who took such a jaundiced view in a reprint from the *Ladies' Home Journal* titled, in a heavy-handed attempt at irony, "Whatever Is New for Women Is Wrong." The article suggested that men had been complaining in a similar vein about the political and social progress of the opposite sex for centuries. Since women were Wallace's primary target audience, he seconded the motion with another reprint, this time from *Woman's Home Companion,* called "Untying the Apron Strings." Yet a third entry aimed at women, and another acknowledgment that sexual mores were changing, was "Love—Luxury or Necessity?," reprinted from the *Delineator,* a fashion magazine. Despite its platitudinous message—that love was the greatest therapeutic force in the world—the article did quote sexual prophet D. H. Lawrence, who claimed that love was something to be learned "through centuries of patient effort." That primal reprint may also provide a clue to DeWitt's detached attitude toward and lifelong silence about his mother: "The mentally sick person," declared author Katharine Anthony, "is wrapped up in himself."

Assorted other articles and fillers in the premier issue also directly or indirectly kept the issue of sex before the reader—for example, Billy Sunday's unsettling piece of advice to husbands: "Try praising your wife, even if it does frighten her at first." The most puzzling of the original "Remarkable Remarks," and one whose meaning was to perplex succeeding generations of Digesters, was evangelist Homer Rodeheaver's observation "One cigaret will kill a cat."

All that, though, was but a token of things to come. In succeeding issues the *Digest* was to publish more and better sex information, and take a more progressive attitude toward sex in general, than any other commercial publication in the English language. Much to the dismay of his father and countless fundamentalist subscribers, DeWitt was also eventually to publish more off-color jokes than any other respectable magazine in history.

Like his sudden onset of passionate journal keeping in 1910, DeWitt's political and sexual philosophy cannot be explained by looking to his earlier writings or behavior for clues. Nothing in his previous notes to himself or in his correspondence hinted at his political or his private sexual beliefs, except for his curious complaint to his mother, while he was still in school, that marriage was a sure recipe for boredom. If anything, Lila's social activism, and the young couple's decision to live in one of the most radical neighborhoods in America, seemingly suggested a predisposition to sympathize with liberal causes.

Moreover, DeWitt's father, Dr. James Wallace, though he voted in favor of Prohibition in 1919, was in general moderately progressive in his political beliefs.

In old age both DeWitt and Lila sometimes liked to claim that working for the *Digest* was a form of ministry, and not a few Digesters were well aware—if somewhat ruefully—that being "a priest for the *Digest*" was part of their editorial lot. But that benign, missionary attitude toward his creation came to DeWitt only much later, when he was in his seventies. Until the very end of his life, he never went to church, refused (unlike Lila) even to identify himself as a Presbyterian in *Who's Who* or other collections of biographical data, and evinced a more or less hostile attitude toward organized religion. What Presbyterian influence there was on the young DeWitt Wallace was at the unconscious level.

Indisputably, though, some of the warring forces within American Protestantism at the time he began his magazine contributed to his enigmatic personality. In the early 1920s the United States was, in numbers and in ethos, still a Protestant country, dominated by the four mainline churches—Presbyterian, Congregational, Methodist, and Episcopalian. Though outwardly homogeneous, Protestantism was in fact at the breaking point. Both the teachings of Darwinists and the so-called higher criticism of Scripture developed in Europe in the nineteenth century were driving a wedge between mostly rural fundamentalists and the more liberal churches of the cities. Conservative-liberal rivalries were especially intense in the Baptist and the Presbyterian faiths, with the northern members of each generally in favor of trying to reconcile the teachings of the Bible with the recent findings of modern archaeology, history, and the natural sciences, while the southern members insisted on a literal interpretation of the Bible.

As a result of this basic disagreement, the Presbyterian church, like the Baptist, had split in two main parts, with the fundamentalists becoming the Presbyterian Church in the U.S., while the northerners were known as the Presbyterian Church (U.S.A.). A professor of Greek and religion in a northern city, DeWitt's father belonged to the United Presbyterian Church, a smaller northern denomination somewhat similar to the Presbyterian Church (U.S.A.). (The two were formally united in the 1950s.) At the national level both northern Presbyterian bodies were also growing increasingly aware of the need to preach another kind of gospel—the social gospel—to America's poor and dispossessed.

In the midst of all this conflict and upheaval were other factors imperiling the primacy of mainline Protestantism—the flood of Catholic immigrants from Europe, a restless Negro population, and a virulent form of postwar nationalism that was hostile to the Russian revolution and any form of radical socialism at home. All those forces were seen as threats to the white Protestant's assumption, heretofore practically a birthright, that America was his country, founded by his mostly British and Scotch-Irish forebears.

Presbyterians in particular were prone to holding such a view. Spiritual heirs of John Calvin, they had been driven from Scotland to America by way of Northern Ireland—like innumerable Puritans, with whom in temperament and beliefs they had much in common—by the English monarchy. More than any other major Protestant church, American Presbyterianism thus saw the United States as its true homeland and was so closely identified with the American Revolution that some members of the British Parliament referred to it as the "Presbyterian revolution."

DeWitt, however, adopted not the Presbyterianism of his enlightened father but that of the southern fundamentalists. The neophyte publisher had intuited the existence of a mass sensibility still deeply attached to God, country, and family and greatly disturbed by all the religious, economic, and racial turmoil in the country. At its ugliest, fundamentalist fear and revolt took the form of the Ku Klux Klan, established in 1915 and glamorized a year later in D. W. Griffith's landmark movie *The Birth of a Nation.* But even at its "best," rural fundamentalism was still passively hostile to Catholics, immigrants, Darwinism, and other cultural and scientific forces threatening Anglo-Saxon Protestant hegemony.

The *Reader's Digest,* from its very first issue, became the secular Bible of this deeply religious and immensely disaffected and fearful majority—three-fourths of whom still lived on farms. Even when its circulation numbered only in the thousands, the *RD* was a mass magazine in sensibility, taking the side of the vast conservative majority on almost every issue. Each month's selection of articles amounted to a personal credo, a manual for reinventing an older and better (namely, white Protestant) America. The mere fact that the magazine was a digest created the illusion that the editors were diligently culling the cream of the current magazine crop without regard for political content. An occasional liberal article further insinuated that, in "cross-examination" fashion, the editors were also dutifully presenting both sides of an issue—even when, as in the case of equal rights for Negroes, there were no two sides. In actuality, though, the *Digest* from the very beginning had a reactionary bias, which the very nature of the magazine camouflaged; and a majority of articles were derived from a relatively narrow range of publications, many of them obscure.

That is not to say, of course, that DeWitt Wallace did not also select articles from some of the major publications of the day. But many of these were also conservative to reactionary—notably the *Saturday Evening Post,* the *North American Review,* and (in its final years) *Scribner's,* which dominated the American scene, routinely profiled captains of industry and great inventors, cursed big government, opposed social and labor reform, and celebrated the virtue of self-reliance. Insofar as the magazines of America had for the past dozen years been DeWitt's real university, his own portable school of life, they probably contributed more to the formation of his conservative temperament and outlook than any other single factor.

Nevertheless, subscriptions continued to come in more slowly than expected. By the fifth issue DeWitt had again lost all hope and briefly returned to St. Paul to look for work. His moods descended on him like "a black cloud," Lila later told friends. Only when she realized that he "liked to worry" did she start "kidding him out of it."

Once a month DeWitt and Lila enlisted the help of the speakeasy customers and girls from a local community club to wrap and address the magazines, which were then transported by taxi to the post office. After each issue was mailed out, Lila and DeWitt celebrated with coffee and griddle cakes at a local Childs restaurant. Despite the low returns, he was late on payments to the printer in Pittsburgh only once during the first five months. After the sixth issue he switched to a plant in Floral Park, Long Island, because of shipping delays.

DeWitt also continued to do most of his reading, selecting, and condensing at the main branch of the New York Public Library. Working in the periodicals room, he transcribed his condensations directly onto yellow sheets of paper. Sitting side by side with him were the homeless derelicts from Bryant Park, which abuts the library, who came in to escape the cold. With amusement, but more often with irritation, DeWitt noted that the librarians had pegged him as just another eccentric.

By fall of the second year, subscriptions were up to 7,000, and DeWitt could afford a Corona typewriter and a foot-powered Elliott stencil-cutting machine with which to make subscription labels.

Around this same time, he and Lila also saw an advertisement on a Village bulletin board for a garage apartment in Pleasantville. Their lease was about to expire, and they needed both more privacy and more room for their growing publication. The notice of a vacancy in the village where they had been married seemed a sign. Immediately, they took a train up.

Stately, plump Pendleton Dudley, a New York public-relations man, was just finishing up a round of golf on the Nannahagen course when a young couple approached to ask about the apartment. Told they were struggling to establish a new publication called the *Reader's Digest,* he good-naturedly suggested they name their own rent for the one-bedroom apartment with dormer windows that sat over a garage. De-Witt and Lila offered $25 a month and later paid an additional $10 for the small stable next door, which they converted into an office. The unheated stable, which had a dirt floor, measured only ten by twelve feet.

———

PLEASANTVILLE, in 1922, was a storybook version of the American small town—spacious homes set far back on wide, tree-lined streets; handsome churches, mostly mainline Protestant, rising prosperously on picturesque corners in the best neighborhoods; and a thriving commercial district anchored by two big banks. Though many of the residents commuted by train to New York, others worked in local shops, schools, and the post office and almost never left their self-sufficient little world. Between May 1 and Labor Day, men wore straw boaters; and there were laws against tying a mule to a tree or playing cricket on Sunday. The speed limit on all vehicles, horse-drawn or otherwise, was fifteen miles an hour.

Pen Dudley lived in an area called Grandview, a modest middle-class neighborhood high up in the surrounding hills. But Pleasantville also had its mansion row, where Joseph Choate, former ambassador to Great Britain, and a state senator lived. The most famous of the town's fifteen hundred inhabitants was asbestos king Harold Manville. Famous in his own way was Manville's playboy son Tommy, who occupied a house elsewhere on the family estate.

On Christmas in 1923 the *Reader's Digest* offered potential readers a special rate of $2.75 for a year's subscription, or $2.50 each for two or more additional subscriptions. Any subscriber who obtained ten new subscriptions got a year's free renewal. The table of contents was also shifted from the inside to the outside cover, where, front or back, it has remained ever since. The logo was reset in Old English, over the capitalized word "service." The legend was modified to read,

"AN ARTICLE A DAY" FROM LEADING MAGAZINES
—EACH ARTICLE OF ENDURING VALUE AND INTEREST
IN CONDENSED, PERMANENT BOOKLET FORM

Among the writers whose work the *RD* condensed in 1922–23 were renowned preacher Harry Emerson Fosdick, journalist Lincoln Steffens, botanist Luther Burbank, novelists John Galsworthy and H. G. Wells, philosopher Bertrand Russell, and poet Gabriele D'Annunzio. DeWitt invented catchy, often alliterative titles with ease—"Burnam and the Birth Rate," "What Is Marriage?" and "What Is a Girl to Do?" But he also continued to run articles of the most reprehensible sort.

Jews, for example, fared even worse than the misshapen immigrants or wily Filipinos castigated in the premier issue. A subsequent article about dishonest tradesmen named only two firms—Gross & Levison (also known as Golden & Markowitz), arsonist jobbers who later resurfaced as proprietors of a retail furniture store. A two-part piece in February and March 1923 titled "The Menace of the Polish Jew" insinuated that Polish Jews in America sided with the Soviets. The provocatively titled "Do the Jews Dominate American Finance?," part of a series on Jews reprinted from the *World's Work,* a Doubleday publication, fatuously confirmed a number of anti-Semitic prejudices: that Jews occupied their "present isolated position" in the community of nations because they lacked "that aptitude for coherence and organization whose ultimate expression is nationality." Author Burton J. Hendrick further claimed that the "Jewish mind" was deficient in two qualities—"the creative faculty and the ability to organize or to cooperate." In short, the Jew was too stupid, too avariciously self-centered, to be a team member who could one day rise to be the director of a large corporation. Proof was that he liked to carry diamonds in his pocket.

———

IN THE SUMMERS of 1923 and 1924, and during Christmas and Easter vacations in between, a young Smith College student named Florence Forth worked part-time for the *Reader's Digest.* Her job was to write letters soliciting subscriptions. DeWitt now obtained lists from church groups, professional societies, and teachers' associations, in addition to women's organizations. Since each letter was to be personalized, Forth was able to complete only twenty to twenty-five a day. Working all alone in the stable, she earned a salary of twelve dollars a week.

DeWitt—or Wally, as everybody now called him, following Lila's less stuffy example—sometimes stopped by, usually to say he was off to visit the printer or make a small correction on one of her letters. He insisted that the letters be written by hand. Many were sent to missionaries, Catholic as well as Protestant, in Africa. Sometimes Wally told her to offer them so many issues free, or to send a sample issue. Forth also kept a primitive file of everyone she wrote to and their replies, though there were no filing cabinets—only brown cardboard boxes stacked on the floor. Wally had knocked a small window out of the wall, and Forth used the foot-and-a-half-wide sill as a desk. A broken-down stool served as her chair. Wally worked upstairs in his apartment when he was not at the library or off on an errand.

To keep warm in the unheated stable, Forth wore galoshes and an old raccoon coat. Wally liked to bundle up in a heavy lumberjack's mackinaw. He also wore the same baggy-kneed trousers and the same shirt every day of the week. Before retiring at midnight, Dudley often observed lights burning in the stable workshop.

That first summer Wally skipped an issue, ostensibly because of the "seasonal preponderance" of fiction in the magazines, and managed to take a vacation, though subscriptions were duly extended by a month. He and Lila also sometimes took long working weekends to Nantucket or the Poconos. Forth recalled that Wally was mostly quiet and very shy and seldom smiled. But never once did he ask if he was giving her too much work, and only kept piling it on. She decided he did not give a "continental" about what happened to other people. Nor did he ever mention Lila, who still worked for the Presbyterian board. For the first two years of the *Digest*'s existence, her salary kept both their household and their struggling enterprise afloat.

The stable did not contain a bathroom, and Forth was not permitted to use the Wallaces' upstairs. One wintry day, though desperate to use the facilities, she waited until returning home at noon. Her mother, enraged, telephoned Wally and informed him that his sole employee would not be returning to work, because of the way he treated her. When he made a crass comment, she called him a sheepherder, adding, "You have no respect for women."

Wally had bought himself a Studebaker convertible, and once a month he drove out to Floral Park to load the car with copies of the latest issue. One trip sufficed. Buck Cornell, a local high school student whose mother owned the boardinghouse where Lila had once roomed, helped Wally wrap the magazines and take them to the post office. Many were complimentary—sent to more ministers, presidents of universities, doctors. Sometimes Cornell was sent into the city on an errand. More than once, after he boarded the train in Pleasantville, Wally got on in Thornwood, the next stop down the line. Cornell watched as Wally walked down the aisle, looking for an abandoned issue of the *New York Times.*

There was a stationery store in Pleasantville called Peter's, run by two brothers. Wally frequented the store to borrow magazines, which he returned the next day. Once he tried to persuade the brothers to buy enough equipment to print the *Reader's Digest,* but—to their later regret—they turned him down because they had no money.

As for Lila, Buck Cornell thought she was outwardly gracious but inwardly "a little snippy."

At the end of the Wallaces' second year of marriage, subscriptions were coming in at a high enough rate that Lila was able to quit her job and stay at home. Another factor was her poor health, though no one was ever quite sure of the nature of her illness. According to the later testimony of one of Wally's mistresses, Lila underwent two abortions, the first of which probably took place around this time.

2

The Presbyters of
Pleasantville

ONE September morning in 1925 a footloose young man four years out of Harvard stepped down onto the Pleasantville train platform. Ralph Henderson had grown up in a remote part of Burma, where his parents were medical missionaries, and later he himself served a four-year term as an organizer for the American Baptist Foreign Mission Society. Now he was looking for a job. He had no prospects and no money except for a few unredeemed traveler's checks.

The night before, at a friend's house in nearby White Plains, Henderson had browsed through a small magazine and learned that its office was "just up the line." Henderson decided to pay a visit. At the country train station, he asked the station master for directions. The man replied that he had never heard of the *Reader's Digest*.

Eventually, Henderson found an American Express agent heaving cartons into a hand truck. The agent told the sandy-haired stranger to walk about a mile up a hill and look for the garage of a man named Pen Dudley. It was a crisp, bright day, and as Henderson walked along he observed a sign put up by the Rotary Club: "Pleasantville, All That the Name Implies."

Passing through a hedge at the top of the hill, he saw a stone garage with a pony stable attached. Standing outside, wearing white linen plus fours and open shirt, was a tall, slender man obviously enjoying a cigarette break. He seemed surprised to have a caller. Henderson explained he had seen the magazine only the previous night, but he liked it and now came in search of a job.

DeWitt Wallace courteously gave his visitor a tour of the crowded office. Two girls were at work cutting Elliott stencils, which contained the addresses of subscribers. The proprietor noted he had just bought a new rack to hold another 100,000—probably more, he added, than he would ever need. Henderson saw there was no room for a third desk.

Outside, carpenters were at work nearby, building a slate-roofed cottage. Having bought some property from their landlord, the Wallaces planned to use its first floor as an office and live in the studio apartment overhead. After DeWitt introduced Henderson to Lila—whom he later described as "blonde, blue-eyed and charming"—the visitor inquired where Hazel J. Cubberley, the other editor listed on the masthead, had her office.

As it was nearly noon, Wally suggested the two of them visit a local restaurant, since Lila preferred to skip the midday meal. Over a plate lunch and a cup of coffee, he talked freely about himself and his magazine. Henderson was also a PK, or preacher's kid, as Lila liked to call her husband and herself, and that formed the basis for an immediate rapport.

Wally revealed that he lived simply and seldom took time off. One of the office girls helped Lila with housework. He himself was publisher, editor, and janitor. Henderson said he was pretty handy with a broom, too. He added that he had written a few pieces for such magazines as *Forum* and *Asia*. Wally proposed that he examine a dozen current publications and see which articles had "usability." Henderson found Wally's manner curiously diffident. Wally spoke in such soft undertones that he was often indistinct, so Henderson frequently had no idea what the man was saying.

A few days later Wally sent a note saying the visit was not unappreciated. Shortly afterward Henderson submitted a magazine report that bore a deadly resemblance to a Harvard term paper. It was never mentioned again, but in late September 1925 the young ex-missionary became the *Digest*'s first full-time employee. Henderson was put on a trial basis for $150 a month—a stipulation never officially terminated. He had no inkling he would work for the *Digest* for half a century and ultimately become one of its most important employees.

Before long the Wallaces moved into their new half-timbered stucco home with its blue slate roof. The new office measured twenty by thirty feet and boasted a high arched ceiling, four desks, filing cabinets, and a bathroom. Henderson's job was to do everything—everything, that is, except editorial work. Soon a fourth person was hired, a young local woman of Portuguese descent named Francesca Quarenghi. Henderson also did janitorial duty after the office closed at 4 P.M. Quarenghi took over the housework for the Wallaces and prepared their evening meal. Later her sister Suzanne also joined the staff, working in circulation.

Lila had a piano and played hesitantly, but in later years Henderson liked to recall that "the click of the Corona and the notes of 'Blue Room' sometimes reached the studio in a mingled sonata." At other times he found himself holding his breath as Lila paused to try again for a missed note.

At the end of the day, Wally occasionally shoved a few desks together as a base for a plywood Ping-Pong table, and the two men slammed away at each other for a hot half hour before Henderson walked back down the hill to his boardinghouse room. Not only was Wally a very good Ping-Pong player, but he liked to play with a cat on the table.

Henderson gained an insight into Wally's direct-mail technique when he discovered that the house journal of the YMCA was regularly delivered to the office. One of its columns was devoted to job transfers with new addresses of YWCA secretaries. Wally suggested that Henderson clip it regularly. When his expression implied that he did not see the point, Wally explained, "This girl, let's say, has just been sent to a strange town. She will be lonely until she finds new friends. A letter—any letter, even a promotion piece—will look very good to her. She'll read every word." And so the *Reader's Digest* mailing list continued to grow, by a few dozen names per month. Henderson noticed that most of the YWCA secretaries he wrote to seemed to become subscribers.

Thousands of other letters were sent out to more general lists—teachers, ministers, social workers. Wally insisted that the envelopes be attractively addressed and asked Henderson to find a woman with a distinguished handwriting. An advertisement was placed in the county newspaper, and several replies were received. Henderson soon learned that genteel old ladies who enjoyed the work were best suited to the task. Every Friday morning he drove to half a dozen homes in the area, carrying cases of envelopes in the rumble seat of Wally's workhorse Studebaker, and exchanged them for those addressed during the preceding week.

Once a month Henderson also transported bundles of brown paper wrappers addressed by Elliott stencil to the Mayflower Press on Long Island. The first time Wally entrusted him with the task, Henderson was too nervous to admit he had never driven a gearshift car—his only experience being a foot-pedal Model T. Nor did he confess that Long Island was as unfamiliar to him as Tierra del Fuego.

To make matters worse, the next morning Henderson awoke to discover that a deep snow had fallen. After figuring out how to shift, he drove for forty miles in second gear into Manhattan, where at the Fifty-ninth Street bridge he bumped into a taxi. Eventually, though, he made it to Floral Park. Henderson never forgot the press run for that day: 16,500.

As the magazine continued to grow, Wally hired yet another full-time employee to help out on the business side. Harold A. Lynch, who bore a striking resemblance to the comedian W. C. Fields, had been assistant rector at St. Mark's-in-the-Bouwerie Episcopal Church in Manhattan and later served at the Episcopal church in Pleasantville. After Lynch's dismissal from the congregation, for adultery, Wally—to be devilish—hired him. Lynch succeeded to the post of business manager, while Henderson became the second person after Wally to work on the magazine's editorial side.

In New York there was a Welshman named Arthur E. Griffiths who handled promotion for the *New York Journal of Commerce*. His wife was a good friend of Lila's. He and Wally had an arrangement: all letters marked "inquiry" were sold to him for fifty cents each. Griffiths was not only credited for any subscription he brought in but also given a substantial credit on renewals. Over a period of time Griffiths' direct-mail effort became a moderately lucrative sideline.

As the operation grew, queries and complaints for Griffiths were constantly getting mixed up with those managed by Henderson and Quarenghi. One day, in frustration, Henderson told Wally that, whatever the cost of his friendship with Griffiths, the operation had to be unified and his authority and ownership made absolute. Wally agreed. Several weeks later he solved the problem by hiring "Griff" to become the *Digest*'s third business manager. Harold Lynch joined Henderson as a jack-of-all-trades and editorial assistant. But in such major areas as printing contracts, the purchase of paper, and relations with magazine publishers, Wally continued to keep his own counsel. According to Henderson, there was no grand design for the *Digest*'s future, "just a man improvising his way against heavy odds."

A critical factor in the *Digest*'s fragile prosperity was that Wally paid nothing for the articles he selected and condensed from other publications—in other words, the entire content of his magazine. This was in marked contrast to his earlier conscientiousness about permissions, back when the magazine was still a publisher's sample. But permissions cost money, and in the meantime Wally had discovered that observing all the niceties of copyright law was a luxury he could ill afford.

Wally's rationale was that usage of material provided beneficial publicity for the magazines quoted. But Henderson soon realized that Wally regarded some magazines as unsafe to use. The least Wally had to worry about, if another publisher discovered that the *Digest* was secretly infringing on its copyright, was demand for payment. Much worse was the specter of a group of incensed publishers getting an injunction—thus effectively halting the *Reader's Digest* in midstride. To make sure that did not happen, Wally for years limited his direct-mail promotions to points beyond a 500-mile radius of New York. That way no editor or publisher was likely to come across the little digest accidentally and discover that it was stealing copyrighted material wholesale. Until at least 1929 Wally paid nothing for his reprints, except perhaps for those taken from the very biggest publications.

There was a precedent for excerpting magazines in digests, of course. The British *Literary Digest* and the American *Review of Reviews* were well-respected journals that were always careful to put quotation marks around verbatim passages and to summarize the rest, though the result was a somewhat disjointed product. Wally avoided such conventions by condensing articles, but the principle remained the same.

Fortunately for the young publisher, nobody paid much attention to the nascent *Reader's Digest.* Two other magazines were also just starting up—*Time,* edited by a pair of young men from Yale named Henry R. Luce and Briton Hadden, and the *New Yorker,* under Harold Ross, a former editor of *Stars and Stripes. Time* had an elaborate masthead, the *New Yorker* none, but both were very much in the public eye. Each was creating a sensation by reinventing the way journalism was written. At its incorporation in 1922 *Time* had seventy shareholders—forty-six of them Yale men and fourteen of them classmates of Luce and Hadden. On March 3, 1923, the first issue of *Time* appeared on the newsstands.

The origins of the *New Yorker* are more clouded in obscurity, but most likely the idea for the magazine grew out of a series of conversations between Ross and Alexander Woollcott, one of the preeminent writers of the day and a luminary of the famed Algonquin Round Table. For financing, Ross turned to a fellow poker player, Raoul Fleischmann, heir to the yeast fortune.

Wally, by contrast, was a loner—up on his hill, forty miles away. What he was selectively reinventing was an old-fashioned, permanent idea of America that bore little resemblance to *Time*'s fast-paced world or the hectic, sophisticated metropolis as seen through the monocle of Eustace Tilley. Rather, the *Digest* was month by month penetrating the largely isolated rural countryside. Unlike other large-circulation magazines, which were directed mostly to an urban readership, it catered to an audience starved not only for information and entertainment but for attention.

If anything, the *Digest* had much more in common with another means of mass communication (the first, in fact), whose golden age was just then beginning—radio. Thanks to Edwin H. Armstrong's recent invention of the superheterodyne circuit and to the enterprise of men like David Sarnoff of the Radio Corporation of America, radio was bringing an unprecedented variety of entertainment, news, and inspiration—just like the *RD*—into America's vast heartland. Sarnoff and Wally were later to become friends and even to cooperate on a *Digest* journalism project.

But Wally did share a few qualities with his more famous contemporaries in publishing. Like himself, Luce was a PK of the Presbyterian variety, and Ross had a similar passion for anonymity even as he edited one of the most visible magazines in the English-speaking world. Wally also shared Ross's fondness for poker. But the two men were not to meet for another score of years, with disastrous consequences for the *Digest*.

While Wally worked, Lila, whose days were spent in suburban dolce far niente, tended to her roses. Yet she did come up with one great original idea—the gift subscription. As Christmas approached, in either 1925 or 1926, she suggested to her husband that a gift subscription should also look special, so she designed a royal purple envelope on stiff, handcrafted paper. A copy of the magazine was inserted into the envelope, which was then tied with a wraparound cord and hand-addressed.

Though the gift subscriptions poured in by the thousands, the Wal-

laces' domestic arrangement almost collapsed under the strain of fulfillment, since everyone, Lila included, worked frantically to send the
announcements out on time. Wally also kept the cost a secret, though
he made a point of congratulating Lila often and profusely. But in the
next year the *Digest* decided to simplify the operation and sent out only
a personalized gift card.

The end of the working day usually found Wally hunched over his
typewriter, following the pencil markings on an edited magazine page.
He condensed as he typed, occasionally adding a connecting passage in
his own words, and did not even make carbons.

L*IKE* the sample issue of 1920, each condensation in those early years
was confined to exactly two *Digest* pages, or approximately 1,300
words—though many were even shorter, to allow for filler or promotional material. Every single piece of paper flowed through Wally's
Corona typewriter. His quota was six manuscript pages per day,
though he often had to abandon his editorial work for other chores,
which meant catching the 9:22 train the next morning and making a
dash for the printer with last-minute copy. Henderson remembered
that Wally enjoyed pacing the station, waiting for the train to come,
because it gave him time to think and exercise.

As early as 1925 Wally tested the *Digest* on newsstands in Cleveland
and Los Angeles. The test showed that single-copy sales would do
well. But he held back for several reasons: the magazine had been
selling itself as a special service to subscribers who might not renew
once they saw it so widely available; and a public display of the magazine might invite competition from publishers with far greater financial resources. Even his source magazines might regard him as a competitor. Then there was the copyright problem.

By 1926 circulation had reached 20,000; in the next three years—
thanks to relentless direct-mail solicitations—it grew an extraordinary
tenfold, to 216,190. Like the stable before it, the studio office quickly
became too small to contain the burgeoning colossus, and Wally was
obliged to rent out the basement and upper floor of the Pleasantville
post office, then two floors of a bank building, then three more floors
of another bank building. As the offices spread, practically anyone in
Pleasantville who wanted a job could get one at the *Digest.*

To help out with the scouring of publications for filler material and short items for the magazine's various humor departments, Wally enlisted the aid of a favorite cousin, Lucy Notestein, who lived in Cleveland. The main branch of the public library in that city was one of the few in the United States with open stacks, which considerably facilitated a search of periodicals. As her responsibilities grew, Notestein hired first one and then several assistants and began to do occasional condensations of books as well. Unofficially in the beginning, and officially later, the Cleveland office of the *Reader's Digest* became the magazine's excerpt department.

Despite appearances, including the battered Studebaker convertible he perversely insisted on keeping, Wally was becoming prosperous, almost month by month. He began sporting tailor-made tweed suits, while Lila bought his ties from Liberty or Sulka. He was tall, strikingly handsome, moved with athletic grace, listened more than he talked, and kept his blond hair close-cropped. The preacher's son was also a chain-smoker and liked to drink and to play poker, usually with Henderson, Dudley, Griffiths, and Lynch.

Wally and Lila rarely socialized as a couple, which was a source of some friction. The gregarious Lila wanted to go out dancing, but Wally was still too wrapped up in his work to permit himself the time and expense of anything more than a very occasional full-dress night out on the town. When they did go out or invite a few friends over for dinner, it was always the same few *Digest* employees and their spouses. Sometimes Henderson brought his mandolin along, and everyone sat around the living room, singing old favorites.

———

THE *Digest* continued to publish political articles espousing conservative to reactionary views. During the Scopes trial in the summer of 1925, it sided with the fundamentalists. An article in the January 1926 issue was titled "The Klan: Defender of Americanism." Author Hiram Wesley Evans, imperial wizard, declared, "A Jew may say or write what he pleases against America and American ways, but if an American voices the least criticism of a Jew . . . the liberals turn to and hound him."

Wally also mastered the art of condensing snake oil. In August 1927 the *Digest* ran an article called "How NOT to Have Cancer" whose message was better body drainage. Anyone who took cathartics regularly need have "no fear of cancer, appendicitis, neuritis, neuralgia, sleeplessness, and a great number of other ailments." Quick and easy remedies for poison ivy, dementia praecox, baldness, meningitis, pneumonia, peritonitis, pellagra, cross-eyes, acne, dandruff, and leprosy were to follow in short order.

Wally was not content to provide his readers with only medical cures and remedies. *Digest* readers were soon told that, with a little spunk and ingenuity, any obstacle could be surmounted. Every issue contained at least one and often two articles that took an ordinary problem—lack of self-confidence, the approach of middle age, "mental atrophy"—and offered a quick and easy but commonsensical solution. Hobbies, for instance, were suggested as an ideal way to keep mentally active. The example of others, both famous and unknown, assured the reader that the accomplishment of some worthwhile goal was always within reach. But the most powerful motivating factor was each individual's untapped inner strength—often rediscovered through prayer. Wally dubbed this category of article "the art of living."

During the 1928 presidential campaign Wally pandered to deep-rooted Protestant suspicion of Roman Catholics. The contest pitted Republican candidate Herbert Hoover against New York governor Al Smith, whose Catholicism overshadowed the fact that he was also a Democrat. Among the articles Wally reprinted was "An Open Letter to Governor Smith," which declared that "dogmatic intolerance is the incontestable right and sacred duty of the Roman Catholic Church." In March 1928 Wally ran an article called "The Heresy of the Parochial Schools," which claimed that Catholic schools stifled independent thought. Even after the election, in July 1929, the *Digest* published "What It Means to Marry a Catholic." A later article resolutely answered in the negative the question "Will America Become Catholic?"

Despite the magazine's pronounced American flavor, as early as 1928 Wally had the idea of starting up an edition of the *Reader's Digest* in London and corresponded with a British news agent named Kimball Root. The agent reported that British publishers were attracted to the magazine's "editorial plan," but he thought that "an American education would be required in people who would reach out to buy the *Reader's Digest.*" He noted that the average reader in England was highly class conscious and did not try to educate himself by "reading beyond his class," in contrast to the average American reader, who avidly read "everything he can lay his hands on that will broaden him and improve his position." But Root did offer to distribute a thousand copies a month on a commission basis. Wally did not pursue the offer.

In every decision Wally made, his principal consideration was to put the *Digest* before as many readers as possible. Thus in 1928 it became the only national magazine to be printed in Braille characters and available at cost to blind readers. Just like his father, struggling to put Macalester College on a secure financial footing, Wally had become preacher and president of his own nondenominational people's university.

Though the *Digest* was not yet on the newsstands, it had already begun to attract imitators. Two in particular caused Wally some concern—*Current Reading,* a Canadian publication which mimicked the *Digest's* typeface and editorial format; and *Sneed's Digest.* Both were given wide newsstand display. But Dr. Wallace could note in one of his many encouraging letters to his son, "You have the most suggestive name—*Reader's Digest.* . . . The new ventures will seem mere imitations. That itself will hurt them from the very beginning."

Even Wally's father had no notion of how successful his son's little magazine really was—that he had just banked a breathtaking $600,000 and would soon double that amount.

Though all of the *Digest's* imitators did eventually die off, more than a hundred were to spring up over time—not only in the United States but in China, Mexico, Canada, Cuba, and Germany as well. Within a few years there were more than twenty in the United States alone, some of them quite specialized. One, for example, was devoted only to stamp collecting; another, to communism.

But finally one imitator, *Fleet's Review,* posed a serious enough threat that Wally took it to court to protect his franchise. The shoe was now on the other foot, and Wally himself had to fend off those stealing his format and editorial mix.

The success of *Fleet's Review* on the newsstands, until Wally forced it to stop imitating the *RD,* also convinced him that he could no longer keep his magazine competitive solely through subscriptions. His first choice as a distributor, the American News Company, was the giant in the business. Wally, however, was unable to come to terms with ANC and blamed the lack of an agreement on the venality of the company's Jewish management.

But Wilbert Smith, president of a smaller distribution company called S-M News, liked the *Digest* and solicited it as a client. Wally took the train into New York to meet with S-M executives, one of whom was Albert Leslie Cole, a stocky, florid thirty-four-year-old bulldog of a man with decided conservative opinions and an insatiable appetite for hard work.

Al Cole's was a typical Horatio Alger–like success story. Born in Chicago in 1894, the son of Albert Channing Cole and Frances Deininger, Cole attended public schools in New York, where his family had moved to, before dropping out at age sixteen. Soon afterward, while walking down a street, he saw a Help Wanted sign in a woolens factory. He was hired at five dollars a week but was told he could not start until the following Tuesday. While waiting for that day to come around, he heard of another job paying the same wage but starting on Monday. So he went to work as an office boy for the Munsey Publishing Company. A few years later he joined the *World Advance,* in time renamed *Popular Science Monthly,* as an advertising salesman.

During World War I, Cole spent a year as an ensign in the navy. He returned to *Popular Science,* became eastern sales manager, and advanced to the position of advertising manager. In 1925 *Popular Science* and *McCall's* magazine joined forces to form the S-M News Company—the initials stood for "Science-McCall's"—and Cole was elected a director. Four years later he was named *Popular Science*'s president and publisher.

Wally still had some doubts about the wisdom of putting the *Digest* on the newsstands. Now, though, his main concern was the reprint fees he would have to begin paying—something he had gotten away with not doing for more than seven years. In April 1929 Dr. Wallace finally persuaded his son that payment to other magazines was necessary because they needed to make all they could and because there was "a certain justice in it." He noted, in unchurchly fashion, "You could not pay for all your articles but you could for several of the best unless the magazine asked an exorbitant price."

Cole thought that the *Digest* had great newsstand potential and did some tests in Cleveland, San Francisco, Los Angeles, and Seattle and on stands operated by distributor Fred Harvey on the Santa Fe Railroad. The tests convinced Wally that putting his magazine on the newsstands was worth the risk of arousing the suspicions of his source publications or inviting more competition.

In April 1929 the *Digest,* which at the time had a circulation of 220,000, made its newsstand debut. S-M News placed 100,000 copies with vendors and sold a phenomenal 62,000, thereby increasing circulation by another 30 percent. A 62 percent sale, high even for an established magazine, was virtually unheard-of for the unpublicized debut of a new publication.

In 1932, the year the *Digest*'s school edition was launched, Wally invited Cole to leave S-M and become the *RD*'s circulation director. Cole declined but proposed that S-M promote the magazine for six months, free of charge, on a trial basis. If the results were favorable, Wally would then have the option of continuing the arrangement for a fee. Cole had recently hired a man named Frank Herbert, former head of promotions for the *Literary Digest*, who would be assigned the project. Wally agreed, with the result that Herbert and Cole began making regular visits to Pleasantville. One of their first creations was a subscription offer for one dollar. They showed it to Wally, who liked it but said he first wanted to show it to Lila. Later he reported back to Cole that she thought it looked like a cheap Sears, Roebuck circular.

"Well, you asked us to help," Cole replied. "At least try it." Wally tried it. In Cole's words, the promotion "sold like hell."

The six-month arrangement was extended, only now Wally paid S-M News a healthy fee—20 percent of all new subscriptions. One day, some time later, Wally invited Cole and Herbert up to Pleasantville for a game of poker. Circulation currently stood above 300,000. But Wally declared that the two men were making too much money. (Assuming Cole and Herbert had brought in a minimum of 50,000 subscribers, S-M would have earned a commission of slightly less than $30,000.) Cole thought Wally was "a goddamned unappreciative fellow" but defended the fee because Wally received 80 percent (or $120,000) of the additional income. Moreover, neither Cole nor Herbert benefited personally. But Wally was adamant and insisted on new terms. Cole refused. All three men quit the poker game feeling testy and unhappy. Cole thought, "That's the end of Wallace."

S-M News continued to distribute the magazine, but the promotions ceased. A year later Wally invited Cole to lunch. When they met, he said he wanted to resume the arrangement. Cole agreed, but only on the original terms. Wally consented. Another factor was that bookkeeper Arthur Griffiths' womanizing had begun to interfere with his work. Wally hoped to replace him with Cole, who along with Herbert now began promoting the magazine again.

Wally made numerous job offers to Cole during those years. With the American economy in collapse—nearly fifteen million workers unemployed, 5,000 banks closed, average personal income down by more than half—*Popular Science,* like many other businesses, was going through very rough times. Cole had reduced his own salary by a third, dismissed the entire art staff, and cut everybody else's salary by 20 percent. Meanwhile, the circulation of the *Reader's Digest* continued to soar. With good reason, Cole once observed, "Wally never knew there was a Depression. Ever."

Wally did, in fact, suffer a few economic reverses as a result of the Depression, but they had no effect on the magazine. Early in 1929 Dr. Wallace cautioned his son about playing the stock market. Over the past six months, he also gently suggested, "the grade of articles in the *Digest* has not kept up quite so high a level of seriousness and importance as they had been, catering a little more to the lighter minded readers. I should set quality over quantity even if your subscription list does not grow quite so fast."

On November 13, 1929, two weeks after the collapse of the stock market, Dr. Wallace consoled DeWitt and Lila, who had lost heavily by buying on margin: "You should religiously avoid that kind of gambling. The losses have been appalling all over the country. It will not have much effect on general business." But on the whole, the letters from Pater—as he often signed himself—were a fatherly mixture of encouragement, reminders to go to church, and praise for the magazine's "high level of excellence."

As the readership of the *Digest* grew, Wally shifted the printing of his magazine from Long Island to the Rumford Press in Concord, New Hampshire, and soon became its biggest client. The *Digest* was now far larger than many of the publications it was excerpting. While gratifying in some respects, the situation was not without ominous overtones. Although by now he had decided to pay his source magazines a reprint fee, Wally knew they might not be so accommodating if they discovered how much newsstand revenue was being siphoned off by the little magazine out in the boondocks. The twenty-five cents charged by the *Digest* was high compared with the fifteen-cent cover price of the *Saturday Evening Post* or the nickel it cost to buy a copy of *Scribner's.* The *Digest* was, on the one hand, draining away their newsstand lifeblood and, on the other, reproducing the best of their editorial material. Wally's problem was to make sure they never got hold of enough information to put two and two together.

It was now that the *Digest* began to earn its well-deserved reputation for secrecy. For the first eight years of its existence, DeWitt Wallace took great care to hide the extraordinary success of his magazine. Since it did not carry advertising, he did not have to submit to an annual circulation audit. There may also have been more necessity than virtue in the *Digest*'s initial decision not to accept advertising. With typical thoroughness, Wally explored the idea of accepting advertisements as early as 1929. A publisher's representative, J. Fred Henry, drew up an analysis of circulation and advertising rates of ten leading magazines that from an advertiser's viewpoint would be considered in a class with the *Digest*. His conclusion: the magazine could sell its advertising at an average page rate of $450 and expect to net $4,898.75 per issue, or $58,785 annually.

But the additional revenue simply did not outweigh the risk of alienating Wally's sources. He knew that by accepting advertising he would also be taking away from them yet another source of revenue— and that might be the straw that broke the *RD*'s back. Even so, the magazine's growth was so conspicuous and meteoric that by 1930 most major magazine publishers, many of them struggling to survive in the wake of the stock market crash of October 1929, now suspected that the *Digest* had a circulation equaling or perhaps exceeding their own.

For a time *Scribner's* even balked at letting the *Digest* reprint more articles, while the *Atlantic Monthly* and other publications considered following suit. The nightmarish prospect of a boycott of the *Digest* by its source magazines seemed more likely than ever.

At this point Wally decided not only that the cheap ride was over but that it would be reckless to try to get any more mileage out of it. Over a series of months he approached his more important source publications and offered them a blanket fee for exclusive rights to reprint for a stated period an article a month in the *Reader's Digest*. Contracts varied in length, and terms were never revealed. The *American Magazine* and the *Saturday Evening Post* at first held out. But Wally paid a personal visit to the *Post*'s presiding editorial genius, George Horace Lorimer, and persuaded him to relent.

Soon the *Reader's Digest*, now up to 112 pages from its original 64, held exclusive reprint agreements with thirty-five American magazines, including all those which had threatened to withdraw. The terms were so generous that many found it not only difficult but suicidal to refuse. Among the publications Wally signed up were the *North American Review, Century, Forum, Woman's Home Companion, McClure's, Collier's,* and *Review of Reviews.* William Randolph Hearst, the one man who had originally had some inkling of the *Digest*'s potential, alone refused to let Wally reprint from any of his magazines. More than anyone else, he understood that the *Digest* was a serious newsstand competitor. But unlike smaller publications suffering from a decline in advertising and newsstand revenues, he was not dependent on handouts from Pleasantville for his survival.

The exclusive contracts had a dual purpose. Not only did they ensure the *Reader's Digest* a plentiful source of material; they all but dealt a death blow to its various imitators, who were now forced to reprint from obscure publications or settle for whatever Wally himself rejected.

As the magazine grew, Wally also hired editors from publications that were falling victim to the Depression. By far the most important editor he hired in those formative years, and perhaps ever, was Kenneth W. Payne, who joined the *Digest* as managing editor in 1930.

———

BORN in Cleveland in 1890, Ken Payne had studied at the Sorbonne and the University of Wisconsin before going into newspaper work. After serving as a war correspondent for the Newspaper Enterprise of London, he did a stint as managing editor of the *People's Home Journal* before winding up as editorial director of the *North American Review.* A once prestigious literary journal, with Henry Adams only one of its many illustrious editors, and Mark Twain and historian Francis Parkman among its contributors, the *NAR* later degenerated into a magazine espousing extreme right-wing views before passing into hate-mongering oblivion toward the end of the 1930s.

As editor of the *NAR,* Payne had been among the first to sign an exclusive reprint contract with the *Digest,* and he was instrumental in encouraging several of his wavering colleagues at other publications to sign as well. At *Scribner's,* in particular, he was in constant touch with Alfred S. ("Fritz") Dashiell, the magazine's managing editor, who kept him posted on management's attitude toward the Pleasantville upstart. Payne then relayed the information to Wally.

Now that the *Digest* had become a major publication, Wally wanted someone in Pleasantville who was not only a skilled editor but a good administrator. Typically, he hired Payne despite the fact that Cole—whose advice on editorial matters was never sought—had once fired him for incompetence at *Popular Science,* where he also served briefly as editor. Wiry, dark-haired, intense, Payne was just forty years old when he started at the *RD.* Moreover, his position as managing editor was in fact a misnomer. De facto, he was the executive editor, charged not only with keeping track of editorial flow and production but with editorial administration. Second only to Wally, he was also the magazine's highest editorial authority and, in the owner's absence, empowered to strike or select an article or filler for reprinting.

With Lila's encouragement, however, Wally was wary of anyone encroaching publicly on his editorial authority, and not until many years later was the injustice of the situation rectified. Nevertheless, Payne proved himself to be not only a brilliant editor and sound administrator—a view widely confirmed in the editorial ranks—but, more important, also someone Wally could trust to advance his reactionary political views.

The *RD*'s publisher had an ulterior motive in hiring Payne—wanderlust. Now that he had money, he and Lila wanted to travel abroad. He even wrote to his father that he was working on a three-year plan that would allow him to spend six months in Europe. Weekend escapes to fancy New York hotels or the Poconos were no longer enough. When a local Pleasantville newspaper profiled Wallace, around this time, its article noted, "His only hobby, besides the magazine, seems to be the taking of aerial jaunts on every conceivable pretext to any point reachable by existing air lines."

As a measure of his confidence in Payne and of the value he put in a top-notch editor, Wally paid his editorial surrogate a salary that very quickly reached $70,000—a sum then paid only to the top executives of the very largest publishing chains. Business manager Arthur Griffiths earned the same amount. In today's terms, those salaries would translate to nearly $420,000.

Between them, Payne and Wally now began to hire the staff of editors who were to help guide the magazine over the next decade. Each editor, along with his wife, was subject to Wally and Lila's considered approval, since it was the Wallaces' view that anyone hired by the *Digest* was hired for life. Not surprisingly, Payne first raided *Scribner's* to lure away Dashiell, a Princeton graduate who had previously worked on the *Baltimore Sun.* A liberal Democrat, which made him an editorial anomaly in Pleasantville, the portly, mild-mannered

Dashiell was officially given the title of associate editor. Unofficially, he became the *Digest*'s first managing editor (a position that, like Payne's, was not recognized on the masthead until many years later).

A number of gifted amateurs and relatively inexperienced editors were also hired, including a young Kentuckian named Maurice T. Ragsdale. Rags, as he was known, was miserable working for Procter & Gamble's soap department in New York. Previously, he had worked as a gandy dancer. After studying stenography, he advertised himself as a male secretary with high-level writing skills. Payne answered the advertisement and hired him. Ragsdale advanced quickly and was named assistant book editor around 1932, serving under Ralph Henderson.

Four other editors with virtually no experience also soon joined the *Digest*—George Grant, a disenchanted lawyer named J. Carleton ("Lou") Dillon, Dorothy Hinitt (who was working behind a gift-shop counter when she met Wally), and Jerome Ellison. Later a young Yale graduate, Harry H. Harper, was hired to act as liaison with the Cleveland office. All shared with Dashiell the catchall title of associate editor.

But Payne and Wally also hired some of the best-known names in American publishing to serve as consultants or contributing editors. One of these was none other than George Horace Lorimer. By January 1932, when he retired from the *Saturday Evening Post,* its circulation had risen to three million and it was the largest weekly in the United States. That magisterial figure, and the place the *Post* occupied in the hearts of the average American, seemed to be mileposts that would never be surpassed by any other publication. Yet Lorimer was only the first in a long line of *Post* editors and other top executives who were to find in Pleasantville, as the *SEP* began its slow, tortuous descent into oblivion, something not unlike a home away from home. Like Wally, Lila, and Henderson, Lorimer was a PK.

In early 1931, feeling that the *Reader's Digest* was in capable hands, Wally and Lila set off on their first trip around the world. In London they stayed at the Savoy. Lila suggested that Wally buy the best grade of kid gloves to carry on their trips around the city. Wally complied and dutifully carried them around for the rest of their stay, one glove in each hand. Later they took the Simplon Orient Express to Paris and Trieste, where they set sail on the steamer *Helouan.* In Alexandria they stayed at the Shepheards Hotel; then they traveled on to Cairo, Luxor, and Bombay.

In their several months' absence, Payne bore down on Lucy Notestein's department in Cleveland, criticizing it for adhering "a bit too conscientiously" to the original when preparing book condensations. He also arranged for an editorial librarian in Pleasantville to oversee all reference work. One reason was to handle the flood of "pestiferous questions" sent in by readers, since answering them contributed to reader goodwill.

Each *Digest* editor—there were still fewer than a dozen—was given his own turf. One looked over *Harper's, Scribner's,* the *Saturday Evening Post,* and the *American Mercury;* another, *Vogue, Liberty,* the *Atlantic Monthly, Collier's,* and *Esquire.* But editors were free to propose articles from those magazines that their chief sponsor overlooked.

One problem no amount of magazine scouting could solve, and that was the toll the Depression was taking on the *Digest's* source publications. With legendary journals like the *North American Review, Liberty,* and *McClure's* dying off, there was a much smaller crop of articles from which to harvest the best, and that bleak set of circumstances struck at the very heart of the *Digest's* identity. No longer could Wally be certain of obtaining necessary material even with his exclusive contracts.

He was far from unprepared, however. Peering into the future of American publishing at one of its darkest moments with something like clairvoyance, Wally had confidently announced to his father the three-year plan that would allow him to travel in Europe for six months while all but his most robust competitors faltered. The first step was to install an editorial and managerial superstructure on which he could rely. With that accomplished, he proceeded to achieve his long-term goal—which was nothing less than the editorial reinvention of the *Reader's Digest* without altering its basic editorial formula.

By now Wally realized that he possessed an extraordinary common touch—a feeling for just exactly what the general reading public wanted. The obvious difficulty was to maintain the illusion that each issue of the *Digest* amounted to a "best of" the current magazine crop. A tough-nosed publisher fighting for his magazine's survival, Wally had decided upon a tack inspired to some and repugnant to others. He was going to make the *Digest* into a "digest"—that is, a magazine that would maintain the illusion of providing its readers with a representative selection of the best of American periodicals but that would actually be doing something altogether different.

To achieve that illusion Wally gradually introduced two new species of articles: the genuinely original article and the reprint that was in fact an article conceived by the *Digest* but first planted in any one of dozens of publications whose ethical concerns, if any, were subordinate to the financial one of merely staying alive.

In the magazine's first decade, Wally had published an occasional original bylined article when the mood suited him. For example, in January 1924 he bent the rules and published an original piece by his father called "Great Gains from the Great War," an ardent litany of the "glorious results" of World War I, including the overthrow of an "imperious Prussian military caste" and a warning to pacifists that a million armed Bolsheviks were waiting to impose communism in Germany at the first opportunity. A similar weighty political think piece, cowritten by Ben Wallace, was another. Such deviations from the formula had obviously been made only to accommodate a relative who thought he had something important to say. But as early as April 1930 Wally began to tinker with the formula itself, testing reader reaction.

In that issue Wally had published an article called "Music and Work." It was unsigned and described as "a special compilation for the *Reader's Digest.*" A compilation called "Music and Health" appeared in May, followed by "Music and Animals, a summary especially prepared by one of our editors," in June.

The *Digest*'s first "official" unsigned original article, debuting in 1931, was "Paging Coolidge, Smith, Baker, and Dawes"; it suggested that America's ex–public officials should be called back to help solve the country's economic mess. But it was not until February 1933 that the first signed original article appeared. Titled "Insanity—The Modern Menace," it was written by a then unknown English instructor at Columbia University named Henry Morton Robinson.

Robinson's article chronicled his visit to "a great State Hospital for the Insane." One paragraph was devoted to a visit to a ward for women suffering from paranoia. "A chorus of wails and hysterical laughter greeted us as we entered the door . . . ," Robinson wrote. "A gaunt caricature of a woman slipped a piece of paper into my hand; it was covered with senseless scrawls, but with a finger to her lips she glided away, signaling me to secrecy as she went."

It was a scene that Wally, who in the beginning personally commissioned all originals, must have been quite familiar with, as a result of having seen his mother in her final years.

———

SOMETIME in 1934 Wally, the loner, met his Tonto. Charles W. Ferguson, a curly haired, amiable young Texan with thick glasses and a remarkable gift of gab, had gone to New York in 1924 to study at Union Theological Seminary and at the New School. After serving briefly at a prosperous Methodist congregation in Dallas, he quit the ministry and began writing for H. L. Mencken's *American Mercury* and for the *Southwestern Review*. Later he became an editor of religious books for the George H. Doran Company in New York.

In 1933 Ferguson submitted to *Harper's* an article called "Business Eats Her Young," which claimed that, in the face of cutbacks, business always sacrificed its future—its bright young men—first. A month later the editor forwarded to Ferguson a check for $12.50, his half of the fee the *Reader's Digest* was paying to reprint the article. Ferguson dropped the authorities in Pleasantville a thank-you note.

Not long afterward, Wally stopped by the office unannounced and told Ferguson that the *Digest* planned to publish original articles and invited him to propose a few. With a shrug, Ferguson agreed, adding slyly, "Though I don't know whether you can pay me what *Harper's* pays me."

"How much is that?" Wally asked.

"Two hundred and fifty dollars," Ferguson lied.

Keeping a straight face, Wally agreed to Ferguson's terms. The *Digest* eventually bought six articles at the asking price, which was in fact several hundred dollars below the standard *RD* fee. Later Wally suggested that Ferguson join the editorial staff.

But Ferguson had just launched the Round Table Press—the imprint chosen for religious books to be published by Doran—and did not feel able in good conscience to abandon it. After another year passed, Wally again invited him to Pleasantville. This time Ferguson accepted and handed in his resignation.

Then misfortune struck. Wally called, full of apologies, and explained that some members of his editorial staff were opposed to the hiring. The two men agreed to meet for drinks at the Commodore Hotel, on Forty-second Street. Ferguson suggested that he keep on free-lancing for the *Digest* instead of trying to find another job.

Wally was impressed that the young man was willing to take such a risk, and they agreed on terms. A month later he called again and announced that the air had cleared in Pleasantville. Although there is no record of what the original objections to Ferguson were, in all likelihood Ken Payne had been opposed to the hiring of yet another relatively inexperienced editor when the Depression was forcing so many veterans into the job market. Though Wally placed great stock in the professionalism of Payne and others, he was to hire a great many more amateurs over the years, balancing them against some of the best-known bylines in American journalism.

Ferguson was given the title of associate editor and put in charge of reading assorted magazines each month for excerptable material. The first item he proposed for condensation was an article in *Liberty* attacking Herbert Hoover. At the top of the page, he wrote, "This article gives Herbert Hoover a well-deserved sock in the jaw!"

Then came his first shock. Having established such warm relations with his employer, he cavalierly assumed they shared identical views not only on politics but on everything else as well. Wally, however, was an ardent admirer of Hoover and had even reprinted several of his articles. As a result, the two men had become friends and Wally sometimes lunched with the former president at his suite in the Waldorf-Astoria Towers, on Park Avenue. Despite Ferguson's faux pas, Wally continued to treat him with unfailing kindness and generosity.

Another reason behind the practice of planting articles was that the *Digest* was getting into specialized areas not being covered by popular magazines. Soon after arriving in Pleasantville, Ferguson was deputized as assistant originals editor and oversaw much of the planting.

The procedure was to approach another publication with an idea for a story, offering to pay the writer's fee and expenses and asking only for the right to "reprint" the article after it was published. The writer was usually chosen from among the *Digest*'s ever-growing pool of approved writers and editors. But planting also served another purpose. Prepublication of an article in the *Saturday Review,* then edited by George Stevens, for example, was its guarantee of validity and authenticity.

Later on, particularly with *Survey Graphic,* under the editorship of Victor Weybright, the *Digest* engaged in what was tantamount to collaboration. Weybright would propose an idea to the *RD,* which developed it into an article and paid for the finished product. *Survey Graphic* then "koshered" the piece, in Ferguson's phrase, by "preprinting"— the term that became the preferred euphemism.

Ultimately, Ferguson got to the point where he was practically giving away articles to other magazines. Once he paid $1,500 for a piece he turned over to the *Christian Century,* whose highest fee was $15. But having the article preprinted in a magazine with a reputation for such high seriousness and conviction made the investment worthwhile. Similarly, the PTA magazine was used for articles on education. As more originals made their way into the *Digest,* it became imperative to place them elsewhere first so that the magazine did not seem as though it were written by roving editors or regular correspondents. Yet, to Wally's mind, the primary consideration behind planting, from the very outset, was to give the articles the validation of a higher editorial authority than the *RD* itself.

Wally closely monitored his editors' productivity, keeping a file for each issue on who had selected the various articles and who was responsible for cutting them. The two tasks did not necessarily go together. A little like his professorial father, he also graded articles either A, B, or C, so whoever garnered the most A's made the equivalent of Wally's dean's list, which was routinely published in the form of an office memorandum.

Despite his close monitoring of editorial productivity, and an attendance sheet tracking each employee's arrival and departure to the minute, Wally was not feared as a tyrant—as Lila came to be regarded by some—and he tolerated disagreements with his own views. He also often answered his own office phone.

Wally's obsession with punctuality, which Lila shared, sometimes produced comic scenes. Jerry Ellison was the odd man out on the editorial staff—an eccentric who occasionally showed up at work wearing lederhosen. Invariably, he also arrived a half hour late to work and was usually late to most editorial meetings as well. In exasperation Wally finally sent him a note, asking whether there was any good reason why he should be late. Ellison waited a full week before answering. Scribbled on the bottom of the returned note was a single word: "No."

———

AS THE MAGAZINE grew, Wally attempted to reduce all of the articles suitable for publication into twenty-five categories, ranging from "Adventure and Exploration" to "Communism" to "Rackets" to "Sex—Marriage, Divorce, Human Relations." Far more important were the magazine's guiding editorial principles, which he had written down as his own criteria when working single-handedly in the periodicals room of the New York Public Library during the magazine's early years. They amounted to the *Reader's Digest*'s three commandments, graven in stone, and were known to every editor:

Is it quotable? Is it something the reader will remember, ponder and discuss?

Is it applicable? Does it come within the framework of most people's interests and conversation? Does it touch the individual's own concerns?

Is it of lasting interest? Will it still be of interest a year or two from now?

Wally also issued a constant stream of memos full of article suggestions, warnings, advice. One of the most curious was a "Confidential Office Memo" to his top editorial staff which noted that some of them "no doubt read an occasional short story or novel." Wally then asked them to ponder the possibility of a monthly fiction supplement to the *Reader's Digest,* perhaps separately bound and containing advertisements to defray its cost.

The memo went on to analyze condensations of short stories Wally himself had made from the October 1934 issue of the *American Magazine,* suggesting that one excerpt seemed to have scientific value and others contained material similar to such *Digest* departments as "Picturesque Speech" ("Mike borrowed a cube of ice from his water goblet and dropped it down Linda's dress"). The memo further warned, "We don't want anyone else swiping the idea, so *please make no reference to this outside the office."*

But Wally had no real interest in fiction, and the proposal—probably issued at the suggestion of Henderson—was never pursued. The hard work and attention to detail paid off. The *Digest*'s net profit for 1934 was $418,000. In a generous mood, Wally decided to offer all subscribers the option of a life subscription for $20. Five thousand took him up on the offer, each of whom received a certificate in gold ink. Many long-lived readers were to receive a more than hundredfold return on their investment.

In another example of his editorial methodology, Wally circulated on November 6, 1935, an original manuscript titled "What Overcompensation Can Do for You," by Dr. Louis E. Bisch, and asked each of seven editors to cut it. He then recirculated the edited manuscript, with each editorial emendation coded according to the respective editor's initials. Maurice Ragsdale made the fewest changes—only one, in fact, for a "savings" of only three words. Ellison made thirteen changes, saving 49 words, and George Grant cut out 51 words in eighteen changes; but Ralph Henderson rewrote a paragraph and saved 59 words. The moral, however, was that the combined condensations of all seven editors reaped a savings of 185 words.

"Obviously, not everyone took the experiment with the same degree of seriousness," Wally gently observed in his report, "but the result has enlightening aspects which I think will interest everyone."

Despite his good work as book editor, Henderson appears to have been in the Pleasantville doghouse for a time. While on board the SS *Majestic* bound for India, a woman named Louise Edgar, who worked briefly as an editor for the *Digest,* wrote to Wally on a subject she knew was "painful" to him. The letter reads like a continuation of a previous conversation, and its subject is the *Digest*'s first employee. Edgar suggested that Wally have a frank talk with Henderson, telling him, "He has not the qualities of imagination, insight & brilliance which are needed; that you have hoped & tried for too long, thinking he might pick up; but that you now know this is based on an inborn quality which, try however hard he may, he cannot get."

In conclusion, Edgar cautioned Wally that it would be "cruel" to retain him on the staff merely out of pity. Fortunately, Wally did not heed his correspondent's advice. Henderson's idea about condensing fiction was ultimately to be the company's salvation.

On January 8, 1935, the *St. Paul Pioneer Press* published an article on corporate salaries, which at that time had to be registered with the U.S. Treasury Department in accordance with the Reserve Act of 1934. Among those listed were the $102,467 for Ken Payne, executive editor of the *Reader's Digest,* and the same amount for business manager Arthur Griffiths. Astronomical as those salaries were at the time, they were less than half the $265,000 being paid to Arthur Brisbane of the *New York Evening Journal.* But Dr. Wallace saw the item and on that same day wrote, "Hey there, DeWitt, hello! Are you there? Do you hear me? Strange things we read? Does it cost such fabulous salaries to get editors and managers for the RD? That is strange publicity to go out to all the world. Is it possible you pay any such salary as above indicates? It looks like madness."

Lila must have thought so, too. On the day after Christmas, 1935, the generous, impulsive editor of the *Reader's Digest* wrote a large-lettered, handwritten reminder to himself that spoke volumes: "Promised LB never to give salary increase, or any bonus, without first getting her approval & consent."

Despite the company's huge earnings and unbelievable salaries, Wally was far from complacent. A memo to his editors titled "Why We Must Keep on Our Toes" compared 1929 and 1935 newsstand sales of thirty-three leading magazines. The circulation of twenty-six had dropped precipitously, with the *American Mercury* sustaining a 75.2 percent loss, *Scribner's* posting a 59.9 percent loss, the *Saturday Evening Post* now down from 1,405,814 to 915,661, for a 34.9 percent loss, and even the *National Geographic* going from 23,501 readers to 10,283.

Only six major magazines showed an increase in newsstand sales: *Time* with a healthy 180.2 percent gain (up to 107,250) and the *New Yorker* up from 45,788 to 61,155, for a 33.6 percent gain. However, all were dwarfed by the *Digest's* circulation in 1935 of 1,457,500, an astounding 400 percent increase from 1929's combined subscription and newsstand sales of 290,000. In 1935 the *RD* was selling an average of 571,600 copies on the newsstand (not to mention another 116,700 to the schools), or more than *Time, Newsweek* (a recent upstart launched with the help of financier John Hay Whitney), the *New Yorker, Vogue, Harper's Bazaar, Popular Science* (all magazines which had shown significant newsstand increases over the past six years) combined. Besides the *Saturday Evening Post,* only three other magazines now outsold the *RD* on the newsstand: *Liberty* (894,346), *Woman's Home Companion* (872,399), and *Collier's* (857,150).

━━

MANY of the early employees and admirers of the *Digest* regarded DeWitt Wallace as the great proponent of the democratization of information and likened him to Henry Ford. The latter put an automobile within reach of the average family. Ostensibly, Wally was the first to provide the public with an even more precious and hitherto inaccessible gift—an education. Wally did, in fact, idolize Ford, whom he was to profile in his magazine more than any other person. However, he did not democratize information so much as create the first mass-market magazine—to be read by people who drove the Model T. Like Ford, DeWitt Wallace did not produce a masterpiece. He invented a genre.

Nevertheless, it was an automobile that was responsible for catapulting the prosperous but still relatively unknown *Reader's Digest* into the national limelight and making it a household name.

One Saturday afternoon in the spring of 1935, Wally was touring the back roads of Westchester County near Armonk in his old Ford—which he had exchanged for his beloved but unsalvageable Studebaker—when he saw at a small garage what appeared to be the remains of a recent automobile wreck. According to the version passed down in an official *Digest* history, he stopped to chat with the tow-truck operator about the heap still attached to his truck. The man explained that another driver missed a curve and plowed into the stricken car, which then rolled over twice. As Wally shook his head over the shape of the automobile, the tow-truck operator said, "You should have seen it before we got the bodies out."

But a version told by his niece Judy held that Wally had driven his own car through a wire-net fence near Brewster and had to send for a tow-truck operator to disentangle the mess. His inattention had been brought on by his trying to light a cigarette.

Either way, Wally got an earful from the tow-truck operator. The next day he entertained his editors at lunch with one ghoulish story after another, including one about a man brought back to life just long enough to die again. Later he decided that if more people could comprehend the full horror of a highway accident, they might drive more carefully. J. C. Furnas, a young writer recently graduated from Harvard, was assigned to interview state troopers and then describe in grisly detail the most horrifying crashes in automotive history.

For the first time Wally felt he had an exclusive, a story no other magazine had ever written about. Also, as one of the very few magazines with no advertising, the *RD* did not have to worry about repercussions from Detroit. Furthermore, Wally alone knew the power he was able to exert since even in the trade the 1.5 million circulation of the *Digest* was a secret.

The result, in the August 1935 issue, was "—And Sudden Death," the title fashioned from a supplication in the Book of Common Prayer: "From lightning and tempest, from earthquakes, fire and flood, from plague, pestilence and famine, from battle and murder and from sudden death, Good Lord deliver us." An editorial note warned that "the realistic details of this article will nauseate some readers."

The piece then described an accident scene that no artist "working on a safety poster would dare depict . . . the flopping, pointless efforts of the injured to stand up; the queer, grunting noises; the steady, panting groaning of a human being with pain creeping up on him as the shock wears off. . . . Minor details would include the raw ends of bones protruding through flesh in compound fractures, and the dark red, oozing surfaces where clothes and skin were flayed off at once."

After "—And Sudden Death" was finished, Wally walked across his lawn one day to Pen Dudley's house and asked his friend whether he wanted to publicize it. Dudley immediately agreed. Proofs of the article were sent to five thousand newspapers and other publications, inviting them—in a twist—to reprint it free of charge, so long as they gave credit to the *Digest*. The article was reprinted in newspapers, in whole or in part, in nearly every sizable American city. Farm, religious, and other periodicals gave it additional circulation, as did company house organs. It was also widely discussed on radio programs, syndicated as a comic strip, and made into a short motion picture. In the Province of Ontario, reprints were mailed out with all official correspondence. The state of Wyoming included it with every set of license plates issued. New Yorkers received it when passing through the Holland Tunnel or over the George Washington Bridge.

Within three months, the *Digest* had distributed more than four million reprints—at two cents each—to more than eight thousand companies, clubs, and civic groups. It became the first of the *Digest*'s public-service reprints, and it marked the time when Pen Dudley took over handling the magazine's promotion.

"—And Sudden Death" also proved the importance of original articles and bore out Wally's contention that they were "an inevitable development, perhaps the most important in the *Digest*'s history."

NOT everyone was caught up in *Digest* mania, however. In a November 1935 issue of the *New Yorker*, E. B. White foresaw a trying situation. He predicted that by 1939 there would be 173 magazines digesting articles from other magazines. Then the digests would begin to digest the digests. Then another batch of magazines would carry the process a step further. The "final mad triumph would come with the boiling down of a Hemingway novel to 'Bang' and a *Scribner's* article on raising difficult children to 'Hit him.'"

White had a point. In addition to the original article and the planted article, Wally also introduced a third new ingredient into the *Digest*'s editorial formula in the midthirties. In the 1934 Christmas issue the editors announced, "The present issue has been increased from 112 to 128 pages, to permit publication from a suitable book. The magazine remains otherwise unaltered." The announcement was followed by an excerpt of Arnold Bennett's *How to Live on 24 Hours a Day*, described by the editors as "a little classic in the science of self-direction."

In fact, Bennett's book had been excerpted in the *Digest* twelve years previously, in the second issue. In the years from 1922 to 1933, there had been ninety-two brief book condensations, though usually of chapters rather than of entire volumes. Among the excerpted authors were British scientist Sir James Jeans and Canadian humorist Stephen Leacock, as well as Stefan Zweig, Lowell Thomas, Ogden Nash, and Lafcadio Hearn. Then Wally, who almost never read them, got the idea of condensing entire books in the back of the magazine.

When he first suggested the idea, Ferguson thought it pretty silly. But Wally was undeterred. He even commandeered Ferguson's wife, Victo, to do the first cut of the most controversial book excerpt ever, Alexis Carrel's *Man, the Unknown.*

A native of France, Carrel had won the Nobel Prize in medicine in 1912 for developing new treatments for wounds. But his latest book was less a scientific than a mystical exploration of racial theories and eugenics. Not a few critics had pointed out that many of Carrel's ideas bore an uncanny resemblance to those also espoused by the National Socialist party in Germany. Carrel shared the assumption of the superiority of the Nordic race, explaining that blacks, Indians, Latins, and "Asiatics" had been "burned" into inferiority by the sun.

Man, the Unknown was causing a sensation both in Europe and in the United States, where it was on the best-seller lists. Among other things it proposed that future generations might elect to kill off their least-desirable types, as was done among pedigree animals, in order to improve the race. Carrel also advocated abolishing prisons and replacing them with "smaller and less expensive institutions" where criminals could either be disciplined or "dealt with."

The September 1936 condensation published in the *Digest* retained some of Carrel's eugenic musings, including this one: "Modern civilization, with the help of hygiene, soft living, hospitals, physicians, and nurses, has kept alive many human beings of poor quality. These weaklings and their descendants contribute, in a large measure, to the enfeeblement of the race. We should perhaps renounce this artificial form of health and exclusively pursue natural health."

Eugenics was an old *Digest* theme, having been explored in the very first issue. Wally was so intent on condensing a portion of the book that he asked Victo to proceed with the cutting even before he had a contract from the publisher. Later he offered Harper & Brothers $1,000 for the serial rights. To Wally's amazement, the publisher refused permission, fearing the condensation might infringe on book-store sales. The book had already been on the best-seller list for more than a year, at one time selling 2,200 copies a week at $3.50 each. By the time of Wally's request it was down to 900.

DeWitt decided to indemnify the publisher and sent Harper & Brothers two checks. One was in the amount of $1,000 for the right to use enough material to fill sixteen *Digest* pages. The other was for $2,500, to be held in escrow with the proviso that, if the book sold fewer copies in the three months after the excerpt appeared, the publisher was to keep the check. During the first week after the installment ran, *Man, the Unknown* set a new one-week record by selling 3,300 copies, and during the next week it sold 4,600.

Controversy, sensationalism, amateur article-writing contests offering $1,000 prizes—Wally knew how to work the crowd. The editorial formula fashioned, then refashioned, over a thirteen-year period had proved to be not merely financially sound but triumphant as well. It was the chatty, upbeat articles, though, minimizing the negative and accentuating the positive, that the *Digest* was perhaps most identified with. The preacher's son filled his magazine with messages of hope and inspiration interspersed with pithy folk wisdom and humor. *Digest* readers were told to believe that faith moved mountains, that prayer and many other things besides could cure cancer, and that even poverty held hidden blessings ("Some poor wretches," claimed one article, "have nothing but money"). That was just what a nation struggling through a Depression wanted to hear.

———

IN THE WANING months of 1936, the *Digest's* veil of secrecy was spectacularly rent by *Fortune* magazine, which had decided to investigate all those rumors about the fabulous wealth of DeWitt Wallace and his little magazine on the hill. Immediate and tangible proof was the dazzling Norman mansion called High Winds, which the magazine's proprietor had just moved into.* When *Fortune* asked Wally whether he would cooperate, he uncharacteristically agreed. But he underestimated the investigative skills of the reporter assigned to the job, and perhaps also the repercussions of all the publicity. On the other hand, he had reason to be proud of his considerable accomplishment and

*See chapter 3.

may have wanted some form of official recognition and even homage, now that the *Digest*'s own fortunes were seemingly secure.

Fortune assistant managing editor Albert L. Furth was assigned to write the unbylined piece. Both Griffiths and Payne were interviewed for the story, as well as Wally himself. The draft manuscript was submitted to Wally for review, and he was invited to make any criticisms he wanted of the "correctness and propriety of any of our interpretations."

Wally permitted a number of inaccuracies to go through, among them that "on the fifth day of the Verdun offensive Sergeant Wallace found himself in a dressing station with an ugly hole through his neck and a piece of shrapnel in his lung." As for the moment when he first thought of the idea of the *Reader's Digest,* he crossed out the phrase "at 2 A.M. on a sheep ranch in Montana"—emphasizing the cut with the words "Please don't"—and substituted "while working with a friend one summer on a ranch in Montana."

He also allowed *Fortune*'s readers to believe that the returns from the *Digest*'s prehoneymoon mailing had been "pretty good" when in fact they had been disastrous. The original manuscript further described him as "tall, lean, thin-lipped and slightly grey, and he is dressed in the tweedy elegance of the English professor with the private income." But Wally deleted "thin-lipped" and also a reference to an earlier illness of Lila's, noting disingenuously that she had not worked at the *Digest* for the past two years. In fact, of course, she had never worked there, but her name on the masthead had to be explained away.

The published *Fortune* profile started off by saying that in the crowded barrooms near Grand Central some "astonishing stories" were being bandied about concerning the *Reader's Digest*—that it was making so much money "its owners . . . don't know what to do with it." Deleted from the published version was the comment that DeWitt and Lila Wallace "are so embarrassed and frightened by the discovery of their Midas touch that they hide their success in furtive secrecy."

The darkest secret of all, Furth wrote in his original copy, was the *Digest*'s circulation. A paper salesman guessed that its print order was close to three million. Finally, there was word that other publishers "ganged together for an embargo on reprint privileges, exacting as their price of amnesty a written pledge by Mr. Wallace that *Reader's Digest* would never accept advertising."

Furth's unpublished version then described the editorial offices in the Mount Pleasant Bank and Trust Company building: "The quiet of the place is startling. The typewriters click, but do not clatter. For an hour at a time no telephone bell rings. Nobody bustles. . . . Only the retching shriek of the noonday whistle on the firehouse nearby causes interruption, and that only because it is time to dash out for the half-hour lunch period."

Rumors around Pleasantville were that "the Wallaces order a community life like the late Elbert Hubbard's Roycrofters at East Aurora [an upstate New York radical commune devoted to the art of printing]. And that the whole town arises at 6:30 A.M. to work from eight until three because the Wallaces believe that a sensible way of living. And that the Wallaces are anonymously Lord and Lady Bountiful to the countryside. . . . As for their wealth—it's true they do not live in a conspicuously grand style—although Mr. Wallace is passionately fond of flying, and has *two* autogiros. . . ."

The surprising thing about all those stories, said Furth, was not that they were cockeyed. The *Digest*'s circulation was not 2,500,000 and Wallace did not own even one airplane, and people in Pleasantville woke up whenever they wanted, within reason. But undeniably all the stories did contain a grain of truth. The true circulation was 1,801,393—"the largest ever achieved by a magazine which contains no fiction or no pictures." Nor had any other magazine costing twenty-five cents ever enjoyed such a circulation, with the sole exception of Hearst's *Good Housekeeping*.

The editorial staff was "nearly innocent of previous magazine experience," Furth noted in his original version, adding that some received six-figure salaries and four-figure annual bonuses. Out of a staff of thirty-two editors, only two had worked on a magazine before. Others had been employed in everything from selling linoleum to designing houses. "[A half-dozen regulars] play poker together every couple of weeks, a thoroughly goofy game in which any card in the deck is likely to be called wild and every pot is settled by a complicated division between winner and loser."

Furth also reported that Wally paid himself only $30,000 a year, though the company's net earnings were $170,516. "A no-nonsense man himself," the unpublished version continued, "he sees no place in Pleasantville for editorial temperament and demands prompt attendance at the office, keeping an absence and tardiness record of the entire staff. But despite such schoolmasterly methods he practically never fires anybody, rarely gives anyone a wigging, and is heartily liked by practically everybody." The few who quit did so because they found life in Pleasantville too restrictive. "Defeatism," Furth remarked, was the only taboo.

Wally's close friend Wendell MacRae, who had grown up with him in St. Paul, took the photographs for the article, including one of Lila studiously reading manuscripts at a desk. Another was a photograph of Wally at his desk, flanked by Payne and Henderson, over the caption "This close and no closer may a camera approach." Wally would not allow any close-ups.

The news of Payne's and Griffiths's salaries stunned not only outsiders but even those in Pleasantville, where the average *RD* editor earned $7,200 a year. By comparison the average salary of the editor of a high-circulation women's magazine was around $12,000.

Moreover, with the newsstand sales divulged, *Scribner's* again refused to renew its reprint privileges. The *Atlantic Monthly* and *Forum,* two of the most respected literary magazines of the time, also threatened to sever their relationship with Pleasantville. Payne proposed that the *Digest* strike back by boycotting all Scribner's books for the book excerpt department. Many other magazines, such as the *New Yorker,* immediately demanded to renegotiate their contracts. Meanwhile, Hearst steadfastly continued to refuse reprint permission. Payne's and Griffiths's salaries were also soon reduced to under $100,000 in order to lower their tax bracket. It was the last time *Digest* salaries were made public for more than half a century.

In due course Wally got sick to death of hearing people attribute the *Digest*'s startling success to "—And Sudden Death." The *Fortune* article also continued to plague him in one way or another for years. Nonetheless, they were the two articles that changed his little world forever.

3

Even the Petunias

ONE day Wally and Lila went to the Fergusons' for supper. During the course of the evening, Victo mentioned how they had locked themselves out of the car the day before. That led to a discussion about how strong car windows were. Someone suggested they were difficult to break even with a hammer. Wally replied, "I'll bet I could break it with one kick."

"Bet you couldn't," he was dared.

Wally went outside, got into the backseat, and put his foot through the window.

Obviously, all was not work in Pleasantville. Wally made sure there was plenty of play. But sometimes not everyone knew what the game was. Charlie Ferguson provided a classic case in point.

In the summer of 1936 Wally asked his associate editor to fly out to Carmel-by-the-Sea, in California, to see Lincoln Steffens, the father of American investigative journalism, who was then in his last illness. The *Digest* had previously reprinted one of his pieces—a ploy that often led to signing up an author for an original. But the trip was no small venture at the time, and Wally himself went to the airport to see Ferguson off, handing him his tickets and a $1,000 bill to cover "incidentals." In addition to visiting Steffens, Wally wanted his colleague to spend another six months roaming around California, looking for stories.

Wally's earnest sidekick never suspected, though, the real reason he was being sent out of town for so long—he was being cuckolded. That was curious because, among the womanizers of the little town of Pleasantville, Ferguson was second only to Wally himself or, perhaps, to Tommy Manville.

Back when he was an assistant minister at the largest Methodist church in Dallas, the Reverend Mr. Charles W. Ferguson had been caught masturbating in front of an open window while watching a group of schoolgirls. The church fired him. At that point Ferguson prudently decided to abandon a career in the ministry and turn to publishing. Yet the incident in Dallas was no temporary lapse but a symptom of a sexual disorder that was later to manifest itself in instances of wife beating and chronic philandering. The personable ex-parson had a dark side that made him the Dr. Jekyll and Mr. Hyde of Pleasantville.

Before Wally hired Ferguson, he and his wife both had to pass inspection by Lila. Getting the final once-over was already a *Digest* tradition, one that was not to vary for another forty years. What was striking, though, was how often Lila failed, and Wally apparently succeeded, in detecting a bad marriage. Particularly in the case of Charles and Victoria Ferguson, Lila also failed to perceive in the young woman one of her most serious rivals for Wally's attentions.

A slight brunette of medium height, Victo was no beauty, drank heavily like her husband, and was born with an extra vertebra that made her appear slightly stooped. But her vivacious personality was immensely appealing to almost everyone—all except Lila, who thought she was vulgar. Wally relished her passion for spontaneous fun. Also, her maiden name was Wallace, and the Fergusons' oldest boy, then eight years old, by odd coincidence was called Wally.

On the night Lila was to meet the Fergusons, DeWitt made arrangements for the four of them to go to a fancy restaurant in New York—an unusual tactic that suggested Wally was out not only to put the Fergusons in the best light possible for Lila but also to make an impression himself on the wife of the *Digest* candidate. Ferguson and Victo were then living in Tudor City, an apartment complex near the East River, and invited the Wallaces to stop by their apartment first for a drink. Lila and Wally arrived dressed to the nines. As they sipped bootleg liquor, Wally sat nervously rocking his leg up and down as usual. Finally, he cross-examined the two Texans about what they most missed about their home state.

The lack of a good Texas-style hamburger, came the reply. Wally had lately been pondering the possibility of a series on the cuisines of different U.S. regions and other nationalities, and immediately his editorial persona took over. What made a Texas hamburger so special, he wanted to know. They tried to explain, a little too enthusiastically perhaps, adding that they had even gone up to Harlem to a place called Texas Hamburgers, which turned out to be no more Texan than knishes and bagels.

However, they had spotted a place around the corner on East Forty-first Street named Riker's, which seemed promising. Caught up in the fervor of their passionate quest, and mindful that hamburger was the quintessential all-American food, Wally banged his glass down on the coffee table and announced, "That's the place we go for dinner! Riker's it is!"

Riker's had only counter service, but the hamburgers were as good as promised. The coffee was pretty good, too, and Wally went away determined to do the series on food. (J. C. Furnas was given the assignment and told to cover every cuisine except Indian, which Wally disliked.) Despite its charms, though, Riker's was nothing like the Plaza or the Stork Club, which Victo, Ferguson, and Lila had set their hopes on.

Later, while in California assigning stories on Charles Laughton or the making of *David Copperfield,* Ferguson never guessed that Wally simply wanted him out of the way for an extended period of time. Nor did he have any suspicions when his boss asked Victo to help him cut *Man, the Unknown,* night after night. Wally himself was the unknown man.

But Ferguson did succeed in meeting with Steffens, who was by then living in his bedroom. Among his other visitors were Max Eastman, Witter Bynner, Carl Sandburg, and the young John Steinbeck, plus assorted labor organizers, professors, and Hollywood types. Ferguson's report on the great muckraker read in part, "Steffens is paralyzed—has been stricken about three weeks. He is all right above the waist and we had a long and delightful session. . . . [H]e wants first to do another article somewhat along inspirational lines . . . based on an incident in the life of his son Pete: the notion of it is that it's not enough to do your best. You've got to do the job or you've failed."

Steffens died that August before he was able to write the piece. Ferguson's consolation prize was Norma Shearer, whom he signed up to do an article called "Reading and Good Manners."

———

MOST of Wally's assignations with Victo and a succession of other women over the years, some of them also the wives of editors, were held in New York's midtown hotels, all of them close to Grand Central

Station and offering the kind of anonymity impossible to find in Pleasantville. The affairs were conducted with such secrecy, and were in such contrast to Wally's effusive devotion to his wife, that few people credited the rumors that now and then cropped up. Those who did know what was going on maintained a loyal and absolute silence. They were not only devoted to Wally but dependent on him for their livelihood as well.

Unlike her husband, Victo was not in awe of the editor of the *Reader's Digest*. Once when she opened the door of her hotel room to welcome Wally, he boorishly began to sing Lila's praises because of something that had occurred just that morning. His lover got dressed and angrily walked out on him. On another occasion she took some pictures at a party where everybody was cutting up and having fun. A few days later Lila appeared at the Ferguson home and demanded the photographs, which she did not want shown around. Victo refused point-blank to hand them over.

Perhaps not surprisingly, the attraction Wally felt for Victo was matched by Ferguson's own lusting after Lila, who was still an extremely attractive, fashionable woman, now in her late forties. But it was one thing to fool around with office secretaries, another to go after the boss's wife. However, when Ferguson drank heavily he became a sloppy drunk. One night he went too far and made a pass at Lila. Wally read him the riot act, ordering him to give up drinking immediately or he would be out.

Ferguson did stop drinking, though lapses were frequent. Later the Wallaces sent him from time to time to the Payne-Whitney Clinic in New York to dry out. Every so often, though, he liked to fly out to Chicago and go on a bender. He frequently went to the Windy City anyway because of his work with the American Library Association, which was headquartered there. He had another reason, too: Ferguson was a bigamist and had started another family.

Lila tolerated her husband's infidelities—though whether as a consequence of a prior private agreement between the two or simply because she accepted his adultery as a fact of their married life cannot be determined. Similarly unknown is whether, at the time, Lila herself indulged in extramarital affairs. One of his problems, and hers, was that she simply did not have enough to do during the day, which was often spent antiques hunting, shopping or getting her hair done in New York, or gardening. A hint of the tension between the two, though, can be discerned in a brief handwritten memo titled simply "Marriage," which Wally wrote to himself on November 11, 1936, a few weeks after the fifteenth anniversary of his wedding:

"1) Consult LB *always* before making dates—never oftener than Mondays, Wednesdays and Fridays. 2) Show affection, thotfulness & without fail when others are present. 3) Don't mention any girls in past. 4) Take initiative in suggesting having friends in. 5) Don't crab abt clothes, [word illegible] etc. when dancing. 6) Drive carefully."

The fifth entry alluded to Lila's one great pastime. She had a passion for ballroom dancing just as Wally was crazy about poker, cars, Ping-Pong, pranks, dirty jokes, and other, more discreet pleasures. At first Wally did not care for dancing. But then Lila presented him with a gift certificate entitling him to a course of ten dancing lessons at an Arthur Murray Dance Studio. Naturally, she went along as his partner.

By coincidence, Victo Ferguson also gave her husband a similar gift certificate. The foursome began going out on the town at regular intervals. Their dancing instructor at Arthur Murray was a handsome young man from Arkansas named Harry Wilcox. He had been an engineer with General Motors before losing his job in the Depression. He danced divinely, and Lila took an immediate liking to him.

Whatever her sentiments about Wally's womanizing, Lila kept them to herself. But over time nearly everyone began to notice that she seemed pointedly to prefer the company of men—possibly because some of the wives were potentially or in fact her rivals.

Everyone also had a theory about why Lila and Wally never had any children. So rife was speculation that, in later years, the Wallaces even disseminated several versions of their own. One popular suspicion, based on Wally's somewhat high-pitched voice, was that his war wounds were really much more serious than he admitted and that, like the American reporter Jake Barnes in Hemingway's *The Sun Also Rises,* he was impotent. That also seemingly explained his flirtatious ways and penchant for dirty jokes—he was only compensating.

On the other hand, Wally told Victo that he made Lila get two abortions. Early in their relationship, according to this story, the two had decided that the *Digest* was to be their only child, on which they would lavish all their love, attention, and energy. That very reason, minus any allusion to an abortion, was later the one Lila herself delicately issued when she chose to address the subject.

Wally was an early supporter of Margaret Sanger, founder of

Planned Parenthood, and gave substantial amounts of money to the Abortion League at a time before such contributions were tax-deductible. The legalization of abortion was also one of the few subjects of conversation that caused the normally detached publisher to raise his voice in anger.

Wally's explanation for the lack of children was that he never wanted to subject the petite, five-foot-two Lila to the rigors of childbirth, for fear she might not survive the ordeal. A less likely but still plausible reason was the memory of his mother's madness and a fear—heightened by his reverence for eugenics—that her illness might be hereditary. In the twenties and thirties, mental illness was often viewed as a shameful blemish on a family's good name. (Bertrand Russell and his first wife chose not to have children out of a similar fear.) That attitude might also further explain Wally's lifelong silence about his mother, who was devoted to him—and his equally long effort to sanctify his father as a struggling martyr for higher education, even though the two hardly agreed on anything.

Late in life Wally was to tell a roomful of startled Digesters that he had undergone a vasectomy when he was younger. Such an operation might have resulted from his wife's refusal to have any more abortions—if she, in fact, had had any—or from his own fear that she might bear him a defective child. Or he may have had the vasectomy—the first such successful operation on a human male was performed in 1894—while still a young man, before he met Lila, when his only motive was to pursue a vigorous sex life without fear of unwanted consequences.

Most likely, however, to judge by Wally's own double testimony, Lila did have two abortions, probably during the early twenties after their move to Pleasantville, and he elected to have a vasectomy soon afterward. Lila's delicate health during those years lends some credence to that theory.

As a young woman, Lila suffered from a severe parathyroid condition. The parathyroid glands secrete a hormone that controls the level of calcium in the blood. An excess of the parathyroid hormone can cause kidney stones and other symptoms such as headache, fatigue, and thirst. For a time in 1929 she was also bedridden with an attack of neuritis. And on a number of other occasions she was hospitalized for reasons never made public.

Many Digesters were of the opinion, regardless of the reason why the Wallaces were childless—or perhaps because they were—that Wally and Lila did not particularly care for children. But Lila once told editor Lou Dillon's wife, Urith, that she and Wally would have loved to be parents. Wally frequently played with the offspring of his employees and once bravely escorted four of them to a circus. Lila reported afterward that he was more worn out than any of his young charges.

The lack of any significant business or editorial responsibilities, the absence of children, and a sporadic social life only increased Lila's loneliness and isolation. Though Wally loved to have fun, he was able to find it in ways that often excluded his wife either unintentionally or by design. For weeks at a time he worked late into the night. On Friday or Saturday nights he liked to play poker. (Once, while he and Lila were traveling in Spain, he even kept a game going for weeks via cable and mail.)

On another occasion Wally and a few other Digesters took a train out west as an excuse to play poker and see a football game in Los Angeles. When the train arrived in Bowie, Arizona, Wally found a telegram from Lila: "Will not let you go anywhere without me again. We belong together always. Shall be all rested and awaiting your return eagerly and most impatiently. More love than ever before."

When Wally did go off again to have some fun with the boys, Lila wrote him, "Make the most of this trip, Sweet Patoot—for I'm not at all sure that I'll ever be able to let you go away without me again!" Replying to Wally's letters home, she admitted to "severe loneliness for" him and promised, "Will celebrate October 15 most enthusiastically on your return."

Sometimes, particularly in the early days when they were feeling prosperous, Wally and Lila escaped together to a New York hotel for an uninterrupted ten-day work binge. They took separate but adjoining rooms and avoided the temptation to waste time chatting by slipping notes to each other under the door. Occasionally, they went out to dinner and the theater. Just as often, he worked and she languished in her room, glumly browsing through a stack of magazines. None of her notes contained a word of excitement. Typical was the message scribbled on a scratch pad of the St. Regis Hotel in New York and put under the door: "I've covered 12 issues of each of these magazines, darlin—and I am a tired baby! Hope there is something useful. Come and kiss me good nite."

If a memo went around from Wally about Lila, it usually regarded the design of the front cover—her one area of expertise. The memos bragged about her in a restrained way, as if issued to please her rather than to advise the staff of something they would surely have known about anyway.

Though Wally and Lila had bought some property from Pen Dudley and built a small house on it, they did not live in the small studio apartment for long. The rapid growth of the *Digest* rendered the downstairs office inadequate shortly after it was finished. Around the time the company's offices were relocated in the business district of Pleasantville, Wally and Lila moved to a secluded six-bedroom house some miles away. The office-apartment was used to entertain visitors, particularly editors or writers who came up from New York. On such occasions a Japanese butler named Yama ministered to the needs of the guests.

When Wally did venture out for a night on the town, he always did it with style. And Ferguson and Victo eventually did get to see New York's best restaurants and nightclubs. Wally made a ritual of leisure, insisting on outfitting himself and Charlie with white tie and tails, complete with malacca cane and collapsible top hat.

In the midst of their revels, Lila was prone to quote a favorite saying to the point of being tiresome. She explained that an Eastern monarch once asked his wise men to invent a sentence that would apply to all situations at all times, and they had come up with "And this, too, shall pass away."

Her frequent citation of the saying seemed to suggest that, faced with the hazards of Wally's behavior, Lila gave him room to roam so long as he had some respect for propriety. So Ferguson, who was aware of Wally's affairs—of all but one—suspected. Like the Eastern monarch, Lila knew that all the other women in her husband's life were only so many passing fancies. She alone had captured Wally's heart. In that conceit, she was entirely correct.

━━━

By *1935* Wally and Lila had amassed a great fortune and decided to build a new home—and not just any ordinary Westchester County mansion but something altogether splendid and magnificent. They bought 105 acres of land in a relatively isolated area in the township of Mount Kisco, about five miles from Pleasantville. The wooded property sat atop a high hill and overlooked Lake Byram. In the distance on a clear day, the Hudson River was also visible. Charles May, a local society architect, was hired to design the new home along Norman lines, while Dolores Risley was chosen as decorator. Lila also hired her dancing instructor Harry Wilcox as construction supervisor.

The project was Lila's salvation, for it gave her something to do. For the next several years she threw herself into all phases of the construction, furnishing, and landscaping of their new home. In anticipation of the move, she had assembled a considerable collection of antiques—mostly American and British.

Plans for the twenty-two-room house called for a massive tower, an elegant winding staircase, and, in the foyer, an immense candelabrum whose pewter leaves resembled the pods of a lily pond. May used stone taken from old fieldstone walls already on the land. He also incorporated pegged studding from the timber of old local barns. An antique English granite mantelpiece was installed in the tower. Workers restoring the mantel discovered an engraved legend that gave the house its name: "High Winds Blow on High Hills." In the rumpus room, which opened onto an Italian garden, Lila installed a pool table and a Ping-Pong table. Also on the grounds were a stable, a fieldstone lookout tower, a swimming pool, and a greenhouse.

It was not long before people began to notice that Lila spent a great deal more time with Wilcox than with her husband. The two conferred together, lunched at fancy restaurants together, inspected sites together. Partly that was due to the public nature of both of their positions. But even so, people wondered. Many Digesters, including Al Cole, thought Lila and Wilcox were lovers.

Risley also had her suspicions but, like Cole, kept them to herself. One day in New York she was asked by someone who Harry Wilcox was. Risley told him. The man said Wilcox was going around saying Lila was his mistress. The *RD*'s decorator got furious. Whether the story was true or not, she thought Wilcox ought to have been more discreet. Another woman with a low opinion of Wilcox was Urith Dillon, who considered him "slimy, dirty, underhanded." Yet she also knew that his position was secure, because if the Wallaces wanted something done that was too unpleasant for them to do personally, Wilcox was the man for the job.

The woman chosen to decorate High Winds had met Lila while she and DeWitt were still living in Greenwich Village. Raised in Persia and China, Risley later chose the distinctive Persian blue slate tiles used on the roof of the house. Afterward Lila adopted the color for her personal stationery and also incorporated it in the interior decoration of any number of *Digest* offices, so it came to be known as "Lila blue."

Risley decorated the entire house—all but a guest bedroom, which Lila wanted to do herself. The result was a very feminine room, with ruffled, criss-crossed curtains and an abundance of fussy frills. When the house was finished, Lila took Wally on a tour of their new home. Asked how he liked everything, he innocently replied that he liked it all—except for that one bedroom.

Neighbors soon began referring to High Winds as the Castle. It had cost Wally and Lila $277,336, or the equivalent of slightly more than $1.5 million in the early 1990s. Its only other occupants were Yama the butler, a spaniel named Topaze, and a Russian wolfhound named Sorvin, which had a habit of running away to the streets of Mount Kisco.

Dillon and Risley were not alone in their contempt for the ex–dancing instructor. The arrogant Wilcox, who loved to intimidate underlings, was for many years the single most despised person in Pleasantville, and even Cole thought he was a "complete crook." Though he found the rumors of an affair between the site manager and his wife amusing, Wally also disliked him. Still, Wilcox provided Lila with companionship. Also, and perhaps more fundamental to his continued presence, he saved Wally's life not long after High Winds was built. The *Digest*'s fun-loving editor, though well into middle age, bought himself a four-seater Fairchild monoplane, took flying lessons, and obtained a pilot's license. While High Winds was under construction, a landing strip was installed in the flatlands below. A favorite pastime was to scare Lila by buzzing their new hilltop home or, when she was a passenger, by cutting the engine and gliding in for a landing.

One time, though, Wally had to make a crash landing. Wilcox, in the right place at the right time, pulled him from the burning cockpit. After that, firing the man would have seemed the height of ingratitude.

THOUGH Barclay Acheson and Wally played golf occasionally in the 1930s, they had grown somewhat apart. The latter considered his brother-in-law—a lanky, mustachioed dandy with a wandering eye—a rather useless fixture because he possessed no discernible skills as either an editor or a businessman. But he had lent the *Reader's Digest* the all-important $5,000 that made the difference between success or failure back in the dark days when the magazine was still located in the basement of a Village speakeasy. When Acheson decided not to pursue a career in the ministry, he was hired as an associate editor and given a big office and generous salary. However, he did no editing to speak of.

On November 8, 1936, after the *Fortune* article appeared, Wally was on the receiving end of a dig from his brother Benjamin:

> We are, if possible, more proud of you than before. I hope they paid you well for the article—or was this one of the articles worked up by the *Digest* and distributed free so as to secure the privilege of digesting & reprinting? . . . It certainly makes the Pater & I out to be pikers—$300 each when you needed $5,000. . . . I don't suppose I'll ever compete with your "tweedy elegance." Do you recall the old days when we worried lest some one with capital sh'd grab your idea & run off with it?

Dr. Wallace was likewise appalled at the wealth of his youngest son, even though the St. Paul press had given him some inkling several years before. "You have given me little idea of what you are worth or what your income is," he remonstrated. Then he dropped a large hint in a postscript: "I am often told that Macalester College is my monument. Would it not be glorious if you both would make Macalester your monument also?"

Already DeWitt and Lila were also showing their philanthropic side, albeit in a rather modest fashion. Most of the Reader's Digest Association's profits were sunk back into the company. In 1936 the RDA donated only $4,418 to thirteen organizations, the largest a bequest of $2,798 to the Near East Foundation and one of $1,000 to the Pleasantville Free Library. The American National Red Cross got a check for a mere $10.

Apart from paying the pensions of three professors, however, Wally resisted giving money to Macalester and even ignored his father's pleas to attend commencement exercises in the spring of 1936, when it had been arranged for both DeWitt and Lila Wallace to receive honorary doctor of letters degrees. Dr. Wallace continued to invite his son and daughter-in-law until the last minute, but Wally simply never replied, and the degrees were conferred in absentia.

━━━

ONE afternoon while High Winds was under construction, Wally invited Ferguson to join him to see how his new house was coming along. During the tour Wally grew excited, pointing out its various architectural features and singing Lila's praises. Ferguson seemed less enthusiastic. Somewhat nettled, Wally repeated his admiration of both house and Lila. Ferguson dutifully echoed those sentiments, but Wally was not convinced of his sincerity. Later the two men drove into Pleasantville for a hamburger and coffee at a local diner. As they drove, Wally demanded, "What do you *really* think about it?"

"I think it's splendid," said Ferguson, feeling cornered, "but it's not the kind of house I'd like to live in."

"What kind of house do you like, then?"

They were passing by some handsome but unpretentious old houses along the way and Ferguson pointed to one almost at random.

"A house like that," he said.

A few months later Ferguson was working in his office when Wally walked in and dropped a set of keys on his desk.

"What are these?" asked Ferguson.

"The keys to the house you wanted," Wally explained. Then he walked away.

Later Wally also built a house for Ralph Henderson and his wife, Clifford, who was a society type and, some thought, standoffish. After noneditor Hazel Cubberley's name was finally removed from the masthead, Henderson's was added. For a time, before Ken Payne came along, Clifford West Sellers was also listed as a fourth editor. But when she left to raise a family, the Wallaces instituted a policy that prohibited a husband and wife from working for the *Digest* at the same time.

That did not prevent Wally and Lila from ignoring that rule whenever it suited their purposes, although remarkably few members of either the Wallace or the Acheson family were hired on either a full-time or a temporary basis at Pleasantville. From the very beginning, they had decided to keep the business entirely to themselves and not invite the participation of relatives as shareholders or as employees. Wally's older brother Ben, the Rhodes scholar who later landed a job as a government bureaucrat in Washington, D.C., in particular resented the fact he had not been issued shares in the company that his $300 had helped underwrite.

As the *Digest*'s fortunes grew, Wally and Lila sent money to nearly everyone in their family and paid for the college educations of literally dozens of nieces and nephews. Ultimately, they also established trust funds for numerous members of the Wallace and Acheson families.

But for many years Ben Wallace turned down the offer of money and even once returned a check with the surly explanation that he and his wife, Katharine, did "not feel like accepting it," since taking the check would only "keep alive the memory of a most unfortunate experience."

Wally and Lila's generosity to their family backfired on another occasion as well. One year Dr. and Mrs. Wallace returned to St. Paul from a winter in California to discover that their son and daughter-in-law had prepared a little surprise for them. Wally and Lila even met them at the train station. But instead of heading for the family home, the four drove to a different neighborhood and pulled up in front of a new stone bungalow. Dr. Wallace and Aunt Miriam were gaily informed that this was their new home, which also came with a housekeeper and new car. Lila herself had decorated the home and chosen all the furniture. Aunt Miriam never forgave her.

While High Winds was under construction, the Wallaces gave their small gabled house to Harold Lynch for a nominal sum—with the proviso that half of it remain a *Digest* office for entertaining guests until High Winds was finished. Lynch's philandering had annoyed Wally to the point where he had not spoken to his editor for more than a year. The ex-priest's morals did not bother his employer so much as the flagrant way he conducted his affairs, which were interfering with his editorial responsibilities.

But Wally liked Lynch's second wife, Mickey, a fiery redhead who had just given birth to twins. Somehow she also found time to make four or five pies for the editors several times a week and bring them over to the office at lunchtime. Wally's favorite was lemon meringue.

After shunning Lynch for so long, Wally had an abrupt change of heart. As if to apologize for his hardness, he impulsively presented him with the gabled house. But when Lynch moved in, he began making additions to the building while the other half was still being used to entertain visitors—which annoyed Wally all over again.

Soon after High Winds was finished, the Wallaces gave *Digest* employees a tour of the grounds. While the rest of the group went ahead, Wally drew Mickey Lynch aside and took her down by the swimming pool. It was bordered with white petunias, but one corner was splotched with scarlet.

"Look," he explained, merrily pointing to those flowers, whose resplendent hue brought to mind Hester Prynne's adulterous badge of shame. "Even the petunias."

II

THE CASTLE

[1937–1944]

4

The Editing Factory

WITH the completion of High Winds, Wally finally had a very special room of his own—the office in his tower, which was reached by a narrow, twisting stairway. Into this sanctum sanctorum no one was ever admitted. Often for months at a stretch, he was wrapped up in his work, emerging in late morning or the early afternoon to visit the office, or else finding time on Friday evening for a few hours of poker.

Lila chafed at having to spend nights listening to the radio or reading a book while her husband worked all alone in his room upstairs. Sometimes he slept up there as well. But even during those furious bouts of work, Wally took time out on most evenings to dance with Lila for a quarter of an hour in the rumpus room. Those fifteen minutes were the terms of compromise. If only momentarily, they took Wally away from his task of building an empire and afforded Lila a respite from her loneliness. Sometimes he also liked to dance after breakfast—an enthusiasm his wife did not share.

Though spartanly furnished, Wally's new office was luxurious in comparison with the workplaces of his employees, who now numbered five hundred and were crammed into fourteen different buildings spread out all over Pleasantville. Parking had become such a problem that the company paid the fine of any worker from outside of town who got a ticket—a courtesy that sometimes cost a total of $60 a day.

Thus Wally and Lila decided to build a new home for their employees as well. In 1937 the Reader's Digest Association bought eighty acres of land in a wooded area known as Lawrence Farms, seven miles north of Pleasantville between Chappaqua and Mount Kisco. Construction began soon thereafter. Harry Wilcox again oversaw construction and later was named supervisor in change of grounds and maintenance. The ex–dancing instructor had a habit of snapping his fingers whenever he wanted anything done.

While construction was under way, Wally experimented in October 1938 with a four-day week for the first half of every month, asking employees to "work like hell" and strictly observe a thirty-minute lunch period. He was trying to condense even the workday. But the noble experiment failed, and the *Digest* soon returned to normal hours.

However, several noteworthy changes of a more permanent nature did take place around this time. Now that the *Digest* no longer had to masquerade as a magazine edited for women by women, Lila Bell Acheson's name on the masthead became Lila Acheson Wallace. And once again, Wally began to investigate the feasibility of launching an edition of the *Reader's Digest* in Great Britain. Most important, he undertook a concerted effort to bring Al Cole to Pleasantville on a full-time basis.

In 1938 Cole was making $50,000 a year at *Popular Science,* plus stock dividends that brought in half as much again. Cole worried that, if he left, the magazine he had helped guide for twenty-three years might suffer serious losses, which in turn would devaluate his stock. As a measure of his esteem for Cole, Wally generously offered him enough money to buy a controlling interest in *Popular Science.* Cole agreed, asking to be paid both a salary and a bonus based on performance. But he added, "I suggest that you fill in the figures."

Salary was not so much a problem as stock and profit sharing. Wally wanted to keep all the stock to himself. For nearly a year the two men haggled almost weekly. At one point Wally and Lila flew his plane down to Miami, where he had obtained his pilot's license, which needed to be renewed. Cole and his wife took a commercial flight down, and for days—when Wally was not racking up flying hours—the men strolled the boardwalk, trying to resolve their differences.

Meanwhile, as a result of Cole's promotional wizardry, the *Digest*'s newsstand sales were increasing at an average semiannual rate of 17 percent. That figure compared with a 12 percent increase for the temporarily resurgent *Saturday Evening Post* and only a 4 percent increase for *Collier's.* In sheer numbers the *RD*'s average newsstand sale of 906,265 was now nudging the *Post*'s league-leading 1,002,286.

By 1939 the luxurious $1.5 million headquarters in Chappaqua was finished and the *Digest* moved out of its scattered Pleasantville offices and into the handsome three-story red brick neo-Georgian building set off by a thirty-two-foot-high cupola. Al Cole, when he spotted the four statues of Pegasus flying to the four winds, quipped, "My gosh! All the vice presidents in one room!"

How Lila got the inspiration for installing a quartet of winged mythological horses in the cupola became a matter of speculation. She claimed she awoke in the middle of the night with a vision of sorts. According to Greek mythology, Poseidon instructed Pegasus to strike the earth with its hoof, causing the fountain Hippocrene to spring forth. Its waters became the font of poetic inspiration. But a local historian jokingly suggested that Lila had gotten the idea from the Mobil service station down the road. By the early thirties the oil company's fire-red flying horse had in fact become a familiar sight on America's highways and thoroughfares. Regardless, Pegasus in a variety of poses was adopted as an official corporate logo.

The decoration of the 91,000 square feet of floor space was overseen by Dolores Risley, who had since married an ex–trolley conductor named Roy Abbott. Because he had also been a bank teller, the Wallaces obligingly made him treasurer of their company. Wally took no interest in the building and did not set foot in it until construction was finished. His only request was that a door be installed connecting Ferguson's office with Ken Payne's, which was next to Wally's. The door was drawn into the plans but never used.

Officially, Chappaqua was a village in the town of New Castle. Despite such technicalities, Wally decided to keep the name of Pleasantville as the magazine's official address. Explained one Digester, "Pleasantville sounds more Digesty. Also it's easier to spell than Chappaqua."

Bordered by lush gardens and plantings, the new RDA headquarters set the style for the campus-like grounds later favored by numerous corporations around the country, though few could boast the collection of original works of art and rare antiques that Lila and Risley installed in the reception room and some of the hallways. For a time, free peanut butter sandwiches with milk were also offered to all employees in the afternoon, because Wally and Lila thought they were healthful. Not only were Digesters like Henry Morton Robinson beginning to resemble sofas—his nickname was Rondo—but their wallets were also growing very fat. Rumors accurately had midlevel executives averaging $30,000 to $50,000 a year, and half as much again in bonuses.

The magazine staff was also growing, fed by all those stories about some of the biggest salaries and best working conditions in the country. Among the editors hired in the late 1930s were Merle Crowell, former editor of the *American Magazine;* Howard Florance, managing editor of the *Literary Digest;* Marc Rose, who had helped found *Business Week;* and Bill Hard, son of well-known ex-socialist muckraker William Hard, Sr.

Across from Wally's office was Grace Naismith, who worked partly as Payne's and Dashiell's secretary and partly as a reader of unsolicited manuscripts. Known as the Pelvic Oracle, she eventually became the magazine's unofficial sex and health editor.

Ferguson, Rose, and Robert Littell, a former drama critic for the *New York World,* worked on originals while J. Carleton Dillon looked after production. In the book department were Ralph Henderson, Maurice Ragsdale, and Harold Lynch. They were assisted by a courtly, red-haired young man named Kenneth Wilson, formerly an editor of *Cosmopolitan.*

In addition to its three dozen editors, the *Digest* also employed three researchers whose offices were in the Chrysler Building in New York, near the main branch of the New York Public Library. By now Lucy Notestein's staff in Cleveland had grown to ten women.

Despite all the rumors, publicity, and genuine flattery in the wake of the *Fortune* article, Wally was determined to recover his privacy and erect a wall of secrecy higher than ever around the new headquarters. Apparently, he had decided that the mild embarrassment caused by the revelation of six-figure salaries, and such things as Lila's previous engagement to be married, outweighed any beneficial publicity.

Moreover, he was temperamentally more comfortable working and living outside the limelight, and stepping back into it momentarily only when it suited his purposes or whim. When *Esquire* asked him to pose for a photograph to run in a "highly dignified" new publication to be called *Ken,* he politely replied that he did not want his photograph to appear in *any* magazine.

Most of the editors seldom saw or conversed with Wally except in passing. Day-to-day editorial business was conducted with managing editor Payne or associate editor Dashiell. With the growth of the magazine, Wally had also instituted a rotating editorship that allowed him to monitor each issue closely while delegating a reasonable amount of equal authority to as many editors as possible.

Every month a different "issue editor" was given the responsibility for selecting the magazine's thirty-one articles, as well as all the filler material, departments, and book excerpt. Crowell, Florance, Rose, and Hard were the main issue editors, each charged with preparing three issues a year.

For a while Ferguson excelled as an originals editor, in one period generating twenty-eight out of sixty-seven. But before long his drinking problem began to interfere with his work and Harry Harper was assigned to oversee that department, assisted by Rose and the new man Bob Littell.

The reading and cutting staff also grew apace, with ten editors whose sole function was to read fifteen to twenty assigned magazines each per month—a task whose lack of intellectual challenge and deadening routine may have been a contributing factor to the alcoholism epidemic in the editorial ranks. Other readers combed through several hundred other periodicals, ranging from specialized scientific journals to company house organs. Upward of five hundred magazines were examined each month. Articles were then graded as either NU ("not usable"), U ("usable"), or P ("possible"). Brief handwritten comments in the margin sufficed when some sort of editorial elaboration was deemed necessary. The reader not only selected and graded but also cut the article, usually to a quarter of its original length, before sending it on to the editor in charge of the reading and cutting staff, who again screened the selections before passing them on to the issue editor for consideration. All articles went into a constantly updated inventory, which also included original articles and plants.

In the editing and condensing process, each editor used a different-color pencil so that the issue editor could keep track of who was cutting or restoring what. By one estimate the magazine staff spent more than five thousand reading hours to find the thirty necessary articles for condensing in any one issue. (The thirty-first article was now replaced by the book excerpt.)

By other estimates, however, Wally had too many editors doing too little work. It was a point on which he was unusually sensitive. Once Victo Ferguson teasingly asked him why there were so many editors when formerly he had put out the entire magazine by himself. Wally angrily defended the need for a much larger staff. But in 1939 he secretly decided to find out for himself exactly how well his editors were doing. Approaching literary agent Paul Reynolds, he arranged for an outside writer to read twenty current magazines and select those articles worthy of *Digest* reprint. He also proposed not to pay the agency directly, for fear that office morale might plummet if anyone discovered what he was up to. A year later Reynolds ran into Wally at a luncheon and asked for an update. He replied that his sub rosa experiment had convinced him that his editors were doing a fine job.

After an issue editor had prepared a typeset dummy or sample issue, it was sent up the line to Dashiell, who could unilaterally kill an article or order a substitution, or even insert an article of his own preference from the inventory. More often the condensations themselves were fine-tuned, with particular attention paid to transitional passages. Rewriting an author's original words, rather than selectively eliminating those deemed nonessential, became commonplace.

The revised and approved dummy issue then made its way to Payne, who had similar powers of discretion, only greater. Payne had promulgated a dictum that had the density of Holy Writ in Pleasantville: "When it is not necessary to change, it is necessary not to change." Payne was generally considered the best "precision cutter" on the staff.

The finished product was then sent to the research department for fact checking, as well as to copy editors and to a lawyer for legal review. Once in page proofs, an article was often condensed further to accommodate new filler or other material.

The final dummy that Wally saw was usually the one that went to press. If he did make a change, it was to propose another article that would fit in better with the editorial mix. He maintained such a close watch over the assignment and purchase of original articles, and the swelling inventory of reprints, that he was as a rule familiar with almost everything that arrived on his desk.

Though the rotating editorship was seemingly a democratic way of distributing authority, it also deliberately pitted the issue editors one against the other. Wally encouraged competition in the editorial ranks, and over time the number of issue editors was to fluctuate up to five or six. Issue editors were judged by how well their issues sold on the newsstands, and they themselves became the objects of lobbying by junior editors. Since the purchase of any original or reprint first had to be approved by an issue editor, sponsoring editors frequently bounced a piece from one issue editor to another. Despite such potential for confusion and conflict, the system worked reasonably well, and advancing to the level of issue editor became the goal of generations of ambitious *Digest* staffers.

However, the title of issue editor was never to become an official one on the masthead. Officially, issue editors were associate editors, though many associate editors—such as Ferguson and Henderson—were not issue editors. Payne, the de facto executive editor, was still listed on the masthead as the managing editor. Dashiell, the de facto managing editor, was still listed as an associate editor. The result of such editorial lumping together was that the names of the two official editors—one of whom, Lila Acheson Wallace, had never edited a single page of the magazine—stood out in stark relief.

Around the time that the new headquarters were begun, the magazine also dropped the *The* from its title and became known simply as *Reader's Digest.* Moreover, for many years the cover of the *Digest* had been a plain, almost severe black and white, embellished at most only with a printer's ornament. When the table of contents was finally shifted to the front cover, the outside wrappers were printed on a heavier stock. At this point the *Digest* began using color—the color of the cover stock. In November 1939 the first illustrations inside the book appeared, simple black-and-white line drawings of an almost Presbyterian plainness.

Though the custom of providing free vitamin-rich peanut butter sandwiches eventually disappeared, shoeshine men continued to prowl the hallways. Furthermore, the dress code required any male in a position of authority to wear a jacket and tie. Music was piped in for fifteen minutes of every hour, and at the end of the workday loudspeakers played "Good Night, Ladies." Employees were allowed two ten-minute breaks per day and a half hour for lunch. Most of the clerical help and lower-echelon editors ate in the large, subsidized cafeteria. Despite a certain regimentation, the working conditions were among the best in the country and were almost certainly a reflection of Lila's enlightened approach to social work a score of years earlier.

A select few of the editors—Marc Rose, Bill Hard, Ralph Henderson, and some others, as well as several favored secretaries—went to a nearby restaurant called the Kittle House, and they also took longer than half an hour. Another favorite hangout was a tearoom called the Maples. After each meal the men threw dice to see who would pay.

———

As the Digest continued to evolve, Wally was responsible for originating the lion's share of the magazine's new departments and ongoing series. "The Most Unforgettable Character I Ever Met" and "Toward More Picturesque Speech" were both his ideas. So later, in March 1943, was "Drama in Everyday Life," which the next month was changed to "Drama in Real Life."

Unlike originals and plants, such additions and innovations were not part of an editorial master plan but were usually the spontaneous outgrowth of a conversation with an author or a group of editors. Any number of other departments were similarly introduced and quickly abandoned, while other series were self-contained. In "Profit by My Experience," one author related how he learned from the Eskimo why it was wise not to be always in a hurry. Another explained why procrastinators cheated only themselves.

The usual procedure for a visiting writer was to take a train up to Chappaqua, where he was met by his sponsoring editor. On the way back to headquarters, they discussed article ideas.

"That's a natural" or "Wally will go for that one" were among the reassuring comments the editor was apt to make about several of the ideas, which the writer then naturally decided to present first. At the cafeteria or restaurant the writer was introduced to Wally and several other editors who were along for the lunch.

The first order of the day was a round of drinks, followed by a round of dirty jokes. One of the few who refrained from the joke telling was Ralph Henderson. Wally sat at the head of the table, opposite the guest. Conversation was mainly a dialogue between host and visitor. The other invited guests were there to eavesdrop or perhaps to put forward a neglected point or bit of germane information. The editors chosen to attend knew that they, too, had been summoned to a command performance.

Then everyone got down to business, and the writer advanced the first few ideas that his editor had assured him were shoo-ins. But Wally seldom liked any of those ideas. By the time lunch was over, the writer had exhausted all of his ideas and Wally was beginning to drum his fingers nervously on the table.

"That's not quite what I had in mind," he would repeat over and over. Turning to the sponsoring editor, he would ask, "What do you think?"

The editor and all the other editors were always in complete agreement with Wally.

"I want something absolutely original," Wally might announce. "I'll pay $15,000 for a great article!"

Instead of inspiring a writer, the mention of this otherworldly sum was likely to depress him even further. He thought of all the things he could do with $15,000 and at the same time realized that his very best ideas were not worth a wooden nickel. The writer's world had never looked bleaker. If no more acceptable ideas were forthcoming, Wally asked, "Were you planning to catch the 2:33 back to town? That's a good train."

A singular exception was the visit of A. J. Cronin, a successful London physician who had turned to writing when his own health broke. His novels *The Citadel* and *The Keys of the Kingdom* brought him literary fame, which in turn brought him one day to lunch with Wally and several of his associates in the small executive dining room off the cafeteria.

During the meal, Cronin casually mentioned a doctor who had vitally influenced his life. Wally suggested he do a portrait of the doctor as the most unforgettable character he had ever met. Cronin not only agreed but set the mold for one of the *RD*'s most famous features ever. When it appeared, in September 1939, "The Doctor of Lennox" was described only as "a memorable pen portrait of 'Dot-and-Carry,' butt of boyhood jokes." Curiously, though, as with the first original article, a visit to a mental asylum, it bore some parallels to Wally's own life and can also be read as a castigation of motherly religiosity and the Presbyterian church.

Known as "Carry," Cronin's childhood friend was a "comically lame," stuttering youth who supported his mother by rising at five o'clock every morning to deliver milk. He received his nickname from Cash, a minister's son, because he was always "dotting along" after the others. Carry hoped to study medicine, but his mother—the widow of a drunken loafer—wanted him to be a minister. So at the age of twenty-four Carry was ordained by the Church of Scotland. At the moment that was to be both his and his mother's greatest triumph, his first public sermon, Carry stammered so badly that he was unable to continue. His poor mother was taken by an apoplectic seizure and died within the hour. Soon afterward, Carry disappeared from his little Scottish town and was never heard from again.

Years later Cronin and Cash, now a member of Parliament, went on a fishing holiday in the town of Lennox in the Scottish Highlands. Circumstances contrived for their landlady to injure her kneecap, and she would see only her own village doctor. Who should show up, "black bag in hand, with all the quick assurance of a busy man," but Carry.

After attending to his patient, Carry turned his attention to his two old boyhood friends. He invited them home to supper, where they were amazed to discover that Carry not only was married to a very pretty woman but was the father of two red-cheeked, healthy children. Over time they learned that the doctor of Lennox was a force for good throughout the countryside, "a man who had refused defeat and won through to victory at last"—just like Wally.

The *Digest*'s second Unforgettable Character was a lovable, harmless, happy-go-lucky German vagrant named Anton, as memorialized in the October issue by his good friend Stefan Zweig. Not so coincidentally, however, the profile appeared the month after France and Great Britain had declared war on Germany. It also set the stage for the single most controversial article printed by the *Reader's Digest* in its first quarter century—the notorious "Aviation, Geography, Race," by Charles A. Lindbergh, an original that appeared in November 1939.

Lindbergh was an admirer of Alexis Carrel, author of *Man, the Unknown,* whose racist views had made a deep impression on him. In fact, the two men even cooperated in the invention of an artificial heart. Lindbergh was also an unapologetic admirer of Nazi Germany—of its people's "energy, virility, spirit, organisation, architecture, planning, and physique," as British diplomat Sir Harold Nicolson observed in his diary. In 1938 Lindbergh had accepted the Order of the German Eagle from Field Marshal Göring, leading Roosevelt to attack him as a Quisling. Lindbergh's article in the *Digest* was little more than a solemn reworking of Carrel's ideas about the white race combined with some of his own flightier notions about the superiority of nations who looked to the skies for their future.

Aviation, Lindbergh wrote, "is a tool specially shaped for Western hands, a scientific art which others only copy in a mediocre fashion, another barrier between the teeming millions of Asia and the Grecian inheritance of Europe—one of those priceless possessions which permit the White race to live at all in a pressing sea of Yellow, Black, and Brown. . . . It is time to turn from our quarrels and to build our White ramparts again. This alliance with foreign races means nothing but death to us."

Warning of the dangers of an "infiltration of inferior blood," Lindbergh claimed that the solution to the problem of preservation of the white race was increased air power, which was mystically allied to "racial character." In his view, only the white race understood the value of putting a premium on quickness of thought and speed of action. By building its air power, the white race—meaning all the countries of Europe and America—would avoid "racial suicide" and defeat the true aggressor, the "Mongol and Persian and Moor"—code words for Asian, Arab, and Jew.

The implication was clear. If the United States did choose to get into the war, it should side with Germany and its Luftwaffe. Though equally European, Britain in Lindbergh's view still put its faith in its navy, while France was similarly enamored of its legions. Neither truly appreciated the mystical symbiosis between air power and racial superiority.

The editor of the article was Wally himself, whom Lindbergh had met at the Engineers' Club in New York, where they first discussed the matter. Both men had long shared an interest in aviation and racial purity. Lindbergh stipulated in a letter to Wally that acceptance of the article meant "that no change be made in text, punctuation, capitalization, or title," and that there be no introduction or reference to this article or to himself. He went on, "Also I would prefer to avoid any unusual form of advertising in connection with the article." In a postscript Lindbergh added that, in the matter of copyright, he preferred "not to restrict the recopying of this article or quotations from it."

As a result the article was given no play and buried in the middle of the book. Two months later it was followed by Anne Morrow Lindbergh's "Prayer for Peace"—in fact, a call for British submission to Hitler's demands. Another purpose of the article was to bolster her husband's flagging self-confidence in the wake of the contempt his pro-German views were provoking in Washington and London. "Prayer" had arrived by messenger in Pleasantville just as the *Digest* was going to press with the January 1940 issue. Knowing the popularity of the Lindbergh name, however, Wally killed two other pieces to make room for the new lead-off feature.

The *Digest* also tried to paint Mussolini in appealing human-interest terms. The Italian dictator, a September 1929 article had noted, "finds no fault with democracy where it can be worked. It won't work in Italy, that's all." Even after Mussolini's conquest of Ethiopia and occupation of Albania, and the signing of an alliance with Nazi Germany, the

Digest in its March 1940 issue reprinted an article from the *American Mercury,* titled "Caesar Grows Old," which melodramatically recounted the time one of Il Duce's children almost died: "He was like a man gone mad. He dropped all work and spent whole days at the child's bedside."

But the *Digest* was also critical of Nazi Germany. Among the articles the magazine published was the exiled Thomas Mann's withering condemnation of the fascist state. Features about the plight of German refugees or the inferior status of German women, many of those articles indirectly scornful of Nazi notions of Aryan superiority, were regular staples. The magazine also published several articles that discussed briefly or at length the Nazi persecution of the Jews.

One of the most famous involved a reprint from a popular fiction magazine called *Story,* which in its September–October 1938 issue had printed a short work of fiction entitled "Address Unknown," by Kressmann Taylor. Never before in the magazine's seven-year history had anything created such a sensation. In ten days the issue sold out. In January 1939 the *RD* reprinted the piece—a haunting exchange of letters between a German Jew named Max, living in San Francisco, and his friend Martin Schulse, a Gentile and former suitor of Max's sister. Martin ignores Max's pleas to help his actress sister get out of Germany, and turns her away when she arrives at his doorstep, pursued by storm troopers. In revenge, Max begins sending Martin a series of letters that convince Nazi authorities that he, too, is Jewish. The final letter is returned to Max, stamped ADRESSAT UNBEKANNT.

Yet the *Digest* persisted in also looking on the bright side of Nazi Germany. Even as late as March 1940, after France and England had declared war on Germany, following Hitler's invasion of Poland, the *Digest* ran a story called "I Married a Nazi," by the pseudonymous British writer Margaret Schmidt, which contained this horrifying passage:

Coming from a democratic country where individuality and personality are tolerated in the female, where one's son is not born to a regime, a uniform, a god and a route, I sometimes feel I'll go crazy. Then I wish to God I hadn't married a German. But then I get scared and crouch down and draw the whole rich Nazism of my husband over my head, and feel as he does—safe, strong, impregnable; a chosen Hitler Woman among a people with a Terrific Destiny.

The Japanese also continued to be seen in a favorable light as late as November 1941. In "Japan Risks Destruction," the *Digest* belittled the notion of a militaristic Japan, noting, "The Mikado's people pathetically long for trade and friendship with the United States."

Presenting both sides of an issue was now an integral part of Wally's editorial philosophy, as though he were conducting a public cross-examination of witnesses for both the prosecution and the defense. Despite his antipathy toward the Roosevelt administration, he even ran an occasional article favorable to the New Deal or to the president himself. But in areas where Wally held strong views—that Nazi Germany ought to be appeased, that labor unions were corrupt, that President Roosevelt wished to assume dictatorial powers—articles reflecting his personal convictions outweighed those that did not by a ratio of three to one. The result of such skewing was an editorial policy masquerading as an impartial presentation of two sides to every story. Articles favorable to an individual or an institution on Wally's enemies list were usually light and anecdotal in nature, while negative pieces tended to be much more substantive.

If the *Digest* did not unequivocally condemn nazism, it harbored no doubts about communism. That was one issue where public dialogue in the pages of the magazine was out of the question, apart from a lone "debate" in the late thirties on the merits of Marxism-Leninism, with the pro position being argued by American Communist party general secretary Earl Browder. (There were similar pro and con exchanges of views on the Ku Klux Klan and the Catholic church.) That kind of tolerance quickly evaporated. As early as March 1941 the *Digest* ran a series of articles by Richard Krebs, writing under the pseudonym of Jan Valtin, on the Red threat, including a condensation of Krebs's book *Out of the Night*. Not long afterward Krebs was exposed as a paid agent of Nazi Germany and an anti-Semite, and his book was condemned as a fraud.

During this time the German Propaganda Ministry frequently reprinted the *Digest*'s antiwar articles or read them over the air. Joseph Goebbels confided in his diary, "An American newspaper, the *Reader's Digest*, . . . has published a sensational article that asserts that the U.S. in the last analysis is unable to undertake anything against the armed forces of the Axis. America's war was a hopeless undertaking and could only result in bleeding the nation white. At least one voice in the wilderness."

Ultimately, George Seldes, editor of the leftist media-watch journal *In Fact,* was to put words into Wally's mouth, saying they represented in substance the instructions he frequently gave to his editors: "We do not want Germany completely defeated," Wally told his editors, according to Seldes's script.

> I think Germany should be beaten up a bit, but I prefer that the American army does it, so that Hitler will learn who is boss in this world.
>
> But I do not want Germany smashed. What will become of the continent of Europe if Hitler is killed and Fascism completely eradicated? The Russians will conquer all of Europe. Therefore our policy should be to whip Hitler to the point where he recognizes we are the biggest power in the world, and then keep Hitler in Europe to police the continent and maintain order.
>
> We also need a little Fascism in the United States to keep this country in order. We need a certain type of Fascism here to keep radicals out and radical systems and philosophies from making any headway, and even attempting to take over the government.

Wally termed Seldes's report "unadulterated lies." But Seldes baited Wally to sue for libel, adding that several *Digest* editors would corroborate his story. Wallace did not sue but retaliated by planting an article in the *American Mercury* that denounced *In Fact* as pro-Communist—which, in fact, was true.

But the controversy did not stop there. Alarmed by the proliferation of *Digest* school editions, the National Council of English Teachers appointed a committee to investigate Seldes's charges. The *Digest* then waged an intense personal-relations campaign, courting members of the NCET's executive board. When the committee delivered its report, affirming that the *Digest* was a fascist publication, the board members rejected it and told the committee to prepare another. *Newsweek* wrote about the second report:

> After 19 months' investigation of the *Digest* as a suitable vehicle for study in English classes, the council's magazine and newspaper committee appeared Thanksgiving afternoon with a sharply negative report. Before its content would be officially disclosed to the 7,000 delegates, the report was emphatically squelched by the nervous . . . council president. . . . On her own, she concluded: "Your executive committee does not care what is in The Reader's Digest."

Seldes and the NCET were not alone in recognizing the awesome potential of the *Digest* as an instrument for shaping public opinion. Though he firmly believed that the United States should stay out of any war in Europe, Wally finally launched a British edition of the *Reader's Digest* in 1938. Two years later, in Havana, the first foreign-language edition was begun with the publication of *Selecciones del Reader's Digest.* Both editions were begun in cooperation with the U.S. State Department as part of its propaganda effort against the Axis powers.*

On the home front there were other wars to be fought. In March 1937 the *Digest* became the first popular magazine ever to discuss syphilis, with an article titled "Combatting Early Syphilis," by John H. Stokes, with a foreword by Dr. Thomas Parran, surgeon general of the United States. In the next issue, Parran himself contributed a follow-up, "Syphilis Can Be Stamped Out," which was first placed with *Survey Graphic,* a third-string general-interest magazine with a minuscule circulation. (Venereal disease, like insanity, fascinated Wally, and he was to return to both subjects repeatedly throughout his active editorial life.) As part of Parran's campaign to eliminate the epidemic, reprints of the article were widely distributed in factories and plants. But when the manager of Swift and Company, a meat-packing company, received the reprint offer, he declined, noting delicately, "I do not believe this is a matter which would be accepted gratefully by our employees. . . ."

Like the syphilis article, "Hope for Victims of Arthritis" advanced a treatment currently being developed by physicians. One of them wrote to the *Journal of the American Medical Association* after the *Digest* version appeared, noting that its title should have been "False Hopes for Victims of Arthritis," since the treatment was still in the experimental stage. The *Journal* itself editorialized, "Those who attempt education of the public in matters of health and disease have a serious responsibility; they do incalculable harm when they [mis]lead the public."

Over the years that pattern was to be repeated numerous times, with the *Digest* selectively advancing a miracle cure based on inconclusive research, followed by complaints from the medical community.

The *Digest* also supported safe driving and cheaper milk, exposed dishonest mechanics and watchmakers, and published comparison ta-

---

*The international editions are taken up at greater length in chapter 6.

bles to show that most cigarettes contained equal amounts of nicotine and tar, despite advertising claims to the contrary. Old Golds, which had a fraction less than the other brands, took out full-page newspaper advertisements announcing, "Impartial Tests Find Old Gold *Lowest* in *Nicotine* and *Throat-Irritating* Tars and Resins. Get July Reader's Digest. Turn to page 5. See what this highly respected magazine reports."

The magazine's mixture of fierce isolationism, humor, warm human-interest stories, and muckraking continued to set new records. At the beginning of 1941 *Business Week* finally announced what had "long been suspected"—that the *Reader's Digest* had "the largest magazine circulation in the world": "The paid monthly figure is 4,100,000 for January, which includes the British edition, printed in London (180,000 copies) and the new Spanish-language edition, 'Selecciones del Reader's Digest,' distributed throughout Latin America (225,000 copies)."

Thus, on the brink of a great world war, the *Reader's Digest* had in just eighteen years become indisputably an American institution.

THOUGH famous names were now appearing in the *Digest* with some regularity, remarkably few of the country's best journalists were lured to write original articles for it—even though the payment rate, up to $2,500 per article, was among the highest in the industry and the challenge of writing two or three digest-sized pages not too daunting. That was partly because the *Digest* harvested one or two recognizable names per issue through reprints or book condensations—a Stephen Leacock piece from the *New Yorker*, a Walter Lippmann column, a story by best-selling novelist Mary Ellen Chase. Other once famous writers—Ida Tarbell, William Hard, Sr.—found in the *Digest*, in the twilight of their careers, a haven from obscurity.

With the war going on in Europe and political passions running high in the United States, nearly everyone in Pleasantville was taking sides. Wally and Payne were adamant America Firsters, which caused hard feelings among those Digesters who were in favor of Bundles for Britain. The political situation also accounted for the absence of well-known bylines over original articles. Famous writers either were not welcome by the policymakers at Pleasantville or did not want to be associated with an organization that was now becoming conspicuously right-wing despite its image as a magazine full mainly of inspirational advice and example.

Beyond that, there was already a certain stigma attached to writing for the *Digest,* where a uniformity of style and simplicity of argument were the rule. The standard apology offered by writers who did work for the *Digest* from time to time was the allure of money.

However, Wally did set his sights on one prominent writer—in fact, one of the most famous in the country. Alexander Woollcott, author, playwright, contributor to the *New Yorker,* and a founder of the famed Algonquin Round Table, attracted Wally because of their mutual interest in words. "Toward More Picturesque Speech," a collection of colorful wordplay or unusual combinations of words, was by now a regular feature either as a filler or a full-page department. Not unexpectedly, Woollcott had himself been picturesquely remembered in the feature on several occasions.

After receiving Wally's invitation to do a series of articles or perhaps a column on language, Woollcott contemptuously told a friend, "Mr. Wallace has destroyed the pleasure of reading; now he is about to destroy the pleasure of writing."

At the time Woollcott was touring the country playing Sheridan Whiteside in *The Man Who Came to Dinner.* Like many a writer, he was desperately strapped for cash. Woollcott consented to do an article and dashed off the first of a series to be called "Lessons in English." But his prolix style did not play well among the word assassins on the *Digest*'s editorial staff, whose job was to pick off as many adjectives and nouns per manuscript as humanly possible.

Wally was by no means in awe of his new contributor. Sensitive to the criticism that all the articles in the *Digest* read as though they had been written by one person, he wrote a memo to his editors declaring the contention baseless. But he did concede that, in any one *Digest,* at least some condensations lacked the distinctive style and flavor of the original. Woollcott's un-*Digest*-like prose would help restore the balance, even though he "spreads his stuff pretty thin."

Yet when Wally asked Woollcott to substitute new copy for the last eleven lines of Lesson IX, the latter complained that they were the best part of the piece, adding petulantly, "I doubt if you really want any more Lessons in English but if you feel otherwise, I am sure that you must have a dozen youngsters underfoot who could turn out samples much more to your taste."

Wally immediately wrote back, "For God's sake, let's get together for a drink the next time you are in New York."

Meanwhile, on March 20, 1939, Wally announced to his editorial staff that business manager Arthur Griffiths had been granted a year's leave of absence and that, effective that day, Al Cole was in charge of the business offices. The memo cryptically explained that Griffiths's "outside activities prevent him from giving the necessary time to the business office." Griffiths had recently abandoned his wife and openly taken up with another woman. Now that the *Digest* was more in the public eye—with Griffiths himself written up in *Fortune*—Wally and Lila wanted no hint of scandal.

Other new names also began to appear on the masthead that year and the next. In 1940 Wally conceived the idea of the roving editor—a catchall category that was conveniently to include, at least initially, writers, consultants, and his brother-in-law. The original three, appearing for the first time on the May 1940 masthead, were Barclay Acheson, Michigan newspaper publisher Karl Detzer, and Paul Palmer.

———

AFTER Ken Payne and Al Cole, Palmer was the most important person Wally hired in the magazine's first quarter century. Until Ed Thompson came along, he was also its most controversial. After graduating from Harvard, Palmer had gone to work for the *St. Louis Post-Dispatch,* where he served as private secretary to Joseph Pulitzer. But Palmer's deeply conservative beliefs did not sit well at that bastion of midwestern liberalism, and he went off to live in Paris, becoming an escort of the famous artists' model Kiki. Palmer was also a championship-level backgammon player, gourmet chef, and disciple of the right-wing Spanish political philosopher José Ortega y Gasset. Tall and handsome, with a well-deserved reputation as a ladies' man, Palmer was unusually restless. Between the ages of seventeen and fifty-seven he was to move at least once a year, collecting sixty different addresses.

At one period, deciding to settle down, Palmer persuaded his then current and very wealthy in-laws—he married five times and later collected his wives' recipes in a cookbook—to buy him the *American Mercury.* H. L. Mencken had resigned the editorship in 1933, by which time its circulation was already in decline from a 1927 high of 77,000. By the time Palmer assumed the helm, in 1935, replacing Henry Hazlitt, the readership stood at less than half that figure.

Palmer reduced the size of the magazine to a digest format, shortened the articles, and halved the price. He also made it over into an ultraconservative, staunchly anti-Communist vehicle, some of whose articles were plants for the much larger but ideologically compatible *Reader's Digest*. Among the frequent contributors to the *Mercury* under Palmer's editorship was Lawrence Dennis, whom *Life* characterized as "America's No. 1 Fascist author" and one of the "two prize examples of native American Fascism." Palmer also published profascist articles by Lord Varney, who had been decorated by Mussolini.

The formula succeeded, and circulation soon doubled. In 1939 Palmer sold the magazine to Lawrence Spivak, his business manager. Eugene Lyons served as editor from 1939 to 1944. One of Palmer's first acts when he joined the *Reader's Digest* was to hire Dennis as a paid consultant. In time Dennis was to be indicted by the U.S. attorney general on charges of conspiracy to overthrow the government. Lyons later became a *Digest* roving editor.

Wally wanted Palmer to be his eyes and ears in Washington. A consummate insider who knew everybody in the capital's most exclusive political and social circles, Palmer was also the kind of man Wally felt he could depend on for sound political advice. As the situation in Europe worsened, he was resolved that the *Digest* would do all in its power to thwart Roosevelt's plan to enter the war on the side of the Allies.

Though Palmer's office was in the Chrysler Building, in New York, he commuted frequently to Pleasantville in order to consult with Wally or other editors. But he also spent a great deal of time in the capital, serving as a one-man Washington bureau. Palmer's responsibilities were to suggest article ideas—usually of a political nature—and, if possible, persuade a conservative senator, congressman, or other official to masquerade as author. The actual writing was done by speech writers, congressional aides, and newspapermen who passed Palmer's political litmus test. However, on occasion—to provide at least the appearance of balance—Palmer also recruited liberals, Democrats, and others to present an opposing viewpoint.

On September 19, 1939, Palmer met with Thomas E. Dewey, Republican district attorney of New York, about putting his name to an article on the European situation. Neither man went into specifics. After reporting on that meeting, Palmer told Wally about a similar meeting with New York's conservative Republican congressman Hamilton Fish, an isolationist and arch-enemy of Roosevelt. Fish, Palmer wrote, "had an extended talk with [German foreign minister Joachim] von Ribbentrop who, he says, talked to him with unusual frankness and candor. . . . [Fish] claims that the Germans have for the past eighteen months been preparing for a five-year war and are now ready to last that long. R. also stated that Hitler had been for six years completely devoted to the theory that England was Germany's natural ally."

As for Nicholas Murray Butler, president of Columbia University and recipient of the Nobel Peace Prize in 1931, he was in Palmer's opinion "definitely a participationist" regarding the prospect of America's entry in the war: "He told me that there was no question of our going into the war in the future—'we are in it now.' . . . I believe he could write as good an article for the participationist point of view as anyone. A possible title: 'America is Already in the War.' "

Later Palmer proposed that journalist Amos Pinchot write an article on how Roosevelt was "reaching for dictatorship." Eventually, the *Digest* arranged for the president's eldest son and close adviser, James Roosevelt, to write a profile. "My Father Is Not a Dictator" was the article originally proposed. Instead, Roosevelt turned in a banal portrait of his father as the head of a "typical American family." Unwittingly, he thereby contributed to the public impression that the *RD* presented a balanced view on every important issue.

Palmer was also concerned with the vast number of European refugees entering the United States, both legally and illegally, and suggested several possible approaches, though he called the matter "a rather touchy one, because of the Jewish angle." Since immigration quotas from Central Europe were already filled, Jews fleeing Germany used Czechoslovakian and Polish visas, which was officially illegal, since those countries no longer existed.

A month later Palmer reported that a source in the Spanish embassy had told him that Franco was demanding all of French Morocco "as his price for entering the war on the side of the Axis." Then Palmer turned to a favorite theme:

A foreigner, an old friend of mine, sat next to columnist Dorothy Thompson at lunch the other day. Throughout the meal, she praised Willkie and inveighed against Roosevelt. Later, he asked her to tell him—because, as a foreigner, he was unfamiliar with our politics—which man, Roosevelt or Willkie, would really be better as a President for the country during the next four years. Miss Thompson thought a moment, and then replied: "Roosevelt." I think there is more of this sentiment in the country than we are aware of. I am told that even economic royalists in the smart social colonies of Southampton and Newport have begun to waver. Formerly violently anti-Roosevelt and enthusiastically pro-Willkie, they now admit frankly that they are going to vote for Roosevelt.

Among the articles that Palmer proposed in 1940 were a friendly profile of Marshal Philippe Pétain, head of the Vichy government, that would draw a parallel between the "Leftish paternalism" that "was directly responsible for the weakening of France" and a piece on "the importance of the science of eugenics," to be followed by other articles on sterilization and "health certificates for those who wish to be married, a movement in the direction of scientific mating, and, above all, clinics and institutes to devote at least as much time to the study of human breeding as is now devoted by the Department of Agriculture . . . to the study of the breeding of hogs."

Palmer also suggested an article on "why aid to Britain is a bad American policy," recommending Lawrence Dennis as the author. "He is an out-and-out isolationist," Palmer commented. "I am not. If I took any side in the present argument, I would be an isolationist. But I do not take any side—I think this country's goose is cooked, no matter what happens. Whether we disintegrate in a losing war, trying to pull British chestnuts out of a world conflagration, or whether we collapse later through internal weakness, seems to me to be an academic question."

Unlike other editors on the staff, Palmer was financially independent—a luxury that allowed him to resign whenever Wally did not go along with everything that he wanted. On August 18, 1940, on stationery of the Metropolitan Club in Washington, D.C., Palmer gloomily informed his boss:

> I have worked hard for you ever since I joined the staff and I have perhaps turned in a certain amount of worthwhile accomplishment: but I have become convinced that I do not really belong on the magazine. I hasten to add that the fault is undoubtedly mine, and not the *Digest*'s. Perhaps whatever talents I may have were better employed at different work. . . . I shall always think of you as the greatest editor and publisher our country has ever produced. . . .

Wally did not take him seriously. Palmer was to resign from the *Digest* far more often than he got divorced. Though four of Palmer's five wives let him get away, Wally refused to accept any of his resignations except on a temporary basis.

Like Palmer, Wally backed Republican candidate Wendell Willkie in the approaching presidential election. Unlike Senator Robert Taft of Ohio and District Attorney Thomas Dewey of New York, who were isolationists in varying degrees, Willkie was a conservative of great personal charm who advocated aid to the Allies. Shortly before the 1940 presidential election, a memo was sent out to all *Digest* employees under the names of DeWitt Wallace, Lila Acheson Wallace, and Ken Payne. It read in part:

> This election may easily have greater consequences, for good or ill, than any other in our lifetimes. . . . You will of course vote as you please. But because some of you may wonder why *The Reader's Digest* supports Wendell Willkie, may we say this: We believe fervently in the sincerity, determination and ability of Wendell Willkie *to unify this nation and to promote the well-being and prosperity of all classes.*

———

SOON after the *Digest* moved into its new headquarters in 1939, Wally issued a decree that the workday was to conclude at 4:00 P.M. sharp, with no exceptions. Knowing that Wally would personally enforce the decree, a number of executives left their offices at the appointed hour and waited in their cars until Wally left for High Winds. Then they returned to their offices and stayed as long as they pleased. But Wally soon caught on to the ruse and made it clear that his wishes were not to be contravened.

Al Cole had never returned home before seven in his entire life, and he was now at a loss how to fill what amounted to half the afternoon. His solution was to obtain from the fulfillment department a list of the names and addresses of all subscribers in nearby towns. Every day at four o'clock he set off on a personal house-to-house tour to interview longtime subscribers, asking them not what they originally liked about the *Digest* but what made them renew their subscriptions. Though he had always liked the magazine, he was unsure about what made it so special. He learned that what most readers liked about the magazine was the art-of-living material they could apply to their daily lives. It was a lesson he never forgot.

When Cole joined the company he brought with him his trusted circulation director, Frank Herbert, who was given a similar responsibility at the *Digest*. One of the young subscription copywriters helping out in the department at the time was Hobe Lewis, who described Al Cole, his first mentor, as a man of great charm, "a supersalesman of the best kind, with high moral principles. He wasn't the way Wally was."

According to the compromise Wally and Al worked out on the latter's remuneration, Cole earned a salary of $50,000 plus incentives. But in a very short time the hard-driving Cole was taking home up to $400,000 a year in bonuses. Finally, the abashed business manager went to Wally and asked for a reduction in compensation—presumably because he was now earning far more than Ken Payne, who was still considered the number two man at the *Digest*.

(As before, Wally continued to give out generous bonuses every year to top employees, the amount depending entirely on his whim. But some bonuses carried a negative message. Almost as dreaded as a pink slip was a bonus of only a few hundred dollars —which was often the prelude to dismissal.)

Like Wally, Cole was regarded as an easy man to talk to but a hard one to get to know. In Cole's case that was partly because he never mixed business with pleasure. His loyalty was also so absolute that no one ever heard him utter a single word of criticism against his employer. On one occasion the two men had a disagreement over policy, and Wally overruled him. Afterward Cole, with a colleague, went out to a restaurant and downed six drinks, which was rare for him. But he did not say a word against Wally and never mentioned the painful subject that brought him there.

On another occasion Cole triumphantly went into Wally's office to report on the latest newsstand figures.

"We've had the best year ever, Wally, the best year we've ever had," Cole said, reading off the top figures.

Wally was reading an article that had gone through two edits, but he was still not sure it was publishable.

"Fine," he answered unenthusiastically.

Taken aback, Cole repeated the gross and net income figures and *Digest* profit after taxes.

"That's great," Wally said impassively. "You always do a great job, Al."

At that moment he decided to kill the article and was trying to think of a replacement.

"I don't think you understand, Wally," said the deflated Cole. He repeated the last figure.

"Just leave them," Wally said. "I'll look at them later."

But as Cole reached the door, he turned and said slyly, "We beat Time-Life."

Wally jumped up.

"We did?" he exclaimed. "We beat Time-Life! Al, that's wonderful!"

———

SOMETIME in 1940 Palmer paid a visit to Earl Browder, head of the U.S. Communist party (and former *RD* contributor), at party head-quarters in New York City. According to a story attributed posthumously to Bruce Minton, at the time a card-carrying party member and journalist on the staff of *In Fact,* Palmer offered Browder any price he wanted in order to write an article for the *Digest* in which he claimed to be a frequent visitor to the White House. When Browder refused, Palmer said he possessed sworn affidavits from Secret Service agents stating that the party head was seen entering a side door of the executive mansion. Despite a final offer of $25,000, Browder declined to go along with the scheme. In 1945 he and Minton were expelled from the Communist party for opposing Stalinism.

Though Wally was never to waver in his contempt for Roosevelt, his isolationist stance toward the war in Europe ended dramatically, like that of most America Firsters, one quiet Sunday morning when Japan launched its devastating surprise attack on Pearl Harbor.

In 1941 American public opinion was just beginning to shift toward intervention. A majority of Americans now expected war and were psychologically ready for it. Interventionist war correspondents such as *Digest* contributor Quentin Reynolds and William Shirer were helping to prepare public opinion with their reports from Europe. Hollywood was also becoming interventionist, as were such influential magazines as *Time* and *Life*.

After the attack, public opinion quickly rallied behind Roosevelt. Within days America was on a war footing, Germany and Italy declared war on the United States, and the conflict in Europe became global.

At the time of the attack, the January issue of the *Digest* was already on press. The next morning, Wally stopped the presses and replaced all six pro-isolationist articles with art-of-living and other noncontroversial features. But tens of thousands of the original January 1942 issue had already been mailed out, so it became the only issue in *RD* history to be printed in two separate versions. Thereafter, the *Digest* became as passionately jingoist as it had been isolationist, though its war fever was always tempered by a lingering ambivalence toward Nazi Germany.

On the other hand, no matter what Roosevelt did, he could never do enough to please the newly bellicose patriots of Pleasantville. As before, the magazine continued to run three articles unfavorable to the administration for every one that could be counted friendly.

As the conflict progressed, thoughtful pieces such as Walter Lippmann's analysis of "U.S. War Aims" became relatively rare. In its effort to stoke war fever, the *Digest* favored realistic descriptions of the wanton slaughter of American prisoners by German and Japanese troops. "I Was an American Spy" told the story of a woman who ran a nightclub in Manila as an American front until she was discovered and tortured by Japanese troops. Shrill warnings about America's internal stability were also staples. Louis Bromfield's "We Aren't Going to Have Enough to Eat," which forecast a U.S. food shortage, was quickly reprinted by the German Propaganda Ministry and attracted widespread international attention. In November 1942 the president was criticized for "not giving America fighting faith that will send us marching." The same issue suggested that a third of the American people were ready for "negotiated peace with Germany's leaders." Similar themes were repeated throughout the war.

The *Digest* adopted an equally inconsistent attitude toward the Jews. For example, the lead article for September 1942 was entitled "The Facts about Jews in Washington," which warned that Jews should "avoid an excessive loading of the government with Jewish citizens." Author of the piece was W. M. Kiplinger, publisher of the *Kiplinger News Letter*, a "service for businessmen," who also noted, "Jews have become concentrated in a few governmental agencies where they are disproportionate, where they are conspicuous for their numbers, where they have intimate contact with the public. . . . This is an error, and it needs to be remedied by the reduction of Jews in these offices."

Yet war correspondent Ben Hecht, who was Jewish, also claimed that the *Digest* was the first major American publication to reveal the extent of the German persecution of the Jews with his February 1943 article, "Remember Us," based on information provided to him by Dr.

Hayim Greenberg, editor of the *Jewish Frontier,* a New York English-language weekly. Hecht—who the following month organized a mass demonstration at Madison Square Garden, attended by 50,000 people, to bring Hitler's "final solution" to the attention of the public—described the grisly specter of 5,000 Jews jammed into freight cars lined with tons of quicklime, 20,000 Jews herded into a field in Silesia and used as targets for Luftwaffe guns, 5,000 Jews burned alive in Cologne, the public hanging of rabbis, Germans forcing old Jews to rub excrement over their head and pray, rape and torture of Jewish women, and other atrocities. According to Hecht, the article "broke the American silence attending the massacre of the Jews."

Strictly speaking, the *Digest* was not the first major American publication to broadcast news of the Nazis' policy of genocide. That grim task fell to the *New York Times,* which in a front-page story on December 18, 1942, reported on a joint declaration by eleven Allied nations condemning Germany's "bestial policy of cold-blooded extermination" of European Jews. The paper also editorialized that same day that Nazi persecution of the Jews was, in the words of a member of the British Parliament, the "greatest single horror in . . . history." Not until August 27, 1943, however, did the *Times* document the Nazi butchery with a chilling table that listed the number of Jews killed according to nationality—thus confirming what the *Digest* had reported on an anecdotal level a half year earlier.

Even during wartime, though, the magazine never lost sight of the need to balance the lurid and emotional with the lighthearted and mildly prurient. True to form, pieces like "Our Wounded Come Home" and "They Walk without Legs" were published side by side with "What English Girls Think of the Yankees" and "Are Yanks Lousy Lovers?"

———

IN MAY 1941 Wally sent a car for Woollcott, who was playing in nearby New Haven. Over dinner at High Winds they discussed a series to be called "Twice Told Tales," including "The Death of Franz Schubert," "The Death of Stephen Foster," and "The Birth of the Battle Hymn." In July, Woollcott handed in the first installment, "Our Lady's Juggler," a maudlin religious tale that Wally declared he showed to his "highly sentimental wife, whereupon a tear was shed as she finished the story. Is that not the ultimate test? . . . Enc. $2000."

The following May, though, Wally had the unpleasant experience of turning down a Woollcott manuscript on Thomas Jefferson and John Adams, informing him that he had "lost sight of a mass audience." Woollcott took the rejection manfully, replying that, even in his present emaciated condition, in which he often burst unaccountably into tears, he "bore up quite well under the shock of getting back a manuscript from an editor for the first time in twenty-four years." He explained, "At the time the blow fell, it occurred to me that a good many which had been docily [sic] published might better have been returned, and I must confess that when you do it at all you do it with great charm."

Some time later Wally invited Woollcott to write a regular Town Crier column, "made up of brief, revelatory glimpses of life in these United States." He added, "Certainly it would become shortly the most widely discussed feature in any magazine. Do you want to try it for a year, at $24,000? Let us make our next meeting the most momentous in publishing history!"

Though the meeting was postponed, Woollcott soon appeared on the masthead as a roving editor. Later, after turning in pieces on Irving Berlin and Stephen Foster, he wrote to say he hoped to corral another famous author to do an Unforgettable for the *Digest:* "I've got Dorothy Parker locked up here [in Vermont] and I think she is at work on a piece for that series. Her instinctive reply to the suggestion was that hateful people were the most unforgettable and she would like to try a portrait of her mother-in-law."

Wally quickly wrote back, telling Woollcott not to let Parker out of his sight until she had written "her greatest masterpiece for the *Digest.*" But two weeks later, after reading her manuscript, he rendered a negative assessment, though the piece had some "memorable touches": "I do not think that one is lifted as one expects to be lifted in reading the sketch. I'm sorry as hell."

On January 23, 1943, Woollcott lunched with Wally and Lila in New York, then stopped at a florist to send a dozen yellow roses to Lila by way of thanks. Afterward he went to a radio studio to appear on "The People's Forum." Midway through the broadcast he collapsed and died.

———

THAT same year the *Reader's Digest* sounded the first notes of the Cold War—at a time when the United States and Russia were on the warmest terms since the 1917 revolution, and 81 percent of all Americans thought the country ought to work hand in hand with the USSR to forge a world peace—with its July 1943 article "We Must Face the Facts about Russia." Author of the piece was Max Eastman, a PK of the Congregational variety, no less, who had previously written an Unforgettable for the *Digest*—conveniently opting to crank out a sentimental remembrance of a parent. Then the renowned ex-editor of the *Masses,* who had recently renounced communism, proposed an article exposing the inherent weaknesses of socialism. Wally immediately agreed.

The result was "Socialism and Human Nature." After it was accepted for publication, Eastman went up to Pleasantville to read the proofs. He had stipulated that he personally sign off on the article, which for the old radical turned reactionary was an event of "momentous importance." American socialism had been in a state of crisis ever since 1936 when a small group of intellectuals, both Communists and fellow travelers, broke with Soviet communism soon after Stalin began his great purge of the Communist party. Many later became hard-line Cold War liberals. Eastman, though among the last of the country's prominent socialists to defect, was ultimately to move much further right than most—propelled all the way by *Digest* money.

When he reviewed the galleys of his article, Eastman was gratified to find his original sentiments, though somewhat compressed, carefully unaltered. After fixing the proofs to his satisfaction, he went home to await the expected hue and cry of betrayal from his old compatriots on the left.

But Eastman had not seen the brash new title invented by the editors: "Socialism Does Not Gibe with Human Nature." Far more unsettling was a sidebar at the entrance to the article. Wally had conspired for Wendell Willkie, arch-capitalist and former right-wing candidate for president, to welcome the old renegade into the ranks of conservative Republicanism.

In his autobiography, *Love and Revolution,* Eastman described the aftermath of the article:

> I was sick for two weeks. The *Socialist Call* held a three-column funeral service: "In Memoriam—Max Eastman." Dwight MacDonald, an editor of *Partisan Review* and one of those who had condemned Stalin in 1936, wrote: "Max Eastman, hero of the old *Masses* trial . . . publishes an attack on socialism which Wendell Willkie implored every good American to

read, and which is the low-water mark to date of such affairs for vulgarity and just plain foolishness."

Though the new title and the Willkie sidebar had made Eastman sick, they did not apparently distress him to the point where he felt either betrayed by Wally or unable on principle to accept another fee from the *Digest*—whose capitalistic rates, after all, were among the highest in the history of publishing. Some time later he once again made his way up to Pleasantville for lunch with Wally and some editors in the executive dining room. During the course of the meal, Wally said, "You write so beautifully that I'm sure you can write for us."

Eastman proposed a series called "Men with Ideas." Wally quickly replied, "I agree to that, and I propose that you become a roving editor of the *Reader's Digest*. We will pay you a living wage, and we won't tell you whom to write about. You pick your own subjects, write as you please"—he paused—"and send us your expense account."

Though he never wrote the series, the ex-radical did become a roving editor, traveling to Latin America, Greece, and Switzerland and remaining with the most powerful voice of American conservatism for the rest of his life.

In June 1941 another roving editor had been added to the staff: Stanley High, a Methodist minister who had been a foreign correspondent for the *Christian Science Monitor* and later editor of the *Christian Herald*. He was followed by William Hard, Sr. Six more were appointed in November 1942. Roving editors specialized: Hard concentrated on politics, Lester Velie on labor problems, Francis Vivian Drake on aviation, High on evangelical religion, Harland Manchester on science, and botanist Donald Culross Peattie on nature. Karl Detzer covered business and community affairs; J. P. McEvoy's beat was entertainment. Robert Littell did literary and historical pieces. Eugene Lyons was the magazine's heavyweight anti-Communist.

Despite their diversity, almost all of the roving editors had one trait in common—they were defectors from the liberal fold. A former speech writer for Roosevelt, High was soon taking potshots at his ex-boss with articles like "Roosevelt: Democratic or Dictatorial?" Hard had been a muckraker for the *Nation* and the *New Republic*. The Russian-born Lyons was assistant director of the Tass news agency in Moscow in the years immediately following the Bolshevik Revolution.

McEvoy had once been known as "the young Debs" for his espousal of socialism.

Most rovers were also uncommonly colorful or eccentric characters. Joseph Patrick McEvoy, abandoned on the steps of the Catholic Foundling Hospital in New York in 1895, was a thrice-married newspaper columnist who also wrote plays, greeting-card verse, and labels for soup cans in a desperate effort to stay solvent. Eventually, he moved to Woodstock, an art colony in upstate New York, where Ben Hecht wrote his first novel in J. P.'s home. One year McEvoy earned nearly a million dollars, mostly from a musical called *The Potters,* which was sold to Hollywood.

"The next found him going about our house at night," his son Dennis later recalled, "extracting coins from the little clay piggy banks which belonged to my sister and me to pay the milkman—credit having been temporarily suspended."

McEvoy also had the unique distinction of writing thirteen articles in twelve months. One winter a grateful Wally told him to take his family on an all-expenses-paid week's vacation. What Wally had in mind was a jaunt to Florida costing about $700. McEvoy, though, who had never gone skiing before, decided to head for Canada with his third wife, Peggy, and their two children. Putting up at a luxurious ski resort, he set about renting skis, hiring instructors, and, in the evenings, closing down the bar. When the bill for $1,700 arrived in Pleasantville, the editorial business manager took it to Wally for approval. Wally stared at the expense sheet for a long moment, then shook his head and said, "This is amazing. I've never seen anything like it. But J. P. is such a fine writer, I can't do anything but okay it."

Another of Wally's favorite roving editors was Lois Mattox Miller, who wrote on health and related topics. After a Miller article on needless tonsillectomies appeared in the magazine, Wally sent her one of his trademark congratulatory notes and asked, "If you ever have your tonsils taken out, can I have them in a bottle to keep in my dresser? I could even love them after your latest wonderful article." Miller later traveled so often for the *Digest* that she felt cheated if she could not visit Europe at least once a year.

Probably the most controversial and colorful of the roving editors was Paul de Kruif, a bear of a man who taught bacteriology at the University of Michigan before joining the Rockefeller Institute in 1920. Later he collaborated with Sinclair Lewis on *Arrowsmith,* afterward insisting that the hero Martin Arrowsmith was partly patterned after himself. In 1926 he published his own best-seller, *Microbe Hunters*. De Kruif's field was medicine, but he was also a crusading sensationalist who unearthed miracle cures for just about everything, sometimes almost every month, on the slenderest of evidence.

One of de Kruif's most notorious articles was "A Working Cure for Athlete's Foot," in which he advised sufferers to swab their feet with a mixture of phenol and camphor. The proposed cure inflamed not only many of those who tried it but also the *Journal of the American Medical Association,* which denounced the article.

That did not put a halt to the *RD*'s medical sensationalism. In its ongoing campaign against syphilis, the *Digest* published de Kruif's sensationalist chef d'oeuvre—"Found: A One-Day Cure for Syphilis," which briefed readers on three physicians "now reporting scientifically upon this epochal one-day treatment of syphilis." Twenty months previously the three doctors had published in the *British Journal of Venereal Diseases* a report on their strictly experimental results, which "should stimulate other investigators to engage in long-term, controlled experiments with a view to the introduction of a more rapid, more certain, less dangerous and costly method of treatment."

Once again, however, the *Digest* had advanced as a sure cure a treatment still in a highly experimental stage. And, once again, the magazine was denounced by members of the medical profession for misleading the public. The *Archives of Internal Medicine* went so far as to complain, "It is too bad no censorship exists to compel conservative accuracy from medical sensationalists."

5

More Ribaldry Than Boccaccio

In January 1940 the *Reader's Digest* provided a rare glimpse of its collective and often boorish sense of humor with the publication of a self-parody circulated among only a very few privileged insiders. The occasion was a phony edition of the real January issue, whose two lead articles were left untouched—"Prayer for Peace," Anne Morrow Lindbergh's clarion call to appeasement; and a glowing profile by John Gunther of Edouard Daladier, the French premier who signed the Munich pact with Hitler.

After that everything went haywire. The masthead lazily noted that the issue was "Edited One Rainy Saturday Afternoon." All the editors were listed by their regular names except managing editor Ken Payne, whose name was replaced by that of Nathan Abernathy, obviously an in-joke; while associate editor Marc A. Rose became Marc A. Rosenblatt. Elsewhere a "Publishers Statement" declared, "The editors are profoundly happy to confirm with deep regret the persistent rumor that *The Reader's Digest* has been sold to a Jewish syndicate. This deal was effectuated in the absence of the previous owners, who will however remain as previous owners."

Toward the end of an article innocuously titled "The Indigestible Czechs," condensed from *Survey Graphic,* author Edwin Muller was describing Czech resistance to Nazi occupation when he began to sound like James Joyce: "Shortly after Hitler moved in, a Czech radio station broadcast a famous Czech fairy tale. It was the story of a greedy giant, King Fierceas Humphrey, with illysus distilling, exploits and all. I know he well. As you spring so shall you neap. O, the roughty old rappe! Minxing marriage and making loof."

The explanation lay in the fact that *Digest* editor Henry Morton

Robinson led a double life. By day he was an editor for the biggest middlebrow magazine in the world. In his spare time he wrote middlebrow best-selling novels like *The Cardinal*. But he also taught English literature at Columbia University and was collaborating with a professor of literature at Sarah Lawrence College, Joseph Campbell, on a seminal exploration into the night world of H. C. Earwicker titled *A Skeleton Key to "Finnegans Wake."* Joyce's difficult masterpiece had been published only the year before the counterfeit issue of the *Reader's Digest* became perhaps the first publication in English to parody it.

The phony January issue also announced that, acceding to insistent requests from agencies, it would henceforth accept a limited amount of "Quality Advertising," and referred the reader to some samples on page 125:

Failing Powers?
Try Dr. Llwellyn's famous
Radio-Magnetic Belt.
New Vim. New Vigor.
Send $1 and Feel 21 again.

———————

Ghoul Writers Bureau

We guarantee to rewrite completely all
copy that we can lay our hands on.

———————

In answering ads, please don't mention
The Reader's Digest

Among the humorous new fillers—and yet another example of the parody issue's ugly Jew-baiting—was this one:

Only ornamental: Everything went well with Rachel, one of my Jewish patients, except that she could not nurse her baby. Appearances to the contrary—very much to the contrary—hardly a drop of milk could we get from her breasts in spite of all our efforts, though we tried for days. One morning I went in to see her and asked at once if her luck had been any better.

"Doctor, no," she said sadly. She paused a moment as if thinking.

"Do you know," she said. "I must be just like one of those darned prohibition bars—"

She tugged at the buttons of her pajama coat, threw it wide open, and cried:

"Look at me, doctor, look! magnificent equipment, and not a decent drop to drink in the house!"

The snickering anti-Semitism was almost certainly not directed at the amiable Howard Florance, who was immensely popular with his colleagues and the only Jew on the editorial staff. More likely, given the equally offensive Negro dialect jokes the *Digest* was fond of publishing in its regular issues, Wally and the other editors thought such humor genuinely funny and—with typical country club hubris—ipso facto not insulting to those whom it poked fun at. Certainly, there was no risk of offending Wally himself, who had published articles far more critical of Jews in the past. At the same time, he was also capable of maintaining a warm relationship with Jewish department store magnate Bernard Gimbel, whom he once professed to admire more than anyone else of his acquaintance.

That same parody issue also gave the *Digest*'s best-known author his comeuppance with a name-dropping satire titled "Lessons in Anguish—XIII," by "Allexandder Wwoollcott," which attempted to answer the question "Is the 'g' in margarine hard or soft?" Pages 112–13 were left completely blank, while article run-ons ran into new, unrelated articles or simply vanished in midsentence. Four pages of photographs in the centerfold—a novelty in its own right—showed a dilapidated clam house offering "2 Quarts Hard Clams 25c" over the ungrammatical caption "The Editors House—your subscriptions will help him modernize it." The centerfold shot of a billboard-ridden highway was captioned "View of the magnificent approach to the New Reader's Digest building."

The zaniness, sheer silliness, and off-color humor of the mock *Digest* was pure Wally—though the timing suggests that it was probably prepared for him as a surprise fifty-first birthday present. Wally not only enjoyed dirty jokes but frequently published bowdlerized versions of those circulating in the corridors of Pleasantville. Several were classics known to every generation of Digesters, but perhaps the most famous was the one originally told to Wally by John Erskine, a popular novelist of the day (and warden of Wall Street's prestigious Trinity Episcopal Church), and later published in the December 1941 issue of the *Digest:*

A young lady, with a touch of hay fever, took with her to a dinner party two handkerchiefs, one of which she stuck in her bosom. At dinner she began rummaging to right and left in her bosom for the fresh handker-chief. Engrossed in her search, she suddenly realized that conversation had ceased and people were watching her, fascinated.

In confusion she murmured, "I *know* I had two when I came."

Nearly every month a smattering of letters arrived in Pleasantville, complaining about the obscene humor (enough to fill a small volume, though *The Best of Reader's Digest Smut* was one title the American public would never see published), not to mention the immodest number of articles about sex. But Wally made even those letters the butt of jokes. After Barclay Acheson joined the staff, all complaint letters relating to off-color humor were passed along to his office. An ostensibly mysti-fied Acheson would then write back saying that as an ordained Presby-terian clergyman he would appreciate having the reader tell him what, what exactly in the story under objection so offended him. The letter would be signed "Barclay Acheson D.D."

But those subscription cancelers were a distinct minority, and the millions of other *Digest* readers loved its earthy sense of humor. Not a few, in fact, submitted jokes of their own.

Yet there was one special reader who liked almost everything about the *Reader's Digest* except its scandalous penchant for telling jokes that had no place in polite society, and that was the father of the magazine's owner. Dr. Wallace frequently visited Pleasantville and on those occa-sions was usually invited to give a lecture to the assembled editorial staff.

Now in his late seventies, a tall, vigorous, distinguished-looking man, with white mutton-chop whiskers, Dr. Wallace was a walking relic of the nineteenth century. One day he sought out Charlie Fergu-son—a fellow man of the cloth, so to speak—to praise several fillers he had enjoyed. But then he added:

"But there are a few others, you know, a very few, but I always seem to find one or two in each issue, dealing with . . . ah—sex, the innu-endo, the unacceptable. No need to explain. Everybody seems to read them first, and one does hear them repeated rather often. Nothing wicked, you understand. But the humor so often seems—well, inap-propriate to a fine magazine and an unfortunate aberration of editorial good taste.

"I find it hard to understand how DeWitt can permit these lapses, not accidentally, but regularly; or how dear Lila Bell somehow lets it slip. I have thought about it often but somehow, as his father, I cannot do more than hint.

"However, in your capacity as DeWitt's assistant—and with your missionary background—you may share my concern. Perhaps you can have more influence than I can properly try to exercise."

But Ferguson knew he could never change a feature so congenial to DeWitt Wallace's taste, or so basic to his editorial policy. On an earlier visit Dr. Wallace had made a similar complaint to Ralph Henderson, who duly passed it on to Wally, much to his amusement.

Not only did the *Digest*'s humor policy remain unchanged, but a few years later—according to a story told by book editor Ralph Henderson—when a suit was brought against *Esquire* magazine for publishing pornography, the defense lawyer read to a jury a string of jokes and challenged them to identify those in the *Reader's Digest* and those in *Esquire*. They could not.

As *Time* magazine later observed, the *Reader's Digest* "dispenses more medical advice than the A.M.A. *Journal,* more ribaldry than Boccaccio, more jokes than Joe Miller, more animal stories than Uncle Remus, more faith than Oral Roberts."

———

VOLUME 1, number 1, of the *Digest* contained only two fillers, one humorous and the other factual. For years afterward, blank spaces were used mainly for subscription appeals and teaser blurbs for forthcoming articles. Yet fillers were commonplace in magazines at the time. Well-established publications like the *Saturday Evening Post* ran a page of short humorous material edited by the likes of Richard Armour, while at the *New Yorker* the fillers at the bottom of columns were almost as popular as the cartoons.

Wally, however, initially took a cautious approach to fillers and humor departments, no doubt because they might seem to detract from the magazine's stress on information and the art of living. But even in his first issue he had included a full page of "Remarkable Remarks."

By 1929, when Lucy Notestein began her operation in Cleveland, fillers and humor departments still accounted for only a fraction of the magazine's content—although lighthearted articles, and others devoted to curious trivia or the oddities and marvels of language, were becoming common. Lucy's father had been a professor of Latin at

Wooster College, and her mother and Janet Wallace were sisters. Lucy William, as Wally called her, was a diligent and conscientious worker, and many of the suggestions for new departments came from her.

One of the first to appear, in February 1930, was titled "Repartee" and consisted of examples of witty ripostes by famous people (John Wesley, on being confronted by an oaf who declared he never made way for fools, calmly stepping aside with the remark "I always do"). Readers were invited to submit examples of their own and were promised five dollars per acceptance. Though the department lasted only a few months, it opened the floodgates.

"Origins," begun in May 1930, also paid five dollars for each example of unusual word origins. It, too, was soon abandoned. "Patter" ran throughout most of 1931 and 1932—two or three pages of jokes. "The Well Known Human Race" (anecdotes about Benjamin Franklin, John D. Rockefeller, and other famous people) appeared in 1931, again promising five dollars for reader submissions, and was soon followed by "Quotable Quotes," "An Album of Personal Glimpses," "Toward a More Picturesque Speech," "Pert and Pertinent," and "Boners."

In addition to departments Notestein also provided Wally with offbeat material for use either as filler or as a brief article—a collection of graveyard epitaphs, for example, or an entertaining list of ways that disputes were settled in China. Initially, until Ralph Henderson took over that function, Notestein was also charged with finding suitable books for excerpting in the back of the magazine. Not surprisingly, Wally's cousin was soon given permission to hire first one and then several assistants, all women. Despite the premium that the *Digest* eventually came to put on excerpts, as they were collectively called, culling them was looked on as women's work.

Even so, Wally expected every one of his male editors to provide him with an informal quota of filler material per month, and those who were lax eventually found themselves reading a memo pointedly asking why they had not lately bothered to submit any fillers. So highly did Wally come to value such editorial popcorn, in fact, that he once remarked in a casual but serious vein that he was thinking of disbanding his Cleveland excerpt department and paying $2,500 per filler.

Wally thought the *RD*'s fillers and various departments about wordplay and language proved so popular because the average reader had a longing to improve his or her understanding of language as a means of communication. In typical practical fashion he did not formulate a lesson plan but merely provided examples month after month that the reader could emulate.

So popular were the filler departments that six days a week the tiny Pleasantville post office was swamped with thousands of reader letters, queries, complaints, tales and jokes, advice, rumors, and remedies—a thundering avalanche of vox populi that had to be sorted, sifted, diluted, until the best of it, like the articles themselves, was judged to be "of enduring value and interest," worthy to be preserved in "condensed and compact form."

But there was more to the popularity of the departments than a simple desire to share information and anecdotal wisdom. Back in the Depression, five dollars was a lot of money. Many people were out of work and could afford the time to browse through magazines and books, looking for suitable submissions. Then there were those who had a very great deal of time on their hands. In the early years numerous filler contributions came from prisoners, with the inmates of the Ohio State Penitentiary setting the pace—an average of one acceptance a month.

Wally also delighted in printing what are now called urban folktales. One such story concerned a hostess who was preparing to give a luncheon. Before her guests arrived, she treated her pet to some of the rich food. After the luncheon was over, she glanced out the window and saw the pet lying dead on the lawn. In horror she telephoned her doctor, who ordered her to tell all the guests to rush to the hospital to have their stomach pumped. Finally, the exhausted hostess returned home—to be greeted by an apologetic neighbor who had accidentally run over the pet with her car but had considerately waited until the party was over to break the bad news.

Over the years variations of that and other stories were to arrive from nearly every country in the world. Finally, in August 1945, the *Digest* reprinted two pages of chestnuts in an attempt to convince readers that the editors had heard them all before. Instead, dozens of contributors wrote in demanding payment.

Among the most often submitted entries for "Toward More Picturesque Speech" (the article "a" was eventually dropped) was Hervey Allen's "His face was as yellow and undecided as an omelette," from the novel *Anthony Adverse*. But the record high was held by George Brooks. Three hundred and two readers submitted a line from his short story in *Collier's*: "The clock hands were closing like scissors blades on midnight, snipping off another day."

THOUGH the *Digest* paid its readers five dollars per acceptance, it also ran another kind of filler for which it paid a thousand times as much money—the celebrity endorsement. Originally, these had appeared on the back cover and usually been ghosted by *Digest* editors.

By the early forties Al Cole had decided that the *RD* required a full-time promotion writer. The lanky, dapper young man hired for the post was Willard Espy, known as Wede to his friends, and later the author of an entertaining series of books on the etymology of words. Before becoming the magazine's first public-relations manager, however, Espy had to pass inspection by Wally.

"He's a nice man," Cole told him reassuringly. "He's not going to bother you." But when they met, Wally fixed the young candidate with a gimlet eye and said, "Tell me, Mr. Espy, of all the articles in the *Reader's Digest* in the past six months, which seemed outstanding to you and could you tell me why?"

Espy knew instantly that he was trapped. Stupidly, he had not bothered even to browse through a recent copy of the *Digest*, had in fact not seen one in years. Wally's displeasure was evident, but he said, "Well, we'll hire you, but on trial."

Espy's trial status, like Henderson's and so many other Digesters', was never officially terminated and he remained on staff for sixteen years. Ten days into his new job, he received a $1,000 bonus. Wally and Lila had just sent around a memo announcing that aside from usual magazine income, they had been "fortunate this year in a 'windfall' from the sale of two books* resulting in a net profit of $72,532." The money was split among Digesters earning less than $250 a month.

Espy soon found himself with one of the most enviable jobs in Pleasantville—a place where most-enviable jobs were becoming a dime a dozen. Espy's was to meet with visiting dignitaries and celebrities, then ghostwrite a brief essay for the inside cover on why they enjoyed reading the *Reader's Digest*. The most memorable was with Albert Einstein. With the war on, Espy hoped to get an endorsement not only of the *Digest* but of the American Red Cross from the eminent scientist, who was then living and teaching in Princeton, New Jersey.

The Reader's Digest Reader, selected by Theodore Roosevelt and the Staff of the *Reader's Digest* (New York: Doubleday, Doran, 1940); and *The Reader's Digest Twentieth Anniversary Anthology* (Pleasantville: Reader's Digest Association, 1941). See chapter 7.

But Einstein refused to endorse the relief agency, because there was a rumor that the Red Cross was separating Jewish blood from the rest. Espy told him the rumor was nonsense. Though Einstein was not satisfied, he treated the impressionable young copywriter so graciously that Espy was overwhelmed by what he saw as an emanation of goodness from Einstein, a "sort of halo."

After their interview Einstein invited Espy to go sailing, but the latter had a train to catch and reluctantly declined. Yet he was so moved by the visit that he began to have trouble distinguishing reality from fantasy. In subsequent months and years Espy vividly reconstructed that day when the two of them went out sailing. They were still chatting about the Red Cross. Einstein had the tiller, and there was quite a brisk breeze. But at one point he threw his hand up to make a point, and the boat veered toward a sand bar. Fortunately, Espy grabbed the tiller and, in his memory, though it never happened, said, "Well, I've saved the unified field theory."

Later he even told the story as though it had happened, until he finally read in a Seattle gossip column a version that said Einstein had actually fallen overboard and Espy pulled him out of the water.

The standard payment to celebrities for their product endorsement of the *Digest* was $5,000. When Espy sent Groucho Marx a final draft of his tribute, the comedian wrote back, "I hope your check is better than your copy."

——

IN ADDITION to fillers, off-color jokes, humor departments, and celebrity endorsements, there was one other thing that pricked people's interest in the *Digest*. Not surprisingly, given the mood of the times and that of the people who edited the magazine, it was sex.

There was probably not a single angle on the topic that the *Digest* did not cover at least once during the twenties, thirties, and forties. Much of the material was, by the standards of a later day, formulaic, predictable, and simplistic. On the other hand, given the legal climate for discussing human sexuality, authors and publishers risked almost certain prosecution if even the driest language threatened to become too explicit. Not until 1935, as a case in point, did the works of pioneer sexologist Havelock Ellis—who was among the first to call for recognition of the "erotic rights of women"—become legally available to the public. The most celebrated paean to Eros in the twenties, D. H.

Lawrence's *Lady Chatterley's Lover,* was to remain known only by reputation to most readers for another three decades.

But there was a rallying point for sexual progressives in the 1920s—birth control, a term invented by Margaret Sanger, a New York nurse who had been appalled by the misery of women among whom she worked in some of the city's poorest sections. In 1921 Sanger founded the American Birth Control League (later to become the Planned Parenthood Federation). The *Digest,* though well right of center in almost every other respect, published year after year a stream of articles on love, courtship, and marriage that often contained an exhortation to every married couple—the stress was always on marriage and monogamy—to make birth control a routine part of their family life.

In the political climate of the 1920s, such editorial support was not lightly given and involved some risk. Like the question of abortion a half century later, birth control was a deeply divisive issue that aroused bitter debate and inflamed passions in every quarter. In 1929 the Sanger Clinic in Brooklyn was raided by police and its files confiscated. Not until six years later did a federal appeals court rule that physicians had the right to prescribe birth control under certain circumstances. Almost certainly—since nothing like a demographic survey of the *RD*'s readership then existed—Wally risked alienating his substantial Catholic readership, much as he likewise invited the wrath of fundamentalist subscribers with all the unseemly humor that he published in his otherwise upright magazine. As a sop to Catholics, anti–birth control articles appeared at great intervals, usually written by a member of the clergy; but the blue humor continued unabated.

Wally also published originals or reprints from politically liberal publications such as *Literary Digest* and *Forum* on such controversial subjects as divorce reform, artificial insemination, and venereal disease. (Many, such as those on sterilization, had a pronounced eugenic undertone.) In a series of articles on "marital pitfalls," Gretta Palmer, wife of Paul, even managed to discuss what is now known as premenstrual syndrome—though without mentioning the word "menstruation." Palmer's treatment was typical of cautious *RD* euphemism:

. . . there are two occasions when a husband's tact, sympathy and self-control are urgently needed, if he is to be an expert in love and life: in the first days of married life, and in the first days of the monthly ebb, when feminine tinder is highly inflammable and an angry retort to an over-wrought wife may be the powder train leading to an explosion.

The underlying message of hundreds of other articles on sex was the same: the husband was to bring patience, thoughtfulness, romance to a relationship, while women were creatures of mystery, fragile conundrums of hormonal chemistry. If anything was amiss in a marital relationship, it was usually up to the husband to fix it. A weekend in the woods was an often prescribed recipe. By the standards of the day, such advice was considerably enlightened. As one *Digest* article noted, "even intelligent married men" were often unaware of whether or not their wives had "ever experienced, in sexual intercourse, the climactic release of nervous tension technically known as an orgasm."

Just as the *RD* was the first large-circulation magazine to publish the word "syphilis," so by daringly (and ever so gingerly) using "orgasm" it was helping to make respectable a word not used in polite society, and considered all but obscene.

The *Digest* was, on the whole, able to take such "liberties" with the language precisely because it was at the same time the most widely read defender of monogamy and other pillars of Victorian morality of any publication in the world. Counterbalancing its calls for divorce reform and birth control were resolutely Calvinistic condemnations of premarital sex, fornication, and adultery. Unmarried women, in particular, were advised never to "go all the way," because (in a non sequitur perhaps fathomable only to *Digest* editors) "almost every man or woman becomes a good sex partner." Similar dubious advice was not uncommon. In a pep talk to a young couple thinking of getting married, a professor of sociology blithely noted, "After marriage, immediate sexual adjustment is not important—it may take as long as a year. . . . Almost all sexual maladjustments are easily cured."

This priggish, Victorian side of the magazine reached its apotheosis in a 1937 original—commissioned, ironically, by Wally—called "The Case for Chastity," by Margaret Culkin Banning, a popular novelist and essayist of the day. A mother of four, Banning counseled young girls to avoid premarital relations because of the unreliability of even the best contraceptives, the high risk of contracting a venereal disease, and "man's preference for a virgin as wife." Even girls who indulged in petting would later experience difficulty in responding to "normal sex relations."

When war broke out, former heavyweight boxing champion Gene Tunney similarly urged young men in the military not to engage in sex outside of marriage, because it was tantamount to being unpatriotic. In "Bright Shield of Continence," in the August 1942 issue, Tunney wrote, "Ordinary athletes . . . realize the importance of continence if they are to keep at the peak of physical form. . . . Can our soldiers and sailors, as the champions of democracy, afford to indulge in sexual promiscuity scorned by most prize fighters? . . . Is this too much to ask of our national crisis?"

With Tunney's article, *Digest* sex advice reached both its nadir and, insofar as DeWitt Wallace and others on the staff intended to set a good example, the height of hypocrisy.

OVER the years Wally's passion for off-color humor grew so legendary that telling the latest joke to the boss became a ritual, at the start of an editorial lunch or a poker game, by anyone wishing to incur his favor. In fact, he even told them himself in his rare public appearances. Accepting a Hawkes Aviation Award, he rattled off three in a row, which amounted to his entire remarks for the evening. The first concerned an innocent septuagenarian who readily pleaded guilty to rape charges as a testimonial to his virility. Wally continued:

[Someone recently asked] who originates the jokes unfit for publication except in the *Reader's Digest*. As an editor I've always been interested in our editorial research trying to determine how rapidly stories circulate, & whether a story is too old, too familiar, to reprint. Surprisingly, we have discovered that in any given group an old, old story will sometimes be new to a majority of persons.

I hope this may be true of an incident I heard ten years ago. A writer from Texas was our luncheon guest and he told this tale. A frontiersman was sitting in a saloon with a prostitute on his knee and drinks on the table. A shooting affray occurred outdoors and a stray bullet plugged the prostitute's heart. With perfect aplomb the man tinkled his glass and called, "Waiter! Waiter! Bring me another whore! This one here's *daid!*"

6

As Thirsty Men Turn
to a Fountain

A PARTICULARLY disturbing proof of how popular the *Reader's Digest* was becoming outside the borders of the United States was a pirated edition printed in Shanghai in the late thirties that undersold the genuine article by half. Wally, the ex-pirate, was being pirated. Protests by the *RD* led to an investigation by the American consulate in Shanghai, which found that the pirating of the *Digest, Parade,* and other publications was an extremely lucrative trade. Unfortunately, there was no legal method by which the pirating could be halted, since China was not a signatory to the international copyright agreement.

Similar indications that the little magazine was beginning to enjoy a big reputation around the world were its healthy sales in Canada and on newsstands in foreign markets carrying English-language periodicals. The next logical step, then, was to publish an edition for readers in Great Britain.

Ten years earlier Wally had looked into the feasibility of a British edition and wisely decided that his resources were far too limited for him to export an edition that promised at best an insignificant return. But by 1938 the *Digest's* circulation of 3,250,000 was the largest of any magazine's in the United States. Rather than entrust an exported edition to a wholesaler, the *Digest* could now afford to set up its own offices and exploit the substantial British market as a natural extension of the American. Delay, in fact, only played into the hands of competitors.

Another important factor was the low editorial overhead. The British edition was to be a reprint of the best of the U.S. edition, minus any material too American to appeal to the average British reader. Plans called for a British editor to act as a kind of issue editor, using the back issues of the American edition as an inventory from which to select suitable articles. However, Pleasantville would still sign off on the British edition, which was also to be called the *Reader's Digest*.

Probably the most important factor, though, was Al Cole, who was intent on putting a copy of the *Digest* in the home of every American and eventually in the home of everybody else on the planet as well. What Wally initially lacked in enthusiasm for anything except the American edition of his magazine, Cole more than made up for. In the spring of 1938, while still a consultant, he and Marvin Lowes sailed for London to meet with distributors, printers, and realtors.

A graduate of Williams College, the thirty-five-year-old Lowes—a debonair, pipe-smoking Anglophile—was thoroughly at home in Europe. After taking his graduate degree at the University of Bordeaux, he had toured the continent on a 5,000-mile bicycle trip. Returning to the United States in 1927, he served for the next eight years as an editor of the *Bookman* and as a free-lance translator. In 1935 he joined the *Reader's Digest* in Pleasantville on the business side. Now, three years later, he was on his way to London as publisher of the company's first foreign start-up.

After determining that production and marketing conditions were favorable to a launch, Cole returned home alone, though typically he did not give Lowes any instructions, since he wanted some time to ponder matters. A few days later, while aboard the SS *Queen Mary,* he wrote and told him to arrange for permanent office space in Bush House, a multi-office complex in Aldwych.

The new publisher and his secretary Jane Pospisil worked furiously in preparation for the launch, sending out more than a million pieces of promotion. On September 3, 1939, Great Britain and France declared war on Germany, which had invaded Poland two days earlier. The first printing in England was a trial run in November 1939, though copies were not distributed. The first real edition came the following month, and it was virtually a replica of the American edition. Ninety-six pages long, it sold for one shilling and contained no advertising, no color, and no illustrations.

The third issue, dated January 1940, contained Anne Morrow Lindbergh's call for British capitulation to Hitler. Though the article generated little interest, by coincidence the British government had recently introduced paper rationing and informed the *Digest* that, because it had not published in England before September 1939, it would receive no more paper. Lowes and Cole complained to the Board of Trade and succeeded in getting a paper ration. Soon afterward Lowes returned to the United States to wait out the war. Pospisil, who had asked the placement bureau for a position with a light work load and no responsibilities, was left in charge.

One result of the rationing was that the subscription list could not be enlarged, merely maintained. Pospisil was not only proofreader, production liaison, and office manager but also head of promotion, keeping a list of would-be subscribers, who were offered a subscription when another subscriber did not renew. In this way the nucleus of an expansion list was built up.

Another problem related to censorship. If any article contravened regulations, the paper ration was imperiled. Pospisil carefully read every issue, later increased to 108 pages, for anything that might displease His Majesty's government. But the paper ration was reduced anyway, even though the censor found nothing to object to.

Another, far more serious problem was the blitz. Soon after war broke out, the magazine's offices in Bush House were requisitioned by the government. Similar requisitions forced it to move three more times—the last bringing it to the Thames Conservancy offices, overlooking Australia House in the Strand. Every evening Pospisil joined other volunteers from the building in a fire-watch patrol whose members helped stuff Christmas subscription renewal pieces as they scanned the skies. All through the war, Pospisil continued to serve as editor and factotum, nursing the newborn through its first years under circumstances that could scarcely have been worse.

━━━

IN *1938,* the year the British edition was launched, Wally and Cole also looked into the idea of publishing a Spanish-language edition but decided not to proceed, because the venture would have been too costly. Negative factors included the expense of translating articles, a dearth of adequate printing facilities in Latin America, high shipping costs, and the seeming lack of a sizable middle-class readership base except in Argentina.

But pressure to publish an edition for distribution throughout Latin America was mounting. Since 1935 an erstwhile journalist-adventurer named William La Varre had tried to interest Wally in the project. Paul

Palmer had also proposed launching a Spanish-language edition, since by now the South American continent was a prime target for Axis propaganda. Publications on the left, though minuscule in circulation, were influential among the intelligentsia and trade unions. Many of the latter were openly sympathetic to the Soviet Union or avowedly Communist. No one in Pleasantville doubted that a Spanish-language edition of the *Reader's Digest* would provide a much needed corrective. But the problems seemed insurmountable. Wally's unenthusiastic attitude toward new undertakings merely complicated matters. The only person who felt passionate about the project, La Varre, did not even work for the company.

The unlikely catalyst for the languishing nonproject was senior editor Charles W. Ferguson. One March day in 1940, without telling anyone in Pleasantville, Ferguson paid a visit to the Cultural Relations Office of the State Department in Washington, D.C. He explained the situation to Assistant Director Charles A. Thomson, adding, "If Secretary [of State Cordell] Hull would write a letter to Mr. Wallace urging him to do it, that would probably turn the trick."

Thomson reported to his supervisor, "I could not be sure whether his was a casual remark or something which he had deliberately planned to say." He also pointed out that several similar publications already existed in Latin America, notably *Ultra* in Cuba and *Síntesis* in Mexico.

However, Dr. Ben M. Cherrington, chief of cultural relations, wrote the *Digest*'s owner, noting that the department was "interested in any initiative which will tend to promote more effective inter-American understanding." Wallace curtly replied that he had no intention of embarking on the project.

A short while later, however, he stopped by Ferguson's office and invited him out for a Coke on the way home. Though the *Digest* had ignored the State Department's gentle nudge, Cherrington's letter had awakened Wallace's social conscience. In his hand was the feasibility study prepared by Al Cole on a Spanish-language edition.

The study asserted that few people in Latin America could afford a twenty-five-cent magazine. Nor had any magazine ever achieved a circulation of 25,000 south of the border. Cole suggested advertising to help keep down costs. At a nearby drugstore Wally and Ferguson sat at the counter. The latter said nothing about his visit to the State Department. The *RD* publisher gave him the report, fingering a paragraph that read, "The likelihood therefore is that, even under optimum conditions, a Spanish edition would at the end of a year reach a circulation of not more than 50,000 copies."

Not very feasible, Ferguson agreed. But he kept a reverent silence while Wally continued to talk to himself, rehearsing a way around the impossible. One of his main worries was that other U.S. magazines might think he was competing with them for advertising dollars. High on the list of potential advertisers were American manufacturers and oil companies with large Latin American holdings or operations.

In the end, though, Wally decided to proceed with a Spanish-language edition on a trial basis, which was to last for an indefinite period of years, after which time the project would be reevaluated.

In June 1940 Palmer informed Cherrington in "strict confidence," "We expect to lose something like $50,000 a year on [the Spanish edition]. If you wonder why a magazine willingly undertakes such a loss, I can only say that Mr. DeWitt Wallace, publisher of *Reader's Digest,* regards the magazine more as a public institution dedicated to patriotic work than as a private property."

But another consideration—one not unappreciated by the State Department—was that money lost in the venture was only subtracted from the *Digest*'s increasingly hefty payments to the Internal Revenue Service.

At the end of the month, Cole and La Varre met with Hull to discuss the venture at length. The *RD* business manager told Hull that the Spanish edition would be a "non-profit publication," which was not literally true. In fact, La Varre—a former gold, oil, and mineral-rights prospector on the Latin continent—expected the *Digest* to be the mother lode he had spent a lifetime trying to discover. From Cole's gloomy perspective, though, being nonprofit and not making a profit were one and the same. His task was not to lose any more money than necessary. To that end, as he explained to the secretary of state, U.S. subscribers would be asked to sponsor charter subscriptions for Latin readers at one dollar a year, with postage prepaid by the *Digest.*

In effect, Cole had devised a strategy to undercut the competition with a below-cost subscription price while enlisting the American people to help pay for that subsidy. The price of an individual copy was similarly cutthroat—the equivalent of ten cents. Like the British edition, the ninety-six-page *Selecciones* would consist of the best of back issues of the American edition, though those of strictly U.S. appeal would be dropped and a few articles of particular interest to Latin America added.

Cole put Marvin Lowes to work on the project, along with a personable young man named Fred Thompson, husband of Lila's favorite niece, Judy, whom Cole had hired at Wally's behest at *Popular Science*. It was under such circumstances that Wally appointed both his brother-in-law Barclay Acheson and Paul Palmer as charter roving editors. The title provided Palmer, who may have thought it up, with a perfect cover. Acheson's duties were less defined. But he was well traveled and needed a job, and the *Digest*'s new international division seemed the ideal place to stick him.

The editorial director was Eduardo Cárdenas, a Colombian who had previously served as the first director of the Editor's Press Service, a news agency tailored to the Latin market. Cárdenas and his staff operated out of the old New York Central Building, on Park Avenue in New York City, translating the U.S. edition directly into Spanish. Self-censorship was mostly limited to disqualifying any article that might offend the predominantly Roman Catholic readership of *Selecciones*—for example, a discussion of birth control or divorce.

In August 1940 the saber-rattling maiden issue of *Selecciones del Reader's Digest* arrived on the newsstands of Latin America—its lead-off article, "This Land and Flag," was an emotional appeal to patriotism reprinted from the editorial pages of the *New York Times*. Other features included one by Frederic Sondern, Jr., "Hitler Looks to South America," which claimed that the loyalties of the five million German immigrants in Latin America, who had begun arriving in force the preceding century, lay first with the fatherland.

Selecciones's success was almost beyond belief. Cole's goal of a circulation of 50,000 in twelve months was instantly met with a sellout of 148,000 copies of the first issue. (The premier issue of a magazine will typically sell less than 50 percent of its run.) In only four months circulation reached 250,000.

In May 1941 Cole dropped a note to Under Secretary of State Sumner Welles, informing him that Lowes was returning to England, where the British edition by now had a print run of 180,000. The *RD* business manager asked for letters of introduction for Lowes to the U.S. ambassador in Lisbon, since the *Digest* was now planning to launch an edition in Portuguese for sale in both Portugal and Brazil. Nelson Rockefeller, coordinator of inter-American affairs for the State

Department, had been among those pressuring the *Digest* to move in this direction.

But there were a few problems. Like the U.S. edition, the Latin American frequently echoed Wallace's pro-isolationist sentiments, thereby playing occasionally into the hands of the Nazi propaganda machine. In the January 1942 issue, for example, *Selecciones* reprinted an August 18, 1941, article from *Life*. "What the American Army Recruit Thinks" ("Lo que piensa el recluta norteamericano") painted a dreary picture of the morale of the typical American soldier, who when he was not quarreling with his companions was usually drunk. All of them, to boot, were allegedly terrified at the prospect of actually having to fight. But *Selecciones* had gone to press with the issue before the Japanese attack on Pearl Harbor the preceding month, and the article—unlike the half dozen pro-isolationist pieces in the January U.S. edition—could not be pulled. Reaction in American diplomatic circles throughout Latin America was one of unanimous horror. The Santiago legation to the State Department noted that the article "could not have been more unhelpful and untruthful, now we are in the war, had it been written by Goebbels."

In 1942 Acheson was named director of international editions and Thompson the business manager. By now the circulation of *Selecciones* had skyrocketed to an astounding one million, easily the largest of any publication in Latin America. The unforeseen growth of the international department also necessitated an addition to the new headquarters building in Pleasantville, which was only three years old.

Though Acheson frequently went to Cole for help, he had begun to complain that the latter was trying to usurp some of his authority—a ridiculous charge, but one that led to a handwritten note from Wally to Cole stating, "Al, you're in charge of the *Reader's Digest* magazine business in the U.S. You have no authority to have anything to do with the international edition, so please stay out of it."

When he received the memo, an enraged Cole went to see Wally, laid the offending piece of paper on his desk, and said, "Wally, I don't know what brings this about. But if you really mean this, you can have my resignation now. Nobody's ever written me memos like that in recent years and I don't think it's fair and I'm very unhappy about it."

"Oh, Lila told me that Barclay said you were trying to take over some of his things," Wally replied. "I know Barclay well enough. For God's sake, forget it." Then he tore the memo up.

While admitting he was no authority on Latin America, Acheson held very definite opinions about what was best for the region. An address based on a recent visit to Central and South America, and given on several occasions before U.S. business groups, outlined his editorial philosophy.

Among other things, Acheson thought the average Latin dictator displayed "greater idealism and a finer patriotism" than dictator-like U.S. political bosses such as Huey Long of Louisiana. Until Latin citizens learned to take responsibility for their own rights and liberties, Acheson held, "the benevolent ruler of an upper class [was] at present best suited to some countries of South America."

In the summer of 1942 the State Department invited the *Reader's Digest* to establish editions on three crucial propaganda fronts—Sweden, Turkey, and Egypt. The Office of War Information (OWI) even offered to publish those editions itself if the *Digest* had no interest, but the offer was declined. Instead, the RD agreed to publish editions in each of those countries and to distribute an English-language edition in India. Not only did it jealously guard its editorial independence, but it also refused an offer of an OWI subsidy. In return the OWI was asked to provide Acheson and Lowes with air priority for an exploratory trip to Sweden on October 3, 1942.

During the flight, Acheson and Lowes walked to the rear of the plane to smoke a cigarette. Moments later the plane crashed over Newfoundland and eleven people were killed—all of them in the forward section. The two men eventually returned to New York and a month later took another flight, this one safely, to Stockholm. Plans were eventually finalized for an edition to be called *Det Bästa ur Reader's Digest* (The Best of Reader's Digest).

———

THE OWI later arranged for similar air priority for Al Cole and Fred Thompson to visit Turkey and Egypt. In Cairo the two men spent several months setting up an Arabic edition and shared a small apartment. Thompson was in the habit of rising at seven-thirty—two hours after Cole, who bustled around every morning in a pseudo-quiet way while his junior colleague pretended to remain asleep. That would continue until seven, when Cole took a shower and began to sing at the top of his voice, effectively letting it be known that the workday could no longer be put off. As soon as Cole got out of the shower, he would say, "Well, now, about that thing we were discussing last night . . ."

Cole figured that an Arabic edition ought to succeed, because there were fifty million Arabic-speaking people in the world, 10 percent of them literate. By his reckoning, the most that an Arabic edition of the *Digest* stood to lose in its first year of operations was $75,000. Once again, as with the Spanish edition, Cole had seriously miscalculated—only this time with less felicitous results.

Initially, *Al-Mukhtar min Reader's Digest* (Selections from Reader's Digest) was a signal success, with demand outpacing the supply of 70,000 copies each month. One Arabic editor called it the "most momentous literary event the Arabs have known in modern times," even though, of that country's so-called literates (who numbered, in fact, only three million), most could do little more than write their name.

Moreover, *Al-Mukhtar* was printed in the language of the educated class and not in the dialect used by the overwhelming majority of Arabs. Also, Arabic tradition called for a book or magazine to read from right to left, or backward by Western standards, whereas the Arabic edition of the *Reader's Digest* read from left to right—no doubt because that seemed more American. But the Arab edition did make one concession to local custom—all articles about sex were excised.

Despite its limited audience and unorthodox appearance, *Al-Mukhtar* reached a circulation of about 150,000 within its first year and was distributed throughout the six Arabic-speaking countries in the Near East—Egypt, Syria, Lebanon, Transjordan, Iraq, and Saudi Arabia—selling at two cents a copy. Because of wartime conditions, plans for a Turkish edition were temporarily suspended.

Cole also arranged for an English-language troop edition of the U.S. *Reader's Digest* to be distributed among American and British forces. The edition was distributed and paid for by both governments. Though the *Digest* made no money on the operation, it was becoming a visible and much treasured commodity among millions of fighting men, who presumably might want to keep on subscribing to it once they returned to civilian life. One in every seven Americans was then in uniform. Troop editions were published not only in Cairo but in Calcutta, Manila, and France, for a combined circulation of 2,000,000. A *Stars and Stripes* edition also appeared in special weekly supplements in the Mediterranean edition of the U.S. service newspaper. A similar supplement was printed in *Maple Leaf,* the Canadian armed-forces newspaper.

By 1943 the circulation of the British edition had reached 206,000, including sales in Australia and South Africa. But its growth was still hampered by severe paper rationing. Plans called for increasing the price and accepting advertising after the war. In the meantime, the British edition was surpassed by the Swedish, whose 300,000 circulation was larger than that of any other publication in the country. *Seleções do Reader's Digest,* the Portuguese edition, had quickly attained a circulation of 150,000 in Brazil, though it was plagued by censorship problems stemming from Portugal's neutrality.

———

IN THE waning days of 1943, the U.S. edition of the *Reader's Digest* made headlines around the country when an article ghosted under the byline of Hugh A. Butler, Republican senator from Nebraska, accused the Roosevelt administration of wasting nearly $6 billion in the furtherance of hemispheric solidarity with its Good Neighbor Policy. The accusations grew out of a trip Butler had taken through twenty Central and South American countries the previous summer.

Boondoggling was a favorite *Digest* theme. Just a few months earlier, in August 1943, Henry J. Taylor had explored it in "Boondoggling on a Global Basis," alleging that U.S. international ambitions were as dangerous as isolationism. The Butler article instantly aroused the indignation of Senator Joseph F. Guffey, Democrat of Pennsylvania, who accused his colleague of being a "catspaw in a bit of journalistic ghostwriting." The *New York Times* of December 8, 1943, quoted Guffey as saying it was unfortunate Butler was unaware of the extent to which "the editors of *Reader's Digest* were using his trust and employing his personal prestige to foist on America and the world a mass of misinformation." Guffey pointed to the *Digest's* "rewrite man" Stanley High as the real culprit. At the same time, Vice-President Henry A. Wallace apologized to Latin America for the "shocking slur."

Wally denied that his magazine made a "catspaw" of Senator Butler, insisting that the article was the senator's and that the $6 billion figure was Butler's own. But the controversy did not die there. It had just begun. Shortly afterward the administration issued a statement saying that the United States had obligated itself to spend less than $1 billion on its Good Neighbor program. Prominent Republicans soon joined in the defense of the policy, including former president Herbert Hoover, 1940 Republican presidential candidate Wendell Willkie, New York governor Thomas E. Dewey, and Alf M. Landon, 1936 presidential candidate. Hoover noted that he himself had ordered American troops out of Nicaragua and Haiti and that the Good Neighbor Policy was in fact "established first by the Republican Administration." All vowed to continue with the policy if a Republican was elected to national office in 1944.

On December 14 the *Times* reported that Tennessee senator Kenneth McKellar, acting chairman of the Senate Appropriations Committee, had found Butler's accusations to be "95 per cent wrong." Total expenditures for the past three years had amounted not to $6 billion but $324,135,000. If the *Digest*'s motives in publishing the article were political, McKellar added, "then these gentlemen [were] putting politics before the successful prosecution of the war and before the best interests of their country." Though Secretary of State Hull also denounced the attack, both the *RD* and Butler steadfastly refused to retract.

The article was also widely criticized in the liberal press in the United States. Both Marshall Field's tabloid *PM* and the *Digest*'s archenemy, George Seldes's *In Fact,* accused the magazine of everything from administration baiting to ambitions for a worldwide cartel based on its policy of planting articles in other publications. In Chile the Communist party organized a boycott of *Selecciones,* which had reprinted the article, while in Washington some members of the Roosevelt administration toyed with the idea of launching an antitrust action aimed at the *Digest*'s policy of sewing up reprint sources with exclusive contracts.

PM had earlier disclosed that José Marie Torres Perona, an editor of *Selecciones,* was a founder of a Franco organization in New York, the Casa de España, "reputedly a link in the vast Falangist propaganda network throughout the U.S.A. and Latin American countries."

Wally himself was sensitive to claims that the *Digest*'s foreign editions promulgated a profascist gospel. To one reader who had accused him of such, he replied somewhat irrationally that—if the charge was true—it was "damned strange" that the State Department bought "5000 copies a month for distribution in Spain (delivered in diplomatic pouches to the Embassy in Madrid)." Spain, of course, as Wally seems to have temporarily forgotten, was a fascist country.

CONTINUING severe production problems with the troop and Arabic editions, as well as the Swedish, finally prompted Al Cole to seek a permanent solution. One of the best production men in the business was Kent Rhodes, a tall, bespectacled man, aristocratic in bearing, who at the moment was working for *Time* magazine on a confidential project with the air force. After talking with Rhodes, Cole persuaded the Defense Department that the publication of the *Reader's Digest* edition for the troops abroad was a significant defense effort.

The Department of Defense agreed to release Rhodes from his commitment, and he was hired by the *Digest* in April 1944. Within a month he took off with Fred Thompson, the two of them posing as war correspondents. Hopping DC-3's, they made their way down to Brazil, crossed the Atlantic in a B-26 to the Gold Coast (modern-day Ghana), and then traveled by rail to Cairo.

After establishing a schedule for putting the magazine out twelve times a year, and not the six that the lackadaisical Cairo office had become habituated to, Rhodes and Thompson toured Palestine, Jordan, and Syria, checking on unit sales with wholesalers. In Ceylon, Thompson arranged to print the *Digest* in an unusual format—a 16-page newspaper tabloid with dotted lines in the form of a cross. After being folded and cut with a scissors, it formed either a 32- or a 64-page edition. Wartime production facilities permitted no other solution.

Moving on to Calcutta, the two "war correspondents" promptly came down with a severe case of dengue fever. Instead of checking into a hospital, though, they traveled on to Bombay and from their hotel beds managed to survey the possibility of an Indian edition. After talking with advertising mogul J. Walter Thompson, who was also in the city on business, they decided the prospects were poor and returned home, much the worse for wear.

Rhodes's next challenge involved getting the Spanish-language and Portuguese-language editions, then being printed by R. R. Donnelley in Chicago, out of the United States and produced locally. On a visit to Cuba, he stumbled on a small storefront printing shop whose owner impressed Rhodes with his sheer drive and willingness to innovate. Over a period of three or four years, the back-street printer managed to build up his press run until he and not Donnelley was printing all copies of *Selecciones* for distribution in Mexico and the Caribbean. Similar arrangements were gradually made in Argentina, Brazil, and elsewhere. In five years Donnelley no longer printed any editions of the *Digest* in Spanish or Portuguese.

While international production problems were being resolved, the centralization of editorial control in Pleasantville occasionally back-fired. In November 1943 the Swedish *Det Bästa* reprinted Eastman's July 1943 article warning that Stalinist Russia was a worse threat to the free world than was Hitler's Germany. Nazi propaganda sources had already translated the article and widely distributed it throughout the country. Its reappearance in an international edition of the *Reader's Digest* was once again a cause for Nazi celebration.

Spain threatened to be a special problem because no foreign maga-zine had ever been printed in that country in the past. A rumor, at once troubling and comforting, was that Franco read *Selecciones* regularly but did not think it appropriate reading material for his people. Through the offices of Catholic Action, the powerful right-wing lay arm of the church, Acheson was able to arrange for a personal interview with Franco. Though the general gave permission for publication in Spain, his subordinates prepared a list of twenty-eight conditions, including one that the *Digest* not publish in any of its editions, Spanish or other, any articles critical of General Franco or of Spain, or any critical of the Catholic church. Ultimately, the magazine merely agreed to observe Spanish law, which meant it could not criticize either institution in Spain.

Another important market was the Finnish. When Acheson first went to Sweden, he was approached by several prominent Finns and asked to start up an edition in their country as well. But the situation in Finland was delicate because the United States had not yet recognized the Finnish government formed after that country and Russia signed an armistice in the fall of 1944. Also it was not known how much freedom of the press the Russians would permit. Eventually, however, plans were finalized to launch a Finnish edition, to be called *Valitut Palat koonnut Reader's Digest* (Bits and Pieces from the Reader's Digest), whose publisher was one of Finland's most famous men, Eljas Erkko, the ex–foreign minister. Unlike the Swedish edition, it avoided the topic of Russia altogether. (The subject was so delicate that issues of the Swedish edition containing articles deemed objectionable by the Soviets were routinely banned in Finland.) The first issue appeared in June 1945 with a printing of 50,000 copies, and circulation soon dou-bled. But as in England, paper rationing inhibited its growth. A Danish edition, *Det Bedste fra Reader's Digest,* was introduced eight months later.

Blueprints for Norwegian, German, French, Italian, and Dutch edi-tions were also being drawn up. In Norway the *Digest* had considerable trouble hiring an editor. Though a number of prominent Norwegian journalists were approached, each refused the position when not given assurance of a reasonably free hand in the selection of editorial material. Some controversy ensued, and the proposed magazine was denounced in the press as one of the most alarming symptoms to date of the ominous trend toward the Americanization of Europe. The editor eventually chosen was the proprietor of a small private language school who had little journalistic experience, but whose docility could be depended on.

A much more prosaic problem facing the *Digest* in every country where start-ups were being planned, with the exception of Norway, was that none had functioning coal mines. That meant paper mills were not operating, despite ample forests. Distribution problems made it impossible to consider a Chinese edition for the time being. Despite the *Digest*'s hostile attitude toward Soviet Russia, Acheson was also hopeful that the *Digest* might someday preach the gospel of capitalism even in the cradle of communism.

BY FAR, though, the most formidable challenge facing the international division in the post–World War II era was occupied Japan. Responsibility for the edition's success or failure lay primarily not with Al Cole or Barclay Acheson but with a man named Dennis McEvoy, whose father, J. P. McEvoy, had once treated himself and his family to a luxurious ski vacation at the expense of an unamused DeWitt Wallace.

Around the time Dennis joined his father on that ski trip, J. P. gave him an encyclopedia set as a birthday present, then sent him off to military school. Later the boy was enrolled in a Spartan-like academy in Germany in order to learn the language. At sixteen he became a copyboy for the *San Francisco Examiner*.

In 1936 J. P. McEvoy set off on an around-the-world assignment for the *Saturday Evening Post*, taking Dennis with him. When the two McEvoys arrived in Japan, they walked right into the middle of the "February 26 Incident," in which half the cabinet was slaughtered by young military officers demanding war. J. P. covered the story from the lobby of the Imperial Hotel, buttonholing guests to find out what was going on. In a clairvoyant stroke that was later to have enormous consequences for the *Digest,* father told son, "The day is coming when there will be a great war between the United States and Japan. A lot of people know European languages, but very few speak Japanese and know the country. You stay here and learn Japanese."

Dennis, by now only eighteen, was left behind in Tokyo, became fluent in the language, and was soon hired as a correspondent for United Press International. In January 1940 the U.S. edition of the *Reader's Digest* published his first article, "Japan's 'Patriotic' Gangsters," a critical account of fascist political thugs. When the war broke out, young McEvoy served in the Office of Naval Intelligence in Southeast Asia.

Dennis McEvoy was a "chunky man with an open Irish face," according to one observer. "He was a karate expert; he could stand on his head and sing an aria from *Pagliacci* and stop his heart from beating for a minute or so at will." Like his father, he was also an alcoholic.

Soon after the surrender of Japan, McEvoy was given priority transportation to Tokyo. By 1946, in his capacity as de facto publisher, he had secured General Douglas MacArthur's permission to print a Japanese edition of the *Reader's Digest*. The editor whom McEvoy wanted to hire was Bunshiro Suzuki, the former editor of *Asahi,* one of Japan's largest newspapers. Before the war broke out, a "patriotic gangster" had attacked Suzuki in his office for his antimilitarist stand, slashing him in the face.

Mateo Okini, the business manager hired by McEvoy, was the former chief of Japanese naval intelligence in China. During the war Okini's plane had crashed over China, and he became a prized prisoner—so prized that he was later kidnapped by American agents and flown to Washington, where he was interrogated by McEvoy and other ONI officials. McEvoy won Okini's goodwill by saving his life. As a Japanese officer, first captured and then kidnapped, Okini felt honor bound to commit hara-kiri. But McEvoy threw a party for him instead, complete with traditional Japanese dishes and geisha girls—and also lots of sake. Touched, Okini forgot all talk of killing himself. Some time later he accepted McEvoy's offer of a job.

The 120,000 press run of the Japanese edition—called, in English, *The Reader's Digest*—sold out within hours at a price of three and a half yen, or twenty-three cents. Within a few years it hit a peak of 1.4 million. Normally, Japanese characters would have required an edition containing 30 to 50 percent more pages than its U.S. counterpart. However, scarcity of paper required it be kept to the same size. That very scarcity contributed to the magazine's popularity. The Japanese were so desperate that Rhodes privately thought the edition would have sold out even if the *Digest* "had printed on toilet paper"—which was the use to which the magazine (like every other newspaper or periodical in the country) was ultimately put.

The *RD*'s purchase of property for its new Tokyo headquarters also amounted to the greatest single real-estate coup in modern Japanese history. Though it involved corruption at the highest levels of government, the company itself was apparently an unwitting party.

One evening McEvoy was entertaining Joseph Dodge, principal financial adviser to General MacArthur and later budget director under Eisenhower. McEvoy complained to Dodge about his difficulty in finding a building to rent at a reasonable rate. Dodge observed that in a war-ravaged country, buildings were expensive but land cheap. However, as the country rebuilt, the reverse became true. Like other foreign companies, the Reader's Digest Association of Japan was prohibited by law from taking profits from the operation out of the country. Other U.S. companies such as Time-Life and United Press International were concentrating their efforts on trying to find ways to exchange yen for dollars. Dodge advised McEvoy to invest in land.

That raised other problems. Foreign companies were also not permitted by law to own property. But in 1946, with Acheson's permission, McEvoy began hunting for land. With a fortune in blocked yen in the *Digest*'s bank account, he decided to buy the very best piece of property in all of Tokyo. What finally struck his fancy was a tract next to the downtown banking district with a guaranteed southern exposure. Unfortunately, the property was also adjacent to the Imperial Palace, overlooking a moat, and owned by Prince Kaya, a member of the royal family. Imperial property was considered especially sacrosanct and off-limits to foreigners.

Using his influence with MacArthur, McEvoy got the general's permission to buy the land if the Japanese government approved the sale. But at the Finance Ministry he was informed that the land had been leased by the prince to an organization called the Green Belt Society. "Green Belt" was the term used to designate the park surrounding the palace, including the big public square in front. McEvoy was told that if he could buy the lease rights from the society, the Finance Ministry would consider giving the *Digest* permission to buy the land itself. But there was yet another legal catch. By law, the property would have to be sold at an auction to the highest bidder.

It so happened that the Japanese minister of finance was a "friend of a friend" of McEvoy. This friend once removed was a lawyer who took out a thick lawbook and opened it to page 780, where he read that if a prospective buyer offered a sum which, in the government's considered opinion, was greater than what could be realized at an auction, then the property could be sold directly.

At the same time, finding out who the principals of the Green Belt Society were was proving to be a conundrum. Everybody whom McEvoy approached turned out to be an intermediary just one level higher than the previous intermediary.

Fortunately, McEvoy was never at a loss for powerful friends in high places. Shigeru Yoshida, the Japanese foreign minister who later became prime minister, was a frequent visitor to the McEvoy home. The next time Yoshida came to lunch, McEvoy complained that he was having no luck finding the principals of the Green Belt Society.

"Oh, you want to meet the principals?" Yoshida asked him.

"And how!" McEvoy replied.

"When would you like to meet them?"

"Well, as soon as I can. I've spent six or seven months trying to find out even who they are. I've been in this country for many years, and I thought I knew my way around, but I'm absolutely baffled."

"They'll be in your office this afternoon at four o'clock," Yoshida replied.

That afternoon, as promised, the principals appeared at the *Digest* office. After some bargaining, McEvoy agreed to buy the lease rights for the equivalent of $15,000. The next day he went to the Finance Ministry to report on his success. The head of the land section asked him what price had been decided upon.

"About $20,000," McEvoy replied.

The official jumped out of his chair, crying, "That's not enough!"

"Excuse me," McEvoy said, "but what, may I ask, is your position? I mean the position of the Japanese government in a private deal made between two private entities?"

The official explained that his position was to protect the Japanese people against exploitation by foreigners. McEvoy started laughing.

"Why do you laugh?" the official asked.

McEvoy explained that any foreigner would have to get up very early in the morning in order to exploit the Japanese. But the official still refused to approve the sale. McEvoy retired to a corner with his lawyer to discuss how much more money should be offered. It was agreed to offer the Green Belt Society another $6,000—still well below the ceiling set by Acheson. The official agreed, lease rights were sold, and ultimately the *Digest* was given permission to purchase the property itself for approximately another $46,000.

Later McEvoy learned that the Green Belt Society was a bogus organization composed of members of the Foreign Ministry, including the head of the land section whose job was to protect the people of Japan from foreign exploitation. "Lease rights" was simply a euphemism for "bribe." The property soon became the most valuable piece of private property in all of Tokyo.

———

As with McEvoy in Japan, the *Digest* also enlisted an ex-soldier to oversee its postwar expansion into France and Germany. But Paul W. Thompson was a professional army officer and brigadier general who had overseen all engineering operations during the Normandy invasion. During the assault he was wounded twice, in the jaw and in the shoulder. By 1946 he was looking for a new career.

While stationed in Washington back in 1940, Thompson—no relation to Fred Thompson—had been assigned to assist Paul Palmer on an article on army engineering. The two men also had something else in common. Thompson had done some writing in the *Infantry Journal.* Later a few of those articles were picked up by the *Digest,* and Thompson found several checks in his mail totaling $1,600, more than he had ever dreamed of.

Using his connections with Palmer, Thompson took a train up to Pleasantville one wintry day in 1946 to meet Wally, who thought the forty-six-year-old ex–brigadier general wanted to do some more writing for the *Reader's Digest.* Thompson thought he was going up for a job interview. The conversation between the two men was cordial but short on specifics. Finally, the question of remuneration was broached. Not being familiar with civilian life, Thompson just took a brigadier's salary and multiplied by three. Wally just stared at the ceiling, looking a little worried, then said writers were not paid a fixed annual sum—and certainly not the kind of money Thompson was asking for.

When the misunderstanding was straightened out, Wally summoned his brother-in-law Barclay Acheson, who invited Thompson home for dinner. A man of medium height, military bearing, and driving ambi-

tion, with a suave manner cultivated in the highest social circles of the
U.S. Army, Thompson was hired in March and sent to Paris as director
of European operations. His mandate was to establish editions of the
Reader's Digest in French, German, Italian, and Dutch. Once again,
Wally had elected to entrust an important job—this time a very impor-
tant job—to an amateur.

Arriving in Paris with a letter of credit and a briefcase full of letters
of introduction, Thompson went to see Harry Hill, a friend of Acheson's and manager of American Express, whose office was in 11 rue
Scribe. Hill offered to rent *Sélection du Reader's Digest* a suite of rooms on
the third floor for six months.

Thompson agreed to the arrangement, thinking he had plenty of
time to find suitable permanent quarters. But the search soon turned
frantic. He inspected basements of department stores, derelict piles on
the rim of the Place de l'Etoile, and even a building on the rue de
Paradis with a curious assortment of sanitary facilities. The city offered
to change the street's name to rue de Sélection, but Thompson sadly
declined, knowing that the street would always be known as the street
of whores.

Then an old military friend, Major General Ralph Smith, the American military attaché in Paris, called to say his staff was moving out of its
headquarters on the boulevard Saint-Germain. The owner of the
building, Countess de Vere, had no inkling he was leaving. Thompson
and his chief assistant, Henri de la Chassaigne, formerly chief of the
Paris branch of J. Walter Thompson, went to inspect the building.
Though Thompson was ambivalent, de la Chassaigne persuaded him
to take it. Thompson later learned that the countess, an American and
the widow of a genuine French noble, lived in New York. Best of all,
the *Reader's Digest* was her favorite magazine. She agreed to lease the
building for 70,000 francs, or $200, a month. In mid-October 1946
Sélection moved to its new home.

The staff consisted of eleven souls, plus Paul Palmer, who had
recently arrived in Paris with a sixteen-cylinder Lincoln Zephyr that
used as much oil as gas—a daunting if not insuperable obstacle to
anyone else in ration-plagued Paris. Thompson liked Palmer, whom he
regarded as one of a kind. The ex-general also doubted whether the
RD's foremost political strategist was a true believer in the magazine's
conservative political philosophy. More apparent was his unerring instinct for what made a good article.

Thompson also admired Palmer's life-style. Though he was much married and a regular at Le Flore and Les Deux Magots, his real lifelong passion was to find the perfect cassoulet. Finally, he pronounced that the best cassoulet was to be found in a little restaurant off the boulevard Saint-Germain.

Though Palmer was not involved with *Sélection* on either the organizational or the operational level, Thompson had been told to provide him with office space and cater to his other needs, which were sometimes not insignificant. Palmer had recently married again, and the new Mrs. Palmer was soon due to arrive in Paris. Since accommodations meeting Palmer's luxurious specifications were almost nonexistent, he decided to move into the *Sélection* office, taking the former rooms of Monsieur le Comte and Madame la Comtesse. But even they did not suffice, and after a month the Palmers moved out.

Thompson's own wife, Friedel, a professional singer from Austria, arrived in Paris a few months later, and they settled into the recently vacated suites. Word of guest rooms on the upper stories soon spread. Barclay and Pat Acheson, Marvin Lowes, Hobe Lewis, and other Digesters were among those who decided to visit Paris and give Thompson the benefit of their advice. Even Al Cole showed up, though he was kept awake at night by the clock on a nearby church which bonged every hour without fail.

Roving editors, too, started to appear in alarming numbers. Thompson usually joined them for breakfast, which was served in an elegant dining room facing the garden. Among the earliest visitors were J. P. McEvoy, George Kent, and hack-of-all-trades Fulton Oursler, Sr., who had recently returned with his wife from Lourdes. Thompson asked whether he thought Lourdes water was really miraculous. Fixing him with an intense stare, Oursler replied, "I would rather die than not believe it."

Then there were all the distinguished guests—most notably, Anne and Charles Lindbergh, who always arrived on short notice. Mrs. Lindbergh enjoyed writing in her upstairs room. Usually, Lindbergh arrived in his tiny *deux-chevaux* Renault, which he ritualistically parked in the courtyard with absolute precision—both the right rear and the front fenders exactly two inches from the wall. Then he would deftly extract his six-foot four-inch frame and lock up.

Occasionally, Lindbergh left on an extended trip, taking his sleeping bag and shunning hotels where he might be recognized. On those occasions he left his car inside the garage, again parking exactly two inches from the wall, but this time setting it up on wooden blocks. Then he disconnected the generator, locked the outside door, and completed the ritual by fitting the car with a tarpaulin.

Marveling over the parked car one day, Thompson decided that it was time to clear out a pile of rubbish in another corner of the garage that had been left untouched. As the pile was being reduced, an automobile began to emerge. It turned out to be a rare Bugatti, which an admiring crowd gathered to watch. Thompson called the Countess de Vere in New York to tell her of the discovery. She was delighted, recalling that she had hidden it so well to keep it out of German hands. As soon as possible, the car was spirited away to be restored.

———

BY 1947 the combined circulation of the *Digest*'s international editions stood at 4,698,000 in nine foreign languages (Spanish, Portuguese, Swedish, Arabic, Norwegian, Danish, Japanese, French, and German) and one English (British Commonwealth and South Africa). At year's end Cole decided to suspend publication of *Al-Mukhtar*. Of those that remained, the most anemic by far was the British. Though paper shortages continued to hamper growth on most editions, the currency-exchange rate was an even more vexing problem. To prop up the postwar economy, the government maintained an artificially high foreign-exchange rate for the pound sterling, thereby confronting American companies with a catch-22—to expand, they needed to supply their colonies with fresh capital. But converting that capital into pounds was costly. Al Cole thought that if the money-supply problem were solved, the circulation could quickly rise to 6 million—an optimistic sentiment as wrongheaded as his earlier gloomy prediction that the Latin American edition might be lucky to sell only 50,000.

Over time editorial difficulties had also arisen. One concerned the question of what to do about articles with foreign settings—a seeming contradiction in a magazine whose main editorial goal was to interpret the American way of life to the rest of the world. Cole and others were fearful that the international editions might not carry enough purely American content.

On the other hand, Wally himself had published thirty-eight articles with a foreign setting in 1922 alone, the year he founded the magazine. The following year saw forty-four articles with settings outside the

United States. As circulation grew and the size of the magazine increased from 64 to 136 pages, the number of foreign settings also continued to rise.

At an editorial conference attended by senior staffers in the international division, the question was explored in depth. Eduardo Cárdenas argued in favor of foreign settings because that way *Selecciones* readers would feel they were keeping up with the world rather than the United States alone. Articles with a foreign background also "build good will in the country they deal with," said Cárdenas. Finally, he argued, they "tend to improve the readability of our magazine in wide areas."

Acheson agreed, but noted, "Scores of important Americans believe that the *Reader's Digest* is America's greatest good-will ambassador. Statesmen and leaders in foreign countries feel exactly the same way about stories that interpret them favorably to our large international audience throughout the world."

He followed up with a long memo to Wally in which he argued that the *Digest* won its big circulation in France not because of any stories it published about that country but because of "the characteristic philosophy and editorial point of view inherent" in the magazine. "France was bogged down in despair," Acheson claimed, "and she turned to us like thirsty men turn to a fountain, because of the courage, faith and hope that radiate from the *Digest* pages. . . . It is this message and not the setting of any article that is the important thing."

Acheson recommended that foreign settings be permitted and articles chosen on their own merits. He also advised that Pleasantville continue to maintain absolute editorial control over all international editions. The proposal carried.

Late in 1947 Acheson sent a confidential memorandum to the State Department. Like other American companies, the *Digest* was still prevented from transferring foreign currencies out of most of the countries in which it published. Acheson declared that the solution involved a choice: either the U.S. government agreed to buy the blocked currency or it granted publishers a dollar subsidy. Acheson preferred the former. He was anxious for the *Reader's Digest* to avoid even the appearance of subsidy, going so far as to insist that no fresh appropriation of government money be made to purchase the blocked currency. Rather, funds were to be taken from existing budgets of the U.S. Information Service or "other existing U.S. government agencies" since a new appropriation "could be fatal to the [*Digest's* publishing] program abroad, by giving the opponents of American policy a ready-made proof of the designs of the U.S. Government for 'cultural imperialism' all over the world, and by appearing to confirm widespread Communist propaganda to the effect that American magazines are not independent but are controlled mouthpieces of the American Government."

Shortly afterward the newly formed Central Intelligence Agency approached the *Digest* and offered to provide it with seed money to set up more foreign offices. Wally firmly turned down the offer. Not only did the magazine have plenty of its own money, he reasoned, but accepting financial assistance from the government would compromise the magazine's editorial integrity.

However, what could not be bought could be obtained in other ways. In succeeding decades, as the country and the world entered the Cold War era, the *Digest* was to become regardless a highly valuable propaganda outlet for both the CIA and, to a lesser extent, the Federal Bureau of Investigation. The year 1947 also saw the establishment of a Washington office of the *Reader's Digest*.

———

HENRI DE LA CHASSAIGNE, Paul Thompson's business manager, had proven to be a man of exceptional talent. Not only had he persuaded Thompson to rent *Sélection*'s headquarters on the boulevard Saint-Germain, but as a former executive for J. Walter Thompson he possessed an insider's knowledge of French publishing that extended to advertising, paper supply, and promotion. Virtually single-handedly he oversaw the production of an *RD* troop edition published in Paris. Yet he never wanted his name on the masthead, despite his claim that he was a count by birth. Thompson suspected that the reason lay somewhere in de la Chassaigne's past, but he never asked.

Then one day Thompson received a call from a high official in the Department of Public Information advising him to spirit de la Chassaigne out of France immediately or risk a terrible scandal involving *Sélection*. Thompson learned that during the Nazi occupation, his business manager had been the head of an office in Lyons charged with deporting Jews to Auschwitz and other concentration camps. Within hours the two men departed in haste for the Italian border, which they reached that very night, with Thompson driving. In Italy, where the pursuit of war criminals was much more lax, the former business manager set up a thriving advertising agency.

Ex–brigadier general Thompson displayed similar latitude toward several former soldiers whom he had once faced on the field. Among those hired for the German edition were two officers who had served under Rommel. One, a former personal bodyguard of Hitler as well, had been captured and spent the war in a POW camp in Kansas. The other, beholding a picture of the RDA home office in Pleasantville for the first time, turned to Thompson and sighed, "What a fine Corps headquarters that would make."

Thompson's willingness to work with ex-Nazis was shared by Wally himself. Soon after the war Radio Free Europe and Radio Liberty (originally, Radio Liberation from Bolshevism) were founded under the auspices of the National Committee for a Free Europe. Along with Henry Luce, Wally sat on the board of the NCFE, which recruited a large number of former Nazis—in a roundup called Operation Bloodstone—to beam anti-Communist propaganda over the airwaves. The *Digest* also led in the forgiveness of Nazis and in June 1948 ran a story titled "The Idiocy of Our De-Nazification Policy."

The launch of the German edition took place in 1948, during the time of the Berlin airlift. German printers capable of handling large pressruns were, like paper, in short supply, but finally Thompson and his associates were able to find a plant in Essen that met their needs. Unfortunately, Essen was in the British zone, and several of the *Digest*'s British imitations were likewise attempting to expand into the German market. As a result, British bureaucracy was wrapping *Das Beste aus Reader's Digest* with all the red tape it could lay its hands on.

Shortly before the first number of *Das Beste* was to be printed, Thompson went to Stuttgart, where the edition was headquartered, to help out with last-minute problems and to join in the celebration. On the day the magazine went to press, he received a call from the plant's owner in Essen. The printer said he had terrible news. British officers had arrived and ordered the presses shut down, because the proper paperwork had not been completed.

Thompson immediately caught a coal train to Berlin, sitting among the coal sacks, and the next morning at eight o'clock was at the office of his old army friend General Lucius Clay, commander in chief of American armed forces in Europe and military governor of the U.S. zone in Berlin. Thompson explained the disastrous circumstances behind his unexpected visit.

Clay picked up the phone, called his British counterpart, and tersely declared that he did not know what formalities had not properly been taken care of, but either the presses in Essen began rolling that very day or he was going to annul the permits of every British businessman in the American zone. Then the two generals went back to Clay's home for lunch. While they were dining, they received a message. The magazine was being printed.

7

Baseball Z and Other Diversions

IN THE DEPARTMENT of practical jokes, the *Digest*'s associate book-excerpt editor Maurice T. Ragsdale was one of the most industrious. He once gave a party for an editor who often boasted of his love of the outdoors. Obligingly, Ragsdale had the party in his backyard in the middle of winter, serving weak ice-cold drinks and a barbecue after sundown. But even he could not top Wally.

When a young excerpt editor resigned in the summer of 1941 to get married and leave Pleasantville, Ragsdale sent out black-bordered invitations to the "Virginia Flory Memorial Party." Taking his cue, Wally arrived at the party in a hearse, preceded by a truck with two loud-speakers attached to the roof blaring funeral music. Dressed in top hat and mourning dress, he also sported his wife's black lace panties and matching bra as arm bands. Wally had bought the lingerie for Lila, who refused to wear the scanty items, because she considered them too diaphanous.

Lila herself showed up moments later in a white convertible, wearing a fluffy chiffon dress. The other partygoers were bewildered because Lila—no longer a blonde now but a brunette—seemed to have dressed merely to go to a party and not as part of a stunt. But they were not sure. One of the women thought she ought to offer a compliment, just in case, and approached to say tentatively, "I like your outfit."

"What outfit?" Lila replied.

Wally also arranged for a series of sophomoric telegrams to arrive regularly throughout the afternoon. When the Western Union delivery boy showed up with the first, Flory read, "Church synod refuses to permit dropping word obey from marriage ceremony. Under circumstances do you think it advisable to proceed with wedding? If so proceed at your own risk. Rev. John Dinwoodie DD."

It was followed by: "When your husband beats you and all the world is dark and gloomy remember that Jesus loves you. Johnny Hell."

The man with an unerring instinct for subtle humor concluded with this clunker: "Sorry but our stock of What Every Bride Should Know is exhausted. May we substitute one of the following volumes: The Physiology of Sex, The Psychology of Sex, The Biology of Sex, Don't Let Sex Throw You, Sure Cure for Insomnia, How to Treat Dogs, Cats, Husbands and Other Pets; Hindu Love Secrets; My Sex Life by Mahatma Gandhi; Sex in Six Easy Lessons. If none of these fills your particular requirements come in and let me advise you personally. Lowell Brentano, Brentano's Book Store."

The party concluded with a hymn sing to the accompaniment of mournful tunes played over the loudspeakers.

Sometimes Wally recruited other Digesters in his pranks. Once editor Lou Dillon, who had a shock of wavy platinum-blond hair, returned from vacation sporting a beard that came in dark red. In those days no one at the *Digest* wore either a mustache or a beard, but Dillon thought it might be fun to be odd man out for a while, particularly because the contrast between blond and red was so striking.

A few days later Wally invited Dillon to meet him in town for lunch. When the latter showed up at the restaurant, he found the boss and half a dozen colleagues sitting around the table, all wearing long beards, droopy mustaches, or wigs.

Just as Wally worked harder than anyone, so he played harder. Lila endured rather than participated in her husband's pranks, some of which seemed punitive or humiliating. Others seemed designed to attract attention lest he be neglected.

A case in point was Wally's airplane. Many of the editors and their wives were terrified at the prospect of getting an invitation from the boss to drive out to the airfield in Armonk and take a trip—something he did almost weekly. Those who sought to curry his favor, which included just about everyone, found it difficult to refuse. Once he flew Dillon's wife, Urith, from Armonk to Montauk Point, on Long Island, and back, then went up the Hudson to Albany before turning around—in all, a journey of some three hundred miles. It was her first and last plane trip.

—

ONE day Wally's longtime friend Wendell MacRae, the photographer, decided to conduct a secret "experiment" with Wally as the unwitting subject. He invited the *RD*'s editor to his Rockefeller Center studio ostensibly to observe him shoot a modeling session. The model was a particularly sexy and sassy young woman named Anita, who was in on the prank. As usual, Wally arrived on time. MacRae set to work photographing the long-legged model in a variety of sheer stockings. When Anita observed Wally staring at her breasts, she said that reminded her of the time she worked as a receptionist. A salesman wanted to see her boss and started peering down her décolletage. She replied, "Well, he's not in there."

After an hour of shooting, MacRae secretly turned the camera on Wally himself and took what many Digesters considered the best likeness ever done of the founder of the *Reader's Digest*—a man wearing a blissful gaze and flushed expression, as though absorbed in a mystical reverie. Only insiders knew that it was really inspired by Anita's long gams and inviting bosom.

MacRae also presented Wally with a modest assortment of photographs that by the standards of the day—those of the average *Digest* subscriber, for example—would have been deemed pornographic. One was a lush close-up of a nude female torso leaning over a martini. The caption read, "Childs Restaurants Now Serving Cocktails." Another close-up showed a rose strategically placed over a woman's genitals with the caption "Gardens of the Nations."

On occasion, after a party at High Winds, Wally liked to sneak out into the darkness, having targeted a certain departing couple. He took pride in remembering what kind of car each of his editors drove. Stealing into the backseat, he curled up in the darkness to enjoy the inevitable postmortem on the party, which invariably included remarks about himself and other Digesters. At the Gate House, to the mortification of his guests, he asked to be let out. Even if nothing uncomplimentary or incriminating had been uttered, his mere presence sufficed to give most couples the creeps. But Wally considered his ghost ride a huge joke, done in the spirit of good clean fun.

As a result of such behavior, analyzing Wally had become an everyday pastime in Pleasantville, particularly by those who knew him well. One Digester thought he suffered from anhedonia, or the incapacity for experiencing happiness. According to that explanation, his propensity for pranks and mischief was only a desperate bid to find enjoyment in something. Others thought his backseat escapades were just his way of wanting to appear ubiquitous. Whatever the reason, Wally's passion for fun—occasionally juvenile, always inventive—was the stuff of *Digest* legend.

Another aspect of his idea of fun was that it usually involved the complicity, willing or unwilling, of beautiful women. Once at a High Winds party, Wally was talking to the tall, long-legged Frances Ellison, wife of Jerry. While the two were chatting, a waitress passed by bearing a tray of drinks. Wally took the tray and held it out at shoulder height.

"Frances," he said, "I'll bet you can't kick this tray out of my hands."

Smiling demurely, Frances looked him in the eye and said, "Of course I can, Wally. But I won't."

"I didn't say you wouldn't," Wally countered. "I say you can't."

The flirtatious badinage continued until she lifted her skirt and with a cancan kick sent the tray flying. Lila immediately closed down the bar.

———

IF WALLY's unpredictability sometimes posed unexpected problems for Digesters, his predictability in other respects was equally worrisome. His and Lila's obsession with punctuality, for example, caused massive corporate anxiety.

In Pleasantville the office working hours had been 8:00 to 3:30; but after the move to Chappaqua they were shifted to 8:30 to 4:00 to accommodate people now arriving from all over Westchester and Connecticut. Wally continued to pay as much attention to attendance and tardiness sheets as he did to his editors' productivity. Anyone more than two minutes late was required to note his or her lateness. Latecomers often received notes politely urging them to arrive on time in the future. On the other hand, employees were expected to depart just as promptly.

Though the lack of absolute punctuality on the part of his employees continued to be a small thorn in Wally's side, no one who had any hope of advancing up the *Digest* hierarchy would ever entertain, for a moment, being one minute late to a party or invitation to supper at High Winds.

One evening, editor Cuyler MacRae, brother of Wendell, and his wife were invited to dinner at High Winds at six o'clock. As usual, they set out well ahead of time but arrived—also as usual—too early to make their appearance. So they drove around for a while, waiting until six o'clock. Pretty soon they discovered that Bill and Rita Hard were right behind them, driving about five miles an hour. Finally, Maurice and Betty Ragsdale showed up at the gate, waiting for six to strike. All three couples arrived at High Winds not only at the same time but exactly on time.

Wally used to carry tiny volumes containing one or several books of the Bible. He disliked wasting time and once claimed he had read the entire New Testament through in one year just waiting for people. In fact, he filled up any idle moment with compulsive reading. Lila once remarked that he could not be in a hotel room for half an hour without reading every line of print in the room and bath, except for the Gideon Bible. He also knew there were three different printed forms for saying grace at Howard Johnson highway inns, and scrutinized the fine print on the back of bar coasters to see who printed them. He even read everything printed on the shredded-wheat box at the breakfast table.

Novels and poetry held no appeal for him. He liked to quote Matthew Arnold's line that journalism was "literature in a hurry." Among Wally's notes was the quip "Things are moving so fast nowadays that people who say it can't be done are being interrupted by those who are doing it."

His favorite writer, curiously enough, was a man in some respects his opposite—the ardent Catholic convert Fulton Oursler, Sr., author of *The Greatest Story Ever Told,* who was described by one colleague as "a forceful person who looked rather like a witch"—an allusion, no doubt, to his penetrating gaze, slight stoop, and shock of dark hair. Oursler joined the staff of the *Digest* late in his career, in 1944, having already written some thirty books, including mysteries under the name of Anthony Abbot, as well as movies, plays, and radio shows.

On the dedication page of his best-selling life of Christ, published in 1949, the busiest storyteller of the day showed he still had a knack for spinning out fiction, albeit unwittingly: "There are two people, man and wife, who in their lives personally and professionally exemplify the teachings of Jesus Christ more completely than any others I know." The Wallaces would not allow Oursler to identify them.

An amateur magician, Oursler once invited Wally and Lila to join him at his Cape Cod home, where he put on a show. For openers he did the "milk pitcher trick," pouring milk into a copy of the *Reader's Digest.* When the fluid disappeared, Oursler announced that it had been "condensed." Next he did a "rising-card trick," giving Lila the queen of hearts and asking her to replace it in the deck. When the card subsequently began to rise from the pack, it bore her photograph— "and was this not proper, since she was the queen of our hearts?"

Oursler was not only a magician but, like many a worthy son of Pleasantville, a shameless sycophant. After divorcing his first wife, he married Grace Perkins, a widely published author and editor of Norman Vincent Peale's *Guideposts* magazine, whom he had met at Alcoholics Anonymous. An offspring of Fulton's first marriage was Will Oursler, author of *The Road to Faith* and other religious potboilers, who in later years was to wage a bitter legal battle with his half brother Tony over the family estate.

Wally's tolerance of the foibles of writers was legendary. After one *RD* writer was accused of assaulting a research girl, he was summoned to High Winds. Everyone expected a royal dismissal. Instead, he emerged with a raise. Wally also defended a writer who had been indicted for misappropriation of public funds.

Then there was Myron Stern, the oldest living free-lance writer for the *Digest.* For some time Wally had been dissatisfied with his work and had not bought anything. Stern's doctor informed him he had terminal cancer. The writer drew up a letter to his lawyer, outlining his dire circumstances and saying he wanted to get his estate in order before he died.

Somehow, the letter to the lawyer was put into an envelope mailed to Wally, while a letter to Wally with yet another article proposal was sent to the lawyer. Many Digesters were convinced that Stern purposely contrived the mix-up. Some were not so sure that he had seen a doctor recently either. Regardless, Wally sent Stern a monthly check for the rest of his life, which to almost no one's amazement did not conclude on schedule.

The opposite of Wally's generosity was his frugality. Among his cost-saving practices was to use both the top and the bottom of a typewriter ribbon. He also liked to resharpen a safety razor on the palm of the hand and stack his fireplace logs at night to make charcoal. He was equally notorious for recycling envelopes, and at lunchtime he often went around to various editorial offices turning off the lights.

Partly as a reflection of his lifelong interest in farming, and partly as a favor to his older brother Bob, Wally bought a farm in Wisconsin in order to grow experimental crops. Bob managed the farm but sometimes had to appeal to *RD* treasurer Roy Abbott because Lila and Wally were too busy to reply. In February 1937 Bob pleaded with Abbott for an answer to his long letter of two months earlier "outlining a program of alfalfa and dairy expansion." Bob wanted his brother, whom he called DeWitt, to invest in milk cows and plant fifty acres of alfalfa in newly plowed ground. To accomplish those goals a $600 check was required. Only after repeated requests was the money forwarded.

Wally, the former second baseman, also remained an ardent baseball fan and frequently invited Digesters to accompany him to games. Even on those occasions, however, he found a way of mixing fun and business—referring to himself as the manager and to the assorted editors accompanying him as ballplayers, whom he then critiqued. Henderson and Ragsdale, for example, were found to be in good form. But Wally worried about Ferguson and Ellison, saying he might have to bench them if they did not snap out of their slump.

Wally's courteousness was also legendary. He never issued a harsh memo. Cuyler MacRae recalled a period when he was serving as an issue editor. Wally would occasionally send him an article. He never said, "Use this." Rather, he asked, "Will this fit your issue?" Once Wally sent MacRae an article concerning children with the attached note "Good piece if this fits your issue."

MacRae sent him a memo back saying, "We have a piece about Danny Kaye and his work with UNICEF that would conflict with this, and I prefer that." Wally then asked to see it. After reading the article, he sent a memo saying, "You're right." MacRae was impressed by Wally's quality of always being as accommodating as possible, and as a result he never felt reluctant to speak his mind.

Another of Wally's qualities was his succinctness. Memos, postcards, rejection letters—all were models of condensation. Even his entry in *Who's Who* was briefer than that of anyone else's at the *Digest*. Sometimes, though, his brief messages contained a big surprise. Wally and Lila were known for vanishing without telling anybody. Once a postcard arrived in Pleasantville informing *Digest* editors that the couple were in Hawaii.

Wally had a habit of occasionally driving over to the airport at Armonk, getting into his plane, and flying off without telling anyone at

the *Digest* that he was leaving. Resorts in the nearby Poconos or Adi-
rondack mountains were favorite destinations, where Wally holed up
with a pile of manuscripts—and sometimes a female companion.

———

BY NOW Barclay Acheson's only daughter, Judy, though thought by
some spoiled and loud, had grown into a young woman of considerable beauty. Soon after her graduation in 1939 from the prestigious
Lincoln School in New York, handwritten invitations on parchment
paper were sent out, announcing the wedding of Judy Acheson to Fred
Thompson, Al Cole's young assistant.

The May nuptials turned out to be the most lavish gala ever held at
High Winds, with horse-drawn carriages bringing the wedding party
back to the house after the church ceremony. Lila was matron of
honor, wearing a gold-colored dress with a train and a hat with a
flowing ribbon. On the day of the ceremony, however, she had not yet
found the right color of ribbon and finally sent her trusted right-hand
man Harry Wilcox into New York to get the desired shade of soft
green velvet. During the reception Wendell MacRae flew overhead,
taking photographs. Later the newlyweds drove off in an Irish jaunting
cart.

As befitted the lord and lady of a grand home, who were sole
proprietors of a still-burgeoning publishing empire, the Wallaces also
moved among the rich and famous as a matter of course. Lowell
Thomas, a relatively recent contributor, invited Wally to be on his
softball team in a game played one August afternoon in 1938 at Saga-
more Hill, the estate in Oyster Bay, Long Island, of Theodore Roosevelt, Jr. Explorer, war correspondent, film producer, and modern-day
Marco Polo, Thomas had been closely associated with the *Literary
Digest,* a newsy forerunner of *Time* that folded that same year. Wally
had quickly signed up its most famous author, and the *RD* eventually
became the sponsor of Thomas's radio show.*

Later Wally and Roosevelt discussed an omnibus volume—Roose-

---

*The *Literary Digest* became one of the first magazines to advertise in the new medium of radio when
William C. Paley, head of CBS, launched the first daily news broadcast of the air in 1928, with the
LD as sponsor. Later the magazine also underwrote Thomas's program. Though an enthusiast both
of radio and of advertising, Wally was slow to take advantage of either at the business level,
preferring to advertise the *RD* in its own pages and to rely on direct mail and word of mouth to
build circulation.

velt was then working for Doubleday, Doran and Company—that the *Digest* might use as a "come on" in subscription renewals. The magazine would produce the editorial, and Doubleday would publish it. The result was the *RD*'s first book collection, *The Reader's Digest Reader,* a collection of articles edited by Roosevelt and the magazine's editors and published by Doubleday, Doran in 1940.

Two of the most celebrated guests to visit High Winds were the duke and duchess of Windsor, who accepted a luncheon invitation from the Wallaces during the 1943 holiday season. When their car pulled up in front of the Wallace home, his former majesty stepped out, beheld the imposing, castle-like mansion, and with tongue in royal cheek observed, "This is what we need—a pleasant little shooting box in the country."

In his thank-you note, the duke noted, "It was also a great pleasure to meet the fine bunch of men, who constitute your Editorial Staff, as well as to see all your employees from whose demeanour one senses their appreciation of the gay atmosphere and comfortable surroundings you have created for them to work in."

Though Wally's correspondents numbered some of the most celebrated names of the day (Winston Churchill, Herbert Hoover, assorted prominent authors), he eschewed political comment, gossip, or other conventions of the prolific letter writer. Relatively few of his thousands of dispatches—thank-you notes, invitations to dinner, congratulatory effusions—made it to the second paragraph. His professional Christmas greetings list included Norman Cousins of the *Saturday Review of Literature,* B. C. Forbes of *Forbes* magazine, John Gunther, Dorothy Canfield, Henry R. Luce, Lester Markel of the *New York Times,* H. L. Mencken, Walter Winchell, Lowell Thomas, and I. F. Stone at the *Nation.*

Pearl Buck was another correspondent. Wally sent her a clipping from the *New York Post* refuting a complaint she had recently voiced to the effect that digests were ruining people's capacity for literature. In a friendly postscript he added, "I do think you are pretty wonderful in every other respect."

She wrote back, "As usual, the newspapers get everything wrong. . . . I am adamant on the subject of digests in their relationship to literature, but I will concede you this point, great or small; for the mass of morons who are not going to read anything, the digests are a benefit." In a mollifying postscript, she added, "I find the editors of digests are like other Christians—one's objections to their creed are dismayingly modified by the fact that they as individuals are so surprisingly pleasant."

Many Digesters did appreciate the "gay atmosphere" noticed by the sad ex–king of England. Some of them even decided to make a home movie about the Wallaces' pleasure dome. The script called for an opening shot of Lila writing to her mother, followed by a close-up of the letter. It read, "Dear Mother: This is the story of my fairy-castle. We call it . . ." Title card: "High Winds." Wally and Lila then proudly showed off the stable, gate, streams, and other attractions, and afterward Judy and Lila went off riding. The camera proceeded to pan to the handball court, Wally's tower, lower pool and terrace, game room, rock garden, and central terrace, until another card asked, "Have you noticed the lake today?" Next came a shot of the "Monk's Garden" with a statue of St. Francis of Assisi amid the roses. Then came another graphic: "Wally's Up to Something," followed by "Lila Hears an Airplane." "Stop It, Wally—You're Frightening the Horses." Lila ended the letter, "With love and kisses from . . . ," followed by a close-up of each member of the family.

As the years went by, Wally worried about Lila because he came from a long-lived family and she from a short-lived one. Despite his fears, she correctly prophesied more than once that she was going to outlive him. After ticking off the names of several men who had outlived their wives and remarried young women, usually their secretaries or another woman with whom they worked, she told Wally, "I'm not going to die and let some young thing run off with you."

Wally had no intention of running off—except maybe once in a while in his airplane. But another form of wanderlust had to do with poker. His favorite poker variation was called Baseball Z, in which nines and hidden threes were wild and a four entitled the lucky player to a base on balls in the form of another card, which could be dealt face down, providing the player chipped in another $2.50.

One day Wally had an inspiration. He wanted to hire a Pullman and head off with some friends for a few days of round-the-clock poker playing. It was to be the first of many such spontaneous expeditions. Asked to look into the price, Cole paid a visit to the president of the New York Central Railroad, got the figures, and reported back to Wally, who had no idea where he wanted to go. Cole suggested a route leading from Dayton, Ohio, where the *Digest* was now printed, to St. Paul, Minnesota.

"We can take some of these guys who have never been to a printing plant before to the McCall plant in Dayton," Cole explained, "and then go see some things in the town you were born in."

"All right," Wally agreed.

On the first night out, everybody got drunk. In the morning, when the train rolled into Dayton, no one was in a mood to visit the plant except Cole and Paul Palmer. At the first whiff of printers' ink, however, Palmer nearly passed out. They immediately returned to the train. When they got to St. Paul, Cole and Ralph Henderson took a long walk while everyone else continued to play poker. Wally never got off the train once.

During the poker games, a chart was scrupulously kept of the winnings and losses of every player. Harold Lynch, in charge of drawing up checks for the editorial department at that time, kept track. A very unlucky player stood to lose a hundred dollars or more during a night. Wally frequently won, much to his embarrassment. But Henderson, his old Ping-Pong adversary, turned out to be a pretty good Baseball Z player, too.

IN *1939* Dr. James Wallace died at the age of ninety. For a brief time thereafter, Wally's contributions to Macalester rose sharply, and over the next few years his total contributions to the college reached $300,-000. Then he stopped giving altogether.

Sometime in late 1940, though no details survive, the family almost suffered another death. This time the crisis involved Lila. From Europe, where he was involved in helping to establish the *Digest*'s international editions, a concerned Barclay Acheson wrote a series of letters home. After the emergency passed and Lila was back in High Winds, "the only appropriate setting for [her] lovely and kindly self," Acheson wrote that he thanked God she "did not take flight—nothing else matters." Lila also received a get-well verse from troubadour Ken Payne, whose three-page poem opened with a long digression on the battle raging in Europe. But part two asked, "What beauty and good can I find?" Proving he was every bit the sycophantic equal of Oursler and Acheson, he answered:

> There's this sea and this sky of ineffable blue
> Like the blue of your eyes . . .

Dear my lady,
There's you!

With America's entry into the war seemingly inevitable, Wally donated his plane to the Canadian government for use in training exercises. It was also no longer possible for the Wallaces to travel abroad. But he still liked to take the train down to New York several times a month to put up at a favorite hotel. Sometimes, after tiring of working on manuscripts, he phoned a staffer to join him. One afternoon while chatting with a writer he suggested:

"Why don't you go over to the Waldorf Towers and have a talk with Herbert Hoover?"

"What for, Wally?" asked the writer, who never wrote on politics. "What's the story?"

"Oh, no story, I guess," Wally replied. "I was just thinking, Hoover's probably just sitting over there all by himself with nobody to talk to. I'll bet he's lonesome."

Around this time Wally and Lila also inaugurated their practice of checking into a suite at the Pierre Hotel, off Fifth Avenue, shortly after Thanksgiving and staying in town through Christmas. Each day Wally spent hours writing hundreds of Christmas cards, every one with a personal message—but always writing against the clock to see how many he could finish in an hour. Lila shopped or visited museums. Several nights a week they went to the theater, often inviting along favored employees and their spouses.

Lila was seeing a lot more of her husband, now that he was advancing into middle age. But she still spent a considerable amount of time with Harry Wilcox. One afternoon he and Lila were driving along Highway 117, which ran behind the *Digest*'s headquarters, when they saw a sign for a new liquor store reading, "Leonard Park Liquors." The next day, at Lila's bidding, Wilcox stopped by the store to persuade the store owner to change its name. He explained that Mrs. Wallace disliked the word "liquors" and thought it lowered the tone of the neighborhood. The owner obliged by putting up a new sign, which simply gave the address, hoping Mrs. Wallace would express her gratitude by buying some liquor from the store from time to time, but he never heard from her again.

Across from the *Digest* grounds was a small stone garage, which Lila fixed up and gave to Wilcox as a home. A girl of about fifteen later showed up at the house and told neighboring Digesters she was his daughter. She stayed quite a while, and her presence gave rise to more rumors because few people believed her. Some even thought she was nastier than Wilcox. Then abruptly she was gone and never seen again.

One spring morning at High Winds, Lila awoke to find Wally standing in the doorway of her bedroom. He was wearing only a hat and carrying a briefcase.

"I've decided that I have had enough," he announced. "I'm running away from home."

Then he vanished. But unlike the disappearing act of Harry's so-called daughter, it was just another prank.

III

THE KINGDOM
[1944–1965]

8

The Talk of the Town

IN THE early forties one of the most acrimonious relationships—"rivalry" would be too strong a word—in publishing circles was that between the *Reader's Digest* and Harold Ross's *New Yorker.* The acrimony, though, was one-sided. Wally admired Ross, reprinted a considerable amount of material from his magazine, and considered the relationship for the most part harmonious and mutually satisfactory. But Ross detested both the *Digest* and its system of planting articles in other publications. It gave him the creeps.

In contrast to the often hostile attitude of magazines like *Scribner's* in the previous decade, those that had survived the Depression were perfectly content to cooperate with Pleasantville in a symbiotic arrangement that seemingly allowed all partners to benefit. The *Digest* now paid well for genuine reprint rights. It also subsidized original articles in its client magazines—not even asking for credit, but only for the right to reprint. In addition to paying the author's first-serial fee and all research costs, it paid a reprint fee to make the transaction "legitimate." Naturally, few free-lance writers complained about getting a double paycheck, while the sponsoring magazine was able to publish an article at no cost.

The *Digest's* stunning largess was in large part responsible for the fact that, for more than eleven years, such a cozy and editorially questionable relationship had gone virtually unchallenged. Some of the most prestigious magazines in the country, including *Harper's* and the *Atlantic Monthly,* willingly permitted their pages to be used for the "preprinting" of articles destined later to be condensed in the *Digest.*

Nowhere in those magazines, moreover, were readers given notice that articles purporting to be original with the respective editors of each publication were, in fact, either original with the *Digest* or paid for with *Digest* money. From the perspective of collaborating editors, Pleasantville simply proposed article ideas they were free to accept or reject. If they ever thought their editorial integrity was being violated, they kept those doubts to themselves.

For competitive reasons only the Hearst Corporation still refused to permit any articles appearing in its publications to be reprinted, or to cooperate in any other fashion with the *Digest*. Other once recalcitrant publications such as *Forum* and Ken Payne's old *North American Review* had disappeared, victims of the Depression or changing times.

Privately, a handful of editors and some others did wonder whether the *Digest* was accruing too much editorial control for everyone's own good. During the Butler controversy, in particular, there was talk—fomented largely by the leftist press and ultimately reaching the floor of Congress—that the magazine was threatening to evolve into an information cartel.

But threats to do something about the *RD*'s monopoly never materialized. Also it was always pointed out that Pleasantville paid for originals in both the liberal and the conservative press, from the *American Mercury* and *Scribner's Commentator* to the *Nation* and the *New Republic*. In fact, the *Digest* seemingly generated articles in all sorts of magazines on just about every topic imaginable—because, after all, its policy was presumably to give its subscribers a sampling of the best of everything. Moreover, the magazine used only a small fraction of what it paid for. Three-fourths of every "plant" wound up on the cutting-room floor.

But Ross felt uncomfortable in his relationship with the *Digest*. The *New Yorker* was one of the few magazines that did not permit the *Digest* to plant articles in its pages in return for a generous fee. But it nonetheless remained a prime source of reprint material, which to Ross was almost as galling. Besides, he had a few scores to settle—among them Wally's appropriation of Alexander Woollcott, with whom Ross had a falling out that he hoped was only temporary. But Woollcott never returned to the *New Yorker* fold—partly, no doubt, because Wally had given him financial independence.

Wally had also tried to kidnap another of the *New Yorker*'s famous writers, E. B. White. In 1936 the *Digest* had reprinted White's "Farewell, My Lovely!" and paid such a generous fee that White was able to switch allegiance from the *New Yorker,* where he had to meet a weekly deadline, to *Harper's,* a monthly. (A classic in American belles lettres, as time would prove, White's nostalgic adieu to his favorite "flivver," a Model T, was one that Wally the inveterate lover of old cars must have particularly relished—thus the generous stipend.) After Woollcott died, Wally tried to hire White as his replacement, which prompted Ross to dash off a note to White saying, "You can have any damn thing you want around this place," in effect, letting him write his own ticket. White returned to his old forum, the opening page of the *New Yorker,* and declined the *RD* offer.

On February 9, 1944, a letter went out to all *New Yorker* contributors, advising them that the magazine had recently decided not to renew its reprint agreement with the *Reader's Digest.* Though the letter was signed simply "The Editors," it bore Ross's unmistakable signature just as surely as his magazine:

> The *Digest* started out as a reprint magazine but grew into something quite different. Nowadays a large proportion of its contents is frankly original with the *Digest* and not presented as reprint material; and of the stuff that is reprinted as reprint material much actually originates in the office of the *Digest* and then gets farmed out to some other magazine for first publication. The effect of this (apart from spreading a lot of money around) is that the *Digest* is beginning to generate a considerable fraction of the contents of American magazines. This gives us the creeps.

In an irreverent tone reminiscent of the magazine's up-front "Talk of the Town," the letter went on to say,

> [The *New Yorker*] has never been particularly impressed with the *Digest*'s capsule theory of life and its assumption that any piece can be improved by extracting every seventh word, like a tooth. . . . Mostly, however, we object to the *Digest*'s indirect creative control, which is a threat to the free flow of ideas and to the independent spirit.

Ross's diatribe was given prominent coverage in the *New York Times* and jump-started a bandwagon of anti-*Digest* criticism. Not only did the letter sever the connection between the country's most sophisticated magazine and the magazine of the millions; it also tolled the death knell of the *Digest*'s planting system with America's best publications, who were stung by Ross's accusation that another creative hand was guiding their own. To atone for its sins, the publishing community cast its former benefactor into the role of pariah.

For eleven years Ross had put up uncomplainingly—in public, at any rate—with whatever threat the *Digest* posed to the free flow of ideas within the somnolent precincts of the *New Yorker*. His contempt for the *Digest* was genuine, and perhaps the most remarkable thing of all was that a man so outspoken had waited so long to speak out. What finally did cause him to erupt had less to do, however, with the *Digest's* octopus-like stranglehold on the magazines of America than with finance, literary politics, and ego.

The tinder was lit as far back as 1936 when Ross read the *Fortune* profile of the *Reader's Digest* and learned that the rubes in Pleasantville had taken him for a sucker. Like everyone else, he had no inkling that Wally was paying out salaries far in excess of what most people in the publishing business were earning. Ross's own salary was reputed to be $40,000, less than half of what a nobody like Ken Payne was getting.

Reading between the lines, Ross also realized that those huge salaries were being at least partly subsidized by the niggardly contracts for reprint rights that the *Digest* had negotiated with its client magazines. Specifically, Wally paid the *New Yorker* $1,800 a year for exclusive rights to condense items from "The Talk of the Town." A two-page condensed facsimile of the magazine's most famous department often appeared as the *Digest's* center spread, even down to reproducing the *New Yorker's* distinctive Irvin typeface.

After the *Fortune* piece appeared, Ross unilaterally and retroactively upped the fee to $15,000 for all previously reprinted and condensed material, and demanded $25,000 a year thereafter for the right to continue to reprint. Henry R. Luce had been similarly motivated to up his fee to $35,000, in return for which Wally had unrestricted access to *Time, Life,* and *Fortune*.

Wally agreed to all of Ross's demands, and for a time relations between the two magazines were once again friendly, at least on the surface. Wally and the *New Yorker's* executive editor, Ik Shuman, were in the habit of lunching every Tuesday. Shuman thought that the other *Digest* editors were some of the most boring people he had ever met, but he held Wally in high regard and in 1940 proposed doing a profile of the *Digest's* editor in chief by Wolcott Gibbs. Wally declined. But Shuman persisted, later writing Wally, "[Gibbs] considers you one of the world's foremost editor-publishers; you have done a unique job, and inevitably there is interest in the personality of the man who achieved something unique."

Wally did not take the bait. He knew that Gibbs had previously cut up another leading editor-publisher—*Time*'s Henry R. Luce. That famous profile, written in a malicious perversion of Timese, ridiculed Luce from his first steps as a toddler: "Headman Luce was born in Tengchowfu, China. . . . Under brows too beetling for a baby, young Luce grew up inside the compound, played with his two sisters, lisped first Chinese."

How Wally might have fared in a send-up of *Digest* condensese was perhaps too unnerving to contemplate. But Wally did say over lunch one day that he wanted to meet Ross, whom previously he had dealt with only through intermediaries or by letter. Shuman agreed to bring the *New Yorker* editor along the following week. That earned him no points with the boss, however. Hearing he would actually have to sit down with the editor of the *Reader's Digest,* Ross got into a typical fit of choler.

The *Digest* was the antithesis of everything the *New Yorker* stood for—a homely little magazine where typographical design was almost an afterthought, the art of editing had been reduced to sentence snipping, and the bland, cafeteria-like editorial fare was served up as a feast of ideas. But for the sake of maintaining good public relations, he went to lunch. Ross's first words, after the two men were introduced, were characteristically antagonistic.

"Well," he growled, "is our stuff good enough for you?"

Ross resented that someone was looking over his shoulder, picking up the best of the *New Yorker* material. By implication, what was not reprinted was somehow less worthy. Ironically, though, the princely reprint fees that Ross had secured for the magazine and its writers had become the worst millstone of all. While perhaps emotionally satisfying, Ross's tough-guy act in the long run only bound the *New Yorker* to the *Reader's Digest* more intimately than ever before. The price of reprinting individual articles had gone up commensurately.

Furthermore, the *Digest* was also in the habit of regularly reprinting just the captions of the *New Yorker*'s celebrated cartoons, on the assumption that the drawings themselves were somewhat less than indispensable. Ross must have felt he was being cannibalized, department by department. Yet he could do nothing about it except complain, because contributors such as James Thurber kept pressuring him to maintain the ties with Pleasantville. As the prolific Thurber—cartoonist, article writer, and occasional contributor to "Talk of the Town"— liked to remind him, the *Digest* paid five times more for reprint rights than the *New Yorker* did for first serial.

Then there was the Woollcott business. Wallace had virtually kidnapped him from the pages of the *New Yorker* and installed him in the *Digest,* paying him $24,000 a year or just about what he paid Ross to reprint anything he wanted from fifty-two issues a year. Ross viewed Woollcott as an apostate. Even after he died, the *Digest* claimed him as one of its own by publishing "The World of Alexander Woollcott"—a selection of his writings accompanied by his portrait.

But in July 1943, the year Woollcott died, the *Digest* also reprinted a profile that had originally appeared in *Harper's* called "Harold Ross and *The New Yorker,*" by Dale Kramer and George R. Clark. In general the portrait was flattering and even affectionate. Among other things, it noted that Ross's middle name was Wallace, that he was of Scotch-Irish ancestry, that he craved anonymity, and that he had a "childish enthusiasm" for practical jokes—four attributes shared by DeWitt Wallace himself.

The article did point out a few of Ross's shortcomings, which besides his famous temper tantrums included confining his editorial staff in cubbyholes "the size of horse stalls" and installing a pay phone in the lobby for staffers to use to make personal calls. In its condensation the *Digest* failed to omit—in effect, seconded the motion on—those and other details that Ross found less than complimentary. On January 17, 1944, *New Yorker* publisher Raoul Fleischmann tersely advised Wallace by letter that the renewal agreement between the two magazines was terminated.

Ross's letter to his contributors followed several weeks later. The lapse in time between the two letters suggests that Ross may only have been trying to justify a de facto situation with some of his more recalcitrant writers. Ross's letter also strongly implies that he himself was coming under increasing pressure not only to continue to allow reprints but to begin "preprinting" as well in the pages of his magazine. Considering what some of the most famous writers in America were subjecting him to, Ross's declaration of editorial independence was all the more admirable—perhaps the most courageous act of his career.

The *New Yorker* announcement further declared:

If the *Digest* wants to publish a magazine of original material, it should do so in a direct manner. We believe it should not operate through other publications to keep alive the reprint myth. We don't want to be in the position of receiving for consideration a manuscript that has already been bought and paid for by some one else, for we regard such a situation as unhealthy. We were willing to be digested, but we are not willing to be first supplied, then digested.

Wally did not reply publicly or privately either to Fleischmann's private letter or to Ross's public one. According to *Newsweek*'s account of the affair, the position of the *Digest* editor was that the magazine "wants to cover a broader field than is possible from routine reprints of ideas generated in other offices, and it has the men and the money to do so."

From the *Digest*'s point of view, however, the controversy did have one happy result. No longer permitted to run a condensed version of "The Talk of the Town," the *Digest* created its own copycat version, "Life in These United States," which was ultimately to become its most popular and best-known department.

—

Ross's letter to his writers generated considerable press coverage and led to a series of "exposés" in other publications—most of them liberal and suddenly alarmed that the magazine with the biggest circulation in the world was at odds with their own political views. But the *Digest* had always been conservative to reactionary, and what its liberal critics meant to say was that the magazine they had once tolerated as a sop for the masses had by its sheer massive circulation become a political voice to be reckoned with.

Shortly after the letter was sent out, the *New Republic* aimed its artillery at Pleasantville and fired away. Bruce Bliven wrote to Wallace, advising him that the magazine would no longer cooperate in the planting of articles. Privately, the *New Republic*'s president was contemptuous of Max Eastman and other renegade leftists who were making a fat living by disavowing their former idealism and old friends. But Bliven's professed reason for refusing to accept any more plants—as disingenuous as it was dishonest—was that the board of directors always assumed that the reading public both knew and accepted such an arrangement. "We find that this is evidently not the case," he now charged.

More to the point, Bliven noted—hypocritically choosing to ignore the *Digest*'s long history of conservatism—that over the past year a "difference of opinion" had developed between the two magazines on "social and political matters." Thus the board, he wrote, "now feels that this rift is wide enough to make it inappropriate for us to cooperate by 'preprinting' articles for you."

Bliven left Wallace the option of continuing to reprint articles from the *New Republic,* however, and expressed the hope that the decision would not interfere with their personal relationship. The annual $1,200 fee was small change to Wally. But any likelihood that reprinted *New Republic* material would turn up anytime soon in the pages of the *Digest* ended with a follow-up editorial a few weeks later in which the liberal weekly ticked off the *RD*'s perceived political and literary shortcomings: the ominously right-wing editorial role of Paul Palmer, Senator Butler's criticism the year before of the U.S. Good Neighbor Policy in Latin America, Max Eastman's shrill tirades against Soviet Russia, not to mention the "tasteless" and "depersonalized" nature of much of the writing.

The same issue of the *New Republic* contained a lengthy article by Richard H. Rovere called "American Magazines in Wartime." Rovere suggested that "when the average American want[ed] to spend an evening improving his mind," he looked at photographs in *Life* or read the condensed articles of the *Digest:*

> No mass magazine has ever taken a consistently dark view of life, but none has gone so far as the *Digest* in celebrating good cheer, and the trend has become more and more noticeable amid the encircling gloom of the last few years. . . . It would like nothing better, I am certain, than to hear of an armless worker, who, running his machine with his feet and hoeing his victory garden with his toes, produced more cartridge shells and bought more war bonds than anyone else in his factory.

In fact, Pleasantville *would* have liked nothing better.

In light of its growing international presence, Rovere worried that within ten years the magazine might have a circulation of 200 million for its "Basic English edition" alone. That wildly improbable prediction served as a high-water mark of liberal paranoia that was to stand for two decades. On the other hand, just a few months later, in November 1944, the *RD* was to reap, in a single day, a staggering 138,676 new subscriptions.

A more thoughtful reason for overthrowing the *Digest*'s editorial monopoly was offered by *America,* a moderately conservative Catholic weekly edited by Jesuits. It declared that Wallace's magazine had assumed "a definite editorial policy" masquerading as an impartial presentation of both sides to a question. Such a "duplicitous" policy, according to *America,* gave the unwary reader the impression there were two sides to every moral issue. It also enabled the *Digest,* through its farming-out system, to become "an instrument for promoting specific social and political editorial propaganda" while at the same time monopolizing public opinion.

Cosmopolitan, Good Housekeeping, and the *Nation,* among other publications, also refused to renew their reprint contracts. By far, though, the most vitriolic attack appeared in the pages of the leftist, pro-union New York daily newspaper *PM.* Since the outbreak of the war, the *Digest* had published a dozen articles about labor unions, almost all of them unfavorable.

Reporter Kenneth Stewart spent more than a dozen tabloid pages drawing his three-part Pleasantville portrait, which was based on two long conversations with Wally and a score of other interviews. After recounting what was known of the *Digest*'s history and Wallace's policy of payment for reprints, Stewart turned his attention to the contract system, using the February 1944 issue of the *Digest* as a test case. From among thirty-eight articles, he found that nine were "frank originals" and seven others "disguised originals" or plants. Two well-known journalists had two articles each—Louis Bromfield, two plants that originally appeared in the *Rotarian* and *Kiwanis* magazines; and Eric Sevareid, an original and a plant credited to the *New Republic.*

Another plant, John R. Tunis's article on the University of Chicago's renewed emphasis on the classics, had originally been assigned by the *Saturday Evening Post.* After finishing the piece and having it turned down, Tunis offered it to the *Digest,* which paid him $2,000. But first it arranged for the article to be published in the *Christian Science Monitor.* The harem favorite, however, was the *American Mercury.* On the average, articles placed there appeared in the *Digest* more than once a month.

By the midforties the *Digest*'s only serious competitor was *Magazine Digest,* published in Toronto. It, too, printed originals and drew on publications not sewn up by the *RD.* According to Stewart, it also got second choice on articles passed over by the *Digest.* Yet the real problem was not its virtual monopoly on reprintable articles but "the possible effect of Wallace's magazine on the whole pattern of American magazine publishing."

The loss of prestige, and even more of valuable resources for plants and reprints, was a serious blow to the *Digest,* but not a fatal one. Wally and his top editors had always looked to their readership, and not to their peers, for acceptance and approval. That approval was evident in an industry-leading subscription renewal rate that hovered near 70 percent. If any readers wrote to complain about the inexplicable absence of articles and fillers from the *New Yorker,* the *New Republic,* and a few other magazines, they were inconsequential in number. Outwardly, the only difference in the *Digest*'s editorial makeup was that credit for reprints began to be given a little more frequently to publications like Norman Vincent Peale's *Guideposts* and the *American Legion Magazine,* which the average *Digest* subscriber probably preferred over sophisticated New York weeklies in the first place.

━━━

THOUGH the *Digest* did not publicly respond to the *New Yorker*'s withering criticism when it cut its ties to Pleasantville, Wally immediately invited Norman Cousins out to dinner to discuss what he perceived as a Communist-inspired "smear" of the *Digest.* His suspicions, though ludicrous insofar as they may have extended to Harold Ross, were not entirely unfounded. In Chile, after all, the Communist party had organized a boycott of *Selecciones.* And in Washington some officials in the administration were again pondering antitrust action aimed at the *Digest*'s exclusive reprint contracts with other magazines.

Wally counted on the editor of the prestigious *Saturday Review of Literature,* and occasional *Digest* contributor, to render a nonpartisan assessment of the situation. What he heard was probably more galling than all that went before—not only because it was more pointed criticism than anything the *Digest* had previously been subjected to but also because Cousins did not have any hidden ideological or personal agenda.

Cousins approached his task as ombudsman with remarkable seriousness. After their meeting he spent days dictating and summarizing the points he had tried to make over dinner. He also reviewed the last thirty issues of the *Digest,* looking for political bias. Overall he was inclined to agree that a smear campaign was probably being mounted against the magazine. But, he told Wally, "I think there is such a thing here as cause and effect. I don't think that anyone can engage in smear tactics over a long period of time, as the *Digest* itself has done, without brooking the same type of thing against itself. I honestly believe that at least seventy-five per cent of the attacks are based on specific abuses on the part of the *Reader's Digest* itself—abuses of good taste and fair play."

One thing Cousins criticized the *Digest* for was its unrelenting attacks on the Roosevelt administration, even taking into account, as Wallace had pointed out, "that the good side is not sufficiently interesting to make for reader interest." Speaking from personal experience, Cousins said, he had found no private organization so guilty of the "bureaucratic bungling and red tape" that the magazine routinely condemned in the government as the *Digest* itself.

Cousins dismissed any notion of Communist involvement in the smear campaign, though conceding, "They are doing whatever they can to discredit you and are whooping it up as the bandwagon takes on momentum." It would be, he cautioned, a "dangerous mistake to assume that the trouble begins and ends with Communists. In writing everything off as an extreme Leftist plot, the danger is that the *Digest* may blind itself to the real opposition."

As for allegations that the magazine showed political bias, Cousins went on, that was "a matter of actual documentation." He concluded that the *Digest* had a habit of using its enormous circulation figures "as the automatic and definitive rebuttal to all criticism." The real issue, he concluded, was that the *Digest* gave too many people the impression it was "trying to throw its weight around." But he added that he thought Wallace's own political views were much closer to center than were those conveyed by the magazine itself, which in recent years had begun to evidence "a conspicuous list to the extreme Right."

Three times in the letter, Cousins encouraged Wally to return the magazine to the middle road of fair play so that it could become "not only the greatest magazine in the world, but also one of the greatest institutions in the world."

But Wally had no intention of returning the magazine to the middle of the road, because it had never been there in the first place. From the beginning he had contrived the political balance strongly in favor of his mostly homegrown, midwestern brand of conservatism, and over the years that conservatism had only deepened and hardened.

Yet unlike Luce or Hearst, he had no desire to dictate foreign or domestic policy in the pages of his magazine. Much less did he share any of Luce's craving for a political appointment or public office. Around the time *PM* was titillating its readers with its report on the secret kingdom of Pleasantville, *Time*'s chairman was meeting with Secretary of State Edward Stettinius about the future of the United Nations; later he spoke with newly elected president Harry S Truman about steps necessary for the final defeat of Japan.

By contrast, Wally's conservatism was less programmatic and more ideological—though the ideology was masked in homely anecdote. And by those same lights, he opposed anything that seemed to intrude on the sanctity of an individual's freedoms—in particular the Red tide of communism that seemed to him poised to wash over the democratic West and drown the individual in the state. Though ignored by intellectuals, the *Digest* had an immense constituency in the working class, unlike the leftist press.

While intellectuals and liberals debated Stalinism, Wally was determined in both the U.S. and the international editions to repeat his simple message over and over again—democracy, based on the free-enterprise system, safeguarded individual liberties. Communism, and by extension any form of socialism, was an abrogation of those liberties and therefore intolerable. Wally's brief flirtation with fascism, which was shared by Luce and many others, was nothing more than a phase of his anticommunism.

Thus, in the waning days of 1944, Wally published what amounted to the most widely publicized and spirited anti-Communist tract ever to appear until then in the popular press, not only in the *RD*'s U.S. edition but in most foreign editions as well, with a combined readership greater than that of any other commercial publication in history. A journalistic ancestor of Aleksandr Solzhenitsyn's *One Day in the Life of Ivan Denisovich,* it was also the first to instill in the public imagination a vivid picture of the Soviet Union as a bureaucratic police state whose "inmates" lived a life of unmitigated dreariness, mediocrity, and fear.

Titled "Report on the Russians," the two-part profile—a second installment was published in January 1945—was written by William L. White, son of the prominent Kansas newspaperman William Allen White and a *Digest* roving editor. White had spent several weeks touring the USSR in the company of Eric Johnston, president of the U.S. Chamber of Commerce.

"There is . . . one marked difference," White wrote, "between inmates of the Soviet Union and of the Kansas state penitentiary at

Lansing, where I have often visited an old friend. Food and clothing in both places are about the same, maybe a little better in Lansing. But should my Kansas friend decide that his penitentiary was not well run, and express the hope that there might be a change of wardens, he would run no danger of being shot if he were overheard by a stool pigeon."

Pravda attacked White for having written the "usual standard production of a fascist kitchen with all its smells, calumny, unpardonable ignorance and ill-conceived fury" and for having abused Soviet hospitality. But the *Digest* permitted the Associated Press to quote from the articles at length, with the result that the gist of White's report was given further publicity in most major American newspapers. The leftist press in the United States had no other recourse but to follow *Pravda*'s example and complain.

———

DESPITE the war drums sounded against the *Digest* by its enemies, however, the biggest onslaught was still to come. Harold Ross had a lot more in store for Wallace than just a caustic note to his contributors. Whether the reclusive editor of the *Digest* liked it or not, he was going to be profiled in the pages of the *New Yorker.* The longest profile ever published by Ross was a six-parter devoted to an even greater object of his contempt—gossip columnist Walter Winchell. But the *New Yorker*'s editor was clearly ready to set a new record.

To wield the hatchet, Ross selected from his pool of writers someone almost the opposite of the formidable Wolcott Gibbs—a virtually unknown staff writer named John Bainbridge, who was still in his twenties. Aware of Pleasantville's reputation for secrecy and the obstacles a prominent reporter might face, Ross wanted someone who could take the time to rummage under every rock and run down every lead. Bainbridge spent two years on the series, traveling to Detroit, Washington, Chicago, and St. Paul. The five-part result was a curious concoction—part straightforward reporting, part middling parody, and part bad fiction. Ross's man was able to poke a few holes in Pleasantville's invisible wall of secrecy, but not to breach it.

The first installment, appearing on November 17, 1945, and titled simply "Wally," opened on a sweeping note:

As a publishing phenomenon, *The Reader's Digest* compares favorably with the Holy Bible. Except for the Scriptures, nothing ever published has been circulated more widely than the *Digest*. Like the Bible, the *Digest* is printed in many tongues and distributed on all continents. . . . Last year the American Bible Society and the British and Foreign Bible Society, the two largest organizations devoted to circulating Holy Writ, together distributed nineteen million volumes of Scripture. During the same period, the *Digest* was bought by more than eleven million people every month.

Bainbridge thought Wallace "the most successful editor in history because he knows probably better than any other man alive what people want to read." Unlike Henry Luce or William Randolph Hearst, however, Wallace had no delusions of grandeur. "He has, if anything, delusions of smallness. To Wallace, most things, including himself, seem smaller than they actually are."

The profile described Wally as "tall, sturdy, and slightly stooped." It noted, "Like Luce, Wallace speaks haltingly and tends to give his auditors the uneasy feeling that he never quite says all he might, but he has little of Luce's austerity." Wally was also the kind of man, one writer who knew both men was quoted as saying, whom if you met on the street you wanted to invite for a drink. Meeting Luce, you said hello and continued on your way.

As for Lila, Wally's "small, mentally adroit, stylish, and eager" wife, her days were spent shopping, visiting New York to have her hair done or taking in a matinee. The most interesting bit of news was that in 1939, five years earlier, Wally's income was $286,011 and Lila's $254,-816, or $540,827 combined. "These figures impress Wallace's colleagues in the publishing business not because they are so large but because they are so small." Bainbridge guessed that the magazine netted $10 million annually.

In subsequent installments, though, Bainbridge was reduced to passing along hearsay, much of it inaccurate—that the scholarly Dr. Wallace disapproved of his son's simplistic brand of journalism; or that a high return on their mailing before going off on their honeymoon had given Wally and Lila the strength to go on.

Halfway through the publication of the series, *Time* reported on the profile, observing that the two magazines had been on the outs for years. As for juicy tidbits, the most scandalous thing the newsweekly could come up with was Wally's age. "*Digest* editors," *Time* confided, "who had wondered how old the boss was, were glad to have that settled." It also passed along Bainbridge's finding that the antinicotine publisher was "a backslider who gets away with a couple of packs a day." The series itself started out briskly enough, but by the third installment, sniffed *Time,* "it seemed like a rambling candidate for *The New Yorker*'s own 'Infatuation with Sound of Own Words Department.' "

But two more installments were still to come. Having run out of anything to report, Bainbridge invented a certain Nikolai Popkov, a "Gadding Editor" of the *Digest*'s Russian counterpart *Minimag,* who reports back to his magazine on the assembly-line journalistic techniques used in Pleasantville. Popkov also conducts imaginary interviews with Al Cole, Harry Wilcox, a young female Digester, and editors Ralph Henderson and Paul Palmer. That evening the Russian visitor traipses up to High Winds: "Before I'm through, I learn that this name [High Winds] is on just about everything, including the bath towels and, down in the stables, the horse blankets."

In his summing up, Bainbridge searched for the secret of the *Digest*'s success, for what made an article of "lasting interest" even though many articles were highly forgettable. His conclusion: it had discovered rose-colored glasses "rosier than anything heretofore known to optical science." Bainbridge also cited the magazine's inspirational overtones and the resounding simplism of its beliefs.

As for charges that the *Digest* was anti-Semitic or anti-Negro, Bainbridge reported, echoing an objection made by *America,*

> The *Digest* has pointed out that some of its best articles have been written by Jews. The magazine has also pointed out that it has printed more favorable than unfavorable articles about both Jews and Negroes. These statements are quite true, but this line of reasoning has struck some observers as ingenuous, since it creates the impression that the *Digest* approaches these topics as though they were questions with two sides.

In the wake of the *New Yorker*'s attack, Wally received a few encouraging words. Saying he thought a vote of confidence was in order, *Digest* regular Lowell Thomas sent a telegram: "You and your lady have done one of the most monumental and impressive jobs since the engineers of ancient Egypt built the pyramids." Bennett A. Cerf, president of Random House, penned Wally a note saying he thought, "as a complete outsider," that if the *New Yorker*'s intention was to demolish him and the *Digest,* "they succeeded only in creating precisely the opposite effect": "I think you emerge from the ordeal as one hell of a guy." Cerf, however, was hardly a disinterested "outsider." Random House titles were regularly selected for condensation in the back of the magazine.

▬

JUST as during wartime so in the years immediately following the war, the propaganda value of the *Reader's Digest*—and, increasingly, its foreign editions—was not lost on politicians, generals, businessmen, and opinion makers. Among Wally's correspondents were Winston Churchill, who made a point of asking that *two* complementary copies of the *Digest* be sent to Buckingham Palace, and Senator Robert Taft and General Dwight D. Eisenhower, both of them already running for the 1952 Republican nomination and courting a man who could deliver millions of votes. At the other end of the entertainment spectrum were Cecil B. De Mille and Billy Rose.

Despite the *Digest*'s mild strain of anti-Catholicism and open support of birth control, DeWitt and Lila even sat down to lunch, at a meeting arranged by Fulton Oursler, with Archbishop Francis Spellman of New York. Wallace was also present at an exclusive dinner party of eight, hosted by General Omar Bradley at the Waldorf-Astoria Hotel, where the guests traded interpretations of current world events and were given a "confidential presentation" of ongoing U.S. Army missions.

After the war one writer who joined the *Digest* was George T. Eggleston, former editor of *Scribner's Commentator,* a New York magazine that had vociferously led the fight against U.S. involvement in World War II. After Pearl Harbor he changed his mind and joined the navy, but was dogged for years by charges of disloyalty. Walter Winchell initiated a letter-writing campaign to demand his removal from the service. Douglas MacCollum Stewart, the publisher, was later tried in federal court on charges of having received $15,000 from a Nazi diplomat before the outbreak of war, but was acquitted. Eggleston's hiring, as well as the prominent role Paul Palmer continued to play in assigning original political articles—often for the foreign editions—was further evidence that Wally's conservatism was in no danger of mellowing.

Just the month before Ross's letter went around to contributors, in fact, Wally had helped introduce a new name to the American and international public—that of Ayn Rand, whose extreme philosophy of "individualism" might have amounted to Wally's creed. In "The Only Path to Tomorrow," Rand defined individualism as follows: "Man is an independent entity with an inalienable right to the pursuit of his own happiness in a society where men deal with one another as equals in voluntary, unregulated exchange." Collectivism, on the other hand, was "the subjugation of the individual to a group—whether to a race, class or state does not matter."

Yet it was sometimes difficult to guess exactly what Wally was after, and there were times when weighty philosophical discussions bored him to distraction. One afternoon Dennis McEvoy, visiting from Japan, received an invitation to join Wally and some guests for lunch in the executive dining room. The other guests included a U.S. general and assorted high-ranking government officials, as well as a smattering of editors. The purpose of the lunch, as always, was to discuss ideas about articles.

Normally very quiet to begin with, Wally was more remote and withdrawn than usual. As the most junior guest present by a good many years, McEvoy also kept quiet. Moreover, he felt a little dazzled by the earth-shaking concepts being so freely and authoritatively tossed about by the eminent specialists. Suddenly, Wally cleared his throat. The entire table fell silent. To McEvoy's surprise, Wally was addressing his question to him.

"Dennis, tell me," he said, "is it true that babies in Japan don't cry?"

McEvoy was stunned, and so was everyone else.

"Well, come to think of it," he stammered, "I don't remember hearing them cry very often."

"Why?" Wallace wanted to know.

McEvoy improvised a theory based on the fact that Japanese babies were breast-fed longer than Western babies and perhaps also had a greater sense of security from being strapped on the backs of their mothers or older sisters. But he offered to look into the matter and give Wally a full report.

"I wish you would," Wally said. "I think it might make a good article."

Though talk of geopolitics and global strategies gradually resumed, it limped along. The participants never recovered from the shock. Wally listened attentively as usual and spoke up again after coffee, reminding his guests that there was just time to catch the 1:25 train to New York.

On another occasion Wallace became enthusiastic about world government. His father had not only been an ardent supporter of the League of Nations but even wrote a book, *The Great Betrayal,* attacking those U.S. senators who blocked American membership in the League. In his own way Wally also considered himself an internationalist, though his internationalism largely translated into making every country in the world as much like America as possible.

In those days he and Charlie Ferguson were in the habit of taking a train into New York one day a week to meet or interview writers, since so many were now clamoring to write for the high-paying little magazine. Ferguson himself saw up to thirteen writers a day, running them "through a chute like cattle." Appointments were in hotel lobbies, coffee shops, or, in the afternoon, cocktail lounges. One writer whom Ferguson took a great liking to was a young Hungarian émigré named Emery Reves, who in 1942 had written a forgettable tract called *A Democratic Manifesto.*

Arriving in America, Reves later became a literary agent and helped organize the United World Federalists, an organization devoted to one-world government. To propagate his political views, Reves wrote another book, *The Anatomy of Peace,* which claimed that political thinking was undergoing a revolution comparable to those wrought in physics by Copernicus and Newton.

According to Reves, capitalism and socialism equally led to fascism. National sovereignty was the cause of all wars. The book called for the creation of a world organization to maintain peace and control the use of atomic energy. Reves also believed that peace treaties between nations and leagues of nations were only masks for power politics. Thus he was opposed to the United Nation's support of self-determination of nations and called for a merging of all nations into a world federation.

The Anatomy of Peace was the first book ever to appear in the *Digest* in three successive installments: in December 1945 and the first two months of 1946. To the third installment Wally gave the declarative title "World Government *Is* the First Step." He also directed editors of the international editions to solicit rousing endorsements of the series from prominent citizens and run them in a box accompanying the final installment.

Before the *Digest* excerpted it, *The Anatomy of Peace* had languished on bookstore shelves. After it became a best-seller, thanks to the serialization, Reves married a New York runway model, moved to

Monte Carlo, and was host to an unending stream of international celebrities. Later he bought the foreign rights to Churchill's memoirs and invested shrewdly, for an anticapitalist, in deflated penny stocks, acquiring Coco Chanel's home in the south of France. Eventually, he forgot all about world federalism.

━━━

LIKE his flirtation with fascism in the late thirties and early forties, Wally's enchantment with the idea of a world federation was an anomaly. Far more typical of postwar *Digest* fare were such early Cold War volleys as "I Don't Want My Children to Grow Up in Soviet Russia," by a Russian émigré who, like William White, also described it as a dreary and dehumanizing place.

At the same time, Henry R. Luce's *Time* and *Life* were urging the United States to enter the civil war in China (Luce's second homeland) on the side of Nationalist leader Chiang Kai-shek, and sponsoring public debate on the advisability of launching a preemptive atomic attack on Russia. Perhaps more than any other two people in the private sector, Luce and DeWitt Wallace were instrumental in persuading the American public to look upon the Soviet Union as not only the enemy but something very like the Antichrist.

(The two men knew each other largely because of Time Inc.'s lucrative reprint arrangement with the *RD*. But any hope of a serious friendship was dashed when Luce and his wife Clare Boothe Luce, a convert to Rome, invited the Wallaces to their Manhattan penthouse for dinner. Repeatedly throughout the evening, Lila—never one to show deference to another woman—pointedly made denigrating remarks about the Catholic church.)

In their desire to fan the flames of anti-Soviet sentiment, both Wallace and Luce frequently sought the services of John Foster Dulles, at the time still an adviser to the secretary of state. A primary architect of the Cold War, Dulles was yet another Presbyterian PK who—like Wally and Luce—had an abiding faith in America's moral transcendence and its responsibility to make the world safe from communism at all cost. "There is a natural or moral law not made by man which . . . has been trampled on by the Soviet rulers, and for that violation they can and should be made to pay . . . ," Dulles once wrote. Alluding to those who advocated the (by implication immoral) policy of containment, he tut-tutted in the pages of the *Digest,* "Some, while perceiving the intolerant and ruthless aspects of Soviet policy, cling to the hope that these aspects are only local or temporary."

Another Cold War favorite of both Luce and Wallace was former ambassador to the Soviet Union William Bullitt, who in 1947 warned in the *Digest,* "Throughout the entire earth, Stalin's forces are on the offense and the democracies are in retreat." William Henry Chamberlain, in an article "reprinted" from the *New Leader,* attributed international tensions to the "fatalistic" belief of Russian's rulers in inevitable combat between East and West.

As for unrest elsewhere in the world, the *Digest* asked in its April 1948 issue, "Must There Be War in the Middle East?" The answer was that sympathy was not necessarily in order for homeless Jews: "Let us remember that the sense of 'homelessness' among many Jews is the emotional root of the more extreme manifestations of Zionism."

Wally also published and was a friend of notorious anti-Semite Upton Close, whom he regularly showered with bonuses, as well as of Joseph P. Kamp and Merwin K. Hart. According to the Anti-Defamation League, Hart was a "professional anti-Semite" who disputed the fact that Hitler killed millions of Jews. It was Hart's National Economic Council that sponsored a ten-dollar-a-plate dinner attended by prominent American anti-Semites at the Waldorf-Astoria on October 26, 1949. Jew-baiters in attendance included Allen Zoll, Conde McGinley, and Kamp. Wally was invited. Though unable and probably unwilling to attend, he sent his apologies and several members of his editorial staff to sit in on proceedings.

As for blacks, when it did not make them the butt of dialect humor, the *Digest* favored de facto segregation and separate but equal rights for them. "A Negro Warns the Negro Press" in January 1944 criticized Negro publications and their "inflammatory attempts to indicate that the Negro gets unfair treatment." In June 1947 Wally published " 'Bones' Hooks and His Modern Pioneers," which praised the efforts of a black former rodeo star to establish all-Negro communities.

And, as usual, the *Digest* had it in for the Democratic administration. In the wake of his decision to drop the atomic bomb on Japan, President Truman received mostly favorable treatment in the pages of the *RD* during his first year in office. But after the 1948 election the *Digest* published nonstop attacks on his farm program, health plan, relations with business, alleged personal extravagance, socialist tendencies, and corruption—eight articles alone on the last topic. The concluding entry was Henry J. Taylor's "Was Corruption as Bad under Harding?" Taylor's answer was no.

The *Digest* was also becoming more conservative about sex. In 1948, when Dr. Alfred Kinsey published the most important book ever written about sexuality, *Sexual Behavior in the Human Male,* there was widespread disbelief that ordinary Americans had so much or so many different kinds of sex. The Indiana University zoology professor had shown, among other things, that many allegedly deviant sex acts were quite common among so-called normal men and women and that homosexual behavior was also far more prevalent than previously believed. The *Digest* was among those who saw Kinsey's work as a threat to monogamy and assigned ex-minister, Eisenhower speech writer, and grand inquisitor of Protestant orthodoxy Stanley High to do a hatchet job.

The article, however, was never published—a victim of High's increasingly chronic depression, alcoholism, and own sexual turmoil. Fulton Oursler also wrote an attack on Kinsey that was so vitriolic that Wally refused to publish it. Oursler called for the book's suppression. Instead, the *Digest* published a "symposium" titled "Must We Change Our Sex Standards?" The anonymous author of the lead opinion— most likely either High or Oursler—declared America all but morally bankrupt, a nation where science "does not recognize any expression of sex as 'abnormal'; except 'maniacal' deeds, pretty much anything is all right." Though Kinsey was not cited by name, others taking part in "A symposium on one of the most vital questions of our times" (the article's overline) included Salvation Army national commander Ernest I. Pugmire ("The harm of such misleading reports is that they become weapons of temptation"), FBI director J. Edgar Hoover ("Man's sense of decency declares what is normal and what is not"), novelist John Erskine, and Boys Town director Father E. J. Flanagan. When the Rockefeller Institute later withdrew its support of Kinsey's research, he blamed not just the *RD* but Oursler personally for working behind the scenes to sabotage his project.

Later High recovered sufficiently to write a textbook example of a Red-baiting Cold War smear—"Methodism's Pink Fringe," which appeared in February 1950. High alleged that a small leftist Methodist group called the Methodist Federation for Social Action had as its purpose "to discredit America at home and abroad, to condemn the American economic system as unchristian, to promote conclusions which give aid and comfort to the Communists." The clear implication was that the MFSA was the official social arm of the Methodist church.

But the MFSA enjoyed no official recognition from the Methodist church and had a membership of only six thousand in a denomination that counted nine million. The *Digest* refused to give the Methodist Council of Bishops an opportunity to defend itself. The council was later obliged to print a pamphlet, "The Reply the *Reader's Digest* Refused to Publish," disavowing the MFSA and reaffirming its commitment to the principles of democracy.

IN THE waning days of 1951, all the adverse publicity generated by the *New Yorker* profile and the assorted attacks on the *Digest* by the *New Republic, PM,* and other publications and organizations came full circle when DeWitt and Lila Wallace made the cover of *Time.* The occasion was the magazine's thirtieth anniversary, still a few months off.

In its tribute, *Time* praised the *Reader's Digest* as "one of the greatest success stories in the history of journalism," noting that the domestic edition of 9,500,000 alone grossed between $25 and $30 million. International editions accounted for another 6,000,000 copies. Wallace was quoted on the secret of his success: "I simply hunt for things that interest me, and if they do, I print them." Wally himself was magnanimously acclaimed "the most successful editor in history"—a remarkable accolade coming from no less an editorial genius than *Time*'s own founder, Henry R. Luce.

Digest contributor Louis Bromfield thought, according to *Time,* that the magazine's main appeal was to "intellectual mediocrity," adding, "Wallace's own 'strictly average' mind 'completely reflects the mentality of his readers,' who like the *Digest* because 'it requires no thought or perception.' " That perceptive but off-the-cuff comment cost Bromfield his status as Wallace's favorite writer, and his familiar byline soon disappeared from the magazine's pages.

"The formula has changed somewhat over the years," *Time* noted, "but it is still essentially the one Wallace hit on in 1920; simplified, condensed articles, most of them striking a note of hope, the whole interspersed with pithy saws or chuckly items. It tries to minimize the negative and accentuate the positive. The *Digest* has always been careful not to burden its readers with somber or brain-taxing articles."

Time also declared that DeWitt Wallace, by now sixty-two, was a "worrier, torn by inner doubts and subject to spells of melancholy"; Lila was "self-possessed and an optimist to the bone." And, the magazine added, the two of them still liked to dance occasionally for fifteen minutes in their rumpus room after dinner. Speaking of the Wallace's great wealth, *Time* approvingly quoted one of DeWitt's oft-repeated sayings: "The dead carry with them to the grave in their clutched hands only that which they have given away." It further noted that the couple were "gradually turning over their stock to a charitable foundation which may run the *Digest.*"

The reference was to the Reader's Digest Foundation, though Wally and Lila probably never had any intention of giving the company to the RDF. Most *Digest* insiders, including Al Cole, assumed that the heirs of the kingdom were Lila's favorite niece, Judy, and her husband, Fred Thompson, Cole's assistant. Lila still doted as ever on Judy, while Fred—tall, handsome, soft-spoken—had earned the respect of nearly everyone for his publishing acumen and personal manner.

Time also tried to render a journalistic judgment on the editor of the world's most successful magazine:

> Wallace thinks of himself as "left of center"; he says most people are middle-of-the-roaders. But most middle-roaders would consider him well right of center. Not a deep or profound thinker, Wallace sometimes originates and runs glib, superficial articles on U.S. and world problems which other top editors would wastebasket. . . . In the main, his political outlook seems to be colored by a nostalgic yearning for the less complicated days of his boyhood, when every man could become his own master without help or hindrance from the Government.

In the long run, *Time* accurately predicted,

> Wallace's greatest contribution to the nation may be found in the cumulative effect of his overseas editions. Invariably, his readership surveys show that articles which U.S. readers like rate equally high with readers everywhere. The *Digest*'s articles—depicting the innate decency, kindness and simple virtues of ordinary Americans, the triumphs of a George Carver or a Helen Keller—have probably done more than all the Government propagandists combined to allay the fears, prejudices and misconceptions of the U.S. in other lands.

9

Hyacinths for
Thy Soul

By the early 1950s many of the *Digest*'s first-generation editors were gone—the chronically tardy, lederhosen-loving Jerry Ellison, who had always been a misfit; Harold Lynch, whose philandering on office time, like that of Arthur Griffiths, Wally could finally no longer tolerate; as well as others like Henry Morton Robinson who had gone off to pursue a literary career. Some, like Lou Dillon, languished in editorial backwaters—which would also have been the fate of Charlie Ferguson had not Wally taken a genuine liking to him and to his wife. Ralph Henderson, who had spent 1944–45 in Burma and India as a "war correspondent," continued as book editor, still aided by Maurice T. Ragsdale. Others of the older generation who were still around included Paul de Kruif and Paul Palmer, whose many resignation attempts continued to meet with failure.

For many members of the *Digest* family, and especially for Lila, the fifties were to be a dark decade. But those personal tragedies contrasted sharply with the company's remarkable rejuvenation on the corporate level—which was all the more extraordinary because it followed so quickly on the heels of the *Digest*'s wartime and immediate postwar expansion, the most spectacular of any magazine's in history, before or after. By the midfifties the winds of change blowing across the fair and pleasant kingdom of Pleasantville reached hurricane force. It was a tempest of the *Digest*'s own making and a testament to the company's amazing ability to reinvent itself over and over again. In the course of the fifties, the *Reader's Digest* was not only to revolutionize the worlds of direct mail and book publishing but also to rewrite the rules for magazine advertising.

That revolution began innocuously enough in 1948 when a young copywriter named Walter Weintz was interviewed by Fred Thompson, assistant general manager, for a position in the *Digest*'s mail-order department. Weintz's previous clients included the Book-of-the-Month Club, Charles Atlas body-building equipment, and Black & Decker tools. He heard nothing for the next few weeks, then got a telegram from Frank Herbert, circulation manager, asking him to return to Pleasantville for another interview.

While Weintz was being interviewed a second time, an older man sometimes wandered in from an adjoining office to snap a question like "How much do you drink?," all the while jiggling coins in his pocket. After getting his answer, he wandered out again. Herbert just grinned and kept talking. Before long the man wandered in again and snapped another question: "What books do you read?" After getting his answer, he wandered out as before.

Whatever answers Weintz gave, they were good enough to satisfy Al Cole. Weintz was hired and went to work for Herbert and Les Dawson, circulation promotion manager. The business side of *Digest* headquarters was dominated by Cole's butternut-paneled corner office, which connected to Herbert's. Beyond that was the office of Fred Thompson, assistant to both Cole and Herbert, where Weintz was given a corner desk.

The wartime boom for the *Reader's Digest* was over. A host of factors—an unwieldy direct-mail operation, population shifts into areas where newsstand sales were still underdeveloped, increased competition from other magazines—had caused overall circulation to drop from 6 to 4.5 million, with newsstand sales plunging from 2 million to 800,000. Wally still opposed advertising for the U.S. edition, and the *RD* was spending an exorbitant amount of money trying to increase its circulation by means of seven different mailing lists, which contained literally millions of duplications. The *Digest* was not yet in any danger of drowning in red ink, like so many once successful magazines before it. But, undeniably, Cole was faced with the prospect of stagnation as the company approached the end of its first quarter century. To reverse the magazine's declining fortunes and regain the momentum of the war years, he somehow had to devise a two-pronged strategy to increase both subscriptions and newsstand sales. There was no other source of income. Cole's genius was to hire men—with some exceptions—of unusual caliber. In Walter Weintz he found someone who developed into one of the most brilliant direct-mail strategists in the country.

Until that time, despite its problems with direct mail, the *Digest* was still getting a 4 percent response on its promotions. This was better than the industry average at the time, only 0.5 percent. And its 4.5 million circulation was still highly respectable. Weintz gathered every promotion letter the *Digest* had ever sent out to do a test—to send out different versions of a direct-mail offer to see which pulled best. He even updated the original letter that Wally wrote to start the *Reader's Digest.* Weintz thought it was a very good mail-order letter and used it as a control. His results showed that the older a letter was, including Wally's, the less well it pulled. The test proved conclusively that a change was in order and that something altogether different had to be developed. But what?

The answer could be found only through more tests. Testing, as Weintz learned, was the basic element of *Digest* business strategy and he was given carte blanche. Cole insisted he adhere to strict budgets on everything else, but never once even proposed a budget for testing. The strategy was dramatically successful. In one year alone Weintz ran four hundred different mail-order tests and soon found ways to nudge the returns from a flat 4 percent to a much more impressive 6 percent, then to an astounding 9 percent, and finally to an almost unbelievable 11 percent. That was still not good enough to satisfy Cole. One day he wandered into Fred Thompson's office and said to his young protégé, "Well, now, the profits on the *Digest* have steadily gone up, and we're the only magazine in existence that's dependent on circulation alone for its income. And we're in an awful squeeze. The squeeze has gotten worse and worse, and we're not making a whole lot of money. What can we do to make money for the *Reader's Digest?*"

The obvious answer was advertising. But Wally's opposition continued. Cole decided to try the backdoor. As early as 1940, the year after he went to work for the *Digest,* he had tried to persuade Wally to change his mind. Even then Cole saw the decision as one of simple economics—the company either found other sources of income or began losing a million dollars a year. At first, the "loss" was merely unrealized income. Only as profits declined and costs soared did a situation arise that Wally could no longer ignore.

The backdoor that Cole intended to use was an English-language Canadian edition headquartered in Toronto. Circulation had grown in

Canada to the point where an edition separate from the U.S. edition was now warranted. As a foreign edition, moreover, it could accept advertising without encountering resistance from Wally. So intent was Cole on bringing advertising into the U.S. *Digest* that he deputized Fred Thompson himself to be general manager of the new Canadian edition. Cole foresaw Thompson not only succeeding him in the long run as business manager but also in the short run becoming the U.S. edition's first advertising manager if and when that time came. For both Thompson and the *Digest,* the prospect of a stint in Canada seemed doubly beneficial.

In the meantime there was still a pressing need to raise cash. Some other revenue source had to be found. Recently, the company had published a volume called *14 Reader's Digest Books,* a collection of supplements from the back of the magazine which sold 200,000 copies at a dollar apiece and made a $35,000 profit. As usual, Wally had split the profit among employees as a bonus. Now he wanted to do another book, sell another 200,000 copies, and make another $35,000 to give away. Cole palmed the project off on Fred Thompson. Busy getting ready to move to Canada, Thompson handed it over to Weintz, asking him to do a test first to see whether there was a market for another book from the *Reader's Digest.*

Weintz did a test and discovered that instead of selling for $1.00, the book could be sold for $1.69. And that instead of selling 200,000, the *Digest* could sell a million copies. And that instead of making a profit of $35,000, it could make a profit of $1 million. What he also learned in the process—a discovery equivalent to finding oil right under headquarters—was that the *Reader's Digest* subscriber list was far more lucrative than previously imagined. With 3.5 million names it now ranked third only behind two venerable mail-order merchandise houses—Sears, Roebuck and Montgomery Ward—yet had never been used to sell merchandise except incidentally.

According to reader surveys, the *Digest's* two most popular editorial features were, respectively, the book condensations in the back of the magazine and the humor sections. The obvious choice for the next book, since the book excerpts had just been published, was a volume entitled *Fun Fare.* But the editors refused to be identified with the project, because it was originating with the business department and not being cosponsored, as usual, by a reputable trade book publisher. As a result, Weintz was also given the job of getting permissions from each contributor to use their material in the book. The *Digest* had decided to pay $10 for each item chosen, assuming the author could be found. But when Weintz's secretary called James Thurber and told him the magazine wanted to give him $10 to reprint one of his stories about dogs, he got very nasty.

"I never talked to such a man," the secretary told Weintz. "You should have heard the language he used! And I offered him $10 for his piece on dogs."

The editors straightened the matter out with the notoriously tight-fisted Thurber (who later called to complain to Wally personally), the book was published, and it sold, as predicted, one million copies and made a million dollars—a sum that did not get divvied up as a bonus. Along the way, Weintz also introduced another direct-mail innovation—the "pictorial envelope." In place of the usual blank wrapper, the solicitation for the book arrived in six million homes adorned with a festive picture of the book jacket showing a clown's mask on the outside of the envelope.

But Weintz also thought that one-shot books were largely a waste of time and that sooner or later the company was going to run out of things it could reprint from the magazine. He wrote a memo to Cole suggesting the company start a book club. Cole replied that the idea had been kicked around before, but agreed to talk to Ralph Henderson about it once again. Henderson had been banging on his door lately anyway.

———

As far back as the second issue, Wally had excerpted a book in the *Digest*—Arnold Bennett's *How to Live on 24 Hours a Day,* and ever since then book excerpts had been a regular staple of the magazine. But book editor Henderson was bothered by two things. In the first place, he had to pass up almost all fiction, because Wally insisted that the magazine was selling facts, knowledge, tools for improving oneself. Space requirements made it necessary to pass up many desirable non-fiction books as well. Wally's proposal back in the thirties for a fiction supplement was never seriously pursued.

But in 1939 a man named Robert de Graff, who had an idea not too dissimilar from Wally's, launched his own version of a pocket-sized series of publications called Pocket Books—ten books selling in soft-cover for twenty-five cents each. The 10,000 first printings of such titles as James Hilton's 1935 classic *Lost Horizon,* Agatha Christie's *The Murder of Roger Ackroyd,* and *Five Great Tragedies by Shakespeare* quickly sold out. Henderson had proof that there was a market for brief, inexpensive fiction, though his idea was still to offer multiple condensed works of longer fiction in a paperback series.

There was also a precedent for offering abbreviated books to the public. In the years before World War II, a book club called Omnibook provided cut versions of full-length works—excerpts, not condensations—using the slogan "In the words of the author." Unlike the *Digest,* it did not construct "bridge work" between passages to facilitate abridgments. But the concept did not prove successful.

In the early forties Henderson again raised the idea that the *Digest* start up a separate magazine comprising at least two book condensations and selling for the same price as the *Digest.* In principle the concept was approved. But the war—with its paper and manpower shortages, and the *Digest's* decision to place all of its resources behind an expansion into foreign markets—put a temporary end to those discussions, and the idea lay more or less dormant until the summer of 1949, when Henderson and Cole again examined the possibility of somehow condensing and packaging fiction.

Books seemed to be the only way out of the company's predicament—its salvation, in fact. Not surprisingly, when Henderson once again broached his plan for packaging fiction one way or another, he received Cole's undivided attention.

After hearing Henderson out, however, Cole decided he was opposed to publishing another magazine. Instead, he preferred a volume in hard covers "to look and feel like a book" and selling at a necessarily higher price. Weintz's experiment had proved that such a product would sell. Also there was some skepticism on the part of others involved in the discussions as to whether each volume of condensed literature should contain only fiction. *Digest* readers, after all, enjoyed the magazine not only for its entertainment value but also for its helpful mixture of factual advice and information. Too much nonfiction, on the other hand, would put a book club in direct competition with the magazine.

An editorial compromise called for the club to publish four 500-page volumes a year (since the potential audience consisted of magazine readers, but not proven book buyers), each containing three different books—a current best-selling novel; a prominent work of nonfiction; and a *"Digest* discovery," either a new book or a classic. None of the selections was to have appeared previously in the magazine. The three-in-one volumes were to sell for $1.89 by mail only. Eventually, Frank Herbert, who had originally proposed issuing the books on a quarterly basis, suggested publishing four condensations per volume, which raised the number of pages to an average of 575. Herbert was later responsible for inventing a nonreturnable box to return unwanted books in, though that unpopular bit of deception was soon abandoned.

And though Henderson has traditionally been credited as being the originator and guiding genius of what eventually became Reader's Digest Condensed Books, it was Walter Weintz who got the ball rolling again. He had demonstrated that the *Digest* live list was receptive to books and could make the kind of money Al Cole intimated was necessary for the company's long-term survival.

But before the book club was given a final go-ahead, Weintz was asked to do another test. Cole and the others wanted to make sure that selling four books a year by mail was a sound idea. Weintz's test presented potential subscribers with the following proposition: "The *Digest* is going to issue books. Would you like to buy one book or would you like to subscribe to four books?" Results showed that 80 percent of those who replied—or 1.5 percent out of a so-so 1.87 percent total return—wanted to buy four volumes a year, not one.

At the time, books were sold by direct mail in three different ways. Readers who ordered full sets of books such as encyclopedias were usually given the first volume free as an inducement to continue ordering the series. Though the number of volumes in a set could run up to twenty-four or more, it was a limited offering, and subscribers were able to purchase the set one month at a time.

The Book-of-the-Month Club, on the other hand, had pioneered the "negative option." Members who joined in return for a free premium agreed to buy at least four selections a year (BOMC counted on an average of five). But they also had the option of returning a card, which accompanied the advance notice of every club selection, declining to make any purchase that month.

A third method, known in direct-mail parlance as the "continuity program," was employed by such publishers as Walter Black's Classics Club, a well-known imprint of the day (and another earlier client of Weintz's). Unlike an encyclopedia, the Classics Club was an open-ended series that contained similar or related titles—in this instance, great works of world literature. Subscribers automatically received one volume a month until they canceled.

Henderson wanted Reader's Digest Condensed Books to be a cross between a continuity program and a book club, and from a direct-mail point of view that was its great strength—an open-ended series of books, each like the last, that formed an attractive set. Weintz devised an offer that gave subscribers the first book free, with the proviso that they agreed to purchase the remaining three volumes in the coming year. There was to be no negative option, yet there was a commitment to purchase.

Though returns on that test shot up to 4 percent, the offer of a free book soon stopped pulling. Weintz then asked himself, "What would be better than free? Maybe people are suspicious of 'free.' "

So he tested "The first book free" and "The first book $1" and also "The first book for 50 cents." Also for 25 cents, 10 cents, 5 cents, 1 cent. He discovered that "Yours for 50 cents" pulled much better than "Yours for $1," and "Yours for 25 cents" better than "Yours for 50 cents," and "Yours for 10 cents" much better than "Yours for 25 cents" but that "Yours for 5 cents" did not pull as well as "Yours for 10 cents" and that "Yours for 1 cent" did not pull as well as "Yours for 5 cents." The reason, Weintz concluded, was that 10 cents was the price people put on their conscience. A dollar was too much, and a nickel so little that they still felt obligated. But a dime was the price of a free conscience. "Yours for 10 cents" eventually drew a total of 18 percent on the original and follow-up mailings.

Gratifying as the high returns were, however, they were also alarming, because they seemed too good to be true. Complicating matters was the lack of any efficient way to keep track of test results. Every day Weintz had to go down to the fulfillment department and copy the figures onto a sheet of paper. Like everyone else, he worried that subscribers might sign up for the first book and then drop out. Tracking returns became such a nightmare that Cole finally agreed to twice-weekly reports on Monday and Friday.

On the next Monday, Weintz took his results down and showed them to Cole and he was satisfied. But the following day he summoned Weintz to his office again and asked to see the test results on the proposed book club.

"Don't you remember, Al," Weintz replied, "we're only getting those results twice a week now. The next report due is on Friday."

"Okay, fine," Cole replied. "Bring me Friday's report today."

After the testing period was concluded, and both Cole and Henderson had conclusive proof that it was time to launch a book club, they went to see Wally. For seven years, ever since the idea had been approved in principle, Wally had subtly mounted a countercampaign of attrition and neglect. Possibly because the idea was not originally his, but more likely because he was interested only in the magazine itself, Wally had resisted Henderson's idea to condense novels and publish them separately. Now, as Henderson and Cole made their pitch, he listened attentively. The two men excitedly explained how the new book club would publish four volumes a year, selling a million copies of each, generating a net profit of $4 million annually. When they were finished, Wally coolly replied that they had overlooked certain points and suggested they make a full-scale presentation in two weeks.

On the appointed day and hour, Henderson and Cole again showed up at Wally's office, this time armed with an easel and charts. But as soon as they began to set up their apparatus, Wally waved his hand for them not to bother.

"You two go have lunch somewhere and get to work on your program," he said. "I won't stand in your way any longer. I've been a damn fool."

The two men politely suggested he had merely been cautious, but left the room feeling vaguely disappointed at not being able to marshal all their facts and figures. Worse, they also still faced the possibility that the figures were somehow wrong and the book club might prove to be a dismal failure.

After getting the go-ahead, Henderson wasted no time. Resigning as *RD* book editor, he recruited two staff members as his assistants—Jack Beaudouin and Agnes Allen. Ragsdale became the magazine's new book editor. In February 1950 the *Digest* announced a new book service to be called Reader's Digest Condensed Books. A few months later the first volume appeared and was sent to 183,000 charter subscribers.

Not surprisingly, the initial selections made by Henderson and his staff were drawn from two best-sellers of the day, Elmer Rice's *The Show Must Go On* and Morton Thompson's *The Cry and the Covenant,* as well as a "classic" example of modern Americana—*The Autobiography of*

Will Rogers. But the *"Digest* discovery" marked something of an editorial departure from the magazine—Alan Paton's passionate plea for racial tolerance and cooperation in South Africa, *Cry, the Beloved Country.* Henderson was among the more moderate editors at Pleasantville, and among those who had little use for right-winger Paul Palmer, who by now had returned to New York from Paris.

Palmer not only continued to monitor the political content of the foreign editions of the magazine but also acted as unofficial co–executive editor with Ken Payne to ensure that the U.S. edition's articles on politics hewed to a sufficiently conservative line. From the very beginning a rivalry arose between the magazine and the book division that reflected not only intramural competitiveness but also a clash of personalities and divergent editorial philosophies. The *Digest*'s conservative orthodoxy was never in any danger of being compromised, and like the magazine itself the book club's nonfiction was designed to publicize famous Americans and promote the American way of life.

But under Henderson the book club remained steadfastly aloof from partisan politics. Wally not only refrained from interfering in the club's editorial operations but forbade Palmer or anyone else on the magazine staff to do so as well.

On average, however, three-fourths of each volume was fiction, so there was little room for much ideological conflict to begin with. Bestsellers pared down to an hour or two's worth of reading remained standard fare. Reader's Digest Condensed Books was the logical and seemingly inevitable extension of Wally's idea to condense magazine articles, and the wonder was that he had not improved on his own memo back in the thirties for condensing only fiction by rounding the formula out with nonfiction as Henderson and his associates eventually did themselves.

But Wally was enthralled by fact—by the doughnut and not by the hole. He believed that information of one kind or another could help a person improve his life, get more fun out of life, make a difference in the lives of others. Fiction held no more interest for him than grand opera, and more than once he liked to boast—though perhaps a little defensively—that he had never read any of the book club's main selections: Henry Morton Robinson's *The Cardinal,* Herman Wouk's *The Caine Mutiny,* Daphne du Maurier's *My Cousin Rachel,* Edna Ferber's *Giant,* Kathryn Hulme's *The Nun's Story,* Edwin O'Connor's *The Last Hurrah,* John Steinbeck's *East of Eden,* and an endless number of similar middlebrow best-sellers. J. P. Marquand, Alec Waugh, and MacKin-lay Kantor were among the other authors who proved to be perennial favorites. The one writer who steadfastly refused to have any of his works appear in condensed form was the language's master of simple, unadorned prose—Ernest Hemingway.

Though Wally showed little interest in the day-to-day operations of the book club, from the start there was a rule that the magazine always had first rights to nonfiction. That also led to a variety of conflicts. As the book club's membership grew, so did the royalties it paid out to publishers and authors. The royalty was calculated according to a formula whereby the main selection garnered the lion's share—a minimum of 25 percent—while the other titles divided the remainder. Within a very short time almost any book selected by Reader's Digest Condensed Books stood to gain more money than if it was "merely" picked up as an excerpt by the magazine, whose fee was considerably less than the average royalty. Publishers and agents eager to make top dollar with their nonfiction properties sometimes found to their chagrin that a book had been chosen not by the book club, where it might earn $50,000 or more, but by the *Digest,* which paid only a fraction of that amount.

Another source of friction was caused by sheer logistics. Since the book-excerpt department had first choice of nonfiction, it also became by that very fact an editorial bottleneck. Normally, a book chosen by the magazine was considered ineligible for the book club. Even on those very rare occasions when the *Digest* decided to excerpt a work of fiction—for example, Edward Streeter's *Father of the Bride*—the magazine also took precedence. A happy exception was Thor Heyerdahl's rousing tale of his voyage across the Pacific aboard a balsa raft. After *Kon-Tiki* appeared in the *Digest,* the excerpt was expanded into a book condensation. For the most part, though, Ragsdale and his staff now found themselves being lobbied not only by publishers and agents but by their book-club colleagues as well.

Reader's Digest Condensed Books proved to be so successful that by the end of its first year it counted 512,000 members and was selling an average of 460,000 copies per quarterly volume—far more than the Book-of-the-Month Club, founded in 1925, and the Literary Guild, which had started up the following year. Some authors were able to win double jackpots by having their book condensed first for *Digest* readers and later served up whole for Literary Guild or Book-of-the-Month Club readers who wanted to devour every last word.

Janet Davis, mother of DeWitt Wallace, here pictured with her three oldest children Benjamin, Helen, and Robert, complained of being "an old, worn-out woman" at the age of thirty. She exhibited symptoms of acute schizophrenia, which her husband attributed to "diabetic tendencies." (Macalester College)

Before the altar of Presbyterian higher learning, Dr. James T. Wallace, DeWitt's father, sacrificed his marriage and the well-being of his family. (Macalester College)

During his sophomore year at Macalester College, Wally (back row, second from left) played second base. Though the team won its conference championship, Wally was asked to leave Macalester because of a prank and spent the summer on the semipro circuit in Oregon and the Dakotas, cheerfully boasting to his father that he was "fielding practically errorless ball." (Macalester College)

Dr. James Wallace and his second wife, Mrs. Miriam Wallace (Janet's sister), in a photograph taken in 1928 or 1929. Known affectionately as "Aunt Maud," Miriam Wallace was Wally's favorite aunt. (Macalester College)

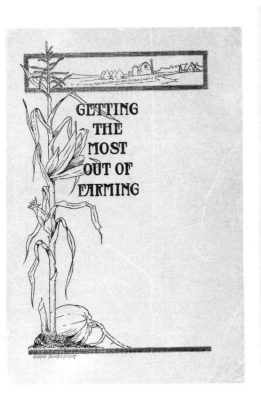

GETTING
THE
MOST
OUT OF
FARMING

THE READER'S DIGEST

THIRTY-ONE ARTICLES EACH MONTH
FROM LEADING MAGAZINES ~ EACH
ARTICLE OF ENDURING VALUE AND
INTEREST, IN CONDENSED AND
COMPACT FORM

FEBRUARY 1922

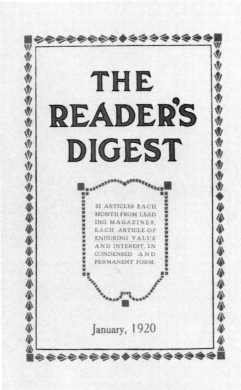

THE READER'S DIGEST

31 ARTICLES EACH
MONTH FROM LEAD
ING MAGAZINES,
EACH ARTICLE OF
ENDURING VALUE
AND INTEREST, IN
CONDENSED AND
PERMANENT FORM.

January, 1920

While peddling *Getting the Most Out of Farming* (top left) out west, DeWitt Wallace got an even better idea. After the war, he produced a prototype (left), which he then offered to any publisher who would make him editor. The first issue of the *Reader's Digest* (right), with Wallace as both publisher and editor, appeared in February 1922.

By 1936 the *Digest* had become one of the most successful magazines in history. Yet its editorial offices continued to be on the top floor of the Mount Pleasant Bank & Trust Co. (building on the left) in the little town of Pleasantville (population 4540). (Wendell MacRae for *Fortune*)

In the office on the left, Ken Payne (in dark shirt) discusses a book excerpt with book editor Ralph Henderson, while next door Wally confers with (from left to right) Charlie Ferguson, Harold Lynch, and Maurice Ragsdale. At the time, the *Digest* had not yet moved to its plush new quarters in Chappaqua. (Wendell MacRae for *Fortune*)

For the benefit of readers of *Fortune,* Lila posed as a conscientious editor, armed with such indispensable tools of the trade as a quill pen. The original caption noted that the *Digest's* cofounder also "edits copy at home, reads manuscripts in bed, gardens, rides horseback." (Wendell MacRae for *Fortune*)

So successful was the *Digest*'s mix of inspiration, earthy humor, and government-bashing that, by 1936, the circulation department was processing 10,000 new subscriptions a day. (Wendell MacRae for *Fortune*)

After the completion of High Winds, Wally often spent months at a time in his tower, which was reached by a narrow, twisting staircase and into which no one was ever admitted. (Roy Stevens, *Time*)

Most of the charter roving editors were uncommonly colorful or eccentric characters. Joseph Patrick McEvoy, whose beat was entertainment, was a thrice-married newspaper columnist who also wrote plays, greeting-card verse, and labels for soup cans. (UPI/Bettmann)

Despite his ardent Roman Catholicism, Fulton Oursler, Sr., was Wally's favorite writer. Oursler's wife Grace served as editor of Norman Vincent Peale's *Guideposts,* a favorite source of "preprinted" articles. Their son "Tony" Fulton, Jr., shown with his sister April in 1949, later rose to become the *Digest*'s deputy editor in chief. (Wide World)

The RDA's business manager Al Cole (left) threatened to resign after Barclay Acheson (right), head of the international division and Lila's brother, complained that Cole was encroaching on his turf. But both were united by a single passion—to put a copy of the *Reader's Digest* in every household around the world. They are shown here in 1951. (Roy Stevens/*Time*)

The *Digest*'s ginger man, Kenneth Wilson, who served as liaison between New York publishers and the home office. (Gordon Hard)

Henderson and the other editors were soon combing up to two thousand books a year, usually reading them first in galley proofs, though surefire best-sellers were often bought in manuscript well before publication. Potential candidates were assigned to readers, both staffers and free-lancers, who submitted brief reports giving a synopsis of the book and noting potential problems that might be encountered in the condensation process, such as significant literary craftsmanship, unusual brevity or great length, complicated plot line, or excessive number of characters. After a book was selected, it was assigned to an editor for a rough cut, though some books were not cut or hardly cut at all. Two works whose relatively short length and literary merit exempted them from an all but nominal condensation were Paton's *Cry, the Beloved Country* and John Hersey's *A Single Pebble,* a book for young adults.

To judge the popularity of their offerings, Henderson and his associates relied mainly on their well-honed instincts. But the *Digest,* with typical thoroughness, had tried to invent a more scientific and rational formula, the so-called Enthusiasm Quotient, or EQ. Following the publication of each volume of the book club, as well as each issue of the magazine, a sampling of several hundred subscribers were asked to rate each book condensation or feature as either Very Good, Good, Fair, Poor, or Very Poor.

Two index ratings were then reported for each selection. The EQ was obtained by multiplying the percentage of readers who answered Very Good by three and the percentage of Good answers by one, disregarding all the Fair answers, and multiplying Poor by minus one and the percentage of Very Poor by minus three. The sum of those figures was the reported EQ. The highest possible index rating was Plus 300, and the lowest Minus 300—a span of 600 points.

The Adjusted EQ Score went one step further by adjusting the enjoyment rating by the actual readership. Thus if an article or book selection obtained an EQ score of 180, and was read completely or in part by 50 percent of the readers, the AEQS was 90.

What rendered the EQ system virtually worthless was that those who read a selection or article only partially were still asked to judge whether it was Very Good or Very Poor. Perhaps for that reason, the monthly EQ scores were widely disregarded by editors both in Condensed Books and at the magazine. Yet the scores continued to be compiled, month after month and year after year, mainly for their curiosity value. One thing the ratings did underscore was the perennial popularity of such *RD* departments as "Laughter, the Best Medicine." Condensed Books's own all-time favorite offering proved to be the Mrs. Pollifax novels of Dorothy Gilman—a series about a grandmotherly woman with a brown belt in karate.

Before publication the condensed version of each title was always submitted to the author for approval. When *Boon Island* was shown to Kenneth Roberts, whose book had been cut down to one-third of its original length, he approved the changes but then began rewriting some of his own sentences. Perhaps America's best-known historical novelist, author of *Rabble in Arms* and *Northwest Passage,* Roberts stopped only when Henderson pointed out that careful readers would accuse the *Reader's Digest* of careless editing.

At first the book department was housed on the second floor of headquarters at Pleasantville. But the department grew so quickly that it soon transferred to a new building on *Digest* grounds and as early as 1951, its second year of operations, began publishing foreign editions as well. Like articles in the U.S. edition of the magazine, book-club selections were not necessarily translated in the same order or combination as they originally appeared, but formed a pool from which new recombinations were made that more closely reflected the reading tastes of British, Spanish, or Scandinavian readers.

As the book club grew, Henderson hired a third assistant, Eleanor Hard Lake, who had written for both *Fortune* and the *Digest* and whose brother Bill was an editor of the magazine. One day Wally stopped her in the halls and asked:

"Eleanor, when are you going to start working for the *Reader's Digest?*"

"But I thought I was, Mr. Wallace," she replied.

"Every person to his own choosing," he sniffed, and walked on.

On one occasion Wally did "interfere" editorially with Condensed Books. Going off on a trip, he had picked up a popular historical novel called *The President's Lady,* Irving Wallace's sentimental account of Rachel Jackson, wife of Andrew. On his return he sent Henderson a note saying that it might have a place in RDCB. Henderson had already rejected the book but ran it on Wally's suggestion, and it became one of the club's fifteen most popular offerings.

Unlike her husband, Lila resolved from the very beginning to take an active role in the book club. In doing so, she knew she would encounter no resistance from Wally, who showed little interest in the editorial operations of the club; and also she had run out of decorating projects. Mostly, Lila confined herself to selecting the covers and approving the overall design of each volume. In addition she made an occasional editorial suggestion. Two of her childhood favorites that soon materialized in condensed form were *Bambi* and William H. Hudson's *Little Boy Lost.*

At the end of its second year, Reader's Digest Condensed Books did a 10-million-piece mailing and collected a million more charter members—an extraordinary 10 percent return. Out of that number, 80 percent were expected to remain in the club when their second volume arrived.

Soon after the books were mailed to the million new members, however, Weintz arrived at work one morning and saw someone he knew. The man looked the other way, pretending not to see him. Weintz walked down the corridor and saw someone else he knew and said, "Good morning." The man stared glumly at Weintz but did not say a word. At the end of the corridor, Weintz met Harry Wilcox, who came up, sadly shook his hand and said:

"Gee, Walt, I'm terribly sorry. It must be a great blow, and I hope you make out somehow, but I'm terribly sorry about what's happened."

"My God, what happened?" Weintz exclaimed.

"Have you gone down to the warehouse and looked?" asked Wilcox.

Weintz rushed down to the warehouse in the basement and there saw 200,000 books returned by customers who were canceling or had changed their mind about joining. Word had quickly spread that Reader's Digest Condensed Books was a giant fiasco, after all, and that Walter Weintz was about to join the reject pile as well.

But Weintz felt relief. He had expected those 200,000 books back— some for refurbishing, to be sent out to late subscribers; most for pulping. However, the political and psychological ramifications of having more books lying around than were contained in some libraries were potentially dangerous. Going back to his office, Weintz called O. E. McIntyre—a subcontractor responsible for the processing side of the company's direct-mail operations—and told him to send some trucks to Pleasantville as quickly as possible.

"I don't know what you're going to do with them, and I don't care," Weintz said. "But we gotta get them out of the *Digest.*"

A truck soon pulled up and carted the books away to McIntyre's Long Island warehouse. Afterward arrangements were made that the truck pick up returned books every day at the Pleasantville post office. Weintz's job was saved—fortunately for the *Digest*. Four years later, membership in the club had reached an unprecedented 2.5 million.

The most important factor in the book club's extraordinary success was the reputation of the *Reader's Digest* as a purveyor of wholesome values, exhilarating reading, and all-around good value—and for that Wally could take full credit. According to no less an authority than Weintz himself, rule number one in any direct-mail campaign was that the product had to satisfy "a need or desire that is harbored in the breasts of men and/or women in commercial numbers." Among those needs, all to his mind met by both the *Digest* and its book club, were "the need for love, security, wealth, success, health, religious faith, amusement and entertainment, popularity, and whatever else it is that brings happiness."

———

AT THE same time that the book club was being launched, Cole and crew were working furiously to pump the magazine's circulation even higher than the 11 percent returns already achieved. Until Weintz appeared on the scene, the *Digest* had been sending out direct-mail promotion pieces in quantities of three, five, or seven million to people on four hundred different lists, and the duplications were, by his description, "horrendous." Among the more bothersome problems was that of subscribers renewing with introductory offers or canceling subscriptions because other subscribers were being offered a better price. A master list was desperately needed, and McIntyre was asked to supply it. His proposal was to create it by taking names directly out of telephone books.

In 1948 a test mailing had proved that the consolidation of lists would be successful. Now, as it had in 1926, the *Digest* turned to little old ladies for help. The women were hired to help compile a master list of 20 million names taken from every telephone directory in the country. Over a period of many months, the women painstakingly searched through more than 55 million names in the various lists, using the entries in the telephone books as reference. Each time a duplicate name appeared on a list, it was scratched out. The new master list that emerged contained just about every published residential address in the country. There was no other list like it anywhere. Using it, the *Digest* was ultimately able to leap very quickly from a 5 million circulation to one of 12 million.

Among the promotion letters that the magazine sent out was one that Weintz's boss Frank Herbert had devised with the help of two New York copywriters, Leo McGivena and Vic Schwab. It began, "Dear Reader: An ancient Persian poet said: 'If thou hast two pennies, spend one for bread. With the other, buy hyacinths for thy soul.' " The letter explained that the hyacinths were the *Reader's Digest.* Potential subscribers were invited to "spend" the penny by returning it to Pleasantville for a twelve-month bouquet. Subsequently, of course, they were billed for the full amount.

A test of the "Persian poet" letter showed that gimmicks worked. Later tests demonstrated that putting a postage stamp in a letter was also effective. In time the *Digest* switched to so-called savings stamps—subscribers who pasted the stamp on their order were given a dollar reduction on the price of a subscription. But in the meantime Weintz had a problem—where to get an awful lot of pennies to mail out to people so that they could buy hyacinths for their souls.

Weintz's assistant was Tom Knowlton, a mathematics wizard who supplied Al Cole with the Friday figures he demanded to see on Tuesday. Knowlton offered to go down to Washington to see William H. Brett, director of the Bureau of the Mint, and ask for 40 million pennies. Since the *Digest* planned a similar mailing for its brand-new book club, it intended to use 60 million pennies in all but had been hoarding the other 20 million over a period of time.

Knowlton went to Washington and met with Brett, who pointed out that he was prohibited from selling coin of the realm to a commerical enterprise. The mint gave money only to the Federal Reserve, which gave money only to member banks. So Knowlton asked, "If you were me, how would you go about getting them?"

The director told him to go see the only people with more pennies than the mint—the companies that operated penny gumball machines, which routinely washed their pennies in an acid bath and sold them in batches of a hundred to banks for $1.02. Knowlton subsequently arranged to corner the New York penny market—40 million pennies in all—at $1.03 per 100. The results of the "Persian poet" mailing were so extraordinary that the following year the *Digest* decided to go with another 100 million pennies. So Weintz called up Brett and asked for an appointment. Brett said, "I'd like to see you, too. You come down to Washington right away."

Knowlton and Weintz immediately flew down. Brett said, "Listen, last year you said you were going to mail 40 million pennies, and you mailed 60 million."

He pulled out a time chart and showed it to them:

"Here's when you started hoarding pennies and here's when you finished. You hoarded 20 million pennies out of the New York market, and I had to ship those pennies in. If there'd been a shortage of pennies, it could have caused all sorts of things. Do you realize how sensitive bankers are to money matters? One banker could have said to another, 'Have you noticed there's a shortage of pennies?' And the other banker could have said to another banker, 'Do you know, money's tight, there's a shortage of cash. People are hoarding money.' And another banker could have said, 'Money's real tight. We better start hoarding pennies ourselves.' And you could have caused a financial panic. It's an election year. Do you realize you could have gotten a Democrat elected?"

Then Brett said, "No more of that. Now, how many pennies do you want this year?"

"A hundred million," Weintz replied.

"Will you take delivery in Denver?"

Weintz asked how much it would cost to move the pennies from Denver to Pleasantville, and Brett gave him an estimate of $20,000.

"You'll save the government $20,000," Brett explained, "because if you take 100 million pennies out of circulation, I'll have to ship them in to replace them. I'll be justified in working this out. You call your local bank and tell them to go to the Federal Reserve and tell the Federal Reserve to come to me, and you'll get your 100 million pennies."

Back in Pleasantville, Knowlton contacted Brinks and Wells Fargo to get an estimate on transporting the 100 million pennies. The figure he received was $130,000.

"That son of a gun," Weintz said, "he deceived us."

He called Brett and angrily accused him of having misled him: "You said it would cost $20,000 to transport 100 million pennies, and it's going to cost me $130,000."

"How are you going to transport them?" Brett asked.

"Armored trucks," Weintz replied.

"We transport them in open flat cars," said Brett. "Don't you realize you can't steal 100 million pennies? Even if you tried to steal a thousand pennies, you couldn't run more than a few hundred yards. Nobody's going to steal 100 million pennies from you. Ship them on open flatcars."

Weintz shipped the pennies by open flatcar, and the bill came to $20,000. They were shipped to McIntyre's plant in Westbury, Long Island, and put in the warehouse, whose floor collapsed under their weight. The floor was rebuilt, the envelopes stuffed with pennies, and the 20 million envelopes taken down to the post office. Officials at the post office refused to accept the mail.

"Why not?" asked Weintz.

"Last year when you mailed your pennies," said the postmaster, "you had the return postage guaranteed on the envelope. This year you don't."

Knowlton had shrewdly figured that dropping the return postage guarantee meant the *Digest* would not have to deal with disposing of "nixies," or undeliverable letters. It cost more to take the pennies out of the nixies than simply to dispose of them. But the postal official gave an explanation:

"Sorry, but this is coin of the realm, and we're not allowed to throw it away or destroy it, and you're going to leave us with the nixies. You're going to get 6 percent nixies on 100 million pennies. That's six million pennies you're going to get back, which is worth $60,000. So we can't accept your mail."

Weintz and Knowlton immediately flew down to Washington again to see Roy Sheridan, head of postal classifications.

"Look," they proposed, "if we write a letter to 542,000 postmasters and promise to take the nixie mail back, will you let us mail the mail?"

Sheridan agreed. The letter was written. The 100 million pennies were mailed out. Some time later a lawyer called Weintz and said, "We're going to sue you for a million dollars because this family I represent received one of your mailings with pennies in it and a little baby saw the pennies and ripped open the envelope and swallowed them. I'm going to sue you for a million dollars."

The matter was settled out of court for a sum considerably less than a million dollars and more than a few pennies. But that did not mark the end of the penny business. Six million nixies had come back as predicted. Weintz asked McIntyre how much he would charge to take two pennies out of an envelope. McIntyre said three cents.

Another of Cole's assistants, who worked for the Boys' Club in

Mount Kisco, suggested the club open the envelopes and split the take with the *Digest*—a savings of two cents over the McIntyre offer.

At this point the *New Yorker* got into the act with a "Talk of the Town" column titled "Husking Nixies," which described the "tide of nixies" inundating the Boys' Club and said that the only worry of the director, a man named Mr. Wall, was "the weight of mail stacked on the clubhouse floor." The article went on, "The process of extracting the pennies has come to be known as 'husking,' and Mr. Wall compares it to opening clams. A good husker can husk up to thirteen nixies a minute; this amounts to $15.60 an hour, or $7.80 for the Boys' Club. At the time of our visit, something over seven hundred thousand pieces of mail had been husked, providing something over seven thousand dollars apiece for the Boys' Club and the *Digest.*"

───

WHILE the penny operation was racking up successes, Cole was meeting with less fortunate results on the newsstand front. The man now in charge of on-site newsstand promotions, former celebrity-endorsement copywriter Willard Espy, knew nothing about the subject, nor was he interested. An advertising campaign devised by Batten, Barton, Durstine and Osborn had proved to be only marginally successful. In desperation, Cole finally sent nearly everyone in the department to visit wholesalers and newsstand operators around the country to see why sales were so abysmal. Weintz went to Texas and learned that the *Digest* was not selling, because *Coronet*—a *Digest* imitator that had once reached a circulation of five million—sat right beside it. S-M News, which still handled distribution, was so efficient that it never had return copies left over. This meant that when the *Digest* ran out at the end of the month, *Coronet* would still be there and begin to steal *Digest* sales.

Though the logical solution was simply to replenish the racks, that involved a host of almost insuperable complications, ranging from lethargy on the part of newsstand "spotters" hired to keep track of sales in major cities to attrition on the part of S-M employees at the warehouse level. Increasing the initial retail quota, on the other hand, entailed numerous risks—notably, increased paper and printing costs. Like other magazine publishers, the *Digest* wanted primarily to sell a greater percentage of its initial pressrun.

Cole decided to get off the small-book display rack and down on the "flat" where the *Saturday Evening Post, Life,* and the *Ladies' Home Journal* were and ask for equal display. Side by side with them he proposed to put four stacks of the *Digest.* That marked the turning point, and sales quickly went from 800,000 back up to 1.5 million. While that was good news, Cole was still mystified why a new magazine called *TV Guide,* with sales of 2.2 million, was outperforming the *Digest* on the newsstands. Founded by Walter H. Annenberg in Philadelphia in 1953, the weekly program guide had grown out of a merger of local guides for the New York, Philadelphia, and Chicago television markets. An investigation by Cole showed that *TV Guide* had also managed to install 22,000 supermarket racks, compared with the *Digest*'s 8,000.

When Cole suggested expanding the *Digest*'s newsstand presence in supermarkets, he was told that women—who accounted for the majority of the magazine's single-copy sales—did not buy the *Reader's Digest* in supermarkets; they bought food in supermarkets. Tests had shown that *Digest*s on display in supermarkets did not sell. Cole sent Weintz and an assistant to Philadelphia, Atlanta, and Los Angeles to visit supermarkets. They learned that supermarket racks containing the *Digest* were in the back of stores and that most of the magazines on those racks were pulp and girlie magazines. *TV Guide,* meanwhile, was all by itself at the checkout counter. Cole approached *TV Guide* and asked if it would agree to a joint display. Not surprisingly, he was turned down. He then went to the A & P grocery chain, at the time the largest in the country, and asked for checkout display and was again rebuffed. Finally, he proposed to pay a fee to any supermarket that allowed the *Digest* to install a checkout rack. The offer was so well received that *RD* supermarket sales immediately tripled, quadrupled, then decupled. Later, when the Safeway chain began to remove the racks for *TV Guide* and replace them with new racks for the *Digest,* the Philadelphia upstart agreed to joint display.

━━━

AMID all the change and growth in the fifties, there was one casualty— the excerpt department in Cleveland, which in 1953 was finally closed down after Lucy Notestein retired. The operation was then transferred to Pleasantville—a move made easier because the Cleveland office had long served as an unofficial training ground for young women who wanted to pursue an editorial career in the home office. However, those who left the all-female environment of Cleveland for the male-dominated precincts of Pleasantville soon discovered that the best and, in fact, only way to advance their career—unless they were content to occupy a lowly slot as an assistant cutter and condenser—was to marry one of the senior editors. One of the most highly regarded excerpt editors was a gangly, attractive Cleveland native named Edie Miller, who married an up-and-coming editor named Hobart Durkin Lewis not long after he divorced his first wife.

By the time the department moved to Pleasantville, it was receiving an average of 37,000 pieces of mail a month, or nearly 500,000 a year. A massive central index kept track of fillers according to line length and subject matter or author, plus variations on the theme. A team of retired editors working free-lance at home supplemented the department's full-time staff of ten, helping to update the inventory, ferret out duplicates, and pare down every month a menu of selections for the issue editor to choose from. Occasionally, a few jokes got retold, even almost word for word, from issues in the twenties and thirties; but that was rare. When such slipups did occur, invariably one or two long-memoried readers pointed out the mistake.

For the most part, though, the central index was amazingly efficient and comprehensive. Some readers became very irate when a submission they thought ideally suited for the *Digest* was seemingly ignored—and apoplectic if they saw the quote published but attributed to another reader. An often-cited example was a Remarkable Remark published in the first issue: "A woman is as old as she looks. A man is old when he stops looking." Wally attributed the quote to a certain Reverend C. B. Preston. But in succeeding decades the *Digest* received countless submissions of the same quotation, variously "uttered by" Ben Franklin, Mark Twain, and many others. The desperation of readers eager to see either themselves credited in print as the sponsor of a quote or a check in the mailbox, or both, kept all three women in the editorial correspondence division busy full-time.

BY FAR the most momentous change in the *Digest*'s history up to that point occurred in 1954 when, after thirty-two years, it reversed its most celebrated long-standing policy and began to accept advertising. In so doing, it also fulfilled a prophecy Robert Fuoss, the *Saturday Evening Post*'s managing editor, had made soon after World War II. During a pep talk to his sales staff, Fuoss had pointed out that, even though *Life* was the *Post*'s main competition at the time and network television was threatening to take off as the hot new national medium, there was a worse threat.

"One of these days the *Reader's Digest* will start taking advertising," Fuoss had warned. "When it does, you *Post* salesmen will wish you were back in the good old days when your stiffest competition was *Life.*"

At the time the *Digest*'s U.S. circulation was still around 4 million, while the *Post*'s stood at a little under 4 million and *Life*'s at 5,369,314. By 1954 the *Digest*'s readership had reached 10 million, while those of *Life* and of the *Post* were in downward and ultimately fatal spirals. For *Post* salesmen, the good old days had indeed never seemed rosier.

Though the *Digest* had never accepted advertising, it had praised the virtues of the medium beginning with its first issue, when Wally reprinted an article showing how advertising had materially contributed to the lengthening of human life by changing the way people thought about their health, food, and hygiene. At least twice a year, moreover, the *Digest* reproduced a praiseworthy advertisement as an example of "Advertising *cum laude.*"

On the other hand, the magazine also vigorously attacked what it perceived as deceptive advertising. As early as July 1943 it had published "Lifting the Cigarette Ad Smoke Screen," based on Federal Trade Commission findings about exaggerated claims for cigarettes. The next month "Taking Dentifrice Ads to the Cleaners" reviewed complaints against half a dozen manufacturers of tooth powders and pastes. An investigation into sensational advertising claims of some cold and headache medicines revealed that their only medically active ingredient was aspirin. One manufacturer sued the *Digest* for libel and lost.

In the ensuing uproar, Wally agreed to be interviewed by the industry's trade journal *Advertising Age*—a prudent expedient since the *Digest*'s international editions were heavily dependent on advertising revenue and advertisers' goodwill. In the interview, he dismissed the notion that the *Digest* was embarked upon an anti-advertising crusade and defended the exposure of abuses by a few advertisers whose exaggerated claims marred the credibility of all advertising.

In fact, sometimes the best advertising a product ever received was a mention in the pages of the *Reader's Digest*. A 1946 condensation of a *Forbes* article about a waterproofing product brought the manufacturer fifty thousand orders and inquiries. In February 1953 an article about a meat tenderizer led to even more astounding results—an average of ten thousand letters a day to the manufacturer for more than six months, or a total of nearly two million letters.

But something very like a crusade against cigarette advertising continued to appear in the pages of the *Digest*. In December 1950 the magazine even resorted to the unusual step of running an editorial titled "About Those Advertisers," which was an attempt to respond to the misuse of the *Digest* name in cigarette advertising and cautioned readers "to appraise with skepticism advertisements—in the press or on the air—of trade-named products which imply RD endorsements. . . . To purchase such products on the basis of a semblance of *Digest* support for claims made in the advertising is to lay oneself open to the possibility of deception." By now any number of cigarette manufacturers, following Old Golds' lead, routinely subverted *Digest* findings on tar and nicotine content by simply touting themselves as lowest in one or both categories.

Despite the vigorous and highly successful campaign by Cole and his associates to rebuild the *Digest*'s circulation beginning in the late forties, by 1954 the magazine—though not the company itself, thanks to Condensed Books—was facing a deficit of more than one million dollars. The enormous postal, paper, and creative costs of the *Digest*'s unending direct-mail efforts, in addition to editorial and other overhead, amounted to more than the income it received from subscriptions and single-copy sales. In almost any other magazine on earth, the difference was made up by revenues from advertising. But the *Digest* did not accept advertising and was now in danger of being subsidized by the book club, which from both a business and a psychological point of view was unacceptable.

Moreover, the problem of introducing advertising in the U.S. edition faced a double obstacle—not only convincing Wally of the soundness of the idea but also not alienating two generations of readers used to reading the magazine without the distraction of big color pictures, on small pages, of Skippy's peanut butter, Dentu-Creme, Ford pickup trucks, and other staples of Middle America. The former hurdle was the more formidable.

In some respects Cole viewed his job as a simple one—to carry out Wally's wishes, whatever they were, insofar as that was feasible. Cole would have moved the earth to make it possible for the *Digest* to continue to run without advertising so long as that was what Wally desired, but by 1954 the business manager had run out of a place to stand. And Wally knew it. Though he was stubborn, he was not unrealistic. When Cole finally convinced him that the *Reader's Digest,* for the first time, might lose money in a fiscal year, Wally capitulated and agreed at least to a readership survey.

Back in 1947, just before Fred Thompson took over the Canadian edition, those readers were polled to see whether they preferred a magazine with advertising to one without but with a higher cover price. Eighty percent of the respondents said they preferred having the magazine filled with advertising over having to pay an extra ten cents per copy.

A survey conducted in the July 1954 issue of the U.S. edition now showed that 90 percent of American readers favored advertising over a cover price increase of thirty-five cents. For thirty-two years the *Digest* had kept the same cover price of a quarter, even though the number of pages had nearly tripled. But still Wally postponed a decision.

One day in early November, Cole and several others from the business side were sitting in Wally's office, talking about various problems. Advertising did not come up, though by now the million-dollar deficit was a foregone conclusion. Out of the blue, Wally said:

"By the way, Al, if you still think we should take advertising, I suppose the first thing we should do is tell the other magazines."

"That settles it then?" Cole asked, taken aback.

"If you still think it's what we should do."

Cole rushed to inform Fred Thompson of the historic decision. By this time Thompson had been brought back from Canada and was, in effect, the advertising director–elect, biding his time until the inevitable day arrived. He immediately rushed down to New York to meet with J. Walter Thompson representatives in order to work on an advertising campaign to announce the news. The firm had recently been hired to replace Pendleton Dudley, whom Lila never liked and who was now halfway out in the cold. (Before he vanished altogether, the *Digest*'s first landlord and patron was reduced to distributing recordings of assorted editors interviewing authors to radio stations around the country. When he died soon afterward, Lila did not attend his funeral.)

The Thompson/Thompson team worked through the night and had the copy secretly typeset on a Sunday afternoon at an odd-job printing shop in Bridgeport, Connecticut. The advertisement never ran, however. News had quickly spread, and orders poured in even before the rates were published.

But Fred Thompson did manage to send out a telegram to 314 agencies, announcing that the *Digest* would accept advertising beginning with its April issue. The page rate was $26,000 for black-and-white, compared to the $20,350 charged by *Life,* whose circulation was second only to the *Digest*'s; or to the $14,600 it cost to advertise in the third-place *Ladies' Home Journal.* Within two weeks the *Digest* received orders for 1,107 pages of advertising, almost triple the amount it could accept for the entire year.

Cole's and Thompson's solution was to apportion space among sixty advertising agencies representing 170 products and services. Initially, the magazine decided to limit advertisements in any one issue to thirty-two pages. Advertisers were selected on the basis of space availability and a suitable variety of products and services. The *Digest* also gave preferential treatment to advertisers in the magazine's foreign editions.

In 1954 the twenty-nine international editions had carried more than 1,500 pages of advertising, representing 2,000 different companies. Most advertisers in foreign editions were big American conglomerates with international operations—U.S. Steel, Texaco, Eastman Kodak, Gillette, International Harvester, Standard Oil, Lockheed, Swift.

Wally also reviewed a number of other magazines and drew up a four-page list of companies whose advertisements he personally approved. He wanted *Digest* editors to write all copy for all advertisements—which, for some advertisers, turned out to be the case. Wally's list included A.C. spark plugs, Bell Telephone, Blue Cross, Chrysler, Eastman Kodak, Ford, General Electric, General Motors, Goodyear, Greyhound bus, Grumman, Hertz, Kaiser Aluminum, New York Life, Pan American, Southern Pacific, Studebaker, Sunbeam, Westinghouse, and Zenith.

Before the first advertisement ever appeared, the *Digest* had confirmed orders for $11 million worth of space. Despite the windfall, the *Digest* still closed out the year 1954 with its first—and last—deficit, though Cole had managed to pare it down to only $500,000.

When the April 1955 issue was published, the new-look *Digest* contained 216 pages instead of 168, and many of those new pages were in full color. Six months later the magazine raised its advertising quota to

20 percent in any given issue—a considerably lower ratio than that of the magazine industry in general, though that restriction was also soon abandoned, as the ratio moved up to the 40 percent mark. The *Digest* became the first magazine to eliminate an extra charge for either a bleed or a second color, to guarantee advertisers a position adjacent to editorial features, and to offer regional advertising editions.

A prohibition against medical remedies—for aspirin, milk of magnesia, antihistamines, and vitamins—was also soon dropped. But the U.S. edition continued to refuse advertising for alcohol and cigarettes, even though both products were widely advertised in the foreign editions. The double standard was insisted upon by Wally personally, even though he had a two-pack-a-day habit and a passion for cocktails. His rationalization was, if not convincing, characteristic:

"I don't have anything against drinking or smoking," he told an interviewer, "but I don't want to feel that we are taking an active part in introducing millions of people to them. Another thing, I have known a lot of writers and other people with drinking problems. Some of them have told me that nothing makes them want a drink of liquor—a drink they shouldn't have—as much as seeing how delicious a high-ball or a martini looks in an ad."

In July 1955 Fred Thompson, only forty years old and already a sixteen-year veteran of the *Digest,* was named advertising director for both domestic and all foreign editions. The only adverse fallout from the decision to accept advertising was the loss of Batten, Barton, Durstine and Osborn. BBDO was also the agency used by the American Tobacco Company, which was upset with the *Digest*'s campaign against cigarettes. When the agency was given a them-or-us ultimatum, it chose to keep traveling down Tobacco Road, even though Bruce Barton and Al Cole were good friends and the advertising executive had written an article for the magazine. Cole was furious.

On the plus side, the *Digest*'s circulation now had to be audited by the Audit Bureau of Circulations. In late 1955 ABC confirmed that for the six-month period ending June 30, 1955, the magazine had a net paid average circulation of 10,236,057. That figure nearly equaled the combined circulation of *Life* and the *Ladies' Home Journal* and set a new record for any publication in the history of type. Only the Bible— miraculously, no doubt—managed to remain the exception.

Keeping pace was Condensed Books, which in due time reached the point where 40 percent of all *Digest* readers were also subscribing to

the book club. Its four million members easily made it—virtually overnight—the largest book club in the world, and the international editions were collectively accounting for millions more.

Among those who wrote Wally letters of support after publication
of the first issue containing advertising was Joseph P. Kennedy, who
said, "I still think, with or without advertising, [the *Digest* is] the great
magazine in the country." Wally, who despised the former ambassador
to Great Britain, ripped the letter in half.

On second thought, however, Wally taped the letter together again
and passed it along to the promotion department with the suggestion
that a "brief" phrase might be usable as an endorsement.

10

Tucking America into
Bed at Night

IN THE early fifties DeWitt Wallace presented a tall, spare figure, though big-boned and physically strong, with a receding forehead. His close-cropped hair, gray now, heightened the impression that he was rather more bald than he was. His tentative, aloof manner, the fact that he was frequently off traveling, plus the many stories about him being handed down to the second generation of editors now coming on board, fueled the growing myth of DeWitt Wallace the enigma, unpredictable genius, and prankster.

There were still no set editorial meetings. As in the thirties and forties, the magazine's internal editorial machinery continued to function with the simple efficiency of a Model T. One team of editors scoured up to five hundred magazines, looking for articles suitable for reprint, while another team assigned originals and arranged for plants. Theoretically, and as expressly stated by Wally and other executive-level editors, a good reprint was valued just as much as a good original.

In practice, however, originals were looked on as stepping-stones in an editorial career while reprints took on the status of a second-class article and were considered the province of those comfortable in their niche. Imperceptibly, the ratio of originals to reprints began to shift upward from 10 or 15 percent to 50 percent, counting plants. Originals continued to be mainly the responsibility of Harry Harper and Howard Florance, while Ferguson functioned as a kind of in-house roving editor without portfolio.

The bias in favor of originals developed even though Wally himself had something akin to real affection for a good reprint. Yet he himself once cautioned his editors not to refer to the magazine as "essentially a reprint magazine" when declining submissions. By the early fifties, as he pointed out, the *Digest* was probably buying more original articles than any other monthly magazine.

The rest of the editorial hierarchy and operation was almost virtually unchanged from what it had been twenty years earlier. The only difference was that Ken Payne was now officially and not just de facto the executive editor, and similar status had been accorded to managing editor Fritz Dashiell. They worked with a team of senior editors that included Marc Rose, Bill Hard, Jr., Bob Littell, Burt McBride, and Walter B. Mahony, Jr. Many of the senior editors rotated as issue editors, and everyone assumed that if Wally ever retired, his editorial successor would come from their ranks.

In fact, though, the man who was to leapfrog over all of them when that time came was not even listed on the masthead. But one afternoon, in the early 1940s, at a party at High Winds, an urbane, well-tailored young copywriter named Hobart Durkin Lewis, known to his friends as Hobe, greatly charmed Lila Bell, and they spent hours talking by a garden wall. Within a few weeks he was advanced to the editorial ranks of the *Digest* itself.

In lieu of editorial meetings, luncheons with authors at the Guest House continued to be the only formal occasions during which article ideas and related business were discussed. When the *Digest* originally acquired the property for its headquarters, there was a colonial-era farmhouse, located a few hundred yards away, that was originally used as construction headquarters. In 1950 Lila transformed it into the Guest House, decorating it with expensive antiques, Oriental porcelain, and paintings, including two Corots. Downstairs were three dining rooms of various sizes, the largest able to accommodate enough guests for a host editor or executive to serve up a lecture as dessert. Upstairs were four bedrooms for visitors, primarily from the company's offices abroad.

Wally usually invited along half a dozen editors to meet with Quentin Reynolds, Billy Rose, Lester Velie, or other well-known authors of the day. Editors also invited their own authors and considered it a feather in their cap if Wally agreed to attend. As formerly, the routine was for the writer to propose several ideas, which were usually turned down summarily. Then a bull session followed. Many writers went home discouraged and empty-handed, but a lucky few left Pleasantville with three or four assignments and the promise of many more.

There was always the prospect of surprise at the noon-hour editorial lunch. On occasion it was the writer who proved intransigent, not Wally. A notable case in point involved a confident, forty-something novelist then making his way—James Michener.

Michener came to the Guest House after receiving a call one day in 1951 from a man whose name he did not at first catch. The caller said he admired the author's work. Only later on did Michener realize that his fan was also in a position to do something about it.

"What was your name again?" Michener asked.

"DeWitt Wallace," said the voice. "I work at the *Reader's Digest.*"

Michener had recently quit his job as an editor at the Macmillan publishing company to become a free-lance writer and travel the lecture circuit—a gamble made somewhat less risky by the fact that a collection of his short stories, *Tales of the South Pacific,* won the Pulitzer Prize in 1947 and had recently been transformed into a runaway Broadway hit musical by Richard Rodgers and Oscar Hammerstein. Even so, he was surprised actually to be getting a phone call from an editor.

"I've been keeping a file on what you do," Wally said, "and you seem to have something to say. I'd be most pleased if you'd come up to Pleasantville and have lunch with me." When Michener hesitated, Wally offered him $2,500 for the honor.

On the train ride up, Michener noticed that the tracks ran by three cemeteries. The first four tombstones he spotted started with the letter *M,* not a good omen. But Wally greeted him warmly, saying how much he and Lila had enjoyed *South Pacific* and that their favorite song was "You've Got to Be Carefully Taught," which showed how racial prejudice was learned through bad example. Michener revealed how he had been accosted by commuters at a train station in New Haven, Connecticut, during the play's tryout and pressured to drop the song, because it was not what people wanted to hear when they went to a play. When Michener reported the incident to Hammerstein, the latter dismissed the suggestion out of hand. Michener, who was not involved in writing either the playbook or the lyrics, thanked him for his decision.

"This is what the play is all about," Michener told Wally. "People are born good and have to be taught to act bad."

Wally agreed with that thoroughly un-Calvinist notion, and then everyone sat down to lunch. But this time the writer turned the tables on the editors. Instead of showing up with a sheaf of article proposals, Michener had arrived empty-handed. All during the meal the half circle of *Digest* editors surrounding him—Wally, Hobe Lewis, Ferguson, and others—bombarded him with one idea after another. Typically, Michener's response was "I think you have plenty of people who could do that much better than I."

Finally, when there was nothing left to talk about, Michener droned on for more than an hour about his observations on trench warfare in Korea. By dessert, painful lapses into silence had become more frequent than suggestions for articles. Ferguson could not remember a more boring session. But Hobe Lewis perceived that the author, though silent and seemingly shy, was really only self-possessed and refused to perform on cue.

"Mr. Michener," Wally finally asked in exasperation, "isn't there anything you're burning to write about?"

"No, Mr. Wallace," Michener loftily replied. "I've never had a burning desire to do anything in my life."

"Wouldn't you like to go to Hawaii and do some stories for us?" Wally persisted.

"Hawaii is the place I'd least like to go," Michener said, explaining how he had already promised the editors of *Life* to do a piece on the island if he ever went—a promise he was in no mood to fulfill.

Lewis thought, "He's pissed on the whole meeting."

Michener, sans assignments, returned to New York, saluting the quartet of tombstones as he went. But Wally summoned Lewis to his office and said, "Keep in touch with that fellow."

A few days later Lewis wrote Michener with seven more article topics. He also proposed another lunch, this time in New York with only himself, Wally, and Michener. It culminated in three assignments and marked the beginning of one of the most long-lived and mutually agreeable partnerships between writer and editor in the *Digest*'s history.

Even so, there were still many more hurdles to be surmounted. For one thing, Michener did not have the least idea how to write something in only a few words, *Digest* style. His first article (apart from a reprint from *South Pacific*) was a snoozer called "Korean Culture," which ran to sixty-four pages, or about ten times the average length. Though the magazine always encouraged writers to treat a subject at full length and leave the cutting to the editors, Michener's offering seemed like an article-sized *Moby-Dick*. Worse, it had a terrible opening. Lewis sent the article back with suggestions for cuts, but Michener found it impossible to reduce his manuscript by more than a few paragraphs. So he asked for a meeting with Lewis.

"If you want to waste your time with me it will have to be with the understanding that I will write the way I want to, in as many words as I find necessary," Michener explained, "and leave to your people the job of cutting. Also, I'm never again going to bother with an opening paragraph, because any of your secretaries can do that job better than I."

To his surprise the accommodating Lewis, as eager as Wally to bring Michener into the fold at any cost, replied, "Cutters and lead-writers we have."

Michener continued to write voluminously and depended on Pleasantville's cutters to make his "inchoate reporting" neat and his "rambling thoughts" concise. As for leads, he soon became accustomed, on seeing an article of his in print, to reading a lead written by another hand, only wishing he had thought of it first. Most of his articles centered around his travel destinations—Hawaii eventually among them. But he was also later to describe for *Digest* readers, in dramatic and thrilling terms, the vigilant role played by the Strategic Air Command in the nation's defense. *While Others Sleep,* an early book that developed out of the article on the SAC, was also a selection of RDCB.

Meanwhile, Michener's career as a novelist prospered, too. *Tales of the South Pacific* was followed by *The Bridges at Tokori, Sayonara,* and *Hawaii.* Each novel seemed longer than the one before, yet the public liked what it read, and each outsold its predecessor. And as earlier, Wally remained a big fan—so much so that he wanted to put Michener on staff and not just have him write for the magazine free-lance. The author always refused, year after year, despite offers that grew increasingly tantalizing but also perplexing. What puzzled Michener was that Wally was a devout Republican, while he himself was an equally ardent Democrat. But Wally had his suspicions. On more than one occasion, Michener found Wally staring at him, only to ask, "You aren't really a Democrat, are you?"

When it became apparent that Michener would never go to work full-time for the *Reader's Digest,* Wally invited him to a restaurant and said:

"Michener, I'm captivated by your approach to life and by what you're trying to do. I exist because people like you can write. Everything I own comes from the skill that some men and women have with words. Obviously you're not going to take a job with me, so let's have this arrangement. You go anywhere in the world you want to go. You write anything you want to write. I don't care what it covers or if it's something that we couldn't conceivably be interested in. We'll pay all your expenses, no matter where you go or what you do. All that's required is that you let us have first shot at what you've written. If we can't use it, you can sell it elsewhere and you won't owe us a penny."

Michener wondered if any writer in history had ever received a more magnanimous offer. The compromise was that he became a roving editor—indisputably, the most successful and prominent of them all. Over the next eighteen years he wrote more than sixty articles, on topics ranging from Japanese rock music and Italian designers to pornography, Nehru, and the art of being a housewife. After his third marriage, the *RD* paid for an around-the-world working honeymoon—a typical Wally gesture. In 1955 alone, Michener's byline appeared nine times.

Unlike those of most other *Digest* writers, his articles on Asia were singularly free of anti-Communist rhetoric. But Michener did support a "tough stand" against communism and called for military aid to Pakistan and Indonesia. He also covered the Hungarian uprising of 1956 for the *RD,* though he had never previously been to Budapest, did not speak the language, and had already written seven long articles that year for the magazine. In Vienna, after the uprising was crushed, he joined another *Digest* contributor, Dickey Chapelle, and crossed the border on several occasions to usher refugees to safety across a rickety wooden bridge over the Einser Canal, near Andau. In March 1957 every edition of the *Digest* carried an excerpt telling of the atrocities inflicted on the Hungarian people. That experience was later developed into a book, *The Bridge at Andau.*

An underlying theme of all the articles was an old conviction of Wally's: the brotherhood of man, a utopian belief that men and women of all nationalities could live together in harmony. "I really believe that every man on this earth is my brother," Michener wrote, exemplifying the *Reader's Digest* at its best. "He has a soul like mine, the ability to understand friendship, the capacity to create beauty. In all the continents of this world I have met such men."

━━━

THOUGH Wally very clearly wanted the magazine to reflect his own political views in the early 1950s, he was faced with the same problems confronting the Republican party at that time—a split between the conservative mainstream and its isolationist right wing, which was traumatized by Truman's stunning upset over Thomas E. Dewey, the liberal Republican governor of New York, in the 1948 presidential election. The *Digest* mirrored that split in a curious way. Its appetite for sensationalism and its borderline-fanatical crusade to expose and publicize the Red menace rendered it a ready-made champion of Joseph McCarthy, an obscure Republican senator from Wisconsin who, in seeking reelection in 1950, hoped to capitalize on the country's fear of subversives in government.

But McCarthyism was only the latest incarnation of anti-Communist hysteria that swept across the country periodically, ever since the first Red scare, in 1919–20. Like other right-wing publications, the *Reader's Digest* saw communism as the paramount threat to the American way of life. Even its hatred of the New Deal stemmed from Wally's suspicion that Roosevelt was leading the country down the primrose path to Stalinist-like socialism.

In other ways, too, the *Digest* both reflected and served to deepen the conservative mood spreading across the country in the wake of the conflict in Korea, the Soviet detonation of an atomic bomb, and the House Un-American Activities Committee (HUAC), which had begun hearings into the loyalty of civil servants in 1947. Apart from radio, the *Digest* remained the single largest and most influential instrument of mass communications in the country—if not among opinion makers, who largely ignored it, then certainly among millions of voters, who in turn often ignored the opinion makers.

In issue after issue the *Digest* supported HUAC or heated up the Cold War with such pieces as "Russia Won't Attack This Year," "How Radical Are the Clergy?" (on Marxist sympathizers in clerical ranks), or "U.S. Dollars Have Armed Russia" (on treason in high places). A regular theme of FBI director J. Edgar Hoover, a frequent contributor, was that nowhere were Communist agents "more everlastingly busy" than in the United States. (Hoover's articles were usually ghosted by arch-reactionary Stanley High or roving editor Frederic Sondern, Jr.) Not surprisingly, the *Digest* also proposed that wiretapping be legalized.

On February 9, 1950, in Wheeling, West Virginia, McCarthy delivered the infamous speech in which he claimed that the State Department was infested with Communists. In his hand he held up a list of their names. Subsequently challenged to provide at least one, he pointed to Professor Owen Lattimore, a member of the faculty of

Johns Hopkins University and adviser both to the U.S. State Department and to General Chiang Kai-Shek.

Along with *Time* and *Life* magazines, whose China-born publisher Henry R. Luce strongly disagreed with U.S. policy toward that country, the *Digest* had routinely denounced the views and questioned the loyalty of Lattimore and other Far East experts. The two publishers, both Presbyterians, preferred the counsel of their own Asia expert, Dr. Walter Judd, a Republican congressman from Minnesota and former medical missionary in China. Judd was a frequent visitor both to High Winds and to Luce's New York penthouse. He was also part of the so-called China lobby in Congress that included McCarthy and other right-wing representatives.

Back in the midforties, the *Digest* had published an article assailing Lattimore's views on how the United States should deal with Red China. His opinions were, in fact, essentially no different from the containment policy later successfully promoted by Secretary of State Dean Acheson and President Truman. The *RD,* though, implied otherwise.

After the article appeared, Lattimore attempted to publish a rebuttal, but the *Digest* denied him space to reply. He then turned to Thomas W. Lamont, J. P. Morgan's right-hand man and a member of United China Relief, a conservative fund-raising group that also included Wendell Willkie and David Selznick. Lattimore had written a letter that he wanted Lamont to put his name to and send to the editor of the *New York Times.* The letter was a refutation of the *Digest*'s charges.

But Lamont, though he deplored the *Digest* article, refused to sign the letter, interpreting it as an appeal to the U.S. government to send military aid to the Communists as well as to the Nationalists under Chiang Kai-Shek. From that point on, Lattimore's name was suspect within the China lobby.

During the HUAC hearings, McCarthy accused Lattimore of inventing the lie that the forces of Mao Tse-tung were mere agrarian reformers. In fact, Lattimore had once edited a journal called the *Institute of Pacific Relations,* which took a progressive line on both China and the Soviet Union. Lattimore had even tried to justify the Soviet purges of 1938. Now under oath, he denied ever having been a Communist and impressively defended himself by claiming McCarthy was serving as no more than a mouthpiece for the China lobby. Lattimore's FBI file was also made available to the committee and seemed to put him in the clear.

McCarthy struck back by subpoenaing Louis Budenz, yet another ex-Communist, former editor of the *Daily Worker,* and occasional contributor to the *Reader's Digest.* Budenz testified he had heard hearsay evidence that Lattimore, though not exactly a spy, was officially responsible for charting the party line that China's Reds were merely agrarian reformers. Though Budenz was unable to substantiate the charge, and Democrats on the Tydings committee later exonerated Lattimore, he was never afterward able to shake off the label of being at the very least a sympathizer.

McCarthy was too extreme ever to be seriously considered as a Republican presidential candidate in 1952. But Senator Robert Taft of Ohio supported many of McCarthy's subsequent accusations—particularly those against Secretary of State Acheson personally and against the State Department itself for "losing" China to the Communists by failing to support Chiang Kai-Shek.

Paradoxically, Wally was also a great admirer of General Dwight D. Eisenhower, then Supreme Allied Commander of NATO forces in Europe. The *RD* publisher was also enough of a realist to realize that the GOP stood a far better chance of putting a Republican in the White House for the first time since Herbert Hoover if Eisenhower agreed to seek the presidency and oppose the colorless Taft for the nomination.

In a larger sense, too, Eisenhower's brand of big-business, antigovernment conservatism more closely reflected the convictions and instincts not only of Wally himself but of Al Cole, who was a powerful behind-the-scenes figure in Republican party politics in Westchester County—at the time the richest Republican enclave in the United States.

Also, the right wing of the party was maneuvering to put California junior senator Richard M. Nixon on the ticket as Eisenhower's running mate. In the same election year that catapulted McCarthy into the nation's headlines, Nixon—who had made his reputation as the HUAC member most doggedly in pursuit of State Department functionary Alger Hiss—had branded his liberal opponent, Representative Helen Gahagan Douglas, as a "pink lady."

As a result of its predicament, the pro-Eisenhower *Digest* became one of the most McCarthyite publications in the country without ever publishing a single article on Senator Joseph McCarthy himself—acting, in fact, as if the most controversial man in America did not exist, and yet routinely fanning the flames of his anti-Communist wrath. At the same time, it continued to publish lofty, thoughtful articles on foreign and domestic policy by Eisenhower—most of them ghosted by William Hard, Sr., Stanley High, or Robert S. Strother, an editor in the international editions. The *Digest* also awarded several college scholarships in his name.

Ironically, its somewhat ambivalent approach caused even the *Reader's Digest* itself to be branded an institution sympathetic to communism by those who wielded a pinker brush. In September 1952 the magazine published a piece titled "Mr. Brown vs. Generalissimo Stalin," by Donald Robinson, which concerned the efforts of Irving Brown, an American Federation of Labor representative, to rid the union of subversives. When far-right columnist Westbrook Pegler read the article, he smelled a Communist plot.

In November 1940 Pegler had sat up with Wallace in High Winds to listen to the presidential election returns. Both were bitterly disappointed by Roosevelt's defeat of Willkie. In his widely syndicated column, Pegler now returned Wally's hospitality with a trademark tirade that accused the *Digest* of a cover-up—specifically, of failing to identify Robinson as a former Red.

The situation worsened when the *RD*'s editorial correspondence department, replying to readers demanding an explanation, denigrated Pegler's "reportorial methods." Incensed, Pegler attacked again. The *Digest* received so much correspondence as a result of the furor that Wally was eventually obliged to draw up a form letter "Regarding Westbrook Pegler's Attack" to be mailed out over his signature. In the letter he thanked those who wrote in for their "frank criticism" of the *Digest* and noted that he had apologized personally to Pegler for the letter sent out by the editorial correspondence department. Declining to take personal responsibility for the offense, however, Wally claimed that the letter was sent out while he was on holiday abroad with his wife. He also regretted the omission of Brown's previous connections and statements during the period from 1928 to 1934, claiming that the *Digest* had not been aware of them.

But he also defended Brown in recent years as "an active fighter against Communism" and "a fully loyal American." Wally went on to quote extensively from five government agencies, whose identities he refused to divulge, supporting his claim.

Finally, Wally insisted that no other magazine had so "courageously and persistently" fought communism as the *Reader's Digest*: "Moreover, we ran many such articles during World War II, when Russia was an ally of the United States. As a consequence, we were bitterly attacked year after year by the leftist press. To be charged now, for the *first time* with having Communist sympathies is more than ironical—it is utterly fantastic."

It *was* utterly fantastic. But then so were the *Digest*'s smear jobs on the Methodist church and Professor Lattimore.

———

As A MONTHLY, the *Digest* rarely had to stop the presses to accommodate late-breaking news stories. An exception occurred with the January 1951 issue, whose lead article "The Right Man in the Right Place" was a celebration of General MacArthur's brilliant maneuver in Inchon. The previous June, North Korean forces had crossed the Thirty-eighth Parallel and swept down the peninsula. Military units from both the United States and the United Nations, under the unified command of MacArthur, had failed for three months to stem the attack and were barely hanging on to the Pusan perimeter. But on September 15, 1950, MacArthur landed a new force in Inchon, the port city of Seoul, behind the enemy line, while at the same time launching a counterattack from Pusan. Panicking North Korean troops stampeded back across their border. MacArthur pressed the attack, meeting minimal resistance, and in October crossed the Thirty-eighth Parallel, intent on reuniting the country.

But by press time U.S. and South Korean soldiers were suffering heavy losses at the hands of Red Chinese "volunteers," who were counterattacking in massive human-wave assaults. MacArthur was in full retreat, and the suspicion that he was perhaps the wrong man in the wrong place was now the stuff of front-page stories and editorial leaders in newspapers around the country.

Though four million copies of the *Digest* had already been printed, Wally stopped the presses and replaced the article with "The Essence of the American Story," a sleep-inducing account of citizen participation in public affairs. In a statement to the press, managing editor Dashiell took pains to explain that the substitution "implie[d] no criticism of General MacArthur."

———

IN THE MAIN, despite the *Digest*'s occasional differences of opinion with Republicans like Senator McCarthy or national institutions such as the Methodist church, the mood of the country and the editorial philosophy of the magazine coincided more nearly than at any time before or since. According to one closet-liberal Digester who took a benign view of the contending philosophies in Pleasantville in the 1950s, the *Digest's* *'Leave It to Beaver,* tucking-America-into-bed-at-night conservatism" won out over its McCarthyite proclivities because "at heart its conservatism wasn't fascist. It was the kind that warned you not to smoke in bed at night."

That was another reason why Eisenhower appealed to the *Digest.* The American way of life in the early fifties seemed fashioned, if not in heaven, then perhaps in Pleasantville itself—at least for white, middle-class Americans.* Amid all the upheaval and turmoil on the international and governmental levels, the country was enjoying unprecedented prosperity, a soaring birthrate, and a religious revival all at once. The hunt for subversives had also given rise to a generation of self-appointed guardians of genuine Americanism—the *Digest* among them—who closely monitored not only the government but also the courts, the universities, the arts, the churches, and almost all other aspects and institutions of national life, looking for anti-American tendencies.

The result was an extraordinary conformity in the country's cultural life. Orthodoxy encouraged uniformity, and nowhere more so than in Pleasantville itself, which by the 1950s had become the prototypical American suburb—a mostly all-white, affluent, conservative community of mostly Protestant Republicans whose vicar was Norman Vincent Peale, a neighbor in nearby Pawling, no less, and a good friend of DeWitt Wallace. Peale preached a gospel—a way of life—called positive thinking. The message found in his best-selling *The Power of Positive Thinking,* published in 1952, was the same that the *Digest* itself had been preaching for thirty years.

"Flush out all depressing, negative, and tired thoughts," Peale urged. "Start thinking faith, enthusiasm, and joy." Those words could have been written by Stanley High, a manic-depressive and alcoholic, on

---

*A 1954 offering, "Meet the Typical American," announced that the typical male stood five feet nine inches tall, weighed 158 pounds, preferred brunettes, baseball, beefsteak, and French fried potatoes, and thought "the ability to run a home smoothly and efficiently [was] the most important quality in a wife." The average American woman, at five feet four inches and 132 pounds, could not "stand an unshaven face" and preferred homemaking to a career. Plus or minus a few inches, those characteristics exactly described DeWitt and Lila Wallace.

one of his good days—and probably were. When he was not hunting for Communists behind Methodist pews or under State Department desks, the tireless High also ghosted for the man who equated a banal godliness with the American way of life.

High was the *Digest*'s liaison with another famous evangelist, whose crusades were drawing tens of thousands to auditoriums and ballparks. Initially, High's intention was to do an exposé on the young Baptist preacher. But after High heard Billy Graham preach, and later met the man, he became first an admirer and then his ghostwriter. He also introduced him to DeWitt Wallace, who was to send Graham's message into millions of homes both in America and abroad.

The bland creed DeWitt Wallace eventually adopted as his own, a mixture of inspirational, positive-thinking platitudes and big-business work ethic, was his compromise in late middle age. It was a set of nebulous Christian beliefs honoring the virtues of patriotism and capitalist zeal as much as God and church, and leaving plenty of guiltless room for the vagaries of private conscience. Benjamin Franklin had also championed such a religion, one that drew from "the essentials of every religion"—not to save souls but to help society found a moral consensus to establish public order. For a later erstwhile Presbyterian, Abraham Lincoln, this so-called public faith became "political religion" and was beneficial mainly in helping to form character. In this version of nondenominational Protestantism, religion was a form of moral excellence.

Yet this distinctly American transmutation of Calvinism was still capable of considerable righteous passion. There were plenty of enemies to consign to hellfire. Surprisingly, though, the *RD*'s most celebrated campaign during the fifties was directed not against Communists, bureaucrats, or Democrats, but against King Tobacco. It was also a textbook illustration of why and how the magazine fastened on some issues and not others to garner publicity. Like government waste or illiteracy, smoking was something that almost all Americans—smokers included—could agree was bad in principle. The only question was how bad. The answer allowed the *Digest* to take the moral high ground without a lot of exertion and to sensationalize its findings with little fear of being publicly refuted or embarrassed.

Furthermore, spokesmen for the tobacco industry, like those in government or education, were inevitably cast in the thankless position of having to defend the seemingly indefensible. It was clever, circulation-building strategy, and the obverse of the *Digest*'s cheerful promotion of self-evident worthwhile goals—keeping young mentally, getting the most out of sex, paying fewer taxes.

Finally, cigarettes were to Wally what liquor had been to his father. But the son's was a bogus Calvinism preached merely for the consumption of a conservative readership predisposed not to smoke to begin with—just as it was also predisposed not to drink, covet a neighbor's wife, or break any of the other commandments that Wally treated with such cavalier neglect.

Around this time Wally gave an interview in which he admitted that the magazine had been vociferously anti–New Deal, but adding, "[The *RD*] will be anti-Republican, too, if we ever get a Republican administration. . . . It's the business of a magazine in a democracy like America to be critical of whatever government is in power."

But the *Digest* could no more be anti-Republican than be pro-Communist. It threw its support behind Eisenhower wholeheartedly, devoting five articles to sing his praises in 1951, and the following year it all but endorsed the Eisenhower-Nixon ticket by running four articles by or in favor of the Republican candidate, and none by or about his Democratic challenger, Adlai Stevenson. It also published its first article on Nixon, "I Say He's a Wonderful Guy," by the vice-presidential candidate's wife, Pat. In the October 1952 issue the *Digest* joined with Nixon to place on Truman's doorstep all the bad press McCarthyism was getting. If McCarthyism was bad, it quoted Nixon as saying, Truman was to blame because he did not cooperate with HUAC and that had led to McCarthyism in the first place.

In November, the month of the election, the *Digest* returned to the still-potent issue of subversion and ran a long interview with Nixon about the trial of Hiss and Communists in the government.

In the final months of the campaign, Al Cole summoned direct-mail wizard Walter Weintz into his office.

"How would you like to take three months' sabbatical from the *Reader's Digest* and work for the Citizens for Eisenhower Committee?" Cole asked.

"I wouldn't like it," replied Weintz, who was a Taft enthusiast. "I wouldn't like it at all."

"I knew you would," said Cole. "I told them you were going to volunteer. Here's the name of the guy to report to. Go down there and get to work right away."

Weintz went down to Washington and "volunteered" to work for the Republican Citizens for Eisenhower Committee. The party's political operatives had chosen "Time for a change" as the campaign slogan. But businessmen were complaining about high taxes, and consumer groups were protesting the cost of living. Cole told Weintz, "There ought to be a campaign theme which will work better than any other theme. Do a test."

Weintz tested ten letters, ranging from "Time for a change" to "Throw the rascals out." One letter pulled three times more than the others, and its theme was Korea—specifically, that it was time to do something to end the two-year-old war, which had already resulted in nearly 150,000 American casualties (and more than a million South Korean casualties). The results were so impressive that Walter Thayer, the head of the Citizens for Eisenhower Committee, flew out to see the candidate. Tests conducted by George Gallup had been saying the same thing, but Weintz's test helped Eisenhower make up his mind. The following week he delivered his dramatic "I shall go to Korea," speech in which he promised to end the deadlock—armistice negotiations were then at an impasse. That speech, if there was ever any doubt, secured his victory.

As its support for Eisenhower demonstrated, the *Digest*'s political outlook, though ideologically right-wing, was not inflexible. Impatient with sustained argument and debate, Wally the pragmatist was more interested in results than in doctrinal purity. The *RD* continued to reflect his lifelong penchant for a "cross-examination" of the issues of the day—for example, by running articles supporting the United Nations and for a time even a few favoring foreign-aid programs. The magazine also showed sympathy toward such objects of McCarthyite suspicion as George Kennan, author with Secretary of State Acheson of the U.S. policy of "containing" the Soviet threat, particularly in Korea. And after the Atomic Energy Commission removed the security clearance of Robert Oppenheimer, "father of the atomic bomb," branding him a security risk, he received moral—if not editorial—support from none other than Paul Palmer. On April 13, 1954, during the height of the McCarthy witch-hunt, Palmer wrote to Oppenheimer, saying he had the "highest regard" for his integrity and adding, "The ordeal which you are undergoing can have only one *just* result—the complete vindication of your good name."

Among other things, the *Digest* proposed self-government for Washington, D.C., statehood for Alaska, and repeal of the Connally amendment, restricting American participation in the World Court. It supported reapportionment and defended civilian control of the Joint Chiefs of Staff. For a time it even came out strongly in favor of First Amendment rights and opposed censorship, proposed higher salaries for federal officials and military personnel, and called for more spending on national parks and federal aid for the improvement of natal care.

Yet all that was to change. As the fifties turned into the sixties and the *Digest* deepened its opposition to labor unions, it finally declared that antitrust laws were passé, complained about the many investigations into big business, and opposed federal aid to education, to highways, to slum clearance, to urban renewal— in fact, to anything. It also fought Social Security (and, later, Medicare). Another favorite longtime target of the *Digest* was the post office. As always, an almost monthly theme was federal waste and inefficiency, mounting national debt, and uncontrolled spending—all of which threatened to bring about national disaster and infringe on civil liberties. Between November 1944 and November 1965, it published more than three hundred variations on that theme alone.

Even the *Digest*'s filler material was often politically tilted, reinforcing favorite biases: "While you're reading these two lines, the U.S. Government will have spent $110,000—if you're a fast reader." "Bureaucracy is a giant mechanism operated by pygmies." "Our Federal Government probably spends as much accidentally now as it did on purpose 30 years ago."

Nor did a *Digest* article necessarily end with its appearance in the magazine. Many enjoyed an afterlife in reprint form. At two cents each, about a million reprints were sold every month, many of them political in nature.

The sea change in the *Digest*'s attitude toward labor unions is illustrative. Though always suspicious of unions as hotbeds of radicalism, the *Digest* had run ten articles generally friendly toward them between 1945 to 1952, plus another eight that were neutral and only nine openly critical. But from 1953 onward—when charges of corruption began to be leveled in the press against the newly elected Teamsters president, Dave Beck—the proportions changed, with only eight friendly and five neutral articles over the next dozen years, compared with forty-nine that were critical. One-fourth of those articles contained attacks on Jimmy Hoffa, Beck's successor. Many of the hostile articles were written by the *Digest*'s "labor specialist," roving editor Leslie Velie, who had previously worked for the *Journal of Commerce*. Hostility toward the unions was also evident in the *Digest*'s articles on antitrust and right-to-work laws. Invariably, any position taken by the AFL-CIO was opposed by Pleasantville.

For obvious reasons, then, Eisenhower was careful, throughout his two terms, to maintain a cordial relationship with the man whose magazine reached more Republican voters than any other publication. When Wally fell ill shortly after the 1952 inauguration, Ike wrote him a get-well note. Later that year the president hosted a stag dinner party for American business, labor, publishing, and education leaders. Among those in attendance was DeWitt Wallace, making his first visit to the White House.

During the two Eisenhower administrations, the *Digest* published a total of fifty-eight articles either bylined by or extolling members of his cabinet and staff. Only eighteen were critical, mostly concerning foreign aid or defense. The majority were general rather than specific in their criticisms.

In January 1956 the *Digest*'s lead article was "Run Again, Ike," even though in the interim Eisenhower had suffered a heart attack. Taking note of the article, *New York Times* columnist James Reston quoted the gist of its argument: "Many people have the idea that an attack of heart trouble incapacitates a man for further active life. And many people have the idea that the Presidency is a 'mankiller.' Both ideas are gross exaggerations."

Reston admitted he was impressed by the *Digest*'s homework on heart attacks. He further conceded that a case could be made that a four-hour day by Ike was better than a twelve-hour day by Adlai Stevenson, who was running against Eisenhower a second time. The main question, however, was "what kind of President he will be from his sixty-sixth to his seventieth years; not whether the Presidency can be made over to fit the President, but whether the President is fit enough after a heart attack to worry through the inevitable crises of the next four years; not whether we like Ike, but whether we love our country." Quoting from a novel by J. B. Priestley called *Rain upon Godshill,* Reston pointedly concluded, "The dangerous man is not the critic but the noisy, empty 'patriot' who encourages us to indulge in orgies of self-congratulation and wishful-thinking."

But wishful thinking was at the very heart of Wally's and the *Digest*'s credo. Later that year he joined Norman Vincent Peale, Harry Emerson Fosdick, and fifty-two other prominent, if somewhat naive, conservative Americans in an open letter to "The Perplexed among Communists," suggesting that they manfully examine their consciences in light of Nikita Khrushchev's recent denunciation of Stalin's crimes: "To err is human. But it is shameful to go on in an evil course and to persist in the betrayal of man's highest ideals, simply because one lacks the courage to go to the bottom and uncover the source of fatal error."

A measure of the esteem both Wally and the *Digest* enjoyed in the public imagination in the fifties was his inclusion in a list of "the world's 100 most important people," from a book by Donald Robinson excerpted in *Look*. In no other decade would either the man or the institution have made the final cut.

—

IN THE forties and early fifties, the *Digest* was supportive, if wary, of the growing but still largely quiescent civil-rights movement. It called for better education, equal opportunity, and greater dignity for the Negro, even though it also frequently expressed the fear that his natural "aggressiveness" might get out of control. By the midfifties, however, as the South seethed with turmoil in the wake of the Supreme Court's historic *Brown* v. *Board of Education* decision, in 1954, to desegregate schools, the rate of articles sympathetic to segregationists sharply increased and was not to abate for more than a decade. Even after Eisenhower in 1957 ordered federal troops into Little Rock, Arkansas, to protect Negro students attempting to enter the public schools, the *Digest* still insisted that "responsible Southerners" would oppose integration until "the moral standards of the white and Negroes, as groups, [were] brought much nearer the same level."

The *Digest* even tried to portray the country's most visible and militant bigot, Arkansas governor Orval Faubus, as a man who "truly likes Negroes." Eisenhower had acted only after Faubus brought the issue of desegregation to a head by calling out the National Guard to prevent Negro students from entering the public schools. Moreover, said the *Digest,* "they like him," and Little Rock had a reputation as "a good town for Negroes."

The only protest against the *RD*'s patronizing attitude came from the colored, as blacks were then called. In the late fifties Wally invited Walter White, executive director of the National Association for the Advancement of Colored People, to lunch at the Guest House. Surrounded by the usual group of editors, Wally stated that the magazine had carried more articles—all originals—than had any other major publication to celebrate the accomplishments of nonwhites. He then cited a number of articles from a prepared list.

White agreed but pointed out that all the stories were of achievements in obvious fields where there was no wall of prejudice but a long period of acceptance of the colored—as actors and athletes, for example. The magazine had failed to publicize colored persons who had made good in business, medicine, and other fields where bigotry was still rife. Wally claimed that the *Digest* would profile any prominent colored businessman or doctor if one could be found.

Later, White arranged for Wally to have lunch with William Johnson, the black publisher of *Ebony* and *Jet* magazines. At the time the latter was turning a profit of $20,000 an issue. White proposed Johnson as an example of a nonwhite succeeding in a field dominated by whites. Not only that, but he had an inspirational, *Digest*-like story to tell. Lacking a college education, he borrowed funds to start up the magazine from his mother, almost the way Wally did, and set up his office in an abandoned Chicago funeral home. A writer was assigned to the story, but the piece did not work out. Not until many years later was the foremost black publisher in the country finally profiled in the pages of the *Digest*.

There was a footnote to the story. In 1942 John H. Johnson, William's father, had launched a publication called the *Negro Digest* selling for three dollars a year, or twenty-five cents a copy, just like the RD. He also copied the *Digest*'s format and design, but for all that the ND went virtually unnoticed, even though contributors had included journalist Marquis Childs, Carl Sandburg, Langston Hughes, and labor leader John L. Lewis.

There were two things that distinguished the *Negro Digest* from the *Reader's Digest*. First, it printed few condensations. Most articles were complete reproductions from both the white and the black press, or even from scholarly publications. Second, the *Negro Digest* was not simplistically upbeat but spoke to an audience that was angry, disillusioned, and disappointed. As Johnson sadly observed, "You couldn't digest that world without digesting the frustration and anger."

In 1947 the *Digest* reprinted one of the *ND*'s editorials, "Time to Count Our Blessings," a rare upbeat exception, which Pleasantville, guardian of the status quo, was quick to capitalize on. Stanley High went out to Chicago to negotiate a price. "What about $500?" he asked. Johnson was shocked into silence, having no idea the *Digest* paid that much for articles. But High misinterpreted the silence and said, "What about $1,000? Would that be all right?" Johnson said yes. High reached into his pocket and pulled out two checks, one for $500 and one for $1,000. Handing over the $1,000, he returned the other to his pocket with a smile.

———

ALL during the fifties the *Digest* continued to involve its readers in fashioning the editorial content of the magazine to a degree unprecedented in the history of publishing, and also to reward them financially to the point that all the contests and questionnaires began to resemble a lottery—which, of course, was the point. One contest, offering $25,000 in prize money, invited postwar Americans to propose ideas for new businesses. Out of 49,000 submissions, 175 were chosen. (Among the suggestions for entrepreneurial readers: hair curling and gadget inventing.)

In February 1955 the *Digest* announced its biggest contest yet for readers, this time offering $2,500 "for unique and authentic personal-experience stories similar in quality and interest" to "Protection for a Tough Racket," by Cordelia Baird Gross, an account of a substitute teacher in New York who by day taught in a school for problem children and by night worked in a nightclub. But the contest seemed less an effort to find interesting tales of ordinary people than a pretext to generate reader interest in celebrity autobiography, since professionals were also allowed to enter.

By the time the contest closed, the *Digest* was swamped with more than seventy thousand manuscripts from all parts of the world. Only thirty-five were published. William Jennings Bryan, Jr., was the first to see his authentic personal experience published, with "My Japanese Brother," followed by *Saturday Evening Post* veteran Nina Wilcox Putnam, with "The Day I Went Fishing with Grover Cleveland." Other winning notables included novelists Mary Ellen Chase and Jerome Weidman and Brigadier General Robert L. Scott, Jr. When the celebrity quotient was factored in, a contestant's chances of getting published became virtually nil.

In addition to contests, the *Digest* loved gore and published it frequently in the kind of explicit detail conspicuously lacking in its articles on sex. In "Once 'Executed,' He Came Back to Save a Nation," a Guatemalan doctor related the massacre of twenty-six political prisoners by the reigning dictator, who then ordered their bodies to be dumped in a charnel-house morgue. Incredibly, doctors later found three of the men still alive and risked their own lives to save them. One became the president of Guatemala. Even that did not top one of the goriest articles in *Digest* history—a 1938 offering called "I Saw a Man Electrocuted," which gave an explicit verbal portrait of the "broiling" of a human being.

———

IF THERE was a worm in Pleasantville's barrel full of American wholesomeness in the fifties, it was the editorial unrest among the *RD*'s international editions. A record of that unrest can be found in a highly secret file, buried deep in the company's archives, that none but a very few have ever been allowed to see. The file consists of approximately two hundred pages—mostly letters and memos between the editors and business managers in the United States and their counterparts in Europe and Asia.

"This document reflected an ongoing quarrel in Pleasantville," according to an editor who has seen the material, "like a discussion in the Vatican about whether the pope was the vicar of God. The bone of contention, and the subject of memo after memo and back-stabbing after back-stabbing, was whether or not the overseas *Digest* should be a faithful reflection of the U.S. edition. It was a control frenzy, mainly by the business people but also by the editors, most of them wanting to keep the colonies down.

"On the other side were the liberators, the emancipators, the grantors of self-governance. They argued that the colonies would flourish better if they were not nailed down and controlled from Pleasantville. Of course, one of the reasons the *Digest* was able to plant itself so successfully in Europe was that it went in right behind the bayonets of the U.S. army. Europe had no paper and we were able to use the paper stocks of the army."

The editorial side considered Dennis McEvoy—then still serving the *Digest* in Japan—a maverick. "At first, because his star was high in the heavens, there was nothing ad hominem. It was all vague stuff about principle. But as he got drunker and drunker, and they needed him less, the memos got much more personal. As soon as possible, they wanted to get rid of him and put the Japanese edition back on orthodox lines." The unorthodoxy of which the Japanese edition was guilty consisted of the occasional article that promoted not the American but the Japanese way of life.

That early revolt in the *Digest's* provinces in the first half of the fifties was thoroughly suppressed, though the question of editorial independence versus centralized control continued to be a sore point and struck at the very heart of the magazine's identity.

The *Digest's* neurotic fear of subversives during the McCarthy years and its relentless celebration of American heroes and institutions during the Eisenhower administration were clear reflections of the philosophy that the American way of life was the best. Inevitably, as the magazine grew in popularity and was exported around the world, Wally and his principal associates came to feel that they were charged with a larger mandate to define, preserve, defend, and publicize the American way of life—much as the Bible did for the Christian way. As many a company executive was later to assert, the story of the *Reader's Digest* in the colonies was every bit as important as that in the home office—if not more so—because the international editions carried the *Digest* gospel around the world and eventually also earned more than half the profit.

The magazine's chief enforcer of American purity of values abroad continued to be Barclay Acheson, who had once claimed that the average dictator in a banana republic possessed greater nobility of soul than the average U.S. political boss. His indefatigable assistant, Marvin Lowes, made more than fifty trips abroad, helping to set up the international editions.

In 1948, in direct response to widespread fears that Italy would fall to the Communists in the elections, the *Digest* started up an Italian edition, *Selezione del Reader's Digest.* Curiously, the managing director of the new edition was not an Italian but Terence Harmon, a former British intelligence officer who had been named editor of the British edition right after the war. A hard-drinking intellectual who boasted that he drank gin in "industrial quantities," Harmon had served as liaison officer with the OSS and was now in a unique position to utilize *Selezione* as a conduit for anti-Communist propaganda originating from both the American and the European intelligence communities. The editor, Mario Ghisalberti, had previously worked for Mondadori, Italy's largest publisher.

Selezione very quickly reached a circulation of 400,000, then 750,000, and in a by now familiar scenario became the country's most widely circulated magazine—though it was frequently denounced by the powerful Italian Communist party as a fascist publication and an instrument of American imperialism. According to some leftist critics, the 1948 Italian campaign marked the first time the Central Intelligence Agency, founded only the year before, got involved in large-scale political propaganda.

Paris was the hub of the *Digest's* international empire, its own cosmopolitan version of Pleasantville. By now, under ex-general Paul Thompson, *Sélection* was the best-selling magazine in France; the book club was equally successful. The Paris bureau was also the central clearinghouse for articles originated in Europe for other foreign editions, and it remained the most popular of all stopover points for Digesters abroad. Given all this activity, and with the difficult start-up years behind him, Thompson felt it was time for *Sélection* to find a permanent home.

The faded mansion on the boulevard Saint-Germain was still owned by the former countess de Vere, who had now remarried an American businessman and resided permanently in New York. As a result, she expressed a willingness to sell. Thompson had the building appraised for the equivalent of $2 million. However, he was not aware of the disinclination prevalent in Pleasantville to own property. The purchase of land in downtown Tokyo had been an exception occasioned by the blockage of currency—a situation that did not pertain in France. In his ignorance Thompson offered the countess—now the very wealthy Mrs. Moffat—$106,000.

As soon as she accepted the offer, he cabled Acheson with the news. Acheson phoned immediately, advising Thompson that he had to renege on the deal, because Wally did not desire to buy that or any other building but only wanted Thompson to devote all his energies to getting the circulation of *Sélection* up to one million.

Thompson said he had shaken hands on the deal and could not go back on it—that if Wally wanted to reverse the deal, he would have to hire a new manager. Acheson later called back and agreed to the purchase. At the closing in June 1950, Al Cole went over to represent the home office. In his pocket was $106,000 in traveler's checks.

Among those employed by *Sélection* to translate U.S. articles into French at the rate of two dollars a page was a young Irishman named Sam Beckett. Maurice Chevalier was also once hired by the Paris editor, to translate Billy Rose's Broadwayese, turning "It was a cinch bet" into "C'était du nougat."

11

"—And Sudden Death"

IN THE SPRING of 1957 Paul Thompson was summoned to Pleasantville to replace the aging Barclay Acheson as director of international
editions. Only recently the two men had cooperated in the launching
of an overseas military edition for U.S. armed forces and their depen-
dents in all theaters. For the ex–brigadier general, however, the promotion was a mixed blessing. In France he enjoyed an American salary
and expense account with numerous tax breaks, a cosmopolitan life-
style, and a corporate independence unique in the *Digest* empire. Not
only did he have a summerhouse near Cannes, but as manager of
international editions he traveled all over the world the year round
without having to answer to Monday-morning quarterbacks in the
home office.

Horrified at the prospect of relocating from the capital of Europe to
a suburban backwater outside New York, Thompson's wife, Friedel,
pleaded with him not to accept. Thompson, though, knew that he had
no choice—that if he refused a promotion, it would be only a matter
of time before he found himself working for someone who used to
report to him.

Many in the rank and file were not looking forward to Thompson's
arrival. Among them was John S. Zinsser, Jr., an editor who worked in
the international division of Condensed Books back in Pleasantville.
The opera-loving, multilingual Zinsser thought the ex-general was a
pushy social climber who could not speak French. Worst of all,
though, for Zinsser and many others, was Thompson's fondness for
writing everything down on his blackboard during a meeting, as if he
were mapping strategy for an assault on a beachhead.

At the conclusion of each meeting, Thompson put everyone's initials on the board and asked a secretary to come in and take a photograph of the final battle plan. Zinsser thought it was all too "nerve-wracking."

The Thompsons moved into a luxurious Italianate villa facing the green and pleasant RDA campus. Its former occupants were Fred and Judy Thompson, and Lila herself had helped design the formal garden in back and plant wisteria. But Paul Thompson soon discovered that he had a more serious problem than the lack of a good office blackboard in his new headquarters. The seventy-year-old Dr. Acheson had no intention of giving up his seat as director of international operations. The younger man settled into a smaller office next door and chafed. Several months went by before he decided he had enough and brought matters to a head by confronting Wally.

Over a series of meetings in the executive dining room, the two discussed his predicament. Acheson also sat in. Privately, the new director thought that his predecessor-to-be had a few good qualities but that his chief asset was being Lila's brother. Forthright and direct in classic military fashion, Thompson made it clear to both men that he had not come over to be Acheson's assistant. Wally, who hated confrontation, cringed. He suggested a compromise.

"We'll make Barclay chairman," he proposed.

Thompson refused to go along. "No," he said, "I want the job that I came here for. But if you change your mind, I understand that, too."

Acheson did finally move out, though Wally insisted on giving him the honorary title of chairman of the international editions. Some months afterward, just before Christmas, he died of a cerebral hemorrhage while shoveling snow. After a frantic search, Acheson's daughter and son-in-law were located in a nightclub in Havana, while Lila and Wally were reached in Palm Beach. On the Saturday after Acheson's death, his body was taken from the undertaker's parlor in Pleasantville to the library of the *Digest* headquarters for a final viewing. The following Monday a memorial service was held in the chapel of Union Theological Seminary, in New York.

Acheson's daughter Judy had always been horrified that her parents spent a lifetime groveling before Lila and her powerful husband De-Witt—that Pat and Barclay "got down on their bellies and crawled before the Wallaces." Judy even admitted doing the same thing herself.

And it was true that all his life Barclay Acheson was in the habit of writing obsequious notes and letters to his sister and brother-in-law, thanking them for year-end bonuses, extra vacation time, profit sharing, special additional bonuses. Like the lowliest sycophant, he expressed his gratitude for their confidence in him and praised Wally's "inspired" editorial policies. He told the Wallaces that the *Reader's Digest* was much more than a magazine—that it was "a great crusade for the finest of American traditions." He expressed "measureless admiration" for Wally's "sanity and genius."

But somehow, according to Judy Thompson, he found the strength to regain his self-respect shortly before he passed away. Even though Lila finally "broke" him, Judy claimed, he found the means to break with his sister for the last two weeks of his life.

One reason Lila treated her brother so imperiously, according to her niece, was the mere fact that the Wallaces lived in High Winds. Acheson called it Lila's "fairy-tale house" and said it was necessary to indulge his sister's royal self-delusions just to make her happy. Also, she disliked his wife, Pat, who had an eastern background and the kind of privileged upbringing that Lila, the preacher's kid, could only dream about. Judy claimed that Lila had once sent her mother, when she was sick in the hospital, dead flowers and stale candies.

Nor was this imperious attitude reserved for members of the Wallaces' immediate family. Lila's favorite niece was only a few years older than the *Digest* itself and from the very beginning had been able to observe the private as well as the public Wally and Lila. In Judy's view, the Wallaces were intensely jealous of other members of the family who did anything notable, exchanged personal friends often—keeping only those who were somehow useful—and were hypocritical in the way they effusively greeted guests to High Winds only to dissect them afterward with annihilating comments. Lila's favorite term of genteel disparagement was to say of a couple, "They are that kind."

What ultimately enabled Barclay Acheson to break with Lila during the last two weeks of his life and regain his self-respect was the edict to vacate his office in Pleasantville once and for all. It was an edict that could have been made only with Lila's approval. Relieved of all authority, Acheson was also relieved of any obligation to continue in his subservient relationship with his sister.

However, there were two very good reasons why Judy did not confront Lila and express the resentment she felt at watching her father abase himself over a lifetime. Like everyone else, she still expected her husband, Fred, to take over the running of the *Reader's Digest* empire, at which time she herself would be installed as the queen of High Winds. Some Digesters believed that, perhaps in anticipation of that day and to make sure it happened, she was also having a clandestine affair with Wally, a charge she denied. But it would take Judy Thompson another nine years before she learned whether her dreams about living in the Castle would come true.

Meanwhile, in time-honored Acheson tradition, Judy herself continued to shower Lila with compliments and praise. Within the year, she and Fred accepted from the Wallaces a luxurious, all-expenses-paid vacation out west. And when Pat Acheson suffered a mental breakdown soon after the passing of her husband, Judy also accepted Lila's money and went along with her instructions to put her away in a sanitarium, where she could receive no visitors and speak to no one on the phone, and whose very whereabouts was kept a secret from Pat Acheson's closest friends. It was there that she died a few years later.

Then an even stranger thing happened. From the time of his death, memories of her dead brother began to be a real presence in Lila's life and thoughts. Though they had never been especially close in life, she had always been protective of Barclay—not only because he knew how to appeal to her vanity but also because, after all, his loan of $5,000 had made all the difference in the magazine's early, vulnerable days.

Yet Barclay Acheson was a relief worker on a Presbyterian salary, and the money had actually come from his wealthy wife—and that money was no doubt the real source of friction between the two women. In any case, Lila had repaid the debt far more generously than Wally himself would have wished.

After Barclay was gone and his wife conveniently out of sight and mind, Lila's isolation increased. Now that she had everything, she began to romanticize the times when she had nothing—when she was just a PK living with her sisters and brother in a humble manse somewhere in the remote Midwest. In her fantasies, that anonymous, interchangeable domicile became her true home, the place where she had known the greatest happiness. Ultimately, that home and the ghost of her dead brother, Barclay, would take over her mind altogether.

———

AS DIRECTOR of international operations, Paul Thompson reported directly to Wally, not to Al Cole. The relationship between Cole and Thompson was barely cordial. The *Digest*'s business manager was among those who resented that a man with no business experience was put in charge of such a vital and lucrative operation. Cole had been willing to make allowances for Wally's brother-in-law, but the choice of the ex-general to succeed Acheson seemed positively perverse. Thompson was no lackey, as his predecessor had been, but headstrong, hard-driving, and ambitious—just like Cole himself, in fact, only a dozen years younger. He was also one of Lila's boys, however, and that always spelled trouble.

All those qualities, along with his new preeminence, now made Paul Thompson a potential rival of Fred Thompson—which was another reason Cole tried to distance himself from his counterpart in the international division. Cole eventually came to know about Wally's affair with Judy. So apparently did Fred Thompson himself. But neither man saw it as an obstacle to Fred's claim to the throne—unless, of course, Lila ever found out.

Moreover, not only did Cole ignore Paul Thompson; he also felt no compunction about trespassing on his turf when the mood suited him. In early 1958, less than a year after Paul Thompson had assumed his new position, Cole wrote to Wally, who was in Phoenix with Lila on vacation. Cole reported that he, Fred Thompson, and Marvin Lowes, the much traveled international troubleshooter, had recently discussed the feasibility of a Russian edition and were in favor of approaching the Kremlin again for permission.

Despite the *Digest*'s evisceration of all things Marxist-Leninist, there had been talk off and on for years in Pleasantville about doing a Russian edition of the magazine. But too many obstacles stood in the way, political and logistical. The *Digest* always went into a country first, establishing a publishing identity and building up a mailing list. Then Condensed Books and other appurtenances of a great capitalist publishing empire were gradually introduced as well.

Nor was the introduction of a Russian edition in any sense a prime example of capitalist hypocrisy—editorially attacking Communism on the one hand while trying to exploit the system economically on the other. The *Digest* took seriously its mission to preach the gospel of free enterprise and individual liberty. The countries most in need of that message were obviously those behind the Iron Curtain. But in previous requests the USSR had shown no interest in enlightening its citizens about life in the West as interpreted by its most widely read magazine.

Predictably, the proposal once again came to nothing, though perhaps the most daunting obstacle facing Cole and his capitalist minions was the mind-boggling challenge of trying to sell a direct-mail product through the antiquated Russian postal system. For that reason more than any other, enthusiasm for the project among other Digesters was always tepid at best.

There was another firing in Pleasantville around the time that Barclay Acheson was deposed, though at the opposite end of the executive corridors of power. Charlie Ferguson's oldest son, Wally, had for nearly ten years worked in the stockroom. Emotionally troubled, he had been unable to earn a high school diploma, but his retentive memory had proven useful in locating items from the *Digest*'s vast collection of printed materials.

Unfortunately, young Ferguson was often plagued by the taunts of fellow workers. Unable to endure their jeers one day, he tried to ram two stock clerks with a hand dolly and was summoned to report to the head of the department. The supervisor decided that Wally would have to be terminated. DeWitt Wallace volunteered personally to perform the delicate task.

With Charlie Ferguson sitting in, Wally explained to the young man in the kindest tones possible that he was being let go, that he would receive a substantial severance, and that the *Digest* was willing to pay for him to enter the Payne-Whitney Clinic in New York for a period of observation. After a moment the older Wally asked the younger if he had anything to say. In a clear, coherent voice, the latter asked if he could remain at the *Digest* for another two months, which would allow him to complete ten years of service and entitle him to be honored as a member of the Old Timers Club. The request was gently denied.

Charlie Ferguson, in an anguished daze, tried to make light of the situation by quoting aloud a line he remembered, attributed to George Washington Duke, father of James Buchanan Duke, founder of the tobacco fortune: "There are three things I cain't understand. E-e-lectricity, the Holy Ghost, and mah son Buck."

DeWitt broke into laughter and made a note of the line, and the two Fergusons left. The quotation made the next issue of the magazine.

Some of the editors murmured that Wallace was being hypocritical and arbitrary in discharging a troubled young man, obviously devoted to the firm, while at the same time publishing so many triumph-over-adversity articles. Unwilling to form a judgment himself about the man whom he perhaps loved more than his own son, Ferguson later asked a

New York literary agent what he thought the incident proved about Wally's character. The agent replied, "That DeWitt Wallace doesn't really give a damn about anything except the *Reader's Digest.*"

———

IN 1953 Al Cole had informed Wally, not for the first time, that he wanted to replace the company's genial but aging treasurer, Roy Abbott, the ex–trolley conductor, who was completely out of his element now that the RDA had grown into an international company. Abbott's chief asset, as even Wally agreed, was that he was married to Lila's good friend and erstwhile *Digest* decorator Dolores Risley. But getting rid of him meant putting one of Cole's men into the chief financial slot, and privately Wally did not think that was such a good thing.

The RDA's outside accountant at that time was Hunter & Weldon, a small but prestigious firm whose other clients included the 21 Club, Toots Shor's, and the Barnum & Bailey circus. Oscar Weldon was an Anglo-Egyptian with a thick accent and a broad suspicion of Al Cole because *Popular Science* was also a client. Knowing Cole's methods of operation, he privately advised Wally not to let his business manager gain control of the RDA's financial operations. Since Cole still worked for a percentage of the profits, Weldon had no doubt the former would put his own best interests first. As a result, Wally informed Cole that he would take care of hiring Abbott's replacement.

Wally and Weldon set about advertising for an accountant whom they would secretly groom as the company's first chief financial officer. The plan was Weldon's. He proposed to hire a young man who, among his other duties, would periodically visit *Digest* headquarters in Pleasantville to perform audits and other services regularly supplied by the firm of Hunter & Weldon. That way Cole and his associates would have no reason to suspect he was really completing a three-year apprenticeship that would allow him to become fully familiar both with the company's financial operations and its management. At the end of that period, Wally had the option to hire him as CFO designate.

The man chosen for the job was Richard Waters, a graduate of Harvard Business School, who had only recently been discharged from the navy. During their interview, Weldon mysteriously informed Waters of the plan without revealing the name of the company whose top financial position he stood to inherit at the end of three years. Waters was willing. Some time later the two men went up to High Winds to meet Wally, who was less than impressed by the young accountant's diffident manner, but hired him on Weldon's recommendation.

Periodically, as agreed, the lumbering, soft-spoken Waters went up to audit the RDA's books. Cole suspected nothing—nor, for that matter, did arch-spy Harry Wilcox. Waters's salary was paid out of the *Digest*'s editorial budget, whose dispersement Cole was never allowed to see. Only the editorial accountant, as Waters later learned, knew that something was fishy.

Once Waters had gained his confidence, however, Wally told him, "We have to accelerate the plan to only two years because Abbott is in failing health."

Thus in 1955 Dick Waters joined the staff as assistant treasurer. For the first few years Cole was hostile, not only because Waters was not his own man but Wally's but also because Waters was wise by now to Cole's ways of manipulating the books. Some of Cole's financial legerdemain, Waters thought, was mind-boggling—never illegal or fraudulent, but certainly leveraged to produce the highest possible bottom line. In 1960 the ulcerous Abbott finally retired from his largely honorary post, and Waters became the RDA's treasurer and first CFO.

The relationship forged over the years between Wally and Waters was in many ways to parallel that between Wally and Hobe Lewis. Waters was Wally's other surrogate son, the one being groomed to look after the business side while Lewis bided his time until he could be named editor. Waters enjoyed the full confidence not only of Wally but of Lila and advised them on their private financial affairs as well as on corporate fiscal policy.

Early on, the new CFO saw that, though Wally ran the company, Lila ran him. Waters also discovered that Wally had no concept of money, nor did he care to acquire one. If he had an idea he wanted implemented, as a courtesy he always asked Waters how much it would cost. But if Wally intended to carry his plan out anyway, Waters's advice was usually ignored. That was another lesson he learned early on: *only* Lila ran Wally.

■

BY THE early 1960s the RDA's cash-flow problems were long gone and the money was pouring in—primarily from advertising revenues, Condensed Books, and foreign editions. In all three areas, the company continued to expand at a rapid rate. But such spectacular growth also brought with it a curious qualification—Wally did not want to make any more profit than was necessary. For a company that boosted big business in a big way, it was a hell of a predicament.

Over the years, just as Wally had modified and reinvented the *Digest* to keep pace with changing times and fend off competitors, so the magazine had in a broader sense outgrown its original purpose to provide its readers merely with "an article a day of lasting interest." During the war a new and larger purpose had come into focus—to publicize and promote the American way of life throughout the world. As it gradually became the planet's most widely circulated magazine, the *Digest* also came to believe that it had an editorial mission that transcended profit.

That mission was not based on any particular utterance emanating from Wally—no sermon on Mount Pegasus, no sending forth over lunch at the Guest House—nor could it be traced back to his correspondence. There was only his exceptional example. Though he never spent much time attempting to articulate the *Digest*'s loftier goals, many of his employees tried to do so for him. Cole had been among the first, telling new employees—almost as if they were disciples— how the magazine helped people get more out of every minute, overcome adversity, and have fun in the bargain.

By the midfifties that interpretation had become familiar wisdom— one part Republican, one part nondenominational Protestant, and two parts Wally, equally the passionate pilgrim of the quotidian and the militant anti-Communist. It had also become an accepted truth in Pleasantville that not just America but the entire world needed to hear this message—that the best way to live life was the good old-fashioned American way.

None of which precluded profit, of course. But as there was enough profit to go around, it seemed pointless to Wally to make any more money than necessary for him to accomplish the remaining goals of his life. Those were, first, to put the *Reader's Digest* into every home in the world, in one language or another, just like the Bible. Already the magazine was going to one out of every four households in the United States and Canada alone and being read, according to pass-along polls, by half the populations of both countries.

Second, Wally wanted to maintain and improve the very special, if paternalistic, environment that he and Lila had created for those who worked in Pleasantville or its far-flung colonies. Finally, and increasingly important, he and Lila wished to devote far more time to their philanthropy. Though they had always been generous in giving to charity, by the late fifties the Wallaces were just on the brink of becoming major philanthropists and two of the most generous individuals of all time.

An ancillary reason for not making more profit was that Wally expected Digesters to heed the magazine's own precepts and enjoy themselves. Workaholics were still frowned on and punctuality and strict adherence to working hours encouraged. A slavish pursuit of profit meant much longer hours for everybody and a lot less fun. Wally and Lila, setting a good example, were off on a world tour by clipper to Honolulu, Hong Kong, Singapore, Bangkok, Angkor Wat, Java, Bali, Manila, and the Philippines. With them, as photographer and companion, was Wally's old friend from St. Paul, Wendell MacRae.

However, that philosophy and the company's cash-rich position also created an unusual tension. By now it had hired some of the most aggressive, ambitious, and highly paid executives in the publishing business. Though the *Digest* was expanding at a steady rate, much of that talent was being prevented from taking a quantum leap, on direct orders from the owner himself. The Reader's Digest Association was kept from making large acquisitions or from borrowing significant sums of money from banks. Perhaps still smarting from the fact that he once had to ask his brother-in-law for $5,000 to get the *Digest* under way, Wally wanted the company to be both self-sufficient and self-reliant.

Another vexing problem facing the company's financial managers was that Wally compounded his lack of interest in profit, as he got older, with an informal, one-man campaign to thwart them at every turn. As a result he allowed inefficiencies to persist indefinitely. Rivalries and intrigues on the business side of the company thus developed under hothouse conditions. Too much talent had too little to do and nowhere to go in an autocratic system ruled by two old men, Wally and Al Cole, whose hand-picked successors were widely believed to be Hobe Lewis and Fred Thompson, respectively. In May of 1959, in a marvel of condensation, Wally announced the promotion of Lewis and three other appointments in a memo that consisted of only thirty-four words:

"HL and HHH have been made Assistant Executive Editors. WBM

and WH have been made Assistant Managing Editors. There will be
no change in the chain of command: KWP

ASD

HL-HHH

WBM-WH."

Ken Payne, Fritz Dashiell, and Harry Harper (HHH) were not too far
away from retirement, and there was never any question that Bill Hard,
Jr. (WH)—as hard-drinking and -working as his name implied but
probably too old as well—was never in contention to succeed as
editor. That left only Lewis and Walter B. Mahony, Jr. (WBM), as
contenders for the editorship. As for Paul Palmer, he was plagued by
ill health. A heart attack had taken him out of the running to succeed
Wally as editor in chief.

An eastern Brahmin—graduate of Deerfield Academy and Am-
herst—"Bun" Mahony was married to a great-granddaughter of Robert E. Lee, had served in the navy during World War II, and rejoined
the *Digest* after Germany's surrender. Mahony came to the *Digest*
through his father, an editor of the *North American Review* whose certificate of indebtedness to the local Sleepy Hollow Country Club Wally
had once purchased. However, as pronounced with a long *a* and ac-
cented on the first syllable, the family's humble Irish surname had a
proper Wasp ring to it—just like that of Adrian Berwick, editor of the
international editions.

Berwick had been recommended to the *Digest* because he had once
served with the Office of Strategic Services—a background in intelligence was considered an impeccable credential at the magazine—and
because he was married to the daughter of the Rhode Island governor.
Virginia Berwick was a great beauty, but her husband presented such a
disheveled appearance that Lila found him repugnant. During the couple's mandatory interview at High Winds, Wally observed the horror
on his wife's face and right then and there offered Berwick a job.

Afterward Lila asked why in God's name Wally hired a man with
dirty fingernails. He replied that her expression seemed to be one of
great pity and compassion, to which she retorted that she was just
being polite. If she was appalled by the Beast, Wally was equally en-
chanted by the Beauty and was probably just looking for a way to avoid
his wife's veto.

Later the Wallaces learned that Berwick, a Jew, had Anglicized his
name. They found out because Berwick's mischievous brother, a

Hasid, sometimes visited the office, conspicuous in black suit and forelocks, and asked to speak to his brother. When the startled receptionist asked who that might be, he replied, "Why, Abraham Berkowitz, of course."

(Neither Mahony nor Berwick quite achieved the pure country club richness of Kent Rhodes, who had executed a complete end run around the name he was born with, Clarence Klink, as hopelessly unsalvageable.)

Though scorned by many of his fellow workers, who considered him punctilious and mean spirited, Mahony nonetheless rose quickly up the editorial ranks by dint of his reputation as a conscientious, productive editor and his extreme loyalty to the Wallaces. Insofar as the *Digest* during the Eisenhower years was becoming formulaic and predictable, Mahony would have done a creditable job as the magazine's ultimate civil servant. But insofar as Wally, now seventy, and his wife doted on Lewis and looked upon him as a surrogate son, the editorial succession was an all but foregone conclusion.

Nevertheless, the company's hands-off approach to big profits gave the various departments within the RDA an unusual organic quality. Almost everything was homegrown—developed in Pleasantville, or very occasionally abroad, and sold through direct mail worldwide. The most important new profit center to emerge—and Al Cole's last major contribution to the company—was the establishment in 1959 of a department to sell long-playing, high-fidelity phonograph records in supermarkets and through direct mail. The idea originated with RCA, which wanted to market generic classical music, popular masterpieces identified by composer but not by performing artist.

The original proposal called for the release of a new record each month by a composer featured in the *Digest*. That idea proved impractical, and it was later decided to create a set of twenty-eight records and sell them in 200,000 grocery stores, 7,000 record stores, and through direct mail.

Cole appointed one of his brightest stars, the mercurial Walter J. Hitesman, to head the new department. Hitesman had taken over the Canadian operation after Fred Thompson was recalled to become advertising director. Except for Thompson, no one enjoyed Cole's favor or confidence more. Hitesman later regretted having gotten involved with RCA, and the partnership was eventually dissolved.

But Music & Records proved dramatically successful, with offerings ranging from *Festival of Light Classical Music* to *Joyous Music for Christmas Time.* In short order, M & R became the company's third-largest money-maker, after Condensed Books and the magazine itself. Later the RDA purchased the assets of RCA Victor's Record Club from the Book-of-the-Month Club and formed a new subsidiary, Reader's Digest Music, Inc.

There were also a few flops, some of them embarrassing to younger executives. A notable failure in 1955 was *TV Reader's Digest,* a weekly half-hour dramatization on ABC based on articles published in the magazine and sponsored by the Studebaker-Packard Corporation. The first episode to be shown, "Last of the Old Time Shooting Sheriffs," from an old Cleveland Amory article, was panned by the *New York Times,* whose reviewer regretted the lack of "qualitative similarity" between series and magazine. Other segments fared no better, and the program was canceled. Later, when Cole proposed that the RDA get involved in something still in the planning stage called cable television, Wally turned him down flat.

Around this time, too, the RDA became embroiled in a curious squabble with its neighbors in Westchester County regarding two fifty-foot billboards lit by floodlights that it proposed to mount on the high ground overlooking the Saw Mill River Parkway. The company thought the signs were an appropriate way to announce the site as the location of the *Reader's Digest* world headquarters, which was second only to IBM as Westchester County's biggest employer.

But local residents said that the signs were advertising—and also very ugly. Curiously, the *Digest* was one of the most outspoken critics of billboard advertising in the country and repeatedly called for the banning of this blight on the nation's highways. Now it not only wanted to join the billboard brigade but chose a particularly scenic stretch of highway to blight. Furthermore, the signs would have detracted from the landscaped grounds and attractive Colonial lines of the headquarters building itself.

The RDA was persistent. After being routinely turned down by the local zoning board on a technicality, it appealed. Local opposition solidified. Neighboring property owners claimed that the signs would "Bronxize" the area. Harry Wilcox asked that the application be amended—to call not for two lighted signs but for one unlighted sign—to meet zoning regulations, then requested a month's postponement. But the appeals board threw out the request, and the issue was dropped.

Not long thereafter, with nary a blush, the *Digest* was back in the business of billboard bashing, urging its readers to complain to their state legislators to protest "billboard slums," which were a national disgrace and a "public nuisance." It was a proposal that many in Westchester seconded and whose espousal by the *Digest* some no doubt thought hypocritical under the circumstances.

———

HYPOCRISY was also at the heart of a much larger issue that the *Digest* had yet to come to terms with, and that was why it accepted advertising for tobacco products in its foreign editions, while the U.S. edition not only refused such advertising but continued to attack the tobacco industry with the zeal usually reserved for its assaults on Communists and subversives.

So persistent was the grumbling, both within the advertising community and among nonsmokers in Pleasantville, that on April 21, 1958, Wally sent a memo to his editorial staff that addressed the *Digest*'s apparent compromise of its integrity. In the memo he blamed any adverse publicity for the magazine, as a result of its policy, squarely on the "ineptitude" of Digesters who did not understand that editorial integrity was in danger of being compromised only if advertising considerations affected editorial content. It would be a serious mistake for any edition of the *RD* abroad to drop an article on cigarette smoking, said Wally, "*if* the piece [was] applicable, lest the article offend cigarette advertisers." To make sure no foreign edition acted unilaterally, he reaffirmed Pleasantville's authority to decide the matter in each instance.

Moreover, Wally added, cigarette smoking was not a "moral issue"—even though, as early as 1952, the magazine itself had claimed that tobacco manufacturers were selling "cancer by the carton." Rather, he insisted only that smoking was an "injurious habit" whose "evil effects on the individual and on his family and in the community generally [were] not to be compared with alcoholism." He continued, "Yet there is no suggestion that liquor advertising be barred from RDIE."

But the pressure from within and without, including the increasingly vocal health lobby, continued to mount. In May 1962 the *Digest* finally announced that its international editions would no longer accept cigarette advertising. The announcement coincided with the publication in the June issue of "Lung Cancer and Cigarettes," which summarized a recent report by the British Royal College of Physicians on smoking and health. The article flatly declared, "Cigarette smoking is a cause of lung cancer and bronchitis, and probably contributes to the development of coronary heart disease and various less common diseases."

The *Digest*'s double standard when it came to billboards and cigarette advertising was mirrored by the sanctimoniousness of its leadership in the area of personal morality. Obviously, the RDA was no different from any other large, sequestered corporation where men and women found themselves spending more time with a secretary or boss than with their respective spouse or lover. But the RDA was also the only *Fortune* 500–size company—it would have ranked 220th if it had been publicly traded—whose foundation rested on the promotion of the wholesome family values that many of its top editors and upper-level executives had flouted from the very beginning.

Two old-timers of unquestionable rectitude, however, were Ralph Henderson and Al Cole. The company's business manager was its pillar of integrity, both personally and professionally. Though not a near-mythic figure like Wally, he was the one person above all others whom Digesters could and did point to as a shining *Digest* success story—an executive who had worked his way up from the very lowest rung—and who was a walking art-of-living article. About the only negative thing people said about Al Cole was that he did not like to spend one more minute than necessary with people who were not members of a small, exclusive group of rich and mostly Republican CEOs, State Department officials, and others in the business, publishing, and political establishment. Cole enjoyed rubbing shoulders with men who ruled empires, and in his last decade that was to become a considerable source of personal and corporate friction. Not hypocrisy but hubris was his abiding sin.

Yet even Cole had approved some questionable business practices, among them Condensed Books's nonreturnable box for returning books in. Eventually, subscriber complaints forced the company to provide a carton with instructions for reuse that were not more complicated than the plot of the novels it contained. Cole further permitted the circulation department to send an announcement to readers whose subscriptions were expiring, informing them their subscriptions would be automatically renewed if an enclosed card specifically instructing Pleasantville to cancel was not received. Moreover, said the promotion piece, the magazine was being offered to subscribers at the "greatly reduced" price of $2.97 per year.

Unwitting subscribers who tossed the notice into the wastebasket without reading it soon began to receive invoices, in addition to their renewed subscription. Dunning notices—a series of twelve in all—were sent to those who did not pay. The first nine were from the *Digest* and the last three from the Mail Order Credit Reporting Association. Eventually, the Federal Trade Commission filed suit against the *Digest,* claiming that subscribers who did not actively renew had in fact not renewed; that the greatly reduced price was the standard subscription price; that the credit rating of nonpaying nonrenewers would not suffer as threatened; and that the Mail Order Credit Reporting Association did not exist. The *RD* later agreed to discontinue the practice.

UNDER Paul Thomspon the *Digest's* international editions also continued to flourish. Paul Zimmerman, a Thompson protégé, oversaw the thriving English-language Canadian edition, while the Japanese and Australian editions reached the half-million mark in circulation. Meanwhile, the London office was working on the "one-shot of the decade," the *Reader's Digest Great World Atlas,* destined to sell in the millions. The book was a first because the concept originated with the London office, not Pleasantville, though Eduardo Cárdenas had published almanacs and similar books for Spanish-speaking readers out of his office in the Chrysler Building.

British Digesters also did the market testing and oversaw artwork. From its inception, because of the common language, the British Digesters displayed more of those good old-fashioned American virtues of self-reliance and independence, and were less susceptible to being treated like children, than non-English-language editors. One British marketing expert, a hard-driving Scotsman named Jack O'Hara, showed such promise that Paul Thompson had him transferred to the home office.

In October 1961 the new Canadian headquarters in Montreal were opened and Wally gave a rare speech, in which he claimed that the *Digest* was the only truly international magazine, published in thirteen languages and circulating in every free nation. "There must be a reason for this phenomenal acceptance," said Wally, going on to enumerate many—notably, that the *RD* chronicled the "stirring achievements and

significant developments in every vital field," illustrated the self-poten-
tial of men and women, and, more than any other mass-circulation
magazine, exposed the evils of communism while portraying the blessings of the free-economy system.

The only serious setback on the international front was due to
circumstances beyond the company's control. In June 1960 Cuba's
new premier, Fidel Castro, confiscated $1.6 million worth of *Digest*
equipment at its Havana plant, which was responsible for printing the
entire Spanish-language edition for Latin America. ("Remember the
26th of July!," published in the April 1959 edition of the *Digest,* only
months after the downfall of Cuban dictator Fulgencio Batista, was
roving editor Georgette ["Dickey"] Chapelle's valentine to the "Castro
movement.") Only the year before, Castro had personally awarded
medals to Herbert L. Matthews of the *New York Times,* Chapelle, and
other credulous journalists who had served virtually as his personal
propagandists in the U.S. media.

Unlike Matthews, however, who in 1967 retired from the *Times* still
refusing to believe that Castro was a Communist, Chapelle was by
February 1961 charging in *Selecciones* that the new Cuban leader was a
Soviet puppet. The people who put out the Latin American edition of
the *RD* had good reason to be upset. The state-of-the-art Goss press
that Castro grabbed was scarcely out of its wrapping. Despite the loss,
Selecciones was back on the newsstands within months—thanks to Kent
Rhodes's iron-fisted efficiency—after headquarters were quickly relocated to Mexico City.

BESIDES the magazine, Condensed Books, international editions, long-
playing records, and the occasional Al Cole brainstorm, there were
other divisions within the RDA empire that both earned a respectable
profit and tried to fulfill the *Digest*'s mission to reach everyone, including those just learning to read and the blind. The educational edition
had a circulation greater than that of the *New Yorker* or the *Atlantic
Monthly,* while the Braille edition, begun in 1928 and supported by the
Reader's Digest Fund for the Blind, was now published not only in
English but also in Japanese, Spanish, Swedish, and German.

For the benefit of blind people who did not read Braille, the company also cooperated with the American Printing House for the Blind
in making twelve long-playing records for each issue of the magazine,

which it distributed to twenty-eight libraries chosen by the Library of Congress nationally and to seventy-two homes and social clubs for the blind. In addition, the *Digest* donated thousands of free subscriptions to federal and state prisons and other correctional and charitable organizations.

All of this hard work, despite its founder's admonition not to make too much profit, paid off handsomely. On July 18, 1960, the *New York Times* reported that the circulation of the *Reader's Digest* had reached 12 million, "the highest in the history of magazine publishing." The three distant runners-up were *Life,* the *Saturday Evening Post,* and *Look.*

The *Digest*'s growth was all the more remarkable insofar as 1961 witnessed the worst recession since World War II. Magazine publishers were particularly hard hit. Uniformly increasing sales and profit seemed things of the past, and rising costs made it difficult for many publishers just to break even. The main culprit was competition from television for advertising revenue. Time Inc. was showing only a minimal profit. Cowles and *Look* were also faltering, while Curtis Publishing was struggling to save the *Saturday Evening Post,* due to debut in a new format in mid-September. *McCall's* had bought the *Saturday Review* for about $3 million, but *McCall's* itself was 41 percent owned by Hunt Foods and Industries, a conglomerate, and that was another ominous trend.

The biggest news in publishing was the announcement by Esquire Inc. that it was negotiating to sell *Coronet,* whose circulation still stood at a healthy 3 million. But the magazine was plagued by rising costs. When the end came and *Coronet* ceased publication, the *Digest* bought its subscription list. Seemingly, all roads leading to and from Pleasantville were paved with gold. No wonder Wally could afford to be so casual about profit!

———

PAUL THOMPSON'S first cousin was Barry Goldwater, Republican senator from Arizona and leader of the Republican right. That was just a coincidence. But Goldwater's political views and those of the *Digest* dovetailed almost exactly. That seemed more like a sign from God. The *Digest* was among the first to know in its heart that Goldwater was right, and it seemed only a matter of time before the magazine promoted his candidacy for the presidency. Even in the election year 1960, when he was not in the running, the *Digest* published five articles by Goldwater, who opposed Social Security, called for the abolition of the income tax, and proposed to sell the Tennessee Valley Authority to the private sector.

Vice-President Richard M. Nixon, another good friend of the *Digest*, was the party's candidate that year, and the magazine spared no effort to ensure his occupancy of the White House for the next two terms. Thus articles by and about Nixon were also staples. In fact, just about any vestige of liberalism, any possibility of a kind word or two about a Democrat, had all but vanished as a new decade dawned. Increasingly, political articles were becoming the exclusive domain of the Washington bureau, headed by Chuck Stevenson, a hard-as-nails conservative of the old school who had come out of the Scripps-Howard chain, wore his white hair in a crew cut, and despised the group of editors up in Pleasantville as namby-pamby middle-of-the-roaders. Month after month the bureau churned out article after article supportive of anti-Communist dictators, among them Spain's Generalissimo Franco, Portugal's Salazar (a "mystic devoted to God" and his native land), and the government of South Africa, whose department of tourism was a major *Digest* advertiser.

In addition to Goldwater's, other nonstaff right-wing bylines appearing frequently in the *Digest* were those of Henry Hazlitt, one of the country's most extreme conservative economists; syndicated columnist and leading McCarthyite apologist David Lawrence; French-born fascist author Bertrand de Jouvenel, dubbed the French Goebbels by the *New York Herald Tribune;* and John T. Flynn, author of *The Road Ahead,* a conservative manifesto similar to *None Dare Call It Treason,* a best-selling anti-Communist doomsday tract by John Stormer. Out-and-out government bashing was the order of the day.

Despite its great wealth and right-wing bona fides, the *Digest* occupied an anomalous position in the conservative movement, whose figurehead, Senator Robert Taft of Ohio, had died in 1953. In the ensuing vacuum, conservatives broke into splinter groups much preoccupied with dogmatic purity. Their leaders ranged from William F. Buckley, Jr., and his "new conservative" *National Review* at the intellectual end to New England candy manufacturer Robert Welch, founder of the John Birch Society. The *Digest*'s populism and its reliance on mostly second-rate writers precluded it from ever being taken too seriously by the Buckley camp, while Welch's denunciation of Eisenhower as a Communist sympathizer—and similar extremist absurdities—made it impossible for the *RD* to support the JBS with any enthusiasm.

As a result, the *Reader's Digest* was ignored by the conservative press just as it was ignored by liberal and leftist periodicals and pundits except for the occasional insult, aspersion, or pat on the head. Everyone, right and left, paid lip service to the *Digest*'s enormous "influence," but nobody bothered to define, or even to care, what that influence was. About the only people who took the magazine's political articles seriously were its subscribers, who now numbered 12 million.

With its enormous conservative constituency—which, like the country itself, was predominantly Protestant—the *Digest* was able to help keep the religious issue alive during the 1960 race between Nixon and his Roman Catholic opponent, John F. Kennedy. Catholics constituted only 26 percent of the population, which meant that Kennedy—not only a Catholic but an eastern liberal—desperately needed to win Protestant votes, particularly in the Bible Belt, which had historically demonstrated a mistrust of, if not animosity toward, Catholics, easterners, and liberals.

Doubtless millions of thoughtful Protestants had legitimate fears that the Democratic candidate might feel obliged to take his orders from a "higher" source than his conscience and the U.S. Constitution—namely, the Vatican. However, there was a fine line between calming fears and subtly playing to prejudice. Kennedy's religion was the only aspect of his campaign that the *Digest* addressed substantively—which it did twice—while at the same time enthusiastically promoting the candidacy of Richard M. Nixon.

Early in the campaign *Life* magazine (whose publisher, Henry R. Luce, also favored Nixon) ran a piece entitled "Should a Catholic Be President?," by maverick Episcopal bishop James A. Pike, who declared that the Catholic faith of a presidential candidate should be a factor only if there were reason to believe that his faith was of the "official" kind and that he would put the wishes of the Vatican first. But if it was of the "unofficial" kind and Americanized, then religion made no difference. Pike was certainly enough of an ecclesiastical sophisticate to know that the distinction was pure wordplay, but held back from certifying Kennedy as an "unofficial" Catholic, even while noting that he had declared his opposition to naming a U.S. ambassador to the Vatican and to granting federal aid to parochial schools.

What particularly bothered Pike was Kennedy's ambiguous stand on "freedom in the distribution of contraceptive information (now focused on the question of our willingness to aid other nations wanting it)." The bishop added that examining a candidate's religion was "not bigotry but responsible citizenship," explaining that he would be similarly concerned about the defense policies, say, of a Quaker.

The *RD* reprinted the article as its lead feature in March. Looked at from one perspective, Pike's essay did to some extent soberly address the issue. At the same time, however, the two most powerful pro-Nixon media organs in the country, once again acting virtually in tandem, had succeeded in sustaining a nagging doubt in the collective Protestant mind about Kennedy's independence from Rome.

In September, as elections neared and Bible Belt anti-Catholicism reached fever pitch, especially in Texas, the *RD* raised the issue again with a two-part "debate": "The Religious Issue in This Campaign," divided into "A Roman Catholic View" and "A Protestant View." The former, by Notre Dame theology professor and priest John A. O'Brien, was a straightforward exposition of the historical Catholic teaching on the separation of church and state. Speaking for the Protestants were Eugene Carson Blake, stated clerk of the United Presbyterian Church, and Bishop G. Bromley Oxnam, former chairman of the Council of Bishops of the Methodist church. Both declared they were "uneasy" about Kennedy's candidacy. While praising him for being "candid and fearless" in opposing federal funds to parochial schools and an ambassador to the Vatican, they criticized him for displaying "political timidity" in not wanting to risk the Catholic church's displeasure by disseminating birth-control information in predominantly Catholic countries.

Like Pike, these two churchmen also pointed out that they were not trying to stir up prejudice but were honestly worried about how the religious affiliation of a candidate might "affect the fulfillment of his official duties." Also like Pike, they justified their doubts with the very same example he used: "Would not Americans ask a Quaker running for President whether his pacifist convictions would prevent him from acting as commander in chief in case of war?"

In fact, as Pike, Blake, and Oxnam all seem to have conveniently forgotten, Nixon was a Quaker. Yet his views on a strong defense were not subjected to similar scrutiny by the fiercely pro-Pentagon *Digest*. For that matter, the *RD* itself shared Kennedy's reluctance to risk

Catholic displeasure by distributing birth-control information in predominantly Catholic (or even Islamic) countries. As always, *Selecciones* and other foreign editions published in Latin America, Spain, and the Middle East avoided all mention of birth control, divorce, and similar sensitive issues.

The same month that the *Digest* debate was published, Kennedy and his advisers finally decided to address the issue head-on. In one of the most dramatic moments of the campaign, he accepted an invitation from the Greater Houston Ministerial Association to discuss his religion. Shortly before the September 12 meeting, Kennedy adviser and speech writer Theodore Sorensen confided to a friend, "We can win or lose the election right there in Houston on Monday night." On the appointed day, Kennedy reassured the Protestant clergy once and for all that "the separation of Church and State is absolute" and that "no Catholic prelate would tell the President (should he be a Catholic) how to act, and no Protestant minister would tell his parishioners for whom to vote." Thereafter the religious issue drew little public attention. But there was more to the story.

In 1944 John Hersey had described the exploits of Lieutenant (jg) John F. Kennedy, commanding officer of motor torpedo boat 109, in a story titled "Survival" for the June 17 issue of the *New Yorker.* But Ambassador Joseph Kennedy regarded its publication in a magazine with such a relatively small circulation as inconsequential. Later he approached Paul Palmer, to whom he had been introduced by *New York Times* columnist Arthur Krock, and persuaded him to condense the Hersey article for the much vaster readership of the *RD.* The profile was condensed and reprinted that same August.

What actually happened, on the night of August 1–2, 1943, was that Lieutenant Kennedy, while on patrol in the Solomon Islands, became involved in a naval action in Blackett Strait between two islands. Through the apparent negligence of both Kennedy and his crew (two men were asleep, two others were lying down, and the radio man was not monitoring his radio), PT-109 was cut in half by a Japanese destroyer—the only such mishap during the war. But Kennedy later displayed great courage in towing his wounded chief engineer to safety by clenching a strap from the man's life jacket between his teeth and swimming for four hours with the engineer on his back. Once on the island, they carved messages on coconut shells and transmitted them by natives back to naval headquarters.

In the original version Hersey, who wrote the article with the cooperation of the Kennedy family, had downplayed the failed military action. But in the *RD* condensation, there was no mention of naval combat at all. Jack Kennedy, son of the ambassador to England, was portrayed as a war hero pure and simple.

In the 1960 election the Kennedy camp distributed hundreds of thousands of the reprints and the American electorate again received a distorted account of the PT-109 incident. Moreover, that was not the first time the reprint had been used by Joseph Kennedy, who as early as 1946 had distributed 100,000 copies of the article to every single voter in the Eleventh Congressional District of Boston during Jack's first campaign for a seat in Congress. The article was reprinted yet again in an eight-page tabloid, 900,000 copies of which were distributed to voters when Kennedy first ran for the Senate, defeating veteran Henry Cabot Lodge, Jr., in 1952. In the presidential election, the reprint worked its charm a third time.

(All three reprints were illegal as well. Ross had initially rebuffed Palmer since the *Digest*, when it bought rights to reprint, kept that right in perpetuity. Also the request to reprint came only seven months after Ross had loudly proclaimed that the *New Yorker* was not renewing its reprint agreement with Pleasantville. However, Ross was eventually persuaded by Palmer to sell the *Digest* onetime condensation rights—though probably only because author John Hersey himself consented to give his reprint fee to the widow of one of the two men drowned in the PT-109 disaster.

(Subsequently, Joseph Kennedy received "permission" from Palmer to reprint the article and distribute it in the Eleventh Congressional District. The widow received no money for the reprint. Most likely, not even token permission was sought from the *Digest*, much less the *New Yorker*, when the Kennedy campaign reprinted the article a second and third time.

(Though doubtless peeved by Joe Kennedy's piracy, Wally was a tireless champion of reprints as a vital part of the *Digest*'s mission to reach as many readers around the world as possible, and he frequently twitted senior editors for regarding reprints as second-class goods. Wally's profound conviction was that, if an article had originally been printed in the *Digest*, it was thereby of "lasting interest" and deserved an afterlife—though preferably at two cents a copy. Ultimately, he would have rightly taken the Kennedy camp's continued reprinting as a tribute to the *Digest*'s unparalleled influence with the American public.)

Jack Kennedy's stunning victory was a great blow to Wally personally and to a majority of the editors at the *Digest*. Kennedy was Democratic, liberal, and Catholic—three very odious traits to those at the *Digest*, which was Republican, right-wing, and mainstream Protestant. He was also Joe Kennedy's son and that made him even worse. But Kennedy's election also created a special problem for Chuck Stevenson in the Washington bureau, because nobody in the new administration would talk to him. The new president's press secretary, Larry O'Brien, thought he was rabid.

Stevenson decided he needed a "liberal" point man, preferably someone young and pliable whom he could send on errands to White House press briefings and interviews. His eventual choice was Bruce Lee, a reporter who wrote the press section of *Newsweek* and had even penned a biography of President John Fitzgerald Kennedy for young readers. Lee seemed to have all the right credentials. He was young, moderate, and obviously acceptable to the Kennedy camp. However, pliable he was not.

Lee soon discovered that he was the only Democrat in the bureau. Worse, he also learned that his curmudgeonly boss expected him to write every story with a conservative slant. Not surprisingly, he found that galling, not because he was a Democrat but because it was so obviously unprofessional. But he had a family to support and, for the time being, did what he was told.

The newest staffer was put to work ghosting articles for congressmen. Not only did the *Digest* pay legislators an honorarium for articles they did not write, but it also ghosted their rebuttals, to be delivered on the floor, if there was any flak in response from the administration. One of Lee's most successful efforts was a March 1964 piece for John Dowdy, Democratic representative from Texas, that listed widespread abuses in the Johnson administration's urban renewal program—in particular, that hundreds of millions of dollars' worth of good housing stock was being summarily condemned as a slum, demolished, then reclassified and sold to urban redevelopers at a fraction of its worth.

When the U.S. commissioner of urban renewal denied the charges and called the author a liar, the congressman rose in the House and read eighteen pages of Lee's ghosted rebuttal into the *Congressional Record*. The commissioner, a former employee of realtor William Zeckendorf, was forced to resign. Coincidentally, in the early sixties, the Wallaces' good friend Laurance S. Rockefeller, at the time head of Rockefeller Center in New York, was also waging a bitter real-estate war with Zeckendorf over valuable Midtown property.

On another occasion Lee ghosted an attack by Senator Robert Kerr of Oklahoma on the high cost of a proposed national health program called Medicare. A few days before the Senate debate on the bill, Kerr walked up and down the aisle of the upper chamber, passing out reprints of the article to his colleagues. It was a very potent method of killing the bill. Medicare was not passed until 1965.

In 1961, around the time Lee joined the bureau, the *Digest* started a press section, reprinting items from a diverse group—the *St. Louis Post-Dispatch,* the *New York Times,* and the *New York Daily News,* among others. Invariably, political opinions were culled from conservative papers. Typical was the *Daily News*'s attack on Kennedy's call for a domestic Peace Corps as just another scheme "to add a lot more jobholders to the federal payrolls." The liberal *Post-Dispatch,* meanwhile, was relegated to discussing ways of saving water. On at least one occasion, a very conservative view attributed in a headline to the *New York Times* was identified in small type at the bottom as a letter to the editor.

The *Digest* also continued to support the defeated Republican candidate, excerpting *Six Crises*—Nixon's bitter memoir, full of recriminations and accusations, covering his early career as a U.S. representative and vice-president—in its May and June 1962 issues. The excerpts chosen charged that Kennedy had during the 1960 campaign been told of U.S. aid being given to a planned U.S. invasion of Cuba. Prior to their publication in the magazine, Nixon wrote to Wally, whom he addressed as DeWitt, saying how pleased he was and adding, "I only hope you do not catch too much 'political flak' from some of my never-say-die critics."

Replied Wally, who by now had begun to contribute to Americans for Constitutional Action, a right-wing group that monitored the voting records of "liberal" congressmen: "We don't worry about 'political flak.' I wish we could carry in every issue of *RD* material as significant as the excerpts from your book."

The Bay of Pigs disaster—the ill-conceived plan for the invasion of Cuba on April 17, 1961—was a favorite *Digest* theme, to which it returned almost obsessively. In November 1962, July 1963, and August 1963, it again ran articles blaming Kennedy for the debacle. Though the president later accepted full blame for the disaster, and was certainly morally culpable for approving the invasion of another sovereign country, the misguided attempt to overthrow Cuban dictator Fidel Castro with a handful of exiles had, in fact, been long planned by the CIA with the explicit approval of Eisenhower, Kennedy's predecessor. Neither the agency nor the former president, two Pleasantville icons, came in for any criticism.

In other pieces the *Digest* also accused the Kennedy administration of allowing the Soviets to sneak missiles into Cuba—in effect, of being indirectly responsible for bringing about the 1962 Cuban missile crisis. Finally, Kennedy's press secretary, Pierre Salinger, summoned Stevenson for a showdown. The offending article was "Why America Slept," an excerpt from a soon-to-be-published *Digest*-sponsored book of the same title—a title bearing a suspicious resemblance to Kennedy's own study of Britain between the wars, *Why England Slept.* Stevenson called Hobe Lewis, the sponsoring editor, who in turn contacted author John Hubbell, an *RD* roving editor, in Minneapolis. A few days later all three Digesters showed up on schedule in Salinger's office.

"Lewis, your persistence in publishing that goddamn book is the last ounce of cooperation you'll ever get out of this place," Salinger fumed.

Lewis was under the impression that the Kennedy administration had never given the *Digest* any cooperation. Taken aback by Salinger's threat, however, he began to hem and haw—not wanting to jeopardize whatever help the White House had lately been offering the *RD*'s Washington bureau. (As Lewis later learned, no such assistance had been extended.) Salinger continued to complain until an assistant informed the group that the president was ready to see them. When they filed in, Kennedy was sitting in his rocking chair, smoking a cigar. Lewis, by now a nervous wreck, blurted:

"Mr. President . . ."

"Knock it off," Kennedy interrupted.

Then he went on to praise Paul Palmer and DeWitt Wallace for helping to burnish his war-hero image and wrapped up the session with a few jokes. As the group was leaving, he added, "Don't worry about all this."

Once outside the Oval Office, Salinger apologized to everyone for having brought them down to Washington. Lewis flew back to Pleasantville. Only hours after he had settled into his chair, the phone rang.

Salinger's office was calling. A secretary had been delegated to ask the delicate question that was behind the tempest in a teapot.

"Mr. Lewis, we do have one request," she said. "We wonder if you could possibly change the title on the book?"

"Sorry," explained Lewis. "It's on press."

Kennedy himself, of course, had modeled his title on Winston Churchill's *While England Slept.*

———

WHILE focusing obsessively on the Bay of Pigs, the Cuban missile crisis, and other problems of the Kennedy administration, the *Digest* (as well as its Condensed Books division) ignored one of the most important books of 1962. In *Silent Spring,* Rachel Carson raised the collective consciousness of America with her warning that pesticides were contaminating the country's ecosystem and food chain. But the *RD*'s response was only to caution, some time after the book's publication, "Many scientists . . . fear that [Carson's] emotional outburst . . . may do more harm than good." On the whole, though, Condensed Books under Ralph Henderson continued to maintain its editorial independence, avoiding the more extreme conservative authors.

At the magazine, however, several different condensations of *Silent Spring* were prepared, in an effort to find a suitable selection, though none ran. A number of major oil companies cast in the role of ecological villain by Carson were major advertisers in the *Digest,* but that was probably not a factor in the editorial decision not to excerpt. The *Digest*'s views and those of the oil companies were in accord to begin with. The more liberal Condensed Books simply decided the book was not an appropriate selection for its readers—though Ken Wilson, the *RD*'s liaison with New York publishers, later regretted the decision.

A much higher priority was the rough treatment of conservative journalists by Bobby and Jack Kennedy. Washington bureau chief Chuck Stevenson was so paranoiac in regard to this subject that he once suspected a man in the office next door of being a private detective hired to spy on him. The man's behavior seemed so obviously surreptitious that sometimes Stevenson stood pressing his ear to a glass against the wall, trying to find out what the man was up to. Finally, Stevenson had had enough and one day confronted his office neighbor in the elevator and asked if he was spying on him. "No," the man replied. "I'm spying on Bobby Kennedy."

Stevenson assigned Bruce Lee to look into the matter. The latter spent months documenting the administration's pattern of spying on reporters they considered unfriendly, primarily Earl Voss of the *Washington Star*. When the article was finally handed in, though, even bureau chief Stevenson was shocked by the allegations of wiretapping, secret surveillance, and transferring of friendly background sources at the Pentagon and the Defense Department to Alaska and Greenland.

"You can't say this about the president of the U.S.A.," Stevenson protested.

"Well, it's true," Lee shrugged.

Just at that moment a secretary rushed in to say that President Kennedy had been shot in Dallas. Stevenson handed Lee back his manuscript and said, "Well, there goes your story."

Two women who avidly followed the details of the assassination were two longtime Digester wives, Victo Ferguson and Urith Dillon. By now Victo and Charlie Ferguson were going through an acrimonious divorce. Victo had evidence that her husband was keeping another family in Chicago, a third in Texas, and possibly even a fourth in California. But it was easier to prove he was an adulterer than to prove he was a bigamist, and so for weeks a pair of private detectives had been shadowing Ferguson and his latest girlfriend, an editor at the *Digest*.

Among the assorted letters from women to her husband that Victo had in hand were a number from someone named Eva Grant. Victo and Urith had no idea who she was except that she had once been a schoolteacher living in Chicago. The two women suspected that Ferguson had met her through his work with the American Library Association, which was headquartered in the Windy City. Then one day, while reading the latest news about the Kennedy assassination, they saw Grant's picture in the newspaper. She was in the paper not on her own account but because her brother Jack Ruby had just shot Lee Harvey Oswald, the reputed assassin of John F. Kennedy, in a Dallas courthouse.

During the three and a half years prior to the killing of Oswald, Grant had managed her brother's nightclub, Club Vegas, a known mob hangout and striptease joint, in Dallas. Ferguson, who had fled Texas some thirty years earlier as a disgraced minister to seek a new career in publishing, now regularly returned to his home state for considerable periods of time. Victo had no idea whether her husband continued to see Grant. But the question became moot late one evening not long afterward when the detectives phoned to say they had photographed Ferguson and another woman in flagrante delicto. A year later Wally's closest friend and future biographer found himself, legally at any rate, a free man.

12

An Unpleasantness in Pleasantville

As HE approached retirement, DeWitt Wallace began to harbor intimations of immortality—and one intimation, strangely enough, was that posterity might not accord him full and unqualified credit for founding the *Reader's Digest*. Increasingly, he became resentful of the legend, which the *Digest* itself had long nurtured, that Lila was a cofounder and coequal with her husband.

Wally had originally put Lila's name on the masthead because he correctly assumed that the *Digest* would appeal primarily to women. When the *Fortune* profile appeared in 1937 and the *Time* cover story in 1951, the legend of the two hardworking young marrieds was perpetuated—how Lila stayed up into the wee hours reading through all those stacks of magazines, helping her husband make selections, and how the returns from that mailing of ten thousand solicitations, just before they went off on their honeymoon, had been so encouraging.

Lila herself told those stories to the interviewers, and so they became part of the official version in the *Digest's* own autobiography, *Of Lasting Interest,* by James Playsted Wood, first published in 1957. Privately, Wally's rather pathetic explanation of why he permitted those modest exaggerations to go unchecked was that he did not want to make Lila appear to be a liar.

In the autumn of his years, Wally became increasingly snappish when anyone referred to Lila in terms that gave her credit when none was due—that downgraded his own role, in other words, as sole founder and presiding genius of the *Reader's Digest*. Typical was an incident involving Stanley High, Norman Vincent Peale's erstwhile ghostwriter, who by now was descending into alcoholic oblivion and the nightmare world of electroshock treatments for depression.

It was Wally's habit in those days to encourage employees to show Lila little attentions—in effect, to fawn on her, appeal to her vanity, and make her feel appreciated. Despite his egotism, he remained as ever the devoted and considerate husband. One day he persuaded High to give a little talk to a small group of *Digest* staffers at an outdoor alcove on the company grounds, with Lila as the guest of honor. Wally sat in, but the more he listened, the angrier he got because High was giving Lila equal billing as cofounder of the *Reader's Digest*. Finally, Wally turned to Al Cole, who was sitting nearby, and asked him to take a walk up to the Guest House. As the two men strolled along, Wally asked irately:

"What the hell's the matter with Stanley High? Lila didn't have a damn thing to do with starting the *Reader's Digest*. Doesn't he know any better?"

"Listen, Wally," Cole explained patiently, "he's trying to be nice to all the women, including Lila. You know the facts and he knows the facts. Don't get mad at him."

"Well," Wally pouted, "I am mad at him. Tell him I don't want him to do that again."

Despite his petty jealousy on this point, however, Wally and Lila were more of a devoted couple than ever. Whenever Gene Doherty, their chauffeur, drove them anywhere, they always sat together in the backseat, holding hands. Once Wood and his wife, Betty, were with Lila in the Guest House, waiting for Wally to join them for lunch. Finally, he hurried in, lifted Lila's foot, and kissed it.

"Oh, Wally!" Lila cried fondly.

In 1961, when a book came out on six famous marriages, Wally and Lila were surprised to find themselves in the matrimonial pantheon, even though they had not been interviewed by the author. The other connubial successes included those of Winston and Clementine Churchill, Alfred Lunt and Lynn Fontaine, oceanographer and naturalist Martin Johnson and his wife, Lelia, Charles and Anne Morrow Lindbergh, and Marie and Pierre Curie. When the Wallaces finally saw a copy, Lila remarked, "At least we're in good company, don't you think?"

Stories about their fierce protectiveness toward each other, and about their often professed mutual love and affection, gradually created a new public image of the Wallaces: a doting couple who lived all alone in the big house. Despite his aloof demeanor, Wally was still known to have an impish streak in him and a continuing passion for off-color jokes. But few put much stock in the stories still in circulation about his past affairs with this one's wife or with certain single women in the office who had a "reputation." Wally and Lila had become like everybody's mother and father—it was hard to imagine them having sex at all, much less carrying on with someone else.

As though to underscore the sacredness of their marriage, Lila had installed Marc Chagall's *The Three Candles* as the centerpiece of her husband's redecorated office. It had recently been done over by Syrie Maugham, society darling and ex-wife of British novelist Somerset Maugham. Painted in 1915, after the artist's marriage to his beloved Bella, the canvas portrayed a bride and groom surrounded by flowers, angels, a pear-domed church, candles, and a wooden fence. It was not only a powerful metaphor for wedded tranquillity and bliss but also a potent reminder to all visitors—not to mention the office's occupant—that DeWitt Wallace enjoyed a similar, if somewhat fancier, domestic paradise up in High Winds.

Maugham also installed in Wally's new office an eighteenth-century English desk containing forty-nine secret drawers—yet another, though perhaps less witting, metaphor for a man who was so enigmatic and secret in his private life.

As for Harry Wilcox, he was now just one of many men—all of them handsome, well-dressed, engaging conversationalists with a streak of cold-blooded ambition—who derived their power from Lila rather than from Wally. Among the latest was the sartorially splendid Bob Devine, who had left *U.S. News & World Report* to become deputy head of the *Digest*'s international editions. But according to Judy Thompson, Lila still relied primarily on Wilcox to be her "spy and confidant," gathering information about what went on in the office, especially as it concerned Digesters' private lives.

Wilcox had plenty to report. So many editors and executives shed their first wives, soon after going to work for the company, that having an affair with a secretary or a colleague was jokingly referred to as a precondition for advancement. In many cases a senior Digester with marital problems sought the Wallaces' advice. Wally and Lila were known to be unusually forthright when it came to marriage counseling. More often than not an editor or executive wanting to trade in a wife was perhaps not seeking advice so much as a signal that he would not be penalized in his career if he divorced a spouse of whom the Wallaces might be fond.

Since Lila was not close to any *Digest* wives to begin with and Wally positively encouraged men in the prime of life to find a wife who would be an asset rather than a drawback, there were few marriages that either of them went to great lengths to salvage.

In contrast to the rash of failed marriages and affairs in Pleasantville, Wally and Lila's union seemed the very exemplar of monogamy—a beacon of fidelity and proof that a long-lived love affair could be the greatest romantic adventure of all. Both were now in their early seventies; few Digesters survived who had personally witnessed another side of Wally. Moreover, his devotion to Lila touched many of those who saw instances of it. Reinforcing the legend of the Wallace marriage was her husband's rage at any slight, real or imagined, shown his wife.

Now that the *Digest* was accepting advertisements, there was a new breed of person around Pleasantville—the slick, hard-nosed salesman, untutored in the courtly ways of the company's upper management and editorial staff. One evening a group of sales representatives were invited up to High Winds for a party. After they left, Lila told Wally that she thought one of the salesmen seemed facile in his appreciation of High Winds and had failed to express the usual thanks and expressions of pleasure when he departed. The next morning an infuriated Wally dashed off a vicious note suggesting to the man that he go back to kindergarten to learn some manners. When the salesman got the note, he went to see Al Cole and resigned.

"Oh, he doesn't mean it," Cole tried to explain. "Like everybody else, Wallace blows his top once in a while. Forget it."

"I can't forget it," the salesman said, "and I can't stay here. I quit."

"You have a real future here, and you know it," Cole protested. "Don't be hasty."

"I can get a job anywhere," the salesman confidently replied.

But it was Cole's policy always to stick up for his men, and this was a man he did not want to lose. He went to Wally and explained. Wally repeated his advice that the man learn some manners and that he would not have Lila insulted in her own home.

"Then we'll lose one of the best space salesmen we have," said Cole.

"Get another."

"I can't get another as good."

"Perhaps I did come on a little strong," Wally admitted. "But he'll get over it."

"He won't. I don't think we can keep him unless you apologize."

"Apologize!"

Wally blew up again. When he calmed down once more, Cole persuaded him to apologize. A meeting was arranged. Wally told the salesman that he had not meant all the things he said in the note.

"No, but you thought them and we'll both remember them," the salesman said. He insisted that his resignation be accepted. A defeated Wally gave the salesman generous severance pay and asked to be used personally as a reference for the next job he applied for.

Wally's determination to defend his wife's honor was surpassed by his desire to pay her public homage, even if that meant occasionally exceeding the bounds of social propriety. One evening in the early sixties, the guests of honor at High Winds were Nelson Rockefeller and his second wife, Happy. The other guests were *Digest* editors and their spouses, including Hobe and Edie Lewis. The liberal governor of New York posed the only serious threat to Goldwater's candidacy in the upcoming Republican primaries. Yet Rockefeller, being a Rockefeller, and Wally had maintained a cordial relationship over the years.

In the midst of the animated conversation, Wally stood up to propose a toast to all men at the table who were accompanied by their original wives. He was the only one. Bowing gravely in acceptance of the toast, he drank the glass empty and sat down. Indirectly, it was also Wally's way of telling Rockefeller—the first divorced man to run seriously for the presidency—that the *Digest*'s sympathies lay with Goldwater.

———

THE household staff at High Winds, with the onset of the sixties, consisted of a butler, two maids, a chauffeur, several gardeners, and one unskilled laborer. The laborer was Wally. On most days his routine was to work in his tower at High Winds late into the night. Whether he slept there or in his own bedroom, he always joined Lila for breakfast in the cheerful Art Deco breakfast nook overlooking the trimmed lawn and rock garden. In an ivy-framed window were two vintage birdcages. Sometimes when Wally was in one of his melancholy moods or conversation lagged, Lila pressed a button and made the cages come alive with mechanical bird song to cheer him up and "have some fun."

Then they did not see each other again until evening, when they often dined alone at home. But they also frequently patronized local restaurants, went into New York to take favored Digesters out to supper and the theater, and regularly hosted dinner parties and other functions—an endless number of them "foodless," according to Judy Thompson—at High Winds.

On the mornings after Wally had put in a night of work, a messenger distributed a blizzard of yellow slips—the fruits of his midnight labor—over the desks of editors waiting for him to approve or comment on a manuscript, a memo, or some other project. He wrote in a clear hand, always in pencil, and each comment was a model of condensation, usually no more than half a dozen words. By eleven he showed up at the office. He was now driving a Ford Falcon and tried to cover the five-mile distance from High Winds to Chappaqua in the shortest time possible, clocking himself against his last best time. (Lila was chauffeur-driven in a white Lincoln Continental that bore a license plate reading "LAW"—a message lost on no one.)

When High Winds was being built, the contractors had laid down a winding asphalt road from the gate to the main residence, and also created a system of auxiliary roads to various parts of the estate, which by now had increased to 136 acres. Barely wide enough to accommodate a jeep and many no more than mud holes, these dirt roads measured altogether about ten miles in length.

As he grew older, spent less time in the office, and left the running of the magazine to others, Wally made the improvement of this network of roads a personal project that bordered on obsession. Like the establishment of the *Digest* itself in the early days, it was a goal he could focus all his energies on and accomplish alone. Single-handedly, he dug up all the rocks for the base, filled them in with sand and dirt, and tamped them down. As a finishing touch, he covered each completed section with leftover oil delivered from the RDA garage, where it was saved and barreled whenever a company car or truck was drained.

After the system of roadways was finished, Wally patrolled the grounds in his jeep, looking for spots in need of repair. It was equipped with a bulldozer blade, shovels, and everything else he might need in an emergency. An obliging guest who persisted in offers of assistance was often rudely rebuffed, and workmen on the estate were strictly forbidden to touch a single pebble.

THE company itself was also in fine form. For its 300-page, fortieth-anniversary issue, in February 1962, the *Reader's Digest* reprised its first cover and reprinted a charter article, "How to Keep Young Mentally," as well as the now legendary sayings attributed to evangelists Billy Sunday ("Try praising your wife, even if it does frighten her at first") and Homer Rodeheaver ("One cigaret will kill a cat"), which Digesters loved to quote. *Time* marked the occasion with a condescending write-up, noting that articles planted in other magazines for reprinting later in the *Digest* now constituted 70 percent of every issue in the U.S. edition.

As for the editorial content itself, *Time* once again pointed to the *Digest*'s "preoccupation with sex," adding, "The *Digest* delights in double-entendre page-enders of fillers, [and] rarely misses the chance to reprint notably daring sex lore from outside authorities." Nor was the newsweekly able to resist taking a swipe at the *Digest*'s stately headquarters overlooking the Saw Mill River Parkway, suggesting that it looked like the "the high school of a particularly prosperous suburb."

Regardless, in 1961 the company's gross advertising revenue, from a magazine that once scorned advertising, was $65 million. From all sources that year, including Condensed Books and a new record club, the company had grossed a total of $155 million.

On the international front the *RD* was now being published in Dutch *(Het Beste uit Reader's Digest)* and in two new Spanish-language editions, in the Caribbean and in Central America—the latter geared specifically to Puerto Ricans. In mid-1964 a Chinese edition was announced, with distribution planned for Hong Kong, Taiwan, Malaysia, Thailand, and the Philippines—all part of Wally's goal to put a copy of the *Reader's Digest* in the hands of everybody in the world, no matter what language he or she spoke.

One language that the magazine was not printed in was Hebrew, but the anemic *Al-Mukhtar* continued to be published in Arabic. It had never made a profit and was published solely as a public service, though its circulation had declined from a high of nearly 150,000 during the war years to less than one-sixth that number now. Then, during the Six-Day War of 1967, *Al-Mukhtar* was forced to suspend publication.

Despite such intermittent obstacles, Wally and Lila made a point of visiting, in their travels, the *Digest*'s far-flung offices, as a convenient destination. Wally used such occasions to boost morale and talk with as many employees as possible. Unfailingly, Digesters from Amsterdam to New Zealand were charmed by the Wallaces' modesty, enthusiasm, and interest in their work.

A visit from the company's legendary founders could be terrifying as well, because it was sometimes unannounced. In one instance that soon became a part of RDA lore, the Wallaces arrived one morning at the company's headquarters in Sydney. Unlike the plush quarters enjoyed by RDA executives in Paris, London, or Pleasantville, the office suite the Australian employees occupied was in a drab section of town. But the executive offices at least had the advantage of opening onto a small landscaped roof garden. However, the garden had developed such an elaborate root system that the staff were taking bets on when the roof would collapse and destroy the expensive electronic equipment in the rooms below.

Wally and Lila had heard about the root system and wanted to check the problem for themselves. One morning the receptionist looked up to see an elderly man and woman asking to see John Cooper, the managing director.

"Who shall I say wants him?"

"Tell him we're the Wallaces," said Wally.

Not recognizing the name, the receptionist conveyed the news to Cooper's secretary. In turn, she instructed the receptionist to find out why they wanted to meet Mr. Cooper. On being asked, Wally replied, "We're just visiting offices of the *Digest.*"

Finally, a clerk was sent down to give the two visitors a tour. Wally and Lila followed him meekly. Cooper, ambling through the corridors, happened to bump into the group and got the surprise of his life.

———

WHILE Wally traveled, worked hard on his road to keep fit and trim, and kept a close watch on the editorial lineup of each issue, the company under Al Cole's generalship prospered on a broad front—advertising and increased circulation revenues, Condensed Books, international editions, school editions, and long-playing classical records marketed through direct mail and in supermarkets—and the *Digest* was also given a facelift.

Over the years the magazine had undergone a number of typographical modifications. Wraparound covers of paintings or of color photographs had been introduced in 1948, with the illustration on the back page extending forward into part of the front cover. Lila's selection of the artwork was, in a sense, an extension of her passion for interior decorating. After working first with Dolores Risley, then British stage designer Oliver Messel, and ultimately Syrie Maugham, beautifying the RDA's worldwide offices, she had finally turned her attention to the homeliest artifact in the kingdom—the *Reader's Digest* itself—and decided it was in need of serious renovation.

The refreshing change from a staid, all-type cover to one featuring colorful depictions of America's national institutions, natural wonders, and small-town epiphanies, usually in the sentimental manner of Norman Rockwell, marked Lila's first significant contribution to the magazine, apart from her sporadic suggestions relating to excerptable material or direct mail back in the early twenties. Her involvement in cover design had also led directly to Lila's role as unofficial art director for Condensed Books when that operation was begun in the early fifties, and there her authority was absolute and in almost direct proportion to Wally's own lack of interest in every aspect of the club.

However, he obviously welcomed his wife's taste in cover art, which not only gave the magazine a more attractive newsstand profile, which contributed to increased sales, but also enhanced the celebratory patriotism of its articles. For a time, beginning in 1957, Lila and Wally even experimented with putting the contents on the back page and a freestanding illustration on the front. Though cover illustrations were eventually discontinued, Lila remained the arbiter for the watercolor to be used on the back cover every month for both the U.S. and the international editions.

In 1962 an even more fundamental design change took place when Kenneth Stuart became art director. Stuart was part of a contingent of *Saturday Evening Post* staffers who had attempted to salvage that magazine with an all-new look, both visually and editorially. The result was a double disaster that offended subscriber loyalists, who missed the Rockwell-era homeyness, and perplexed would-be readers, who had no more idea what the magazine was supposed to be about than its editors did.

Stuart was hired by the *Digest* when the Curtis Publishing Company, which owned the *Post,* decided on yet another revamping of the troubled magazine, hired a new team of editors and designers, and moved the operation from Philadelphia to New York. During his nineteen years at the *Post,* according to one critic, the magazine always "looked like a seed catalogue." But in Pleasantville that was a plus because something very like a seed catalog—Wally's first publication, *Getting the Most Out of Farming*—had been the *Digest's* progenitor.

The hiring of Kenneth Stuart marked the culmination of Lila's quiet remodeling of the *Digest*. If not nearly as extensive as the *Post*'s, the visual overhaul was still just as traumatic for some subscribers and editors. Moreover, Lila's influence over the magazine seemed to be growing just as Wally's role began to recede—the slack being taken up by "Lila's boy" Hobe Lewis.

Even though hers was a strictly visual influence, it was to affect the overall appearance and identity of the *Digest* as much as the first advertisements had in 1954—a move that Lila had strongly opposed on aesthetic grounds. Though she lost that round, she refused to compromise when her back-cover domain was threatened. Once, at a party for advertisers at High Winds, Wally was told that Coca-Cola had just bid $18 million for the back panel for the entire year. Hurrying over to Lila's side, he gave her the good news. Looking straight at him, she replied, "I bid $19 million."

Stuart charmed Lila with his flair, both personal and professional. Unlike the average gray-suited Digester, he had personality and knew how to dress. He also had a vision for the *Digest* that coincided with hers. To make way for Stuart, longtime art director W. O. Woodbury was abruptly forced out.

One of Stuart's first moves was to introduce Granjon for body type and Baskerville for display. He also began to illustrate stories, either with a color drawing or with a photograph. Occasionally, the watercolors on the back cover alternated with a reproduction from one of the Wallaces' growing collection of French Impressionist masterpieces.

Executive editor Ken Payne did not always see eye to eye with Lila on artwork. For decades he had diplomatically refrained from disagreeing with her on any matter she felt strongly about. Payne's diplomatic skills, in fact, were almost as legendary as Lila's willfulness. But finally he felt he had to object to the almost revolutionary look Lila was imposing on the magazine he had edited for so many years. Lila became furious and gave him a severe bawling out. After the blowup, Payne went straight home and told his wife, "Ruth, we're going to Florida. *Now.*"

That very day they left for Florida, though Wally later tried to get hold of his longtime editor and patch things up—to no avail. Not long afterward Payne found himself replaced by Lewis.

Payne's poor relationship with Lila had been exacerbated when his sister took an ocean voyage and happened to mention to another passenger that her brother Kenneth Payne was the man most responsible for the success of the *Reader's Digest*. The passenger, unknown to Payne's sister, was likewise the sister of someone famous at the magazine—Lila Acheson Wallace, no less. When she got a report of the conversation, Lila was not amused.

In the latter days of his tenure, Payne grew increasingly disturbed that he was never going to be named editor. Now in his early seventies, he had for years waited for Wally to announce his own retirement. But that day never came, and now they were both too old. And Payne, though ultraconservative, also never liked sharing power with arch-reactionary Paul Palmer.

Around the same time that Payne departed under such unpleasant circumstances, managing editor Fritz Dashiell was shunted over to General Books, where he became editor of special projects. He was succeeded by Harry H. Harper. Next in line was the new assistant managing editor, Bun Mahony, who routinely worked seven days a week now that Wally was no longer around to send people home at 4 P.M.

Though Payne later managed to salvage something of his relationship with the Wallaces and performed a few minor editorial tasks, working out of his home with the title of senior editor, his career was effectively ended. He died in 1962, bitter at the way he had been treated after so many years of loyal service.

———

OTHER *Post* staffers besides Kenneth Stuart who made their way to Pleasantville in the wake of that troubled institution's latest upheaval were Ben Hibbs, the revered, longtime editor in chief, and Bob Fuoss, his successor, who had accurately predicted that the *Post* would really start having problems the day the *Reader's Digest* began taking advertising. Even the illustrious George Horace Lorimer served for a time as a *Digest* consultant.

Both Hibbs and Fuoss were assigned menial editorial jobs at the *Digest*. The fifty-seven-year-old Fuoss was installed in a handsome office, given a secretary, and put to work editing a series of children's books. Hibbs was occasionally asked to ghostwrite an article for Eisenhower or some other dignitary. For his trouble, Eisenhower was paid $25,000 an article—at the time, the *Digest*'s highest rate. Fuoss soon resigned in disgust, complaining to a friend that, in something more than forty years of experience, the *Digest* managers were the only people he had ever dealt with who turned out to be "completely untrustworthy." Fuoss had been promised a chance to play a significant editorial role in Pleasantville. But those who constituted the *Digest*'s inner editorial circle had no intention of giving either of the once highpowered *Post* editors an inside track.

———

THOUGH Wally was still vigorous in his old age, working on his road, traveling to Hawaii two or three times a year with Lila, and playing an active though no longer pivotal role in the editorial operations of the *Digest,* he also knew he had to plan for the day when neither of them would be there to run the company. Increasingly, also, both of the Wallaces were becoming far more preoccupied with their philanthropic endeavors, now that they ranked among the wealthiest couples in America. Though they kept an exceedingly low profile with their charitable gifts—Wally's mainly to Macalester College and other educational institutions, Lila's primarily to the arts—they also had to ensure that their philanthropy would, after they were gone, continue along the guidelines they established.

Most important of all was the question of who would inherit the Reader's Digest Association after the Wallaces passed away—a question on nearly everyone's mind now that they were both in their early seventies. Though they had made generous provisions for literally dozens of nephews and nieces, cousins, and other members of the Acheson and Wallace families, no one expected Lila and Wally to divide the company among their relatives.

What seemed to observers to make a lot more sense—in fact, what was the only solution imaginable—was that Fred and Judy Thompson would inherit at least a controlling interest in the company, if not the whole thing outright. But Lila and Wally never hinted to anyone what they had in mind, and kept their own counsel. It was almost as if they had a secret and were going to reveal only a little of it at a time.

In 1961 Wally had quietly begun appointing certain chief business executives and editors to vice-presidencies. Several of those appointees first learned of their elevation only when a colleague pointed out their new status on the masthead, or they learned about it from a friend.

A few days before Christmas 1964, at a luncheon for top editors and senior management in the Guest House, Wally announced almost casually that he and his cofounder had decided to create the office of president and that they were appointing Hobe Lewis to the position. Lewis was also to hold the title of editor in chief, while DeWitt and Lila became cochairmen. At the time the fifty-five-year-old Lewis was executive editor and a vice-president. Though he had some premonition that he might eventually take on a greater role in the running of the company, he was as stunned by the announcement as everyone else. The same announcement also named Harry H. Harper a vice-president and executive editor and Bun Mahony a vice-president and managing editor.

Though it was tacitly understood that Wally would remain an active editor at some level, most of the editorial staff were relieved that the company would continue to be run by someone on the editorial and not the business side. The momentous changing of the guard received scant notice in the *New York Times,* however, which reported merely that Lewis "did some traveling" with former vice-president Richard M. Nixon during his unsuccessful presidential campaign against John F. Kennedy. In that capacity, said the paper, Lewis served as a deputy of the Wallaces.

The appointment of Lewis to the presidency turned out to be only a warm-up. Almost exactly a year later, Wally again surprised the small, insular world of the Reader's Digest Association—this time shaking it to its very foundations with an executive reorganization unlike anything in its previous forty-three years. It amounted to his second revolution, the first being his radical decision to change the magazine's editorial mix, in effect upgrading it from a reprint magazine to a magazine of originals, plants, and genuine reprints. A third upheaval did not occur until 1984, three years after his death. What Wally had up his sleeve, as he entered his seventy-seventh year, was stunning proof of his determination to steer the RDA into the future with no regard for family sentiment, the advice of his closest confidants, or conventional corporate wisdom.

On Christmas Eve, Al Cole traditionally hosted a lavish party in the fireplace room of a local restaurant called Nino's. As usual, on December 24, 1965, the magazine's upper-level employees on both the editorial and the business side began arriving late in the afternoon. After the party was in full swing, Wally arrived alone, although he had not been expected to make an appearance. Cole greeted him warmly. Wally asked for everyone's attention. All the partygoers assumed that the boss was going to wish them a happy holiday before heading back to High Winds. Instead, he said that he had an announcement to make.

First, he declared that Al Cole was going to vacate his position as general manager as of the beginning of the new year. Second, he named Paul W. Thompson as his replacement. Then he appended a few kind but vague words about Fred Thompson—that his talents would somehow be put to good use and so forth. That very day Fred had been discharged from a New York hospital and was still recovering from a bout of hepatitis, though he managed to make it to the party.

Everybody in the room was thunderstruck—above all, Al Cole, Paul Thompson, and Fred Thompson, none of whom had been consulted in advance or had any premonition of the shake-up. Some people wondered whether Wally had become confused and named the wrong Thompson. Cole immediately stood up and said, "Wally, this is the worst thing you've ever done to me."

Walter Hitesman and Dick Waters, staunch allies of Fred Thompson, likewise arose and announced their resignations. The dispossessed nephew-in-law just sat at a table with his head down, too stunned to speak. Hobe Lewis, who had not been consulted about the changes either, was equally dumbfounded. But Paul Thompson, hearing the negative reaction to his appointment, overcame his own surprise, stood up, and in a defiant voice said to Wally and the crowd, "I accept."

Wally left immediately for home. Cole and a few others stepped out into the night in a daze. The cold was no more bitter than their own feeling that Wally had betrayed them—betrayed their loyalty, betrayed an obligation to Fred Thompson, who by right of marriage and proven business acumen was the Wallaces' rightful heir, betrayed the future of the RDA itself by handing it over to the care of an ex-general held in low esteem by most of the magazine's fiscal mavens. Only production chief Kent Rhodes went over to the new business manager to shake his hand and say, "I'm with you."

The very next morning, Christmas Day, Paul Thompson drove to High Winds. He was in a state of high agitation and had to see Wally to make three demands—in effect, three preconditions before he actually took over.

No one at the RDA had any doubt that Lila had a strong hand in the Christmas Eve massacre, as it was already being called. Some speculated that she felt Cole had already received too much credit for the great success of the *Reader's Digest.* Unceremoniously removing him at this juncture made it clear that the company belonged solely to the Wallaces and that they could do with it as they pleased, without regard for the wishes of anyone else; that its success was due, above all, to Wally's editorial genius; and that everyone else's contribution, even Al Cole's, was of a secondary, subordinate, and derivative nature.

Lila had never been as impressed with Cole as Wally was. Once, harking back to the time when the disgraced Arthur Griffiths was business manager, she grumbled to Ralph Henderson, "I wonder who really was the smart one there." She had also played a role in bringing Paul Thompson to Pleasantville from Paris. Even though he eventually was responsible for forcing Barclay out, she liked the diplomatic, deferential Thompson immensely. Cole was still a vigorous seventy-two, and the *Digest* did not have a mandatory retirement policy. Obviously, he looked forward to running the business side of the company for several more years, even if he could not name his own successor. His dismissal—which was also tantamount to telling Fred Thompson that he had no future in the company, and which was made public at a party hosted by Cole himself—seemed not only precipitous but designed to humiliate.

Paul Thompson sat down with Wally and Lila on Christmas morning and told them what he wanted: first, that the RDA institute immediately an automatic and mandatory retirement policy for employees reaching the age of sixty-five, himself included. At the time, he was sixty. Thompson's argument was based on military policy. He wanted younger employees to be able to advance at an orderly rate without meeting resistance at the top from an entrenched gerontocracy. Privately, he also foresaw the possibility that, in five years' time when he himself reached sixty-five, neither Wally nor Lila might be alive. A mandatory retirement policy was also a preemptive way of ensuring that there would be no more such high-echelon massacres, with himself as one of the victims.

Second, Thompson insisted on being given the title of executive vice-president. It was a title that Cole himself had never held. Paul Thompson wanted there to be no doubt as to his authority.

Finally, he demanded that he move into Al Cole's own butternut-paneled office.

"You mean Al can't stay in his office?" Wally asked, perplexed. "But we're all a family."

"This is even more important than the other two," Thompson replied.

Lila teased the new business manager about his insistence on a retirement policy and suggested that he might have many more years of work left in him when he reached sixty-five—an opinion Al Cole would have roundly seconded. But in the end Thompson got his way. Lila and Wally saw the common sense of his three demands and agreed to all of them. Wally said he would telephone Cole and give him the rest of the bad news.

When Thompson returned to work on the first day of the new year, 1966, he discovered that Cole's office was completely bare. The file drawers were empty. He had ordered his secretary to destroy all of his records, so that not one scrap of paper remained to show that a man named Albert Leslie Cole had worked his heart our for thirty-three years to make the *Reader's Digest* the world's most widely read magazine.

The firing of Al Cole marked the beginning of an estrangement between the ex–business manager and Wally that was to last for almost fifteen years, until both were very old men and Wally near death. Though Cole did not turn his back on the RDA—he loved it and Wally too much to make an absolute break, and was soon put on a $30,000-a-year retainer for life—he was not so worried about the company's welfare that he took it upon himself to confer with his successor about the transition of power. The two men never met once to discuss the momentous change in the RDA's business administration. Cole went home to sulk, and Paul Thompson assumed his new duties with characteristic self-confidence.

On the first day of the new regime, Walter Hitesman and Dick Waters paid separate visits to the new executive vice-president, retracted the words they had uttered in a moment of heated emotion, and offered to work as hard and loyally for Thompson as they had for Cole—if that was what Thompson wanted. He accepted their offer. With Fred Thompson now out of the picture, Hitesman, another favorite of Lila's, had decided over the holidays that he himself might someday take over the running of the company. Waters now entertained similar hopes.

In his first administrative act, Thompson established an executive committee and offered Cole the chairmanship, which he accepted. Thompson was a member ex officio. His second act was to send Fred Thompson into exile. The *Digest*'s advertising director was transferred to Australia, taking along with him his wife, Judy, and two sons. Charles D. Hepler, one of the company's original four salesmen, was named as his replacement.

Only two years later did Fred Thompson realize that he had actually been fired that Christmas Eve. When that moment finally dawned, he resigned from the company, returned to the United States, and took a job with *Family Circle.* Later he joined the *New York Times,* where he eventually became advertising vice-president. During his tenure at the *Digest,* perhaps Fred Thompson's most remarkable achievement was that he never made an enemy and was one of the most popular and well-liked people in the company—despite and not because of his relationship with the owners. As affable as he was talented, he maintained his friendships with many of his former colleagues even after he left the company.

But Lila and Judy remained forever estranged, and therein lay the real reason for the abrupt firing of Al Cole and the banishment of his protégé to one of the company's remotest provinces. Some months earlier Lila had found out about Wally's alleged affair with her tall, blonde, blue-eyed niece.

One night after a party at High Winds, according to several reputable sources, Wally had arranged to meet Judy in one of the bedrooms of the Guest House. Somehow there was a mix-up, and Lila learned of the assignation. Fred and Judy were summoned back to the house, and there ensued a row lasting for hours that Wally's nephew and private secretary Gordon Davies described as "terrible."

Judy had compounded the problem by writing a series of scurrilous letters to several of Lila's sisters, reporting on her behavior; and, of course, word had got back to the mistress of High Winds.

During that marathon argument late into the night, long-simmering resentments and family problems were also thoroughly aired. The Thompsons accused the Wallaces of having misled them for years into thinking they were going to inherit the *Reader's Digest* empire, all the while planning something else. Lila was annoyed at Judy's habit of wandering through the rooms of High Winds as if its mistress were already dead, telling people how this and that was going to be changed after the Thompsons moved in. Lila thought Judy not only presumptuous but, even worse, tactless enough to imply that Lila's taste in decor was less than impeccable.

However inured Lila might have become to Wally's infidelities, she obviously drew the line when it came to her own niece. Things were said that night that could never be forgiven or forgotten; and perhaps, in a larger sense, for all the indignities she had suffered during her life, Lila needed to be appeased. Whatever her original relationship with Wilcox, his status was now—and had been for years—nothing more than that of a favored employee and confidant. Wally, meanwhile, continued to live by a double standard that permitted him to roam while remaining the "devoted husband." No matter how broad-minded she had been once upon a time, Lila had had enough.

Since Judy's husband was not only Cole's man but also Wally's, Lila, like Salome, demanded the head of Fred Thompson on a platter. Wally finally had to render to his wife the most valuable thing he possessed—the power to determine the future of the company. At the same time it was the worst possible blow she could deliver against Judy. By the almost unanimous consensus of the RDA's money managers, it was also a decision not in the best interests of the company. Nevertheless, Paul Thompson always insisted afterward that he acted unilaterally and without consulting Wally and Lila when he sent Fred Thompson off to Australia.

With the departure of Al Cole and Fred Thompson, and the RDA now under the leadership of Hobe Lewis, and with a new business manager in place, the company was off to yet another new beginning. Inevitably, though, there was also a certain amount of postmortem analysis, particularly on the managerial level. Stunning as Wally and Lila's move had been, it also undeniably reflected a growing disenchantment with the aging Al Cole.

In the opinion of assistant treasurer Bill Cross, for example, Cole was more a "sales type" than a "true business type." Not only had he always been basically an advertising salesman, but he felt frustrated working for a private company. The *Digest*'s business manager was among those who had tried to persuade Wally to take the Reader's Digest Association public—in the first place because Cole himself had options on half a million shares, but also because he knew the company could expand at a much faster rate if it could amass a great amount of capital through a public offering.

However, once RDA counsel Barnabas McHenry explained to the

Wallaces what a prospectus was, and what they would have to disclose, they not only refused to go public but began an intensive search to find a way to keep it private forever. Since they had no heirs, the only solution was to give the company to charity—though, in a typical Wallace twist on things, he did not want the charities to run the company, which spelled only bureaucracy and stagnation, but vice versa. Keeping the RDA private, yet charity owned, seemed a legal impossibility, if not an outright contradiction in terms, in light of IRS regulations. Yet Wally was intent on finding a way to keep the company from becoming just another publicly owned conglomerate after he and Lila were gone.

According to Cross, moreover, many of the problems the *Digest* was experiencing in the latter part of Cole's career were a result of his increasing frustration. "He was running around with high-powered businessmen from other companies who were swapping success stories," said Cross, "and Al wasn't able to show those guys what a big man he was. He was trying to hit a home run in the later stages of his career."

One of Cole's most damaging long foul balls was the RDA's misguided attempt to sell record players door-to-door. "We had five hundred salesmen," said Cross, "selling crummy RCA Victor portables for huge amounts of money on the installment plan. It was depressing. Also a disaster. We were all ashamed of the thing. But Al wouldn't quit."

Thompson quickly moved to end the project. However, Cross also took a dim view of the new business manager and executive vice-president, even though he had a tremendous track record. In Cross's opinion, the European operation on which Thompson had built his reputation was a "can't-lose game" to begin with, so anyone smart enough not to foul things up too badly was going to look good. Thompson's tendency to surround himself with yes-men also earned him little respect among the company's money men.

To make matters even worse, Thompson's passion for blackboards and diagrams had only grown with his ascendancy. One of his protégés was Judson Bryant, a chartist and ex-military man like himself. Bryant churned out hundreds of charts and graphs, as Thompson continued to imbue the conference room with the air of a war room and each project took on the overtones of a military campaign.

In subsequent years Judy liked to boast to people, including Hobe

Lewis's wife, Edie, about her affair with Wally. Edie and the others assumed her intention was to get back at Lila by spreading the report as widely as possible. But later, after her husband became an executive at the *Times,* she changed her story. Though admitting she and Wally used to meet regularly in New York hotels, she claimed it was only because he was lonely and eager to talk with someone who would not gain financially by knowing him—a curious excuse insofar as the one who stood to gain most financially from Wally was Judy herself.

The transition of editorial power from DeWitt Wallace to Hobe Lewis also marked the end of the *Digest*'s hands-off attitude toward American politics and its entrance into the mainstream with a vengeance. Pleasantville offered just too slow a game for Lewis. Even being the golf partner of Richard M. Nixon, who was already plotting strategy for his campaign to win the Republican nomination and then the presidency in 1968, was not enough to satisfy Lewis's appetite for adventure and the limelight.

IV

INTERREGNUM
[1966–1976]

13

The Sun Prince

THE YEARS stretching from roughly 1966 to 1976 brought the *Digest*'s worst nightmare—an America that bore no resemblance to the Pleasantville of the mind that it had sought to sow in Middle America for more than four decades. But those years also witnessed the magazine's greatest triumph—its role as the mouthpiece of the Silent Majority and the single richest and most powerful champion of Richard M. Nixon in the private sector. At the very least, the *Digest*'s editorial, financial, and strategic contribution to Nixon's election has been greatly underrated. More likely, it was indispensable.

So intimately were magazine and presidency bound together, moreover, that in the wake of Nixon's resignation and disgrace, not only the country at large but the diehard, passionately pro-Nixon outpost in Pleasantville was rent and shaken to its very depths. By 1976 the *Digest* was wallowing in its own saga of shame and scandal, one with national repercussions, which Wally and other executives were quickly able to sweep under the red-white-and-blue Pleasantville rug as if nothing had ever happened.

All that was due primarily to one man, Hobart Durkin Lewis, whose editorship coincided with those tumultuous eleven years, and who was the first person after Wally to leave his invisible signature, like a watermark, on the pages of the magazine. That signature was a virtual facsimile of Wally's. If during the forties and fifties a number of *Digest* editors came to look on DeWitt Wallace as a father figure and themselves as his sons, that sentiment was unilateral. The only person on the editorial side Wally looked upon as a "son" was Hobe Lewis, who shared many of his personal and editorial traits.

Hobart Durkin Lewis was a New York–born, Princeton-educated copywriter with the advertising firm of N. W. Ayer in Philadelphia when he first got the idea that he wanted to go into publishing. Among Ayer's accounts was *Fortune,* which Lewis handled. Once a month he took a train up to New York to meet with editor Eric Hodgson, and after a while the enterprising copywriter asked for a job. Hodgson explained apologetically that there were no openings.

Some time later, in 1940, Lewis saw in the *New York Times* a position advertised by the *Reader's Digest:* "Young writer wanted. $8000 a year." He applied, only to discover that the position was for a circulation subscription editor. Lewis fancied himself a serious writer, having already published a number of short stories in *Esquire,* the *American Mercury*—where his editor was Paul Palmer—and elsewhere. But common sense told him not to let the high-paying opportunity pass.

On Hodgson's recommendation, Lewis was hired by Al Cole—beating out fifteen hundred other applicants—and put to work. But first, as usual, Cole spent an hour instructing Lewis on his first day on what the magazine and Wally were all about.

"We appeal to the best instincts of mankind," Cole told him. "We want to improve mankind, or rather help them to help themselves. Wally's hooked on self-help, and every article has to have some uplift in it."

Lewis progressed rapidly, through promotions to the international editions, to the editorial ranks of the *Digest* itself, with a two-year stopover at the excerpt department, in Cleveland. While in the Midwest he had to fight a long-distance war with Judy Thompson, who for a time wanted to establish a rival excerpt department in New York and close down the one in Cleveland. Not only was he a diligent worker, but he was also the most skillful among the editors in currying favor with Lila. Getting to be one of "Lila's boys" was a guarantee of something in Pleasantville—either instant favor, followed by cursory dismissal, or a professional lifetime of her powerful sponsorship and blessing.

When Lewis divorced his first wife and began to date excerpt editor Edie Miller, he was momentarily in the Wallaces' doghouse because Lila was not fond of her at all. He even tried to get his first wife to take him back. But later Lewis and Miller were married, and Lila's attitude toward the new Mrs. Lewis softened. After all, she had also dated Paul Palmer, that old charmer and roué, when he was between marriages;

and the equally dapper Lewis wore suits handmade in London by Turnbull and Asser. For that matter, Lewis never forgot what Lila was wearing the first time he met her—matching shocking-pink turban and shoes and a bright blue dress.

In the monocultural environment of Pleasantville, Lewis's urbanity and sartorial flair immediately differentiated him from his mostly inter-changeable peers. Moreover, when he put his mind to it, Lewis was a great editor—every bit as good technically as Wally, and positively brilliant at writing headlines and captions. But Wally had an authentic common touch. It came naturally. With Lewis it was an acquired and somewhat restless skill.

Upon his elevation to the editorship, Lewis quickly outgrew the parochial life-style and limited responsibilities that had traditionally gone with the job. Being editor of the *Reader's Digest* was not his life but a door to the bigger world outside Pleasantville. After forty years in the wilderness, the *Digest* was about to get a taste of the promised land— the Oval Office, Hollywood, Broadway.

To at least one colleague the new editor in chief was the Sun Prince. His reign was to be long and, on the whole, prosperous, if only because it was difficult for the *Digest* to lose money even when it spent reck-lessly, as it was to do frequently over the decade ahead. But the day would come when the Sun Prince flew too close to the sun, and a darkness fell on Happy Valley.

EVEN after the great row at High Winds, after Lila found out about Wally and Judy Thompson, the Wallaces seldom if ever disagreed, much less argued, in public. But the business of Judy Thompson still rankled. Particularly in winter, when the Wallaces stayed at their suite at the Pierre, they continued their practice of inviting high-ranking *Digest* editors and executives out for an evening of dinner and theater (Trader Vic's was a favorite restaurant). After a second martini had loosened her tongue, Lila was known to direct the conversation around to her niece, reviling her with catty remarks while the guests squirmed uneasily.

There was no such thing, of course, as being one of "Lila's girls." Not a single woman in the *Digest* family, whether employee or spouse, enjoyed anything close to an intimate relationship with Mrs. DeWitt Wallace. By now there were some women who had worked their way up to the lower editorial tiers. Gertrude Arundel was head of the research department, and Vera Lawrence oversaw excerpts. But members of these two departments were considered second-class editorial citizens. Notable distaff associate editors included Audrey J. Dade, Helen Hector, and Grace Naismith. All were eventually to achieve the rank of senior editor, and Dade became assistant managing editor.

But neither they nor the generation of female editors that followed were to advance any further. Though paternalism and sexism were pandemic in the American workplace in the years before Betty Friedan's *The Feminine Mystique* sounded the alarums of revolt, the conditions in Pleasantville provided an extreme example of male intransigence and patronization.

The most blatant gender discrimination occurred in the editorial trainee program run out of the research department in New York. That department and the magazine's library had always been housed in Midtown Manhattan, because researchers needed to trudge to and from the main branch of the New York Public Library, on Fifth Avenue and Forty-second Street, and to other archival resources in the city. In 1965 the *Digest* moved its research department to the thirty-fourth floor of the Pan Am Building, over Grand Central Station. New house counsel William Barnabas McHenry and his staff were also quartered there, as was Kenneth Wilson, liaison and chief negotiator with New York publishers for both the *Digest* and Condensed Books.

The overwhelming majority of researchers were women, a preponderance of them graduates of a Seven Sister college. An unspoken policy at the *Reader's Digest* was that a young female hired by the research department could expect to stay there for the length of her career, or perhaps move laterally into the excerpt department. A few young men were also hired as researchers, but everyone understood they were really part of the editorial trainee program lately devised by management to make its young recruits more professional—just like those at the hated *New Yorker*, in fact, and a lot less like the "gifted amateurs" once ridiculed in that magazine's pages.

Whether as a result of that policy or simply because the type of young woman the *Digest* tended to hire at that time had little interest in a career to begin with, the research department for many years had a reputation as a cushy place for debs and postdebs to set up lunch dates, cocktail parties, and Junior League functions. Male researchers were paid a significantly higher salary. But, the argument went, they had themselves and their families to support, while the debs-cum-researchers used their paychecks for cab fare and other incidentals and paid their rent with the interest from their trust funds.

Yet the debs acquitted themselves well, and over the years the department became a highly professional operation and a legitimate source of pride within the company. Occasionally, a hoax got through, most notably "The Man Who Wouldn't Talk," a 1953 story about the exploits of a Canadian citizen named George DuPre, who claimed he had worked for the French resistance in World War II. DuPre's death-defying heroics in the service of democracy were written up by *Digest* superhack Quentin Reynolds, whose fat-cat Westchester life-style and alcoholism had destroyed whatever native journalistic skepticism he had once possessed, and a book version was later published by Random House. Soon after publication, a Canadian newspaper exposed DuPre, who as it turned out had never even been to France.

But such slipups were the exception. With a passion for accuracy that sometimes verged on the sublimely ridiculous, and in some ways rivaled and perhaps equaled that of its vaunted counterpart at the *New Yorker,* just two blocks away, the research department checked an average of two thousand facts from an average of 450 sources in every issue.

But the *Digest*'s research department also had an Achilles' heel, a fatal flaw that over the years permitted literally hundreds of fact-checked falsehoods, distortions, and half-truths to creep into its stories. That flaw was the Washington bureau, or rather the way in which it was able to manipulate the verification of facts to its own political ends. If the bureau was opposed to a piece of welfare legislation or favored a proposed Pentagon defense contract, the researchers were directed by a Washington staffer to check their "facts" with a congressman opposed to the one or a Defense Department bureaucrat supporting the other. Frequently, given the bureau's propensity for ghostwriting, author and source were one and the same. (Many ghosted articles carried names invented just for the sake of putting a fresh byline into the magazine, or as a way of distancing the bureau from the piece in question. Such fictitious bylines were known as "stiff names," a play on "ghost.")

A textbook example was bureau chief Chuck Stevenson's May 1964 castigation of the Area Redevelopment Administration, an aggressive antipoverty federal agency designed to provide technical assistance and financial aid to blighted areas. Unusually lengthy at 4,500 words, like many articles aimed at favorite *Digest* targets, particularly in an election year, Stevenson's latest adventure in underhandedness followed a familiar formula. The title, as so often, was a rhetorical question: "Is This the Way to Fight the War against Poverty?" The answer, equally formulaic, praised the idealism inherent in any war against poverty but laboriously tut-tutted the waste of taxpayer money and the usual bureaucratic snarl. The ARA subsequently complained that Stevenson's article contained twenty inaccurate or misleading statements of fact. An independent third party confirmed that fourteen of his indictments were inaccurate and that in only six was Stevenson possibly correct.

James Daniel's September 1961 "Let's Look at Those 'Alarming' Unemployment Figures" caused Ewan Clague, director of the Bureau of Labor Statistics, to complain that he had never read "a short article in which so many inaccurate statements were presented in support of such unwarranted conclusions."

Daniel refused an invitation to testify about his article before the congressional Joint Economic Committee. His article charged the U.S. Employment Service with manipulating statistics to make the unemployment situation appear more dire than it was. But a study by an independent committee of economists and statisticians of the methods used by the Bureau of Labor Statistics found Daniel's charges to be groundless. Secretary of Labor Arthur Goldberg also wanted to write a rebuttal to the article, but his request to the *Digest* was ignored.

On the other hand, two of the most ambitious and successful projects undertaken by Arundel and her staff was the research for two of Cornelius Ryan's war books, *The Longest Day*, on D-Day, and *A Bridge Too Far*, on the fall of Berlin. Ryan was one of Wally's favorite writers. At a Guest House luncheon one day in the late fifties, he invited the author to choose any subject he wanted to write about—much as he had done for Michener—and the *Digest* would lavish on him all the money and research support he needed. Ryan replied that he had always wanted to do a book on the Normandy invasion.

Wally was enthusiastic. In short order, fourteen researchers were dispatched to search war records in five different countries. In addition, the research department sent out three thousand questionnaires and interviewed seven hundred participants or eyewitnesses. Though the research bill mounted into the hundreds of thousands, Wally's matchless generosity was such that he still wanted no payback. Ryan's book was published by Simon & Schuster and became a huge bestseller. All Wally asked for was first-serial rights—the right to publish an excerpt from the book in the magazine and also in Condensed Books before any competitor. For that privilege the man who underwrote the book paid an additional $150,000. There was simply no concern about the bottom line.

By the time Ryan got around to doing his second book, Bruce Lee—the liberal nobody else in the Washington bureau wanted to touch with a ten-foot blue pencil—was given the thankless task of going through all the army's classified materials on the siege of Berlin that were housed in the National Archives. To get access to the files, Lee had to be given top-secret clearance—via a straightforward application to the army with a ninety-day waiting period and no string-pulling assist from the *Digest.*

Several months later John Toland came in to research *The Last 100 Days,* his own book on the fall of Berlin. Lee moved quickly to block him from access to the Ryan-*Digest* material.

"I've been here for nine months," he told the archivist. "All the material is flagged and cross-referenced. The *Reader's Digest* has put a lot of time and money into this. I'm just not going to let him look at it."

Had the archivist not acquiesced, Lee would have been prepared to take off all the flags and cross-references. For the next five months, while he finished his research, Toland and his wife sat in one cubicle glaring at Lee through the glass, while he glared back at them from another. It was Lee, in fact, who unearthed the materials for Ryan's central thesis—that the American troops under Eisenhower could have taken Berlin. As a result, the Simon & Schuster contract was rewritten and the focus of the book changed from the Red rape of the city to the advance of the Allied forces.

———

JAMES MONAHAN was a fat, bespectacled, two-pack-a-day senior editor with a mission: to bring the American tobacco industry to its knees, just as other Digesters, smokers one and all, had tried before him. Though it was not quite enough to get him to quit smoking personally, Monahan had accumulated an impressive amount of the latest scientific data proving that cigarettes were a leading cause of lung cancer and heart disease.

Monahan was married to roving editor Lois Mattox Miller, a steady, highly professional, nonsmoking health writer whose work reflected a much more responsible approach to issues of health and medicine than had prevailed during the heyday of Paul de Kruif. Following the uproar in the medical community in the wake of de Kruif's irresponsible home remedies, trotted out as the latest in scientific research, the *Digest* had embarked on a course of fence mending with the medical community. Wally himself was eventually to apologize in the pages of the *Journal of the American Medical Association* for "our having caused embarrassment to the already busy doctors" often "overwhelmed and besieged by patients—many of them desperate—who have just read of some treatment and feel they should have it, willy nilly." But he also reminded the doctors that the *Digest* had "opposed attempts of government and do-gooders to socialize" the profession.

Before long, many of the *Digest*'s articles on health were being reprinted from *Today's Health,* a magazine sponsored by the AMA, and occasionally from the AMA *Journal* itself. But that did not stop the magazine from publishing articles like "A Sure, Swift Way to Take Off Weight." Fad diets, like wholesome sex trends, were among the magazine's near-monthly staples and resistant to a responsible editorial cure.

In July 1954 Monahan and Miller's article "The Facts behind the Cigarette Controversy" had provoked greater public interest than any other *Digest* article since Senator Butler's attack on government spending in Latin America a decade earlier. It had reviewed the findings of researchers at such institutions as the Memorial Center for Cancer and Allied Diseases, in New York, the American Cancer Society, and the U.S. Public Health Service, and was the first head-on, frontal assault on the tobacco industry supported by scientific evidence and published in a popular consumer magazine.

Two more articles followed in 1957, again written by Monahan and Miller and again based on laboratory tests of filter-tip cigarettes. After "The Facts behind Filter-Tip Cigarettes" appeared in the July and August issues, showing that Kent filtered cigarettes contained less tar and nicotine than other brands, the sales of Kent skyrocketed. According to a page-one story in the *Wall Street Journal,* Kent sales shot up 500 percent between May and August alone, while shares of the manufacturer A. P. Lorillard rose six points. When columnist Dorothy Thompson asked for a packet of Kents, she was told, "You won't find a carton in town. All sold out. *Reader's Digest.*"

Yet again, as in the case a decade earlier with Old Golds, the end result of a *Digest* crusade against cigarettes was that in the public eye it appeared to be condemning most brands but touting one or two that were less harmful than others. That was certainly the effect the articles had on Wally. He also switched to Kents.

During that same period Monahan was also a prolific author of books—many of them ghosted, in true *Digest* fashion, for people too busy to write their own, or whose story coincided with the magazine's conservative political views. Typically, such books—like Connie Ryan's—were published by a major trade house, with the *RD* asking only for first-serial rights. A case in point was Tom Dooley, the young navy doctor from St. Louis who went to Laos in 1954 to work with refugees fleeing from the Communist regime of Ho Chi Minh in North Vietnam. Ironically, years earlier the *RD* had published a profile of Ho as a patriotic revolutionary exiled in Paris and enamored of Jeffersonian democracy.

Dooley's story was a virtual gift from heaven—an idealistic, devoutly religious American, working in one of the poorest and most oppressed regions on earth, who was single-handedly holding back the Red sea in Southeast Asia with his thumb. Monahan's two assistants were editorial trainees Walter Hunt and Fulton Oursler, Jr. Hunt was a refugee from Standard Oil's house organ, while Oursler, son of Fulton, Sr., was just recently out of the army. With help from the research department, Monahan polished Dooley's *Deliver Us from Evil*, the *Digest* excerpted it, Condensed Books published a condensed version, the book itself became a best-seller, and for the first time Americans began to pay attention to a place—formerly a French problem—called Vietnam. Hunt and Monahan later wrote another of Dooley's books.

By the midsixties, though, Monahan was back in the frontline trenches of the Great Tobacco War, ankle-deep in tar and nicotine. In the evenings, after all the other employees had gone home, he and Oursler visited various desks, emptied the ashtrays, and then measured the length of the butts to determine how far down the average cigarette was smoked. Monahan had also hired Foster D. Snell Inc., consulting chemists and engineers, to survey thirty filter brands on levels of tar and nicotine. The results this time showed that Carleton cigarettes contained the lowest, followed by Marvels, Duke of Durham, True, and Montclair.

The beleaguered but ever wily tobacco industry promptly publicized the findings yet again. Carleton and Montclair were products of the

American Tobacco Company, producing 130.5 billion units a year. At the time, True was still being test-marketed in only ten cities, and after Monahan's article appeared the advertising agency hired to promote it had to quickly develop a national advertising campaign based around the message "Hold on, we're coming!" Said a spokesman for Lorillard, makers of True, "The demand has not only been phenomenal but tremendous."

Occasionally, Wally popped into Monahan's office. The Sky Club on the top floor of the Pan Am Building was one of his favorite lunchtime hangouts. As Condensed Books had an office on another floor, there were plenty of excuses for him to wander through the halls—usually unannounced. But in Monahan's case, Wally was less interested in chatting about his pioneering series, and all the publicity it was generating for the *Digest,* than in sneaking around to grab a spare pack or two of cigarettes that had not been consigned to the laboratory. At the time he was trying to give up smoking and had to hide his habit from Lila.

———

WHEN the *Digest* began accepting advertising, in 1954, Wally had proposed—as a way to ensure quality copy—that the text be written by editors of the magazine. Eventually, to some extent, editorial copy writing did become a practice at Pleasantville, though for appearance's sake the editors hired to perform that task were retired rather than still on the payroll. Given Wally's enthusiastic attitude toward advertising as yet another conduit of information, no hypocrisy or breach of ethics was probably involved, at least insofar as he personally was concerned. But the net effect, to which Wally was almost willfully blind, was to erode the editorial credibility of the magazine itself and to blur the line that separated copy written by advertisers from copy edited by editors.

Senior editor Sam Schreiner's most vivid impression on arriving at Pleasantville was that the usual tension between the editorial and the business sides of most publishing enterprises was "almost totally absent"—in contrast to Harold Ross's dictum that advertising representatives were forbidden even to set foot on the *New Yorker*'s editorial floor.

In fact, so blurred was the division between *Digest* editorial and advertorial that editors were often drafted as hosts or tour guides for visiting advertisers. Nor were editors and writers prohibited from accepting free weekends at the hunting and fishing lodges of wealthy businessmen. In return, those same editors and writers were expected to address advertising conferences and stockholder meetings throughout the country, and even around the world.

A typical instance of editorial/advertising collusion occurred in an *American Legion Magazine* reprint in May 1965 called "Coping with Crank Phone Calls," which offered advice to people bothered by unwanted calls. The most obvious suggestion, that they ask the phone company for an unlisted number, was not given. The *ALM*, a longtime favorite source for planting, had begun its article with the statement "It may be that you need an 'unlisted' or a 'non-published' number." AT&T was a major advertiser in the *Digest* and had a long-standing policy of discouraging unlisted phone numbers as bad for business. Obligingly, the *Digest* removed precisely what Wally claimed good advertising ought to provide—sound information.

The very next month the *Digest* reprinted an *Esquire* article on American gasolines, but condensed away all references to advertising gimmicks used by the oil companies, such as Shell's platformate or Texaco's claim that it tailored all of its gasolines to different climatic conditions around the country. The *Digest* also added a new final paragraph: "But whatever you pay, you can be sure that you are getting one of the best bargains in industry." Needless to say, oil companies such as Shell and Texaco were major advertisers, especially in the international editions.

That September an article titled "How Good Are American Cars?" answered unequivocally that they were "the best buys in the world today." To the question "What Are the *Real* Causes of Auto Crashes?" it had in April 1964 answered that poor maintenance, bad driving, bad highways, and a lack of seat belts were the main causes—not unsafe cars. The question "Are Cars as Good as They Used to Be?" was in the February 1964 issue given an answer that Cadillac, Chrysler, Oldsmobile, Rambler, Mercury, Pontiac, and Ford—all of which had full-page color advertisements in that issue—wanted to hear: American cars were better.

The *Digest* was becoming not merely an advertising medium but a huckster for American business. According to the liberal *Changing Times, Digest* editors as a matter of policy "always show advance proofs of the text to advertisers if the story conflicts with advertisers' interests." More often, the proofs were leaked by advertising salesmen eager not to displease a client—a common enough occurrence in magazine publishing in general. What distinguished the *Digest* was not that it was especially beholden to the advertising department. If the *RD* did abridge and mend its text from time to time to please an advertiser, it was not because it feared any loss of income. Rather, more startlingly, as instance after instance demonstrated, it was simply because *Digest* editors agreed that big business was right, and tailored their text accordingly.

—

IN 1965, like a plague of twenty-year locusts, the left-liberal press decided to invade Pleasantville once again. It was not a conspiracy and did no serious damage, since by this time the *Digest* was immune to almost any kind of criticism and sniping. The plague amounted to little more than a small dark cloud passing over the kingdom's otherwise perpetually blue sky.

The cloud became noticeable in the March 13, 1965, issue of the *New Republic* when columnist TRB (Richard Strout) claimed that conservative opponents of the Supreme Court's recent one-man-one-vote ruling were mounting a counterattack and getting powerful support from the *Reader's Digest.* That ruling had set the stage for a redressing of political power between the states and the cities in a country that had become 70 percent urban. With their power base largely in rural areas, conservatives hoped to dilute the reform, according to TRB, by enacting a constitutional amendment permitting each state "to decide whether one of the two legislative bodies could be apportioned on a basis of something other than people—cows, maybe, or acres."

TRB went on to note that Reo M. Christenson, a political scientist at Miami University in Ohio, had recently analyzed the *Digest* in the *Columbia Journalism Review* and discovered that it had published "more than 300 articles" on variations of the theme that "federal power is a menace to the liberties of every American, great and small." Christenson's conclusion was that, "beyond cavil," the *Reader's Digest* was "staunchly Republican."

Though that was obviously not objectionable in itself, said Christenson, he thought teachers using the magazine's school edition ought to warn students "of its bias, its partisanship, and the dubious character of its reporting on the Washington scene." A more serious objection was the *Digest*'s refusal to publish letters to the editor rebutting its biased reporting. Two causes for liberal alarm, concluded TRB, were the *Digest*'s having recently been awarded the Medal of Freedom by the right-wing Freedoms Foundation and its attack in the March issue, then on sale, on the "federal one-man-one-vote heresy." Such a rule, according to the *Digest,* might lead to "legislatures under the raw control of metropolitan vote-getting machines."

Professor Christenson's "Report on the Reader's Digest" in the winter 1965 issue of the *CJR,* to which TRB alluded, was not only the first in-depth journalistic analysis of the magazine in twenty years. It was also the first disinterested retrospective—*pace* any Pleasantville paranoia—since Norman Cousins had undertaken a private review of the magazine as a favor to Wally back in 1944.

The occasion for Christenson's article was the recent announcement by Wally and Lila that after forty-two years of guiding the magazine they had decided to step aside and assume the honorary posts of cochairman. The article's focus was an examination of the *Digest's* public-affairs material in the postwar era. Recalling an observation made by the liberal Catholic weekly *Commonweal* in 1944 that the *Digest* was then the most powerful vehicle for the printed word in the American hemisphere, Christenson claimed that the same was still true twenty years later. *Commonweal's* rejoinder was also noted—namely, that "the millions of people who depend largely on the *Digest* are in danger of intellectual malnourishment and ideological deficiency diseases." Christenson found no reason to revise that verdict either.

Like other critics before him, Christenson reproached the *Digest* for maintaining the pretense of offering its readers a "cross section of magazine opinion" when, in fact, 70 percent of its articles, "including a high percentage of those dealing with public affairs," were either staff written or plants. "These practices help insure that the *Digest* offers its own philosophy, not a sampling of American opinion."

What followed was a lengthy critique of two decades' worth of public-affairs articles to assay their "reportorial accuracy." Christenson found, not surprisingly, that a dominant editorial theme was that "federal officials are congenitally extravagant, that deficit spending and the national debt threaten disaster, that federal taxes are an insupportable burden, that the federal bureaucracy bungles and botches as it bloats, and that federal power is a menace to the liberties of every American, great and small."

Christenson offered the following general assessment:

> The typical *Digest* reader is exposed to more worthwhile literature than would be the case if the *Digest* were not on the scene. . . . And it helps

youngsters develop reading habits—a service of no mean importance. It is a pity, though, that a magazine that in so many respects has demonstrated its ability to meet the tastes and needs of millions of Americans should have its usefulness so seriously impaired by editing so obsessed with the wickedness of Washington under Democrats that it countenances or encourages shoddy and politically biased reporting.

The TRB and *CJR* pieces were only the preliminaries. The main event appeared in the March–April issue of *Fact* magazine, where the *Reader's Digest* became the object of criticism that passed over from alarm and ridicule to loathing and derision—some of it wildly unfair, some of it irrefutable, all of it confirmation that the zeitgeist of the sixties and the *Reader's Digest* were on a collision course. Just as the magazine was the perfect embodiment of the Eisenhower fifties, so it was the epitome of almost everything that the counterculture then brewing in Haight-Ashbury and New York's East Village found repugnant in American culture and politics.

Ralph Ginzburg, publisher of *Fact,* had the unenviable distinction at the time of being America's most notorious pornographer, having published four issues of a glossy quarterly devoted to erotica called *Eros*—exceedingly tame by later standards, but shocking enough to some sensibilities in the early sixties that Ginzburg was eventually required to serve eight months in prison.

Fact, equally brief-lived, was his revenge against the narrow-minded, puritanical forces that had put him there—the magazine was published while he appealed his sentence. The names on its prominent list of contributors ranged from Saul Bellow and Art Buchwald to Westbrook Pegler and Pierre Salinger.

Foremost among Ginzburg's Calvinist persecutors was "The Pleasantville Monster," as the article by journalist Warren Boroson was provocatively entitled. Ginzburg made it his cover story, using as artwork three monkeys covering their eyes, ears, and mouth with large type reading out of the logo, "Fact: *Reader's Digest* is dishonest, ignorant, irresponsible, John Birchite, anti-Jewish, & anti-Negro." The lead illustration accompanying the article itself depicted a Janus-faced Republican saying out of one side of his face, "We need a little Fascism in the United States," and out of the other, "Pesticides, Cars, Drugs Safe! Safe! Safe!" Fact: Ginzburg was as good at sensationalizing his message in a few words as Wally was.

Ignoring the fact that the RDA ranked only eighth among U.S. media giants, Boroson claimed, "What AT&T is to telephones and what General Motors is to cars, the *Reader's Digest* is to magazine publishing." Proof was that one out of every three literate Americans read the *Digest* and that only the Holy Bible was more widely read. Everybody read it, from Ronald Reagan, the Republican party's latest right-wing banner-waver, to Walt Disney, Chiang Kai-shek, and J. Edgar Hoover. But hardly anybody knew it for what it really was—"a dishonest, hypocritical, reactionary, irresponsible, ignorant, arrogant, money-grubbing swindle sheet": "For the *Digest* is not only the most colossally successful magazine in the world; it is also the world's single most powerful literary instrument of ignorance and evil."

What followed was a reprise of the *Digest's* troubles with the Federal Trade Commission and the American Medical Association, its attempt to put up a billboard while at the same time attacking the industry, and its hypocrisy over cigarette advertising. Boroson reported:

> The *Digest* makes a big smug fanfare about how self-sacrificing it is in refusing cigarette and liquor advertising. What it *doesn't* mention is whether the ban on alcohol and tobacco goes for all 29 editions and not just the American one. For enlightenment on this I wrote to Hobart Lewis, the *Digest's* new president, and his reply was: "In some countries a limited amount of liquor advertising is accepted. In no country is cigarette advertising now accepted."

Only three years earlier, of course, the *Digest* had announced with great fanfare that it was no longer accepting cigarette advertising in its international editions and forecast a loss of $17 million over the next nine years. Suspecting that Lewis was dissembling, Boroson bought two current foreign editions, *Das Beste aus Reader's Digest,* the German version, and *Valitut Palat koonnut Reader's Digest,* the Finnish version. He discovered not only that the magazine's editor in chief was being less than candid but that the *RD* was publishing as much liquor and tobacco advertising as ever:

> In the [German version], I lighted upon full-page ads for Malteserkreuz brandy, Polar Pure rum, Black & White Scotch whisky, Henkell wine, Pott rum, Jacob Stück Scotch whisky, and Wissoll brandy—more ads for liquor than for any other product. In the latter edition, besides Ballantine Scotch

whisky and Aalborg brandy advertisements, I discovered full-page ads for van Kemp cigars, Meester Henk cigarillos, Meester Hans cigars, and Philip Morris, Viceroy, Kent, and Newport cigarettes—more ads for tobacco than for any other product.

Unaware that the magazine had already reversed itself, Boroson drily observed, "Of course, it may be that the *Digest*'s ban on tobacco and alcohol in its domestic version is motivated by a genuine concern for Americans, but if so I cannot help feeling its discriminatory policy is carrying America First a bit too far."

Getting to the nitty-gritty, Boroson chastised the *Digest* for its hypocrisy in sexual matters, always railing against pornography and yet "forever slobbering over it." He went on to identify the magazine's chief antipornography writer, O. K. Armstrong, as a convicted tax evader—and thus "a fitting choice for the *Digest*'s Guardian of Public Morals."

It was the pot's turn to call the kettle black. Warming to his task, Boroson pointed out the *Digest*'s fondness for the off-color joke, then observed that it also published "some of the steamiest advertisements around." In the February 1964 issue an advertisement for Cannon stockings allowed the reader to "peep up a woman's dress," while one for Helene Curtis bath oil portrayed "a woman, from behind, naked down to her behind." In that same R-rated issue, a third advertisement, for Perma Lift, showed "a beautiful blonde bursting out of her bra, the nipple of one breast clearly outlined and the other breast buried in the naked bosom of a little girl." Boroson admitted:

> You have to have a heart of stone not to feel somewhat sorry for the *Digest* in one respect. I mean, when a magazine has run articles entitled "Sex on the Campus," "Too Much Sex on Campus," "Sex in the Classroom" (twice), "Sex Standard in Moscow," "Sexual License: Key Soviet Strategy," "Russia's New Line on Sex," "The Sex Story for Children," "What Not to Tell a Child about Sex," "How Parents Can Help Adolescents Understand Sex," "The Boy and Sex," "What Wives Don't Know about Sex" (twice), "What Husbands Don't Know about Sex," "How Men Feel About Sex," "What Do You Know About the Sexes?" "What the Sex Manuals Don't Tell You," "The Pastor Speaks of Sex and Marriage," "The Mystery of Sex," "Romance Vs. Sex Appeal," "Fiction and Facts about Sex," "Let's Stamp Out S*E*X," "I'm Sick of Sex" (I believe it), "A Woman's Response in Sex Relations," "Sex as a Nazi Weapon," "The Sex Relationship

in Marriage," "The Sexual Relationship in Marriage," "Don't Expect Too Much of Sex in Marriage," "What Is Sex Education?" "Sex Competition," "S-x and the Film," "Perfume and Sex Appeal," "Must We Change Our Sex Standards?" (twice), "Sex Appeal on the Air," "Sex Madness," "Sex Life After Middle Age," "Sex and the Teen-age Girl," etc., it's got to be rather hard-pressed for a new angle.

After cataloging the *Digest*'s sins, Boroson asserted that his main complaint was the magazine's dishonesty in both its advertisements and its articles. "When you come down to it," he concluded, "even the name is a lie. The *Reader's Digest* is not primarily for readers. Nor is it primarily a digest. (For that matter, the *Digest* isn't even situated in Pleasantville anymore . . .) [It] stopped being a magazine for readers in April of 1955." In that month the *RD* began accepting advertising for its U.S. edition.

About the only charge Boroson did not level against the *Digest* was that it had once published two articles by a notorious pornographer—namely, Ginzburg himself. When he was just out of college, he wrote two articles for the magazine—one on long-lived politicians and the other on the draft. The former was planted in *Esquire,* then edited by Arnold Gingrich, who later hired Ginzburg as his second-in-command.

A short while after the *Fact* article was published, an obviously hostile BBC crew arrived from London to prepare a documentary on the *Digest*'s forty-fifth anniversary, in 1967. With the camera trained on Lewis, the interviewer—no doubt primed by the *CJR* and *Fact* articles—wanted to know why the *Digest* was so obsessed with secrecy, a subject the other critics had not touched on. Lewis sidestepped the question and rambled on instead about the magazine's upbeat philosophy, calling it a "Puritan philosophy" based on "the work ethic and the perfectibility of man."

The result, grumbled the BBC commentator, was that people read the *Digest* comfortable in the knowledge that each issue was like the last—no nasty surprises. Worse, it saw a solution to every problem and "heroism rather than misery in every disaster."

—

IN *1966,* when Ronald Reagan was running for governor of California, the *Digest* invited him to a gala Guest House luncheon in his honor. As the Republican party's new right-wing standard-bearer, Reagan was a *Digest* darling and benefited frequently from articles either explicitly favorable to his campaign or critical of the policies of the Democratic incumbent, Pat Brown.

At the time, though, Reagan was still more famous for having been a Hollywood actor than for his opposition to state welfare, federally subsidized medical care, and similar Pleasantville anathemas. The women of the *Digest* were particularly excited at the prospect of his visit, and most of the spouses of the top editors and executives arrived for the event wearing their best dresses.

While Reagan was getting ready in one of the guest rooms upstairs, Wally and Lila, early as usual, mixed with the invited guests. Wally noticed how fashionable all the women looked and called on them to come forward and strut their stuff one at a time. He began with Lila, who obediently modeled her designer dress, doing a mock version of a runway stroll. Then one after the other the women were summoned to parade, turn, and strike a pose, while Wally made goggle-eyes and applauded. Many of the women waited in dread, hoping they would not be invited up, yet having no choice but to heed his call when it finally came. Eventually, Reagan descended the stairs and the floor show ended.

During his after-dinner talk, the future governor railed against the promiscuity of America's youth, citing as an example the time he once went to see a basketball game at the University of California at Berkeley. After the game was over and all the students had left the gymnasium, he went around picking up used condoms and collected fifty-seven that had apparently been put to use during the game. Wally loved the story, and contributed to Reagan's campaign. But he had also discovered a new form of fun—serving as an MC at impromptu employee fashion shows.

Not long afterward Wally cut a picture of a revealing dress out of a magazine and circulated it among the women on the editorial staff, suggesting this was the kind of garment he admired and would not mind seeing adopted by one and all on dressy occasions. Thereafter the fashion-show game became a much more regular and explicit form of entertainment at retirement dinners and other office get-togethers, usually at the Guest House.

In the new version, Wally became the designer and fitter of women's fashion. Often Lila was the first "customer," to warm things up. Wally's first order of business was to appraise his wife's figure, often with cupping gestures of his hand, and playfully show it off from many angles. Then he took measurements, shaking his head in comic incredulity and making it clear that professional scruples forbade him from touching. Each patch of the dress had to be imagined and laid on its proper place. After the dress was sewn together, it needed to be tucked here and there and to be contemplated from a distance every so often.

Then other couples were urged to follow suit, with the husband serving as designer while his wife played at being a wealthy customer to be waited on obsequiously. Wally also made it clear that his and Lila's version was not merely to be matched but to be topped. Sometimes he ordered partners to switch and rematched men and women who were not married to one another.

His admiration of the figures of some female retirees went a step further. One day he stopped by unexpectedly to visit a recently retired but still very attractive associate editor at her friend's New York apartment. During the visit he made a sexual advance by putting his hand on her breast and was strongly rebuffed.

Word of Wally's tasteless, boorish, but all too typical, behavior was spreading not only around the office but also around the villages of Westchester. People wondered whether the games were meant to humiliate and punish Lila or whether the two of them—both known, after all, for their fondness for the risqué—found the game genuinely amusing. Some thought Wally's long-rumored obsession with women was getting a little out of hand. Others even questioned whether, at the age of seventy-six, he was still completely sound of mind.

Wally knew exactly what he was doing. He was having fun and not making any apologies about it. He was equally canny when it came to work. Though no longer editor, or even officially an honorary cochairman along with Lila, Wally kept a tight control on the masthead, and names were added or subtracted only at his direction. But one evening at a dinner party at High Winds, a young editor went up to Wally, who was talking to Lewis, and asked how long a person had to be at the *Digest* in order to get his name on the masthead. Wallace replied, "Why don't you ask the editor in chief?"

After the young man left, a stunned Lewis asked Wally whether he now wanted him to make that kind of decision. Wally replied, "Sometimes."

14

One Bright Light amid the Encircling Gloom

ONE EVENING in the early seventies, while on assignment in Hollywood, *RD* editor Tony Oursler was invited to the home of United Artists producer Arthur P. Jacobs to meet a mystery guest. And therein lay a much larger tale. Like Dante in middle age, the Reader's Digest Association, now under the leadership of Hobe Lewis, had come to a dark wood where the straight way was lost.

Only recently the RDA had decided to get into the movie-making business. Oursler was dispatched to the film capital because he had once ghosted the draft of Lillian Gish's memoirs and because his late father was the author of that mogul masterpiece *The Greatest Story Ever Told.*

Oursler's liaison at UA, the RDA's business partner, was David Chasman. When the two men arrived at Jacobs's sumptuous Hollywood home, the producer introduced Oursler to his actress wife, Natalie Trundy, and offered them a cocktail but said they would have to drink it quickly. That was because as soon as their other guests arrived they would all sit down to dinner. Just as Oursler and Chasman were handed their drinks, the doorbell rang.

"Gulp them down," said Jacobs.

Then he went to answer the door. Moments later Groucho Marx appeared in the room, walking with a cane and supported by his companion Erin Fleming. Jacobs introduced Oursler as an editor for the *Reader's Digest*. Still holding Oursler's hand, Groucho reeled backward and an expression of mock pity clouded his face.

"What a tragedy," he stage-whispered, adding, "You poor boy. That's the worst thing I've heard today. Tell me, how did it happen?"

At the dinner table, Groucho returned to his theme:

"So . . . how *did* it happen? How did a nice boy like you ever become an editor at a place like that?"

"Well," Oursler began, "to make a long story short . . ."

"Congratulations," Groucho interrupted. "Did you rehearse that? Or is it fresh from the hearse?"

"My father was an editor at the *Digest,*" Oursler managed to say, after the laughter died down, "and after he died . . ."

"Ah, I see. It's a *genetic* disease. Have you seen a doctor?"

"No, sir."

"Sir? Did he call me *sir?* Have I just been knighted or am I just benighted?"

The conversation soon veered into other directions, but at one point Groucho returned to the *Digest* and asked Oursler, "Is it true all your writers are midgets?"

As desert neared, Oursler felt emboldened to ask, "Groucho . . ."

"He got the name right. I'm de-*knighted* to make his acquaintance. Yesss?"

"Have you ever read the *Digest?*"

"I wanted to," Groucho replied. "I really did, but a friend warned me off. He read it for a month. An article a day. He loved it, he said, but nights, he suffered from . . . *short*comings."

After the laughter again died down, Groucho revealed that the *Digest* was a "secret resource for comedians" because they had all stolen jokes from it. He went on to applaud the *Digest* art of the one-liner.

"But last month you carried condensation one step too far," he continued. "You published one of my jokes and then sent me a condensed *check*. The bank teller wouldn't cash it. He said he couldn't count that low."

Oursler nicely riposted that the board of editors, after careful consideration, had agreed that Groucho was to get "half of what we pay Bob Hope."

This time Groucho laughed the loudest.

Oursler's odyssey had begun a short while earlier when Hobe Lewis and New York celebrity agent Helen M. Strauss, neither of whom knew anything about the movie business, sat down to lunch to talk about exactly that. The RDA had just undergone yet another executive shake-up, this time leading to the forced retirement of business manager Paul Thompson. Treasurer Dick Waters, production head Kent

Rhodes, marketing virtuoso Walter Hitesman, and Lewis, among others, decided they could no longer tolerate Thompson's military style of leadership and failure to move the company forward in any significant way. Though the RDA's growth had been steady, they looked on the ex–brigadier general as a caretaker who had failed to take full advantage of the *Digest*'s brand-name recognition and apple-pie status with the American public. A delegation went to see Wally, whose attitude was, as always, cruelly Darwinian—let the managers fight it out among themselves, and the strongest and best would survive.

As a result, scarcely six years after Thompson had taken over the top position, the old warrior gracefully resigned under pressure. Fortunately, as a face-saving gesture, he was able to point out that the resignation coincided with his sixty-fifth year. Yet most insiders believed he had every intention of staying on—thus the coup—despite his insistence, on taking over from Al Cole, that the RDA institute a mandatory retirement policy. That policy had never been implemented except when it suited Wally's purposes—which it now did. Though Thompson lived just across the company campus, he faded away without even an offer of the chairmanship as a consolation prize.

Editor in chief Hobe Lewis now became the company's first chief executive officer—further evidence that Wally did not want anyone on the business side running the company. The courtly Rhodes and the abrasive Hitesman, once good friends and now rivals, advanced to the posts of first vice-president and executive vice-president, respectively. But Lewis's closest ally on the business side was Dick Waters, an ambitious maverick who had his sights set on eventually becoming chairman.

Soon afterward Lewis was having lunch with Strauss, an agent with the William Morris Agency, whose clients included *Digest* superstar James Michener. In recent years the need for wholesome entertainment had never seemed more urgent. A sex revolution unlike any seen in Western civilization in four hundred years was sweeping across Europe and America, and it was largely being spawned by magazines—competitors with the *Digest* on its own newsstand turf, in particular *Playboy* and *Penthouse*.

Worse, those same magazines were already slouching toward Hollywood. *Playboy*'s Hugh Hefner was bankrolling a bloody version of Shakespeare's *Macbeth*—all the more lurid considering that Sharon Tate, wife of director Roman Polanski, had only recently been stabbed to death in a sensational ritual murder by followers of Charles Manson. Violent movies like *Easy Rider* and *Dirty Harry* were the big box-office hits. With the Disney studio in disarray following the death of its founder in 1966, family-oriented entertainment had become such an unpopular commodity that the American Baptist Convention finally had to distribute *The Cross and the Switchblade,* a movie about a minister who tamed New York street gangs with a Bible.

Over lunch Strauss mentioned that her friend Arthur B. Krim, head of United Artists, was making a family-style movie called *Tom Sawyer* and looking for a coproducer. The previous credits of executive producer Arthur Jacobs included *Dr. Dolittle* and *Goodbye, Mr. Chips.* When Lewis expressed an interest, Strauss arranged for him to fly out to Hollywood to view the first rushes. Lewis liked what he saw—a wholesome, high-adventure, predigested vision of an unspoiled America, only set to music. Even more, he loved rubbing shoulders with moguls and movie actors.

After talking things over with Waters and Wally, Lewis told Krim that the RDA would agree to be coproducer and assume half the $2.8 million production cost in return for half the profit. In June 1972 United Artists and RDA officially joined forces to present a series of films designed to appeal to family audiences—despite the fact that UA had built its critical reputation on such serious non-family works as *Fellini Satyricon, Sunday Bloody Sunday,* and Ken Russell's *Women in Love.*

Lewis thought the *Digest* could well afford to gamble. Condensed Books, the fattest cash cow in the Pleasantville pasture, continued to set new records. On January 1, 1966, the magazine had raised its circulation guarantee to 15.5 million; the following year it raised it by another million. The October 1964 issue had set a new all-time record for advertising revenue, which only continued to climb. Even after Wally and Lila had given away millions to their charities, there was plenty of small change left over.

From the very beginning, it looked as though Lewis and Waters had the golden touch. *Newsweek* paid a visit to the *Tom Sawyer* set, describing Oursler as the "reserved, tweedy assistant managing editor" who served as the "magazine's eyes and ears," and talked about its serious commitment to family fun. The RDA's man in Hollywood himself delighted in his glamorous new life-style—reading scripts aboard a 707, answering the telephone at his table in the Polo Lounge, watching rushes in a darkened room, and deciding that, yes, Jodie Foster would make an ideal Becky Thatcher.

Tom Sawyer, starring Johnny Whitaker as Tom and Celeste Holm as Aunt Polly, opened at Radio City Music Hall to long lines despite tepid reviews. According to an ecstatic UA spokesman, the Reader's Digest logo affixed to a movie "practically guarantees that people all over Middle America will come to see your picture." To prod Middle America along, the *Digest* ran a seven-page article on the movie in its July issue to coincide with its national release. It also published a piece of wishful thinking called "Are Dirty Movies on the Way Out?" At a big party in the lobby afterward, everybody got tight and hilarious. A triumphal Lewis approached Krim and announced, "Arthur, tomorrow we're going to start making *Huck Finn.*"

Almost immediately, though, the RDA began to experience difficulties receiving a proper accounting from UA on what kind of profit the first picture was generating. Though the figures were published every week in *Variety*—in its first twelve weeks at only two theaters, *Tom Sawyer* had grossed more than $2 million, or more than two-thirds of its production cost—the *Digest*'s net share remained a mystery number always out of reach of the company's accountants, who knew how to play the same game in magazine publishing but had no idea what their counterparts in Hollywood were up to.

Undeterred, Lewis pushed on. After all, *Macbeth* had in the meantime proven to be a $3 million disaster, while *Penthouse*'s Bob Guccione was sinking five times that amount into an X-rated debacle called *Caligula.* Though all three publishers were moving out of their usual areas of expertise, only the RDA seemed to have found the right formula. Getting a proper accounting of the film's profits was, for the time being, a mere detail.

Halfway through the filming of *Huck Finn,* producer Jacobs died unexpectedly. Unperturbed, Krim informed Lewis that the RDA would have to pay Jacobs's widow the full amount remaining on his contract. That was how business was done in Hollywood, Krim explained. Lewis concurred. The RDA paid.

The cost overruns continued to mount. Finally, the movie—another musical—made it into the theaters. Nobody liked it, nobody went to see it. *Tom Sawyer* eventually turned a modest profit. Nobody cared. *Huck Finn* had cost the company millions. The lowest point for Lewis came when Wally dropped by his office one day and said, "Lila and I were walking down the street the other day and saw *Huck Finn* on the marquee, so we went in and there were only twelve other people in the audience with us."

Even Lewis had to agree that the film was as terrible as *Tom Sawyer* was good. But he was still smitten with Hollywood. The problem was that he needed a producer whom he could trust. Helen Strauss, then in her seventies, seemed the ideal choice, even though she had less experience than Oursler. Strauss became chief of the RDA's new movie and TV department. Together she, Waters, and Lewis decided to make a movie out of Charles Dickens's *The Old Curiosity Shop*.

Kent Rhodes, Waters's assistant treasurer Bill Cross, and other fiscal conservatives in Pleasantville were alarmed when they heard the news but were powerless to stop the Lewis-Waters-Strauss star-struck express. They grew even more concerned on hearing that Strauss and Lewis wanted to call the film *Mr. Quilp,* after the hideous dwarf who played the villain. At the last moment, in an effort to breathe some life into the film, the title was changed back to *The Old Curiosity Shop*. Dickens's tearjerker, despite Anthony Newley in the lead role and a happy ending obligingly provided by Pleasantville, lost $4 million anyway.

But Lewis was not a quitter. Subsequently, he called Strauss again to say he had recently been reading *The Memoirs of Sarah Bernhardt* and wanted to make another musical, called *The Incredible Sarah*. Strauss thought it was a wonderful idea. British actress Glenda Jackson was cast in the starring role. The best part came when Lewis and Waters got to fly over to England, where the movie was being filmed, to see the rushes. They liked what they saw, but *Sarah* bombed anyway and millions more were lost.

Though frustrated and disappointed, Lewis was still not ready to give up. He and Waters had also recently become involved in backing a Broadway musical. The editor in chief had heard at a cocktail party that a play heading for New York was looking for a backer. The next day he called Waters and suggested they and their wives drive up to East Haddam, Connecticut, that weekend to see the play at the Goodspeed Opera House. Waters agreed and proposed they take his car.

Waters's driver was named Walter. On the appointed evening, with Walter at the wheel, the foursome drove up to Connecticut. An ex–sanitation driver, Walter was not only on overtime but had also been promised dinner money and a ticket to the show. That promised to be a special thrill because he had never seen a play before in his life.

After the play was over, Walter picked up his party on schedule. June Waters and Hobe Lewis thought the musical was so corny that the American public would never go for it. But Edie Lewis and Dick Waters were enthusiastic. Finally, to settle the argument, Hobe asked, "Walter, what do you think?"

"I thought it was great!" Walter exclaimed.

They drove the rest of the way home in silence. The next morning, Lewis phoned Waters and said, "Well, what shall we do?"

"You heard the vote," Waters replied.

"Yeah, three to two," Lewis said. "Walter wins."

The RDA decided to back the musical, and *Shenandoah*, based on a 1965 movie starring James Stewart, went on to become a modest critical success. Though it had been years since Broadway had seen a hit on the order of *Hello, Dolly, Fiddler on the Roof*, or even *Zorba*, Waters and Lewis thought the Great White Way had never looked rosier. Later they agreed to back another musical and gave David Susskind nearly $500,000 to produce *All Things Bright and Beautiful*, based on James Herriot's best-selling memoir about his years as a country veterinarian in between-the-wars England. The book had also been one of Condensed Books's all-time best-sellers, and the stage version had been playing to full houses in the British Isles, in Canada, and in Australia. If anything looked as though it were going to turn a bright and beautiful profit, *Bright and Beautiful* did.

But the RDA did not understand Broadway accounting procedures any more than it understood Hollywood's and never recouped its investment on *Shenandoah* either. Meanwhile, Wally was becoming increasingly agitated. Though he did not like to make excess profit, losing so much money was another matter. To an interviewer doing a story on the company's branching out into other areas besides publishing, he had bluffed, "We do as we damn well please, and that's close to ideal."

But the loss of millions upon millions was also making him very angry. Once a week he called assistant treasurer Cross to ask, "Did we get our money back on *Shenandoah* yet?"

Cross's answer was always no. After *Bright and Beautiful* flopped, Hitesman, Rhodes, and Cross were finally able to persuade Wally to forbid Lewis and Waters to produce any more movies or plays. Oursler was summoned home.

———

MANY of the RDA's problems in the seventies stemmed from money—too much of it. As a privately held company, it was prevented from raising fresh capital through the sale of public stock. All ventures had to be financed through cash flow or short-term loans. Wally refused to allow the company to incur any significant debt. Fortunately, beginning in the midsixties that cash flow had become a veritable Niagara and the RDA was up to its neck in black ink.

For that very reason, Wally adopted a hostile attitude toward superfluous profit, which he abhorred almost as much as making none at all. Though any number of new projects were begun during this period, the RDA's founder had to be convinced that the job could not just as readily be done by the *Digest* or another division already in place. Precisely that philosophy had given Lewis and Waters a ready-made excuse to get into the entertainment business—it was the one area in mass communications not being exploited by the RDA.

The chief difficulty facing Pleasantville in many of its new ventures was that they had nothing to do with direct mail, a field in which the RDA had demonstrated something very like collective genius. Though figures and other information regarding the worldwide mailing list were guarded with the utmost secrecy, the RDA direct-mail machinery was among the largest, most efficient, and most profitable in the world—as attested by its annual postage bill, which in the United States alone ranked among the five heftiest.

Alluding to the company's demonstrated direct-mail clout, Hobe Lewis liked to boast on public occasions that the RDA felt that retailing was "100 years out of date." With one out of every four families in the United States getting the magazine, it seemed only natural to exploit the list by selling it as much merchandise as the market would bear. The fabulous success of Condensed Books and a long string of blockbuster specials seemed to prove the point.

But there was a problem with direct mail. It was boring, unless you happened to be a copywriter. As a result, Lewis's sensible, hard-nosed talk belied an expansion policy that sometimes bordered on the willful or perverse, but did serve to keep the company CEO amused. Too much of the diversification had nothing to do with direct mail. A full quarter of the company's various offshoots were now involved in enterprises the RDA had not been in only a few years earlier.

Typical of the blind alleys the RDA was chasing up was its attempt to create an electronic educational system in cooperation with Sylvania Electric. Even further afield was Pleasantville's effort to sell mutual funds in West Germany—a test market that the company eventually hoped would extend around the world—in cooperation with the Boston-based investment firm of Loomis Sayles.

Even direct mail had its problems. Though marketing surveys were extraordinarily dependable for the most part, they were not foolproof. Enough people, for example, had ticked off the "would buy" column to justify publishing a lavishly illustrated volume on national landmarks called *Treasury of America*. But when it was published, an unhealthy number of them defected to "no interest." An attempt to mass-market previously published direct-mail titles like the *Complete Do-It-Yourself Manual* at such unorthodox retail outlets as hardware stores also ended in failure.

Yet there were money-making exceptions—notably, the QSP (Quality School Products) division, which helped children raise funds for their school, Scout organization, or baseball league by selling magazine subscriptions, record albums, candy, and even place mats door-to-door. Another remunerative area was the RDA's overseas study-travel programs for teenagers, marketed through local boards of education via the Foreign Study League, which the company purchased from the Transamerica Corporation for an undisclosed price.

But book publishing held a special, almost mythic attraction for the company. It had not only been the first but remained the most lucrative of all the RDA's nonmagazine ventures. For that matter, Condensed Books was even beginning to edge out the *Digest* itself as the most profitable division within the company. With the extraordinary success of the book club and specials at their back, upper-management Digesters, led by Lewis, assumed as a matter of course that the great Pleasantville engine could climb every mountain, ford every stream. For proof, they had only to read the magazine's own never-say-die exhortations published in just about every issue.

Other publishing ventures that the RDA was currently involved in, though with less spectacular results, ranged from a standard college dictionary and dictionaries for high schoolers to the Cassell's line of foreign-language dictionaries and an annual called the *New International Year Book,* an illustrated compendium of information on a variety of subjects. In 1965 the company commissioned Elizabeth L. Post, granddaughter-in-law of Emily Post, to publish a revised and updated version of *Emily Post's Etiquette: The Blue Book of Social Usage.* Later the RDA also published an Emily Post cookbook.

Thus it seemed only natural for the RDA to get involved in trade publishing, the last book frontier and the most glamorous. The rationale behind the decision was that Special Books still appeared to be a largely underdeveloped resource. In order to exploit the immense book-buying public that did not purchase its books through direct mail, the company proposed buying up a well-established, highly regarded trade publishing house and selling the RDA's direct-mail titles directly to bookstores. Conversely, new titles generated by the house could be sold through direct mail. While perhaps sound in theory, the idea proved disastrous in practice. As the mandarins of Pleasantville kept forgetting, publishing was an art, not a science. The books sold by the RDA through direct mail had almost nothing in common with books sold in bookstores. Trade publishing involved not only a different distribution system but different editorial standards and practices.

In 1966, however, the RDA was still a wide-eyed neophyte when it entered the world of commercial publishing by acquiring Funk & Wagnalls and its affiliate Wilfred Funk Inc., which included a line of reference books, encyclopedias, dictionaries, general fiction, and nonfiction. Prime mover in the negotiations was the expansion-minded treasurer, Dick Waters, and at first the acquisition seemed a bright feather in his cap. Dr. Wilfred Funk had long been editor of one of the *Digest*'s most popular features, "It Pays to Enrich Your Word Power," which was later taken over by his son Peter.

The grand plan was for all titles to carry both the F & W and the RDA imprint, with the former distributing to the trade and the latter selling the same product through direct mail—primarily F & W's strong backlist of dictionaries, reference books, and special encyclopedias. Its best-known book was the *Funk & Wagnalls New Standard Dictionary of the English Language,* last revised in 1963, though F & W also published books on such *Digest*-friendly topics as weaving, mythology, and travel.

The year after joining the Pleasantville family, Funk & Wagnalls published the massive, 2,094-page *Reader's Digest Great Encyclopedic Dictionary.* But that proved to be just a little too much word power for *Digest* readers, and the book bombed. As it turned out, none of the other F & W reference works proved very popular with Middle America either.

Funk & Wagnalls also published regular trade books. One of these, scheduled for publication in 1968, was a work by Samm Sinclair Baker titled *The Permissible Lie.* An advertising executive with seventeen books to his credit, Baker argued that the advertising industry was engaged in a multitude of underhanded practices. When advance copies were sent out for review, the book was harshly criticized by advertising trade journals. Word soon got back to Hobe Lewis, editor of the largest advertising print medium in the world, with estimated annual advertising revenues of $68 million, that advertising agencies were very unhappy. Over the objections of F & W editors, Lewis peremptorily ordered Baker's book to be canceled.

Baker's agent Perry H. Knowlton, president of Collins-Knowlton-Wing Inc., immediately cried foul, charging that the cancellation, just weeks before publication, was the first known instance of corporate book censorship in the history of publishing. When the *New York Times* called up for an explanation, Lewis truthfully claimed that Baker's book did not "jibe" with the philosophy of the *Reader's Digest,* but declined to elaborate on what that philosophy was. However, he denied that the *Digest* was engaged in any form of censorship, adding only that the book did not meet the company's editorial standards. Later he told *Time* magazine, "Advertising is good for business, and business is good for the country."

Baker, a former president of the Donahue and Coe advertising agency, complained that he was informed that the book was canceled because it was "contrary to the best interests" of the *Digest:* "I was told that the *Reader's Digest* believes that advertising is good for business and that business is good for the country. The implication was that it was almost an unpatriotic book."

Baker later found a publisher in World Publishing, a subsidiary of the Times Mirror Company, which itself quashed an advertising campaign for the book around the theme "The Book That *Reader's Digest* Suppressed." The reason given to Baker by "horrified" Times Mirror officials was that such a campaign would have been in "bad taste." Baker himself interpreted that to mean "bad business," because World often sold reprint rights to the *Digest.*

In 1970 the entire editorial staff of Funk & Wagnalls was fired. Declared Lewis, "*Reader's Digest* will exert tighter quality control over Funk & Wagnalls." Tighter control meant publishing two books about Lewis's golf partner, President Richard M. Nixon. But F & W continued to lose money regardless. One of the most serious problems the

RDA encountered was trying to determine what a browser in a bookstore was likely to purchase. Its questionnaires for readers, hyacinths for their soul, EQs, and all the other paraphernalia of direct-mail promotion had no relevance. Poor distribution also continued to plague the operation. Ultimately, the RDA's solution was to unload F & W and start up Reader's Digest Press, publishing about twenty titles per year in cooperation with major New York publishers, which already had large, efficient distribution operations in place. Moreover, the emphasis was to be on quality, not on mass appeal.

Meanwhile, the *Digest* had named its first publisher—advertising sales director Charles Hepler. The *RD*'s circulation now stood at an astounding 17 million in the United States alone, and advertising revenues were soaring. Hepler's chief salesman was Richard F. McLoughlin, only thirty-nine. Money was still no problem.

━━━

DESPITE its breakneck international growth, the company did have some unexpected competition, both at home and abroad, from an unlikely source. In January 1967 the USSR commenced publication of a magazine called *Sputnik,* which bore a suspicious resemblance to the *Reader's Digest.* Company executives were not amused by this sincerest form of flattery, and their howls of protest reached all the way to the Kremlin—for all the good it did them.

Published in Russia by the Novosti press agency and printed on high-quality paper in Finland, where the Soviets could use Finnish currency acquired as reparations following the 1939–40 Russian-Finnish War, the pocket-sized *Sputnik* aped not only the editorial format but also the international cloning of the *RD*. In all, three editions— English, Japanese, and Russian—were exported to the United States and fifty-eight other countries. Like the *Digest, Sputnik* contained a potpourri of articles condensed from Soviet journals and newspapers, many of them illustrated in four-color—a visual improvement over its dowdy American counterpart.

Conspicuously absent, for the most part, was the conventional Cold War propaganda that the *Digest* thrived on. Chief editor Oleg Feofanov claimed that the magazine's purpose was to "make money, not propaganda." Simple, *Digest*-style headlines soft-pedaled articles like "Why Divorce in the U.S.S.R.?" and "Is Space Exploration Worthwhile?" A dialogue entitled "The Beauty of Women" even went the *RD*'s fondness for the risqué one step further by illustrating it with drawings of nudes, a rare thing in Russian publications and absolutely, positively *nyetski* in Pleasantville.

Perhaps even more shocking were letters from readers offering criticism and suggestions—a right denied to 100 million readers of the American *Reader's Digest* and its international editions. Heavy-handed Soviet saws, though, needed sharpening: "A man can survive anything but his own death." "Some mice pride themselves on not eating cats." Editor of the Kremlin copycat was Gennadi Gerasimov, later to become a well-known Soviet spokesman and head of the Foreign Ministry's Information Department.

The first Soviet magazine ever to go commercial, *Sputnik* was a grand success—everything, in a manner of speaking, that Pleasantville could have wanted in a magazine except that it was not owned by the RDA and did not exactly promote the American way of life. The first printing of the London edition, numbering only 5,000 copies, sold out in three days. The much larger Japanese, Russian, and American editions, still piddling by RDA standards, met with similar success.

Two days after *Sputnik* appeared on America's newsstands, the State Department—at the RDA's bidding—complained to the Soviet embassy that continued distribution of the publication in the United States depended on Soviet permission to allow the *Digest* and the *New York Times* to circulate freely in the Soviet Union. And therein lay the story behind the story.

Since 1956 the U.S. embassy in Moscow had been permitted to distribute 62,000 copies of *Amerika,* a Russian-language monthly prepared by the USIA. Two thousand were given away at the embassy, and the rest were, in theory, sold. In return the Soviet embassy gave out in the United States 2,000 copies of its own English-language *Soviet Life* and tried to sell the remaining 60,000 through newsstands. This handsome but stodgy publication faced overwhelming competition, while *Amerika* encountered no such opposition from Russian journals.

In an effort to prevent the United States from scoring a decisive propaganda victory, the Soviets tried to limit the distribution of *Amerika* to an equal number of sold copies of *Soviet Life*. When that tactic failed, the Kremlin simply decided to put out a sprightlier magazine and took its cue from America's best-selling publication. The result, to the chagrin not only of the *Digest* but of the USIA, was that *Sputnik* instantly succeeded in outshining and upstaging its true competitor—*Amerika.*

Eventually, in order to ensure continued distribution of its new launch in the United States, the Soviets proposed to State Department officials to allow the *RD* to circulate a "self-censored" Russian-language edition of 200,000 to be sold freely in Russia. Meanwhile Bob Devine, deputy general manager of *RD* international editions, rushed off to Moscow and other East European capitals to discuss the possibility of a *Reader's Digest* in Russian, Polish, Serbo-Croatian, and other languages. Nothing came of either proposal, mainly because the USIA and other government agencies took a dim view of allowing the *RD* to become a quasi-official instrument of propaganda, even though it had been exactly that ever since World War II.

A few years later, with *Sputnik* continuing to flourish, the Russians decided on a more frontal assault on the propaganda front. Like its CIA counterpart, the KGB was actively involved in subsidizing books and magazines throughout the sixties and seventies and almost certainly was behind the publication in Moscow of a book called *Fabrica Izhi i illuzy* (The Factory of Lies and Illusions), subtitled "An Introduction to the American Propagandistic Magazine Industry," by G. A. Golovanova. The factory in question was the *Digest*.

As its heavy-handed title suggested, the slender paperback took a typical Cold War line on the *RD*'s support of American foreign policy and big business, its perpetuation of political stereotypes and socioeconomic myths (capitalism), its advertising standards and hypocritical emphasis on moral uplift. But no one in Pleasantville, including Wally, Hobe Lewis, and other top editors, ever heard about it. If they had, it would only have given them a big laugh.

———

DESPITE its nearly unbroken string of failures, the *Reader's Digest* did bankroll one big winner in the midsixties—which was all the more remarkable because Richard M. Nixon was a politician with a reputation for being a loser, and a sore one at that. The *RD* and Nixon went back a very long way—all the way to the time he was still a student at Whittier College and entered the Southern California Extemporaneous Speaking Contest, sponsored by the magazine. Contestants were required to read every article published in the *Digest* in recent months, then speak extemporaneously on an article selected at random. The topic assigned to Nixon was "Youth of 1933," and he won handily.

Later, while stationed as a lieutenant in the navy in the South Pacific in 1944, Nixon—not yet a father—did some research on how to plan a family. Among the items he clipped was an article from the *Digest* on which he scribbled several notations: "No danger in first baby after thirty . . . more intelligent if older parents (only because of environment). Nursing better than bottles." Two years later the Nixons' first child, Tricia, was born.

By the time the *Digest* published "I Say He's a Wonderful Guy," by Pat Nixon, in 1952, the magazine and the Republican vice-presidential candidate had already forged a strong bond based mostly on the anti-Communist zeal and rhetoric they shared. But Mrs. Nixon's article was also the first in a string of media reconstructions of her husband's public mythology, each containing a small but telling alteration of fact. In the article, for example, she claimed that their courtship had lasted for "almost three years," while, in fact, it was only one and a half years long; and that Dick Nixon "spent almost four years in the South Pacific," when his overseas duty actually amounted to less than fourteen months.

Even so, Al Cole and Wally also thought Nixon was a wonderful guy, and it was they who in 1960 asked Lewis, then an executive editor, to be their eyes and ears in Washington during Nixon's unsuccessful run against Kennedy. Lewis's friendship with Nixon, and with his family and such friends as Bebe Rebozo and Bob Abplanalp, dated from that time as well.

Even after Nixon lost the election, by less than 1 percent of the vote, the *Digest* resolved to keep his name and face before the public. It did that in several ways—first, by publishing, during the sixties, a total of eleven articles by Nixon, or an average of more than one a year. In 1962, Hobe Lewis invited him to Pleasantville to discuss foreign policy while the defeated Republican standard-bearer was running for governor of California—a race he also lost.

But the *Digest* not only did not give up on him but continued to serve as his only significant public forum. A 1963 Nixon piece called for the liberation of Eastern Europe and a "complete change of direction . . . in U.S. foreign policy," with a goal of "nothing less than to bring freedom to the Communist world." Implicitly, the article was also critical of Eisenhower for not having helped the Hungarian uprising in 1956.

In August 1964 Nixon returned to the *Digest,* attacking Lyndon Baines Johnson, Democratic candidate for president, in "Needed in Vietnam: The Will to Win." The article amounted to a preview of his own 1968 platform plank and fully articulated his Vietnam policy:

"Every military man with whom I talked privately admitted that we are losing the war. But every one of those men believes that it is possible for us to win it . . . and win it decisively." The good news was: "We have an unparalleled opportunity to roll back the Communist tide, not only in South Vietnam but in Southeast Asia generally, and indeed in the world as a whole."

Nixon's gloomy forecast, if America did not exhibit that will to win, was for the fall not only of South Vietnam but of Laos, Cambodia, Thailand, Malaysia, Indonesia, the Philippines, Australia, and Japan. Roving editor and right-wing novelist Allen Drury, who joined the *Digest* after resigning from the *Washington Post,* echoed Nixon's hard-line approach in "The Dangerous Game of Let's Pretend." Drury accused the U.S. government of timidity and claimed that it was "fantastic that we should so consistently argue ourselves out of the unflinching firmness which may well be our salvation."

In subsequent articles Nixon returned again and again to the same theme, arguing that there was "no substitute for victory" and that "to negotiate in Vietnam would be negotiation of the wrong kind, at the wrong time, at the wrong place." Articles on welfare reform and economic development in the ghettos attempted to poke holes in President Johnson's Great Society, which in Nixon's typically hyperbolic pronouncement had now become "the most lawless and violent [nation] in the history of free peoples."

In its November 1964 election issue—with Arizona Senator and right-wing standard-bearer Barry Goldwater as the Republican party's candidate—the *Digest* ran an article by Nixon titled "Cuba, Castro and John F. Kennedy." Nixon charged that a small group of "liberal" White House advisers persistently gave "incredibly bad advice" that strengthened the enemy, that the Democratic administration had followed a "weak-kneed" foreign policy in Cuba, that the country had been "humiliated, frustrated, outguessed and outmaneuvered at every turn," and that the United States must fight the Cold War more steadfastly rather than follow the Johnson-Kennedy course. Publication of the article was timed to reach subscribers a week before the election and was virtually a condensed version of Goldwater's foreign policy. Two other articles in the same issue, by Dr. Walter Judd, keynote speaker at the Republican convention in 1960 and Wally's longtime China hand, were further paraphrases of Goldwater's domestic and foreign policy.

After Goldwater lost, a disconsolate Tony Oursler pulled down the blinds in his office and sat in the darkened room with a candle on his desk. But there was one bright light amid the encircling gloom. Over the next few years the *RD* almost heroically persevered—more than any other private U.S. institution—in keeping Richard Nixon's name before the public and in preparing the way for his second coming, in 1968. Not only did it sponsor some of his well-publicized foreign travels, but after candidate Nixon entered the 1968 primaries the company plane, *Pegasus,* regularly transported him to speaking engagements and political rallies.

Some Digesters also suspected that the company's immense mailing list—which was never rented out to anyone, for any reason, under any circumstances—was provided to Nixon's election committee for fund-raising and other purposes, but that charge has never been proven. By this time Hobe Lewis had become, in the words of *Time* magazine, one of "a small group of intimate friends, men with whom [Nixon] dined, shared his deepest thoughts."

As a presidential candidate, Nixon was obliged to resign his assorted honorary chairmanships, including that of the Boys' Clubs of America, whose annual board of directors dinner was often used as a political platform. Nixon's successor was Al Cole, who by now was also chairman of the Advertising Council as well as an extremely influential and powerful Republican fund-raiser. Though still estranged from Wally, Cole acted as Lewis's éminence grise, and the consensus in Pleasantville was that, when it came to politics, the editor in chief did whatever the ex–business manager told him to do.

Also dispatched to Washington during Nixon's second run for the presidency was ex–Washington bureau staffer Bruce Lee, who spent a considerable amount of time with Lewis, the candidate, and his entourage. Lee's assignment was to ghost a book for Nixon, who wanted it to dwell on his sympathy for the plight of black people because he himself had known bitter poverty during his childhood. Lee told Lewis, "I can't write that book. And it shouldn't be written."

Lewis asked why. Lee explained that Nixon was going to win in the border states anyway, that he was not going to get any more black votes, because the blacks did not believe him, and that if he wrote a sob story then white voters were not going to believe him either.

"You're a fucking liberal," Lewis replied. And for the next six months, Lee was in limbo. Lewis was furious with him. Nixon's people brought in speech writer Patrick J. Buchanan to write the book, but the project was eventually abandoned.

On the night of Nixon's crucial primary victory in Oregon, a new member joined that intimate, clubby group of friends, and Lewis for one was less than pleased. After a J. Walter Thompson executive, Bob Haldeman, became chief of staff, the campaign became an all-business, no-nonsense proposition. The talkative, convivial Lewis called Nixon's private secretary, Rose Mary Woods, and asked bluntly, "What happened? The fun's gone."

Nevertheless, the *Digest*'s October 1968 election issue continued in the magazine's tradition of packing articles with a Republican slant. Typically, Democratic candidate Hubert Humphrey received no mention whatever. Nixon, though, weighed in with an article inspiringly titled "Let a New Day Dawn for the U.S.A.!"—a condensation of his acceptance speech at the Republican National Convention the previous August. Washington bureau staff writer John Barron seconded the motion with yet another cookie-mold diatribe against federal waste and bureaucracy whose only purpose was to establish an anti-administration mood.

After Nixon's landslide victory, Lewis discovered that all the fun had not gone out of being a friend of the president after all. Apart from flying off to Florida on *Pegasus* to play golf with Nixon, Rebozo, Abplanalp, and others, Lewis was also a guest at the wedding of the Nixons' daughter Tricia to fellow Princeton graduate Edward Cox. Others invited included J. Edgar Hoover, Red Skelton, Rebozo, Warren Burger, various cabinet members, Billy Graham, Norman Vincent Peale, Art Linkletter, and Ralph Nader—with one exception, the last (Cox had worked briefly as a "Nader's raider"), a veritable hall of fame of *Digest* contributors. Conspicuously absent from the ceremony was anyone from Congress.

Nixon and the *Digest* also continued to cooperate on matters great and small, almost on a *Mi casa es su casa* basis. Nixon wrote a preface to a collection of White House Sunday morning sermons being published by the RDA. More significantly, during the administration's battle to gain congressional approval for a new antiballistic missile program, presidential assistant Charles Colson approached former U.S. senator Henry Cabot Lodge—Nixon's 1960 running mate—to front for a pro-ABM article for the *Digest* to be written by Charles J. V. Murphy, a veteran *Digest* author. Lodge's home state of Massachusetts was a center of liberal opposition to the project.

In the summer of 1970 the *Digest* published Lodge's "A Citizen Looks at the ABM," which stressed the importance of the program in the proposed arms treaty then being discussed with the Soviets. Coincidentally, Lodge was appointed ambassador to the Vatican at around the same time.

Afterward a reprint of the article formed part of a brochure sent to twenty thousand editorial writers, veterans, and others in the eight states where the ABM was in trouble. When the program finally came to a vote in the Senate, it managed—just barely—to squeeze through.

15

Campus Comedy

IN LATE 1964 a young man named John Wulp applied for a job as an editor of the *Reader's Digest*. Wulp was no typical applicant in Oxford broadcloth and penny loafers just out of an Ivy League school, but an artist and weaver, with a history in the theater. A refugee from the artsy life in Nantucket, this former editor on a small magazine was broke and desperately in need of a job.

The *Digest* was intrigued by Wulp probably because he was the closest thing to a hippie anybody in Pleasantville had ever seen. That same year the formation of the free-speech movement at the University of California at Berkeley climaxed a period of student discontent with the administrative bureaucracy of the university specifically and with the way America was in general being run by government and big business. After California's governor ordered six hundred policemen to arrest protesting students, as Jerry Rubin later observed, "the war against Amerika in the schools and the streets by white middle-class kids thus commenced."

As campus rebellion spread, students around the country were soon protesting unpopular tenure decisions, mandatory ROTC programs, curfew, dress codes, and invitations to members of the Johnson administration to speak to students. At the same time, the counterculture was on the brink of moving out of its East and West coast ghettos and exporting its blend of Oriental mysticism, hallucinogenic drugs, protest music, and nontraditional diet across the country. The slow, uphill struggle of the civil-rights movement and President Johnson's steady escalation of the war in Vietnam, both of which had already resulted in too many early deaths, gradually became the new focal points of student unrest as it moved off campus and into the streets. The *Digest*'s Washington office, of course, had no doubt about where to lay the blame—squarely on the Kremlin's doorstep, as usual.

Although Wulp had longish hair, he was polite, well spoken, thoughtful. He was hired, though only after being put through thirteen interviews. The last was with the old man himself, DeWitt Wallace, who still interviewed all editorial candidates. Wulp found the experience very touching. Staring down at him from the wall was a Mathew Brady photograph of Lincoln. Wally had decided that Wulp was an intellectual and asked, "Why don't intellectuals like our magazine?"

Wulp did not know the answer, but somehow managed to acquit himself and was put to work in Condensed Books. The experience soon led to an unexpected bonus—the reinvigoration of his own artistic aspirations. After visiting High Winds, he began to romanticize the Wallace household and life-style as a Gatsby-like magnet for the wealthy, the powerful, and the talented. Hanging from the walls were Impressionist masterpieces. Equally intoxicating were Syrie Maugham's decor, houseguests like Martha Graham or the Nelson Rockefellers, and even the fact that Lila's jewelry was not store-bought but commissioned.

Every evening Wulp returned home and painted furiously, for the first time able to take himself seriously as an artist, because his fellow Digesters were buying everything he painted. Among those who purchased a Wulp watercolor or oil were Hobe Lewis and Paul Thompson, though Pleasantville's best-known art collector refrained. Wulp also introduced up-and-coming editor Ed Thompson to his friend LeRoi Jones, the black playwright and revolutionary who had recently changed his name to Amiri Baraka.

There was just one problem in his new paradise. Unlike most of the editors, business executives, clerical workers, secretaries, and just about everybody else in Pleasantville, Wulp was opposed to the war in Vietnam. The majority of Digesters were disappointed that Goldwater had been so resoundingly defeated by Lyndon Baines Johnson in the 1964 election. But they supported the president's decision to escalate the war, especially when he authorized the new army commander, General William C. Westmoreland, to send U.S. troops into combat for the first time, at Danang.

Even so, novice book condenser Wulp felt distinctly comfortable in the paternalistic Pleasantville milieu, even managing to convince himself that the *Digest* was essentially a liberal magazine and institution in a larger, less political sense and particularly in its employment policies. It was a conviction from which he was never to waver—not even five years later, when the war in Vietnam had become such a divisive issue both in the country at large and in the hawks' nest where he worked that the peacenik of Pleasantville felt he had no alternative but to resign.

—————

ANOTHER young man who joined the *Digest* around this time was Ric Cox, a graduate of the journalism school at Southern Illinois University at Carbondale. Cox was hired as an editor of the *Campus Courier,* a newspaper supplement the *Digest* intended to sell to campus newspapers around the country. The supplement seemed an ideal vehicle not only for advertising directed at the youth market but for the *RD*'s conservative political message.

Previously, apart from its school edition and the occasional diatribe against Communists on campus, the *Digest* had mostly limited its editorial material on colleges to "Campus Comedy." Introduced in 1961, it was the first new department in six years.

Senior staff editor Roy Herbert was initially the project editor for the *Courier.* He had come up with the concept and with his wife, April, put the prototype issue together on their living room floor. After the supplement got the go-ahead, it was turned over to Jeremy Dole, a former *Playboy* editor who used to write the copy about the playmate of the month's favorite hobbies and the qualities she liked in a man.

The *Digest*'s publicity apparatus already serviced 400 college newspapers—as well as 1,250 commercial newspapers, 350 editorial writers, 90 women's-magazine editors, and 150 Washington-based reporters—with a continuous stream of news releases. Each month the collegiate press received a press kit based on current *Digest* editorial material plus filler items. A similar kit went to 90 college radio stations. *RD* publicity also rained down on hundreds of trade magazines and business newspapers, 240 television stations, and 500 commercial radio stations—the latter with brief commentaries on *Digest* articles narrated by announcer Hugh Downs.

To facilitate its ability to sell national advertising in the supplement, the *Digest* in March 1966 purchased the National Advertising Service Inc., representing about 800 college newspapers with a combined circulation of 3.3 million, for an undisclosed price. NASI was then re-named the National Educational Advertising Services (NEAS). Just when everything seemed to be humming along, the howls of student protest were heard in the world's biggest ivory tower, high on a hill in Pleasantville. Though 81 student papers had already signed up for the *Courier*, the nation's most prestigious and largest universities—led, ironically, by those in the Ivy League, where a majority of *Digest* editors had gone to school—viewed the supplement as an unwelcome intrusion into academe.

One concern was about advertising revenues—that *Digest* salesmen working for NEAS would henceforth concentrate on selling for the supplement and not for the papers themselves. The bigger concern, though, had to do with the editorial content of the supplement, as exemplified by the sample issue being shown around. The editor of the *Daily Pennsylvanian* called it "just another *Reader's Digest*" that did not address "substantive issues that college students are interested in." Other campus papers that rejected the *Courier* were the *Daily Princetonian*, the *Yale Daily News*, the *Columbia Spectator*, the *Harvard Crimson*, and the *Michigan Daily*, at the University of Michigan.

However, the *Digest* pressed on, and by the following April claimed NEAS was halfway to reaching its goal—a 500,000 circulation. The *Crimson* fought back, editorializing that it was not the paper's policy "to print the opinion of people not on the staff of its pages." The *Spectator* was particularly active in drumming up opposition and said the *Courier* "would lessen the quality of the paper." But the traditionally conservative *Dartmouth* decided to use it, dubbing the controversy "a little piece of paranoia, a little bit of the pompous Ivy League attitude—the attitude that the college newspaper is above [the *Digest*]."

But most of the nation's major college papers were unanimous in their opposition. Soon after Cox went to work in Pleasantville, the *Digest* folded the project, and he was transferred to the magazine's copy desk.

———

IN *1968*, dubbed by William Manchester "The Year Everything Went Wrong," January began with the capture of the USS *Pueblo*, followed by the Tet offensive. In March, President Johnson dramatically announced he was not seeking reelection. Days later Martin Luther King, Jr., was assassinated while standing on the balcony of a Memphis motel. Early in June the nation was traumatized a second time, with the assassination of Robert Kennedy. In August an army of 24,000 police and National Guardsmen guarded the Democratic National Convention while demonstrators rioted outside.

When the schools opened, riots at Columbia University climaxed five years of student turbulence. *Oh! Calcutta!* brought nudity and a nose-thumbing attitude toward bourgeois morality to the stage. Feminists were organizing a group to be called the National Organization for Women. Nixon was campaigning for the presidency and looking to win.

That same year, in the never-never land of Pleasantville, conservative *New York Times* war correspondent Hanson W. Baldwin reported in the March issue of the *RD*, "The allies are winning, and the enemy is being hurt." Nixon, in a piece condensed from *Foreign Affairs*, defended the American presence in Vietnam as a bulwark against communism. In April an article titled "Let's Close Ranks on the Home Front" criticized war protesters who acted against their country's best interests. Richard H. Sanger, a former foreign-service officer, answered in the affirmative the question "Is Insurrection Brewing in the United States?"

In an article timed to coincide with Martin Luther King's march on the nation's capital, Washington bureau staffer William Schulz declared, "One thing is certain; whether or not all of the protestors' plans materialize, the nation faces international humiliation as a result of the Washington campaign. Communism's world-wide propaganda apparatus is set for a field day." At the time only a handful of blacks worked at the *RD*, none in an editorial or senior position. Each day they sat apart at a table in the cafeteria, "separate but equal," and did not dare protest.

In the art-of-living category, a March reprint from *Time* was titled "The Difficult Art of Being a Parent." In April: "Why Students Turn to Drugs," by Anonymous, who had been there. Septuagenarian Pearl Buck, in a piece reprinted from *Family Weekly*, "The Pill and the Teenage Girl," asked rhetorically, "What is the sex act when it is nothing but release or sport? It is nothing—it is less than nothing. It becomes tiresome and even disgusting."

The June issue revealed results of a Gallup poll authorized by the *Digest* and claiming that 27 percent of all soldiers and marines who had served in Vietnam were either willing to return or had already volunteered to do so. August's "What Every Husband Needs," by Hannah Lees, from her book *Help Your Husband Stay Alive,* told wives that what he needed was mothering.

A November offering by Marilyn Mercer, "*Is* There Room at the Top for Women?," noted prophetically, "Full integration of women into business would mean, ultimately, changing some of our most deep-rooted ideas about sexual roles. And this is something that has never happened before in the civilized—and uncivilized—world." It had never happened in Pleasantville before either, and the time was soon coming when Digesters would discover they harbored some of the most deep-rooted sexist notions in the entire country.

———

To COUNTER growing antiwar sentiment in the United States, Wally wanted all Digesters to put a decal of the American flag on their automobiles. He made it a personal campaign. Employees received little notes discreetly tucked into their pay envelopes informing them that, unless they had a special reason, the company would appreciate it if they put the enclosed decal on their automobile. Security guards toured the lot and took down numbers of license plates of those cars that did not oblige, and in the next pay envelope there would be another reminder. Few held out.

Wally also took the campaign nationwide. In the February 1969 issue the *Digest* launched a "Fly This Flag Proudly" campaign and inserted detachable flag decals in 18,441,369 copies of the magazine. The unmistakable message was that the magazine supported Richard Nixon's war policy abroad and his law-and-order policy at home. Editorialized founder DeWitt Wallace, "The display of the flag is one way to show that we know what a privilege it is to be an American. Don't you get a thrill when you see the flag flying outside a post office, a factory, or an office building? I do."

In a follow-up survey, the *Digest* established that 78 percent of its readers removed the decal from the issue and half of those put it to use. Countless civic, religious, school, and business organizations as well as thousands of individuals ordered another fifty million. Before long, ten million cars and five million homes were sporting the *Digest* flag decal, and it became the Silent Majority's most visible and potent symbol of where its sentiments lay.

In Pleasantville the infinitesimal antiwar contingent was increased by one when a young man named Kenneth G. Gross was hired in October 1969 as an associate book editor. At the time the magazine was striving to recruit younger editors who could reach the youth market. Gross qualified because he was thirty and had written for *Esquire,* then the savviest publication in the country, and also for the *Nation.* Though the latter was regarded in Pleasantville with only slightly less suspicion than *Pravda* was, *Digest* executives were in a bind. Surveys showed there were relatively few readers between the ages of twenty-five and thirty-five. The gambit to lure younger readers by means of the *Campus Courier* had failed, while the magazine's most concentrated readership was among the over-fifty, Geritol generation.

Only hours after going to work, Gross asked John Wulp, who sat across the hall, about all the automobiles in the parking lot plastered with flag decals. Wulp, whose car was flag-free, replied, "It's your first day at work here and you haven't got a flag yet? Your future here is going to be blighted."

Gross later put a flag on his car—though not the *Digest* flag, but a flag with a black hand and a white hand joined in the background. On the front bumper was a moratorium sticker.

On the same day a petition was circulated among editorial employees at the magazine to protest the war in Vietnam and support the moratorium. A dozen or so had signed. Immediately taking Gross for an ally, Wulp showed him a memo he had sent to Lewis objecting to an article slated for the December issue entitled "No Surrender" and calling for a rededication to the war and signed "The Editors." The memo outlined several objections to the article.

After a series of compromises, Lewis arranged for the piece to be slightly modified and re-signed "An Editorial." Editorials were so rare that they usually ran only during moments of great national crisis—the entry of the United States into World War II, for example. With the country deeply divided over the war, Lewis now thought the moment opportune to deliver a similar appeal to Americans to unite behind their president—though, in fact, the "editorial" amounted mainly to a preview of Nixon's November 3 war speech calling for "Vietnamizing" the war. But Wulp did win a moral victory. For the first time a *Digest* editor had gone beyond merely voicing a negative opinion on an article and succeeded in having it altered after it had been prepared for publication.

Thereafter the magazine changed its policy and did not circulate controversial pieces well ahead of publication; higher-up editors did not want rebellious editors editing them. But the stage had been set for a much more dramatic confrontation.

On that same first beautiful autumn day, Gross was gazing out his window at the trees when he began to hear what sounded like church music. He rushed across the hall to poke his head into Wulp's office.

"What's that?" he asked.

"You mean the music?"

"Yes. The music."

"Oh, that's the carillon."

As if the contents of the *Digest* and the manicured grounds were not supplying enough inspiration to her employees, Lila had recently installed an electronic carillon in the cupola which could be played either manually or automatically. It went off twice a day, at noon and at closing time, for fifteen minutes—and sometimes longer on special occasions. Wulp explained that for military visitors the carillon performed "The Caisson Song," the Marine Corps hymn, or Sousa marches. Then he took Gross's arm and marched him down to the cafeteria.

In succeeding days Gross was further struck by the drowsy ambience of the place and the fact that Wally's and Lila's offices were preserved almost as shrines, since neither showed up much any more. Gardeners labored endlessly over the flowers, which seemed only to embellish the funereal hush that hung over the place. The editorial pace was almost somnambulistic. In their biweekly reports on their activities, which were circulated among Wally, Lewis, and other higher-ups, editors simply noted that they were "reading." Some editors liked to boast that, à la Flaubert, they often spent two or three days searching for the mot juste for an article.

Another thing Gross quickly learned was that almost everybody was reduced to his or her initials, and he became KGG. A rare exception to that rule was John Edwin Wulp, who for reasons of company hypersensitivity was condensed to JW.

By November, in the wake of the Vietnam moratorium, the first word of the My Lai massacre was beginning to leak out. Gross was sitting with Tony Oursler when they heard. Oursler, visibly upset, said, "Let's not jump to any conclusions."

A young editor who had served in Vietnam rushed into the office, waving a copy of that morning's *New York Times.* He fairly shouted,

"They should take these guys and shoot them. They should take the guys who did this thing and shoot them right in the head."

"Look, let's not jump to any hasty conclusions," Oursler again insisted. "So far we really don't know anything for certain."

"This blackens our entire effort," the veteran said. He repeated that the perpetrators should be shot in the head.

"Okay!" Oursler shouted, angry. "Let's just forget it for now!"

Lunch in the days that followed was particularly strained, and tempers were lost more than once. The war seemed to be focusing everyone's attention on an unwanted subject. Gross found that many of the more creative types at the magazine had outside interests. One editor, who wrote for "Sesame Street" on the side, buried himself in his free-lance work. Another wrote romantic novels.

Winter came and snow covered the ground. One day Gross, Wulp, and a third editor were talking about the war in Wulp's office.

"You see," said Wulp, leaning back in his chair, "I believe that the way we can best influence things around here is to get someone like Norman Vincent Peale to support our view."

Oursler popped his head in the door.

"We're trying to find some way to get out of Vietnam," Wulp informed him. "We're trying to help the president end this bloody mess."

Oursler's face clouded over, but he simply walked away. Moments later he returned with a cup of coffee in his hand. By now he privately despised Gross as a liberal viper in the Pleasantville henhouse.

"Listen," he said, flushing. "You people are paid to read and judge books, not to sit around here talking about the war in Vietnam. We have plenty of editors who do that." Then he walked away again.

Gross's first assignment—and a strong inducement for him to remain at Pleasantville—had been to edit a book on the murders of three civil-rights workers during the 1964 Mississippi Summer Project. Several members of the Ku Klux Klan were charged with the slayings, and the case dragged slowly through the courts. The writer was the *Digest*'s Don Whitehead, author of *The FBI Story*, who had been given exclusive access to FBI files on the case. The book ran to 90,000 words, and Gross's task was to reduce it to 10,000 for publication in the February 1971 issue of the magazine.

Gross found Whitehead's manuscript "staggering." It was obvious that the FBI had informers planted at virtually every stage of the plot, and the story of the murders was chilling. But Gross had problems with the manuscript.

"Can I do rewriting?" he asked Oursler.

"If it needs it," he replied.

Whitehead had treated the dispute between King and Hoover at some length, coming down heavily in favor of Hoover, whom King had charged with ignoring the needs of civil-rights workers in the South. Gross boiled the dispute down, but much of the pro-Hoover sentiment was restored by Oursler. At that point Gross began to think of resigning. He consulted Wulp on the matter, but Wulp had something else to complain about.

"I've just heard," he said, "that there is an article on Vietnam that they haven't circulated. It's for the February issue and hasn't been circulated yet!"

Already it was mid-December. Normally, anything prepared for publication in February would have been circulated in late November. Moreover, the rumored piece was scheduled as that month's lead feature. Wulp and Gross tried to get hold of a copy. But the issue editor pleaded ignorance. Then they discovered that the story had been shown only to editors who were considered politically compatible. Some time later, though, Wulp walked into Gross's office and threw the proof onto the desk.

"Just look at that crap!" he shouted.

Gross looked. The title read, "From Hanoi—With Thanks." The overline: "A chilling study of how American antiwar demonstrations give aid and comfort to the enemy in Vietnam." The unsigned report was labeled a compilation. An editorial introduction told readers that the excerpts from speeches and reports broadcast over Hanoi Radio that followed were a sampling that showed Hanoi was depending on antiwar protests in the United States to win the war.

Gross and Wulp hastily copied the pages and distributed them throughout the building. The headquarters were bedecked with Christmas wreaths; workmen were installing Christmas trees in the lunchroom and along the corridors. But instead of the approaching holidays, everyone was talking about the so-called compilation. Everyone was also mindful that Christmas bonuses were due. The prospect of mounting another campaign to get the article killed seemed futile in light of the last effort. Gross asked Wulp what he proposed to do next.

"I don't know," Wulp said. "I'll have to start thinking about leaving, I suppose. What are you going to do?"

Gross returned to his office and wrote a memo to Lewis supporting the right of Americans to dissent without having their patriotism called into question. But Lewis was in Washington with Nixon. Within days a dozen similar memos arrived on the editor in chief's desk, among them one from Wulp. Soon afterward a shock wave passed through the office when word spread that he had also sent in his resignation.

Lewis asked him to reconsider. He also offered to negotiate some of the objectionable wording. But Wulp found the entire tone offensive. In the interim Gross and Wulp had learned that the compilation had been prepared with the assistance of the North Vietnam desk of the State Department.

After listening to some of Wulp's objections, Lewis changed "well-meaning citizens" to "sincere, well-meaning citizens." Instead of "A Compilation," it became "A Documentary Report." Instead of "A chilling study of how American antiwar demonstrations give aid and comfort to the enemy in Vietnam," the lead overline sentence read, "A study of how American antiwar demonstrations serve to prolong the war."

Wulp quit anyway. Gross and others discussed joining him in a mass resignation. But only one editor, Elizabeth Dempster, followed suit. For the others there remained that prospect of the Christmas bonus.

Undeterred by the two staff resignations, Lewis also canceled an article by Cornelius Ryan on the Hué Tet massacres and issued a memorandum to the editorial staff dated December 10, 1969, in which he strongly defended the two February articles in question.

A few days later Gross resigned. Recently, there had arisen rumors he was going to be transferred to New York. "People who make trouble are usually sent to New York," he was told. He spent his last two weeks in the Pan Am Building. On his final day, a senior editor near retirement came to pay a visit. He had been hostile to Gross at first, but their relationship had warmed.

"I think you behaved well," he said, as they stood looking out the window on the thirty-fourth floor. "But you must remember where you are. These people aren't interested in what you think or what you believe."

In contrast to the pastoral splendor of Pleasantville, a spectacular sunset spread over New York harbor. The closing of the day and of Gross's brief career seemed to fill the room with melancholy.

"It's not easy," the editor said sadly. "There are a great many things that you have to swallow. A great many things. I tried once. During the

Second World War. We had a great fight about the America Firsters. But it was brought home to me, and brought home quite forcefully, that it was their magazine. It doesn't belong to us, you see."

———

THE MAN to whom the magazine belonged had little use for America's war protesters, but he never lost his admiration for John Wulp, the *Digest*'s token intellectual, who decided on leaving Pleasantville to get out of journalism altogether and return to the theater. It was also an old love of Wally's, and he contributed generously to Wulp's new ventures. But there was one problem that neither personal friendship could transcend nor money solve, one heartache that was to remain with Wally for the rest of his life, and that was the chaotic state of affairs on one college campus in particular—Macalester College.

Such was Wally's devotion to his alma mater that when he received books inscribed to him by authors or publishers hopeful of getting their book accepted by the magazine or book club, he tore out the page bearing the inscription and sent them to James Holly, the college librarian. Holly never knew what to do with the books, since most were not worth the shelf space. But it did not seem tactful to refuse them, considering what the great man in Pleasantville was doing for the small liberal arts college in St. Paul.

By the midfifties it seemed almost a coincidence that Wally's father had once been president of Macalester or that the college had Presbyterian roots. Wally the individual and Macalester the institution, the twin offspring of Dr. James Wallace, had taken separate and widely divergent paths. Like many small midwestern colleges, Macalester had become not only an attractive oasis dedicated to the liberal arts but a modest outpost of liberalism as well. If Wally recognized the discrepancy, he kept it to himself. He wanted to remold the college in his own image. He nearly succeeded. Wallace's great wealth made him, never mind who actually held the position, the de facto president of the college, just like his father.

One thing that Dr. Wallace had never had to put up with, though, was student rebellion and revolt. Despite Wally's vigilance and extravagant generosity, the unthinkable happened. Macalester College got caught up in the campus revolution. The tumult culminated in April 1970 with the appearance of yippie Jerry Rubin at a liberation rally timed to coincide with the eve of the annual stockholders' meeting of the Minneapolis-based firm Honeywell, which had numerous contracts from the Defense Department to develop and produce weapons. Sitting out on the tree-lined campus were a thousand or more students, including hundreds of flower children wearing headbands and face paint. It looked like Woodstock all over again. Worse, it was all being subsidized by Wallace money.

Wally had not always taken an intense interest in Macalester. Back when his father was still alive, the college's most successful dropout had given the college two separate bequests, amounting to $407,865, to establish a scholarship fund in Dr. Wallace's name and to pay for the pensions of three professors. In late 1939 and in 1940, after his father passed away, Wally gave a total of $662,000. But for the next ten years he gave nothing. Then came an isolated gift of a quarter of a million dollars. In 1956, though, the devoted son read an account of his father's struggle to establish the college—in Wally's words, "the suffering, acute and prolonged," that Dr. Wallace's lifework entailed— and Wally was shocked. From that moment on, he determined to fulfill his father's dream.

By the midfifties the college's enrollment was up to 1,800. As though trying to make up for his lack of understanding as a youth, Wally endowed professorships in Dr. Wallace's name in history, religion, and political science, as well as the Barclay Acheson Professorship of International Studies. In 1965 the Janet Wallace Arts Center was dedicated. Among the works of art sprinkled over the campus was a bronze drinking fountain by Isamu Noguchi that had once graced *Digest* headquarters in Tokyo.

When Wally resumed his giving to Macalester, its president was Dr. Harvey M. Rice, who assumed the post in 1958. Wally donated to Macalester both as an individual and through various companies and funds, including the Wallace Suspense Fund for the occasional bit of fun. (Some of his extravagances included buying new band uniforms, installing closed-circuit television, and inviting Dorthy Carnegie, widow of Dale, to lecture faculty and students on how to win friends and influence people. Lila also contributed, costuming the cheerleaders and underwriting a performance of *The Taming of the Shrew*.) Once a year Wally called on a number of prestigious publishers in New York, armed with figures on how much the *Digest* had paid in the previous twelve months in reprint fees. He then delivered a well-rehearsed solicitation for a contribution to Macalester College. Though the plea was tactfully made, implicit was the threat of punitive action.

In 1968 Rice was forced to resign over a personal matter. At the time, Wally's salaried educational consultant was Paul H. Davis, a wealthy conservative from Los Angeles who had made his fortune by playing poker—always a good credential so far as Wally was concerned. Davis's recommendation as Rice's successor was Arthur Flemming, secretary of health, education, and welfare in the Eisenhower administration.

Flemming agreed to accept the post on several conditions—that he be paid a token honorarium of only $1 a year, that Macalester declare an open-admissions policy, and, most important, that Wally establish a special fund of $7 million. In return, Flemming promised never to ask for more money again to make up any deficits at the end of an academic year.

Despite his Eisenhower credentials, Flemming was a radical in Republican clothing. One of his first priorities was to ensure that 10 percent of all Macalester students came from minority groups. Within a few semesters, black students—many from the Deep South—had established a strong presence on the campus. Macalester paid not only their tuition, room, and board but also their traveling expenses—two round-trips home a year, at Christmas and Easter. Flemming even approved a $100-a-year cosmetics supplement for black female students.

Though still estranged from Wally, Al Cole remained a trustee of the college and in March 1970 visited Flemming, advising him that all the permissiveness on campus and the obscene language in the student newspaper, *Mac Weekly,* were causes of grave concern.

In particular, Cole said he disapproved of the college's acceptance of eighty-two black and other disadvantaged students with full student aid. Flemming countered that he hoped to offset the budget deficit caused by the disadvantaged students by applying to the federal government and several foundations for aid. The bottom line, though, said Flemming, was that—contrary to his original promise to Wally—over the next three years the college needed $4 million more in additional aid. After reading Cole's report, Wally sent Flemming a three-word reply: "Go to hell."

By now Macalester was supporting, with Wallace money, 150 disadvantaged students, white as well as black, at a cost of $800,000 a year. Though that was a major factor in the college's budget, another was the high salaries paid to Macalester professors, whose income was in the top 10 percent in the academic world. It also peeved Wally that Flemming had abolished majors in journalism and religious education.

But he did not dispatch reporters from the Washington bureau to see if Communists perchance were behind the conspiracy to squander Wallace money. Instead he sent Paul Davis.

Meanwhile, in early May, a group of Macalester students traveled to Washington to protest the war and the recent killing of four bystanders at an antiwar demonstration at Kent State University. At the same time, Hobe Lewis asked roving editor James Michener to write a book on the fatal shootings, which the RDA and Random House would copublish. That summer Michener moved to Ohio, where a team of *Digest* researchers had been investigating the story almost from the beginning. Later he was assisted by student interviewers hired through Kent's School of Journalism.

Using his motel room as headquarters, Michener researched and wrote the book concurrently and later tried to hand his files over to the FBI, but was turned away. Some of the people at Kent State thought he was working for the FBI as a front man and avoided him. For Michener and the RDA it was just another best-seller, people thought, though he had donated $100,000 to the school, twice what he expected to make from the book, precisely to protect himself from such an accusation.

In March 1971 the *RD* printed the first of two installments from Michener's book, later published as *Kent State—What Happened and Why*. Michener claimed that Kent State was a hotbed of revolutionary activity (just like Macalester), where by his guess 80 percent of the student population had tried marijuana. Jerry Rubin had once attracted two thousand students at a rally (just as he had at Macalester).

Sounding like an honorary member of the Washington bureau, Michener suggested that the Kent State incident had been planned by outside agitators. Both the FBI and the President's Commission on Campus Unrest later attributed the "primary cause" to Nixon's announcement that he had ordered the bombing of Cambodia.

Two Kent State speech professors later tested Michener's work for accuracy by distributing two hundred questionnaires to people named or quoted in the book. Their conclusion: it contained "inexcusable errors of form and substance. . . . The vast majority of the inaccuracies consisted of Michener having people describe things they did not witness, of Michener having them use language which is not characteristic of them, and of Michener embellishing or distorting what people did say or do."

During his interviews Michener had not taken any notes or used a tape recorder, relying instead on his "Germanic memory." His conclusion on Kent State: "President Nixon's Cambodian speech had minimal effect upon [the great majority of students], but a profound one upon the radicals, who would have approved nothing he proposed."

Michener blamed everyone—National Guardsmen, students, demonstrators, faculty, college administrators, the community, local police, governor—in effect, all of American society. He refused to accept the fact that the enraged guardsmen had agreed among themselves to open fire and were guilty of either manslaughter or murder. Later he opposed a federal grand-jury inquiry into the killings, saying it would do more harm than good.

Journalist I. F. Stone characterized Michener's book as "bullshit, right down Nixon's alley," but *Time* and *New York Times* columnist Tom Wicker praised it for its overall balance.

Meanwhile, Paul Davis's confidential report on Macalester had been delivered to Wally on June 21, 1970, and examined both the history of his gift giving and the question of whether the *RD*'s founder had an "obligation" to make additional gifts. Davis noted that of the $35 million already given, $20 million was in irrevocable and perpetual endowments producing more than $1 million a year. Another $1.4 million in the Macalester Wallace Reserve awaited his instructions. According to Davis, Wally had no legal, moral, or ethical reasons to continue giving to Macalester.

Wally stopped giving to the college in January 1971 and refused to make a public comment. At the end of the spring semester, Flemming resigned, having served as president for only two and a half years. But that was not the end of the problem. Davis convinced Wally that "financial skullduggery" was still going on at the school. Just as Harvey Rice and Flemming had diverted Wallace funds with the collusion of Macalester treasurer John Dozier, according to Davis, so Dozier and the new college president, Dr. James A. Robinson, were perpetuating the pattern of fund diversion and "political trickery."

Davis listed six options, from doing nothing and letting the diversions continue rampantly to complaining and bringing about a temporary halt to the diversions, to going to St. Paul and proving the diversions, in which case Robinson might quit or be fired. But Davis's own recommendation was that Wally either hire a Minneapolis attorney or auditor to gather the facts or else release Macalester from all restrictions and permit it to operate the High Winds Fund (a private Wallace foundation, run in tandem with the Lakeview Fund) in whatever manner it thought advisable, while Wally himself retained control of the Wallace Reserve Fund.

Wally replied in a note scribbled in the margin, asking for proof of recent diversions. On August 17, 1973, Davis wrote a confidential letter to Carl B. Drake, Jr., a Macalester trustee and head of St. Paul Companies, noting that the fund had dropped from $1.6 million to less than $400,000 and demanding to see proof that either Wally or Davis himself had authorized the withdrawals from principal, as Drake had alleged the day before by phone. Davis also worried that other Macalester-operated funds "might be suffering from unauthorized invasion."

John Driscoll, president of the Rock Island Corporation in St. Paul and chairman of the Macalester board of trustees, sent Davis a blistering reply not long afterward, saying he resented and rejected the suggestion of a cover-up and warning that if Davis persisted in his charges the matter would end up in court. Moreover, Driscoll added, the conditions of continued donor control surrounding the Wallace Reserve Fund violated both the spirit and the letter of federal gift-tax laws. "If the Internal Revenue Service was aware of your continued attempts to control these funds on behalf of Mr. Wallace," he wrote, "I believe it would place the tax treatment of these gifts in serious jeopardy."

To avoid a confrontation with the college, Davis resigned as Macalester's paid consultant. In his parting shot, he quoted anonymously two of the nation's top foundation executives, who claimed, "Macalester College doesn't have a chance of being one of the dozen or so private colleges which are needed and can be significant in pure liberal arts."

So much for DeWitt Wallace's vision and dream, $35 million later. Perhaps because he feared public scandal, and perhaps also because he was plain fed up with Macalester, Wally did not persist in trying to find out whether there had been any unauthorized diversions, as alleged by Davis. Only with the beginning of the fall 1976 semester, when Wally was eighty-seven years old, did he finally resume giving to Macalester, in recognition of the college's improved financial management.

16

Wally's Monster

THE MEDIOCRITY, strangeness, and pathos permeating life at the *Reader's Digest,* and Wally's own fading years of public service, were nowhere better illustrated and personified than in a young, hypnotically charming six-footer named Harry Morgan. If the urbane, ambitious Hobe Lewis was the son Wally in middle age never had, Morgan was the grandson Wally the lonely grandfather figure doted on—a fresh, eager, hyperaltruistic, well-mannered kid who seemed too good to be true, and probably was.

But Morgan was not only Wally's godson but his creation, his "Frankenstein's monster." The comparison is not too far-fetched. In Mary Shelley's tale an idealistic student of philosophy discovers the secret of imparting life to inanimate matter. After collecting bones from a charnel house, he manufactures a humanlike being and gives it life. The creature, endowed with prodigious strength, inspires loathing in whoever sees it. Lonely and miserable, it finally turns on its creator.

Harry Morgan's misfortune was to be discovered, while still a young man, by DeWitt Wallace, the idealistic philanthropist, who sought to transform him into an instrument for spreading American goodwill and *Digest* benevolence around the world. Propelled by superhuman energy and a vaulting ambition to be just like his creator, Morgan very nearly beat Wally at his own philanthropic game. Almost everyone in Pleasantville came to despise him. Lonely and miserable, he grew estranged from the man who had fashioned him out of sheer money and was nearly destroyed by the villagers.

In the end, creator and creature formed an uneasy truce, both cognizant that each had tested the very limits of manipulative behavior. The story not only offers a revealing textbook case of the inner workings of the *Reader's Digest* but also illustrates on a number of levels Wally's deepest concerns, his vulnerabilities, and the *Digest*'s own enduring editorial and philanthropic agendas.

Morgan was still a teenager growing up in California in the early fifties when he initiated a correspondence with the first lady of American altruism, Eleanor Roosevelt. In 1953, when Holland was struck by terrible flooding, the budding Good Samaritan spent his summer vacation helping in the relief effort. Later he joined the air force. While stationed in Dayton, Ohio, he spent his free time giving talks before civic groups. After raising $2,000, he used the money to treat his Dutch friends to a visit to the United States. Meyer Berger, the Pulitzer Prize–winning columnist for the *New York Times,* later wrote a story about Morgan's project. That led to a meeting with Clarence Hall, a senior editor at the *Digest.*

President Eisenhower had recently launched People-to-People, a high-minded plan to promote world peace that was short on specifics. Eisenhower's idea was for individuals, acting on their own initiative, to help bring about understanding between people of different countries. But six months later the *Digest* was unable to find a single individual who was actually doing anything to improve international goodwill.

Bright-eyed Harry Morgan, however, struck Hall as just the sort of person the president ordered. In the February 1958 issue, the first of four articles on Morgan appeared—a number that eventually earned him a place in a pantheon of *Digest* heroes whose only other inhabitants were Henry Ford, Thomas Edison, and Dwight D. Eisenhower. The article generated two thousand letters from readers, plus cash donations amounting to $5,000. With the consent of his commanding officer, Airman Morgan decided to keep the exchange program going and call it Ambassadors for Friendship. One of the letters he received was from DeWitt Wallace, who asked to be kept posted on his work.

After receiving his service discharge, Morgan enrolled at Rutgers University. At the invitation of Colonel Edward Eagan, chairman of the People-to-People sports committee, he flew to Europe over his summer holiday and selected four young athletes to visit the United States. When the quintet returned, Morgan's pen pal Eleanor Roosevelt threw a party for them at her estate in Pawling, and the next evening Eagan and his wife, Peggy Colgate Eagan, gave another at their home in Rye, New York. Sitting next to Morgan was DeWitt

Wallace, though neither recognized the other's name. Wallace and Eagan, who was also New York State boxing commissioner, planned to attend a boxing match at Madison Square Garden later that night. Over supper Wallace learned that Morgan was about to set off with his four visitors on a cross-country tour of the United States, camping out in national parks, as part of the president's People-to-People program.

"That's terrific," said Wally, who had taken much the same tour himself as a youth. "This would make a great *Reader's Digest* article."

Morgan replied that the magazine had already done one. Wally looked at him and said, "What do you mean, they've done one?" While Eagan waited impatiently, the *RD*'s publisher then cross-examined the guest of honor at length about his various activities.

A few days later Morgan, a fraternity brother, and his four guests set off, spending eleven weeks speaking at Rotary clubs, living with farmers, and camping out. When Morgan returned to New York in late August 1959, he once again contacted the *New York Times*. Meyer Berger had since died, so he was put through to Seymour Topping, the newspaper's former correspondent in Bonn, who said he could use a good story.

Immediately after the interview, Morgan—who was also president of the student body—left town to attend a conference. On his return he found half a dozen messages under his dormitory door: "Call DeWitt Wallace," "Call Gordon Davies." Morgan called Davies, Wally's private secretary, not knowing that Wallace was the man he had met at Rye. After lecturing him for not promptly returning the call, Davies gave Morgan the number to High Winds.

When Wally answered, his first words were "I wrote you a letter in 1958 saying keep in touch, we want to know more about your work. And now you've let the *New York Times* scoop us."

Morgan did not know what he was talking about. After calming down, Wally went on, "You and I have got to get together for lunch and talk. How are Thursdays for you?"

"On Thursdays I have to take fundamentals of calculus again," Morgan admitted. "I flunked it the first time."

"You know," said Wally, his mood softening, "I used to cut classes I didn't like once in a while."

They arranged to meet at twelve o'clock at the Pinnacle Club in the Socony Building, on Forty-second Street, the following Thursday. When the young student showed up, Wally introduced him to Leland

Stowe, a Pulitzer Prize–winning journalist, who only minutes earlier had accepted a position with the magazine as a roving editor.

"We're going to hear some interesting things about this young man," Wally said to Stowe during the introductions. "Why don't you join us for lunch?"

The annual six-month roving stint with the *RD* permitted Stowe to teach journalism the other half year at the University of Michigan in Ann Arbor, so he was in a mood to celebrate. Over lunch, after quizzing Morgan about what he and his guests did that summer, Wally turned paternal and asked, "What does a young man in his early twenties with the air force behind him, another year of college ahead of him, what do you want to do with your life?"

Morgan answered that he hoped to find work helping other people, perhaps with the State Department or the United Nations.

"What?" Wally exclaimed, choking on a cracker. "All that bureaucracy, committees? I'm disappointed in you."

"But I've got to live," Morgan explained. "And I like working with different nationalities."

"I know a man who wants to offer you a job," Wally continued. "But if you have the United Nations and the State Department on your brain he might not be too excited. Now what would you really like to do?"

"I guess what I'm doing now," Morgan shrugged, thinking perhaps someone had written the *Digest* a letter, offering him a job. "But there must be some strings attached."

"There's one string," said Wally, "and here it comes. Harry, if this were to work out, whatever you do with your life you must always believe in what you're doing and *have fun.*"

Morgan still did not know that the editor of the *Reader's Digest* was also its proprietor. But he observed tears welling in Stowe's eyes. Wally reached over and shook Morgan's hand.

"You've been hired," he announced. "Put me down for Thursday lunch. For the whole year. Cancel your calculus class."

Then he went over to a telephone, called Clarence Hall, and arranged for the *Digest* to do a second article on Ambassadors for Friendship. Later Morgan learned that his $3,000 student loan had been mysteriously paid off. Every Thursday thereafter, editor and student met at the Pinnacle Club. Wally told him how he met Lila, and all about Macalester, and began paying him $500 a month. To earn his salary, Morgan gave a talk at Macalester that by Wally's calculation was surely worth $5,000. Morgan's usual speaking fee was $15.

Finally, Morgan wrote a letter to Lila Bell, fulsomely congratulating her for having such a wonderful husband. Later she asked to meet the young man who had so captivated her husband. The lunches on Thursday also served to keep Wally occupied while his wife was having her hair done across town at the River Club, and usually the two men were the only ones left in the dining room. On the appointed day when Morgan was to be introduced to Mrs. Wallace, Wally—who was trying to stop smoking—asked Morgan for a Kent. When the latter declined, he angrily summoned the waiter and ordered two packs of cigarettes. Opening one, he proceeded to smoke nearly the entire pack.

While visiting the men's room before leaving, Wally complained, "If you hadn't been smoking those damn cigarettes I wouldn't have taken them. Now I've got to meet Lila Bell at the Park Lane Hotel and she's going to know it immediately."

Pointing to a shelf of toiletry articles, Morgan said, "Why don't you gargle and spray this stuff on you and she'll never know."

So Wally gargled and sprayed and then asked Morgan to smell him. Morgan pronounced him odor-free. Then the two went over to the River Club. When Wally went up to kiss Lila, she immediately said, "Wally, you've been smoking. And why are you wearing all that cologne?"

Abashed, Wally gestured toward Morgan and said, "It's his fault. He got me into this whole mess."

Lila revealed how she had put Morgan's letter in her treasure book and that she wanted to meet his fiancée, Catharine Johnston, a Smith College art history graduate and beatnik artist living in Greenwich Village. A few Thursdays later, Morgan and Johnston, the Wallaces, and Fred and Judy Thompson gathered in a Manhattan restaurant. Wally was wearing a ten-gallon Stetson hat and cowboy boots. Inevitably, at one point, Lila's and Johnston's conversation turned to art. Soon they were engaged in a heated exchange, and Morgan heard Lila say, "Well, darling, I don't really think you're right. You see, I *own* the painting."

"Mrs. Wallace, you own the painting," Johnston coolly replied, "but I *studied* the painting, and this was my field."

Morgan thought, "There it goes. The job is gone, finished."

Wally changed the subject, but the atmosphere at the table had turned frosty. Everyone tried to talk about something, except for

Johnston and Lila, who maintained a stony silence. But three days later Lila wrote a note apologizing to Johnston and admitting she was wrong. The two women were to become fast friends.

Shortly after Morgan and Johnston got married, they headed off for Macalester College in St. Paul. At Wally's direction, President Harvey Rice had invited him to join the staff as special assistant to the president in charge of international programs. The second article on Ambassadors for Friendship had since generated fifteen thousand responses and nearly $100,000 in donations. Wally felt vindicated because some Digesters had grumbled about running yet another profile of Morgan, especially as the lead. With so much money in hand, Wally also decided to incorporate Ambassadors for Friendship as a nonprofit corporation.

A few weeks later the Morgans and the next group of students from abroad set off on a cross-country trip. It was also the Morgans' honeymoon. Every other night they called Wally at High Winds to tell him what they had done, seen, and eaten and whom they were staying with. At the end of summer the Morgans settled into their new home—the top floor of the International House on the Macalester campus.

In late September 1960 Macalester trustee Al Cole visited the college. While the two men were chatting, Cole asked if he had any ideas for a special project, because Wally had intimated he had some extra money lying about. Though caught off-guard, Morgan blurted out that, by coincidence, he did just happen to have a great idea in mind. Cole was so impressed by his enthusiasm that he invited Morgan to return with him to Pleasantville the next day and pitch it to Wally. Morgan panicked. "I've got twenty-four hours to come up with the best idea of my life," he told his wife, "or I'm going to be fired."

She reminded him of an idea once proposed to Morgan by Broadway columnist and TV host Ed Sullivan, who had suggested bringing foreign journalists and writers to America so that they could write about their experiences afterward. Later he devoted one of his "Little Old New York" columns in the *New York Daily News* to Morgan, comparing him to Father Keller of the Christophers, whose motto was "It is better to light one candle than to curse the darkness." If only Morgan devoted his energies to the working press, Sullivan declared, millions of people around the world could learn what America, warts and all, was really like.

Morgan returned with Cole to Pleasantville, and the following day the two of them met with Wally in his office. Morgan revealed how he wanted to bring twelve foreign journalists between the ages of twenty-one and thirty-one to the United States for twelve months and let them work, study, and travel in depth. But Wally was not impressed.

"What happens at the end of twelve months and six of these twelve people decide they hate us?" he asked. "For the rest of their lives they're going to write ugly things about the United States."

Morgan replied, "Wally, here you are, a man who's built this great empire all over the world, and people compare the *Reader's Digest* to mom, the Bible, and apple pie—that it's one of the glories of America; and here you are afraid of what people are going to write about us? I'm ashamed of you."

Wally loftily responded that, if Morgan so passionately believed in his idea, he should have no trouble raising the money on his own. Cole just shook his head. And that was the end of the meeting. Depressed, Morgan took the train back to New York. But en route he resolved to raise the money. He also believed in a Greater Power and prayed, "Just teach me what I ought to know."

On arriving at the Wentworth Hotel, on Forty-sixth Street, where he was staying, Morgan rummaged through the yellow pages to get ideas. Under "Airlines," Pan American World Airways had the biggest advertisement. He promptly telephoned and asked to speak to someone in marketing. By an extraordinary coincidence, Juan Trippe, the company's founder, picked up the phone. When Morgan breathlessly tried to explain his problem, Trippe invited him to meet with PR director Sam Pryor. Morgan dashed over, pitched his idea, and left with a promise that Pan Am would provide free round-trip airfare for a dozen journalists from as many countries around the world.

Back at his hotel, Morgan called Bill Headden, the head of Standard Oil of New Jersey, who had helped underwrite Morgan's cross-country honeymoon trip. Headden promised him all the gas, tires, and car parts he needed.

Thrilled by his two successes, Morgan returned to St. Paul. George Romney, chairman of American Motors in Detroit, later agreed to supply the journalists with five Rambler station wagons. Then Morgan called the National Cash Register Company in Dayton, where he had once been stationed, and asked to speak to Stanley Allyn. The chairman listened politely for a moment, then suggested that his caller contact the company's charitable contributions committee.

With trademark hubris, Morgan answered, "Mr. Allyn, I'm ashamed of you. You're the chairman of one of the largest international companies in the world. I thought if anyone would be interested in an idea about better friendship between countries it would be you. I'm sorry to take your time."

Cowed, the chairman replied, "Don't hang up. Please keep talking. I've got plenty of time."

Morgan talked for half an hour, proposing the company give each journalist a thousand dollars in spending money, or $12,000 in all. Allyn, who was leaving for Europe that night, agreed to take up the matter with the charitable committee on his return. When Morgan countered that a good idea ought not to be "penalized" by being put on hold, Allyn wearily suggested that Morgan call him the next morning at his hotel in New York. At the very least, said the CEO, he wanted to talk things over with his wife.

At this point Morgan felt he held the upper hand. Reasoning that it was easy to say no over the telephone, he took an overnight flight and arrived in New York the next morning. At five minutes to nine, he phoned Allyn from the lobby of the Waldorf-Astoria. Allyn asked how the weather was in Minnesota.

"It was fine when I left last night."

"Left? Where are you calling from?"

"I'm in the lobby."

There was silence on the phone. Morgan explained that Allyn would probably not think very highly of a young salesman who tried to sell a sophisticated computer system to a banker over a phone twelve hundred miles away.

"Well," Allyn sighed, "I'll tell you right now I'd fire the bastard. Come on up for a cup of coffee."

Over the next few hours, the two men discussed the idea in depth. When the question of money finally arose, the NCR chairman revealed that he and his wife had decided to give $3,000 apiece. Morgan was overjoyed, much to Allyn's puzzlement.

"That's the trouble with young people today," he said. "They're always satisfied to get half of what they ask for."

As Morgan put on his coat, the chairman continued, "By the way, there are two words in my vocabulary that probably have meant more to me than anything else. What does a young man in 1960 think of the word 'challenge'? What does 'challenge' mean to you?"

Morgan gave him a dictionary definition, and Allyn only shook his head and said, "That's not going to get you very far."

"What's your definition?" Morgan asked.

"You're in a big city where a lot of things can happen," Allyn continued, "and I challenge you to go out and find someone who's going to give you $6,000 to match mine so you can go home with what you came for. That's what I call a challenge."

Morgan accepted the challenge and shook Allyn's hand. The chairman walked him to the bank of elevators, and while they waited Allyn asked, "And what does the word 'incentive' mean to you?"

Morgan gave him another dictionary definition.

"That won't get you anywhere," Allyn said, shaking his head.

"What's your definition?"

"Well, I've challenged you to find someone, tell them your dream, and ask them for $6,000 to match mine. And Harry, if you don't raise another $6,000, I don't ever want to talk to you again. You don't get my $6,000. That's incentive."

The elevator door opened and Allyn said, "By the way, don't use my name to get in any place."

The door closed and Morgan descended to the lobby.

"What the hell," he thought. "I had the money almost in my hand, and then he starts talking about challenge and incentive."

As soon as he reached the lobby, Morgan headed straight for the yellow pages. Years earlier he had read an article about Thomas Watson, Sr., founder of IBM, who had once worked for NCR. On a hunch, he walked over to the IBM executive offices and asked to see Arthur ("Dick") Watson, director of world trade. Told that an appointment was necessary, Morgan asked if he could sit in the reception room on the off chance someone else might cancel. Three hours later a sympathetic secretary finally showed him into Watson's office.

"Mr. Watson," Morgan began, "I've got only fifteen minutes to convince you to give me $6,000 for something that I believe in. And if you don't, I'm going to lose $6,000 this very day."

Watson walked around to where Morgan was standing, shook his hand, and said, "Young man, I suggest you sit down in that easy chair over there, because you've got the most serious problem I've heard all day."

That broke the ice. Morgan told Watson about Allyn's challenge and incentive, adding parenthetically that he did not use the NCR chairman's name to get the appointment. He also recounted his meetings with Wally and Juan Trippe, and the promises of help from Bill Headden and George Romney. Thoroughly entertained, Watson picked up the phone and called the Waldorf. Again the Greater Power arranged for Allyn to answer. The two men chatted and joked for a moment.

Then Watson said, "I've got this man from Macalester College in my office, and what's this idea of you putting him through this torture? A good idea is a good idea. And by the way, before Mr. Morgan leaves my office I'm giving him a check for $6,000. You'd better not skip the country without giving him the money you owe him, too."

Back on the sidewalk, Morgan felt exhilarated. Returning to his hotel room, he phoned Wally, who did not know he was in New York.

"I've been working on this journalism project . . . ," Morgan began.

"What project was that?" asked Wally.

"The one where you told me to go out and raise the money."

"But what are you doing in New York? And why didn't you call me to get permission to come up here? We can't have you running all over the country."

Morgan told him about his conversation with Juan Trippe and his meetings with Allyn and Watson.

"Where—where are you now?" Wally asked, agitated and excited. "This is unbelievable."

Morgan was summoned to Pleasantville and the next day told his story at the Guest House to Wally, Al Cole, and Hobe Lewis. Wally asked how much more money he needed to raise. Morgan proposed to fly down to Atlanta and talk to the chairman of Coca-Cola.

"Stop," Wally fumed. "Don't raise another nickel. This started out as a *Reader's Digest* project, and I don't know if you messed up enough, but this is *a Reader's Digest program!* All these other companies are getting involved and I think that's fine. But don't get anybody else involved."

Morgan later sat down with public-relations director Sterling Fisher to work out the details. Fisher suggested that Morgan select journalists only from countries where the *Digest* had foreign editions. Some weeks later he embarked on his first trip around the world to pick candidates for the Foreign Journalists Institute, which like Ambassadors for Friendship was to be carried out under the auspices of Macalester College. Wally arranged for Morgan to raise a few more dollars from David Sarnoff at NBC, and Fisher put him in touch with the U.S.

Information Agency, which provided some background assistance. And it was decided to let Coca-Cola get a taste of the project, too.

In due course, Morgan and twelve charter visiting journalists from around the world toured the United States in five fire-red Rambler station wagons. At the end of FJI's first year, Wally threw a farewell party for the journalists at the St. Regis Roof, off Fifth Avenue, and personally invited the presidents of every supporting company to attend. Fisher later proposed that Morgan rename the project the World Press Institute.

Despite his success as an emissary of American and *Digest* goodwill, Morgan was not satisfied. Though he lacked any training in journalism and had never written or edited a single article, he wanted more than anything else to be a *Digest* editor. Wally encouraged him in his ambition, but cautioned that he needed more journalistic experience—to be provided by the WPI—before he was reassigned to Pleasantville.

After five more years went by, Morgan's wife finally declared that she had not gotten married to live on a college campus in the Midwest. Morgan persuaded Wally to make him a senior editor—much to the alarm of most other editors, who saw Morgan as a publicity-hungry, self-promoting impresario of idealism who shamelessly traded on his friendship with the Wallaces to travel around the world for a living. They also had no doubt that his ultimate goal was to become editor in chief, succeeding Hobe Lewis when that day arrived. The question came down to what the qualifications for being an editor were any more—being able to commission and edit an article successfully, or going beyond all that and living it.

The grumbling finally reached such a level that Al Cole had to intercede and inform Wally of all the rancor toward Morgan in the editorial ranks. Wally compromised by grandly "demoting" Morgan to roving editor.

━━━

AMONG those especially wary of Morgan was senior editor John Allen, who was out of the same mold—an extrovert do-gooder, a jovial, pudgy glad-hander who wore his virtue on his sleeve. When Wally or Lila was on the grounds, Allen was known to wander conspicuously among the flower-bordered walks in search of a stray piece of litter he could triumphantly snatch up just as one of the Wallaces came into view.

Like Morgan, Allen thought he had a shot at someday being editor in chief. But the highly visible altruism of the two men made their rivalry unique. Most of the other contenders were traditionally divided between old guard and Young Turks. The former were led by Bun Mahony, the humorless, passionately loyal managing editor. Among the up-and-comers—many of them close friends despite the often bruising competitiveness of their circumstances—were senior staff editors Ed Thompson, Roy Herbert, and Tony Oursler and Washington bureau editor Ken Gilmore. If there were any dark horses in contention for the chair currently held by Hobe Lewis, they existed only as figments of their own imagination—or possibly, for brief periods of time, of Wally's, since after all he had a track record of being unpredictable. And as events were to prove, he still had a number of stunning surprises in store for just about everybody.

Allen was a Young Turk, too, of course. He and senior editor Ed Thompson co-owned a ski lodge, and their children played together. As an editor, Allen was also highly industrious. But Allen's ace was that he was the son-in-law of Norman Vincent Peale, Wally's favorite preacher and good friend, and that fact put him in a position to advance his candidacy not just on the editorial front but through the backdoor of good works and positive thinking, which Wally was such a sucker for and which Morgan perhaps thought he had all to himself.

There were other parallels between the two men as well. After serving as a Japanese translator for the Marine Corps in the Far East, Allen enrolled at Yale. On graduating, he became Los Angeles correspondent for *Time*. After a stint as a schoolmaster, he interviewed with the *Reader's Digest* and was put to work condensing books for its book-excerpt department. Soon he moved on to cutting and condensing articles and to working on originals. But the change in venue was not enough to salvage a troubled marriage. Like many another Digester, Allen became a free agent not long after embarking upon his career in Pleasantville.

Though not a religious man, Wally regularly liked to listen on Sunday evenings to Norman Vincent Peale's sermons broadcast from Marble Collegiate Church, on Fifth Avenue, over radio station WOR. One day in the early sixties, Allen was assigned to work with an author named Arthur Gordon on a profile on Peale. The former invited Allen to hear Peale preach. Mrs. Peale was away at the time, so the duty of liaison for the two Digesters fell to the Peales' youngest daughter,

Elizabeth, then a student at Mount Holyoke. She and Allen began dating and were later married.

In due course Allen was to find himself embarrassed occasionally on Monday mornings when Wally wanted to discuss Peale's Sunday evening sermon and Allen had not always heard it. But one Monday morning Wally called up Allen and said, "I don't think we have enough religion in the magazine. Why don't you contact a lot of people, and we'll have a series on 'What Religion Means to Me.' "

Allen duly informed the other editors of the series. On Tuesday morning, promptly at 8:30, Wally phoned again and said, "You know that idea on religion? I've been thinking about it. I think it's pretty stupid, so forget it."

Morgan and Allen soon found themselves locked in pious *mano a mano* simply as conduits of Wally's noble impulses, not editorial genius, and on the face of it the former had the upper hand. It was Morgan whom the Wallaces took along on their vacations—an extremely rare privilege. It was Morgan whom rumor said the Wallaces were going to adopt, making him officially the son or grandson they never had. It was Morgan who aroused envy, contempt, and perhaps a little nervousness in just about everybody. Allen, especially, was consumed with jealousy.

Around this time, Wally's close friend and biographer James Playsted Wood was at work on a revised edition of the *Digest*'s officially sanctioned history, *Of Lasting Interest.* There Wood obligingly wrote for the edification of the public that Wally saw Morgan as "a vibrant young man with a dream" and as "someone he could form and guide, adding his experience to the youthful energy of sharp-eyed and ambitious youth."

Privately, though, Wood thought that the two biggest mistakes Wally had ever made were, on the institutional level, giving money to Macalester College and, on the individual level, promoting the career of Harry Morgan. It was a view that few *RD* insiders would have disagreed with.

Despite the relocation back east, the Morgans' marriage soon failed. Morgan moved in with one of the few people who had befriended him in Chappaqua—Harry Wilcox, who still lived in the house given to him by Lila years before. Now there were two Harrys for everybody to worry about. Digesters called them the odd couple.

17

Where There Is Beauty, There Is No Crime

BY THE EARLY SIXTIES Syrie Maugham's place at the *Digest* was taken by a young, very handsome, flamboyantly homosexual interior decorator named Bill Kennedy—sometimes called Wild Bill Kennedy for his outrageous dress and behavior, as well as such accessories as a bronze Bentley. Kennedy captivated Lila utterly. He was witty, charming, urbane—and besides that, he had a sense of fun that was becoming an extremely rare commodity among the gray-flanneled legions of Pleasantville.

An example of Kennedy's idea of fun was to invite Wally and Lila down to Greenwich Village, the *Digest*'s first home and by the sixties a prime staging area for hippies, radicals, and just about anybody at the other end of the political and cultural spectrum from Pleasantville. For the occasion, Kennedy outfitted the septuagenarian Wally as a "hippie" in tight leather pants and Lila as a bohemian floozie. Hoping they blended in with the often outrageous street scene, the trio wandered the Wallaces' old neighborhood, looking at all the oddly dressed people.

Kennedy was now in charge of decorating new *Digest* offices around the world—making sure that he always used Lila's favorite colors—Persian blue, pale rose, and celadon green. He also refurbished several rooms in High Winds and designed the new offices in the Pan Am Building, in New York. It was only natural, then, that in 1964 Lila appointed Wild Bill to oversee the restoration of Boscobel, one of her first major forays into the world of philanthropy.

Built in 1804 in the neoclassical style of Scottish architect Robert Adams by States Morris Dyckman, the son of early Dutch settlers,

Boscobel was situated in upstate New York near Peekskill and had fallen into ruin. In 1961, after the last member of the Dyckman family died, the land was condemned for a public park and the decaying sixteen-room mansion sold to a wrecker for $35. At literally the last moment, with the help of state police, a preservation committee managed to save the house and appealed to Lila for help.

Lila pledged $750,000 to have the house dismantled and reconstructed farther up the Hudson valley, on a site overlooking the river opposite West Point. Just upstream were three of the most famous homes in America—the Vanderbilt and Mills mansions and the home of Franklin Delano Roosevelt at Hyde Park, now all open to the public. Boscobel, whose name means "beautiful woods," was to make a fourth.

After the house was put back together again, Kennedy was given the commission to refurbish the interior. He and Lila shared a passion for American antiques, and the assignment seemed not only logical but felicitous. No one doubted that he had impeccable taste. One thing he did not have, and no one thought to ask about, was any concern for historical authenticity in the period restoration he was about to undertake. Boscobel had been an elegant example of the Federal period, but for Kennedy the main thing was to fill the house with rare, expensive, and beautiful things just so long as they were American and roughly from the early nineteenth century, give or take a hundred years.

As work proceeded, the costs ran up astronomically—far beyond the initial projections and alarmingly like those of the government boondoggles the *Digest* was forever castigating. One day James Wood mentioned to Lila that he heard that the latest figure was two million dollars.

"Don't tell Wally," Lila replied, "but it's nearer three."

When Boscobel, fully restored and redecorated, was dedicated and opened to the public, Nelson Rockefeller praised it as one of the most beautiful homes ever built in America; and Averell Harriman called it "a unique and unsurpassed triumph of the early American builder's art." But over time, as architecture and antiques buffs, local historians, and other restorationists joined the ranks of visitors, they began to notice something peculiar about Boscobel. It did not look like a Federal showpiece at all. Everyone even agreed that it probably looked a lot better. For the time being, however, no one said anything. Lila had spent millions, and to voice any criticism would have seemed ungrateful.

AMONG Lila's other early philanthropic interests were the Martha Graham dance company, the Metropolitan Opera, and the Metropolitan Museum of Art, three of New York's glitziest cultural pillars. Lila was both magnanimous and creative, donating a building on East Sixty-third Street for Graham's School of Contemporary Dance, underwriting the production of several operas, and helping the museum restore and mount a permanent exhibition of its major collection of Egyptian art.

Wally did not share his wife's enthusiasm for grand opera, and he thought that most people connected with the arts were phonies. Lila agreed with her husband when it came to Rudolf Bing, general manager of the Metropolitan Opera, whom she found odious. Yet she had a weakness bordering on a schoolgirl crush for museum director Thomas Hoving, who could charm her out of anything—and often did. Kennedy and Hoving were typical of the kind of man Lila favored—hucksters of the arts with a gift of gab and a genius for flattery.

Graham was altogether different—an artist first and a fund-raiser second. Also, she was a woman, and Lila seldom got along with any woman who presumed to meet her on terms of social equality. Lila's support of Graham's company, then in its heyday, was a logical extension of her own lifelong passion for dancing. Moreover, Wally enjoyed going to see modern dance and ballet, which he appreciated for its athleticism.

The two women had a falling out when Lila insisted, as a condition for further financial support, that Graham give up her career as a performer and devote herself exclusively to choreography and the running of her company. At the time, the early sixties, Graham was drinking heavily. Lila's advisers thought that Graham was too old to be a performer any longer and that she was not using wisely the money provided her. Graham eventually retired as a performer, and Lila continued to supply the troupe with funds, although their friendship had come to an end.

Lila and Wally kept completely separate bank accounts and had separate foundations. They did not tell each other what they were doing except incidentally. Corporate counsel William Barnabas McHenry, who also handled the legal end of the Wallaces' charities, thought Lila was the better philanthropist because she had "flair." Wallace, by contrast, "sort of worried things to death, like Macalester."

McHenry was an associate with the prestigious New York law firm of Lord Day & Lord when, in 1957, he was assigned to the RDA as corporate counsel. At first his duties were routine—vetting each issue of the magazine, approving contracts, overseeing litigation. But in 1962 McHenry persuaded Al Cole that the RDA could save money by employing him directly.

Before long, though, McHenry had alienated Cole and others higher up in management. Particularly alarming to some was the RDA counsel's undisguised social ambition—his relentless quest to work his way into New York's most exclusive circles on the Wallaces' coattails. Worse, from his enemies' point of view, he succeeded in a remarkably short time—hobnobbing, as Wally's and Lila's stand-in, with the Rockefellers and their illustrious ilk.

Fortunately for McHenry, his early years with the RDA also coincided with the great upheavals of 1965–66, when Lewis became editor and Paul Thompson took the place of Al Cole as business manager. Thompson admired McHenry, who like himself had outsider status—his offices were in the Pan Am Building—and promoted his career within the company.

In addition to guiding the Wallaces through the thickets of tax law relating both to themselves as individuals and to the RDA, McHenry helped establish the Wallaces' major funds, drew up their separate wills—filed in three different states to foil would-be will breakers—and soon became, after Laurance Rockefeller, Lila's most trusted adviser on the arts.

McHenry's rise to power was all the more remarkable in that neither Wally nor Lila seemed to care for the man personally—a view shared by many Digesters, one of whom found him to be a man of "Dickensian odiousness." Another saw him as a superannuated prep-school sophomore, always sporting a bow tie and flaunting his Princeton and Columbia Law School degrees. On the other hand, he also had several supporters within the company, including treasurer Dick Waters and his assistant William Cross.

But the Wallaces disliked mixing with New York society and art types and serving on boards even more than they disliked McHenry, whose service in that respect proved invaluable. Also, as Cole glumly came to realize, the house lawyer—as the man most intimately familiar with Wally's assorted tax and other legal affairs—simply knew too much to be fired.

The Wallaces derived money from two sources for their philanthropy. The first came from the dividends paid on a large block of stock owned by the RDA Foundation set up in 1938. But they also simply took income out of the company, as much and whenever they wanted. For the last two decades of their lives, they were to devote themselves almost exclusively to charity. And with their enormous wealth, they became in a relatively short period two of the most generous and unpredictable philanthropists in the world—and also, on occasion, two of the most gullible and exploited.

That exploitation had begun in the early sixties when Lila contributed heavily to the Korean Little Angels, a children's dance troupe, and hired out Philharmonic Hall in New York for a performance. Later she learned that the Little Angels were a fund-raising front for the Unification church of the Reverend Sun Myung Moon and withdrew her support.

The Wallaces also worked in such secrecy, or aversion to publicity, that their charitable work remained known only to a rather small group of people, and then mostly in New York. Up until the 1960s Lila's only previous appearance in the public limelight occurred in 1954 when she was invited to sit on the board of the New York Central Railroad.

As philanthropists, Wally and Lila manifested an often touching humility and genuine altruism that transcended the occasional pettiness and vanity of the private person. Wally also showed an obstinacy that struck at the very core of his relationship with his father. He was determined to elevate a fairly obscure and liberal St. Paul college to national prominence. That intensely narrow focus on education—he also gave millions to other small schools and colleges—was in part the reason why his philanthropy went largely unnoticed. In 1963 he had approvingly quoted Horace Mann: " 'To make money immortal, invest it in men.' Mrs. Wallace and I believe no other investment yields greater dividends of satisfaction than one made in behalf of liberal arts colleges."

They had plenty to invest. A May 1968 *Fortune* survey ranked DeWitt Wallace among the thirty-one wealthiest men in the United States—not in the same billionaire class as J. Paul Getty and Howard Hughes, but rubbing $200–$300 million shoulders with the likes of S. I. Newhouse, Joseph P. Kennedy, David and Laurance S. Rockefeller, and John Hay Whitney, and a hundred million or so above such pikers as Doris Duke and J. Seward Johnson.

In those years Wally endowed scholarships in more than two hundred schools and colleges around the country, including another alma mater, Mount Hermon, in Northfield, Massachusetts; and aided youth-leadership programs in such organizations as African Student Aid, Junior Achievement, and the National 4-H Club. In 1973 and in 1974 he also donated money to the Association for Voluntary Sterilization.

Lila did not share her husband's investment philosophy. She was quite content to let her husband have Truth all to himself. Rather, except for relatively small gifts to the American University in Cairo in honor of her late brother or to her own alma mater, the University of Oregon, she preferred to give money to Beauty.

"I'm most interested in beauty," she once said—naively, as events would prove. "Where there is beauty, there is no crime. I cleaned up the entrance to the Metropolitan Museum."

———

WHAT money Lila did not give away to museums and to opera and dance companies she spent in other ways on beauty—in the acquisition of French Impressionist masterpieces and antique furniture. Over a period of years that collection eventually became, in the opinion of the art critic of the *New York Times,* "the country's most valuable outside the Rockefellers' at Pontico Hills."

Among the masterpieces in the Wallaces' collection, all of it accumulated by Lila, was a *Water Lilies* by Monet, a huge work executed in 1918 at his home in Giverny and one of his last paintings of a favorite subject. Lila paid $25,000 for it in 1961. Other acquisitions included Monet's *Landscape with Orchard and Figures; Dancers,* a pastel by Degas; the 1924 bronze sculpture *Gulls,* by Gaston Lachaise; the bronze bust *Jester,* by Picasso; *Portrait of Jeanne Hébuterne,* by Amedeo Modigliani, which cost $1 million in 1966; *Landscape at L'Estaque,* by Paul Cézanne; *Chartres,* by Maurice Utrillo; *Sailboat at Poissy,* by Maurice de Vlaminck; *Thatched Roofs at Auvers,* by Vincent van Gogh, painted only a month before the artist's suicide and acquired in 1961 for only $20,000; *Flowers in a Vase,* also painted in van Gogh's last days and bought in 1963 for $200,000; and *Anemones and Mirror,* by Henri Matisse.

Lila's philosophy of buying paintings was to "fall in love" with them. She once explained, "I'll go down to Knoedler's and they'll have something that they think I should look at. . . . If I wake up the next morning and say, 'Lila, you don't really need it,' then I don't buy it. But if something says, 'Lila, you can't live without it,' then I buy it. It's really that simple. A painting is like a husband. If you can live without the man, why marry him?"

It was a philosophy perhaps inherited from her artist mother; and Lila treated her favorite paintings, those she kept at High Winds, just like men she could not do without or whom she did not want to share. Never once was High Winds opened to the public.

The finest painting in the Wallace collection was Monet's *Nymphéas,* which hung in the dining room, though Lila's favorite was Renoir's *Young Woman in Blue Going to the Conservatory,* an 1877 profile of a fashionable young Parisian, which she had acquired in an unusual way. One evening in the midsixties actress Miriam Hopkins phoned. In desperate need of money, she offered to sell the Renoir to Lila at a price far below its current market value on condition that she received the cash within forty-eight hours. It was Hopkins's only valuable remaining possession. Lila agreed to buy it sight unseen, and two days later *La Jeune Fille* was prominently hung over the fireplace of the drawing room in High Winds.

The son of Georges Braque also once found himself strapped for cash and sold Lila several of his father's paintings on short notice. Al Cole had frequently complained that Lila's expenditures on art—the unheard-of $20,000 on van Gogh's *Thatched Roofs,* for example—were a drain on the company's cash flow; and that was another source of friction between the two. But Lila told the younger Braque she would sell the paintings back at the purchase price if he later so desired. Braque was not normally a painter Lila admired, and she had bought the works literally to be charitable. Then, to be uncharitable, she installed one of the Braques in the corridor just outside Cole's office.

As the collection grew, the RDA offices in Pleasantville, New York City, and elsewhere were transformed into galleries with collections rivaling those of a medium-sized museum. Lila believed that great art was something to be appreciated "not only in moments of solitude, but also in our flying minutes of busyness as we go about our daily lives." Besides Chagall's *Three Candles* in Wally's office and Pierre Bonnard's *Stage Design* in her own, there were a Utrillo and a van Gogh in the reception room; and elsewhere Blatas's *La Place au Ceret* and Redon's *Pegasus,* as well as works by Toulouse-Lautrec, Soutine, Vuillard. With the beginning of the art boom in the midsixties, the value of many of those works soared into the hundreds of thousands, then even breathtakingly higher.

Yet security was so lax that on one occasion art director Kenneth Stuart, to prove a point, joined a group of visitors taking a tour of the office and grounds. Before the visitors departed, Stuart managed to carry out, under his raincoat, a masterpiece worth at least his pension; he later displayed the work (Picasso's *Jester,* fittingly enough) to Cole as proof that the RDA quickly needed to do something to protect its fortune in art. In short order a state-of-the-art security system was installed.

On another afternoon an editor was walking along the corridors when a colleague told him he had just overheard Wally asking where that particular editor sat. Hurrying back, he reached his office just moments before Wally appeared outside the open door. He did not enter but stood staring at something hanging on the wall outside.

"I just wanted to see what more than a million dollars looked like," he finally explained.

When Lila was just beginning her public career as a philanthropist, a woman editor in the London office provided a perceptive word portrait of the mistress of High Winds. The editor was struck by Lila's delicacy, and noticed her ability to handle any subject lightly.

"Wallace was probing me pretty seriously," the editor wrote to a friend,

> but Lila would somehow "lift" the weight of his questions. I envied her this ability of being able to inject yeast into dough. It was all part of her charm—a very feminine trait. And her laugh. She had a very potent, musical laugh. Even in later years, when I met her fairly frequently, and she might say something a little bitchy about someone or tell a slightly blue story, she would frame her comment in laughter.

Lila also always appeared beautifully groomed and dressed. In those days she favored sapphire and crystal David Webb earrings and Mainbocher clothes, as well as cherry red lipstick to match her thinning auburn hair, which was dyed every week.

"But over the years I noticed that occasionally, when moved, she would be spontaneously simple, just like a young girl," the editor went on.

One evening at a dinner party at Charlie Ferguson's house, where I made the fourth, he served us a delicious, old-fashioned, ordinary stew. Ferguson's table wasn't big enough to hold all the dishes, so we sat around and ate our stew on our laps. Wally and Lila adored it, and suddenly she said: "Oh Wally, isn't this lovely? I haven't enjoyed a dinner so much since we were first married! Do you remember?"

It was the first time I saw the other face of Lila Acheson Wallace. The charm she exerted then was true and deep, springing from the heart and not from cleverness.

Shortly after Boscobel was renovated to resemble the fashionably tasteful home of a New York interior decorator with unlimited funds, Wally announced to his employees that a special fund of $500,000 was being put aside which the firm would contribute to worthy causes. The employees would decide to which ones. Wally wanted as many Digesters as possible to become more personally involved in philanthropy.

The top 750 employees were asked to fill out a form, designating six charities to receive their share of the pie, and return it to the company treasurer. Checks were then issued in the specified amount and transmitted to the employee, who mailed them out with an explanatory letter. The experiment was a first in the history of philanthropy and was written up in the *New York Times* and elsewhere. Wally hoped that other corporations would soon emulate the RDA's democratic example.

The program stipulated that an agency receiving funds be nonprofit, that an employee not benefit personally, and, most especially, that a donation to a college not be applied on the tuition of a relative. Furthermore, employees were discouraged from trying to curry favor with either Lila or Wally by contributing to a favorite Wallace charity such as Boscobel or Macalester.

But according to Bill Cross, at the time the assistant treasurer, employee-designated donations proved to be a disastrous idea. No one involved—employees, donees, or even the Wallaces themselves—ended up looking very good. Those on the initial short list were supposed to keep the matter confidential and did not. And at least two abused the privilege by substituting RDA donations for a portion of tuition charges for their children in private schools. The Westchester Council of Social Agencies also criticized the plan as "an unwise dissipation of charitable funds" and recommended that the money be turned over to the Westchester County United Fund.

Meanwhile, the clamor raised by employees excluded from the program eventually forced its expansion, and by the third year the program included the entire staff. Then things began to fall apart. Instead of transmitting the checks along with a letter, many simply sent them out with no explanation. Soon the treasurer's office was deluged with calls and letters of inquiry. Literally hundreds of checks never cleared and were presumably not mailed. Many of the calls from ministers, fire departments, and preparatory schools were to this effect: "Mr. and Mrs. A gave RDA donations, but Mr. and Mrs. B did not. Were they eligible?" Eventually, Wally and Lila scrapped the program, though mainly because most Digesters were simply turning the money over to their church.

In early 1967 Lila again tried to give away money and caused a ruckus—this time the ruffled feathers belonged to peacock Rudolf Bing. After attending a matinee at the Metropolitan Opera's new home in Lincoln Center one Sunday afternoon, Lila had joined mezzo-soprano Risë Stevens for a chocolate sundae at O'Neal's Saloon, across the street.

Stevens was cochairman of the opera's national touring company, which had only recently announced the cancellation of its third season, for financial reasons. During their tête-à-tête, Stevens was gloomy to the point of tears because the third season was 90 percent booked—compared with 66 percent the two previous years—when Bing canceled it. As Stevens well knew, Lila had earlier supported productions of Massenet's *Werther* and Wagner's *Parsifal.* Trying to console Stevens, Lila asked, "Would a million help?"*

Though it was too late to salvage the season, the overjoyed Stevens hoped that the touring company could resume its activities in 1968–69. She had always believed that it needed three seasons to prove itself. But when Bing heard of the pledge, he angrily summoned Lila to his

---

*Unlike her husband, who often dribbled his money out, Lila liked to give away a million dollars at a time. Previous million-dollar gifts had gone to a local YWCA in Westchester County and to a $36 million U.S./Egypt/UNESCO fund to move the 3,200-year-old Abu Simbel temple from the Nile valley to a higher site in order to make way for the Aswan High Dam. The Egyptian government, as a token of its gratitude, later presented her with a 4,000-year-old gold chalice, which became her favorite receptacle for cocktails—martinis, of course. The chalice's previous owner, Nefertiti, had used it when she resided in Abu Simbel with her husband, Ramses II.

office, then kept her waiting ten minutes. When she was finally shown in, he did not invite her to sit down but instead coldly launched into a lecture.

"Mrs. Wallace," he intoned, "I understand that you've agreed to help Risë in a situation, and you realize, of course, that Mother Met is the most important thing. If large funds start going to that little touring group, other funds directed to Mother Met will be shifted by people living in St. Louis and other parts of the country."

"Really, Mrs. Wallace," he went on, "we can't do things that way. We can't have the road company taking away money that Mother Met herself needs so badly. After all, the road company is merely going to tour the provinces."

Lila drew herself up and said, "I don't know about you, Mr. Bing, but I come from the provinces."

And without another word she left the room. Waiting for her in the limousine outside was Harry Morgan, who now frequently accompanied Lila into town on Thursdays. A furious Lila told him, "I have no use for that man. He's rude and crude, a real Austrian Jew. And, you know what? In a few weeks he's going to call me and say, 'Mrs. Wallace, about that gift . . .' And you know what I'm going to tell him? I'm going to tell dear Mr. Bing that I've *spent* it."

A few weeks later Bing did call about the money. In view of the opera's recent costly move to Lincoln Center, he hoped Mrs. Wallace would see fit to turn her gift over to the parent company instead of the touring troupe. But Lila told him the money was spent, and so the touring company was suspended. As a sop, she later gave Mother Met $300,000 to stage a new production of Mussorgsky's *Boris Godunov.*

———

THOUGH Wally did like to dribble his money out, he also knew how to give away a million dollars at a time—if not with his wife's flair, then with a low-key sense of the dramatic that was equally the stuff of legend.

A favorite charity of Wally's was Outward Bound, which appealed to his athleticism and sense of adventure. One afternoon the founder of the wilderness-based program, Josh Myner, gave a talk to a group of New York business and community leaders, among them Wally. As the two men were descending in the elevator afterward, Wally handed Myner a crumpled envelope, almost as an embarrassed afterthought, and hurried away. When Myner looked inside, he found a check for $1 million.

In 1968 Lila gave another one million dollars—her fourth million-dollar gift in recent years—to underwrite construction of Lincoln's Center's Juilliard School of Music library, which was named in her honor. Later she gave five million dollars to the school's capital fund-raising campaign.

The following year, when she was already more than eighty years old, Lila also provided the money for renovating the Great Hall and Plaza of the Metropolitan Museum, on New York's Fifth Avenue, adding her own distinct touch—flowers in the niches in perpetuity: forsythia in February, quince branches in March flown in weekly from Amsterdam.

"DeWitt always wanted to know how much she spent on the 'continuing gift,'" Hoving later admitted. "She never told him." At the time it cost an estimated $100,000 a year to keep the Great Hall constantly in bloom.

Shortly after the renovation was completed, Gerald Van der Kemp, curator of Versailles, entered the Great Hall one morning and saw coordinator Chris Giftos on a stepladder, arranging a great vase full of flowers. Giftos told him that Lila Wallace was responsible. Van der Kemp was then involved in raising funds to restore Monet's gardens at Giverny and decided to get in touch with her. Fortunately for Van der Kemp, Monet was Lila's favorite painter.

One of Wally's and Lila's most trusted consultants was art dealer Daniel Wildenstein, who reassured them of the value of the Giverny restoration. Eventually, with Wallace money, those immortal gardens were also restored—tulips, larkspur, and peonies in the spring; sweet-pea, snapdragons, and foxglove in summer. Arches and trellises were draped with clematis and climbing roses. As a reporter noted at the time, "The gardens that had captivated Lila Acheson Wallace on canvas were restored to ebullient reality."

———

IN LATE 1969 Harry Morgan decided he had come to a dead end, personally and professionally. His marriage was over, and he also felt overwhelmed by a sense that all he had accomplished in life was due to the munificence of DeWitt and Lila Wallace. At thirty-five he resigned as the associate executive director of the Reader's Digest Foundation, a post he was given after his career as a roving editor came to nothing.

Another motive was that he no longer had any hope of even becoming director of the RDF and succeeding Sterling Fisher. Assistant PR director Bob Devine had been given that plum assignment, and it was almost axiomatic that no two of Lila's boys ever got along.

One thing Morgan did have, though, as a result of all his traveling and moving in New York's most exclusive art and social circles was plenty of contacts. Among them was Broadway producer David Black, whose hits included *Ready When You Are, C.B.,* and, off Broadway, *The Knack.* Black was in the midst of mounting a new production, a musical based on Lewis Carroll's *Alice's Adventures in Wonderland,* reinterpreted and updated as a cautionary tale about the drug culture of the sixties. Morgan mentioned the play to Lila, who asked for further details.

The following Thursday, Morgan and Lila had lunch with Black at the River Club. Over her second martini, Lila agreed to become the principal backer. Before leaving, she asked Morgan to stop by High Winds the following week to accompany her to a local bank to make arrangements.

The next morning, Morgan got a call from Wally, who was furious—accusing Morgan of getting Lila drunk and trying to persuade her to spend so much money on a sleazy Broadway play with naked women running around on the stage.

"You're taking advantage of a dear and personal friendship," Wally went on, "and this sleazy Broadway producer . . ."

"That's David Black," Morgan interrupted. "He's got credentials, he's a lovely human being, and you should meet him."

Wally further explained that there were tax considerations involved in any underwriting and that neither he nor Lila was interested in making a profit from the play in the first place. Morgan revealed he had already talked with the president of Northfield Mount Hermon, Wally's alma mater, about the school's receiving any profits. At that point Wally became interested.

"Well, if Lila wants to take a flier on Broadway," he concluded, "I hope the two of you have some fun."

Two hours later Morgan's phone rang again, and Barnabas McHenry was on the line, saying he wanted to meet Morgan and Black for lunch the next day, adding that the producer should bring his lawyer.

When the four of them met, McHenry accused Morgan of having

gotten Lila drunk, but offered to pay Black $25,000 to take care of "difficulties." Black insisted that Lila had not been intoxicated and was bound by an oral contract. When Morgan agreed, McHenry kicked him under the table and told Black he had twenty-four hours to think over his offer. But under no conditions, said McHenry, was Lila going to get involved in the play. Then he left.

Convinced that Lila was not inebriated when she agreed to back the play, Morgan tried unsuccessfully to reach her at High Winds. Finally, he arranged for a letter to be hand-delivered. Late that evening Wally phoned and said, "You just leave my wife alone. She can't sleep."

In the end *Alice* fell through. Morgan and the Wallaces became estranged. Later Wally called Harry Wilcox, who was still Morgan's house mate, and instructed him to deliver an envelope from headquarters to High Winds. The envelope contained 50,000 shares of company stock in Morgan's name. Wally tore it up.

———

IN THE early seventies Lila and Wally received another shock when a former employee of New York's Knoedler Gallery confidentially informed them that Wild Bill Kennedy had defrauded the couple of hundreds of thousands of dollars, and perhaps millions. The prestigious East Side gallery was one of Lila's favorites, and its own transactions with the Wallaces were beyond reproach. But the Knoedler employee had dealt with Kennedy during the refurbishing of Boscobel and other projects and eventually discovered that the decorator was buying antiques and artwork through a dummy company that he wholly owned and controlled. This dummy company in turn resold the items to the RDA at a markup of 50 percent and more.

The former Knoedler employee, after retiring and waiting five years, decided he could no longer in good conscience remain silent. He wrote to Lila, telling her how he admired her charitable work. He then went on to reveal that Kennedy once purchased a painting from Knoedler's for $200,000, then resold it to her for $300,000 instead of merely adding the usual 15–25 percent markup. Lila always initialed invoices without questioning the price, because she trusted Kennedy. But that painting was one of the few that did not appreciate in value.

Kennedy had continued to be a frequent guest at High Winds, particularly when Wally was out of town. Lila indulged him and thought he was pretty. In turn, Kennedy acted in proprietary fashion, showing guests the various rooms as though he were lord and master of the house and pointing out which pieces were "his"—that is, which he had bought. Nor was Lila's devotion reciprocated. Frequently, when he showed up at High Winds, he would ask someone, even those closest to Lila, "Well, is the old bitch in today?"

After a brief investigation Kennedy was summarily fired. McHenry also had some of Lila's other artwork examined by Sotheby's, and it was discovered that, at one time or another, she had purchased a fake Gauguin, a fake Toulouse, a badly restored Renoir, and a fake Picasso.

Around the same time, Harry Wilcox, the ex–dancing instructor and Lila's oldest confidant, was also fired. Although Al Cole and others loathed him, the original Harry had managed to remain a company fixture for thirty years. In recent years he had also assumed the unofficial position of corporate host, greeting and escorting celebrity visitors like Arthur Godfrey when they came to Pleasantville to wave at the employees and have lunch in the Guest House.

But during an audit of the company's bus service for its employees, treasurer Dick Waters had discovered a discrepancy of $125,000. Wilcox was in charge of selling employees their weekly two-dollar bus ticket and had been skimming the proceeds for years. When Waters confronted him, Wilcox blamed an assistant, whom he subsequently fired. The assistant then turned around and implicated Wilcox, who insisted on taking his former colleague to court, where he was convicted of embezzlement. Wilcox seemed vindicated.

But other vendors in Pleasantville and surrounding townships had become fed up with Wilcox's skimming and provided Waters with affidavits attesting that the RDA's plant manager had regularly been demanding a 10 percent kickback on all services and sales. Though knowing he was treading on dangerous ground, Waters wrote a confidential memo to Wally, with no copy to Lila, supplying him with indisputable evidence that Harry Wilcox was a crook. Despite this second blow, Wally and Lila responded generously and allowed Wilcox to announce his retirement.

The loss of Kennedy and Wilcox under such sordid circumstances was compounded by the fact that by now it had become fairly obvious to everyone that Kennedy's restoration of Boscobel had been unsatisfactory from a historical point of view. Sometimes in 1977 Boscobel was emptied and its furnishings auctioned. After the interior was properly rerenovated at RDA expense, at a cost that by then had reached eight million dollars, Lila was brought once again up the Hudson River to view the home. As she toured the rooms, she whispered quietly to a companion, "I know this is the way it's supposed to look. But I can't help thinking it looked better before."

18

Drowning in a Sea of
Pabulum

A PROBLEM for many of the bright young men and the occasional
woman who, in the 1970s, wanted to make a career with the *Digest* was
that life at headquarters, Wally's corporate paradise, was a little too
claustrophobic. Pleasantville seemed too dauntingly insular—not just
too Republican, but too stuffy, unsophisticated, positively rural.

Wally had always been cosmopolitan in his way, of course, and so
were Paul Palmer, Hobe Lewis, and a few others. But the majority of
editors were suburban provincials, completely cut off from the New
York publishing community, and many of them conspicuously second-rate talents to boot. Too much originality and creativity would
have been a liability in Pleasantville, where much of the work consisted
of picking out, cutting, and condensing other people's ideas—a relatively simple operation that, perhaps as an outgrowth of a mass inferiority complex, had evolved over a generation into an elaborate ritual.

In fact, condensing an average 3,000-word article to one of about
1,300 words had by now come to involve one of the most fatuously
laborious editorial bureaucracies ever visited upon so little in the history of publishing. Up to ten editors cut, condensed, chiseled, checked,
rechecked, pruned, polished, repolished, finessed, and plucked every
last superfluous syllable until an article had arrived at its irreducible
essence—or so everyone who belonged to the cult of condensation
liked to think.

Others, the brighter ones, never saw what the big deal was all about
and thought that a couple of editors and a few good fact checkers were
enough to handle just about anything. After all, the *Reader's Digest* was
not in the same literary league with that other temple of high editing—

the *New Yorker.* One facile young editor found it impossible to spend more than two hours on a cutting job that was rated a ten-hour chore. At the time, the editor in charge of cutting and condensing was associate editor Audrey Dade.

After she gave the apprentice cutter an assignment, he proudly returned it that very morning, expecting a congratulatory pat on the head. Instead, he was reprimanded for doing sloppy work. The next time Dade gave him an article to condense, he let it sit on his desk for three days, then spent two hours cutting it. Dade began to value him as one of the best cutters on the staff.

According to senior editor Samuel Schreiner, a majority of *RD* editors, not having much editorial experience elsewhere, were probably not even aware that their situation was unusual. Also, *Digest* editors bore scant resemblance to the "ink-stained wretches" of legend. High salaries, bonuses, profit sharing, and, in some cases, stock ownership made all but the most creative content to parboil articles into literary pabulum day after day, decade after decade.

Not surprisingly, the brighter editors generally tended to drift upward from cutting and condensing to assigning originals—which now accounted for 70 percent of the editorial content. And as before, the magazine also rotated each month among four, five, or six issue editors, who reported to the executive editor. An issue editor was not only in the most challenging, interesting, and rewarding editorial job in Pleasantville but also in a bruising competition for the post of editor in chief.

In 1974 the most talented and energetic of the younger editors on the Pleasantville campus, and also one of the most ambitious, was Edward T. Thompson—no relation to either of the *RD*'s other two prominent employees of the same name. A passionate sailor and skier, the blond, boyish Thompson was also immensely popular with many of his co-workers, though some found his abrupt, almost gruff manner intimidating. A graduate of the Massachusetts Institute of Technology, with a degree in chemical engineering, Thompson had worked as a petroleum engineer for four years before becoming an editor of a magazine called *Chemical Engineering.* In 1956 he joined the staff of *Fortune,* where he earned a reputation as one of the most prolific writers in the magazine's history. Four years later he was hired by the *Digest.*

Though he lacked an Ivy League degree, which by now had become almost a sine qua non on an *RD* editor's résumé, Thompson did have one advantage over the other editors of his generation—apart from his atypical background, popularity, and sheer drive. In their common effort to curry the favor of Hobe Lewis, no one else could boast of being the son of Edward K. Thompson, the managing editor of *Life*. As a result Thompson *fils* was routinely able to entertain the *Digest* editor in chief with the latest details of all the Luce living going on at Time-Life Inc.

When Lewis finally did name Edward Thompson an issue editor, though, the timing was less than auspicious. That same month, Thompson and two other editors, Roy Herbert and Walter Hunt, had planned a ski trip to St. Anton, in Austria, along with their wives. Unwilling to cancel the trip, Thompson decided to make it a working holiday and stuffed the entire dummy issue, containing all of his editing, into a briefcase. At the Zurich airport on the way home, he absent-mindedly left the briefcase at a ticket window. For a frantic fifteen minutes, the six Digesters raced through the terminal, searching the waiting area and ready to tackle anybody who looked suspicious. After the briefcase was retrieved, Herbert laconically observed, "Well, at least it shows he can delegate authority."

Herbert also had several claims to fame—one being that he bore a striking resemblance to British movie actor Laurence Harvey. Moreover, Herbert's father, Frank, had been for many years the magazine's stellar circulation manager and protégé of Al Cole. After graduating from Princeton and serving in the army, Roy had approached his father and asked for help in getting a job as an editor at the *Digest*.

"I can get your foot in the door," Herbert, Sr., replied, "but I can't put your ass in the chair."

The foothold sufficed. Though members of the same family were officially banned from working together at the *Digest*, Wally bent those rules just like any other when it pleased him. Roy was assigned to the copydesk and worked his way up. He had been at the *Digest* only a few years, however, when his brother Frank, Jr., publisher of the *Atlantic Monthly*, died quite suddenly. The day the obituary appeared in the *New York Times*, Wally called Roy and asked if he knew whether Frank's widow was being taken care of financially. Roy gratefully replied that his brother's widow was being provided for through a generous pension plan.

Herbert had done his own first issue back in September 1967—an experience that left him euphoric. At the time the only other regular issue editors included managing editor Bun Mahony and assistant managing editors Bill Hard and Cuyler MacRae. Herbert thought he eventually had a clear shot at the top job. He had not only seniority over Thompson but administrative experience under his belt as well. However, even though the two men became good friends, it was a case of the tortoise and the hare. Despite Herbert's long head start, Thompson gained on him quickly.

Yet another talented young editor under Lewis's command was Kenneth Gilmore, a graduate of Brown University who later worked as a copyboy on the night shift of the *Washington Post*. Affable, easygoing, and studious-looking behind thick spectacles, Gilmore was hired by Chuck Stevenson in 1957 and quickly became his protégé—the man whom the Washington bureau chose to groom as a future managing editor who might eventually have a shot at the position of editor in chief. After serving a stint as a staff writer, he succeeded Stevenson as bureau chief in 1966.

Unlike most Washington editors, Gilmore cultivated editorial friendships in Pleasantville and eventually achieved both insider and outsider status concurrently. Along with Thompson, Herbert, and Tony Oursler, Gilmore was considered one of the four contenders for the title of editor in chief when Lewis retired—unless, of course, that post went to crusty Bun Mahony, who was dependable if nothing else.

But Mahony was what Wally, Ken Payne, Paul Palmer, and Hobe Lewis were not—dull. Herbert had a drinking problem—a factor that made him, in just about everyone's mind but his own, the dark horse. Oursler was a Roman Catholic—which was perhaps not an insuperable problem in his case, because both of the Wallaces were extremely fond of Fulton, Jr. On the other hand, most odds makers were willing to wage good money that Wally and Lila would never permit the *Reader's Digest,* the most visible and influential mouthpiece of non-denominational Protestantism in Christendom, to fall into the hands of a papist. There is little doubt that, had he converted to something more socially acceptable such as the Episcopal church, Oursler would have been the front-runner. Since that was not a viable alternative, only Gilmore—a Presbyterian PK, no less—remained in a one-on-one race with Thompson.

But then, all of them, even Mahony, were in a one-on-one race with the tall, blond, abrasive Thompson, whose only conceivable drawback—a reputation as a ladies' man—was probably not much of an obstacle.

Perhaps the most eccentric of the Younger Turks in Pleasantville was Dan O'Keefe, described by one associate as "a sophomore science nerd—very bright, but painfully shy." He was also widely regarded as Wulp's successor as resident intellectual, a man with strange interests in things like magic and philosophy who read books with an Enthusiasm Quotient of zero. O'Keefe had edited *Achievement* magazine, the national publication of Junior Achievement, to put himself through college. With his lifelong enthusiasm for the visions and altruism of youth, Wally read the magazine regularly and offered O'Keefe a job upon his graduation.

None of the other editors had Thompson's panache, energy, and flair. Once roving editor Joe Blank, who specialized in writing about hurricanes and other natural disasters, was in New Orleans to do a story about Hurricane Camille. At the airport he learned that every available automobile had been rented out to relief workers and government officials. In desperation Blank phoned his editor Ed Thompson back in Pleasantville to see if he knew anybody who could lend him a car. Thompson's reply: "Buy one."

——

ONE OF Thompson's most industrious writers was a roving editor named Jim Miller, who had two distinctions. He was among the first nonpartisan investigative journalists to begin writing for the *Digest;* for that very reason, he also played an indirect role in Thompson's downfall.

At the age of forty Miller had quit his successful career in public relations and decided to become a writer. He had only one contact in magazine publishing, but it was a good one—Hobe Lewis, then the executive editor of the *Reader's Digest.* Back in the days when Miller was representing clients like RCA, he would pitch an article by the president of the company, get Lewis's okay, then ghost it.

Tiring of that game, he determined to start writing under his own byline, and Lewis obliged by giving him plenty of work. He also advised Miller to get a specialty. Soon he became the *Digest*'s single most productive writer, turning in up to ten articles a year—mostly on environmental issues.

When Lewis was promoted to editor in chief, he handed Miller over to Thompson, at the time a relative newcomer. Miller, though, was relieved to have a new editor in Pleasantville. A common complaint about the editor in chief—one shared by Miller—was that Lewis never returned phone calls or answered letters and in general seemed too distracted by other business to spend much time with his writers or editors.

Ed Thompson, though, turned out to be splendid. Miller found him to be just the opposite of Lewis—hardworking and also very acute. After reading an article, he immediately called up to discuss it. He was also willing to fight for an article in an editorial conference and not just go along with majority opinion. Best of all, he came up with article ideas of his own and sent along clippings with suggestions or leads to his writers.

The conservation movement was just gaining momentum in the early sixties—what Miller thought of as its second wave, under Jack Kennedy, after Teddy Roosevelt had first championed the cause of preserving America's wilderness despite the vigorous opposition of western developers.

Despite his early idealism, Miller soon found himself embroiled in a microcontroversy in which he was accused of being not the champion of tougher laws to protect the environment, not the fearless opponent of big-business interests, but exactly the opposite. Miller's accuser was J. Anthony Lukas, the *New York Times*'s heavyweight investigative reporter, writing in [*More*], a short-lived journal of press criticism.

In February 1969 Miller had published "America the (Formerly) Beautiful," which painted a bleak picture of how the United States was systematically destroying its landscape and natural resources. The "two main villains" responsible for the ecological mess, according to Miller, were population growth and "government agencies assigned to manage our resources." But Lukas contemptuously pointed out that "industries—the major polluters—were mentioned only incidentally and no offending companies were named."

What really galled Lukas, though, was not so much Miller's article. After all, it was perhaps unrealistic to expect "hard-nosed, investigative reporting from a magazine which brings us such journalism as 'Behind the Boom in Tropical Fish.' "

But for September 1971 the *Digest* was planning an advertising supplement called "Environment '71," in which big U.S. business was invited, at a cost of $59,965 a page, to "tackle all phases of this large, complex and urgent problem." In Lukas's translation that became a way for American industry to "buy space to counteract mounting public concern and protest about environmental pollution." Moreover, the advertisements were to appear as advertorials designed to increase big business's "believability."

Miller was convinced that the *Digest* was not selling out to big business. By then he was the magazine's chief environmental reporter and had never been put under any pressure from Lewis or anyone else to downplay industrial pollution. In Miller's opinion, Lukas simply had a visceral dislike of the *Reader's Digest*. Full of self-righteous indignation, Miller complained to the editors of [*More*] that he had, in fact, named New York utility Consolidated Edison by name in the cited article. He then went on to list a half-dozen other articles in the *RD* which had "pointed the finger," in Lukas's phrase, at specific U.S. companies. Though he later conceded he was not impugning Miller's journalistic integrity, Lukas stood by his condemnation of the *Digest*'s "quasi-journalistic venture into corporate image-making."

Then the situation got worse, and Miller discovered that Lukas had a point. In 1973 the United States sent massive aid to Israel in its devastating attack on the combined forces of Syria and Egypt during the Yom Kippur War. In retaliation the Organization of Petroleum Exporting Countries (OPEC) announced that it would not sell oil to nations supporting Israel and increased its prices by 400 percent. With U.S. domestic oil production also dwindling, some schools and offices closed down and long lines began to form at service stations around the country.

Assigned to write a series on the much publicized energy crisis, Miller chose first to concentrate on natural gas. He concluded that the so-called shortage was manufactured by the industry by means of phony production statistics. Though unpopular with the Washington bureau, the article ran.

Miller then turned his attention to the oil industry. After he handed his article in, the Washington bureau turned a copy over to the Department of the Interior, which Miller scorned as little more than a front for the oil industry. Subsequently, an Interior Department press agent wrote a refutation of Miller's thesis. But Thompson, the former petroleum engineer, defended the piece and Lewis published it without any substantive changes.

Yet the squeeze was on not only from the Washington bureau but from the advertising department. In January 1975 the intimate relations between advertising and editorial were all but consummated when a team of *Digest* advertising representatives and editors, including Ed Thompson, flew to Vienna to meet with OPEC officials and pitch to them a global, multilingual advertorial ranging in cost from $1.87 to $4.53 million, depending on such factors as the number of international editions in which the advertisement ran. The purpose of the advertorial was to help the organization polish its worldwide public image and counteract charges that its fivefold increase in the price of oil was responsible for inflation and worldwide recession. As Lukas was among the first to suspect, the *RD* was pioneering yet another late-twentieth-century phenomenon, corporate image making.

In the end OPEC elected not to advertise in the *RD,* because it found the cost excessive. But the *Digest* did win a consolation prize. In February it began running another yearlong monthly series of advertorials, this one explaining the American economic system. The biggest advertorial campaign in history, costing $1.2 million, it was paid for by 150 corporate members of the Business Roundtable, most of them *Fortune* 500 companies. Another member was the RDA itself. The article-like advertisements were created by *Digest* editors under the aegis of former advertising salesman Dick McLoughlin, who by now had risen to become director of magazine operations. Later the RDA paid more than $100,000 to have each article in the series, which it described as "a mini-course in economics," reprinted in fifty college newspapers.

Like much of the magazine's editorial content, the advertising message simplified facts and emphasized the inspirational. "Whatever Happened to the Nickel Candy Bar?," the first installment, ignored the causes of the recession then gripping the country. Instead, employees were encouraged to increase their efficiency in the workplace: "You have, we have, in our hands, in ourselves, the means to produce not just cars and books and songs and bread, but an entire way of life and economic environment second to none."

With the publication of the Business Roundtable advertisements, the wall separating *RD* advertising and editorial—never very sturdy to begin with—developed a major fissure. In the long term it also signaled the beginning of the end of editorial independence in Pleasantville. A subtle shift was taking place. Unlike Wally, who had always resisted every kind of encroachment on editorial autonomy, both

Lewis and Thompson were wheeler-dealers who courted the business side. If each was able to maintain his editorial independence, that was mainly through his force of personality and the unique protection he enjoyed from Wally himself.

But in the process, editorial sovereignty itself was abdicated, and editors were positioned to become the accomplices of the business side. Inevitably, the next step, sooner or later, was editorial subservience—after Wally was gone and an editor came along who lacked Lewis's or Thompson's style.

━━

BY THE midsixties all of the well-established international editions of the *Digest* were finding it increasingly difficult to reprint only American material, because the inventory of usable articles had been depleted. Nevertheless, the RDA was as reluctant as ever to grant even limited editorial autonomy to its outposts. Editors—whether in Pleasantville or abroad—who worked on the foreign editions were regarded as a species of second-class citizen. Some were also perceived as saboteurs, intent on subverting Pleasantville's highly centralized control and themselves choosing what their readers ought to read—namely, something besides Americana.

During the emancipation struggles of the late fifties, Adrian Berwick, editor of the international editions, had thrown in his lot, if somewhat lukewarmly, with those who felt that viable cultures existed outside the United States. But for the most part, according to an associate, "he was a rhino in his own patch, a turf builder."

As a result of the growing dispute over editorial autonomy, Paul Palmer had resigned as executive editor, taken the title of senior editor, and gone first to London and then to Paris to oversee the creation of the first European originals primarily for foreign use. The results were mixed. Palmer, at sixty-five, was sick and frail—no longer the bistro-haunting boulevardier, the Washington journalist who knew everybody in the administration, but the kept man of Pleasantville, an aging society gadfly who spent his leisure time judging dog shows. Soon after returning to the States, he resigned for the fifty-sixth and last time.

Another *Digest* compromise—and journalistic first of sorts—was the "adaptation." U.S. articles were simply adapted for foreign consumption. That, too, proved to be only a brief stopgap. Finally, foreign editors were permitted to assign articles to writers on subjects of their own choosing. But all articles had to be approved by an American editor in Pleasantville, which also reserved the right to edit all articles originated in a foreign language. As a result each foreign original was first translated into English, then reviewed and edited before being washed back into the original and published. Foreign editors occupied the peculiar position of being able to assign but not accept or edit an article. Then they were accorded the privilege of publishing it.

Sometimes, though, foreign editors got a little help from allies back at the home office. One such ally was Bruce Lee, who after finishing up his research on Cornelius Ryan's *A Bridge Too Far* had transferred to New York, working under Ken Wilson in the Pan Am Building. Lee's new job was to help select book excerpts for the international editions of the magazine. For the French edition one month Lee chose a recently published biography of Napoleon. In routine fashion the entire book was then translated into English, cut to the proper length, translated back into French, and in due course published in *Sélection*. An astounding 500,000 copies were sold on the newsstands alone—a figure that did not sit well, however, with the powers in Pleasantville.

Lee got into a fair amount of trouble because he was accused of promoting French nationalism instead of American ideals and figures like George Washington. Mahony was among those particularly upset. Even Wally summoned Lee and said to him, "I appreciate the zeal, but perhaps it's excessive."

England still occupied an uneasy place in the *Digest* international orbit. Pleasantville thought the British edition was "hideous," according to one transatlantic insider. Unlike the U.S. edition, however, which was ignored everywhere except in Middle America, the British edition was regarded in the United Kingdom as a major national publication fully involved in the country's political and cultural life. The same was also true of the German edition.

But the semi-autonomous British division was troubled by internal strife and poor management and was unable, for a long period, to capitalize on its advantages. By the midsixties the circulation of Condensed Books in Great Britain had reached a high of about 500,000, but then it plummeted to only 60,000 before it was eventually turned around.

By the early seventies the war of independence was flaring up on several fronts. In 1968 Maurice Ragsdale had retired as the *RD*'s book editor. Among his more successful projects was working with

Gordon Prange on his history of Pearl Harbor. A professor of history at the University of Maryland, Prange had been on MacArthur's staff in occupied Japan and for nineteen years had labored on his book, interviewing every known survivor of the Japanese attack. *At Dawn We Slept,* later a nonfiction best-seller, was the result of his heroic labor, though Prange died before he was able to finish the book, leaving two research assistants to complete it. Ragsdale engineered a section called "Tora! Tora! Tora!," which became the basis of the movie of the same name.

Ragsdale's place was taken by Tony Oursler, a staunch defender of the need to impart American values to Arabs, Buddhists, and Latin American Catholics. But Oursler had inherited a British-born assistant named Jeremy Leggatt, once described by a friend as "the most disenchanted man in Christendom." The acid-tongued, multilingual Leggatt not only was emotionally involved in creating genuine native editions but also thought it commercially the more viable thing to do. He chafed at the idea of choosing a biography of American evangelist Billy Graham for the edification of Spanish Catholics.

As the climate for emancipation seemed to improve, Ragsdale came out of retirement and joined Lee in an effort to create autonomous book departments operating out of the Pan Am Building, in New York, and not answerable to Pleasantville. But their bid for independence was firmly repulsed. Lewis, Mahony, Oursler, and Wally, in particular, simply could not tolerate the idea of foreigners determining their own material or editorial philosophy—one that was not a faithful reflection of Pleasantville's in every detail. In 1972 the defeated Ragsdale retired again and moved to London with his wife, Betty, a former fiction editor of *McCall's.*

Ragsdale's two retirements also bookended the departure from the company in 1970 of his former boss and the *Digest's* oldest employee, the venerable Ralph Henderson, who had stayed on well past the company's so-called mandatory retirement age of sixty-five. During the big shake-ups of 1964 and 1965, Henderson had made way for his chief assistant, Jack Beaudouin, who became CB's editor in chief, while the book club's founder became editorial director. In his distinguished career Henderson had accomplished what no other high-ranking RDA employee before or since could claim: he had established the company's most lucrative division, Condensed Books. Also, like Fred Thompson, he had made no enemies.

Leggatt, meanwhile, was put in charge of selecting the book excerpts for the international editions and told to behave himself. By now 70 percent of the readers of the U.S. edition were women. While that made life relatively easy for Oursler and his staff, Leggatt found that trying to divine the reading tastes of different nationalities was a form of literary roulette. In the first place, it was difficult to ascertain the sex of a CB subscriber in European households, where subscriptions were traditionally put in the man's name. Then there were complications like that in Britain, where more men than women subscribed and where those women who did were far more interested in adventure tales than their American counterparts were.

Thus a story like *Breaker Morant,* about the court-martial of three Australian soldiers accused of atrocities during the Boer War, had wide appeal in the United Kingdom but relatively little in the United States, India, or Japan. By the same token, Leggatt assumed that another work, about the massacre in Amritsar, in which a group of Gurkhas and Sikhs fired into a crowd during the independence movement in India under Gandhi—would be of interest only to Indians. Yet it was also popular with the Taiwanese, and even the British picked it up.

Then along came Alain de Lyrot, another emancipator. A French count whose title dated back to the time of the Crusades, de Lyrot had studied as a young man at Columbia University, in New York, before joining the Paris bureau of the *New York Herald Tribune* in 1958. Later he accompanied de Gaulle to Algeria during that country's revolt against French rule and was dramatically rescued from a hostile mob by guerrillas.

Eventually, de Lyrot became European bureau chief of the Copley News Service, an American-owned news syndicate with close ties to the CIA and the FBI. Given such an ideal résumé, it was only a matter of time before de Lyrot was hired by the RDA. In January 1966 he was appointed editor in chief of *Sélection du Reader's Digest.*

By this time the French operation had achieved an almost unrivaled preeminence among international editions. *Sélection* enjoyed a million-plus circulation, the largest in France, while CB subscriptions were up to nearly 800,000 per volume.

Despite such success, new CB editor in chief Jack Beaudouin took it as an almost personal affront that the American titles he regularly selected for the U.S. edition were consistently turned down by the French. As a result there was constant bickering between Paris and Pleasantville. But astute marketing and Gallic chauvinism proved an unbeatable combination. Ultimately, the French book club succeeded in obtaining for itself a unique quota—three of the six selections per volume could be by French authors. However, all other international editions remained predominantly American in content.

After de Lyrot was named to replace Adrian Berwick as head of the international editions, the Frenchman found himself in another war of independence. Reassigned to Pleasantville, he teamed up with Leggatt to propose the establishment of a separate and independent book-excerpt department for overseas. Again the uprising was crushed and de Lyrot sent down, like Ragsdale, Lee, and others before him, to defeat. "Pleasantville," grumbled de Lyrot, "is the corpse of an amazingly powerful monarch."

The editorial succession and continued American orthodoxy of the book division were assured one day in the early seventies in the form of a walk-in—someone who simply showed up at Pleasantville to apply for a job. Walk-ins were seldom hired at the editorial level. But as Barbara Morgan was being interviewed, Beaudouin happened to pass by. Morgan, a bright, well-turned-out young woman, was hired on the spot as an associate editor for the international editions. Beaudoin did so without consulting Noel Rae, editor of the international editions, and brought her up to introduce her to the staff.

For the next two years Morgan apprenticed under Rae. Gradually, however, she realized there was a power vacuum in the U.S. edition and transferred over. Both Beaudouin and Joseph Hotchkiss, the new CB executive editor, were nearing retirement. The likely successor as editor in chief was John Zinsser, CB's first international editor, who had by now taken the place of Ken Wilson as head of CB's liaison office in New York. But Zinsser himself was not that much younger than Hotchkiss and therefore not likely to hold the top post for more than a few years before he, too, reached mandatory retirement age.

In the bookish, masculine environment of the CB offices, Barbara Morgan, with her expertly applied makeup and stylish clothes, stood out as an anomaly. Later Beaudouin's first wife, like himself an alcoholic, died suddenly when she fell and hit her head on the corner of a table. Her husband found her the next morning lying on the floor with the TV set still on. Morgan jokingly speculated that Beaudouin knocked her down.

Before long, though, she became much more canny about good corporate mores, and also got involved in several of Wally's favorite charities.

———

SIX YEARS after purchasing Funk & Wagnalls, the RDA sold off its backlist and got out of trade book publishing altogether—though not for long. In 1972 RDA treasurer Dick Waters decided the company needed another tax dodge. The solution was yet another book division, to be called Reader's Digest Press, whose modus operandi was to enter into a series of individual per title partnerships with various publishers and share editorial and production costs as well as profits equally. The RDP provided the editorial product, and houses like Simon & Schuster, Doubleday, Random House, and Harper & Row distributed. Though the new imprint did not sell directly to bookstores, it did market the books through direct mail. Titles were also eligible for selection by Condensed Books. The man selected to head the new division, headquartered in the Pan Am Building, was also the most qualified—Bruce Lee, champion of editorial autonomy for the international editions.

Despite Lee's liberal track record, Lewis gave him complete latitude to publish what he wanted. As a result, on more than one occasion, the RDP publisher found himself going against official *Digest* policy. Yet even then, Lewis stood behind him, as happened with *We Almost Lost Detroit,* by John G. Fuller.

An eerie forerunner of the movie *The China Syndrome,* Fuller's book accused Detroit Edison of colossal and potentially catastrophic mismanagement in the construction of its Fermi nuclear reactor. Fuller showed that the plant had not only been poorly designed and built but had almost suffered a meltdown when it was first turned up to full power.

As it happened, Walter Krister, head of Detroit Edison, was a good friend of Lewis. The uproar came from a different quarter. Former secretary of state William P. Rogers called Lee and insisted he be shown the material. When Lee expressed curiosity about his interest in the book, Rogers revealed that he was representing Detroit Edison. Only then did Lee realize that he was skating over very deep political waters.

Lee consulted with Lewis, who asked him whether he could prove his case. Yes, replied Lee. "Conclusively."

Fortunately, Lee had also been in touch with a civilian in charge of nuclear-reactor review for the Pentagon. That individual had gone on record from the beginning that the plant was unsafe. He also reviewed the manuscript and pronounced it 100 percent accurate, even writing a letter offering to testify to that effect at any time.

Undeterred, Rogers sent Lee a letter threatening both a libel suit and an injunction against publication of the book. At that point *We Almost Lost Detroit* was at the bindery. But Lee did not tell that to Rogers. What he did tell him over the phone was:

"Don't think you have any hope of stopping the book or seeking damages. For your information, these are the people I've lined up to testify that the book is true." He then reeled off a list of names.

Replied Rogers, "You're a smart young son of a bitch. I'll get you if it's the last thing I do."

The venom in his voice was so great that Lee just sat there and thought, "There's only one thing to do. If he's going to come in with an injunction, he'll come in at the warehouse. So we'll ship from the bindery."

The plan worked, and the books were shipped successfully. But a month and a half later, Lee got a call from an apoplectic Charles Hepler, the magazine's publisher. Westinghouse and General Electric had pulled a series of advertisements on safe nuclear power, worth $1.5 million. Lee was summoned to Pleasantville to explain himself.

At this point Lee knew that "knives were flashing in the dark." It was very dark and very dirty, and he knew pretty well where the knives were coming from. In particular, there was a lot of pressure from former secretary of defense Melvin Laird, who had recently joined the RDA as senior counselor,* to recall the book and get rid of Lee. But Lewis never wavered, nor did Wally. Lee proved to them that he had his case nailed down so tight that "nothing wiggled." Rogers never got his injunction. Copies were also just vanishing from the bookstores, though Lee never did figure out how many were bought by readers and how many by Detroit Edison, Westinghouse, and other members of the nuclear club.

Later Lee published *Desperate Bargain: Why Jimmy Hoffa Had to Die,* by veteran *Digest* roving editor Lester Velie, who was the first to claim that the former Teamster head was the victim of a gangland execution ordered after he became a liability to gangsters.

Over a period of time Lee also began having trouble getting what he

*See chapter 20.

considered proper accountings of sales. Each publisher had a different formula, and there was no way to get a single contract that all publishers could agree on. In 1976, despite several succès d'estime, the RDP issued a statement that all titles then in production would be published but that the future of the operation was undecided. Once again the company was abandoning trade publishing. The following year all existing contracts were sold to McGraw-Hill, and Lee resigned from the company.

19

I Am Joe's Headache

IN THE LITTLE WORLD of Pleasantville, who parked where was a big problem. Employees now drove in from three counties and three states, filling up acres of parking lot every morning. Over the years one surrounding hill after another had been flattened and asphalted to accommodate commuters. The most distant, and also the most elevated, was called by some editors the Acropolis.

On Wally's orders Digest policy all through this expansionist period had been to ban reserved parking spaces for company officers. With his mania for punctuality, he preferred parking to be on a first-come, first-served basis. Soon after becoming president, however, Hobe Lewis set up a new system. One morning in September 1966 early risers found eighteen parking spaces in the first row of the parking lot nearest the main building marked "Reserved." Pride of place belonged to DeWitt Wallace, followed by Al Cole, then Lewis himself.

Wally did not like the implied elitism of the new parking system—that company executives, even if they showed up late for work, were no longer penalized. On days when he visited the office, he frequently parked in any reserved space he felt like. Once a new guard saw him pull into Harry Wilcox's space and ordered him to move. Wally obediently backed out. Some thought that the incident was proof of Wally's lack of self-confidence; others saw it as a sign of his humility; to others still it proved that he always looked for an amicable settlement to a dispute but that there might be retribution later on.

Part of the problem was Wally's extreme reticence—another of his personal enigma variations. He was known simply to call any department in the company without going through a secretary. More than

415

one secretary hung up on the presumed prankster. It compounded the problem that some Digesters, particularly Tony Oursler, excelled at imitating Wally's high-pitched voice and halting manner of speaking.

Another of the parking elect was senior editor Roy Herbert. Oursler was at the time an associate editor without a parking slot. One day Herbert's car was being tuned up at the garage. He and Oursler had driven for a long lunch to a place called Murphy's in the village of Mount Kisco. After a cocktail-enhanced meal, they finally wandered to the parking lot. Hearing brakes screech, they looked up and saw a flawlessly maintained 1940 Chevrolet come to a halt. Fixing them with a beady eye, Wally repeatedly revved the engine, then sped off, tires peeling. Oursler, driving a Mercedes, spun out in hot pursuit. Two passing cars slowed down just enough to allow him to careen onto the highway. Then he managed a glimpse of Wally turning a sharp right at the next corner into Highway 117.

Weaving in and out of trucks and cars, Wally and Oursler raced down the crowded five-mile stretch leading back to the office. Oursler's goal was to overtake his boss, and he drove like a man obsessed. Both men passed everything on the road, with Wally still in sight as Oursler swerved into the headquarters entrance. As they approached the reserved parking section, they saw that Wally had parked in Herbert's space. Oursler had a choice—park in slot number 1 or drive to the Acropolis.

Wally was walking toward the main building when the two tardy editors skidded to a halt to consider the dilemma. He waved genially as if nothing had happened. It was another Wally conundrum—what did his behavior really mean? Perhaps it showed how Wally liked to clown around to dramatize his feelings about something—in this case, parking. Or possibly lateness. Or it may have been one more step in his circuitous way of finally coming to a decision about the parking lot. At the RDA there was a saying that a decision was what you made when you did not know what else to do.

Some time later Wally called on William May, president of the American Can Company, which was located a short distance from Pleasantville. When their meeting was over, as May walked Wally back to his car, the latter noticed there were about forty cars parked under the building, but none reserved for May or other executives. People parked according to what time they arrived, just as had been the case in the *Digest*'s early days. Wally was delighted. As soon as he got back to

Pleasantville, he called in treasurer Dick Waters, told him what he had seen, and issued an order that all "Reserved" signs be removed at once.

Waters pointed out that in the case of American Can, unlike that of the RDA, all of its executives were in one small building and its manufacturing site was elsewhere. There was also wisdom in having reserved slots, because top editors and executives often invited important guests to Pleasantville and took them out to lunch instead of to the Guest House. Having them hike all over the parking lot was a waste of time. Wally was not convinced, but did not insist that the order to rescind be issued.

A few months later Wally chanced to run into an editorial employee named Jim McCracken, who had been hired as an associate editor, only to discover that the editorial ranks were already heavily overstaffed. The temporary solution was to make him an editorial accountant. Years passed. Meanwhile, McCracken proposed a series of articles about the various body parts of a forty-seven-year-old man named Joe who was well past his prime in just about everything. The catch was that each article in the series be told in autobiographical form and incorporate the latest in medical research.

Though Wally seldom thought in terms of a series, he liked the idea immediately. But instead of assigning the first piece to McCracken, Hobe Lewis and Wally turned it over to a writer named J. D. Ratcliff, whose specialty was popular science. Joe's heart told its story in January 1967, and it proved so popular that Ratcliff was immediately assigned to do another and McCracken's dream of a series became a reality. The series soon gave a new dimension to an old *Digest* category—the art of living longer—and was itself the longest the magazine ever ran, thirty-three articles in all. Five years after the first Joe article appeared, the series had been expanded to include several parts that Joe did not have but Jane did, beginning with her breast.

Wally did not reward McCracken with a bonus, as he often did with articles that he enjoyed. Instead, he merely issued a memo praising the series. Privately, he told McCracken that he would be rewarded, but months passed and no money came. Finally, McCracken sent a discreet note to Wally, reminding him of his promise. Along came a handwritten voucher from Wally authorizing payment to McCracken of $2,500, the average price of a *Digest* article. McCracken eventually had to write out the check himself and get it properly signed.

Ratcliff, in the meantime, continued to write about Joe's prostate,

Jane's ovary, Joe's kidney. For the British edition, Joe became John; he was Georges in French, Peter in German, Harry in Dutch, Old Joe in Chinese. Reprints of the articles soared into the millions and another 100,000 boxed sets of thirty-three reprints were sold at ten dollars each.

But there was one part of Joe's anatomy whose autobiography the *Digest* had yet to publish. It was a touchy subject. Finally, the problem was resolved. The *Digest* invented a new euphemism, and "man gland" entered the language in November 1970. The man gland was Joe's left testis.

One afternoon Wally and McCracken met in a corridor as they were both leaving the building for the parking lot. Wally asked McCracken, "Where do you park?"

McCracken pointed to the Acropolis.

"Depends on what time I get here," he admitted.

"You mean you don't have a space assigned?"

"No."

Perhaps because his conscience bothered him, or perhaps because he was only looking for the least pretext to abolish reserved parking, Wallace fumed, "Then nobody does."

Reserved parking had come to an end, and an order to that effect went out the next day. And, as usual, everyone began to ponder the psychology of the edict. One writer told his editor, "I think your man Wallace is a tyrant who wants everybody else to be democratic."

———

GENIAL Jim McCracken was not the only *Digest* editor who felt that promises made to him when he was hired were never kept. Former *Saturday Evening Post* editor Bob Fuoss, assigned to edit children's books, had resigned in disgust shortly before Joe came along. Another malcontent was Pulitzer Prize–winner Leland Stowe.

Fifteen years after he had been hired, Stowe wondered why none of his articles ever got published, even though the *Digest* had bought dozens and kept inviting him to Guest House luncheons. In his 1965 Christmas greetings to fellow ex-Poster Ben Hibbs, Stowe complained that his byline seldom appeared any more in the magazine. Hibbs, still a *Digest* senior editor, replied to Stowe's complaint in a long confidential letter of his own, agreeing that the *Digest*'s habit of assigning and buying far more material than it used was a discouraging one for writers.

Hibbs himself had almost resigned the previous fall, but Lewis asked him to stay on because he was former president Eisenhower's ghostwriter. Stowe replied in equal confidence that, after one of his articles finally appeared in print, Wally had written in his Christmas card, "One is not enough. Don't you agree?" Stowe found that "as a Yule greeting that was especially hard to take" and sent Wally a four-page list of all the articles he had written that were not used. Wally did not reply. When a few years later another Stowe article was published, a forgetful Wally wrote another congratulatory letter to Stowe and said, "It's a mystery to me why you don't produce more articles."

This time a thoroughly frustrated Stowe sent Wally two packages of articles that the *Digest* had purchased but never used, along with a long letter of complaint. Nothing happened. Later the still-riled Stowe calculated that the RD wasted up to one million dollars a year—not to mention the "psychic cost" to writers—by buying articles it never used.

The editorial bureaucracy castigated by Norman Cousins in 1944 had within twenty years grown to monstrous proportions—a bloated logjam of reprints, originals, book excerpts, and fillers numbering into the hundreds of thousands, with more being added every day by too many editors with too little to do and too much money to spend.

———

EVEN highly successful authors, whose inspirational subject matter seemed ready-made for *Digest* consumption, had their troubles fitting into the scheme of things. A case in point was Doris Lund, whose book *Eric*—recounting the death of her twenty-two-year-old son from leukemia—became a best-seller and a selection of Condensed Books. Lund's father, Don Herold, was a celebrated cartoonist who both wrote and drew for the *Digest* in the thirties and forties. After raising four children, Lund decided to try her hand at writing children's books. Fate intervened when Eric was stricken and died four and a half difficult years later.

As a way of dealing with her pain, Lund wrote a brief account of her son's courage in the face of death and sent it to the *Swarthmore College Bulletin*. Subsequently, a New York publisher asked her to write a book about the experience. To Lund's great surprise, *Eric* became a best-seller. Later the *Digest* bought it for Condensed Books for $50,000, and Lund was given a fancy luncheon at the Guest House, which struck her as a "scary place, like the entrance to a sanatorium." The high protocol of a Guest House luncheon, as formal as a state dinner, was based on two canons. The first, applicable only to Digesters, was never to express a negative opinion. The second rule, applicable to all, was one drink per customer. Even though Lund found all the editors amazingly complimentary, the situation was stressful and she was desperate for a second drink. Finally, one of the editors, seeing her predicament, said, "Have one."

Lund replied, "I love you," and did.

She next proposed writing about her father as an Unforgettable Character. Everyone agreed, and eventually the article was written and published. After that the honeymoon ended, and Lund discovered it was harder to get an article published in the *Reader's Digest* than to secure a second drink at the Guest House.

Lund's editor was Dan O'Keefe, who asked her to write an article about serendipity. The talent of making fortuitous, accidental discoveries seemed right up Pleasantville's alley, but numerous writers had tried and failed. One reason was that O'Keefe asked for a twenty-page outline—roughly three times the length of the proposed article, even though he was the author of a pamphlet for authors titled "What Is a *Digest* Outline?," which encouraged a "mean length" of two pages.

After much labor Lund handed in the outline. O'Keefe sat on it, analyzed it, dissected it. He wrote her rambling philosophical editorial notes. Finally, he returned the outline with revisions. Lund felt she had been handed back some lifeless thing full of holes and was being asked to breathe some zest into it. Yet she persevered. She turned the article in. O'Keefe went off on vacation. On his return he wrote Lund a long apologetic letter, saying he had drunk too much when he wrote some of the letters, and accepted the piece on serendipity.

Even when the *Digest* was being nice, Lund found the experience unnerving. Once O'Keefe sent a limousine to pick her up for an editorial luncheon at the Guest House. A long black Cadillac pulled up in front of her house, and Lund settled herself in the backseat. When they got to Pleasantville, Lund asked the driver, "Aren't we a little early?"

"I was supposed to bring you ten minutes early so that you get to wait," the driver explained.

"They soften me up," she observed.

"Right," he replied.

And Lund did feel softened up. She waited the ten minutes, thinking there was something awfully unfriendly about such an attitude. Finally, O'Keefe and the other editors came along. That day he wanted to showcase Lund because she had proved to be one of his more successful writers, whose articles consistently earned high EQ ratings with readers. Over lunch she was given four more assignments.

Lund's career at the *Digest* came to an end in the service of a good cause. She proposed doing an article about the Candle Lighters, an organization that provided helpful information about drugs, diet, where to obtain a wig, and the like to families with a seriously ill member. Lund was aware there was a "certain horror" about writing for the *Digest*—that it was always necessary to apologize to sophisticated friends about it. Yet no other magazine was half as effective in promoting a good cause.

O'Keefe was confused and thought she was writing about Compassionate Friends, a support group specifically for parents whose children had died brutally—usually by suicide or in an auto accident. Though a mourning group, it was not the same as Candle Lighters. Only after O'Keefe got the assignment okayed did Lund discover the mix-up. She insisted on doing the article she had originally proposed, but O'Keefe convinced her that the issue editor was crazy about doing an article on Compassionate Friends. The compromise was to do an article on both organizations. The result, after much labor and too many revisions, was a bomb.

After the article was rejected, O'Keefe invited her out to lunch, insisting they sit next to the restaurant's kitchen door to prevent any lurking Digesters from overhearing their conversation. He wanted to know why the article got into such trouble. Lund explained again that the two organizations were totally different. Then she asked a second time to do an article just on the Candle Lighters. He agreed. It took her two years, but she felt it was the best article she ever did. The article also provided the organization with the most publicity and support it had ever received. But the experience left Lund a burnt-out case, and she decided never to write for the *Digest* again.

A man who enjoyed a considerably happier experience at the *Digest* was Alex Haley, who back in the early fifties was a young black navy cook and struggling writer. After submitting a story to the *Digest,* Haley was surprised to receive not a form rejection slip but a personal letter from an editor saying the piece was not quite what the magazine needed. Encouraged, Haley kept submitting articles, and each was returned with the same personalized rejection.

In 1953, after being discharged from the navy, Haley was given his first writing assignment. A magazine called *Park East* asked him to do a piece about Harlem. Haley spent four months researching and writing; he was literally typing the final draft of the twenty-four-page article when he received a letter from *Park East* informing him that it was suspending publication. So he mailed the manuscript to Pleasantville, knowing it would come back.

It did come back, only this time with a longer letter. The editors said they could not use the article as written, but had marked points of interest if he wanted to submit a new outline. All the marked passages were about people in Harlem who had created successful businesses. Haley was ecstatic.

The article went through eight revisions, but finally, in June 1954, the *Reader's Digest* published "The Harlem Nobody Knows," Haley's first big break in print. Years later he wrote "Mr. Muhammad Speaks" for the issue of March 1960, which led to his first book, *The Autobiography of Malcolm X,* the ghostwritten life of the controversial Black Muslim leader, who was assassinated the year after the book was published, in 1964.

After that Haley had no idea what to do next. One Saturday he was strolling in Washington, D.C., and happened to pass the National Archives. He wandered inside and on an impulse asked to see the census records of Alamance County, North Carolina, for the year 1870. In the microfilm room he threaded a tape through the machine. As he adjusted the old-fashioned handwriting, the lines of names, ages, and occupations seemed to become almost animated. Haley felt as if he were standing on the side of a dusty road in Alamance County, where his forebears were born and raised, looking as all the people went by. And then, in the fourth roll of film, Haley saw the entry "Murray, Thomas, blacksmith."

While growing up in New York State, Haley had often heard his grandmother and great-aunts talking about their father, Tom Murray, the blacksmith of Alamance County. Seeing Murray's name on the rolls brought him stunningly back to life. Next came the names of Haley's great-aunts with whom he used to sit on his grandmother's porch in Kenning, Tennessee. Yet their ages were listed as twelve, eleven, and six, which just seemed impossible. Haley could not believe that his crusty aunt Liz had ever been six years old. Right then and there he decided to trace his family back to Africa.

A short while later Haley was invited to a lawn party at the RDA and introduced to Lila. Though he proved to be completely tongue-tied, Lila was characteristically gracious. When they parted she said, "If I can ever be helpful to you, let me know."

Haley spent the next three years researching his family's roots. Then he wrote a letter to Lila, explaining how he was developing his story and what he was trying to do. Lila directed him to meet with several editors, including Oursler and Ferguson. Subsequently, they invited Haley to lunch at the Guest House. Later the editors conferred in little groups and told Haley they would get in touch.

A few days afterward *RD* editor John Wulp, at the time the magazine's in-house intellectual, was surprised to receive out of the blue an outline of the book. Also enclosed in the packet was a note from Wally asking for Wulp's opinion on whether the *Digest* ought to finance the book. Wulp wrote a letter back urging the company to become, in effect, Haley's patron. Later he felt he had almost personally commissioned what became *Roots,* one of the best-selling novels of all time. Oursler, however, was the book's official sponsor.

Two days after Haley's visit he was informed that the *Digest* had decided to give him $1,000 a month for a year—a veritable fortune. In addition, the magazine was also willing to cover his travel expenses to anywhere in the world. From Haley's point of view, that was the pivotal thing. The *Reader's Digest* was making it possible for him to follow his family's story to England, to France, and especially to Africa. Without that support his book could not have been written.

Haley spent twelve years researching and writing *Roots,* finally finishing it one summer in St. Paul while staying at the International House with Harry Morgan. When it was published, to considerable commercial and critical success, earning him in the process a Pulitzer Prize, Haley again met with the editors as guest of honor at a Guest House luncheon. Afterward he was taken to the Westchester airport, where he was greeted by two pilots wearing Pegasus-shaped pins on their lapels. Haley was the only passenger. "We're ready when you are, sir," one of them said.

As the plane took off, Haley looked out the window at the countryside below, remembering the early days, the rejections, the years of work. Suddenly, a thought came into his head—that he felt closer to the *Reader's Digest* than to any other institution. Though he had never finished college, it had become his alma mater.

▬

THE *Digest* was the people's university of Middle America and Alex Haley's alma mater, but many Digesters had a difficult time agreeing on an appropriate corporate mythology. Before the presidency of John Fitzgerald Kennedy made Camelot a byword of American pop culture, a handful of romantic-minded employees had viewed life at Pleasantville in terms of similar enchantment and sublime calling. Though they never pressed the comparison too far, there were enough passing similarities to satisfy the beclouded imagination of an editor, his feet propped on the desk and a glass or two of noon-hour wine still working its potent magic.

At such moments the *Digest* seemed like a suburban Avalon presided over by a wise Arthurian monarch. Gathered around him were journalist-knights set to do battle with the enemy. Among the most treacherous was the Red Knight of communism. Another foe was the Purple Knight of uncondensed prose. The greatest adversary of all, the one who had destroyed untold millions of lives down through the ages and always threatened to unseat even the worthiest opponent, was the Black Knight of doom and despair. The Excalibur-like sword that every Digester was given to wield was forged with unalloyed optimism—a pure and steadfast belief that no individual ever lacked the means to surmount any of life's problems, no matter how insignificant or catastrophic.

Moreover, the *Digest* also inhabited a purely mythical place called Pleasantville—a postal figment of the public imagination, so far as the magazine's actual location was concerned, for more than thirty years. Insiders also had no trouble matching up many of their contemporaries with the spectral figures of legend. Among the more obvious choices were the usurping nephew Modred and the sorcerer Merlin.

Even the rare teetotaler might have found himself driven to such whimsical distraction as he whiled away the interminable afternoon condensing an article called "New Hope for the Dead" from 3,000 to 1,300 words while taking care to retain the substance and flavor of the original, and making sure that the three *Digest* watermarks showed through as always: that it was quotable, applicable to the reader's daily life, and of lasting value.

"New Hope for the Dead," of course, was another mirage—the one article of articles that would have met those criteria in spades. But it was even more ephemeral than the daydream of Camelot—a newsstand headline jokingly invoked by a generation of Digesters to symbolize in exaggerated terms what the magazine's so-called art-of-living franchise was all about—the promise of triumph over every form of adversity. Since the magazine's founding, readers the world over had been told how to overcome just about every ailment, disease, or discouraging word known to man this side of paradise, from hemorrhoids and cancer to a conjugal sex life that was all sizzled out.

Then along came the life-after-life testimonials of people who saw themselves dying on operating tables or in automobile accidents, only to be brought back at the last moment to the land of the living, and the *Digest* was finally able to guarantee its readers even immortality. In its October 1974 issue the *RD* ran a first-person article by Victor D. Solow called "I Died at 10:52 A.M.," on how his heart stopped for twenty-three minutes and he later emerged a "new 'I.'" In January 1977 came the book excerpt from *Life after Life,* a best-selling collection of similar testimonials by Raymond Moody. "New Hope for the Dead" was no longer a joke.

The search for a mythic corporate identity proved more difficult, however. After Camelot was stolen outright by Jack Kennedy, some editors proposed Tara, the mist-enshrouded plantation in Margaret Mitchell's antebellum Southland, which had all the right credentials—a harking back to a time and place that seemed the beau ideal of American life. Pleasantville did have, after all, a sort of Old Dominion setting; and the interior of Maison Lafitte, Wally's favorite restaurant, just down the road, had been used for several interior scenes during the shooting of *Gone with the Wind.*

Still others likened the company to a monastery, the Vatican, a fortress on a hill, Peyton Place. But Kent Rhodes, the RDA's head of production, had the best name of all. He called the *Digest* "Mother."

THE *Digest* was also a monthly traveling road show, just like those that used to tour the small towns of America a century earlier, using a mixture of flimflam, sex, and snake oil to draw the crowds.

As before, Wally continued to have something of an obsession with venereal disease, particularly syphilis, which the *Digest* was the first among popular American magazines to discuss in detail. One day he scribbled a memo on a yellow sheet of paper to Grace Naismith, the Pelvic Oracle, which read in its entirety, "Dear Grace: Do many girls in college, or older women in 'respectable' circles, have gonorrhea or syphilis? Greetings & fond regards. Wally."

As a result of that memo, Naismith wrote two articles that brought America's most respectable readers up to date on the country's two most disrespectable sexual diseases.

For the most part, though, as Wally grew older the magazine took an increasingly negative attitude toward sex, even though it continued to publish as many articles on the subject as ever. "The New Case for Chastity" and "A Girl's Right to Say 'No!' " were typical titles. Marya Mannes's "The Power Men Have over Women" announced in its first sentence, "They [men] are not necessarily brighter, but they usually have us where they want us. Like a man with a dog." Heavy reader response led to a collection of letters a few issues later titled "The Power Women Have over Men," which was summarized by one simple, irrefutable truth: "The power of women over men is 'No!' "

The *Digest* also underwent a sea change on such issues as divorce reform and abortion—partly a reflection of the country's deepening conservative mood, which it had helped to shape. After a particularly forceful article promoting abortion reform was published in the late sixties, for example, actress Loretta Young sent Lewis a letter protesting that she was horrified by the piece. Enclosed was a prolife "letter from an unborn fetus" to its mother, mourning the lost opportunities for love and joyful sharing that the two were destined never to share.

John Wulp, who was given the piece to edit, was amazed at how the magazine often took a liberal stance, then got terrified by what it had done and published another article to counteract what had gone before. Increasingly, though, even the token liberal piece was becoming a near-extinct journalistic species. When it was published in a subsequent issue, the fetus letter signaled the *Digest*'s new approach to one of the country's most divisive issues.

Conservative as the *Digest* was, it still offended readers for whom it was not conservative enough. When the magazine condensed Desmond Morris's *The Naked Ape,* many readers who held to the creationist theory canceled their subscriptions. In a small Wisconsin town citizens complained to the school board about the use of reprints of "I Am Joe's Prostate," "I Am Joe's Man Gland," and "I Am Jane's Breast" in the classroom. Even birth control, a favorite *Digest* theme, was no longer risk-free, though articles on the subject had always provoked dissenting letters. Catholic readers were greatly disturbed when the *Digest* recruited liberal theology professor and priest John A. O'Brien of Notre Dame University to write an article saying that Pope Paul VI "followed the wrong advisers and made a mistake" in his recent condemnation of all methods of birth control.

When "Parenthood Should Wait" was published, in February 1969, it was followed up in June by a compilation of angry letter extracts entitled "Parenthood Should *Not* Wait!" And, as usual, every issue also generated letters complaining about the off-color humor, only now there was no Barclay Acheson, D.D., to write back asking whether the offended reader could explain what, what exactly was so offensive about the joke in question.

———

HARRY MORGAN left the *Digest* in late 1969 to make it on his own, going to work for Alvin Yurick, a former vice-president of the Ford Foundation who was then running the Academy for Educational Development. It was during this time that Morgan became estranged from the Wallaces over the *Alice* affair.

Yurick's ambition was to found an international correspondence university tied in with the Famous Writers School, with branches all over the world and a U.S. campus that students came to for their last semester. His partner in the project was Jacqueline Grennan Wexler, the ex-nun and president of Hunter College, and Morgan had been hired—he thought—to get publicity in various countries through his connections with World Press Institute alumni.

Summoned one day to a meeting with Yurick and Wexler, Morgan was advised that New York State law required the school to have $500,000 in the bank before accreditation could be granted. As Yurick explained, the money was proof that the school was not a fly-by-night operation. Morgan said he thought that should be no problem, since the Famous Writers School looked as if it was going to make a big profit.

But Yurick told Morgan that things did not operate that way and that, furthermore, one of the reasons he was being paid $50,000 a year—$30,000 more than he had been making at the *Digest*—was his connection not to the WPI but to the Wallaces, who were known to be interested in education. Morgan's heart stopped. Somehow he managed to say he thought he had been hired because of his international contacts and all-around creativity.

Yurick and Wexler informed him they could get people with those credentials anywhere. They wanted him to go to the Wallaces. Morgan said he did not know whether he could do that. Minutes later he walked out onto the street and phoned a friend to come and get him. For the next several months he suffered through a period of deep depression, not seeing anyone and convinced that any success he met with for the rest of his life would depend on his knowing the Wallaces and that he himself was worth nothing.

Finally, he pulled himself together, went to see *Digest* business manager Paul Thompson, and told him his problem. Thompson inquired whether he had any money, and Morgan said the divorce had left him broke. Later Thompson arranged for Morgan to receive $15,000. Morgan asked his banker to send him a check for $1,250 every month for twelve months, no more and no less. Then he went on sabbatical, visiting Europe and Russia, but having no contact with the Wallaces.

The year was nearly up when one morning, while sitting in his New York apartment, Morgan received an unexpected call from Wally. Wally talked as though nothing had happened, saying he was having lunch that day with Mrs. John J. McCloy, head of the Girls' Clubs of America and aunt of Condensed Books editor John Zinsser. He and Morgan agreed to get together. Around two-thirty Wally showed up, gave Morgan a big hug, then walked around inspecting the apartment—looking in the refrigerator, opening closets. "Well," he pronounced, "it looks as though you aren't headed for the poorhouse yet."

Then he sat down. Morgan anticipated a let's-let-bygones-be-bygones speech. Instead Wally said, "Harry, I've got to ask you something. When are you going to get off your ass and do something wonderful so we can do another article about you in the *Digest?*"

Stunned, Morgan managed to tell him how he was working on a project to send high school and college musicians to Iron Curtain countries as part of a cultural-exchange program. Wally suggested he visit Pleasantville and talk to the editors about a fourth article. There was no mention of *Alice.*

"We ought to go out and celebrate," Wally announced, getting up to leave. "Lila Bell is downstairs in the car with Gene, and the three of us are going to go have the biggest and best chocolate float we can buy in New York."

They went downstairs, and Morgan could see that Wally was trying to play the part of peacemaker. He told Lila that Harry had invited them out to find the biggest and best chocolate float in New York. Lila kept looking down, and finally she reminded Wally they had a dinner engagement. However, she added that Morgan could come out to High Winds some evening and have his chocolate float there. Wally looked at his watch, then said, "Harry, I know you're busy. But can you work something out—tomorrow maybe?"

Morgan was not busy at all. He went up to High Winds, and the three of them had chocolate floats and renewed their friendship, and over the next several years Wally contributed more than one million dollars to Harry Morgan's various projects to encourage world peace and understanding among nations. Also from that time on, Morgan became in effect a private employee of Wally and Lila, but not of the RDA, and in addition to his salary they sent him tax-free gifts several times a year.

But in the early stage of their reconciliation, Morgan had no luck in interesting any of the editors in a fourth article. All were cool to the idea because they were tired of what they perceived as Morgan's manipulation of Wallace and his years of traveling around the world on *Digest* money. Ultimately, Wally himself arranged for a lunch at the Guest House, where he sounded out a group of editors about a fourth article. Senior editor Ed Thompson was particularly hostile to the idea.

"But this is a different approach," Wally argued. "This article could stand on its own."

All the other editors were in agreement with Thompson, and the article seemed doomed. But Wally drew Morgan aside and told him he was going to get Hobe Lewis to recommend a writer.

"If Hobe recommends a writer," Wally explained, "they can't say this is an article I pushed for, because I'm sure you don't want an article put in just because I said so."

Lewis picked senior editor Bob O'Brien, whom he often used for pet projects. O'Brien wrote an article called "Harry Morgan's Impossible Dream." After reading it, Wally called Morgan on the phone and said, "Harry, I think this may be the best article we've done, but I'm staying out of it."

Though the article was bought, obviously to please Wally, it was punted from one issue editor to another for more than a year. Finally, Tony Oursler selected it. Morgan immediately called Oursler to thank him and was told, "Harry, this is an article that Wally would run if he were running the magazine, and someone's got to do it. I'm thrilled that I can be the one."

When the article was published, in February 1974, Wally invited Morgan to High Winds to celebrate. A small box at the end of the article invited readers to nominate amateur singing or musical groups to participate in the cultural-exchange program. Fifteen thousand nominations poured in—"every grandmother in America," in Morgan's words, "nominating a grandchild's marching band." After that the program really began to flower. For their part, *Digest* editors prayed that they had finally, once and for all, seen the last of Harry Morgan.

———

ON JANUARY 28, 1972, Joe's magazine celebrated its fiftieth anniversary in the White House at a white-tie party hosted by Nixon and his wife, Pat. Highlight of the thick anniversary issue was a long interview with the president. At the reception Wally announced that he was going to support Nixon for reelection no matter who ran against him, adding, "I've often thought we'd have a utopia in this country if every community adopted all the advice we offered from time to time."

Among the hundred or so blue-chip guests were Secretary of State and Mrs. William P. Rogers, Secretary of the Treasury and Mrs. John B. Connally, Attorney General and Mrs. John N. Mitchell, and Secretary of Commerce and Mrs. Maurice H. Stans. Others included Dr. and Mrs. Billy Graham, Mr. and Mrs. Norman Vincent Peale, Mr. and Mrs. Al Cole, André Kostelanetz, Lionel Hampton, Dr. and Mrs. Sidney Hook, Colonel and Mrs. Frank Borman, Mr. and Mrs. Hobe Lewis, Fred MacMurray and his wife, June Haver, Mr. and Mrs. James Michener, Mr. and Mrs. Bob Hope, Merrill Lynch president Donald T. Regan and his wife, and Mr. and Mrs. Laurance Rockefeller.

Nixon acted as master of ceremonies and after dinner, in the East Room, awarded Wally the Medal of Freedom. Then the president announced that the Ray Conniff Singers would entertain the group, adding, "If the music is square, it's because I like it square."

Just then one of the singers, a young woman named Carol Feraci, raised a placard reading "Stop the War, Stop the Killing." At the same time she shouted out to the president, sitting with his wife in the front row, "You go to church on Sunday and pray to Jesus Christ. If Jesus Christ were in this room tonight you would not dare to drop another bomb."

The group then performed its first number. Afterward Conniff turned and said to the audience, "The beginning of this program was as much a surprise to me as everybody." Among the clearly hostile audience there was much shuffling and many additional groans and boos. Someone shouted, "You ought to throw her out."

Conniff told Feraci that it would be better if she left, and she did. A few days after the incident, Nixon phoned Conniff and reassured him that he was not upset with him personally.

20

Indigestion

LILA AND WALLY frequently accepted invitations to dinner at the homes of favored employees, and one evening they drove up to Pawling as guests of John and Elizabeth Peale Allen. Before dinner Wally and Allen walked across the highway to visit the Allens' neighbor, a dairy farmer. Wally wanted to compare modern farm equipment with that of the farms he had worked on in Montana. A few days later Wally wrote Allen a note asking him to find out from the farmer what he would feed deer. "We have these deer that come around, and I like to feed them."

Allen checked with the farmer, who recommended calf starter. Allen memoed the information back to Wally. The next day another terse query arrived through the interoffice mail: "Where can I get some calf starter?"

Allen offered to get Wally a ton of calf starter from Agway in Bethel, Connecticut. Though it was illegal to feed deer in Westchester County, since it tamed them, the calf starter was delivered, and in due course Wally sent Allen a check.

A year later Allen got a memo asking him to inquire how much the farmer paid for calf starter. Allen learned that the price varied quite a bit, but that a person could mix it with corn, which was cheaper than calf starter. Allen duly informed Wally, who was relieved to know he was not being cheated by the Agway people. He wrote back saying, "Next year I'm going to mix it 50/50."

Allen could only shake his head. After all, he knew this was the same man who had recently slipped a million-dollar check to the head of Outward Bound. But Allen also knew that, despite his generosity as a philanthropist and employer, Wally was cheap when it came to spending money in other ways and even embarrassed by his wealth.

On more than one occasion, when Allen was showing visitors around High Winds, Wally went along and at the end of the tour told his guests, "You realize this house was built at the height of the Depression. There were all these Italian stonemasons building Kensico Dam, all of them very inexpensive, so that I don't think High Winds really cost more than a tract home would today." It was an unconvincing bit of ingenuity, but charming.

Equally touching was his devotion to his deer. He was as protective of them as he was of his road—in fact, too protective. Members of the Bedford Riding Association frequently went riding over local estates, including High Winds. One day two cocker spaniels accompanying their masters on a jaunt ran off and found their way into the shed where Wally was chopping wood, down at the far end of his road. Enraged by the recent molestation of deer on his property by wild or unleashed dogs, Wally—who had shown a fondness for animals all his life—tied the two pets to a post and beat them to death with a chain. When the owners of the spaniels threatened to bring suit, he settled out of court for a little less than $100,000. The affair was kept very hush-hush, but word began to get around that part of Westchester, and more particularly at RDA headquarters in Chappaqua, that the old man of the mountain was getting to be very strange in the head in his old age.

——

In 1972 Harold H. Helm, who had served as the company's banker for twenty years, asked Wally, "What's going to happen if anything happens to you?"

The reply was, as usual, a question: what did Helm think he should do. Helm knew that Wally did not want the Reader's Digest Association to go public. So he suggested that Wally pick a handful of friends and trusted employees and ask them to be the voting trustees of the Wallaces' stock. Together Wally and Lila owned 100 percent of the RDA's voting stock.

Helm's first suggestion for an outside director was Laurance S. Rockefeller. Wally authorized Helm to approach the philanthropist, who was not only a personal friend of the Wallaces but also an adviser on their own charitable giving. Rockefeller was reluctant at first to become involved with a privately held company. Helm told him, "The *Digest* is an institution, and this is a public trust that nobody ought to turn down."

Rockefeller relented, and he and Helm were later named the first outside directors of the RDA in July 1973. At seventy-two, Helm was still active as chairman of the directors' advisory committee of Chemical Bank, while Rockefeller, sixty-three, served as chairman of the Rockefeller Brothers Fund. Other charter trustees of the Wallace Trust, as the group controlling the company's voting stock was christened, included Wally and Lila, Kent Rhodes, Walter Hitesman, and Dick Waters.

The Wallaces were now spoken of only in the most reverential tones. Wally had the label of genius attached to him, though many of the editors were unsure what the nature of that genius was. Every so often he would call up one of the new editors and ask him or her to come down for a chat. That prospect was alarming to a great many people who had never met a living legend before, much less one who held such absolute power over their own fate. One editor literally had a nervous breakdown in her office because she knew she was going to be summoned by Wally at any moment. Every day she dressed in her best finery, but the call never came. Finally, she snapped.

When such a summons did arrive, the neophyte usually heard a polite, diffident voice on the other end of the line saying, "This is Mr. Wallace. Could you spare me a few minutes?" At first, the conversation never seemed to be about much. Wally sat in his big wing chair, his face half in the shadows, so that the nervous visitor never quite got to see the old man's features without seeming rude. While seeming to be chatting about nothing very much at all, Wally skillfully conducted an interview that told him everything he wanted to know about the new employee.

One April evening in the early seventies, Wally and Lila were dining downstairs at High Winds. As Lila often did, she wore her favorite piece of jewelry—a large, jewel-encrusted, Pegasus-shaped brooch given to her by her husband. The Wallaces always felt secure despite the isolation of their home, especially since a new security system had only recently been installed. But outside a car drove by, slowing down just enough to allow a young man trained as a gymnast to roll out. Quickly, he retrieved a ladder previously hidden nearby.

Then he climbed into Lila's second-story bedroom, whose location he knew in advance, and made off with most of her jewelry, worth an estimated $165,000. Upon discovering the theft, Lila called the police, who suspected but were never able to prove that one of the men who helped install the security system was an accomplice of the burglars.

In truth, Lila felt more relief than distress. Her favorite brooch had not been taken. Her only concern was the loss of a piece given to her by Rockefeller—a bird-shaped brooch set with jade and lapis lazuli—in gratitude for her generosity to the Bronx Zoo's World of Birds. Without his knowledge, she later secretly had it duplicated.

Wally continued to be an absentee owner in many respects. Though often traveling and spending his winters not at the Pierre, as formerly, but in Arizona, he was enough of an erratic presence to keep all on their guard. Usually, when he strayed from his tower, it was to pursue his almost fanatical one-man campaign to keep overhead and related costs down. Among the orders issued from High Winds was a directive to the Guest House to stop giving away cigarettes to guests and to replace pricey cashews with peanuts.

Showing up at unexpected hours at headquarters, he also still liked to roam the halls, turning off the lights in unoccupied offices. One memo to the staff complained that the electric bill for the month of January was up more than $10,000 over the previous year. Habitual offenders were likely to return from lunch hour to find a personalized memo in Wally's own hand reminding them of company policy about turning off lights in unoccupied rooms.

Another of his enduring obsessions was punctuality, and even after a half century the RDA continued to keep attendance records. Every week Wally was sent copies of hand-filled records from department heads. He had become the cranky, protective patriarch of an immense family whose grown children ran the business but still had not learned the greatest of all *Digest* lessons—how to get the most out of twenty-four hours a day, only eight of which were reserved for work.

The most important concern of all in Wally's old age—apart from worrying about what would happen to his company after he died—was protecting its good name. Memo after memo reflected his fear that the company was moving too quickly in too many areas without fully taking into account the effect such actions might have on the *Digest*'s reputation for quality and dependability. When Walter Hitesman, backed by Jack O'Hara and Hobe Lewis, proposed selling digital-radio clocks by direct mail, Wally asked, "How much a feather in *RD*'s collective hat is it to be promoting such a sale, so far afield from our established activities?" The first mailing on the radio had resulted in a profit of $750,000. Unimpressed, Wally complained, "But should the desire to make money ever come first in our calculations? I don't think so."

That lesson was completely lost on Hitesman, one of the company's more aggressive and flamboyant wheeler-dealers, who was looking to repeat his fabulous success as head of Music & Records by marketing a host of other products. Hobe Lewis had long ago learned his lesson. But the one who did take Wally's words to heart was Jack O'Hara, who revered Wally and was to become the most ardent believer in his no-profit-just-for-its-own-sake philosophy.

WHAT the *Digest* did not talk about was frequently far more interesting than what it did. In the early fifties it had ignored Senator Joseph McCarthy but not McCarthyism. While condemning student riots and the drug culture of the sixties, the *Digest* all but refused to recognize the Peace Corps and the rare idealism of a rare generation. It ignored *Silent Spring,* Rachel Carson's environmental manifesto, and it had almost nothing good to say about such other folk heroes of the sixties as consumer advocate Ralph Nader, the Beatles, and Dr. Spock. In 1968 a visitor from Mars, reading only the October issue of the *Reader's Digest,* would never have suspected that a Democrat named Hubert Humphrey was running for president.

In the election issue of October 1972, the *Digest* decided to mend its ways and at least acknowledge the existence of Democratic contender George McGovern. Typical, though, was a quote from London's *Economist:* "As they see it, the South Vietnamese have less to fear from Hanoi than from the election of Sen. George McGovern." Another negative item from *Newsweek* suggested that if Senator McGovern succeeded in his proposal to withdraw American troops from Europe, Soviet Russia might take over Europe.

President Nixon's name, of course, was omnipresent in that reelection issue—as if it had been published not by the RDA but by the GOP. Among the pro-Nixon pieces was Secretary of the Treasury John B. Connally's "A Time for Toughness in America," while Washington bureau staff writer Eugene H. Methvin declared that Nixon appointees were finally beginning to set America on a true course, and added portentously, "Today the Supreme Court appears almost exactly poised between opposing Constitutional philosophies. Your vote this November may well tip the balance."

The Republican drumbeat finally became so relentless that Wally himself began to sense the *Digest* was overloading its pages with articles too obviously pro-administration and ordered a reduction in their number. He also proposed reprinting an antiwar article by Clark Clifford, Johnson's former secretary of defense, who had told the president the war was hopeless. But on that issue Lewis prevailed upon Wally to change his mind.

Of all the *Digest*'s many sins of omission, the most significant by far was its steadfast and ultimately hysterical refusal to acknowledge the Watergate scandal just beginning to break in 1972. Throughout 1973, during the televised hearings of a special Senate committee in which former White House counsel John Dean implicated Attorney General John Mitchell and other members of the administration in an attempt to tap the telephone of Democratic headquarters, the *Digest* still refused even to mention what had become the biggest news story in a decade.

Instead, the magazine continued to batter away as usual at Washington bureaucrats, Communists, union leaders, IRS agents, environmentalists, Democrats, college students, and the Mafia. Yet, while cynically cataloging every conceivable ill and abuse known to civilization, it refused to diagnose the cancer in the nation's capital.

During this period Nixon paid his second visit to Pleasantville. The president had to visit his dentist in New York and phoned one Monday morning to ask Lewis if he could stay over at the editor in chief's Bedford home. Lewis, of course, was delighted. On Wednesday the Secret Service arrived to run telephone lines, check out the blood supply in the local hospital, and install a special switchboard in Lewis's garage. Several agents also covered the toolshed window with brown paper, then went in and never left until the visit was over.

On Friday, Nixon arrived by helicopter with his doctor, valet, and military aide, and Lewis hosted a dinner party attended by former New York governor Thomas E. Dewey, Wally and Lila, and Al Cole. That night the doctor and military aide were obliged to share a bedroom because the third bedroom was also crammed with electronics. For weeks and months afterward Hobe Lewis was the most celebrated man in Westchester County.

Only in February 1974 did the *Digest* finally make an oblique passing reference to Watergate when John Connally, in the press section, was quoted in a reprint from the *New York Daily News:* "When there's a loss of confidence, do we want a President to resign? . . . Shouldn't we be patient enough to let the system work its will through the judicial processes of the country?"

What that translated into, so far as Nixon's friend Hobe Lewis was concerned, was a desperate hope that no one would discover that the shadow of Watergate reached all the way to Pleasantville. Frequently, even urgently, as the fast-breaking story unfolded on the front page of the *Washington Post* and elsewhere, investigative reporter Carl Bernstein—who with his partner Bob Woodward broke the story—had called Lewis, only to be told he was out of the office, out of town, out of the country. Woodward's unnamed source within the administration, code-named Deep Throat, had told him to "follow the money." One thing Woodward and Bernstein had been able to verify was that one branch of the money trail led to Hobe Lewis. What Bernstein did not know, however, during some of those frantic calls to Pleasantville, was that Lewis was indeed out of the country—in Switzerland, in fact, putting $100,000 in cash into a secret account that could not be traced.

The Watergate tapes—the secret recordings Nixon made of his conversations in the Oval Office—had already revealed that during a key Watergate cover-up meeting on March 21, 1973, the president told his White House counsel John Dean, ". . . a million dollars. And you could get it in cash. I, I know where it could be gotten." But no one had ever answered the question of where Nixon could get that million dollars in cash.

Nixon also discussed money on April 17, 1973, as the cover-up was beginning to unravel. "Legal fees will be substantial. . . . But there is a way we can get it for you, and uh—two or three hundred thousand dollars. . . . No strain. Doesn't come outta me."

In that same conversation, Nixon continued, "I didn't, I never intended to use the money at all. As a matter of fact, I told B-B-Bebe, uh, basically be sure that people like uh, who, who have [been] contributing years are, uh, favored."

Who, though, was ever favored? No one had ever said. Lawrence M. Higby, an aide to White House chief of staff H. R. Haldeman, had testified that the latter told him that $400,000 was available for legal fees from a cash fund controlled by Nixon's friend Charles G.

("Bebe") Rebozo. Yet government investigators were never able to identify anything except the $100,000 that billionaire Howard Hughes gave Rebozo, who testified that after keeping the money for three years he returned it to the Hughes organization.

That $100,000 had triggered investigations into both Rebozo's and Nixon's personal finances, but no charges were ever brought. In the special prosecutor's files were the results of two investigations, never made public, which focused on unanswered questions about Nixon and money—many of them concerning favors to large corporations in return for political contributions. Woodward claimed that the prosecutors knew that Nixon and his longtime secretary, Rose Mary Woods, had collected $100,000 in cash at the White House in November 1971. At Nixon's direction Woods kept the money in her safe for about eighteen months and returned it in June 1973, within several days of the return of the Hughes $100,000—or several weeks after the IRS had begun an investigation into the source of the money.

The prosecutors further learned that Saudi Arabian businessman Adnan Khashoggi kept an account in Rebozo's Key Biscayne bank. Two separate cash withdrawals of $100,000 from that account—one in May 1972 and the second the following November—could never be traced. At the time of the withdrawals, Khashoggi was lobbying to get a presidential endorsement for a multibillion-dollar plan to permit American capital to be paid in advance for Saudi oil reserves. According to Woodward, the $100,000 kept by Woods in her safe was given by Minnesota millionaire Dwayne O. Andreas—the "soybean king" and good friend of Al Cole—who told the investigators the money was an early 1972 campaign contribution.

All that amounted to no more than a footnote to the Watergate story, Woodward conceded. But on June 27, 1976, the Sunday edition of the *Washington Post* bannered a six-column headline: 4 YEARS AFTER WATERGATE, MONEY QUESTIONS LINGER. Woodward had taken up the money trail again. Bookending the article were photos of Rose Mary Woods over the teaser caption "$100,000 kept in White House" and of Dwayne Andreas with "$125,000 in campaign contributions."

Woodward now reported that Andreas made another secret contribution to the Nixon campaign—$25,000 in cash given through Kenneth H. Dahlberg, a Nixon fund-raiser in the Midwest, in the form of a cashier's check made out to Dahlberg and deposited into the bank account of one of the Watergate burglars. The trail left by that check provided investigators with their first concrete evidence linking the burglars and the Nixon campaign committee.

Within six days of the burglary, Nixon knew that the existence of that $25,000 made him a vulnerable target in the FBI's investigation of the affair. He then ordered the cover-up by directing the CIA to divert the FBI, since an investigation of Dahlberg could lead to Andreas. Woodward speculated that Nixon might have been motivated partly by a desire to conceal the existence of the $100,000 in Woods's White House safe. Nixon's chief aides certainly knew that the $25,000 also came from Andreas.

Two days before he ordered the cover-up, Nixon met his chief fund-raiser, Maurice Stans, and his campaign manager, John N. Mitchell—both of whom, incidentally, had attended the *Digest*'s fiftieth-anniversary party in the White House, only months before the break-in. John Dean later testified, "Stans was concerned about the Dahlberg check. I was informed because it was in fact a contribution from Mr. Dwayne Andreas, whom I did not know, but I was told was a longtime backer of Sen. Hubert Humphrey. Neither Stans nor Mitchell wanted Mr. Andreas to be embarrassed by disclosure of the [$25,000] contribution."

At his trial Haldeman testified that he knew the $25,000 was from Andreas. But he claimed that the real purpose of the cover-up was to save Andreas from any embarrassment—that the CIA and FBI had perhaps been used politically, but not in any effort to obstruct justice. Nor was there any indication that Haldeman initially knew of the $100,000 in Woods's safe. Later he and Nixon discussed whether to turn that money over to the Watergate defendants, but rejected the idea.

The tape transcript of that conversation led investigators to learn from Woods that there was another $100,000 given by Andreas. Since the money was kept after the election, Watergate prosecutors decided that Nixon never intended to use the $100,000 in the 1972 campaign. Moreover, the money was not on Woods's secret list of early contributions, though the $25,000 via Dahlberg was. How did Andreas manage to get that $100,000 to Nixon?

According to Woodward, in 1971 Andreas contacted one of his golfing partners, Hobe Lewis, editor in chief of the *Reader's Digest* and a personal friend of the president: "Lewis put Andreas in contact with

Woods and the $100,000 was soon delivered personally by Andreas to the White House."

In June 1973, when Nixon and Woods decided to return the money, according to Woodward, "Woods asked Lewis—and not Andreas—to come to the White House. She then gave him $100,000 in cash—all $100 bills in 10 packets of $10,000 each. According to the sources, Lewis then had Woods inform Andreas the money had been returned."

In a recent interview, Woodward wrote on June 27, 1976, Lewis

> confirmed the details of the transaction and said his role was "perfectly innocent." Lewis said that he took the cash home and then several days later called Andreas and asked to borrow the money. The loan was confirmed by a letter which Lewis said he sent to Andreas. In addition, Lewis said that he later signed a formal promissory note for the $100,000 loan, which has not been paid back.
>
> The transaction involving the $100,000 did not violate any law because there was no evidence that the $100,000 was anything more than a political contribution which was returned and then loaned to another person.

According to Barnabas Henry, "Hobe would do anything Cole told him. Nixon didn't have anything to do with the *Reader's Digest* until he came to Wally for money. Al was a big Nixon person. Wally got into substantial tax problems as a result. It was Al Cole's fault."

After Lewis got the money back, there arose the problem of what to do with so much cash. The solution was simply to say that Lewis had personally borrowed the money from Andreas. Ultimately, it was deposited in a Swiss bank. But Lila was embarrassed and mortified by all the publicity.

"That's not the way it should have happened," she complained to friends. "Hobe Lewis is getting too big for his britches."

In December 1973 Rebozo was ordered by a Florida judge to provide the names of those who maintained accounts in the bank's small trust department. The bank had complied with other subpoenas relating to the investigation but declined to furnish the names of the trust account holders. The bank and the Dade County prosecutor later reached an agreement to turn over records of any accounts held by Nixon, who was a large depositor at the bank. The prosecutor also sought information on other depositors, including H. R. Haldeman and John D. Ehrlichman, former assistants to the president; DeWitt Wallace; Nixon's brother Donald; and Lynden O. Pindling, prime minister of the Bahamas.

The prosecutor refused to comment on his reasons for seeking the bank records and stated only that his office was attempting to learn whether there was information in the bank that would aid them "in the investigation of the conspiracy that began on Key Biscayne on March 30, 1972." On that date former attorney general John N. Mitchell and other aides had approved the plan to break into the Watergate apartment and office complex.

McHenry thought Lewis was headed for jail. Ultimately, the stress got to the point where Lila had to undergo an operation for a perforated ulcer. Fortunately for Lewis and the reputation of the *Reader's Digest,* however, the grand jury was dismissed. But he had fallen out of favor with Lila, and it was only a matter of time before he was gone.

———

IF THE *Digest* was looking for presidential favors in return for its contributions to the president, they were almost certainly related to the company's colossal postal bill. Almost all of the *Digest*'s operations were conducted through the mails—magazine subscriptions, Condensed Books, sweepstakes, Music & Records—and for years the RDA had vigorously lobbied for relief and a reduction in rates. In December 1973, with Washington paralyzed by the Watergate affair, Nixon's chief domestic adviser and former secretary of defense, Melvin R. Laird, resigned, saying he believed that the House of Representatives should vote by March 15 on whether to impeach the president.

Laird, whose resignation had been expected for some time, also announced he was taking a position with the Reader's Digest Association. Like John Connally, Laird had urged the president the previous summer to release the Watergate tapes and other papers, a step Nixon had taken only in recent weeks after his credibility was destroyed. Laird's position at the RDA was that of senior counselor for national and international affairs, but his chief responsibility was to act as a lobbyist, based in Washington, on the postal front.

As a result of the Wallaces' IRS problems and the business over the money in Rose Mary Woods's safe, their contributions to the Republican party were drastically reduced. In 1972 they had legally contributed $100,000. Gerald Ford, Nixon's vice-president, received only $9,050 when he ran for election in 1976. In Wally's view Nixon was "guilty" of a cover-up, and Watergate was "a very sad and tragic event in American history."

Lewis himself claimed that he had begun to break with the White House after the Christmas bombing of Cambodia. He also declined to contribute to a Nixon defense fund, and spoke with the president after his resignation only once.

"The Wallaces, the Al Coles, Lewis all fell into the same trap I did," Billy Graham subsequently explained. "All the time I had any association with Nixon, he was a perfect gentleman. For example, he never used foul language, and I never saw him drinking. Lewis told me the same thing."

Ed Thompson later commissioned T. H. White to write an excoriating attack on the Nixon administration. "I know you have to do it," Lewis told Thompson. "Just do what's right and tell the story as it is."

In April 1975, with Lewis as editor in chief, the *Digest* bit its tongue and published the first of two installments of *Breach of Faith: The Fall of Richard Nixon,* published by Atheneum but initiated by the *RD,* which split the advance and profits. The magazine had come 180 degrees from Pat Nixon's 1952 article "I Say He's a Wonderful Guy."

———

HOBE LEWIS had reached the so-called mandatory retirement age in 1974, but Wally allowed him to stay on indefinitely. The reasons were obvious. The Watergate situation was still in a state of extreme flux, the grand jury in Florida was still impaneled, and there was no way of knowing whether the good name of the *Reader's Digest* was going to be dragged through the headlines of the nation's newspapers. Wally was extremely displeased with Lewis, but thought it more prudent to keep him in Pleasantville on salary than to put him out to pasture and beyond his day-to-day control.

Then, suddenly, Hobart Lewis was removed as editor in chief and banished to an office in the Pan Am Building. In mid-November 1976 the company further announced that Lewis had reached the mandatory retirement age (he was, in fact, sixty-seven) and was vacating the chairmanship at the end of the year.

"I always thought that Hobe Lewis didn't exist," said one writer when he heard the news, "and now he doesn't."

Lewis's sudden departure had been the result of a last straw that broke the back of Wally's patience. In true *Digest* tradition, going back to the early days of Harold Lynch and Arthur Griffiths, it was yet another case of *cherchez la femme*. "She was an extremely feminine and attractive woman of a certain age," according to one observer, "feminine in the sense that she was always heavily scented and there was much rustling of gowns in everything she wore."

Lewis had always been a womanizer, which was never much of a problem so long as certain unspoken rules were observed. One was not to let social pursuits interfere with work. Another was never to spend company money on girlfriends. Lewis, plagued by domestic problems and a recent prostate operation in addition to the unfavorable publicity surrounding his connection with Nixon, had virtually abandoned his role as editor in chief. His only memorable achievement, in the twilight of his career, was to drink champagne from the shoe of retiring managing editor Audrey Dade. Thompson, Oursler, Gilmore, Herbert, and Mahony kept the engines running efficiently, however, alternating as issue editors and assuming increased executive responsibilities.

One day the woman in question appeared suddenly on the scene, out of nowhere, and soon there were stories that she had once been married to an English lord, once worked for *Time* magazine as a researcher, once been an interior decorator. The one story everybody believed was that she was Hobe Lewis's latest infatuation. Though not on salary, she was getting money as an RDA consultant. The RDA was also paying the rent for her swank Manhattan apartment. Each month the check was paid out by treasurer Dick Waters, who also approved Lewis's expense accounts. Over a period of time, Waters could not help noticing that whenever the CEO went off to London, Switzerland, or Paris, his girlfriend always followed after. The two expense accounts were like a road map of their affair. All the money Lewis was spending on the woman raised more eyebrows among insiders than anything else because, after all, many of the top married editors and finance people had girlfriends. But they did not give them RDA money.

Making matters worse for Waters personally were the tearful phone calls he regularly received from Edie Lewis, asking where Hobe was and when he was coming home to see his children.

In due course Lewis sent out a memo asking that someone handle the output of good ideas coming from the woman. At one point Dan

O'Keefe was her handler. But nearly everything that she sent seemed wide of the mark by a considerable margin; when O'Keefe managed to beg off, she was inherited by Walter Hunt, editor of the magazine's book-excerpt department.

On one of his frequent visits to London, Hunt obliged Lewis by taking the woman out to lunch, along with several others involved in the British book operation. It was mutually agreed that every month she would read through a number of books sent in by publishers and make her recommendations for condensation. But the arrangement soon collapsed when the woman refused to go into the London office to pick up the books, insisting they be sent to her by limousine instead.

In November 1975 Lewis instructed Tony Oursler, who was issue editor, to publish an article by the woman. It was on an esoteric subject that Oursler had no interest in, but he followed orders and put it on the story list. When Wally saw the title, he called Oursler and asked him what it was about. Oursler told him. Wally then said, "I don't want that in the *Reader's Digest."* Oursler replied, in effect, "I don't either, but Lewis wants it in." Wally then asked who the author was.

"Someone whose name I don't know," replied Oursler, though the woman had also written several articles for the British edition, and he might have seen her name there.

Wally was infuriated. In short order Lewis was removed as editor and told to report to work in New York, where for the time being he continued to act as chairman—always an honorary post. When Wally informed Ed Thompson that he was the new editor in chief, he asked two questions. Thompson had been attending a circulation meeting that morning in the basement with senior business management when the phone rang. Kent Rhodes picked it up, then went around and whispered in his ear that Wally wanted to see him.

Thompson went up to Wally's office. Wally rambled on about charities for a while, and Thompson had no idea why he was there. It suddenly became clear when Wally said, "Well, as editor in chief, you're going to need to know these things."

Thompson asked him to repeat what he just said.

"Yeah," Wally replied. "You're editor in chief as of today."

Then he asked, "Can you get along with Mahony?"

Thompson said they were two very different types of people, but he promised to try. Wally's next question was "You can get rid of [Hobe's girlfriend], can't you?"

"Sure," Thompson replied.

His first task as the new editor in chief was to write a letter to the woman, whom he had never met, firing her. Getting rid of Mahony proved a little more difficult. Wally, meanwhile, strode down to the office of the head of the copydesk, Clarice Fontaine, picked up a proof copy of the latest masthead, and with a red pencil drew a line through Lewis's name.

"There goes the editor in chief," he said. "There goes the CEO."

Then he walked out.

V

CIVIL WAR
[1977–1984]

21

The Fab Four

THE *Digest*'s new editor in chief, Ed Thompson, was not like his predecessors, DeWitt Wallace and Hobart Durkin Lewis, in the least. His abrasive personality was in sharp contrast to Wally's diffident, enigmatically polite way of approaching people and problems. Once, an editor who was partly crippled went to see Thompson and said, "I've got a problem." Quipped Thompson, "Yeah. You've got a gimp leg. What else?" The editor did not take offense. Most people treated Thompson's bluntness, and his frequent bursts of temper, as a mask. Those closest to him thought he was really a "pussycat"—thoughtful, considerate, loyal to friends and subordinates—who was only trying to hide his insecurity.

Thompson's editorial style was also different from Wally's and Lewis's, which had been more or less identical. Though a good Republican, he was not a dogged party loyalist like Wally, Lewis, Al Cole, and so many other Digesters. Nor did he have the "common touch," his finger on the pulse of Middle America—though nobody else in Pleasantville did any more either. The *Digest* was by now a formula magazine produced by Ivy Leaguers for the consumption of people with whom they had virtually nothing in common either in educational background or in socioeconomic status and life-style.

The one common bond between editors and readers, though, was their political conservatism. Over several generations the *Digest*'s editors had astutely cultivated the largest conservative constituency in the country. For every "opinion maker" who read *Time,* the *New York Times,* or the *Washington Post,* there were ten or more subscribers whose chief source of political information was the *Reader's Digest*—and they made their opinion count where it mattered the most, in the ballot box.

Thus when Ed Thompson was faced with covering his first presidential election as editor in chief, he decided, for the first time in *Reader's Digest* history, to approach it evenhandedly. In its issue of October 1976, the *Digest* ran a "debate"—parallel answers to the same questions—between Republican incumbent Gerald Ford and Democratic contender Jimmy Carter. The only newsworthy item in an otherwise banal exchange of opinions concerned taxes. Ford proposed giving "greater tax relief" to families earning $8,000 to $30,000 per year. Carter said he favored a "truly progressive tax rate," which would have higher-income families pay a higher portion of their income in taxes. But the most remarkable aspect of the debate, which went unreported in the press, was not the content but the rigid fairness and lack of bias shown by the editors.

Under Bun Mahony the Democrats would have been shown no such quarter. For that matter, he scarcely showed any to his new boss. Dray horse to the winged Pegasus, Walter B. Mahony, Jr., had spent his lifetime in the service of the *Reader's Digest,* working virtually around the clock seven days a week. By dint of such dedication he had risen to become executive editor and a vice-president. Upon his promotion, four editors had been appointed to fill his position as managing editor, leading a subordinate to complain, "A horse race like this sure makes it hard on us ass-kissers—we don't know which one to kiss."

Many old-timers assumed Mahony would be the next editor in chief when Lewis retired. So did Mahony himself. Perhaps he was indirectly encouraged in that belief by Wally himself, who often discussed the editorial succession with various top editors, asking questions about this or that one's skills, managerial abilities, personal foibles. That was standard Wally practice with almost everybody. Yet it would have been out of character for him to tell Mahony that he himself would get the job, even though he was in effect the acting editor with Lewis always wandering off to Hollywood, Key Biscayne, or Europe. Moreover, Lewis himself had a low opinion of Mahony's abilities and had recommended Thompson as his successor.

Nevertheless, Mahony had reason to believe he was the logical heir apparent by reason of his age and experience. At the very least, he may have expected to be given the editorship as his honorary due. When the position went to Thompson instead, the *Digest*'s faithful servant could scarcely believe it—literally not even conceding to Thompson himself that he possessed the authority Wally had so traitorously invested him with.

Though he despised Mahony as a mere fact checker, Thompson at first tried to accommodate his executive editor. Among the first orders of business were salary data. Mahony controlled that information, yet when Thompson asked for the file, the resentful Mahony refused to hand it over. Thompson again requested the information. When he was rebuffed a second time, Bun got burned. Firing him was out of the question, because of his superhuman loyalty to the company and to the Wallaces personally. The new editor in chief solved the problem by sending him into exile in the offices in the Pan Am Building. There he was set to work as a lowly editor for General Books. The memo announcing his departure was cosigned by Thompson and Wally.

For a time Mahony perhaps hoped simply to outlast Thompson and be brought back as the *Digest*'s savior. Though very improbable, such a scenario was not entirely out of the question. Thompson was by far the best of the available candidates, but he was not an ideal choice. When Hobe Lewis had been tapped as editor, he was so much like Wally that he amounted to a young alter ego. No other candidate was really ever in contention.

Thompson's closest rivals, whom he also considered good friends, were Tony Oursler and Ken Gilmore. Yet their rivalry underscored another reason why Mahony may have suspected that Thompson would not last long. By now the Washington bureau was nearly thirty years old. True, it was not much of a journalistic presence in Washington. It was all but ignored by the capital press corps and almost never invited to major press functions. And bureau staffers did not mix much with other D.C. correspondents, much as Digesters in Pleasantville kept apart from the publishing community in New York.

Yet the *Digest*'s bureau was very much a presence in Pleasantville, and it had lobbied hard for one of its own—Gilmore—to be appointed editor. Not only did he meet their political specifications, but he had administrative experience, having served for a number of years as head of the D.C. office. Wally had discussed the editorship with Gilmore, and for a time it had seemed to be a race between him and Thompson. Gilmore even seemed to have the advantage, because there was another problem with Thompson—probably the biggest chink in his armor—and that was his reputation as a ladies' man.

That had also been true of Wally and Hobe Lewis, of course, but times had changed. Wally had removed Lewis as editor because of a woman. And Wally's own philandering in earlier years was one thing; what he expected of his successor, now that the magazine was by far the largest promoter of family values in the world, apart from a church or two, was another. In the last months of Lewis's tenure, while all the liabilities and virtues of the various contenders were endlessly discussed in the corridors of Pleasantville, the "morality question" was frequently raised in connection with Thompson.

Wally was concerned about Thompson's reputation—though, as it turned out, not that much. He was fond of the man personally, readily perceived him to be the brightest of the lot, and was satisfied that Thompson's conservatism was genuine. As an editor who always played with a wild card or two up his sleeve, and who hated rigidity and conformity, Wally was also aware that even his beloved *Digest* had become predictable and too one-sided.

In Thompson, Wally recognized the one editor strong enough to stand up to the Washington bureau—an opposition he desired not because he was himself particularly displeased with the bureau's work but because he believed in intramural competition as a prime font of creativity and renewal. Another important factor in Thompson's selection, particularly where Lila was concerned, was that he was a family man, father of five children, and married at the time to his second wife, Nancy Cale, a former *Digest* researcher and ex-deb.

Finally, perhaps more than any of the other candidates, Thompson knew how to have fun. He was an ardent sailor and skier whose Vermont chalet was popularly referred to as "Ed's beds." Not only at the office, but socially, four of the editors—Thompson, Gilmore, Tony Oursler, Roy Herbert—competed in friendly fashion. After Thompson became editor, they were sometimes referred to as the Fab Four, after the Beatles. Though Thompson was very much the undisputed head man, in a broader sense the future of the *Digest* lay in the hands of every member of this close-knit quartet. That was because, rather than proceeding to eliminate those nearest to the throne one by one, like a good Machiavellian, Thompson invited his three senior colleagues, three of his good friends, to join him in plotting the future course of the magazine of which he was now the editor in chief. Though at one level he was insecure, at a much deeper level Thompson had enormous self-confidence, and he also placed great trust in his fellowman.

And that pointed to another trait people noted in Ed Thompson—his naïveté. Did he really think—his colleagues wondered in hindsight—that his three closest rivals, his three good friends, were simply going to accept their defeat at his hands as if the editorship of the *Reader's Digest* were no more than a tennis trophy? Was Thompson so ignorant of the human heart that he knew nothing of treachery, envy, resentment?

ONE of Tony Oursler's admirers was a fellow Digester who once upon a time had loathed the man.

"People who worked for him called him Fulsome Oleo," the colleague recalled, "with a voice that was deliberately Nixonian. Quite insane, but because he was slightly insane I kind of liked the guy. One time I was looking out the window, and there were Fulton, Walter Hunt, and Maurice Ragsdale's widow, in the pouring rain, all under umbrellas, scattering Ragsdale's ashes in the gardens in back that face on the old parkway."

According to researcher Chris Kirby, Oursler was Pleasantville's "resident Attila the Hun—right-wing, very opinionated, dangerous. You didn't know where you stood with him. He could really cut you down. Also he knew how the political system worked at the *Digest* inside and out. He was a real *Digest* product. But he was also a smart guy—perhaps the toughest issue editor to work for. He'd come back to you with question after question after question on an article you thought you had thoroughly researched. He'd come up with a new angle and really bust your chops on it."

"Oursler disapproved of Ed Thompson," observed associate editor Gordon Hard, son of veteran editor Bill Hard, Jr., "and would say things about Ed behind his back. He'd cluck about Ed's peccadilloes—thought it made a bad example. I felt he was talking about Ed to the Wallaces. As a moralist, he disapproved of Ed for moral reasons; and also, like a lot of people, he wanted to be head of the *Digest*.

FOR a time, while Gilmore was still a staff writer, Lila had been concerned that he was not married. A wife was simply seen as a necessary social adjunct in Pleasantville's social circle, which extended to the capital, and no editor or executive of any consequence was a bachelor. Lila's apprehension eventually got to the point where Wally summoned Gilmore for a man-to-man talk, encouraging him to go to YWCA dances to meet nice girls.

Gilmore was in no hurry, however, and only some years later, at the age of thirty-two, married Janet Dunseath, a graduate of Sarah Lawrence College, whom he had courted for two years. Yet more than one Digester observed that, soon after getting married, the friendly, easygoing Gilmore executed a 180-degree personality change and became an intensely ambitious executive type who had clearly set his sights on becoming editor in chief.

Gilmore had always been industrious, and from the very beginning was a favorite of bureau chief Chuck Stevenson. In 1962 his young protege coauthored with James Monahan *The Great Deception: The Inside Story of How the Kremlin Took Cuba.* The bureau specialized in KGB horror stories, and early on Gilmore—whose sister once worked for the CIA and whose brother was a USIA official in New Delhi—developed a taste for cloak-and-dagger spy stories. Later he edited a book on the KGB written by his bureau colleague John Barron.

(In fact, of the Fab Four, only Roy Herbert seemed to have no special interest in espionage. Thompson also had a sibling in the CIA—his brother Colin, who once visited the Pleasantville offices in the hope of persuading the *Digest* editor to kill a piece the agency was not pleased with. Thompson refused. Most passionate of all the KGB watchers in Pleasantville was Tony Oursler, though unlike Gilmore and Barron he confined himself to editing, not writing—in particular, editing books and articles that took an increasingly debunking view of CIA activities. Ultimately, Gilmore and Oursler were to have a serious falling out as a result.)

In 1973 the goal envisioned by Stevenson was achieved when Ken Gilmore was named an assistant managing editor and moved to Pleasantville. Two years later he was appointed managing editor.

Curiously, though, Gilmore had in the meantime grown to be considered "a sort of flat tire" by some in the Washington office, according to one bureau staffer. "People in Pleasantville saw him as obliging, honest, and straight. But in the D.C. office he was regarded as a lamebrained, spineless character. So when he left to go to Pleasantville, that obviously meant he was on the inside track, but no one in Washington ever believed he would make it."

Gilmore was still a freshman on campus when Wally personally appointed him to be issue editor for the November 1975 issue—his first. Tall, easy-going, personable behind thick horn-rimmed glasses, the newcomer conscientiously sifted through hundreds and hundreds of articles in the bloated inventory, reviewing those passed over time and again by his predecessors. As subsequent events were to prove, he had a pronounced taste for platitudinous art-of-living.

Not long after Thompson was made editor, he invited Gilmore, de Lyrot, and Dimi Panitza to join him on a fact-finding mission through Israel, Jordan, and Lebanon to see firsthand what was happening in the Middle East and to visit the staff of the Arabic edition. All four toured the war zone wearing bullet-proof vests and stopped to pose for a picture during an interlude in the fighting.

After Alain de Lyrot retired, Gilmore was put in charge of international editions. Someone expressed the view that his successor was a rather straight-shooting, low-key person. De Lyrot's reply: "He's one of the most ruthless, ambitious people I've ever met."

But in Pleasantville, for the moment, the photograph of the four vest-clad editors also served as an apt metaphor for the ceasefire in editorial warfare signaled by Thompson's elevation to the post of editor in chief. Gilmore, who had been in no special hurry to marry, knew how to bide his time.

THERE was another editor who by reason of his relative youth, temperament, and editorial stature was by rights an honorary fifth member of the Fab Four. Yet Walter Hunt was too prematurely avuncular, too constitutionally cautious, and too inexperienced in working with writers and articles to entertain any serious notions about one day becoming the top man. As editor since 1972 of the magazine's monthly book excerpt—an important responsibility, since that feature was usually at or near the top in reader popularity in almost every monthly poll—he also enjoyed an independence unique in the ranks.

Two others who faded from the field of contenders were John Allen, Peale's son-in-law, and diligent, self-effacing Roland Strand, a highly professional technician but not a man possessed of a grand vision or much ambition. Neither had ever been made an issue editor, which for Allen—who had aspirations of becoming editor in chief— was a particularly bitter blow. Later Wally offered him a position as head of the Reader's Digest Foundation, which after reflection, and talking the matter over with Barney McHenry, Allen declined. He subsequently realized that McHenry had wanted control over RDA philanthropies for himself.

After Thompson was made editor in chief, he sidetracked Allen into public relations. Thompson regarded his old ski partner as an editor who blew with the wind and was too desperate to please—personality traits which did not fit into the more professionalized editorial staff he was trying to assemble. Though PR suited Allen's extrovert sensibilities, he chafed because the slot was a distinct comedown from that of senior staff editor.

Despite his teddy-bear appearance and demeanor, Allen had a barbed sense of humor. Nor was his overbearing geniality purely genial. He could be hard on certain non-Wasp employees. Some Digesters thought that, after being bumped off the editorial track, he performed his duties as head of public relations somewhat halfheartedly.

PEOPLE now often came up to Thompson and said things like "Gee, I can't wait to see how you're going to change it." His standard reply was "If you see it change, I've gone too fast."

Despite such protestations, Thompson did early on make a number of changes both large and small. By 1976, reprints from other magazines had fallen into such low repute that nearly 80 percent of the *Digest*'s contents was original material, including plants. That figure was all the more astounding because planting itself had all but ceased and most of the originals were simply presented as such, without the fig leaf of "preprinting."

The only reason that planting endured as long as it did was that it balanced the rapid growth of original articles. Planting helped give the *Digest* at least the appearance of still being a reprint magazine. But the time did come, early in his reign, when Thompson quashed planting altogether.

Thompson was also determined to introduce more and better investigative journalism into the pages of the *Digest* and not just round up the usual suspects month after month—Communists, union leaders, Democrats in Congress. In July 1977 he achieved some success in a low-key article titled "Skin Cancer: The Avoidable Killer," by Donald Robinson, when the *Digest* broke the story that President Lyndon Johnson had undergone a secret operation for skin cancer while president.

Subsequently, the president's widow, Lady Bird Johnson, told the *New York Times* she had no knowledge of such an operation. His personal physician, Admiral George G. Burkley, insisted that the so-called cancer actually consisted of small sunspots and callus-like growths called hyperkeratoses which had been removed from the back of Johnson's hands. He added that the keratoses contained no evidence of cancer.

The issue became a minor media event not because anyone thought the president's health had ever been in serious jeopardy but because the *Digest*'s story raised the question of whether secrecy had been maintained on a medical matter. Ultimately, the question was resolved—and the *Digest* vindicated—when a navy official confirmed that Johnson did have secret surgery for skin cancer on his ankle, even though the surgery had not been entered into Johnson's log for the date of the surgery, October 16, 1967.

Another change instituted by Thompson in the early years of his editorship was the addition of two departments, "An Encouraging Word" and "Notes from All Over"—the first in a decade. The use of filler material was also reduced—from a high of 1,887 separate items in his first year, for an average of 157 fillers per issue, to a low of 1,573 in 1982, or 131 an issue. About 50 percent of those published were submitted by readers. Overall reader submissions in a typical year continued to be astronomical. In 1978 alone, more than 385,000 pieces of mail, or about 1,500 per workday, arrived in Pleasantville from readers eager to sell the *Digest* a joke, filler, or anecdote.

On a more informal note, Thompson reintroduced the wearing of casual clothes, particularly on warm summer days—sports shirts for men, simple dresses for women. As always, fashion at Pleasantville was dictated by trends among top management. During the regime of the well-tailored Lewis, editors feared being embarrassed if summoned unexpectedly to a conference where they might have to sit in short sleeves while their boss presided in his hand-tailored suit.

By far, though, the biggest change instituted by Ed Thompson related to advertising. Early on, Thompson asked the founder for his views on finally accepting liquor advertising in the *Digest*. Wally replied that his only concern was the good name of the magazine. But he did not come right out and forbid liquor advertisements. In March 1978, during a party thrown by the *Digest* advertising staff to celebrate its best first half in history, word came that Wally had decided to lift the magazine's prohibition against beer and wine advertising. Since revenues were up 16 percent, to $32.4 million, for the half, there was obviously no economic necessity behind the decision. The *RD* simply cited changing times.

The decision to consult Wally on the question of advertising was unavoidable, given the magnitude of the change in policy. But it was the last time his advice was sought on anything of consequence. Increasingly, *Digest* policy was being made, on large issues and small, by company executives who often simply chose not to inform the founder and owner of some inevitable project or policy change he would only have needlessly held up. Even as he moved into advanced old age, the Reader's Digest Association was shifting into the post-Wallace era. Some insiders even thought Wally had begun to grow a little bored with the *Digest,* after more than a half century, and in a larger sense that was true. Details no longer concerned him as they had in the past, nor was it possible for him to keep up with all developments in the company's vast international operations.

Yet he continued to receive regularly updated inventories of articles purchased by the *Digest*—still his only real love—and it was simply not possible for anything to appear in its pages, whether relating to editorial, advertising, or other matters, without his knowledge and approval.

———

UNLIKE Wally or Hobe Lewis, editor in chief Ed Thompson did not run the RDA absolutely, but was obliged to share power with a co-equal on the business side. His partner in publishing was John A. O'Hara, an intense, dark-haired Scotsman known as Jack to his friends, who had once upon a time hoped to spend the remainder of his corporate career in Mexico—so much so that he had twice refused Walter Hitesman's offer to return to the United States to take over CB/SS (Condensed Books Single Sales). O'Hara and his family also thought it wise to keep at arm's length from all the political turmoil in Pleasantville.

The RDA's international troubleshooter, the Dr. Fix-It of marketing operations on four continents, had joined the *Digest* back in 1961. During his original interview with Terence Harmon, chairman of RDA Ltd. of London, O'Hara was cautioned, "If you join, you must understand you will have to determine by osmosis what the company wants because you will not be told by DeWitt Wallace."

Hired for a midlevel position in the company's direct-mail operation, O'Hara was put to work with Victor Ross, whom he later came to revere as a "genius" of marketing. At that time the London office of the RDA was one of the company's stellar successes, employing 350 people. The British edition enjoyed an extraordinary one million circulation, the largest of any magazine in the United Kingdom. Few people, including O'Hara himself at the time of his hiring, were aware it was an American-owned publication.* There was no highly centralized command issuing a stream of memos and bulletins. The RDA Ltd., like its U.S. counterpart, depended on strong individuals to understand what Wallace wanted.

O'Hara also worked with Peter Glemser, head of General Books and the London office's number two man, who virtually invented the technology that enabled a publisher to determine the market for a book before it was published. Glemser's brilliant stroke was to "pretest" the "publishability" of a book by means of random questionnaires designed to determine the degree of reader interest. A form letter asked readers to tick off the subjects in which they were most interested—history of man, camping, gardening, Bible dictionary, great scientists, world atlas. Respondents were then requested to indicate their level of interest in another column, where the choices ranged from "would order" or "might order" to "some interest" or "no interest."

After the questionnaires were returned and collated, Glemser and his associates made their decision to produce a book on the basis of availability of material and projected production and translation costs, since the plan also called for marketing the book in as many countries as possible, including the United States. The result, published in 1963, was *The Reader's Digest Great World Atlas,* which ultimately sold in the millions in many languages, became the forerunner of a long string of successful books, and created the pattern for similar operations in the United States and elsewhere. In some places, such as South Africa, the book even sold more than 100 percent of its print run because respondents ordered multiple copies and the book had to be reprinted—a rare postmarketing procedure.

Though direct-mail wizard Walter Weintz had proposed, back in 1950, that a book club be established because publishing one-shots

---

*It was a point of pride (and certainly of amusement) among Digesters that readers of foreign editions did not know that the *Digest* was a U.S.-owned magazine.

was an inefficient use of the RDA's mailing list, the company had not abandoned specials. Rather, in order to get as much mileage out of the list as possible, Al Cole and Wally had set up an informal specials departments run, at first, by *RD* managing editor Fritz Dashiell after he relinquished his post. Before long the RDA had gone beyond cannibalizing past issues of the magazine and was exploiting the *Digest* name to sell anthologies of mystery or Bible stories or titles like *Our Human Body—Its Wonders and Its Care.*

But the spectacular success of *Great World Atlas* soon led to far more ambitious plans to publish books designed with international appeal and a minimum of translation hassle in mind. Early sequels included *Marvels and Mysteries of the Animal World* (1964), *Great Painters and Great Paintings* (1965), and in 1966 the first *Reader's Digest Almanac.*

In 1963 O'Hara transferred to the almost nonexistent international book division in the United States, which was closely monitored by Wally. Like Condensed Books, it was a fiefdom whose growth and direction he wanted to make sure remained within certain editorial parameters. At the time, Wally was still reluctant to allow the United States to produce similar megabooks designed for international consumption. When Walter Hitesman tried to convince him that the RDA should do a book on gardening, Wally replied that the American public already had too many such books from which to choose.

O'Hara's task was to unify and simplify the RDA's worldwide marketing systems. As pretesting technology evolved, respondents in the "would order" category were subdivided into categories—"mothers," "handymen," "nature lovers," and so on. Those respondents were then sent another, more specific questionnaire, until finally the RDA felt reasonably confident that it could market a book through direct mail and be assured of an international sale well into the millions. But O'Hara had been on the job for only eight months when he was summoned by Paul Thompson.

"You're going to Stuttgart to solve problems, get special books going," Thompson told him. O'Hara, who expected to return to London, knew none of the key people in the German office and was full of misgivings. What was their attitude going to be toward an outsider? What exactly was the assignment? But he accepted, and asked Thompson for a letter to the managing director outlining his authority and role. "If you don't know what to do," Thompson merely replied, "you're not the man for the job."

Once in Germany, O'Hara found that the position was all-embracing—magazines, books, records, promotions, product development. His German colleagues proved to be especially hardworking and efficient. Four months later Thompson and Harmon showed up in Stuttgart for a review. At a luncheon attended by all the company's top officials, Thompson pulled out the letter he had written four months earlier—before O'Hara had asked for it—which outlined his authority and role. While everyone watched, Thompson tore it up.

That incident was to remain in O'Hara's mind the perfect illustration of what the RDA was all about. Employees were expected to read Wally's mind. Those who were tuned in could.

After leaving Germany, O'Hara returned to London as head of Condensed Books, coordinating editorial, promotion, and marketing. A year later he moved on to Canada to oversee marketing operations, then was named managing director of the Australian and New Zealand editions for eighteen months. From January 1970 to November 1972, he was in Mexico, where he found the operation in a terrible state because of inflation and closed down the Brazilian, Chilean, and Argentine companies.

Then one day in 1973 circulation director Gordon Grossman called and told O'Hara that this was the last call. Paul Thompson, O'Hara's original mentor, was now gone, and there was no one in Pleasantville to look after his interests. Hitesman had also been forced into early retirement by his enemies—primarily Kent Rhodes and Dick Waters. (The ouster of Hitesman so upset Wally that three weeks later he apologized to Laurance Rockefeller, the RDA's new trustee, for having accepted the resignation.) Yet another big upheaval on the business side—still more fallout from the firing of Fred Thompson—seemed in the offing. Like Paul Thompson before him, O'Hara realized that if he did not move to Pleasantville, he would shortly be working for someone who used to work for him. Later he talked to Lewis, who asked him to take over international operations.

Years later, after Lewis himself was exiled to New York, he proposed to Wally in a long memo that O'Hara become president. The office had been vacant since Lewis's departure, and jockeying and lobbying for the position among upper-management people was intense. At the same time, the only advice Lewis had given to his successor Ed Thompson was "Don't let them make you president." In the event, production head Rhodes succeeded to the office for a one-year term. The title was his reward for a lifetime of service with the company, and Wally had previously asked O'Hara whether he would mind the wait. O'Hara said he did not.

Meanwhile, with Thompson's appointment, there was widespread sentiment that Pleasantville needed new blood not just on the editorial side but in the business ranks as well. Rhodes and treasurer Dick Waters, the company's two highest-ranking executives, belonged to the generation of Paul Thompson and Lewis. Rhodes was set to retire, but Waters clearly wanted to run the company.

As a result, Cross, O'Hara, Ed Thompson, and Recorded Music head George V. Grune banded together and told Wally they could no longer work with Waters. His erratic track record, they argued, ranging from Funk & Wagnalls to Hollywood, had been less than impressive.

Just a few months previously, Wally had urged each of the five and a few others to sign up for an Outward Bound expedition into the Colorado wilderness to improve teamwork and leadership. But all Waters could envision was himself halfway up the side of a sheer cliff, with his life in the hands of Cross on the ledge above, dangling a rope. Not liking that prospect, the embattled treasurer sent an assistant in his stead. No doubt troubled by similar suspicions, all the others did likewise.

After receiving the anti-Waters delegation, Wally summoned his treasurer, whom he had hired long ago on the recommendation of his outside accountant Oscar Weldon, to High Winds. The two men remained very close. Secretly, Lila also still depended on Waters to funnel her a couple of hundred thousand dollars every now and then to spend on a painting she did not want Wally to know about. But if Waters's colleagues refused to work with him, that would present a serious problem. No specific charges were discussed.

"You have a job here as long as you want," Wally promised.

But Waters—like Paul Thompson, ousted in a similar coup years earlier—knew he was through. In typical fashion, Wally was not choosing sides but letting Digesters fight it out among themselves. Having no other option, Waters resigned to become associate dean of the Harvard Business School, his alma mater.

Thus on January 1, 1977, Jack O'Hara received the appointment as president and head of the RDA's vast business operations. Wally told him, "Very few men deserve to be made president." Significantly, though, he asked Ed Thompson to make the announcement personally—a subtle, two-edged message to the editor that, unlike Lewis, he was not worthy to be made president but shared with him equal executive billing. Rhodes, at the same time, was made chairman, while Lewis departed from the company altogether.

A year later President O'Hara also got the nod—to Thompson's chagrin—to become the company's next CEO. It was a position the editor in chief wanted for himself. Lewis had held both positions, three in fact—CEO, editor in chief, and, after Hitesman was forced out in 1973, president. Most Digesters thought Thompson was slated for the position, owing to his demonstrable flair for business and to the *Digest* tradition, as quasi-hallowed as that at the *New Yorker,* of having an editor in the top slot.

But the board of directors, according to outside director and former Chemical Bank chairman Harold Helm, thought that the forty-nine-year-old O'Hara had "the best-rounded background." The mandate it gave the new CEO was to transform what had essentially been a one-man show for fifty years or more into a conventionally organized and operated corporation.

The main factor behind O'Hara's selection was the growing importance of the RDA's nonmagazine and foreign operations. Recently, the company had surpassed annual sales of one billion dollars, with foreign editions of the *Digest* alone accounting for 17 percent of that amount. Hardcover books, both domestic and foreign, contributed another third of the sales total, with foreign sales providing a relatively higher profit margin, thanks to lower editorial and production costs and, in some cases, to a stronger foreign currency. Records, music tapes and cassettes, audio equipment, educational materials, QSP (the school fund-raising program), and such assorted items sold through the mail as globes and commemorative stamps now collectively accounted worldwide for the remaining third.

The appointment of Britisher Jack O'Hara was also a quiet signal that the RDA, the world's largest purveyor of the American way of life, had become a truly global company and that it was now in the business of packaging not merely a national but an international version of right-wing Americanism through its profiles of American figures, staunch support of American foreign policy, and espousal of conservative positions on a variety of other issues.

There was a problem, however. While Thompson was no editorial alter ego of DeWitt Wallace, O'Hara was very much in the mold of

Wally the old-fashioned, or perhaps merely unfashionable, anti-entre-preneur who saw no need for the company to make more profit than necessary. Thompson and others in the company, especially former advertising salesmen George Grune (O'Hara's replacement as director of Books & Recorded Music) and Richard McLoughlin (director of magazine operations), thought the company's future lay in diversifica-tion. In particular, Thompson wanted to focus on nonmagazine opera-tions both in the United States and abroad and saw the biggest oppor-tunity for growth in Japan, Korea, and Latin America.

O'Hara, though, who had a reputation as a skillful manager, thought his first priority was to review the RDA's operations and recommend changes in procedures. To that end he brought in a team of outside consultants, who after several months remained baffled by the way the company's unorthodox management system worked and who de-parted, in the words of one Pleasantville executive, "with a nice fee and their tail between their legs."

Nevertheless, O'Hara did gradually begin to straighten out the lines of authority. Thompson, of course, remained unquestionably in charge of all editorial operations and was accountable to no one but the board—meaning, in other words, only to Wally himself so long as he lived and, presumably, to no one at all thereafter, since the board was perceived as little more than a rubber-stamp operation.

On the business side O'Hara became the only man since Wally retired to whom all operations reported directly. According to one vice-president, attempts at long-range planning and budgeting had previously been "a pulling-something-out-of-the-air kind of thing" and performance reviews had been done "on the back of an enve-lope." O'Hara introduced tighter procedures and tougher cost con-trols, instituted the RDA's first job-evaluation program, hired a spe-cialist to teach supervisors how to manage, and, like Thompson, scheduled more frequent staff meetings.

To emphasize his authority, O'Hara also decided that the office which had earlier suited a Hobe Lewis, a Walter Hitesman, and a Kent Rhodes was not big enough. After evicting or displacing several editors from their offices, the new CEO created along the front corridor a new, improved executive office for himself that was exactly the same size as Thompson's.

Yet the future ownership of the company remained a mystery. Looking into its crystal ball, *Business Week* declared, "The trust's beneficiaries are known only to the Wallaces, their legal and financial advisers, and perhaps no one else. What does seem clear is that the trust's purpose is to assure the continued publication of the *Digest* as a privately held enterprise."

THE long-simmering feud between Pleasantville and its far-flung colonies over the question of editorial independence came to a head in 1977, the second year of Ed Thompson's reign, when the new editor in chief convened the *Digest*'s first worldwide editorial conference, at the Jackson Hole Lodge, in Jackson Hole, Wyoming.

As in the days of Hobe Lewis, most American editors still opposed emancipation. Led by Oursler and Gilmore, they believed that when DeWitt Wallace founded the *Reader's Digest,* he created a homespun, plain-talking, not-a-word-wasted, pocket- or purse-sized magazine that spoke in the idiom of America itself. They boasted that in its fifty-odd years it had become not only a national but a global institution, the real voice of America, tickling the world's funnybone with chuckle-packed anecdotes and then scaring its pants off with another revelation about international communism. Inherent in that message was the role of the United States as global peacekeeper, exemplar of democracy, and nondenominational Christian missionary to unbelievers. Not surprisingly, decentralization and multiculturalism, the leitmotifs of the Jackson Hole meeting, struck conservative Digesters as threats to the very identity of the magazine.

But the legacy and spirit of Maurice Ragsdale, Bruce Lee, Alain de Lyrot, and other would-be emancipators lived on in the hundreds of foreign editors, the RDA's own miniature United Nations, who thought the time was now ripe for decentralization. For them the *Digest*'s uniqueness lay not in its Americanness but in its universality. Admittedly, DeWitt Wallace had started out advocating some very old-fashioned American concepts of human nature, politics and art, sex and humor, education and the work ethic. But that vision had transcended its origins. Not the average Middle American, but Everyman, was now the common reader.

Proof was that the *Digest* was now published in thirty-two editions in thirteen languages, with an estimated worldwide readership in excess of one hundred million people—more than the population of most countries. Implicit in the simmering rebellion in the colonies was the view that the latter-day America Firstism of the RDA was anachronistic, as was its white, Anglo-Saxon, right-wing Republican orthodoxy.

In his welcoming address Thompson stood before the scores of editors from around the world and said, in effect, "Let a hundred flowers bloom. Let diverse schools of thought contend." But Tony Oursler, an admirer of Churchill, when he heard Thompson's summons to cultural pluralism in the pages of the *Digest,* complained to a colleague, "Bang go the colonies." Other conservatives, particularly those from the Washington bureau, such as right-wing firebrand Bill Schulz, who had succeeded Gilmore as head of the department, were incensed. Immediately after the talk, the right-wingers met in ad hoc sessions to figure out how to batten down the hatches again. Some thought their best hope lay in bringing in Cold Warrior Melvin Laird, whose name was the most prominent one on the magazine's masthead, now that he was senior counselor. Though Schulz was cynical about Laird's "standard Rotary speech," as he called it, it was better than nothing and might dampen the sudden enthusiasm about emancipation.

Laird agreed to address the conference and the next day stood before the same sea of expectant delegates from around the world. With blundering insensitivity, he began, "I've just been on a tour of Europe for the White House. The only country in the Western alliance that has a chief executive is the U.S.A. All the others are politicians."

Laird's blindered glorification of the United States and patronizing ridicule of other countries, even its Western allies, hit his audience like a hand grenade. Afterward Lin Tai-wi, the corpulent, tough-minded editor of the Taiwan edition, stood up to complain. In a voice choked with rage, she said, "My country has always had to deal with Western barbarians." She went on for a full three minutes, then collapsed in a heap and was fanned by her acolytes.

Raul Singh, the editor of the English-language Indian edition, also stood up. "Mr. Laird," he said, "your speech has taken me back to John Foster Dulles." But then he stopped, realizing he was already in dangerous territory. Later Ko Shioya, editor of the Japanese edition, politely disagreed with some of Laird's views.

Thompson himself was virtually oblivious to all the upheaval, commotion, and occasion for joy and consternation that he had caused. Walking away from the hotel ballroom after Laird's speech, he was approached by an editor who worked in the international editions in Pleasantville. Realizing that "something amazing" was happening, the editor said:

"Good God, Ed. Do you realize Laird just lobbed a bomb among all those people?"

"What bomb?" Thompson replied. "I didn't realize anything."

"It was like total schizophrenia," the editor later recalled. "All of the overseas editors were furious and felt insulted by this man Laird, who looked like an overgrown turtle. But on the other side were the Americans who didn't understand what had happened, or why Raul or Lin stood up and got hysterical. They probably thought she had too much to drink."

Later, at the Jackson Hole editorial summit, the *Digest*'s Washington bureau, traditionally the guardian and dispenser of the company's holiest right-wing writ, was also criticized for being so rigidly conservative. Shaking with rage, Bill Schulz stood up. Invoking the editorial legacy of DeWitt Wallace, he proclaimed that the bureau would never betray its mandate to promote the deeply conservative political philosophy of the company's founding father.

Washington staffers were paranoid in regard to what they saw as the "pinkos" in Pleasantville, according to a bureau insider, "which was ridiculous. There were no pinkos. Some were center-of-the-road Democrats, but others were very conservative, like Oursler. Yet there did come a point when the *Digest* stopped supporting the U.S. war effort in Vietnam. That caused tremendous trauma for the hard-liners."

The editors of the international editions were now free to assign articles without receiving authorization from the head of international operations—none other than ex–Washington bureau director Ken Gilmore. However, Gilmore still signed off on the editorial content of all foreign editions of the magazine and had the authority to kill any article he disapproved of and replace it with another of his own choice.

22

Cold War Hothouse

IN THE EARLY 1980s the *Digest* ordered a new computer system for its editorial offices in Pleasantville. Among those brought in to design and install the system was a young woman intrigued by the special printer reserved for the Washington bureau.

"The people in Washington were suspicious to the point of paranoia," she recalled. "Not only did they have a hit list of people they wanted to malign, but any political article had to be cleared by the bureau. So a four-way hookup was established between Pleasantville, Donnelley printing, PPI [a data base], and the Washington bureau.

"The *Digest* was not only tricky but cheap. It had initially put in clunky, poor equipment, so that they outsmarted themselves. The bureau's special printer at Pleasantville was installed in an out-of-the-way place and a message devised to alert campus editors that Washington was making corrections. The message was 'You have something waiting.' That was the euphemism for messages from Washington, which usually came late at night, when everyone was gone home, and they were also very long. Whenever the printer jammed and beeped, which was often, everyone knew Washington was on the line, furiously revising something."

In good weather, this same woman was visited by her mother, who lived nearby, during the noon hour. While eating lunch, they sat in the car in the parking lot, "watching all the zombies and making fun of them, seeing which one looked most like Dr. Strangelove."

Of particular interest was all the *Digest*'s dis (discarded) data, which the computer expert was never allowed to see. She knew only that in the basement there were "acres and acres" of such material, since the *Digest* had been computerized since the early sixties.

"And there were always these very secretive types in trench coats who went into the basement to use its records. The company had a record of everyone who ever subscribed to the magazine—all color-coded according to different parts of the country, and other data on age, sex, financial history, reading habits, your profession, what kind of car you drove, the neighborhood you lived in, and anything else pertaining to a customer's profile. There was so much information about those fifty million Americans, in fact, that nobody was allowed to work in marketing until after he or she had been with the company for six or seven years. Then the *Digest* began to feel comfortable with you and allowed you to do some travel. They were just suspicious of everyone."

Uncomfortable with the corporate environment, she decided to resign.

"I got out. I knew that nothing quite worked that way. Something was wrong. I also felt that my phone was being tapped after I left. I kept getting calls at home from people asking to talk to someone at the *Digest,* even though our number was completely different from the magazine's. Why was that? I got pretty scared for a while. It was a creepy place."

For all the prettiness of the grounds and buildings, the *Digest's* headquarters in Chappaqua was described by many people, both visitors and employees, as creepy, scary, spooky. The company's penchant for secretiveness, the long shadow cast by the Washington bureau with its close ties to the CIA and the FBI, the uncertainty about what was going to happen to the *RD* after the Wallaces died—all contributed to the slightly unreal atmosphere that seemed to pervade RDA headquarters, at least to those who presumed themselves not to look like Dr. Strangelove.

Yet a curious thing was happening at the *Digest* under Ed Thompson—it was becoming at once more liberal and more right-wing, like a rubber band being stretched at both ends. The liberalizing trend was reflected less in anything so radical as an article or two espousing Democratic doctrine than in a tendency no longer to adhere to a rigid ideological line, to present more than one point of view, and to criticize once sacred icons—Richard M. Nixon, for example. More precisely, the magazine was being transformed into a genuinely dynamic conservative publication—one with incomparable financial, research, and other resources—willing to place a greater premium on objectivity and investigative journalism than on partisan politics.

In an effort to get to the bottom of assorted spy-related and other stories, for example, the *RD* was routinely filing Freedom of Information Act (FOIA) requests with the CIA and then suing the agency in court when those requests were summarily turned down. On several occasions, notably concerning Captain Nikolai Artamonov, also known as Nicholas Shadrin, the *Digest* launched a full-scale suit for agency records.

Shadrin was a Russian naval officer who defected to the United States in 1959 with his Polish fiancée and later obtained a midlevel position as an intelligence analyst for the Pentagon. In 1966 he was approached by the KGB, which was ostensibly interested in reconverting him into a mole. Shadrin went to his superiors, who asked him to begin providing his new KGB handlers with FBI-fed information about American intelligence operations. In 1975 Shadrin and his wife went to Europe on assignment, using a skiing trip as cover, to meet with KGB officials on the front steps of a church in Vienna. Then he vanished. His frantic wife repeatedly demanded an explanation.

One ex post facto rationalization was that Shadrin had been sacrificed as part of a larger intelligence operation. But there was a lingering suspicion within the intelligence community that the CIA had fallen into a trap and blundered. Amateur spymaster Tony Oursler, in an attempt to uncover the events leading to Shadrin's disappearance, forced the issue in a costly series of FOIA suits against the CIA, FBI, and Department of Justice that dragged on for years.

Oursler "did not become a dissident right away," according to one editor who worked with him. "He did not start attacking things he regarded as shallow like the FBI and the CIA until after Thompson became editor in chief instead of him. Then he became a rebel—to embarrass Ed."

Ultimately, the *Digest* won a Pyrrhic victory in its FOIA litigation involving Shadrin. The CIA released several hundred heavily censored documents, while withholding thousands more. As a result, for all its trouble, the *Digest* learned virtually nothing new, and the Shadrin case remained unsolved.

At the same time, such litigation served only to widen the breach between Pleasantville and its Washington bureau, which remained defiantly protective of the agency. Politicized, partisan, and paranoid, the bureau had been serving as a primary conduit for CIA and FBI propaganda, self-promotion, and disinformation since the days of Allen Dulles and J. Edgar Hoover. As a result senior members of the bureau looked on Thompson, Oursler, and their lukewarm conservative ilk with all the venomous animosity that right-winters in the fifties reserved for Alger Hiss and other pinkos in the State Department.

———

FOR the first thirty years of its existence, despite a recent spate of tell-all books by ex-agents Victor Marchetti, James Agee, and others, nothing substantive had ever been published on the murky relationship between the CIA and the media. In October 1977, however, former *Washington Post* reporter Carl Bernstein electrified media watchers everywhere with his sensational claim that four hundred American journalists, including correspondents of the *New York Times,* CBS, and a dozen other organizations, had secretly shared and sometimes provided operational assistance to the CIA over the past twenty-five years.

Among the individuals who worked closely with the agency, according to Bernstein, were C. L. Sulzberger, foreign-affairs columnist for the *Times;* brothers Joseph and the late Stewart Alsop, both of whom wrote nationally syndicated columns; and CBS chairman William S. Paley. Bernstein also accused the upper management of Reuters, UPI, the *Miami Herald,* and the Hearst chain.

In the ensuing uproar, executives at NBC and ABC news, the *New York Times,* AP, *Time,* and *Newsweek* said they were unable to uncover any evidence that their employees had maintained confidential relationships with the CIA over the past quarter century. Sulzberger adamantly denied the accusation (though it was later confirmed by his own newspaper). Iphigene Ochs Sulzberger, widow of Arthur Hays Sulzberger, the late publisher of the *Times,* added that her husband had once told her that the CIA had approached the paper and asked to use it as a cover and that he had refused.

The *Digest,* then as now not considered a major player in the media, did not merit even a mention by Bernstein. Yet at the time the RDA enjoyed an intimate relationship with the agency perhaps unmatched by any other major American communications giant, with the exception of Time-Life.

On the official level, Hobe Lewis, like Arthur Hays Sulzberger, had been approached by the CIA with a similar offer. Some believe that, unlike Sulzberger, he agreed to cooperate, a charge Lewis has denied. In the late sixties, for example, the *RD*'s editor in chief walked into the office of treasurer Dick Waters, accompanied by two men whom he introduced as agents of the CIA. After informing Waters that he had passed a background check, Lewis revealed that the CIA wanted to put some of its agents on the *Selecciones* payroll in Peru—an arrangement that might eventually come to Waters's attention.

Waters agreed to go along with the plan. But two months later the liberal press in Peru was in an uproar over CIA infiltration of universities and other national institutions. Though *Selecciones* was not implicated, on that occasion, its newest staffers quickly departed.

The CIA had also approached Harry Morgan with an offer of financial assistance when he was running the World Press Institute and traveling around the country trying to raise money. He declined. The only person he later told about the incident was Wally, who assured him he had done the right thing. But Morgan did notice that several of the dirt-poor West African journalists who joined the WPI program, especially those from Nigeria and Ghana, suddenly had a lot of money by the time they returned home.

In 1975 the Church committee—a special Senate committee headed by Idaho Democrat Frank Church that had been established to investigate the past activities of American intelligence agencies—began looking for evidence of illegal or improper CIA activities. A consultant to the Church committee named Fred Landis, a specialist in propaganda analysis, interviewed former CBS Moscow correspondent Sam Jaffe, Jr., who had been keeping a file on CIA-media ties. Jaffe suspected that the relationship between the agency and the *Digest* extended beyond that of propaganda outlet and was institutionalized. What CIA propaganda the *RD* did print, according to Jaffe, was merely the result of disgruntled former agents expressing their views through the medium of sympathetic editors.

Landis himself suspected that the *RD* had at least the appearance of an institutional relationship with the CIA and was involved in four areas of intelligence gathering: photography, which seemed to be an unnecessary adjunct of the magazine's art and editorial departments; editorial research for articles that were never printed; market research and polls; and special projects.

When Marxist-Socialist Salvador Allende was elected president of Chile in 1970, according to Landis, the *Digest* sent a reporter to remote areas of the country to investigate industrial accidents in the country's copper mines. Previously, a Finnish newspaper had accused a *Digest* employee of being a CIA agent for taking photographs of a copper mine. Though the reporter's research never resulted in a published article, the CIA soon afterward organized a strike among Chile's copper workers. In Landis's view, this was a classic example of psychological warfare—workers striking against a workers' government.

———

THE *Digest* had, of course, started up many of its foreign editions in cooperation with the State Department as part of its war effort. But material support from the government almost certainly went no further than accepting priority status for paper shipments and using the air force and other service-controlled transportation facilities to distribute the troop and other editions.

Furthermore, the *Digest* had specifically declined the offer of a subsidy from the U.S. government for an international edition. But unofficial editorial cooperation was another matter. After the war many of the international editions continued to serve as prime fonts of anti-Communist propaganda—in particular, *Selecciones,* the Latin American edition, and *Selezione,* the Italian, which had been begun in direct response to the threat posed by the Communist party in the 1948 national elections.

Besides Terence Harmon, the former British intelligence officer who had started up the Italian edition and later been named general manager of international operations, a significant number of other *Digest* editors on the foreign editions also had backgrounds in intelligence or propaganda-related operations—notably, Dennis McEvoy and Mateo Okini in Japan; Eduardo Cárdenas, first director of *Selecciones,* who had previously managed the Editor's Press Service, identified by ex-agent James Agee in his book *CIA Diary* as an agency proprietary; Alain de Lyrot, editor of *Sélection* in France; André Visson, also of *Sélection,* an editorial jack-of-all-trades who had once worked for Radio Liberty, also a CIA proprietary; and Adrian Berwick, who had once headed the Office of War Information's Overseas News and Features Bureau.

Many others on the U.S. edition were alumni of the OSS, the Office of Naval Intelligence, or other intelligence-related government agencies. These were men drawn to Pleasantville not as part of any official understanding between the magazine and the CIA or FBI, but simply because the *Digest* was a good place to work and offered an atmosphere that was, for true Cold Warriors, ideologically congenial. All during the fifties and sixties, after all, with Wally's open approval and encouragement, J. Edgar Hoover used the Washington bureau much as if it were his own personal PR firm.

But in such a climate it was perhaps inevitable that some Digesters—particularly editors and staff writers in the Washington bureau, as well as free-lancers handled by the same office—would enter into a much cozier relationship with both the FBI and the CIA. Over the years the *Digest*'s bylines on espionage-related activities amounted to a veritable Who's Who of CIA upper management and fellow-traveling journalists.

The years just before and after the publication of Bernstein's exposé, for example, had seen a curious string of coincidences relating to *Digest* contributors and the world of espionage. In 1975 journalist Edward Hughes, on assignment for the *RD* in Lebanon, was detained by security forces and accused of being a member of an Israeli assassination squad that killed three Palestinians in Beirut in 1972. Hughes, not a *Digest* regular, called the charge "a load of rubbish" but was ousted from the country.

In early 1976 the Ford administration began planning a thorough revision of its program for dealing with international terrorism. New approaches emerged at the end of a confidential two-day conference sponsored by the State Department which drew two hundred specialists from four countries to Washington. Reporters were banned from the conference on the ground that the participants "could talk more frankly," explained a State Department official after ejecting a reporter. But two journalists were allowed to remain as participants: Eugene H. Methvin, of the *Digest*'s Washington bureau, and Robert Moss, an editor of the *Economist,* whose CIA connections had recently been disclosed in the press.

Toward the end of 1978 the *Digest* also ran a posthumous article by David Holden on the Middle East. The year before, Holden had been shot to death in Cairo, and headlines in the British press had linked him to the CIA. The *Sunday Times* later sued the CIA to obtain Holden's file. One CIA report noted that Holden had been sent to cover Allende's Chile for the *Digest* and that he was a close friend of John ("Dimi") Panitza, a Bulgarian-born aristocrat who headed the *RD*'s Paris bureau.

Two other old *Digest* hands were Professor William E. Griffith and

Charles J. V. Murphy, a former reporter for *Fortune,* both of whom played percussion in the magazine's anti-Communist marching band. In his *Rolling Stone* article, Bernstein identified Griffith—along with Zbigniew Brzezinski, then professor of political science at MIT, and CBS News president Richard Salant—as a member of a four-man "supersecret CIA task force which explored methods of beaming American propaganda broadcasts to the People's Republic of China."

Griffith had been the agency's main liaison at Radio Free Europe until 1958, when he left to join MIT's Center for International Studies—then sponsored and partly funded by the CIA. As an *RD* roving editor, Griffith traveled frequently to Asia, Europe, and particularly Africa, where he was routinely accorded priority VIP treatment by the local U.S. embassy or consulate. Griffith's academic specialty was guerrilla counterinsurgency.

The *New York Times,* in its subsequent investigation into CIA media operations, learned that Murphy, while on the *Digest*'s payroll, was asked by Allen Dulles, after he left as CIA director in 1961, to help him write his memoirs. Murphy was actually given office space in the agency's headquarters, though that arrangement was terminated soon after it was discovered by Dulles's successor, John McCone. Another close CIA friend of Murphy's was James Jesus Angleton, former head of counterintelligence.

The *Digest*'s broad relationship with the CIA extended even to editorial apprentices. On two separate occasions in the midseventies, while the agency was under intense public scrutiny owing to the revelations in Bernstein's article, the *Times*'s series, and other media exposés, researcher Chris Kirby was assigned the task of fact checking an article whose main purpose was to serve as a CIA halo. In both cases the pro forma procedure was identical. Accompanying Bill Schulz in the first instance and Gilmore in the second, Kirby was ushered through five layers of security at agency headquarters, in Langley, Virginia, until he and his companion reached the inner sanctum—the office of CIA chief William Colby.

During both meetings, the normally reserved, cerebral Colby became expansive and talkative. After details of the article were verified, a perfunctory process lasting about ten minutes, the conversation turned to CIA activities around the world. Though no expert in espionage and counterinsurgency, Kirby realized that much of Colby's discourse covered information not on public record. After about an hour and a half, the senior Digester thanked Colby for the briefing and, trailed by his "researcher," departed.

—

INDISPUTABLY, the Washington bureau's heavyweight, the man with the best sources in the CIA, FBI, and other government agencies, its farthest-right ideologue and most prolific author, was John Barron, who reminded some people of a revivalist preacher. A protégé of Ken Gilmore, Barron had formerly worked at the *Washington Evening Star* with Jeremiah O'Leary, the godfather of Washington's conservative journalists. Previously, Barron had served with the Office of Naval Intelligence. While stationed in Berlin, he held the title of officer in charge of clandestine operations.

Among Barron's early articles for the *RD* was a 1968 election-year propaganda piece called "Time for Reform in the IRS," which castigated the agency for the "vicious pressures" used by collectors that degraded them and taxpayers alike. In 1974 he published his first full-length work on Soviet espionage—*KGB: The Secret Work of Soviet Secret Agents,* a fervent account of Russian infiltration of assorted sanctums of Western intelligence and policy-making. The information had been leaked to Barron by J. Edgar Hoover, who did not want the Soviets to open a consulate in Chicago. So predigested was the research that, after delivering the manuscript to the publisher (the Reader's Digest Press, then being run by Lee), Barron flew off to visit various European capitals and other destinations simply to leave research tracks.

The *New York Times* later declared that the CIA had an "operational purpose" in assisting Barron with the writing of the book. (Hobe Lewis, too, suspected a close link between the agency and Barron, but with characteristic insouciance never bothered to investigate.) Some agency critics speculated that the book was also the CIA's response to Agee's *CIA Diary,* which contained two appendixes listing the names of, respectively, CIA officers and front organizations. Barron's book contained a fifty-one-page appendix returning the favor.

Though *KGB* was widely ignored, it did attract the attention of a man named Ilya Wolston, who found his name in a list, elsewhere in the book, of Soviet agents allegedly indicted on or convicted of espionage-related charges. The phrasing of the paragraph resulted from a collaboration between house counsel Barnabas McHenry and Barron but reflected the latter's belief that Wolston was dead.

Not long after the book appeared, the allegedly dead alleged agent, who lived in Barron's hometown of Washington, D.C., showed up with a powerful D.C. law firm behind him and sued the *Digest* for libel.

The suit, which had profound repercussions for the publishing industry, turned on the right to privacy because no one had written about the man for more than twenty-five years. Lee later discovered that Barron had been "somewhat ingenuous in revealing his sources" and that McHenry had made a judgment call. Representing the RDA was former special counsel to the president Joseph Califano, whom the company had been keeping on a $1,000-a-month retainer for years. McHenry finally decided to put him to work.

Wolston, in fact, had been arrested a quarter of a century earlier, but never indicted. In 1958 he pleaded guilty to criminal contempt of court for failing to honor a subpoena issued by a grand jury investigating Soviet espionage. Wolston was the nephew of Jack Soble, who did plead guilty to espionage charges. Just before Wolston was to testify before a grand jury, however, his wife and doctor announced he had suffered a nervous breakdown and was unable to appear in court.

The lower courts, holding that Wolston was a public figure, granted summary judgment in favor of the *RD*. Wolston appealed. In June 1979 the case went to the Supreme Court, which overturned the ruling, saying there was no such thing as an involuntary public figure, as the *Digest* had claimed in its defense.* The Court further agreed that Wolston was entitled to a trial. As a result of the ruling, the *Digest* settled with Wolston out of court for a substantial six-figure sum.

Another person who took notice of the book was ex-CIA agent Joseph Burkholder Smith, who later revealed in his own memoir that the agency had sent Barron a Soviet defector with a story it had simply made up. According to Smith the "CIA then assisted John Barron with material for his book *KGB: The Secret World of Soviet Secret Agents.* He also used our story."

Despite those small embarrassments, Barron flourished as the magazine's Coldest Warrior, becoming in the process the closest thing the

---

*In order for a public figure—generally, anyone who has been in the news in the recent past—to collect damages in a libel suit, he or she must prove "actual malice" on the part of the defendant. The *RD* argued that Wolston, at the time of his criminal conviction, was ipso facto a public figure, in which case Wolston would have to prove Barron acted maliciously. A six-member majority of the Supreme Court disagreed that Wolston was a public figure, arguing that an individual who has not sought publicity is not required to prove "actual malice" on the part of the defendant when suing for libel.

Digest had to a nationally prominent journalist, or at least one whose name was recognized by people other than *RD* subscribers. Like Oursler, Barron was an expert in espionage. Unlike Oursler, he did not have to sue the CIA to find out what he wanted. Both the agency and the bureau were only too willing to feed him information on KGB activities that was unobtainable anywhere else.

The trademark sensationalism of routine, bureau-sponsored KGB horror stories and other cloak-and-dagger tales seldom made them newsworthy. An exception was a May 1976 "signer"—*RD* slang for a ghostwritten piece—by former defense secretary Melvin Laird, claiming that the CIA had in recent years twice foiled assassination attempts on elected U.S. officials and that the agency had thwarted plans to kill prominent American Jews with letter bombs. Laird was under contract to front for four articles a year; many were ghosted by Barron.

In the same article, Laird revealed that the CIA had also uncovered military preparations by one non-Communist government to invade another. "Details cannot yet be made public," Laird confided. "But we quickly and privately brought the countries together, laid out the facts, induced them to negotiate. C.I.A. espionage thus prevented a war."

Subsequently, Laird refused to identify the objects of the bomb plots but said the CIA learned that two cars containing Soviet-made explosives had been left in midtown Manhattan on March 4, 1973, while Prime Minister Golda Meir of Israel was visiting the city. The cars contained enough explosives to "kill everybody within a 100-yard radius." A Senate Intelligence Committee spokesman later confirmed that it had asked the CIA what procedures had been followed in releasing such information and whether intelligence sources had been compromised.

A liberal in the Pleasantville office who took a cynical view of leftist characterizations of the *Digest* as a media puppet of the CIA was associate editor Gordon Hard. The preponderance of *RD* editors, both in the United States and abroad, with OSS, ONI, or similar backgrounds was explained, according to Hard, by the fact that many journalists had worked in intelligence during the war. Leftist scenarios that had Dimi Panitza or Dennis McEvoy in something out of a spy novel were all "wrong, misleading, circumstantial."

Even so, Hard himself was appalled by what he felt was the *Digest*'s acceptance of CIA handouts at face value. A particularly galling instance was an article bearing Laird's byline and describing how the

USSR was cheating on the Strategic Arms Limitations Talks agreement of 1972, by which the two superpowers promised to limit offensive nuclear weapons. Laird claimed the Soviet Union was not dismantling its equipment fast enough and that American spies had found out. Hard double-checked the story with Paul Warnke, a SALT negotiator, and Warnke told him, "Mel is peddling that story all over town. I just wish he'd stop. He knows it's not true. The Russians aren't taking apart that base because the weather's too cold, and they can't move their trucks around up there. They told us beforehand they weren't going to do that on time. We said okay. They're going to do it next spring. We have those problems, too."

When Hard confronted Barron, who ghosted the piece, with Warnke's comments, Barron just shrugged and said, "Well, that's what Mel said. That's what Jamie [Angleton] said."

Barron also served as a principal unofficial fund-raiser for the CIA, haranguing the Democrat-controlled Congress in the pages of the *Digest* whenever a cutback in agency funding seemed imminent. As a string of cautionary tales of KGB deceit and sordid success always made clear, a reduction in the CIA budget, at the hands of liberal legislators, was more or less apocalyptical for America and Western democracy.

Not only did Barron like to report on spies, but he liked to play one. In London he once went to dinner at a respectable hotel restaurant, then afterward experienced a mysterious, life-threatening constriction of the throat. British doctors were able to save his life by injecting him with cortisone, a drug the Soviets were not very familiar with at the time. Barron later decided there was a KGB contract out on him and someone had reached the chef.

Later, when he was flying regularly to Bangkok to do a story on Cambodian genocide, Barron always took the precaution of booking five different tickets on five different days on an international flight. On each of the appointed days, his wife drove him to the airport, and Barron reconnoitered. If his suspicions were in any way aroused, they returned home. Only at the very last minute, if it seemed impossible for a KGB agent to hop onto the same plane, did Barron decide to board.

In Bangkok, Barron hooked up with Anthony Paul, head of the *Digest*'s Hong Kong office and a WPI alumnus. Paul was an Australian and something of a maverick, a good friend of Ed Thompson who thought Pleasantville was an unspeakable place, full of pompous people who were racist and xenophobic—"Americanists," in his term, rather than patriots. But he knew his way around Asia and would prove a valuable assistant. Barron told Paul he had passed a security check and later introduced him to a local KGB agent—an amiable drunk whose cover was correspondent for the Tass news agency.

The Barron-Paul collaboration ultimately resulted in *Murder of a Gentle Land*, published by Reader's Digest Press in 1977 and widely excerpted in the *Digest*'s international editions. The book was among the first to reveal the extent of the wholesale slaughter of Cambodian civilians—Barron and Paul put the figure at 1.2 million in a population of 8 million—under the brutal regime of the Khmer Rouge.

The authors' central thesis—that a tiny group of Paris-educated fanatics ("nine men at the top") had decreed the systematic massacre and starvation of the population—was challenged by leftist critic Noam Chomsky, who held that the deaths were the result not of official policy but of civil war.

The debate over the extent of Communist atrocities in Cambodia later even made the movies. In *The Killing Fields,* based on *New York Times* foreign correspondent Sydney H. Schanberg's book of the same name, the character of Schanberg—played by actor Sam Waterston—has recently returned to New York after his tour of duty, leaving behind his friend and photographer Dith Pran. At a press awards dinner, Schanberg is asked by a reporter how he would respond to the accusation that he and other (liberal) journalists underestimated the brutality of the Khmer Rouge and thus shared responsibility for what happened in Cambodia.

"We made a mistake," Schanberg replies.

"There's been a lot of refugee stories lately in the *Reader's Digest* about conditions in Cambodia," another reporter interjects, in an obvious allusion to the Barron-Paul articles.

"What's the matter?" asks Schanberg. "Don't you believe them? Maybe in this instance the *Reader's Digest* happens to be correct."

Over time the relationship between Barron and both the FBI and the CIA developed into a mutual-aid society. For example, the FBI fed Barron information on a spy case and then, during the trial, deposed him as a professional witness and even, on occasion, invited him to sit with the prosecution. Barron was also the man who usually handled Soviet defectors in the media once they had been thoroughly debriefed by the CIA and were good only for propaganda purposes.

Lila's favorite niece, Judy Acheson Thompson (right), and her husband Fred expected to inherit the kingdom of Pleasantville. Instead they got an even bigger surprise. The woman at left is not identified. (Gordon Hard)

Reader's Digest world headquarters, Chappaqua, New York, 1951. *(Time Magazine)*

At the time this photo was taken in
1951, the *Reader's Digest* was the most
successful magazine in history. Yet its
proprietors and editors were virtually
unknown (from left to right): Ken
Payne, Marc Rose, Ralph Henderson,
Lila Wallace, Paul Palmer, Wally, and
Fritz Dashiell. (Arnold Newman, *Time*)

TIME

THE WEEKLY NEWSMAGAZINE

THE DeWITT WALLACES
With scissors, paste and sunrises, 15,500,000 customers.

Boris Chaliapin

DeWitt and Lila make the cover of
Time Magazine in 1951 (© 1951 *Time
Magazine*)

Harry Morgan was the grandson Wally, the lonely grandfather figure, doted on—a hyperaltruistic, well-mannered kid who seemed too good to be true. (Macalester College)

On the *Digest*'s fiftieth anniversary in 1972, President Richard M. Nixon awarded the Medal of Freedom to DeWitt and Lila Acheson Wallace at a celebrity-studded dinner at the White House. Looking on is Pat Nixon, whose "I Say He's a Wonderful Guy" launched the *Digest*'s sixteen-year marathon effort to get her husband elected president. (Wide World)

Under the editorship of Hobart Durkin Lewis, the *Digest* witnessed its greatest triumph—its role as the voice of the Silent Majority. *(Time Magazine)*

Corporate counsel W. Barnabas McHenry once confided the secret of his success at the RDA: making no friends but "a hell of a lot of enemies." (Marilyn Yee/*New York Times* Pictures)

Executive editor Walter B. ("Bun") Mahony, the *Digest*'s ultimate civil servant, refused to accept the fact that he was not named editor in chief. Later he was demoted to copy editor for general books. (Gordon Hard)

After serving briefly as head of the Voice of America, Kenneth Y. Tomlinson returned to Pleasantville, where he succeeded Kenneth O. Gilmore as editor in chief. (USIA)

The RDA's most ardent, and perhaps only, apostle of DeWitt Wallace's corporate gospel—no unnecessary profit, always put the interests of the subscribers first—was president John A. ("Jack") O'Hara, depicted here in a line drawing by Doug Jamieson.

An ex-Marine who still jogs daily, chairman
George V. Grune oversaw the transformation of
the RDA from the largest mom-and-pop
publishing company in the world to an
international communications giant. (Duke
University)

The first thing Barron liked to do when he got hold of a defector was take him to the supermarket. "Barron would watch him, this Russian, his eyes bulging, crossing himself and genuflecting, and saying, 'My God, this abundance!'" observed one bureau insider. "Then Barron would take him home and play hymns. People laughed at all this, talked about the Barron apotheosis, the defector confronted with rows and rows of cans and stereo systems. That was Barron's shorthand for the conversion of an admitted believer in Marxism-Leninism to someone who could go whole hog for the free-enterprise system."

——

AT A New York City rally in support of Poland's Solidarity movement on February 6, 1982, left-wing critic Susan Sontag asked rhetorically, "Imagine, if you will, someone who read only the *Reader's Digest* between 1950 and 1970, and someone in the same period who read only the *Nation* or the *New Statesman*. Which reader would have been better informed about the realities of communism?" She went on to include herself among those "on the so-called democratic left" who had "willingly or unwittingly told a lot of lies" about communism in order not to aid and abet "reactionary" forces.

Like Paul Palmer, Sontag equated communism with fascism, calling it "successful fascism . . . fascism with a human face," and challenged leftists to abandon "many of the complacencies of the left . . . to abandon old and corrupt rhetoric." Sontag, in short, was asking her listeners to believe that the *Digest*'s dire warnings about communism had been right all along.

Leftist critics reacted swiftly: Noam Chomsky attacked "apologists for U.S. state terrorism," James Weinstein declared that the regime of General Pinochet of Chile was more repressive than that of Poland's General Jaruzelski, and Edward W. Said drew attention to the mistreatment of the Palestinians. The tyranny of Stalin was old news and no longer relevant.

In a postmortem on the affair in *Harper's* magazine, critic Walter Goodman noted that what particularly irked Sontag's critics was "her reference to the *Reader's Digest,* a magazine nobody reads apart from its 30 million [worldwide] subscribers. For someone on the intellectual Left to utter a kind word about the *Digest* was stupefying; the magazine is not merely reactionary, it is also lower middlebrow. It runs articles about pets."

Setting aside the question of whether communism and fascism were one and the same, Goodman suggested that the comparison between the *Digest* and the *Nation* more readily lent itself to documentation. To that end he had gone to the library to sample articles about the Soviet Union, Poland, and related matters in both magazines from the end of World War II to the era of Solidarity. He found that for the *Digest,* beginning around 1946, "the threat to peace came exclusively from Stalin's Russia," whereas for the *Nation* it came from German revanchists, British imperialists, residual fascists, and anti-Communists in Washington.

Citing the *Digest*'s 1946 excerpt of KGB defector Victor Kravchenko's *I Chose Freedom,* Goodman suggested that its tale of KGB control over the private lives of Soviet officials at home and abroad seemed "mild, as though one were to accuse the Guatemalan military of jostling." Yet the *Nation* displayed virtually no interest in such works by defectors except to suggest that they were ideologically suspect. Contributor I. F. Stone, for example, had made excuses for Stalin's arrest of sixteen Polish leaders in 1945 and three years later defended the 1939 Stalin-Hitler pact that had doomed Poland.

From the very beginning of the Cold War, of course, the *Digest* had described Russia as a dreary, dehumanizing place. But that was not what readers of the *Nation* were learning from Alexander Werth, its correspondent in Moscow, who once reported that hairdressers and manicurists were "among the busiest people in Russia now," adding, "I heard more gay laughter in the streets of Moscow than in any capital of the West."

Goodman, for his part, chastised the *Digest* for its often apocalyptic tone. "A steady diet of the *Reader's Digest* could cause indigestion. The magazine's warning drums heightened the beat of the national pulse. There were no calls for holy war, exactly, but a Salvation Army spirit resounded through its pages."

The controversy did not stop there. The *Nation* offered to reprint Sontag's Town Hall speech, explaining that the left's attitude toward communism was among its central concerns. Sontag accepted the offer but asked to revise the original speech for publication. The *Nation* agreed. When the text arrived, the editors noticed that some of her remarks had been deleted. One omitted passage concerned Sontag's celebrated contention that readers of the *Reader's Digest* between 1950 and 1970 were better informed about the "realities of Communism" than were those who read only the *Nation* or the *New Statesman.*

Meanwhile, the *SoHo News,* a New York alternative newspaper, had published an unauthorized transcription of Sontag's remarks. Media critic Alexander Cockburn, writing in the *Village Voice,* accused the *Nation* of "hypocrisy" for the apparently self-serving omission. The *New York Times* implied the same in its own story about the literary contretemps.

The *Nation* responded in an editorial, informing Cockburn, the *Times,* and its readers that the omission was Sontag's own; that it chose to publish her remarks in the first place because she had promised to talk explicitly about the magazine's coverage of communism in those decades; and that, furthermore, it thought her message was "simplistic" to begin with.

As for the merits of the comparison between itself and the *Reader's Digest,* the *Nation* said it left to others "the pleasurable task of analyzing our editorials and articles of thirty years ago." But it decided as a public service to let its readers know what they had missed by not being exposed to the *Reader's Digest* from 1950 to 1970.

First, there was the "helpful vocabulary." Communists, for example, were referred to as "Red slave drivers and sadists," while Soviet policy was "the Kremlin's harvest of hate." The *Nation* also derided the *RD*'s "bold forecasts," such as that in "Why Red China Won't Break with Russia," as well as repeated predictions of the imminent collapse of the Soviet empire. Typical "foreign policy analysis" was encapsulated in the title of an article by David Lawrence: "Is Peaceful Co-Existence the Answer?" No, said the *Digest,* it is "the counsel of despair." Finally, there were all the "menace-from-within reports" by J. Edgar Hoover, Max Eastman, Whittaker Chambers, and others.

On a "more serious matter," the *Nation* expressed disapproval of the lawsuit filed by Sontag against the *SoHo News* for copyright infringement and pointed out that it was involved in a copyright infringement case of its own. The plaintiff in the case happened to be, once again, none other than its natural adversary—the *Reader's Digest.*

——

IN EARLY *1977,* six weeks after he left the White House, former president Gerald Ford and his wife, Betty, signed a series of complex deals designed to earn them at least one million dollars for their memoirs— rather less, however, than the two million being offered to former secretary of state Henry Kissinger for a similar package.

Representing President Ford was Norman R. Brokaw of the William Morris Agency. One of the major players in the megadeal was the *Reader's Digest,* which had bought a half stake in the president's book and even obligingly arranged for one of its Washington staffers, Trevor Armbrister, to do the ghosting.

But what started out innocently enough as just another high-profile publishing partnership wound up as a major headache that required the ministrations of a divided Supreme Court before the *Digest* got any satisfaction—and it was cold comfort at that. As frequently seemed to happen when something disturbed Pleasantville's equanimity, leftists were blamed.

While Ford was still in office, another agency executive, Owen Laster, head of the literary department, had contacted Chris Chase, an actress turned author whom he represented, about ghosting the memoirs of Betty Ford. After Chase agreed, Laster sent Mrs. Ford a copy of Chase's recent book *How to Be a Movie Star.*

Later, in a hallway conversation, Laster was chatting with an assistant agent named Marsha Higgins, who suggested Armbrister for the president's book. Higgins represented the *Digest*'s roving editor, who had written books about the USS *Pueblo* incident, the murder of union leader Joseph Yablonski, and the House of Representatives. Armbrister himself called a few days later to tell Higgins he would be interested in collaborating on the Ford memoirs and was told he had already been nominated.

The former president later met with Chase and Armbrister and approved of both. Meanwhile, Laster had narrowed his list of prospective publishers to five. One of the people he talked to was Erwin A. Glikes, vice-president and publisher of Harper & Row, who later telephoned around to get an idea of paperback, first-serial, and book-club possibilities. One of the people Glikes talked to was Ed Thompson, Armbrister's boss, who was enthusiastic about the project.

The next day Thompson met with Glikes, and they shook hands on a deal to share costs and profits equally. A contract was not signed until several weeks later, after President and Mrs. Ford had signed their own contracts. Laster then flew to Palm Springs to confer with Ford, bringing with him a detailed outline of what Glikes and Thompson expected from the book. In particular, the *Digest* and Harper & Row wanted Ford to focus on his dramatic selection as vice-president after the resignation of Vice-President Spiro Agnew and to describe the circumstances leading to his decision to pardon President Nixon.

President Ford approved both the editorial outline and a fee of $100,000 to his ghostwriter. Mrs. Ford reached a similar understanding with her publisher and ghostwriter. That accomplished, the Fords began construction of a fifteen-room Spanish-style hacienda next door to old friend Leonard K. Firestone in Palm Springs, where they intended to settle. Ford's former press secretary, J. F. terHorst, later criticized his ex-boss for becoming a millionaire through "huckstering and hustling and merchandising the presidency."

While writing the book, Armbrister conducted some two hundred interviews with the former president and also tried to use Ford's own words wherever possible, but in some instances the language was purely his own. The editor for the book was *Digest* managing editor Ken Gilmore. In the finished book, titled *A Time to Heal,* Ford acknowledged, "[Armbrister] interviewed me for hundreds of hours, then assisted me in the assembling and writing of these recollections." Previously, the RDP had also published former secretary of the treasury William Simon's similarly titled *A Time for Truth,* a hard-line conservative manifesto calling for the creation of a "counter-intelligentsia" to challenge the liberal domination of the media, universities, and foundations.

Though the *Digest* was half owner of the Ford memoirs, it agreed to pay $35,000 for the license to publish selections of the book in its issue of May 1979. *Time* magazine agreed to pay another $12,500 for first-serial rights for its issue going on sale April 16, 1979, timed to coincide with the shipment of *A Time to Heal* to bookstores. All was on megaschedule, as planned, when a fly named the *Nation* magazine landed in the ointment. In its issue of April 7, 1979, the 30,000-circulation weekly, which operated at a loss, scooped the *Digest* and *Time* by running a 2,250-word article titled "The Ford Memoirs, behind the Pardon," which revealed all the juiciest details in Ford's book relating to his pardon of Nixon.

Winthrop Knowlton, the outraged chairman of Harper & Row, characterized the *Nation's* action as "a rip-off of an author who was a President of the United States." Spokesmen for the *Digest* and *Time* were equally indignant. Adding insult to injury, critic John Leonard, writing in the *New York Times,* declared the book to be the literary equivalent of a WIN button—a reference to the "Whip Inflation Now" buttons that became a national joke and symbolized Ford's ineffectual war against stagflation.

In a statement *Nation* editor Victor S. Navasky loftily urged Harper

& Row and the *Digest* to "be sensitive to our First Amendment rights," though he declined to exercise that right himself by refusing to divulge the details of how he obtained an advance copy of the book. After *Time* canceled its plan to publish and withheld its $12,500 payment, since the *Nation*'s close paraphrase of the passages in question preempted all the news value in the excerpt, Harper & Row and the *Digest* turned around and sued the *Nation* for infringement of copyright. The case, tried in U.S. district court in Manhattan under Judge Richard Owen, was to become a landmark in copyright law.

In February 1983 Judge Owen ruled that the *Nation* had violated federal copyright laws by printing "what was essentially the heart" of the Ford book. The court also struck down the magazine's claim that the article was fair usage protected by the First Amendment and ordered the *Nation* to pay $12,500 to Harper & Row and the *Reader's Digest*.

In an editorial protesting the ruling, the *Nation* pointed out that friend-of-the-court briefs on behalf of the magazine had been filed by the *New York Review of Books,* the *New York Times, Scientific American,* the *Progressive,* and the Reporters Committee for Freedom of the Press. The *Times* brief listed a number of occasions when it ran news stories prior to publication from such books as White House counsel John Dean's *Blind Ambition,* Nixon's own *Memoirs,* and presidential assistant John Ehrlichman's *Witness to Power,* among others.

All that proved, according to the editorial, that the *Digest* and Harper & Row were placing commercial interests over the First Amendment, and the *Nation* therefore intended to appeal. In another editorial it had bitterly complained that Judge Owen "literally consigned the First Amendment to a footnote."

In November of that same year, the *Nation* had its day in court. Overturning the $12,500 judgment, Judge Irving R. Kaufman of the U.S. court of appeals wrote, "We do not believe it is the purpose of the Copyright Act to impede that harvest of knowledge so necessary to a democratic state. . . . We do not believe the act was intended to chill the activities of the press by forbidding a circumscribed use of copyrighted words." The ruling was front-page news in the friend-of-the-court *New York Times.*

In May 1985 the case was again back on the front page. The RDA and Harper & Row had appealed to the Supreme Court, which ruled that the *Nation* had violated copyright. Associate Justice Sandra Day

O'Connor, writing for the majority, ruled that by using generous verbatim excerpts the *Nation* "effectively arrogated to itself the right of first publication" that went beyond fair usage. The *Nation* had to pay up. However, the *Digest*'s victory was only Pyrrhic. Although Betty Ford's *The Times of My Life* made the best-seller list and garnered much critical praise, her husband's *A Time to Heal* was a flop with readers and reviewers alike.

———

IN THE *1980s* the two most sensational, controversial, and ultimately questionable cautionary tales of KGB deceit and terror involved two men, named Arkady N. Shevchenko and Mehmet Ali Agca—the one an under secretary at the Soviet mission to the UN and the other the would-be assassin of Pope John Paul II.

The men shared several singular qualities, apart from being at the center of lively and often acrimonious debate on the role of the CIA in its convoluted war of media disinformation and deception with the KGB. Under the hidden hand of the CIA and other Western intelligence agencies, each man also underwent a remarkable public metamorphosis and reemerged a person altogether different from the seemingly simple individual he had been before.

In their new, improved, and much sensationalized revisionist identity, both Shevchenko and Agca were also provided a dark new, KGB-shrouded past—Shevchenko as a CIA supermole and Agca as a radical leftist tool of the Bulgarian secret police, a KGB client. Not so coincidentally, each man first received his new identity in the pages of the *Reader's Digest*.

In 1978 Shevchenko had defected from his post, under mysterious circumstances, and later that year signed a $600,000 contract with Simon & Schuster for a book tentatively titled *From Captivity into Freedom*. When the manuscript was finished a year later, Simon & Schuster head Richard Snyder and editor in chief Michael Korda agreed that it did not contain enough new interesting material on the USSR to merit publication and sued for the $146,875 already advanced.

In December 1980 Shevchenko was deposed by Simon & Schuster lawyers and kept to the story of his defection as related in the manuscript. The book was next sent to Steven Frimmer, editor of Reader's Digest Press, who had the same opinion of it as Korda and Snyder. Before returning it, though, he handed the manuscript over to Washington bureau reporter Henry Hurt, who interviewed Shevchenko for twenty hours to see whether, perhaps with his collaboration, the defector could add any substantive new details. Hurt had no success, and Shevchenko decided to give up on the book.

Three years later, in 1984, Shevchenko's lawyer forwarded a copy of a new manuscript to an editor at Alfred A. Knopf. This latest version, titled *Breaking with Moscow,* had all the elements of a thriller, beginning with a new section called "The Reluctant Spy," which portrayed the author as a supermole whose career was now peppered with car chases, safe houses, spy equipment, and assorted dangerous missions.

Several of the original chapters had also been beefed up with dramatic verbatim conversations with Soviet leaders, including Khrushchev digressing at length on Castro, China, and Dag Hammarskjöld. In a new last chapter, "The End of the Game," Shevchenko outlined his flight to freedom.

Almost effortlessly, the book hit the best-seller lists, propelled by a *Time* cover story, a segment on "60 Minutes" touting Shevchenko as the CIA's most successful supermole ever with a rank equal to Al Haig's when he served as deputy to Secretary of State Henry Kissinger, and a movie deal. The book also received an unqualified recommendation from Leslie Gelb in the *New York Times Book Review.*

Significantly, the man chosen to demolish Shevchenko's credibility was none other than conservative journalist Edward Jay Epstein, a *Digest* contributor.

In late 1975, shortly before he was named editor in chief, conspiracy buff Ed Thompson had hoped to pin the Kennedy assassination on the KGB and told Epstein he could put him in touch with a defector who claimed to have seen the Soviet agency's secret files on Lee Harvey Oswald.

Among Epstein's earlier works was *Counterplot,* which criticized New Orleans district attorney Jim Garrison for pointing an accusing finger at the CIA. That book led to *Inquest,* a probing postmortem on the Warren Commission that ultimately exonerated both it and the CIA in the matter of a cover-up.

Thompson told Epstein that another Soviet defector, Yuri Nosenko, had walked into the offices of the Washington bureau and offered to tell his tale. In his 1974 *KGB: The Secret Work of Soviet Secret Agents,* RD editor John Barron had discussed Nosenko's KGB career in some detail and even alluded to his revelation that two panels of Soviet psychiatrists had examined Oswald at the behest of the KGB.

Now, apparently, Nosenko was coming forward once again, this time to reveal everything he knew about Oswald's two years in Russia.

An officer of the KGB's Second Chief Directorate, which oversaw Soviet counterespionage, Nosenko maintained he had been Oswald's control in Moscow in 1959 and reviewed Oswald's entire KGB file before defecting in 1964, two months after Kennedy was shot. Both an unexpected and an unwanted gift, the defection caught the CIA off guard and aroused the suspicions of some within the agency that the KGB hoped to sow confusion and discord among members of the Warren Commission.

After agreeing to take on the project, Epstein interviewed Nosenko in January 1976 and found the ex-KGB officer's answers inconsistent. Donald Jameson, a CIA contact helpfully provided by the *RD* and a close friend of Nosenko, assured Epstein the problem stemmed from Nosenko's unsure command of English.

Epstein then contacted James Jesus Angleton, who had been ousted earlier that year as a result of disclosures of illicit CIA activities (such as conducting a massive spying campaign against American citizens, in violation of the agency's charter) by Seymour Hersh in the *New York Times.* Angleton asked Epstein why he thought Nosenko finally decided to tell his story after so many years. So far as he knew, Epstein replied, Nosenko had simply walked into the Washington office of the *Reader's Digest* and befriended an editor there. Unknown to Epstein at the time, John Barron and Nosenko were friends. The *Digest* editor had even attended the latter's wedding.

"I know that a journalist might not want to look a gift horse in the mouth," Angleton told Epstein, "but did you assume he walked in on a whim?"

Epstein then learned that some defectors had contractual obligations to the agency. Nosenko, as he later discovered, was indeed under contract to the CIA and had been authorized to contact the *Digest.* Such approved contacts were called briefs.

Jameson turned out to be a CIA consultant whose job was to bring Soviet-bloc defectors like Nosenko into contact with journalists so that they could deliver their authorized briefs. That was how the CIA planted news stories in magazines and books. The CIA was also active in writing entire books and publishing them under the defector's name. *The Penkovskiy Papers,* a Doubleday best-seller in 1966 (and *Digest* book excerpt), had been the most successful to date.

When Angleton and Epstein next met, Epstein suggested that even though the story was authorized by the CIA and perhaps even censored, that did not mean it was untrue. Angleton agreed: "What that means is that the agency has now decided to go public with Yuri Nosenko. I would expect that his autobiography is already in the works."

Jameson, in fact, had already mentioned the book to a *Digest* editor.

"Why shouldn't his story be made public?" Epstein asked. "What was wrong with his information?"

Angleton explained, "Up until the time I left the agency, all reports based on what Nosenko said carried a label I had insisted on. That label specified 'From a source whose *bona fides* have not been established.'"

By this time Thompson was becoming concerned that Epstein was spending more time questioning the authenticity of a source than looking into the assassination. But the *RD* editor was also willing to proceed with the Nosenko investigation even though it might seemingly discredit another *Digest* book for which Nosenko had provided information—namely, Barron's *KGB*.

Epstein never did resolve the question of Nosenko's authenticity. When Epstein's book *Legend* (edited by Tony Oursler) was finally published, several years and $500,000 later, it hewed to the Angleton line that all the known facts about Lee Harvey Oswald amounted to no more than a skillful cover story or "legend" concocted for him by the KGB.

As a result the breach between Pleasantville and its pro-Nosenko Washington bureau only widened. The bureau had perhaps hoped that Epstein—whose own conservative bona fides had seemingly established him as a journalist the CIA could count on—would, in effect, act as its surrogate. But unlike Thompson, Epstein had been unwilling to accept at face value the information the agency provided him.

The situation became worse with the publication of Shevchenko's revised memoirs of his career as a CIA supermole. They set the stage not only for a twenty-one-gun media salute but also, when the smoke cleared, for Epstein's masterful unmasking of the author in the pages of the *New Republic*. After ridiculing Shevchenko's new "Le Carréan" guise, ex-Digester Epstein demonstrated in irrefutable detail how the author's career had been "spun out of formulaic spy fiction or invented out of whole cloth."

Shevchenko's new identity had made its trial run in a 1983 book by

John Barron called *KGB Today: The Hidden Hand* and based on interviews with another alleged Soviet defector, Stanislav Levchenko, whose cover had been a position with a Russian foreign-affairs magazine published in Tokyo. In an arrangement it had used with Barron before, Epstein declared, the agency dispatched Levchenko, who was under contract to the CIA, to "hand-deliver" to Barron "certain particulars about the Shevchenko case." As Epstein admitted, that was the same procedure the CIA had used when he was researching *Legend* and the CIA sent him Yuri Nosenko. Levchenko now revealed that Shevchenko had been a CIA superstar.

Epstein wondered why Barron had been so credulous when the CIA had previously sent him a defector whose story later had proved to be wholly fictive. The obvious conclusion was that, as with *The Penkovskiy Papers,* the CIA had simply manufactured a self-congratulatory tale of agency victory and ignominious KGB defeat. Barron, for whatever reason, elected to publish it and even submitted portions of the book to the CIA for review.

Barron's second KGB book was edited by Ken Gilmore and published by the Reader's Digest Press—an imprint resurrected mainly to distribute right-wing tracts emanating from the Washington bureau. That same year the *Atlanta Journal,* in a series on CIA infiltration of the media, noted that in the fifties and sixties Time-Life Inc. had enjoyed an extremely close relationship with the intelligence agency. But now some CIA watchers saw the *Reader's Digest* "as gradually achieving that 'most favored' status granted by the CIA."

———

Further proof that the CIA and the *RD* were bedfellows was provided by one of the magazine's crustiest roving editors—Rome-based Claire Sterling, who specialized in sensational unmaskings of the KGB's darkest deeds. Years earlier, in *The Terror Network,* Sterling had claimed that the Kremlin was secretly funding, training, and supervising a worldwide network of terrorists wreaking deadly havoc in Western Europe and elsewhere. After Secretary of State Al Haig cited the book in a get-tough speech given on the day he took office, it was briefly a cause célèbre. Much to the chagrin of new CIA director William Casey, however, Sterling's thesis was later thoroughly discredited by an independent agency-appointed panel.

In September 1982 Sterling was back on the offensive, with an even more sensational charge. After spending nine months investigating the plot to kill Pope John Paul II, Sterling declared she was convinced that Mehmet Ali Agca, the Turk convicted of the assault, was not a fascist-fringe extremist acting on his own, as was widely reported in the press. Rather, the twenty-three-year-old Agca had received extensive support from a Turkish gun-running ring controlled by the Bulgarian secret service, "one of Moscow's principal surrogates for terrorism and subversion."

That same month Agca had been sentenced by a Rome court to life imprisonment. The major media considered the case closed. Agca had in fact mentioned Bulgarian connections in his statements to Italian police. According to Sterling, Italian officials assumed the pope had been shot because he supported Solidarity, the Polish trade-union movement. Yet secret bank accounts, Sterling asserted, had been established for Agca as early as 1977 to finance his terrorist activities. In the year preceding the assassination attempt, he had allegedly spent at least $50,000 traveling around Europe without cashing a check. Solidarity was not formed until late 1980.

In a subsequent book-length account of her investigation and the worldwide controversy engendered by the *Digest*'s publication of her findings, Sterling glossed over the exact circumstances leading to her decision to investigate the case. Whether the inspiration was her own, or came from her editors at the *Digest,* who happened to be Bulgarian-born Dimi Panitza, head of the Paris bureau, and Ken Gilmore, or perhaps was a happy suggestion from yet another source, was vaguely left to the reader's imagination: "I was lucky," she wrote, "to have had the chance [to unmask the Western conspiracy of silence on the assassination]. It isn't every day that a reporter gets an offer like the one I had from the *Reader's Digest:* take as long as you like, go wherever you please, spend as much as you must to get as close to the truth as you can."

The reason why the Italian government, the Catholic church, and various Western nations had conspired to suppress the evidence of a Soviet plot was also a "long story" that Sterling subsequently decided she could explain "only in part" even though, in the wake of her accusations, that was precisely the point and she had world enough and time. For empiricist Sterling, the "how" was "easier . . . to explain" than the "why."

Regardless, Sterling's article on the plot to kill the pope, published in the September 1982 issue of the *Reader's Digest* and in its international editions, amounted to yet another sensational *j'accuse* from the right-wing *RD*/CIA axis aimed at proving, contrary to official agency doctrine, that the KGB's hidden hand was conducting a vast symphony of deception that Western democracies were too deaf and distracted to hear.

At first Sterling's article received only scant attention in the media—a brief page 12 Reuters item in the *New York Times;* and two days later a Soviet denial on page 7. The *Times's* own five-man research team was not mobilized to follow up. That same month NBC reporter Marvin Kalb broadcast a news special that made similar claims about Agca's Bulgarian connections. It, too, was widely ignored.

On December 16, however, four months after the *Digest* press kit on Sterling's article had been sent out to the media, political columnist William Safire gave the theory his official blessing in the *Times*. The logic was Cold War simple. Ex-KGB head Yuri Andropov was now top man in the Kremlin. In August 1980 the Solidarity-backed strike among Polish dockworkers in Gdansk had reached the critical stage. Dissent and freedom threatened to break out in nearby Ukraine. The solution was obvious: kill Polish-born John Paul II, Solidarity's most prominent supporter. But first establish a plausible denial by getting the Bulgarian secret service to carry out the dirty work.

Two days later the *Times* responded in an editorial, and the battle was joined. "Killing a Polish Pope would not have made Poland less rebellious," the editorial pointed out. Moreover, political assassinations were "as dangerous to the user as the victim." Nor had the Italian police any corroboration of the theory. The fact that Agca obtained the Browning revolver used in the assassination attempt from within Bulgaria's flourishing underworld of arms smugglers did not prove Bulgarian complicity either.

Meanwhile, the newspaper of record launched its own investigation. Six weeks later, in a front-page story, the *Times* reported that, though Agca had spent several months in Bulgaria, there was still no proof the government itself had anything to do with the shooting. Even the Reagan administration, usually quick to attack Soviet misconduct, had adopted a cautious attitude toward the assassination theory.

On the other hand, Sterling's thesis did gain some believers, including former national-security adviser Zbigniew Brzezinski and former secretary of state Kissinger. Support for the theory, according to the

Times, came from Paul B. Henze, a former CIA station chief in Turkey and an aide to Brzezinski, who worked as a consultant to the Rand Corporation. The newspaper claimed that Henze was hired by the *Digest* to investigate Agca's background and that some of his findings were incorporated into Sterling's article.

Ed Thompson later wrote a letter to the editor admitting that Henze—a friend of Washington bureau editor Kenneth Y. Tomlinson—had been hired to prepare a "preliminary" background report on the attempted assassination, but denying it was ever shown to Sterling in any form.

Ultimately, three Bulgarians were arrested and tried in Rome on charges of conspiring with Agca to assassinate the pope. For the next three years, off and on, the controversy played out in the media, especially in the left-wing and right-wing press, each accusing the Reagan administration, Italian government, Catholic church, *New York Times,* and dozens of other players, large and small, of a cover-up. Then the three men were acquitted for lack of evidence, and Sterling's tarnished big-bang theory of KGB connivery, like so many other *Digest*-sponsored brouhahas, died with a whimper.

23

God Is My Copublisher

WHAT the Lord giveth, about 800,000 words of divine revelation in English translation, the *Digest* decided in 1976 to take away—to cut its number one competitor down to about two-thirds its usual size, by excising close to 320,000 words. It was to be the ultimate act of condensation—not to mention the Bible's first major revision in 2000 years. In the process the *Digest* even generously provided Holy Writ with 20,000 or so new words—those damnable connecting passages again—that had not been imparted to the original inspired authors. The result was a publishing disaster—Condensed Books's biggest flop, which some faithful *Digest* readers suggested was literally the work of the devil.

Editorially, though, the Reader's Digest Condensed Bible was a brilliant concept, brilliantly achieved, and without doubt the company's greatest and most unsung triumph. If fundamentalist passion worked against it from the right, misplaced snobbery defeated it from the left. Discriminating readers who regarded condensed versions of the world's literary masterpieces as desecrations saw in the Condensed Bible a similar lower-middlebrow travesty, even though the Old and New Testaments—viewed strictly as literature—contained more repetitious passages, more tiresome irrelevancies and inferior passages, more lack of cohesion, than any other great book by God or man. The RDCB was a blessing to people who always intended to read the Bible but got discouraged after the eighteenth or nineteenth "begat."

In consequence everyone at either end of the religious and intellectual spectrum ignored the one authentic "condensed masterpiece" produced by the publishing empire of DeWitt Wallace, its reverent and skillful homage to the only publication with more applicability, quotability, and lasting value than itself.

The idea for the Condensed Bible grew out of a series of discussions among Condensed Books editor in chief Jack Beaudouin, executive editor Joseph Hotchkiss, and special-projects editor Herbert Lieberman. After getting tentative approval from Wally, the CB division conducted a prepublication survey of prospective subscribers, describing the proposed condensation in general terms and inviting readers to check, as usual, the "would order," "might order," "some interest," or "no interest" box. "Would order" got the most checks, and that led to the final go-ahead.

But CB analysts ignored what the test-marketing results were really saying—that the "would order" column constituted only a lukewarm majority and that *Digest* loyalists were in general not eager to buy a Condensed Bible in the quantities that the company was accustomed to. Among the book club's articles of faith was an almost fanatical aversion to risk. Its prepublication surveys had become so refined that, with few exceptions, it could deliver million-copy best-sellers one after the other like no other publisher in the world. Yet the Bible, the world's best-selling book, looked like less than a blockbuster in the hands of the world's biggest direct-mail marketer of books. That illogic led *Digest* executives to assume there must be some mistake.

There was a second early warning that something might be amiss, and again Pleasantville chose to ignore it. Letters began to trickle in from *Digest* readers who interpreted the Scriptures as the literal word of God and viewed the proposed project, which they had heard about through the grapevine, as blasphemous. Many of those letters cited chapter and verse to make their point, usually Revelation 22:18–19:

"I give this warning to everyone who is listening to the words of prophecy in this book: should anyone add to them, God will add to him the plagues described in this book; should anyone take away from the words in this book of prophecy, God will take away from him his share in the tree of life and the Holy City."

In most editorial operations, the tastes and convictions of the editors determined what was to be published or not published. But the very raison d'être of Condensed Books, as underscored by its prepublication surveys, was to ascertain the tastes and convictions of its readers, who acted as a kind of collective editorial board, and to publish accordingly. Yet once again their will was ignored. CB executives rationalized that controversy had met Jerome's translation—the so-called Vulgate—in the fifth century and the King James Version in 1611, not to mention the Revised Standard Version in 1952, so it was only natural that some controversy was going to attend their own undertaking as well.

As if alienating the fundamentalists were not bad enough, the senior editor of the Bible project was John Evangelist Walsh, who had previously written a life of Victorian Catholic poet Francis Thompson and a study of the bones of Saint Peter. The committee formed by Walsh—including three recent retirees and four younger editors, both male and female and of assorted religious faiths—worsened the RDA's predicament by recommending that it condense the Jerusalem Bible, a product of mostly Roman Catholic scholarship. The recommendation was overruled. As a national forum for Billy Graham and Norman Vincent Peale, as one editor admitted, the *Digest* "just couldn't go to market with a Catholic Bible."

Ultimately, the committee settled on the Revised Standard Version (RSV) of the King James Authorized Version published in 1952. Bruce M. Metzger, professor of New Testament language and literature at Princeton Theological Seminary and chairman of the continuing RSV committee, was hired as an adviser. (Ironically, in German Metzger's name means "butcher.")

By early January 1979 the *New York Times* had heard of the project and called Pleasantville. In a brief item an unidentified *Digest* editor confirmed that a condensed Bible was in the developmental stage, adding boastfully, "I know it's an extraordinary thing to think about, but we've condensed the 'Odyssey' and the Russian novelists, and there's no reason to think we can't do the Bible."

Before long, bad Condensed Bible jokes were making the rounds—the Ten Commandments reduced to five, Moses' forty-year sojourn in the desert squeezed into a three-day, two-night package tour of the Sinai, the story of Noah's ark pared down to that of an old man in a rubber raft with two wombats. The *Times* even weighed in with an editorial wondering tongue-in-cheek whether the *Digest*'s editors intended to blue-pencil "a few of the a-time-fors out of Ecclesiastes" or take the song out of the Song of Solomon. In a humorless letter to the editor, Ed Thompson reprimanded the *Times* for "criticizing a work in progress without having read a line of it." Already the RDA was getting nervous.

On Walsh's desk was a fifty-page confidential document detailing how modern editorial techniques were to be applied to the Bible. According to the document, condensing the word of God was to be achieved mainly by:

(1) Cutting repetitious words. For example, 2 Kings 19 was repeated verbatim in Isaiah 37. (2) Cutting repetitive thoughts, primarily in Ezekiel and in the letters of Paul. (3) Eliminating duplicate versions of incidents reported more than once, such as those in Jesus' life related by Matthew, Mark, and Luke. (4) Cutting material of no modern relevance, such as genealogies, geographies, and historical and architectural details. (5) Cutting down on mere rhetoric or any overabundance of words that resulted from Englishing the original. Simplifying "answering them he said" to "he answered."

(6) Nevertheless, preserving the sound of the RSV, so some words cuttable on the above five grounds were to be left in if deemed essential to maintain an elevated tone. (7) Adding words to conclude a sentence or to provide a connection, especially when a very wordy passage was reduced to a very few. (Walsh estimated that no more than 5 percent of the condensation was added material—but 5 percent of 480,000 words was more than the combined length of the five epistles of Peter and John.)

The actual work of condensation took three years. One rule was that no editor could condense a passage without consulting at least three Bible scholars' commentaries on that passage. After the first condensation was made, it was put through a "check cut," which amounted to a second condensation. Then Walsh looked it over, before sending it to Metzger for final review. Condensation operated on two levels—block cuts involving long passages, and line-by-line work.

First to go were the Old Testament genealogies, including a list of all the descendants of Noah and most of the generations recounted in 1 Chronicles 1–9. Next went the ritual laws of the Pentateuch—typical of those passages Walsh thought were of "reduced relevance" for modern readers. The number of psalms was greatly decreased so that Psalm 23, which was left intact, became Psalm 13. Many of the warnings and lamentations of the prophets were also eliminated. By the time the editors were finished, nearly half the Old Testament had been chucked.

By contrast, only one-fourth of the New Testament was reduced—notably, Paul's rhetorical repetitions in his epistles and his Old Testament citations in the lengthy letter to the Hebrews. The shortest gospel, Mark's, ran almost at full length. Even the words of Jesus himself were reduced by 10 percent, though the Our Father was left untouched. Where there was ambiguity—whether Jesus fed four or five thousand people—the ambiguity was retained. Snipped, though, was the remonstrative passage of Revelation 22:18–19.

In September 1982, to much fanfare, the Reader's Digest Condensed Bible was finally published—a hefty, 767-page tome distributed through the trade by Random House, though mail order would account for the bulk of sales. Yet only a month earlier, Thomas Nelson Publishers, the world's largest publisher of Bibles, upstaged the launch by issuing a New King James Version of the Bible—an effort that involved a 130-member international team of scholars and cost an estimated $4.5 million.

The corresponding figure for the RDCB was never revealed, but by now the *Digest* knew what it should have known seven years earlier—that the truncated word of God, as handed down to John Evangelist Walsh on Mount Pleasantville, was not going to play very well in Peoria. Only an estimated 500,000 copies—a paltry number by Condensed Books standards—had been printed. Already it was a write-off.

Reviews were mixed. Norman Vincent Peale obligingly described the new condensed version as "reverently innovative." *Newsweek*'s religion editor Kenneth L. Woodward praised the condensation's readability but noted that some Bible students wondered whether there were "more than merely technical reasons for excluding one passage rather than another." A case in point was the chapter in Genesis devoted to Judah's illicit liaison with his daughter-in-law Tamar. Jewish theologian Arthur Cohen pointed out that the result of deleting so many psalms and regulations was a Christian product "worthless as a Bible for Jews."

That was the good news. Jerry Falwell, head of the Moral Majority, in Lynchburg, Virginia, spoke for a much vaster constituency—the *Digest*'s own—when he complained, "To condense something that God has written gives unusual powers to human beings. . . . I would suggest that they stick to condensing books by men."

▬

IN FEBRUARY *1980* the *Digest*'s traditional animosity toward the Kennedy family culminated in a withering attack on the youngest political member of the prominent Boston clan, Edward M. Kennedy, Jr., Democratic senator from Massachusetts, who only weeks earlier had embarked upon his long-delayed quest for the Democratic nomination for president. An article in the *Digest,* timed to appear in the midst of the Iowa "caucus" primary, the first in the nation, offered new evidence that Kennedy lied about what happened on the night of July 18–19, 1969, when he drove off a bridge with Mary Jo Kopechne, a young campaign worker. More than any other single reevaluation of the so-called Chappaquiddick affair, the article in the *Reader's Digest*— "Chappaquiddick, the *Still* Unanswered Questions," by senior editor John Barron—dealt the Kennedy campaign a devastating blow from which it never recovered.

For a time Kennedy's presidential prospects had never seemed brighter. Among the factors contributing to his decision to seek the nomination were President Jimmy Carter's collapsing popularity; a perception that Kennedy himself had survived the incident at Chappaquiddick, now ten years in the past, with his reputation intact; and a fear that California's popular Democratic governor, Jerry Brown, might also seek to capitalize on opinion polls showing that the American public thought that Carter's domestic and foreign policies were both aimlessly adrift. A Gallup poll indicated that Kennedy could win the nomination by a two-to-one margin. Various media around the country were also encouraging him to throw his hat in the ring.

Meanwhile, members of the *Digest*'s Washington bureau, like conservative Republicans everywhere, thought the New Right's charismatic standard-bearer, former California governor Ronald Reagan, was in a position to defeat Carter if he survived the Kennedy challenge. A revival of religious fundamentalism and changing U.S. demographics, both of which coincided with the editorial content and with the over-fifty readership of the *Reader's Digest,* were profoundly altering the mood of the country.

At the same time, movements like Jerry Falwell's Moral Majority were calling for prayer in public schools and a broader definition of pornography while opposing passage of the Equal Rights Amendment and abortion on demand. All were near-monthly themes in the pages of the *Digest,* the trusted bible of Middle America and of all those retirees in Florida and Arizona. As in the fifties the mood of the country and the editorial philosophy of the *RD* seemed to be converging.

Moreover, like Nixon, the former Hollywood actor turned politician had been also been receiving financial and editorial support from the *Digest* for years before he sought his party's nomination—in fact, from the very beginning of his political career. By *Digest* standards, Reagan seemed poised to become an even more ideal president than Nixon, not least because he actually read the magazine—one of his favorites.

Not only was Reagan the quintessential reader, but he even served as an unofficial mouthpiece of the *Digest*'s editorial philosophy, borrowing its anecdotal style to make his points and from time to time citing the magazine as an authoritative source. If Reagan was going to face any serious opposition from the Democratic quarter, it could come only from the one man who possessed even more charisma, at least by association, than Reagan—Edward M. Kennedy. Thus he had to be destroyed.

The weapon of choice was Barron's meticulously researched piece, which argued persuasively that Kennedy had not only left the accident scene, as he admitted, but also left a girl behind to die and lied about it. Barron's story enjoyed widespread play in the press and was considered a disaster by the Kennedy camp. In addition, the *Digest* heavily promoted the article by distributing a lurid reenactment of the accident to TV stations and advertising the article in a variety of media. In America's family-oriented heartland, the message was heard loud and clear.

At the inquest Kennedy testified he had gone to a party on Chappaquiddick Island arranged by his cousin Joe Gargan and lawyer friend Paul Markham. Among the six unmarried women in attendance was Mary Jo Kopechne. Sometime after 11:15 P.M., Kennedy and Kopechne allegedly left the party for her hotel in nearby Edgartown, even though she did not bring her hotel keys or purse. Veering off the main road, he took a dirt road over a narrow, guardrail-less bridge that spanned a small pond. The car careened off the bridge and landed upside down in seven to ten feet of water. The heavyset Kennedy was able to escape through a window and swim to the surface, whereas the slender Kopechne remained trapped in the car.

Kennedy claimed he then walked a mile and a half back to the cottage instead of calling for help at a nearby firehouse. Kennedy, Gargan, and Markham returned to the pond, where they again tried in vain to rescue Kopechne.

Though the island's ferry had shut down for the night, the ferryman was obligated—as a sign on the slip clearly stated—to ferry anyone at any hour across the 500-foot channel to Edgartown. Yet Kennedy chose instead to swim the channel while fully clothed. Back at the Shiretown Inn, where he was staying, he talked briefly with the manager and asked the time, which was 2:25 A.M. Kennedy, who was wearing dry clothes, told the manager he had been awakened by a party next door to his room.

The following morning the upturned Oldsmobile was discovered by fishermen and Kopechne's body recovered. Her head was thrust up and back as if seeking a pocket of air.

Kennedy testified that he did not report the accident, because he lacked the "moral strength" to call Mrs. Kopechne, and instead "tossed and turned" all night. But no one at the inquest accepted Kennedy's contention that he and Kopechne had left the party as early as 11:15. A deputy sheriff on patrol said he saw the senator's car at an intersection at 12:45 A.M. and observed two passengers.

Kennedy also judged he had been driving at twenty miles per hour when he crossed the bridge. But a series of scientific tests paid for by the *Digest* determined that Kennedy—the first person to drive off the bridge in forty years—had actually been traveling between thirty and thirty-eight miles per hour.

The *Digest* also paid for a scientific analysis of the tidal currents in Poucha Pond, where Kopechne drowned, and found that the current was "not so strong as to constitute an insurmountable obstacle." Kennedy claimed that the strong tide had made it impossible for him to reach Kopechne, even though he was a strong swimmer, who later allegedly swam across the 500-foot channel.

Barron reported, too, that when Gargan and Markham returned to the cottage after having supposedly left Kennedy, no one noticed that their clothes were wet, nor did they have any bruises, though at the inquest Kennedy said Gargan had been severely bruised.

Barron concluded that no genuine attempt had been made to rescue Kopechne, especially if the accident happened after 12:45 and Kennedy was seen neatly dressed at his hotel at 2:25 A.M. Even if the accident occurred at 12:50, Kennedy still had to walk back to the cottage to fetch Markham and Gargan and then somehow get to Edgartown, go to his room and change, and appear downstairs by 2:25.

Moreover, according to Barron's piece, a certain Mr. Ballou claimed he saw three men crossing the Edgartown Channel in a small boat around 2:00 A.M. Also, Gargan and Markham had told the girls at the cottage that they were looking for a boat. Later a young boy on the island claimed that his boat had been used during the night and tied up in another place.

Barron hypothesized that Kennedy, Markham, and Gargan had decided to let Gargan take the blame if the car was discovered, while Kennedy established an alibi, and that they had perhaps returned to Chappaquiddick the next morning only to see whether the accident had been discovered or whether perchance the tidal current had swept the vehicle into Cape Poge Bay, where it could disappear entirely.

Subsequent stories in the *Washington Star* and the *New York Times* raised similar questions and all but sealed Kennedy's fate. The senator characterized the *Digest* article as "dead wrong" and "shoddy" and organized a team of admiralty lawyers and oceanographers of his own to refute the magazine's assertion that he lied when he testified that during the post-midnight swim a strong north-flowing tide exhausted him and nearly swept him out to sea. According to the *Digest,* the tide was flowing southward into the relative safety of the harbor.

The American public believed the *Digest.* Opinion polls suggested that only 22 percent of the public thought Kennedy was telling the truth. In the New Hampshire primary, Kennedy fell behind Carter by 10 percentage points. In the Florida primary on March 11, Kennedy was crushed. Meanwhile, Reagan was emerging victorious in primary after primary. Jacqueline Kennedy Onassis later convened an extraordinary meeting of top Kennedy aides and old family friends to discuss how to extricate Teddy from the race honorably and preserve the family name.

Oddly enough, the inspiration for the piece had come not from within the Washington bureau but from editor in chief Ed Thompson.

ONLY months after taking on Ted Kennedy, the *Digest* again made national news, with an attack on another alleged fraud on the American scene—the church of Scientology, whose faithful inner core of "thieves, shills and spies" the magazine claimed was destroying untold numbers of innocent lives. NBC followed soon thereafter with a similar attack—yet more evidence that the two organizations were being fed from the same source.

Bylined by Washington-bureau staffer Eugene Methvin and appearing in the May 1980 issue, "Scientology: Anatomy of a Frightening Cult" portrayed founder L. Ron Hubbard as a near-psychotic whose aides scrubbed his office daily for a "white glove" inspection and rinsed his laundry in thirteen fresh waters. The FBI, Methvin further confided, had noted in its files that Hubbard "appeared mental."

Methvin then revealed the cult's brainwashing techniques—a process called auditing that allegedly left one recruit in a "zombie-like trance" in which she carried out the commands of her superiors and that allegedly caused another to drown herself. He further disclosed that the IRS had once turned up nearly three million dollars in cash on Hubbard's 320-foot yacht and that he accused the World Federation for Mental Health (WFMH), in league with the FBI, CIA, certain elements of the media, and other groups, of persecuting him. The obvious conclusion, said Methvin, was that cults like Scientology were nothing but rackets masquerading, in an abuse of the First Amendment, as religions.

Unlike the Methodist church, however, the church of Scientology did not simply rebut the article, in high-minded fashion, with a press release, on the assumption that readers who wanted to bother could then judge the issues for themselves. Hubbard also hit the *Digest* with a multimillion-dollar libel suit. At the same time, loyal aides were set to work to see what they could uncover about Methvin and his presumed connection to the WFMH—which, in fact, Scientologists *did* believe was behind the persecution of their organization. The church of Scientology is opposed to all forms of psychiatry and to all varieties of mind-altering drugs.

The first thing the Scientologists discovered was that, when Methvin and his wife had purchased their home in a Washington, D.C., suburb in 1967, they were assisted by attorney James J. Bierbower, whom former CIA agent James Agee later identified as one of a group of lawyers the agency used in connection with its proprietary holdings.

In the midsixties, at the time of the house sale, Bierbower was serving as vice-president of Southern Air Transport, one of the CIA's most important airline proprietaries. Some months before the closing, Methvin had published a puff piece in the *Digest* on the American Institute for Free Labor Development (AIFLD), a CIA-controlled anti-Communist labor union—also exposed by Agee—that was especially active in Latin America. Methvin, who joined the Washington bureau in 1965, got his start in journalism working for *Orbis,* an ultraconservative journal of opinion published by ex-CIA official William Kintner and Stefan Possony, director of the Hoover Institution and Methvin's media godfather. In 1967 the *New York Times* revealed that *Orbis* was funded by the CIA.

In 1966 the CIA was also conducting Operation Chaos, designed to discredit the antiwar movement on college campuses. That same year the *RD* published Methvin's "How the Reds Make a Riot," which it claimed was based on "four years of research," even though the author had been on staff for only about a year. A few years later, in a speech to the Georgia Press Institute at his alma mater, the University of Georgia, Methvin tipped his hand by stating flatly, "Truly if the atomic era of megaton bombs is too important to be left to the generals, journalism is too important to be left to journalists."

Scientology also discovered that Methvin sat on the advisory board of an organization called the American Family Foundation (AFF), whose other members included Dr. Louis Jolyon West, a California neuro-psychiatrist who had in the midfifties helped conduct some of the CIA's earliest and most notorious secret research on LSD and mind control. During that period West had administered a lethal dose of LSD to an elephant. The purpose of the AFF was to formulate effective methods to deprogram members of "cults" such as Scientology.

The AFF's principal benefactor, moreover, was the Scaife Family Charitable Trust, whose trustee was right-wing millionaire and CIA groupie Richard Mellon Scaife. The Pittsburgh-based Scaife, heir to the Gulf Oil and Mellon fortunes, had been identified by the *Pittsburgh Post-Gazette*—and by numerous other publications—as having "at least one demonstrable link to the Central Intelligence Agency."

That link was Forum World Features, a Third World news agency based in London during the early seventies and set up with funds provided by the CIA and British intelligence and laundered through Scaife. The man who ran Forum World Features, until it was sold off in 1975, was Brian Crozier, a well-known fixture on the radical right, who also contributed frequently to both the *Digest* and its Latin American edition, *Selecciones.* Crozier later became an editor for the *Economist.* Among his protégés was Robert Moss, the only other journalist, along with Methvin, who in 1976 was permitted to attend the State Department's confidential two-day conference on international terrorism.

For years before Methvin's article appeared, Scientology had been engaged in a vigorous, if largely ignored, exposé of CIA experiments in biological warfare and drug-induced mind control. Most of the accusations were for the consumption of the faithful in the church's own publication, *Freedom.* But by 1979 the nation's press was beginning to take notice. The *New York Times* carried an item on Scientology's analysis of army and CIA documents, obtained through the Freedom of Information Act, that showed that both government agencies had conducted bacteriological and chemical tests on New York City streets and tunnels in 1966. Similar articles soon appeared in the *Washington Post, Omni,* the *Nation,* and other publications. When *Freedom* then revealed that the CIA had also sponsored open-air tests of whooping-cough bacteria in Florida in the midfifties, leading to an outbreak that killed twelve people, the findings were again publicized in the *Post* and other papers.

Scientology also exposed the agency's use of soldiers as guinea pigs in its experiments with the drug BZ, a hallucinogen up to one hundred times more powerful than LSD, as part of its study on riot control. And once again the nation's newspapers followed up with news stories, while the *Los Angeles Times* weighed in with an editorial, titled "The Abandonment of Humanism," which accused the Pentagon of committing offenses "that deny the common bonds of humanity."

Then in March 1980, only months before Methvin's article appeared in the *Digest,* the church of Scientology chronicled the agency's Baltimore-based development of a machine called the Biogen, capable of breeding microorganisms in large quantities for use in biological warfare. As before, the church's FOIA-obtained findings were widely reported in the press.

Just the previous January, Methvin had written a ringing denunciation of the FOIA for a conservative journal of opinion, the *American Spectator.* In that article he also opposed a new draft charter for the FBI prepared by the outgoing Carter administration that would have severely limited the bureau's authority to carry out domestic intelligence operations. A subsequent FOIA disclosure showed that FBI and CIA surveillance of the church of Scientology over the years had resulted in more than 200,000 pages of paperwork.

A further, far more intriguing entanglement was the CIA's political-action staff's work with Moral Re-Armament (MRA), an interdenominational politico-religious movement founded by Frank Buchman that thrived during the Cold War deep-freeze of the fifties and sixties. In 1967 DeWitt Wallace through the Reader's Digest Foundation gave

MRA $190,000—the largest sum by far given by the RDF to any organization of any kind that year. Boscobel Restoration, by comparison, received only $150,000 that year, while the recipient of the third-highest amount, Harry Morgan's World Press Institute, was awarded $46,500. Every other arts organization or educational institution blessed that year by RDF bounty received a comparative pittance—the Metropolitan Museum of Art, for example, only $500.

Obviously, the *Digest* was either laundering CIA funds or Wally had elected to give an unusually large amount of money to a cause that inspired a momentary enthusiasm. In any event, the CIA's arrangements with MRA provided the agency with covert channels to the leaders of Asia, Africa, and Europe, where the movement was for a time particularly popular.

In addition to infiltrating the elites of each country, the CIA also required the services of a worldwide front organization that would bring them into contact with the masses. With that in mind, the CIA had approached Hubbard, whose organization the agency hoped would serve as the low road to MRA's high. But that tidy plan came to naught when Scientology's founder and the CIA had a severe falling-out.

Though Scientology's information gathering on Methvin failed to implicate the WFMH, the circumstantial evidence overall suggested that the *Digest* was once again serving as a mouthpiece for the CIA, this time to attack an increasingly high-profile critic of the agency and destroy its credibility. In that capacity Methvin succeeded spectacularly. From 1980 onward Hubbard's church of Scientology—until then considered little more than just another loud fringe organization—became synonymous with the worst excesses of mind control, the very label the church had sought to pin on the CIA. To add insult to injury, the church's suits against the *Digest* were also later dismissed.

—

"*The* monthly for people who hate to read," sighed Mary McGrory in her *Washington Post* column for November 23, 1982. "You have only to study the transcript of Ronald Reagan's last news conference to see that the staple commodity of the dentist's waiting room is, to him, a bible, even though he's on the airwaves this week pushing hard for the real Bible."

In the November elections nuclear-freeze plebiscites had passed in eight states. At a news conference soon afterward, Reagan categorically declared that the Soviet Union was pulling the strings on the nuclear freeze, which was being manipulated by "those who want the weakening of America." Asked for evidence, Reagan said there was plenty, some of it even published by the journalism "fraternity."

Pressed to be specific, the president cited an article in the *Reader's Digest* by John Barron. In an effort to give Reagan's reading list greater respectability, White House press secretary Larry Speakes later divulged that Reagan had also perused *Commentary* and the *American Spectator* on the same subject.

"He could not quite bring himself to name his favorite publication," McGrory continued, "perhaps because he senses that not all reporters share his faith in its infallibility. A few sentences later, he slipped in a reference to 'intelligence matters,' and nobody in the administration seems able to back it up. But when he has the Reader's Digest, he doesn't need intelligence reports. The hot item in the October issue, 'The KGB's Magical War for "Peace,"' was enough for him. It's a hard-breathing account about how the KGB is pulling the wool over the eyes of millions of innocent Americans who support the freeze."

Among the "dupes" were Harvard's George Kistiakowsky, who had helped develop the atomic bomb, as well as Nobel laureates Owen Chamberlain, Hans Bethe, and Herbert C. Brown. "Geniuses they may be in their field, but do they read the Reader's Digest? Probably not. They have cut themselves off from information by which their president sets great store. You understand the depths of the president's belief in the Digest when you see how he discounts material from other sources."

It was the first time as president, but not the last, that Reagan had invoked the world's most widely read magazine as an authoritative source, even though in subsequent open congressional testimony neither the CIA nor FBI would allege that Soviet agents were manipulating the nuclear-freeze movement.

Reagan was an old admirer of Barron, in fact. In early 1981, while away on business, the journalist had received several messages at his office from the White House. When he returned the calls, he was put through to the president, who congratulated him on his latest book, *MiG Pilot,* which Reagan had just finished reading. The president said he was recommending that his vice-president, George Bush, and the members of his National Security Council also read the book because "it shows what Russia is really like."

So highly did Reagan regard the *Digest* as an authoritative source that, only two weeks after his November news conference, he cited the same article again. On December 6, the president met with antinuclear activist Dr. Helen Caldicott in the White House for an informal discussion on nuclear arms. The meeting was arranged through Reagan's daughter Patti. But as the meeting progressed, Dr. Caldicott, an Australian pediatrician affiliated with the Harvard Medical School, grew shocked as much by the president's rhetoric as by the gist of his argument. Reagan declared that the Russians were "evil, godless Communists," and quoted material showing how they had orchestrated the nuclear-freeze movement. Moreover, said Reagan, opponents of nuclear proliferation were KGB dupes.

"That's from the *Reader's Digest,*" Dr. Caldicott said.

"No, it's not," Reagan replied, shaking his head; "it's from my intelligence files."

At the conclusion of the meeting, an angry Reagan refused to shake his visitor's hand. Later Dr. Caldicott found the material cited by the president in the *RD,* as she had suspected.

Intermittently, throughout the next eight years, Reagan was to repeat the performance—the only difference being that in the future he overcame his embarrassment and went out of his way to mention the *Digest* by name.

The next year Reagan named *Digest* editor Kenneth Y. Tomlinson, who had transferred from the Washington bureau to Pleasantville, to head the Voice of America. Before accepting the appointment, however, Tomlinson made a point of asking Ed Thompson whether he thought it was a good career move. Thompson got the impression that if Tomlinson did leave to take a position in government, he was leaving the *Digest* for good.

But there was never any question among the other top editors and among the Washington bureau's increasingly powerful friends on the management side of Pleasantville that the appointment was anything but an interim step on his way up the editorial ladder. In the fall of 1982 Tomlinson was sworn into office by Charles Wick, head of the USIA.

—

AT ED THOMPSON's next worldwide editorial conference—at Gurney's Inn, on Long Island—the question of who controlled Washington stories stood high on the agenda. With Reagan in office, the bureau had gone from being the capital's perennial outsiders to semi-insiders with warmer White House and cabinet relations than with any previous administration.

Yet editors in Pleasantville continued to assign articles that the bureau thought fell in its realm. Thompson had established that division of labor from the very beginning of his editorship when he and Jeremy Dole, and not two bureau editors, conducted the "debate" with President Ford and Democratic contender Jimmy Carter in 1976.

Environmental writer Jim Miller continued to be a major headache. Miller now occupied the unique, and dangerous, position of being the only free-lance writer covering people and topics that the Washington bureau considered its turf. He was spending half his time in the capital and practically living at the Madison Hotel. Despite such proximity, the bureau knew he was a writer it could not control.

Every time Miller submitted an article, back would come bitter, personal memos to Thompson from Washington—usually written by Washington bureau senior editor Ralph Kinney Bennett—attacking the piece. Gilmore's hand was also evident.

Miller then had to take time out from his regular research to refute the refutation, which required further research. From doing his homework, Miller knew that Bennett's refutations were, in fact, hand-me-downs from the PR departments in the Justice and Interior departments and in other government agencies.

A Miller's tale that particularly vexed the bureau was one on the troubled nuclear plant in Browns Ferry, Alabama, which on June 28, 1980, failed to shut down during routine maintenance. Earlier in the year it had been plagued by a series of malfunctions, and critics feared another Three Mile Island nuclear catastrophe. Miller charged the General Electric designers and operators with incompetence and the TVA and the Atomic Energy Commission with gross negligence.

Predictably, the Washington bureau tried to get the piece killed. At the same time, advertising salesman Dick McLoughlin showed the article to the management of General Electric, a major advertiser. After McLoughlin returned to Pleasantville, armed with the company's refutation, there was a conference at which Ed Thompson presided. Miller had to defend the article to McLoughlin line by line. No changes were made. Thompson ruled that the article should run.

With Gilmore's backing, Bill Schulz finally won a concession from

Thompson that henceforth any article proposal normally coming within the bureau's purview would be sent to D.C. for review. To Thompson's credit, though, Miller never once lost an assignment.

In May 1983 Thompson threw his biggest and best editorial bash— the Third Worldwide Magazine Editorial Conference, at Loew's Monte Carlo Hotel, with 108 participants. Thompson reminded the Digesters that the magazine had been breaking a number of big stories "through an increased emphasis on investigative reporting."

But, he added, "deep down, that's not the prime reason readers read us. The *real* reasons are the dramas, the humor, the articles on how to get along with your wife, the need to fight for freedom. These are the service pieces of a basic order. And the *Digest* is a service magazine."

It was to be his last hurrah as editor in chief, though no one knew it at the time, and his most important point was to reaffirm the *Reader's Digest*'s commitment to what eventually became his undoing—the art of living. At the same conference, Gilmore reaffirmed the same point: "We cannot be what we are not. Let's never inadvertently sound as if we're ashamed of our help-humanity, upbeat philosophy. That may be the strongest card in our deck."

Arch-liberationist Alain de Lyrot, executive editor on the international side, boasted that the editorial content of the global editions had achieved "a degree of variety, sophistication and impact unrivaled in international publishing." By 1983 the international editions were originating more articles, more adaptations, more pickups, and more reader-contribution programs than ever before. The hundred flowers were blooming.

De Lyrot reported to Ken Gilmore, who now held the title of executive editor. Tony Oursler, doing similar duty for the domestic edition, held the same title. However, their promotions had been attended by a pointed vote of no confidence in Roy Herbert, the fourth member of the Fab Four, whose drinking and lack of administrative ability were making him an increasing liability. Hurt and angry at being overlooked, Herbert tried to quit. A heartless boss but good friend, Thompson dissuaded him from leaving precipitously; and an arrangement was made, sometime in 1982, for Herbert to stay on the books until he reached retirement age.

Around this same time Thompson also gave O'Hara an unsealed envelope. Inside was the name of the person the *RD* editor in chief thought should succeed him in the event he got hit by a truck. Thompson's choice was Jeremy Dole, by now one of three managing editors, along with Peter Canning and Mary Louise Allin. Ironically, Dole had been a protégé of Lewis and was not close to the man who nominated him as his successor.

—

THE nondenominational Protestantism that the *Reader's Digest* preached for over half a century has often been described as "muscular Christianity," and the phrase is apt. God was a stern, Jehovah-like figure made in the image of rural patriarchs who sat at the head of the table in millions of small farms across America—men with little time for frivolous pleasures (poker, for example), and who expected their sons and daughters to rise before dawn to do their chores. It was a simple, rule-bound faith with no use for ritual and not much patience for doctrinal niceties.

The *Digest* reflected this form of unadorned Christianity in numerous ways—by glorifying the virtues of capitalism, which was the great engine of muscular Christianity, and by having as little to do as possible with religions like Catholicism, whose ritual and intellectual debate were traditionally regarded by Bible-based Protestantism as the vanities of prideful men. Muscular Christianity's arch-enemy was communism—a perverse, mirror-image atheistic Calvinism spawned by the devil himself as a cunning way to undermine the free-enterprise system and install the Antichrist at the head of the table.

Soon after World War II the *Digest* had energetically begun to promote the gospel of patriotism and anticommunism as preached by its most ardent champions—notably, Norman Vincent Peale, pastor of Marble Collegiate Church, on New York's lower Fifth Avenue; and a young southern evangelist named Billy Graham. America's most famous preacher of the day, Bishop Fulton J. Sheen, was never given a forum in the magazine. Appearances by prominent Catholics in the pages of the *Digest* were mostly limited to an occasional anti-Communist tirade by New York's powerful conservative archbishop, Francis Cardinal Spellman. Similarly, the Cold War's most publicized martyr, Jozsef Cardinal Mindszenty, Catholic primate of Hungary, was profiled twice in four years. Another popular Catholic, Tom Dooley, was likewise publicized in the *Digest* only for his anticommunism. Jewish religious authors were as conspicuously absent from the pages of the *Digest* as rabbis at a country club.

If American Protestantism had no Cold War martyrs, though, it had the next-best thing—scapegoats. In the early fifties the *Digest* had first gone after one of its own with Stanley High's low blow, "Methodism's Pink Fringe." In the seventies and eighties the magazine revived this species of religious McCarthyism in all-out holy war not only against the perceived weaklings in the muscular Protestant camp but also against those quasi-religious cults that had abandoned Christianity altogether.

For its first victim the *Digest* chose the most prestigious Protestant organization in the world, the World Council of Churches. Back in 1971, during the height of the Vietnam protest movement, Clarence Hall had flayed the WCC as a Communist front that aided American draft dodgers to flee to Canada and Sweden. A decade later the *RD* returned to the attack with an August 1982 article provocatively titled "Which Master Is the World Council of Churches Serving? . . . Karl Marx or Jesus Christ?" Written by roving editor Joseph A. Harriss, the article claimed that the WCC condoned violent solutions to social problems, particularly in the Third World, and had contributed funds to African liberation groups working for the overthrow of the white regime in South Africa.

The article received considerable play in the media, particularly the religious press, and occasioned a lengthy defense by the WCC, which complained about the *Digest*'s "nationalist spirit," which was "in fundamental conflict with the basic principles of ecumenism." But the church organization did concede that it was "not a pacifist organization" and did send money to South African liberation groups seeking "the violent overthrow of white regimes in Southern Africa."

The controversy had scarcely quieted down when the *Digest* returned to the offensive in its January 1983 issue with "Do You Know Where Your Church Offerings Go?" and answered it in the subtitle "You'd better find out—because they may be supporting revolution instead of religion." This time the *RD*'s target was the National Council of Churches (NCC), an ecumenical organization composed primarily of four mainstream Protestants churches—United Methodist, Presbyterian, Episcopalian, and United Church of Christ—that had come into prominence in the sixties for its role in the civil-rights movement.

According to the *RD,* members of those denominations were unwittingly "supporting revolution instead of religion" through their Sunday offerings, a part of which were earmarked for the NCC—

which, like the WCC, in turn allegedly handed the money over to revolutionaries. A month later CBS's "60 Minutes" joined the attack, with Morley Safer going over much of the same ground. Ironically, leftist critics of the NCC had accused it of collaborating with the CIA.

Newsweek, Washington Post columnist Colman McCarthy, various religious scholars and dignitaries, and most highbrow religious journals rushed to the NCC's defense. NCC officials themselves admitted they were openly supportive of Third World liberation movements and critical of U.S. foreign policy. But *Newsweek* noted that only 0.2 percent of all churchgoers' Sunday contributions were forwarded to NCC headquarters, on New York's Riverside Drive, the "God box." McCarthy wrote that the *Digest* article and the "60 Minutes" investigation, rather than being "independent journalism at its investigatory best," instead "uncritically aired some charges advanced by a new conservative group called the Institute on Religion and Democracy," which he characterized as "an upstart conservative faction bent on smearing its opponents." He added, "Its grumblings about the council's replacement of 'revolution for religion' are absurd, unless feeding, housing and educating the world's poor are revolutionary deeds."

Not much was known about the IRD, which had served as the article's primary source. A relatively new, privately funded political organization consisting of only six members, it sought to be the neo-conservative movement's frontline counteroffensive in the religious theater. The liberal Catholic weekly *Commonweal* thought there was "a certain comic quality" to the IRD phenomenon insofar as a self-appointed group of half a dozen persons, two of whom had no previous record of any church activity, had established themselves as the body to which the leaders of the nation's churches were now accountable.

On the other hand, even its defenders admitted that the NCC was a sprawling, almost ungovernable bureaucracy whose membership had been steadily shrinking since 1965, partly as a reflection of the decline of mainline Protestantism itself. The Presbyterian faith had already lost nearly a fourth of its four million members in the previous quarter century. Also the NCC was ridden with internal strife—though, in that respect, it was just like the *Reader's Digest.*

Another thing the NCC was criticized for was its $80,000 contribution to a literacy program begun by Nicaragua's Sandinistas—a small amount, however, when compared with the $3 million given by the U.S. government. Ironically, part of the NCC budget derived from royalties paid by the *Reader's Digest* for its use of the RSV Bible. In his own inscrutable way, God had arranged for money earned by the *Digest*'s Condensed Bible to wind up in the hands of the world's poor and oppressed.

24

You Will Receive
$1.75 Million

AFTER WHIZ KID Walter Weintz left the RDA in 1958, at the age of forty-two, because he had no more worlds in Pleasantville to conquer, there was a vacuum in the promotion department—a lack of that inspired and sometimes crazed brilliance that fueled the biggest and most successful direct-mail operation in the world.

The vacuum was soon filled by a twenty-six-year-old Princeton graduate and Fulbright scholar named Gordon Grossman, who not only improved on his predecessor's 11 percent returns but eclipsed them altogether with returns that sometimes soared into the stratospheric 50 percent level—and even higher. The device—crazed, brilliant, and perhaps diabolical—that Grossman used to accomplish that feat was to become a commonplace of pop culture in every country with a postal system. Mailboxes around the world have not been the same since. Grossman invented the publisher's sweepstakes.

After being hired by the RDA the year Weintz left, Grossman first tried his hand at market research and copy-writing before finding his niche in product management, or the tailoring of new products to fit different segments of the market. Working seven days a week, night and day, he quickly made a name for himself as the company's marketing wunderkind. The RDA's vast direct-mail operations now extended from circulation maintenance and renewal to development of new book products and magazines to Condensed Books and Music & Records. Grossman's expertise soon made him much sought after by the heads of all those divisions, and his ascent up the corporate ladder was meteoric. In 1966 Paul Thompson named him director of circulation.

By 1972 Grossman, then only forty years old, had become marketing director and his domain extended to all consumer-marketing operations, both international and domestic.

Then, like Weintz before him, he abruptly resigned in 1974 because he had reached a corporate plateau. Another changing of the guard was in the offing, with Thompson due to leave, and for Grossman there was no way to go but straight ahead—which in the bruisingly competitive financial corridors of Pleasantville was the same way as down.

Grossman regarded Thompson primarily as a good caretaker who had gambled by naming him circulation director. But Grossman also knew that too many people were lined up ahead of him—Jack O'Hara, Dick Waters, Bill Cross, George Grune, Dick McLoughlin—and that he did not have a shot at being named president in the foreseeable future. More to the point, Grossman was loyal to Walter Hitesman, who had spearheaded the company's marketing of long-playing records both in supermarkets and through direct mail and who later became president of the RDA. When Hitesman was forced to take early retirement, Grossman followed. With considerable clairvoyance, he foresaw a long period of confusion and did not want to spend his days "covering [his] ass."

It was for his invention of the publisher's sweepstakes, while still a junior executive in his twenties, that Grossman was chiefly esteemed by his peers in circulation and promotion. As a marketing device, the sweepstakes changed forever the way major magazine publishers conducted direct mail. And though its demise was often predicted on the ground that the very ubiquity of a sweepstakes solicitation rendered it no more effective than ordinary junk mail, the *Reader's Digest* continued to refine it in the most primitive and effective way imaginable—by upping the prize money and giving out more prizes every year.

Grossman got the idea for the sweepstakes in 1960 when the magazine was looking for a new way to increase response to magazine mailings, especially for Condensed Books. In an Oldsmobile showroom he saw a "lucky number" promotion for a car giveaway and was inspired to attempt a variation to sell magazines. Traditionally, the *Digest* was used as a lure—some like Bill Cross called it a loss leader— to obtain names for the mailing list, which was then used to market more lucrative products such as books and records. A newsstand test proved quite successful, and in the following year there was introduced through direct mail a sweepstakes contest that in hindsight proved to be too complicated. In fact, it was a huge flop.

Undeterred, Grossman and circulation director Les Dawson devised a simpler contest. At the same time, they merged it with another promotion piece that used a token. People who received the promotion in the mail were asked to place the token either next to a box that said, "Yes, I want to subscribe," or one that said, "No, I do not want to subscribe." There was no reason for anyone to mail back a no response, but having it there increased the yes responses.

The revised contest offered subscribers two token choices: "Yes, I want to enter the contest and subscribe," or "No, I do not want to subscribe but I want to enter the contest." The test on that version in 1961 ran well beyond an 11 percent return.

Dawson and Grossman then spent the next six months convincing *Digest* lawyers that the sweepstakes did not violate gambling laws. Wally, though not opposed to a full-fledged contest, was not enthusiastic about it either. He was concerned that *Digest* subscribers, whether potential first-timers or renewers, not be taken advantage of. But once he was persuaded of the sweepstakes' apparently extraordinary effectiveness and of its legality, he gave his go-ahead.

Al Cole was Grossman's principal supporter. The contest was exorbitantly expensive by the standards of the day, with a "rollout" or payment schedule of $999,000 and a top prize of $50,000. Dawson and Grossman had convinced Cole that the only way to do it right was to give away a fortune. Both circulation executives wanted the rollout to be $1,000,000, but Cole thought that advertisers might object to such a figure—an "irrational" fear, in Grossman's opinion. As it turned out, though, everyone agreed $999,000 looked better in print anyway.

The extraordinary response to the sweepstakes revolutionized direct-mail promotions and rendered the 11 percent return obsolete among the big players in magazine publishing. Moreover, as the circulation of the *Digest* marched upward by the millions, the payback to the company was threefold—an increase in advertising revenues and in larger markets both for Condensed Books and Music & Records, not to mention a host of other RDA promotions, for products ranging from clock radios to maps.

Unfortunately, there was a downside. In 1970 the Federal Trade Commission took exception to Wally's benign view that consumer rights were being protected in the sweepstakes and issued a cease-and-desist order. The FTC had received numerous complaints from consumers claiming they had been tricked into subscribing to the magazine with the false promise that they would win a prize or money. The FTC agreed with these claims. Though the RDA vigorously protested, it eventually consented to an order preventing it from "using or distributing simulated checks, currency, 'new car' certificates' or . . . any confusingly simulated item of value" in its sweepstakes solicitations.

In 1973 the RDA decided to test that consent order by including an item labeled "Travel Check" in a new sweepstakes. In 1974 it went one step further by enclosing an item identified as a "Cash-Convertible Bond." All sweepstakes copy was closely monitored by Wally, who on one occasion in 1974 even wrote to Jack O'Hara with five different proposed changes in the promotion copy. Wally had become convinced that the sweepstakes not only did not really fool the public but were a way of saving or creating new jobs at Pleasantville.

The contest between the FTC and the RDA reached a critical stage in mid-1975 when the government agency filed suit in U.S. district court in Wilmington, Delaware, charging that the *Digest* had unilaterally broken its 1971 consent order and was continuing to use deceptive practices in the sale of magazine subscriptions. In particular, the FTC objected to the distribution of millions of simulated checks, some of which were marked "$100 a Month for Life" and others "$2000 a Month for Life." After fifteen years the courts were going to decide whether the *Reader's Digest*, which had always kept suspiciously mum on the subject of gambling, was engaged in that practice itself. Wally, the old cardsharp, was betting he held the winning hand.

———

ANOTHER game was starting up in Pleasantville that year, and Wally thought he held all the aces in that one, too. He was wrong. The feminist movement had finally begun to catch up with the *Digest*. In 1964, shortly after the start of the sweepstakes, the Equal Employment Opportunity Commission (EEOC) had been created to fight discrimination in the workplace. In areas where feminists were particularly active, such as publishing, the EEOC was soon instrumental in bringing suit in federal court against employers it deemed were discriminating against women. Two notable suits against *Time* and *Newsweek* led to widespread reforms within the industry.

But the women of the *Reader's Digest,* in far-off Pleasantville, re-mained for the most part unaffected by and uninterested in the fray. Few had risen high in either the editorial or the managerial ranks, and those who had did not desire to rock the patriarchal boat. Corporate mores called for women to dress and think conservatively, accept their mostly low-paid menial or secondary positions with good grace, and look after their male bosses—in effect, to be a species of office house-wife. It was a role the majority of distaff Digesters did not despise.

The company's role model for women was, of course, Lila Acheson Wallace—who, though she wielded enormous power within the com-pany and now had a reputation in her own right as a patron of the arts, still saw her primary role as that of wife and helpmate to DeWitt Wallace. Following Lila's example, many of the *Digest's* female editors and secretaries aspired to nothing higher than the post of wife of a company executive, since it offered women in Pleasantville not merely more money but also greater social prestige than anything else did.

Al Cole's secretary and second wife, Peggy Winston, was perhaps the most successful example of male-track upward mobility. But Hobe Lewis, Bill Hard, Ed Thompson, and John Allen had also taken a second, or sometimes third, wife from within the company. (The all-time winners in the matrimonial sweepstakes were Paul Palmer and roving editor Donald Day, several of whose five wives, respectively, were also *RD* writers or editors. Among Day's works was *The Evolution of Love,* a thoughtful history of sexual customs.) Overnight, *Digest* women who "married up" went from being minor functionaries to being the wives of powerful men invited to sit down to dinner with Wally and Lila at High Winds. Yet making those same women, or any woman, the equal of men went deeply against the *Digest* grain, and so the reforms taking root in the New York publishing world were not merely ignored but viewed with disdain by Wally, Lewis, and the boys.

Moreover, Wally himself continued to engage in a form of mass sexual harassment perhaps unprecedented in American corporate his-tory. Women continued to find his "fashion shows" demeaning and humiliating. Once, at a Guest House party for World Press Institute journalists, he rounded up a number of single female staffers as part-ners for the young men from abroad. Before heading to High Winds, Wally spoke to the assembled guests:

"Young men, I'm going to give you a good piece of advice. These girls are here for only one purpose—so that you can have some fun.

And to you girls, I'm going to tell you that these men have a reputation for being fine men in their countries. If you are going to be raped, you might as well relax and enjoy it."

One of the young journalists at the party later remembered that by nightfall the Guest House had been turned into a love nest, with couples having sex "upstairs, downstairs, outside. Some guys came in with mud all over them."

The number of women who worked in Pleasantville was considerable—over two thousand. The *Digest* chartered more than twenty buses to import workers from upstate New York and Connecticut, more than 90 percent of whom were women and 75 percent of whom were married. The highest-ranking woman in the company was assistant managing editor Mary Louise Allin.

One woman in Pleasantville radically different from all the rest was Pat Tarnawsky, a writer and marathon runner who worked in Condensed Books. Under her maiden name, Patricia Nell Warren, she wrote novels with pronounced homosexual themes, including *The Front Runner,* later regarded as a classic in modern homoerotic literature. Senior editor and fellow runner Peter Canning read one of her novels and was shocked. In a land of immovable objects, she was an irresistible force, and she had little use for Wally, Lewis, and the boys, and for all the timid women in the company to boot.

Apart from Tarnawsky, the only feminist ferment in the small world of the *Reader's Digest* was among the mostly female researchers in the Pan Am Building, in Manhattan, who were exposed by dint of geography to the rising tide of women's liberation. Also, with their Seven Sisters education, they tended to be better educated than the average woman at the home office. Among them was Susan Smith, a Vassar graduate who joined the company the same year the EEOC was created.

One evening in 1970 longtime department head Gertrude Arundel and several of her researchers were attending a cocktail party where the conversation turned informally to the topic of whether there was discrimination against women at the *Digest.* Some pointed out the obvious segregations—in the all-male Washington bureau, the almost all-female research department, the male monopoly at the top of the masthead, the lack of female roving editors. Other women thought they were being treated just fine. Arundel herself took the Pleasantville line that the women of the *Digest* had nothing serious to complain about.

But somebody mentioned Tarnawsky's name, and Smith decided to get in touch. Thereafter, the two women began to discuss ideas and discrimination regularly. Tarnawsky's consciousness-raising dated from the time she ran in the Boston Marathon—before women were officially allowed to enter—and she had been kicked, pushed, and insulted for twenty-six miles. Smith agreed to research whether the *Digest* might be violating any of its female employees' rights. She also got in touch with Harriet Rabb, a law professor at Columbia University who had successfully represented the women who marched against *Time*. Said Tarnawsky, "We have to run around the track one more time."

It was a practice, around then, for editors from Pleasantville to visit the research department occasionally to discuss editorial and other matters on an informal basis so that the researchers would not feel isolated. The talks were held in the small library, which contained only six chairs. Originally, the women researchers sat on the floor and the few males occupied the chairs. But as the *Digest*'s feminist movement blossomed, the males soon found themselves sitting on the floor and the women standing or sitting. One night executive editor Ed Thompson himself showed up.

"Listen, you broads," he said, and then went on to defend the *RD*'s pay scale and advancement policy for women, though a little halfheartedly. Someone asked why a woman had never been named to any of the top editorial positions at the *Digest*.

"Because there was never a woman who qualified," Thompson replied.

Smith thought, "That never stopped any of the male editors from advancing." But she remained silent. Smith had also written a memo to Thompson asking for a promotion. He replied with characteristic bluntness that she was not good enough to deserve a promotion, and added that women in general did not work out in Pleasantville. Rabb, when she saw the memo, was delighted. She considered it "hot"—incriminating.

Editor in chief Lewis never went down to talk to the researchers. But Jeremy Dole, the ex–*Playboy* editor, sensed that the women were unhappy and sent out invitations reading, "Just to let you know we love you," for a Valentine Day's party at the Yale Club. In those days that still-unliberated male bastion required women guests to shuttle behind a screen on entering or run into the open palm of the doorman.

However, the party was a great success, and the researchers were grateful for Dole's gesture. Despite his tough-guy posturing, Thompson was well regarded by the researchers, who recognized that he wanted justice and fairness for them even when he sometimes put his foot in his mouth.

Meanwhile, for a brief time, articles on women became more popular in the pages of the *Digest* than articles on dogs. Hobe Lewis's editorial policy seemed designed to counter the growing tide of feminist sentiment not only across America but in Pleasantville itself. Female as well as male writers were enlisted in the struggle. Elsieliese Thrope's May 1972 piece, "But Women *Are* the Favored Sex," bleated, "If Women's Libbers win their war, they will certainly lose the peace."

Over the next several months Tarnawsky and Smith bravely took their campaign public, even though they knew they were committing career suicide. Tarnawsky made a number of speeches to groups of women in Pleasantville, explaining that she felt that discrimination against their sex was the result of cultural factors and not a conscious policy by management. She hoped that Wally and Lewis, as reasonable men, would recognize the gross injustice of the situation once they were presented with evidence showing that women were being paid considerably less than men for doing the same work.

At the first big meeting organized by the feminists, more than a hundred women showed up. Later a number of volunteers drew up a white paper that listed instances of injustice as well as demands for remedy. The paper was sent to Hobe Lewis in the form of a memo, and copies were circulated among top editors and touched off a series of lower-level meetings and considerable debate in the corridors and cafeteria.

After four weeks with no reply, the women began to get restless—and insulted. They felt that Lewis, Wally, and the others were laughing at them, patronizing them. To make matters worse, a group of five hundred *Digest* women signed a statement saying they bore no grudge against the company and thought it a fine place to work. By the end of the tenth week, Lewis still had not replied. Despite the recent gains made by women at *Time* and *Newsweek,* it was obvious that the male hierarchy of the *Reader's Digest* was not going to give an inch.

At this point a small group of activists from Pleasantville and New York held a secret meeting to discuss strategy. Father Andrew Mullins of St. Bartholomew's Episcopal Church, a few blocks north of the Pan

Am offices, made the parish hall available. At the meeting the women decided to file suit. Mullins also gave the women use of the church's printing facilities and, subsequently, of parish premises for a press conference when the suit was announced in 1973.

When Wally first heard of the legal action, he cried out, "But we love our girls!" The suit weighed heavily on the magazine's founder, who was disturbed by the women's seeming lack of gratitude. He was also annoyed that he was being perceived as a male-chauvinist culprit and that the company's generous employment policies were being rejected as deficient.

The suit entailed the taking of an endless number of depositions, many of them lasting up to five hours—all on company time. Legal fees were mounting. Harriet Rabb and her students—all frequent visitors to campus headquarters—were investigating, keeping records, writing subpoenas designed to bring in necessary information.

Shortly after the suit was filed, Wally summoned one of the ringleaders, an editor named Elaine Franklin, to his office. Franklin was elated, hoping that the summons meant a break in the stalemate. She was a relatively new member of the editorial staff, having worked for the *Digest* only three years, and had been hired without first being reviewed by Wally. He knew of her only by reputation.

When Franklin entered the room, Wally did not walk halfway to greet her as he often did with visitors, though she still thought he seemed friendly. But when she reached his desk, he also did not invite her to sit down. After a mumbled hello he asked her straight off to tell him what was on her mind.

Taken aback, Franklin sensed that Wally felt personally offended. But she did not want to let the opportunity pass. Standing there, she explained that some women working for the company wanted to make a career in publishing and therefore deserved not only equal pay for equal work but also an equal opportunity for advancement with men so that they would have the same dignity and status.

Warming to the subject, she could not discern whether Wally was listening attentively or wearing a mask of indifference that allowed him to think his own thoughts. When she was finished, he came around from his desk and spoke: "Do you know you've got fire in your eyes when you get excited?"

It was half question, half exclamation. Then he bowed and motioned toward the door with a gesture of dismissal, while murmuring that she must tell him more some other time. Once outside the office, Franklin could do nothing but laugh—partly in outrage and disbelief, but partly in contempt.

Smith v. *the Reader's Digest,* a class-action suit filed under Title VII of the Civil Rights Act of 1964, was finally ordered to trial in the spring of 1977 before the U.S. District Court of the Southern District of New York. In her brief Rabb called not only for equalization of salaries and retroactive additional pay for women who earned less than men in comparable positions but also for an end to discriminatory hiring, placement, and promotion policies. The plaintiffs also protested such demeaning practices as keeping a record of the number of visits female clerical staffers made to rest rooms and the length of stay. Perhaps most shocking, not a single woman whom Rabb interviewed before filing the suit had ever worked up the nerve to ask for a raise.

The unique defense mounted by the RDA only deepened the collective outrage and disbelief of the feminists. The company declared that under the First Amendment it had a right to hire whom it pleased, including only men, to carry out its editorial policies—just as a women's magazine had a right to have only women as editors and a magazine for blacks had the right to hire only blacks as editors.

By now the struggle had lasted seven years. With every passing month it became clearer that the company's case was hopeless. Yet the RDA showed no intention of backing down or making an out-of-court settlement. Then, late one Sunday afternoon—the day before trial—Wally called treasurer Dick Waters and told him to settle. Waters immediately called chief *Digest* negotiator Martha Farquhar—a competent in-house lawyer, though the use of a female lawyer was obviously a ploy on the part of management—who at that moment was visiting Rabb at her offices at Columbia.

On November 5, 1977, the RDA made front-page news in the *New York Times* when it formally announced it had agreed to pay 2,600 present and former employees more than $1.5 million in settlement of a suit brought by eight women four years earlier. Past and present employees were to get lump-sum payments ranging up to $5,500 each. In addition, the salaries of those still working for the company were adjusted by as much as $8,000 a year. Women were also promised more high-level jobs. Earlier that year NBC had agreed to similar terms for its women employees.

Fully half of the women had asked to be dissociated from the suit, and many did not want to cash their share of the settlement when they were eventually presented with a check. Lila Wallace's secretary, Dorothy Little, after finding herself $3,000 richer, was furious. She told Lila she did not want to accept the money, after all the Wallaces had done for her and other women in the company. But Lila the ex–social worker replied that the settlement was something both she and Wally had agreed to.

"It hurt," Lila said. "But if you don't cash the check, it'll just be divided up by those others."

___

ANOTHER lawsuit involving the *Digest* about this time was the suit by Harold Courlander and Crown Publishers against Alex Haley, the *Reader's Digest,* Doubleday, the ABC Network, and the *New York Post.* Courlander was the author of the 1967 novel *The African,* published by Crown. In a suit filed in U.S. District Court for the Southern District of New York, Courlander and Crown claimed that Haley's *Roots* was "copied largely" from Courlander's novel and asked that further marketing of the book and TV presentations be enjoined. Haley later settled out of court, paying Courlander a substantial six-figure sum. Nevertheless, the man who had so eloquently thanked Lila Acheson Wallace for making it possible for him to research his book remained a *Digest* roving editor, and his Pulitzer Prize was not rescinded.

___

THE CASE of the FTC versus the RDA dragged on for five years. In the meantime, however, sweepstakes promotions had been wholeheartedly adopted by Madison Avenue and were being used not only by other publishers but by Avis, TWA, the National Easter Seals Society, and others. The popularity of the sweepstakes, also known as giveaways, was assisted by a couple of recessions and rising unemployment. The Direct Mail Advertising Association estimated that advertising mail accounted for 30 billion pieces annually, or 160 pieces for every man, woman, and child.

The chances of winning anything were still remote—in the case of the *Digest,* 20,564,000 to 1. Even so, that left plenty of winners. As of February 1977 the *Digest* had awarded $12.2 million to 781,514 individuals, half of whom did not subscribe.

Despite the ubiquity of sweepstakes, in July 1980 Chief Judge James L. Latchum found in favor of the plaintiff and ordered the *Digest* to pay civil penalties amounting to $1.75 million for violating a consent decree obtained by the FTC in 1971. Ignoring last-minute requests to keep secret information under seal, Latchum also released data suggesting that the RDA had a net worth of $325 million. The after-tax profit for the 1976–78 tax period was more than $37 million, while the RDA's gross revenues exceeded $475 million. The fine, based on that net worth, was the largest ever for a violation of this type.

The RDA appealed, but in August 1982 the third U.S. Circuit Court of Appeals upheld the lower court's ruling. The RDA then took the case to the Supreme Court, which in January 1982 let stand without comment the ruling and fine.

Having lost in the courts, the RDA now decided to use diplomacy and persuasion. By this time not only had the novelty of the promotion worn off, but the number of complaints to the FTC had fallen sharply. In a series of negotiations with the FTC, *Digest* executives attempted to persuade the government that sweepstakes were really just harmless games.

The strategy worked. In October 1983 the FTC reversed itself, agreeing that the use of the word "sweepstakes" in its promotions was "harmless puffery" that did not mislead consumers. It further agreed that the *Digest* could also use the word "lucky" in its promotions.

In an unusual addendum in the *Federal Register,* FTC commissioner Michael Pertschuk emphasized the real point of the suit—not so much whether the sweepstakes were illegal or deceptive, but that the *RD* had flouted the consent agreement. Like the women of Pleasantville, the FTC only wanted a little respect.

25

The Men Who Would
Be King

IF THE WARRING COURT of Pleasantville had a Rasputin, it was corporate counsel William Barnabas McHenry, playing his role as philanthropic savant and financial confessor to Lila Acheson Wallace's increasingly spacey Czarina Alexandra. While a handful of the nobles wanted to give him a poison pill, they could not agree on the formula.

The resourceful house lawyer really had no need of allies, much less of admirers. Once he was asked by a business acquaintance for the secret of his success at the RDA. McHenry replied, "I never made one friend but a hell of a lot of enemies, and that has made my success." Though the remark showed typical bravado, McHenry was also shrewd enough to know that, in the volatile atmosphere of RDA office politics, any alliance could ultimately prove fatal.

Like Al Cole and others before him, Ed Thompson frequently told Jack O'Hara and others that the RDA's counsel was "incompetent" and urged that he be fired. O'Hara agreed, at least up to a point.

It especially galled Thompson how a legal hybrid called a supporting organization, or SO, had been set up for each of the charities that were going to inherit the RDA after the Wallaces died. Eight of them—Sloan-Kettering Memorial Hospital, Macalester College, Hudson Highlands (a New York State environmental group), the New York Zoological Society, Community Funds, Lincoln Center, the Metropolitan Museum of Art, Colonial Williamsburg—owned no voting stock. Two funds established in the names of DeWitt and Lila Wallace, which owned all the voting stock, and a smaller fund associated with Macalester rounded out the ownership.

Half public charity and half private foundation, the SO allowed each beneficiary to own stock in a for-profit corporation. The board of each SO generally comprised two representatives from the RDA, an equal number from the charity itself, and one or two outsiders.

Through an oversight on McHenry's part, the contractual arrangements between the RDA and the SOs neglected to inform them how they could dispose of their stock. For a time each of the charities—though none apparently understood the situation—had the option to sell its RDA stock on the open market rather than back to the company. That potentially disastrous state of affairs had led to a great deal of scrambling in the legal department. The head of each charity had to be gingerly approached and informed, in effect, that the RDA wanted to make an amendment to the contract without revealing exactly what it was.

Despite this legal nightmare, no one, not even the owners of the company, quite knew how to get rid of McHenry. While the nobles killed one another off, McHenry endured, even thrived. Indeed, he boasted that he had survived every change in business administration and had nothing to fear from the latest crop of executives up in Pleasantville.

McHenry did not like to use an expression twice. One of the few he liked to repeat, apparently forgetful of all the problems it had caused at Macalester, was "There are very few problems in this world that can't be solved by money." Boasting about the famous people he met as the Wallaces' envoy was another habit. Once he sat next to Jacqueline Kennedy Onassis at a dinner party—a moment he was especially proud of. Another encounter with celebrity involved former vice-president Nelson Rockefeller, who on the night of January 26, 1979, had gone to his town house on West Fifty-fifth Street with his "assistant," Megan Marshack. While the two were having sex, Rockefeller suffered a heart attack.

In a panic Marshack called a girlfriend, who phoned McHenry. At his direction the two women dressed Rockefeller and called the police. Rockefeller was dead on arrival at the hospital. Though some details of Rockefeller's death and Marshack's cover-up eventually leaked out, McHenry's role was known to only a very few higher-ups at the *Digest*. His loyal service in the family cause was one more reason why he enjoyed the gratitude and appreciation of the RDA's powerful trustee Laurance S. Rockefeller.

Not surprisingly, McHenry regarded few of the other RDA employees as his social equals. The RDA house counsel belonged to the small, ultra-exclusive social circle in Manhattan devoted to the arts and fund-raising. He insisted that the legal department remain in the Pan Am Building in part because he did not want to spend any more time in Pleasantville than necessary. Kent Rhodes, when he was chairman, grew tired of people asking him at charity balls and opening nights whether he knew Barney McHenry. Rhodes's standard, irritable reply: "Yeah, he works for me."

McHenry also had to deal with his old nemesis Al Cole, who had unsuccessfully tried to get him fired on several occasions, only to find himself thrust out into the cold one dismal Christmas Eve at a restaurant called Nino's. In the intervening dozen years or so, Cole had become a nonperson at the RDA, even though he still served both as a consultant and as a trustee. But the former post was meaningless because nobody consulted him about anything, and the board of trustees never met, for the simple reason that Wally and Lila did not like meetings.

During this period Wally and Cole remained estranged, exchanging Christmas cards but not seeing each other socially. The only significant exception had occurred during the Macalester troubles when Cole, as a college trustee, reported to Wally on his talk with then president Arthur Flemming. At another point Cole, ever the deal maker, tried to interest Wally in buying *Redbook*. Wally coldly turned him down.

However, sometime around 1978 Wally suffered the first of several minor strokes. Cole went to see him, and from that time on Wally began to draw him back into life at Pleasantville. Cole returned more than willingly. Wally perhaps wanted his once most trusted adviser, now in his late seventies, to counsel him as the RDA moved inexorably toward the post-Wallace era.

In that connection Cole one day asked the founder who the executors of his will were. Wally replied, "I don't know, Al."

"For God's sake," Cole exclaimed, "you don't know who the executors of your will are?"

"No, I don't," Wally admitted.

"I think you better find out," Cole advised him.

"Where do you think the will is?" a befuddled Wally asked.

"Hell, I don't know where your will is," Cole replied. "You must know. Don't you have a safe-deposit box somewhere?"

"Oh. I guess I have. Maybe it's upstairs."

"Well, I think you'd better get it."

"All right," said Wally. "I'll get it."

The next day the two men had lunch, and Wally brought the will along. Cole learned that Barnabas McHenry was the sole executor.

"Wally, that's the greatest mistake you could possibly make," said Cole, "to have one executor of your estate of this giant business. It's most unfair to the employees of the company."

"Will you be one?" Wally asked.

"Well," Cole replied, "I don't want to be, though I will if you want. But there are others who ought to be on there instead."

"I want you to be on it," Wally insisted.

"I think you ought to appoint O'Hara and Thompson," said Cole. "They're the two people who are running the company, and if you appoint them, then at least McHenry can't steal the place."

"Why don't I fire McHenry?" Wally asked. "I've never had any use for him anyway. And neither does Lila."

"Don't do anything about McHenry," Cole said. "You've got problems here, and you can't tell what they'll be. Don't get that fellow trying to be as nasty as he could be."

"Can't I fire him?" Wally asked again.

"No, you can't," said Cole.

McHenry possessed potentially incriminating information not only about the Wallaces, of course, but about Cole as well. The lawyer knew that the ex–business manager told Lewis to serve as Nixon's bagman. Wally's greatest vulnerability lay with his philanthropies, which he often used as a cover to pad the retirement or compensation packages of favored employees. No one ever doubted the sincerity of his motives when he arranged for Digesters to serve on the boards of organizations to which he gave money. But honorariums, free travel, and other perquisites—many of them nontaxable—were often involved. Another of Wally's tax-evading ploys was to arrange for the children of privileged Digesters to travel abroad courtesy of the RDA's Foreign Study League.

Cole also thought McHenry had the Wallaces "scared" because some of their charitable contributions, though made with the best of intentions, would get them into trouble with the IRS if it ever found out. A case in point was Lila's contribution to the Korean Angels, operated by the Unification church of the Reverend Sun Myung Moon. McHenry, according to Cole, convinced the Wallaces he was able to ensure that the contribution remained tax deductible despite Moon's own troubles with the IRS. Some, like Harry Morgan, suspected that McHenry simply cowed the Wallaces, saying they ought to die with their good name intact.

A further reason for not stirring the legal waters was that both Wally and Lila were beginning to exhibit unmistakable signs of senility. In various subtle ways McHenry had intimated that any attempt to oust him would result in a huge, protracted lawsuit and in horrible publicity for the *Digest.* Yet he also regarded most members of senior management as would-be corrupters and perverters of the Wallace legacy. The Wallace manqué had come to believe that no one understood the Wallaces' philanthropic instincts half so well as he himself.

Wally did agree to adding the names of O'Hara and Thompson to his will, but he still wanted Cole to be listed as an executor as well. Shortly afterward both O'Hara and Thompson invited Cole to lunch and told him McHenry had threatened to go to court and prove that Wallace was non compos mentis if Cole were listed as an executor. Since Cole had no interest in being listed anyway, he agreed to drop out.

In due course Jack O'Hara and Ed Thompson were named coexecutors of DeWitt Wallace's estate, which controlled 50 percent of the company's stock. The terms of the will called for the entire estate to pass on to Lila, if she survived him. O'Hara and Thompson were also named coexecutors of Lila's estate. McHenry remained a coexecutor, as well as the executor of the various trust funds and other personal matters that the Wallaces had set up for relatives, friends, and a few close employees.

The new arrangement seemed to diminish McHenry's power and to enhance that of the company's two chief executives. Another clause in the two wills called for coexecutors O'Hara and Thompson to control 50 percent of the voting stock of the Reader's Digest Association after both Wally and Lila died. That meant, theoretically, they were both invulnerable so long as each remained loyal to the other.

But the new arrangement also put the enemies of Thompson and O'Hara on short notice. The balance of power was now being measured out in a corporate hourglass—containing, figuratively, the lifeblood of DeWitt and Lila Acheson Wallace. If there were to be any palace coups, they would have to occur before Thompson and O'Hara inherited even greater powers and the mantle of invincibility.

ONE afternoon in the late seventies, Jack O'Hara went up to High Winds to report informally, as he did from time to time, on how the company was doing. Wally was always especially interested in the foreign editions of the magazine. On that particular day O'Hara was troubled by the declining fortunes of the Danish edition. A loss of several hundred thousand dollars had been projected for the coming year, and O'Hara had come to ask whether the RDA should close down its Danish subsidiary.

After a brief discussion, Wally went over to his desk, wrote out a check for the amount of the projected loss, and handed it to the company CEO. O'Hara got the message. Wally simply did not want the RDA to become a bottom-line communications giant like Time Inc. In his view the *Digest's* highest priority was to serve the American public and, in a larger sense, the whole world with information and inspiration offered at the lowest possible cost.

O'Hara did not deem this a naive view, only a singular one, which was to be borne home to him over and over again: the RDA existed not only to make money but to perform a service to people. If a new project was to be initiated, or a well-established division terminated, the operative question was always the same: what was in the best interests of the worldwide readership of the *Reader's Digest?*

Thus every time an increase in the cover price was proposed, Wally resisted—not always successfully. He found the very concept of price testing abhorrent. He also wanted subscribers who paid in installments to pay the same amount—with no interest or handling charge—as those who paid all at once. The result was that the RDA acted more like a nonprofit, public-service corporation than any other *Fortune* 500–size company in the world.

That state of affairs also meant sometimes hiding facts and figures from Wally. For example, the German company, one of O'Hara's many former homes, was enjoying considerable success on all fronts—magazine, books, recorded music. Yet O'Hara knew he could not tell that to Wally, who would regard so much profit as obscene. On more than one occasion when he demanded to know where all the money was coming from, he ordered a reduction in price, whether in the cost of a subscription, a book, or a record. The minimum necessary profit, Wally instructed O'Hara, meant selling everything at the lowest possible price. Half the time he went up to High Winds, it sometimes seemed to the company president, it was to justify the price of a record album or a book.

Despite such constraints, O'Hara did not find it impossible to run the business with adequate profit. The big problem lay with other executives, primarily in marketing, who viewed Wally's philosophy with amused condescension. The result was that O'Hara stood virtually alone, his finger in the dike, holding back the flood tide of diversification, growth, and the full marketing exploitation of the *Digest*'s 100-million-name mailing list, the world's best and largest.

Wally's second priority was his employees. He looked upon all Digesters as members of one big extended family and instructed O'Hara to distribute free turkeys to everyone at Thanksgiving—another corporate first, at least on such a scale, and one that stood for years as a symbol of how quirkily benevolent the RDA had become, and how cavalierly indifferent to the bottom line. Employees also continued to get Fridays off in May, days now referred to affectionately as "Wally days." Moreover, he directed O'Hara to bring the international companies up to U.S. standards, especially regarding pension and health plans.

On the other hand, Wally and Lila seemed indifferent to the rank and file's acute case of collective anxiety. Nobody had any idea whether the company would eventually go public or remain private. Going public meant change, accountability to stockholders, a loss of the RDA's unique identity as an organization that put service before profit. But remaining private suggested that the company would continue to be the frustrated giant of direct-mail publishing—the feisty champion of a free-market economy that was forbidden to practice fully what it preached. It was almost as if Wally had invented a perverse, capitalistic form of communism just for his employees.

Worse, it seemed to be working. In 1979 the RDA reached a milestone by becoming a billion-dollar company. Domestic circulation had climbed to 18.3 million—a figure which, for advertising and other reasons, had been stabilized for the past five years and which was exceeded only by that of *TV Guide*. Worldwide the magazine boasted 100 million readers in thirty-nine editions, published in fifteen different languages. After several flat years advertising was also sharply on the increase, though both *TV Guide* and *Time* garnered a greater share of the market.

The third priority was charity. Whatever was left over was to be given away. Increasingly, though, the choice of which charities received how much RDA money was being made not by Wally, or by Lila, but by Laurance Rockefeller, who dominated the board of trustees. Many top Digesters were annoyed that four million dollars of RDA money had gone to Colonial Williamsburg—the first major gift to the historic Virginia village that did not come from a Rockefeller. But it *was* Rockefeller money, in a sense. With Wally and Lila in their dotage, Rockefeller had suddenly been given indirect control of a vast philanthropic fortune. Toward that end he found a more than willing ally in Barney McHenry. Excluded from the philanthropic decision-making process, O'Hara was obliged to rubber-stamp the major bequests engineered by Rockefeller as representative of the will of the trustees.

Despite or perhaps because of the atypical situation he found himself in, O'Hara the Britisher tried to model himself personally on Wally, the old-fashioned American. Temperamentally, the two men were opposites. Like Thompson, O'Hara was abrasive, gruff, prone to bursts of temper. But his public profile resembled the founder's. O'Hara knew that DeWitt Wallace did not like people who aggrandized themselves. Wally himself, in O'Hara's view, was not so much secretive as exceedingly private, a man who shrank from self-publicity.

O'Hara thus gave no interviews during his entire reign, with the exception of one to *Business Week* shortly after his appointment. As a result of that and Thompson's own low-key public profile, the RDA's reputation for secrecy persisted, both in the mind of the public and in the corridors of Pleasantville itself. Adding to that aura, apart from the Washington bureau's breathless peddling of CIA-spun tales of Soviet conspiracy and intrigue, was the mystery of what was going to happen to the company after Wally and Lila died. Not only did the reporters from *Business Week* come away with no answers to that question, but hardly anyone in Pleasantville knew either.

O'Hara and Thompson knew, of course, but were not authorized to release that information to anyone. And they learned the fate of the RDA only when, after being made trustees, they arranged to have lunch with the company's two cofounders specifically to find out what the ultimate provisions of the will were. It was a delicate question, but it had to be broached. Finally, O'Hara managed to blurt out that he wanted to ask something relating to the company's future. Lila gave him a cold look. "We may deign not to respond," she replied.

But she and Wally did respond, and that was how the editor in chief and the president of the Reader's Digest Association were told the company's most closely guarded secret—that eleven charities would inherit the kingdom of Pleasantville. Wally also gave instructions that the company remain forever private and High Winds become a guest house for visitors.

Two of the most powerful dissenters to Wally's less-is-better philosophy were Condensed Books and Recorded Music director George Grune and director of magazine operations Richard F. McLoughlin, two former advertising salesmen who typified the "new breed" of employees that began to appear in Pleasantville in the midfifties when the magazine elected to accept advertising.

A burly but still muscular former marine who rose at dawn to jog and work out before reporting to work an hour early, Grune joined the RDA in 1960, later became manager of the Pittsburgh office, then marketing director of the U.S. edition of the magazine. Tall, soft-spoken, forever flashing a salesman's ready smile and handshake, he had assumed his present post in 1976 and the following year was elected to the board of directors. The nondescript McLoughlin—a grown-up version of the clean-cut boy next door—joined the company in 1956, became advertising sales director in 1969, and like Grune was elected a director in 1977. In early 1980 Charles Hepler was forced out as publisher and replaced by McLoughlin, who also continued as director of magazine operations.

Though Grune and McLoughlin often operated in uneasy tandem, the former was seen as the stronger and more ambitious. He had pressured O'Hara to sell a variety of merchandise and later urged that pocket calculators be given away as a premium to new subscribers. O'Hara refused. Grune appealed to Wally, who also said no. Despite the setback, Grune continued to enjoy the support not only of Cole but of board members Laurance Rockefeller and Harold Helm, who admired the ex-leatherneck's gung-ho drive.

Privately, both Cole and Rockefeller were of the opinion that the RDA should become exactly the communications giant Wally did not want it to become. Cole had even tried to get Wally to take the company public, while Rockefeller's ulterior motive was to generate as much profit as possible for the charities that were going to become the RDA's owners after Lila's death. If Wally was guilty of naïveté, it was in assuming that Rockefeller and Helm, the two arch-capitalists whom he had appointed as outside trustees, would embrace his eccentric vision of a publishing empire that took such a cavalier attitude toward good old capitalistic profit.

Nonetheless, in a company of the RDA's size, complete creative stasis was impossible—some new ventures were inevitable. The two most notable during this period involved a magazine start-up and an acquisition. Both were disasters. They were headed by the most ardent apostles of expansionism, by Dick McLoughlin and George Grune, respectively—though, in the latter's case, with less than characteristic enthusiasm.

When Madison Avenue first heard that the pokey, old-fashioned RDA was actually considering the launch of a new magazine, its first in fifty-six years, many observers were skeptical. After all, in recent years the company had considered and then abandoned plans for publications in such areas as do-it-yourself, health, sports, retirement, and business. Talk of yet another magazine, this one to be called *Families,* left most advertising agencies believing it would join the others in never-never land.

Moreover, despite its impressive record of achievement with the magazine, condensed books, and records, the RDA also had a history of failure that seemed to point to a moral—namely, that what the company did best, and what was its basic strength, was to repackage the creativity of others. Whenever it tried to be creative itself, it flopped miserably, as witness its misadventures in Hollywood, its failure to produce successful family entertainment for television, and the stillborn *Campus Courier.* Added to all that was a failed television magazine begun in Germany and a misbegotten women's magazine in Spain, not to mention the Condensed Bible.

In January 1980 the RDA had bought 20 percent of *Book Digest* from Dow Jones & Company in exchange for direct-mail and other subscription sales assistance, distribution expertise, and the like. Only six years old, *Book Digest*—a monthly literary review—had been acquired by Dow two years earlier for $10 million and currently enjoyed a circulation of one million and advertising revenues of almost $5 million.

Soon after the RDA took an equity position in the publication, however, Dow moved to reduce circulation dramatically, to 400,000, by sharply increasing the subscription price. Advertising rates were also slashed to less than half. Dow's rationale was that 400,000 faithful subscribers were of better quality (higher income and education) than one million who simply elected to subscribe because the price was low. The RDA, which thought only in terms of mass marketing, was aghast. Squabbling over lines of authority quickly intensified, and eventually the RDA sold its share of the company back to Dow. Though no significant financial loss was incurred, the psychological repercussions were depressingly familiar—the RDA was trapped inside a mass-market web of its own making and unable to sell anything besides its general-interest, lowest-common-denominator magazine, condensed books, and generic music.

There was one bright beacon of hope, however. The usually reliable product-testing department had determined through random questionnaires that there was a market niche for a new publication whose editorial content was focused somewhere between that of *Parents* magazine and that of women's service magazines. Further group and one-on-one interviews at shopping malls confirmed the rosy prospects of a magazine tentatively titled *Families*—a standard-size monthly for busy parents, primarily female, who wanted only one magazine to give them tips on how to raise children while still enjoying a great sex life and looking glamorous.

After getting the go-ahead from Wally, *Families* was launched in October 1980 with an initial print run of 400,000 and Jeremy Dole at the editorial helm. But Wally, his mind almost gone by now, had little understanding of what the RDA was really up to. Publisher McLoughlin and advertising director Lynn Mapes had also successfully persuaded Madison Avenue to take the venture seriously—so much so, in fact, that the launch set a new record, sixty-seven, for most advertising pages for a maiden issue of a consumer magazine. Only two weeks earlier the previous record—sixty pages—had been established when Time Inc. launched *Discover,* a monthly devoted to science.

In the rush to publish, however, the RDA abandoned its traditional marketing strength—direct mail—and chose instead to sell the entire first issue through single-copy sales on newsstands and supermarkets. Heavy premiums paid to wholesalers and retailers ensured prominent display but eroded profit. The strategy called for publishing the magazine originally as a quarterly and then converting it to a monthly at an opportune time.

High newsstand sales based on a quarterly—not monthly—newsstand life, and overly optimistic projections of advertising revenues, eventually persuaded the board of directors to give McLoughlin approval to go to a monthly format, beginning with the November issue. Within five years, predicted a jubilant Mapes, circulation would reach two million.

Twenty-one months, nine issues, and sixteen million dollars later, *Families* was folded. The recession of 1981–82 was partly to blame. Advertising had dropped to an average of only forty-two pages an issue, while circulation remained substantially below the guaranteed 600,000. But market analysis was also seriously to blame. With the Condensed Bible, the RDA had simply underestimated the public's aversion to tampering with Scripture. *Families* represented a miscalculation of a different sort—identifying a niche in the market that did not exist. Once again the company had failed by straying not only from its direct-mail strengths but also from its mass-market base. O'Hara, who had supported the project from the beginning, bore the brunt of the blame.

While *Families* was being launched, O'Hara also arranged for the RDA to take a 51 percent equity position in the Source Telecomputing Corporation, a supplier of electronic services—data banks, games, electronic mail—to owners of home computers, for $3 million. Based in McLean, Virginia, Source had 7,000 subscribers and annual revenues averaging between $150,000 and $200,000. The RDA's plan was simple to the point of simplism—to make the same service available to the *Digest*'s 18 million subscribers, or at least to those of them who owned a home computer, even though the company had not done sufficient research on exactly how large that market was.

The RDA soon learned that it had bought a can of worms—a company teetering on collapse with millions of dollars in debt, hundreds of customers infuriated over poor service, and the two founders suing each other in court.

Undeterred, Pleasantville in December increased its holdings to 80 percent, at the cost of another $1 million, then paid off Source's debts of $2.56 million. Meanwhile, the RDA had still failed to determine whether there was a mass market for Source services. A further complication was that the data-bank field was already overcrowded, with nearly fifty other companies offering similar services, mostly to computer buffs. The RDA then compounded its folly by trying to market not only the information service but also a French-made computer for between $500 and $700.

In June 1982 Grune was given the biggest task of his life—to snatch Source from the ashes of bankruptcy. By now the company's investment had reached nearly $20 million, with annual losses ranging up to $7 million on revenues of $8 million. Internal factionalism also remained a significant problem.

The main difficulty with Source, as Grune quickly realized, was that it embodied an idea whose time had come too early. Nearly everyone expected home information services to become a big business eventually. But in 1982 the home personal computer was still a relatively rare commodity. Moreover, usage rates were high. Perhaps most important, Source faced a formidable competitor in CompuServe, which had several advantages—a commercial time-sharing business and a popular sex line that allowed customers so inclined to "talk" to one another anonymously and uninhibitedly. Those advantages steadily translated into CompuServe's growing dominance.

Grune was a tough, able administrator who quickly succeeded in paring costs and improving service. Putting the company on a profitable footing proved a more elusive goal, however. Ultimately, his plan was to sell Source, and in March 1983 he persuaded the Control Data Corporation to take a position in the company. For the time being, though, the RDA continued to maintain a controlling interest in its electronic white elephant.

Despite such ventures as *Families* and Source, and despite the limitations imposed on the company by its idiosyncratic owner, many industry specialists thought that the RDA's domestic market was saturated and criticized the company for not exploiting the *Digest* name—and especially its priceless mailing list—more aggressively in other areas.

O'Hara and other executives met those criticisms, somewhat haplessly, by saying growth and greater profits were not a priority goal. Publicly, even CFO William Cross was obliged to claim that profits were "secondary" to providing a good product at a reasonable price and to "making this a good place to work." Privately, all were at their wit's end.

26

———

The Final
Condensation

ONE DAY in 1979 Wally and Harry Morgan were having lunch when Wally said, "Harry, I need your help. We've got to work on Lila because she's becoming a recluse. She's staying at home, and I'm afraid she's going to start using a walker and I don't want her to use a wheelchair, because that'll be the end. Now, Lila's the most interesting woman in America and there are a lot of people who would like to know her, but she refuses to see people. You know a lot of interesting people. I'd like Lila to have some new friends."

Morgan then happened to be sitting on the board of directors of the New York City Opera Company, whose newest member was the recently retired coloratura Beverly Sills. Chairman John Samuels had previously told Sills that Morgan had worked closely with DeWitt and Lila Wallace, and Sills in turn asked Morgan if there was any way she could meet the two philanthropists and patrons of the arts. Morgan offered to set up a lunch. A few days later he phoned Wally and said he was reporting on his effort to bring some new friends into Lila's life.

"That's great," Wally said. "What have you got on?"

Morgan suggested that Lila have lunch with the opera star Beverly Sills.

"Good, hang on. Hang on," Wally said. "Don't hang up."

After going off to see Lila, he reported back that Lila was excited about the opera star's coming all the way from California for lunch, but thought it a terrible imposition. Morgan asked what he meant.

"You said she's coming from Beverly Hills."

"No, Beverly Sills, the opera singer," Morgan said, talking loudly into the phone.

"I heard you the first time," Wally said, "and if she's going to be in town anyway, then Lila will see her. But don't have her make any special trip."

"Beverly Sills!" Morgan shouted.

"Right. When is she going to be in town?"

They made a date for Lila to meet the opera star on Thursday at the River Club. The lunch went off as scheduled, and afterward Sills related to Morgan that the experience was one of the highlights of her life. She added that Lila had promised to give the opera company one million dollars to start a fund to encourage American singers.

Later Sills tried to call Lila and got no answer. She asked Morgan for the private number to High Winds, which he was reluctant to give out, since he did not want a repeat of the *Alice* affair. He gave her instead the name of someone who had the private number, and Sills called that person and got it. But she could still not get through to Lila. Weeks went by, and Sills told Morgan that Lila's behavior did not seem compatible with the woman she had lunch with at the River Club.

Later Sills heard that Barney McHenry had advised Lila that the Metropolitan Opera Company would be upset if the rival New York City Opera Company received a one-million-dollar gift from the Wallaces. It was an almost identical replay of Lila's attempt to give a one-million-dollar gift to Risë Stevens, only to be thwarted by Rudolf Bing. McHenry, who served on the board of the Met, advised Lila that a gift to the New York City Opera Company would be an indication she had lost faith in the Met. The smaller company never received the million dollars, and Sills never heard from Lila again.

The Sills affair, McHenry's growing influence over the Wallaces' philanthropy, and their increasing isolation and reclusiveness were only some of the signs that life was getting stranger and stranger both at *Digest* headquarters, in Chappaqua, and at High Winds, in Mount Kisco, five miles away. Overworked and under great stress, President Jack O'Hara began to fear an assassination attempt on his life.

O'Hara's paranoia, though mostly induced by anxiety and his cold-turkey attempt to give up drinking (he had switched from cocktails to caffeine—twenty-four cups of coffee a day), was not entirely irrational. Following the publication of several articles on terrorism, the Paris office of *Sélection* had received several threatening phone calls; and a bomb was later defused in front of the Rome office near the Spanish Steps. A deranged Mexican citizen even sent DeWitt Wallace an unintelligible death threat, though one the FBI took seriously enough to check out. Nothing was turned up.

In such an atmosphere of treacherous infighting, foreign peril, and emotional strain, O'Hara finally decided he no longer wanted to keep his office in the front, along with the other top executives', and ensconced himself in a back office with a private corridor and two-story drop so that no one could climb into his office and waste him in his prime. Though editor-in-chief Thompson, who did not feel at all threatened, occasionally twitted O'Hara about his siege mentality, no one else dared.

O'Hara's physical isolation was matched, in an odd way, by that of Wally, who now spent much of his time in his tower. Over a period of several days in 1978, he went through his files and burned them one by one in the fireplace, including all of his confidential files on his editors. Finally, chauffeur Gene Doherty persuaded him to stop for reasons of safety. The two put the remainder of the files into several cardboard boxes to be disposed of later.

From time to time, though, Wally still liked to patrol the office hallways, poking his head into doorways to chat with people about their work. Many were startled to find the emaciated founder standing in their doorway, but he seldom left without murmuring some form of encouragement or commendation. Yet it was obvious to all that Wally's questions were becoming increasingly unintelligible and that his gaze often drifted off into the distance as he listened to the answer.

He also jotted down a few pages' worth of reflections, a Pealesian summing-up of his philosophy of life:

"When you have philosophy 'This too will pass' you are on highroad to a self-made cure," he wrote, echoing Lila's own favorite creed. "Many fearful people have no deep interest in life. Vitality! Harmony! Confidence! Realize that you are a part of the Eternal Life Principle! . . . Temperance brings tranquillity & self-command. . . . Nobody can change the law. Whatsoever a man soweth, that shall he also reap. . . . *Sex* Sexual dissipation is often a frantic escape from a feeling of inferiority." Finally: "The greatest Kingship is the royalty of self-control, & the greatest conquest is the mastery of self."

Wally's last adventure was a 1977 white-water rafting expedition down the Green River in Utah. Former chairman Kent Rhodes made all the arrangements through Josh Myner, head of Outward Bound. The group of old-timers who went along—mostly the remnants of

Wally's poker group—called themselves the Ancient Mariners. At the last minute Cole had to drop out, after coming down with a cold. The following year Wally wanted to make the trip again. But Lila had been bitterly opposed the first time, so Rhodes told him the water was too low.

Still, Wally and Lila did manage to get out together on occasion. One day they went into the town of Mount Kisco to shop. Lila, who had always favored designer clothes, was unknown to most local merchants and no longer dressed so elegantly as before. Wally, as usual, had put on whatever was at hand. Lila spotted a pair of shoes in a window and wanted to try them on. The store owner, seeing them walk in, assumed they were just another local couple. When a young salesclerk approached, Lila asked to see the shoes.

Since they were expensive and the old woman did not look as if she could afford them, the salesclerk brought another pair instead. Lila graciously replied that, though they looked nice, she preferred to try on the ones in the window. Wally, meanwhile, began cross-examining.

"Do many people from the *Digest* come in here?" he asked.

"Oh, yes," the clerk replied. "Lots of customers from there."

As he continued to ask questions, she wondered whether he worked there himself—whether he was a guard or something.

"Do you work for the *Digest?*" she asked.

He smiled. Lila looked at him and smiled. Then she said, "It's ours."

Early in March 1981 Wally was taken to the Columbia Presbyterian Medical Center, in Manhattan's Washington Heights, to be operated on for an abdominal obstruction. His recovery was slow, and he later contracted pneumonia. When the doctors saw that death was imminent, they made arrangements for him to return to High Winds so that he could die at home. On his last evening in the hospital, however, he received two unexpected visitors.

Judy and Fred Thompson were returning to their Manhattan apartment after a weekend in the country and remembered that Wally was in the medical center just above the West Side Highway. On an impulse they decided to pay a surprise visit and let bygones be bygones. Wally was asleep as they entered the room.

A passing nurse explained that Mr. Wallace was restless and would awaken shortly. The Thompsons sat down to wait, having been given permission to stay. When Wally finally did wake up, he sat upright, dangled his legs over the edge of the bed, and asked for his plaid robe.

Then, putting his hands on the shoulders of a diminutive Asian nurse, he stood up and did a clumsy Highland fling. Just then a resident walked in and ordered the exhausted Wally back to bed. The doctor also wanted the visitors to leave, but Wally pleaded that they be allowed to remain as a reward for his recent good behavior. The doctor replied that Wally was going home the next day and that was his reward.

"That's a sentence, the way I feel now," he replied. "Not a reward. I feel worse than I did when they brought me here. And since I came of my own accord, you can at least let me have some privacy with my kin. That's a blessing I have at home."

The doctor obligingly withdrew. Wally wanted to discuss the Thompsons' sons—what they were doing. He had heard they were going into business and congratulated them, adding, "I'd have gone into business myself if I had thought I could succeed."

Even as he lay dying, Wally was being enigmatic. The Thompsons did not know whether he was being ironic or had forgotten that he founded the *Reader's Digest*. Later that evening, after his visitors went home, he told the resident, "Tell Lila not to worry. I'll be sending her flowers in the morning."

The next day—March 30, a Monday—he was taken to High Winds, where he died late in the afternoon. His last hours were difficult. In attendance were chauffeur Gene Doherty and his wife, as well as a nurse and Wally's nephew and private secretary, Gordon Davies. A prolonged death rattle and a worsening of phlebitis added to Wally's suffering. The official cause of death was pneumonia. He was ninety-one years old and the *Reader's Digest* itself less than a year short of sixty. At the time of his death, the magazine he founded was the most widely read in the world—its name instantly recognizable in every literate country. Yet Roy William DeWitt Wallace, in death as in life, was known only to a relative few. He had also outlasted two generations of *Digest* editors, with a third at the helm.

In the *New York Times* his obituary was accorded respectful back-page status. A much bigger, front-page story was the attempted assassination that same afternoon of President Reagan by a troubled young assailant hoping to impress movie actress Jodie Foster, who had played Becky Thatcher in the RDA's only successful film, *Tom Sawyer.*

The next morning a memo signed by both O'Hara and Thompson informed Digesters of the passing away of the company's founder. "A man who at the age of 88 went on white-water raft trips, still made major decisions about the affairs of a billion-dollar corporation, and continued to carry on a vastly fulfilling love affair with his wife of nearly 60 years—such a man need not be unduly mourned. . . . With Shakespeare, we say: 'We shall not see his like again.' But we add to that: 'Thank heaven we did see his like, knew him, and benefitted so greatly from his wisdom.' " The memo further announced that the offices would be closed the following Monday and that the memorial service would be private. It also requested that no flowers be sent.

The memorial service at High Winds was attended only by the RDA inner circle—top members of management and editorial and their spouses, members of the board, Gordon Davies, Harry Morgan, and Gene Doherty—as well as by those who had left the company but still had strong ties, Fred and Judy Thompson, Paul W. Thompson, Kent Rhodes, and others. Before the service began, George Grune and McHenry's wife, Fanny, tried to walk through the rooms. Lila's private secretary, Dorothy Little, shooed them out. Though slight in stature and retiring in manner, the fiercely protective Little—who had formerly served as Paul Thompson's secretary—was at home in the most rarefied circles of power and feared nobody.

The service was a simple one, and Wally's longtime friend Norman Vincent Peale gave the eulogy.

"I don't suppose that even though we loved him devotedly we'd say that DeWitt Wallace was perfect," Peale told the mourners. "Who among us is? But he was about as near to it in my book as anybody could be because he loved people. His objective was to serve his readers."

Peale then recalled how, when Wally began the *Digest* in 1922, America was in turmoil. Traditional morality, he said, was under siege from the likes of F. Scott Fitzgerald, Rudolph Valentino, Sinclair Lewis, and H. L. Mencken.

"Into this kind of a civilization," said Peale, "came a young Galahad, who believed in what? In the United States of America, in American freedom, in free enterprise, in goodness, in decency, in morality. And that filled a need because that's what the people wanted to believe. The man that lived in this house and looked out over these hills of Westchester, of him it may be said he saved America. It's not too much to assert. He was of the stuff of which America is made, its best."

During the service there was concern that Lila might break down.

Even before Wally died, however, she had begun to address and refer to him as her brother Barclay. When the nurse brought her down to the living room where the service was held, Dorothy Little sat with her and held her hand. As people came up to pay their respects, Little told her in a whisper who they were. But at one point during Peale's eulogy she leaned over to tell Little, "I wish Mother were here to hear what they were saying about Daddy. Isn't it so nice?"

After the service, Gene Doherty took Lila on a long drive. When they returned to High Winds, she refused to get out of the car. So they took another long ride, and when they returned she still refused to leave the car. Finally, she consented, though making it clear she knew that Doherty had made a mistake. When she instructed him to take her home, she meant the home she had lived in before she had everything. Later she often spoke of not being in her true home and asked frequently about her daddy.

Wally's body had been cremated, and the next day Barnabas McHenry went alone into the rose garden and strewed his ashes, as the *Digest*'s founder had requested. Though, also at his behest, there was to be no epitaph, Wally had once facetiously proposed the only one that seemed fitting: "The final condensation."

A week after Wally's death, the *Times* produced an editorial eulogy of its own entitled "American Digest," which took a more measured note of his passing. "There is a peculiar kind of ability," said the editorial, "usually defined as 'having a finger on the public pulse,' which can make its possessor if something less than an artist something more than a merchant. Louis B. Mayer and Henry Luce were pulse-takers of that kind, and so was DeWitt Wallace, who conceived and edited the *Reader's Digest* and who died last week. All three, perhaps inadvertently, are partially responsible for the American self-image. Trying to reflect it, they also helped create it."

As usual, though, there was a dissenting voice. One of Wally's oldest enemies—the equally long-lived George Seldes, leftist journalist and founder of *In Fact*—reviewed the life and career of DeWitt Wallace in the pages of the *Nation*. Seldes complained that, though the newspaper of record did acknowledge that some people considered the *Digest* "culturally middle-brow and socially conservative," nowhere in this *"nil nisi bonum* national tribute to the great man did anyone suggest that . . . the *Digest* was a repository for Wallace's political and social prejudices and hatreds. Without exception, these views were far right."

Ironically, Seldes's attack came at a time when a majority of the people in power at Pleasantville only wished the *Digest*'s editorial credentials were so impeccably reactionary.

——

OLD *Digest* hands frequently made the pilgrimage up to headquarters just to see familiar faces and wander the hallways. Bun Mahony, though now retired, still stopped by the office to pick up paper, pencils, and other office supplies—a last, paltry perk appropriated by a man forgotten but not gone. After his reconciliation with Wally, Al Cole also showed up several times a week. As a result he became a kind of listening post for all sorts of complaints from both the editorial and the business sides. After a while what he heard began to bother him a great deal.

One of the people who had Cole's ear was James Stewart-Gordon, a short, barrel-chested, self-professed former professional wrestler and husband of Faith Stewart-Gordon, who had inherited the Russian Tea Room from her former husband. Stewart-Gordon was also a freelance writer with unprecedented access to Wally and High Winds. But according to a Digester with intimate knowledge of both the Pleasantville and the Washington editorial offices as well as the covert byways of the U.S. government, Stewart-Gordon had "very deep contacts. One day nobody ever heard of him, the next day he was a regular at High Winds. And if you want to find who put him so close to the throne, you have to look at the Washington bureau and at the United States government itself. Both were very unhappy with what was happening editorially in Pleasantville."

What the CIA and FBI did not like was the liberal drift of the *Digest* under Ed Thompson. Not only was the magazine becoming less receptive to their own media spin on national and international events, as laundered through the Washington bureau, but frequently both organizations were themselves becoming objects of criticism in the *Digest*'s pages.

Wally enjoyed Stewart-Gordon's rousing adventure stories immensely, even though they were notoriously difficult to fact check. Once a frustrated issue editor, reviewing an article full of names, places, and events the research department could not verify, circled Stewart-Gordon's byline and asked—little suspecting the truth— whether that, at least, was accurate. (Stewart-Gordon's real name was

Bogardus, though the rest of his past is shrouded in mystery.) Regardless, for a while Wally was even a weekly regular at the Russian Tea Room, where Stewart-Gordon often acted as a greeter of the restaurant's rich and famous clientele.

Ed Thompson was not even remotely suspicious of Stewart-Gordon, but eventually terminated his relationship with the *Digest* because his work was not up to standard. In retaliation Stewart-Gordon prepared an editorial analysis of every issue of the *Reader's Digest* edited by Thompson. When the file became thick enough, he showed it to Al Cole, waiting by his listening post. The file claimed to demonstrate that the magazine was not running nearly enough of the kind of positive, how-to-get-ahead articles that had inspired readers for more than a half century, but was becoming—what was even worse than liberal —*negative.* John Allen was another who whispered in Cole's ear that the *RD* was running "medical scare articles" and heavy political pieces that made Thompson feel "big."

At one point Cole and his second wife, Peggy, even visited the public library in Bridgeport, Connecticut, to look up old issues of the *American Magazine* to see what kind of art-of-living articles it had contained. So impressed was Cole that in mid-1982 he asked Thompson out to lunch and suggested he hire somebody simply to rewrite and update the articles as a way of saving the *Digest*—which otherwise, he intimated, was going to go the way of the *American* itself, which had also faltered under a new editor who began tinkering with the original formula.

———

IN THE WEEKS, months, and years following Wally's death, High Winds became something of a haunted house, filled with the ghosts of Barclay, Wally, and Daddy, whom Lila alone could see but whose presence others could sense in one degree or another. A new butler and his wife had looked after the Wallaces in recent years, though his indifferent service and her uninspired cooking earned them both the hearty contempt of RDA management. When the butler developed a brain tumor and could no longer care for Lila properly, the burden of physically looking after Lila and superintending the grounds fell on Doherty and his wife, as well as on a series of nurses. The burly, red-haired Irishman was devoted to Lila, and it became a common sight for him to squat before her and say, "All right, Mrs. Wallace. Let's go." After she put her arms around him, he hoisted her on his back and delivered her to a wheelchair or divan. In her last years Lila was crippled by arthritis and unable to walk.

But she was still able to drink her martinis out of the 4,000-year-old Egyptian goblet etched with lotus leaves on the sides. On occasion Dorothy Little also arranged for Lila, who always loved classical music, to be entertained. In the spring of 1984, for example, the Omega Ensemble, a four-member chamber group, went up to High Winds to play Chopin for the two women—his scherzo in B-flat minor, a fantasy impromptu, a nocturne.

There was a bitter rivalry between Doherty and McHenry over who really was in charge of things at High Winds, and who had Lila's best interests at heart. As in the past, the family—including Judy Thompson and Gordon Davies—stayed away. Doherty worked not for the *Digest* but for the Wallaces, though he assumed he would become a company driver after Lila died. He despised McHenry as a social-climbing, power-hungry lawyer using the Wallace fortune to make a name for himself in New York society. McHenry regarded the chauffeur, who was named in Lila's will, as a nuisance he would have fired in a minute if he had had the authority. But it was McHenry who hired the nurses and acted as a kind of remote-control nanny while at the same time overseeing Lila's ongoing philanthropic work and taking care of routine legal affairs for the company.

Doherty was also frequently on the phone with Harry Morgan, complaining about all the "shenanigans" going on at High Winds. Later the chauffeur and his wife paid a long visit to Morgan in New Jersey and claimed that ermine coats, jewelry, and other items were missing from the house.

In Lila's last years all the decisions about whom to give money to were made by Barney McHenry and by her secretary, Dorothy Little. While Lila was still in possession of her faculties, she had arranged for Little to become a cosigner of the Lila Acheson Wallace and High Winds funds through which she gave money to charity. McHenry had been similarly empowered. After Lila was no longer able to sign her name, Little's signature became mandatory. As requests for money came in, they were collected for Little, who drove down to High Winds from her home in Vermont two or three times a week. The part-time secretary then identified those institutions whose requests seemed worthy of a grant and scribbled a brief note to McHenry in the margin suggesting an amount—usually only a few thousand dollars, though sometimes more.

McHenry then reviewed Little's suggestions, as a rule agreeing with her and arranging for the checks, which also needed his signature, to be drawn. After a year or so the RDA board stepped in and required that all requests get its approval. But none of the Wallace foundations operated according to standard guidelines. According to one close observer at the time, they operated "out of McHenry's hip pocket."

In the early 1980s British landscape architect Sir Peter Shepheard took an interest in restoring the gardens at Charleston, the country house of Bloomsbury luminaries Vanessa Bell and Duncan Grant in Sussex. McHenry, who spent a month every year in England, became involved in the project and agreed that Lila Acheson Wallace would pay for the restoration. On his trips abroad he also frequently bought art for the *Reader's Digest* collection. His acquisition of paintings by Bell, Grant, Roger Fry, and Dora Carrington became the largest concentration of Bloomsbury Postimpressionism in the United States.

Later McHenry helped to restore I Tatti, the quattrocento villa that art historian and critic Bernard Berenson created as an homage to Tuscan art, architecture, and landscape. McHenry was also known to hand out grants of $15,000 at a time to theater groups or other organizations he admired, even if they had not applied for them.

In the grand Wallace tradition, though, McHenry's most significant bequest was eight million dollars to the Metropolitan Museum of New York to build a new wing to house contemporary American art. At one level Lila might have approved of the gift, had she been in possession of all her faculties, since the Met, along with Boscobel, was one of her two favorite charities. On the other hand, she had very old-fashioned and very pronounced ideas about what constituted beauty and art. The irony that the money was being used to build a showcase for abstract and postmodern art—the kind of beauty she never had any use for—was not lost on Digesters who knew what was going on. McHenry encountered no serious resistance from the board of directors, because, though it was the higher body, it took its orders from the board of trustees,* whose most

*The board of directors officially decided on all aspects of corporate policy, but all voting stock was owned by Lila Acheson Wallace, whose proxies sat on the board of trustees. As a result, trustees were able to dictate policy much as DeWitt Wallace had while still alive, even though they did not sit on the board of the corporation itself.

powerful member was Laurance Rockefeller. Like McHenry, Rocke-feller also sat on the museum's board.

Another gift that McHenry and Rockefeller engineered was seven-teen million dollars to Colonial Williamsburg. That grant—far larger than the Wallaces' previous gifts to the historic settlement in Vir-ginia—alarmed and angered any number of people in Pleasantville, notably Al Cole, who thought it was "the wrong thing to do."

But Cole held Rockefeller in low esteem because he did not under-stand publishing and never said "anything that makes any difference." What especially bothered Cole, though, was Rockefeller's relationship with McHenry. The ex–business manager claimed he found it impossi-ble to have "any respect for Laurance," because his favorite was McHenry. Cole also harbored a similar opinion of another outside director, banker Donald Platten: "He doesn't know anything either," Cole said of him. "Doesn't say anything." Bill Cross shared his opinion that neither Rockefeller nor Platten knew anything about publishing.

Cole went so far as to confront Rockefeller and say to him about McHenry, "He's the most terrible man I've ever met. If I had anything to do with him, he'd be out of here so damn fast, he'd never know where he's going. And Wally had no more use for him than I did."

But Rockefeller and McHenry belonged to a mutual back-scratching society Cole was powerless to dissolve. In the disarray created by all the factionalism on both sides of the executive corridor, however, Cole did have enough leverage to unseat the one man he thought most responsible for the *Digest*'s myriad troubles—editor in chief Ed Thompson.

McHenry also had no use for Thompson and did everything in his power to stir up discontent and deflect attention from himself. More-over, Rockefeller was unkindly predisposed toward Thompson from the beginning of his tenure, owing to a minor slight. Soon after being installed as editor in chief, Thompson wrote Rockefeller a letter, invit-ing him to lunch to discuss his views on the future direction of the RDA. But the secretary had spelled Laurance's name with a *w* instead of a *u*. Rockefeller had testily replied to the effect that a man in Thompson's position at least ought to know how to spell the name of one of the company's trustees.

In January 1984, with Lila's condition worsening by the day, the RDA underwent a major management reshuffle as Pleasantville execu-tives positioned themselves for an endgame. With support from Cole and Rockefeller, George Grune was named publisher, while Dick McLoughlin was appointed director of new business planning and operations. Both Grune and McLoughlin proposed speeding up the company's growth through a series of acquisitions and new ventures. Bill Cross, who had serious differences with both Grune and McLoughlin over their expansionist plans, became director of administration and finance.

———

ALL THIS TIME Ed Thompson thought he had the best job in the world. He occupied Wally's old office and revered the magazine's founder as a "genius" who "always went to the heart of things. He was kindly, but he didn't tolerate fools gladly. If you were a fool, he let you know about it pretty fast." The same was true of Thompson as well.

The most visible change in the *Digest* during the eight years of Thompson's tenure was that twenty-five out of thirty articles were now illustrated, compared with only five or six about a decade earlier. Thompson thought the magazine had gained more "visual vibrancy." Otherwise he did not think the magazine had changed much over the years. As he told an interviewer around this time, its main concerns were the "basic human emotions of love, fear, hunger." He added, "We want to help people help themselves, either with their personal life or business life or community life. The world changes and we change with it, but we're not trying to change the basic makeup of the magazine." In short, Thompson was dedicated to preserving the art of living.

Yet some, like O'Hara, thought he was restless because just editing the magazine was not enough of a challenge. Only recently, in fact, Thompson had formed a new subsidiary, Reader's Digest Entertainment Inc., and named former Disney executive Jeffrey S. Grant as president. Like Hobe Lewis before him, Thompson hoped to parlay the *Digest*'s reputation, creative resources, and editorial materials into wholesome family entertainment, aiming at such markets as network, cable, pay TV, and syndication. Also like Lewis, he was preoccupied with noneditorial matters, even though he never did get the title of president.

Bill Cross perceived a similar discontent on Thompson's part. In the days before Thompson became editor, Cross used to make up the editorial budget. Once or twice a year he sat down with executive editor Harry Harper or, later, Bun Mahony and went through it. The editorial budget was not a budget per se, but a projection of expenditures, and the review was mostly a rubber-stamp operation. Thompson took a much more active interest in cost projections. Not only did he know what he wanted to spend money on, but in Cross's opinion he also showed no inclination to keep the expenditures to a reasonable level.

What particularly vexed the chief financial officer (CFO) was Thompson's buildup of the editorial staff to 220 people, which in Cross's view led to conspicuous waste and not enough work to go around. After all, Thompson himself had mandated that 50 percent of the magazine—up from 30 percent—be reprints.

Thompson was also in the habit of flying to Europe, Latin America, or Asia three or four times a year on the company plane, convening international editorial conferences, renting yachts, and in general acting in a grandiose manner—an unforgivable sin in the eyes of the cost-conscious CFO, particularly in the wake of the severe 1982 recession.

Cross also thought Thompson was losing control of what was going into the magazine. Things were being published that many members of top management or the board found deeply disturbing—articles that were real downers, like the horror story about a baby whose face was burned away. Other articles—not to mention cartoons and illustrations—seemed to be in direct contravention of the *Digest*'s traditionally patriotic, right-wing philosophy. Rockefeller was particularly disturbed by a drawing selected for an award in a *Digest*-sponsored art contest for high school students. The prizewinning drawing, which was reprinted in the magazine, showed the Statue of Liberty up to its neck in trash. Rockefeller thought that it was outrageous to desecrate one of America's most revered icons in such a manner and then to compound the folly by publicizing the drawing in the magazine that above all others told the world what the United States was all about.

Another upsetting example of how the *Digest*'s philosophy was being perverted was a cover illustration that showed a group of people admiring the statue *Prometheus Unbound* in Rockefeller Center. One of the onlookers was a flasher, exposing himself to art, a notion that art director Kenneth Stuart considered hilarious. But Rockefeller, Cross, and numerous others on the board or in the highest editorial echelons of the company were not amused.

Nor was the discontent confined to the business side; it extended to the editorial. For some time a group of five or six very senior editors—at the level of Gilmore and Schulz—had been privately complaining to O'Hara, Cross, and other executives about Thompson's wayward editorial philosophy, lack of editorial control over and even disinterest in the *Digest*'s editorial content, and other perceived failings.

As things were coming to a head, O'Hara kept reassuring Rockefeller, Cross, and the others that he was going to sit down and have a heart-to-heart talk with Thompson. On one occasion the O'Haras and Thompsons even went down to Bermuda together. O'Hara looked forward to the trip because, he told everyone, it provided the perfect occasion for the two chief RDA executives to take a long walk on the beach and see if things could be worked out.

But the moment for raising some of the more difficult questions about Thompson's leadership never presented itself. Subsequently, there was another meeting with O'Hara, director of international product marketing Thomas Esencourt, and executive assistant Norman Racusin. The three went off with Thompson to have a talk, which also turned out to be not very substantive. On several occasions the blunt-mannered Cross offered to confront Thompson directly. O'Hara discouraged him, saying, "Your relationship with Ed is good. So you stay out of it. Ed and I will work things out."

Though it was Jack O'Hara who finally brought matters to a head, Rockefeller was prepared to do whatever was necessary if the company president did not act soon. The catalyst was Al Cole, who had been persuaded by Stewart-Gordon that the *Digest*'s art-of-living selection was not what it used to be, and who kept pushing O'Hara to act.

How was Ed Thompson really doing? A confidential memo circulated by Ken Gilmore and Tony Oursler to the editorial staff reported on an analysis of *Digest* reader polls presented to the board of directors in late 1982. According to the two editors, the analysis contained "both encouraging and challenging information." It also contradicted the file compiled by Stewart-Gordon.

The report was titled "What Do the *Digest*'s Readers Like to Read?" The once simple answer to that question was "Whatever DeWitt Wallace liked to read." And it was still true, said Gilmore and Oursler, that whatever the editor in chief and his staff liked to read was what "interests and excites our readers."

The report further noted that the most enjoyed and best-read feature of the magazine was "Laughter, the Best Medicine," read by an average of 87 percent of all readers every month. In descending order, the next most popular were "Life in These United States," "Humor in Uniform," "Campus Comedy," "Word Power," "News from the World of Medicine," and "All in a Day's Work." Oursler and Gilmore pointed out that all of those departments were popular not only for their entertainment value but also their brevity and regular appearance.

All articles fell into thirty-one categories, such as "health and safety," "animals," and "biography." But the category called "ordeals" (such as that of the baby whose face was burned away) won the number one ranking year after year. Runner-up categories included "inspiration and good works," "crime," "family and children," and "mystery and suspense."

According to the report, the single most popular article published in the past five years was "They've Killed My Daughter Twice!," which appeared in the January 1981 issue and told the story of a young woman who recovered from an accident caused by a drunk driver, only to be later killed by another drunk driver. As ever, the second most popular type of article after dramas was the dog story. "Any article about a dog almost always ranks among the top five articles in an issue." At the low end of reader enjoyment for 1982 was a twenty-six-page condensation of Henry Kissinger's *Years of Upheaval,* which garnered a below-sea-level EQ of only 26.

The crucial question in the report was "Are readers responding more favorably or less favorably to our editorial content?" Oursler and Gilmore nevertheless found that there had been a steady, across-the-board increase among all segments of the *Digest* audience, both in readership (the percentage of those who "read all" of an average article) and in enthusiasm (how well they liked the article). In 1976 the average "read all" figure was 52 percent; by 1981 it had reached 54 percent. Moreover, the average EQ in 1976—when Thompson took over—was 157, and by 1981 it had reached 168.

Looking for common denominators for a successful article, Oursler and Gilmore emphasized that articles eliciting emotional involvement—"whether it's laughter or sorrow, confidence, endurance or love—do *far* better than even those very popular pieces that inform, instruct or advise." Though the *RD* intended to continue to publish "exposés of criminals, mindless bureaucracy and corruption," it preferred to emphasize the good news over the bad because the editors believed that the average reader's greatest appetite was for inspiration that would "nourish his heart and spirit."

Despite such a glowing report card, Thompson stood no chance of remaining editor in chief once O'Hara joined forces with Cross, Rockefeller, Cole, Harold Helm, Gilmore, and the others. And yet another player had decided to join the game—Cole's erstwhile protégé Fred Thompson, who had taken it upon himself to study a number of recent back issues. He, too, later reported to Rockefeller that the editorial direction of the *Digest* was not what Wally would have wanted.

As matters were coming to a head, Washington editor Nathan Adams arranged for a secret meeting with Cole and several discontented editors from the bureau at the former business manager's winter home in Hobe Sound, Florida. Adams insisted that Thompson be replaced by Ken Gilmore, to which Cole replied, "Over my dead body."

The bureau malcontents and Cole, acting as unofficial surrogate for the board of trustees, were later able to agree on Gilmore as a compromise candidate. Attending the second meeting, at which Gilmore was confirmed as choice of successor, was former editor in chief Hobe Lewis, who also had a winter home on the island.

On the morning of March 19, 1984, a Monday, an unsuspecting Ed Thompson, accompanied by his third wife, Susie, arrived early at headquarters. An ex–*Digest* editor who had worked her way up from researcher before retiring, Susie often visited Pleasantville to chat with friends. Normally, Ed Thompson would have preferred taking the day off. He and Susie had just returned from an executive fact-finding trip to Mexico, and he was plagued by a case of turista. But Jack O'Hara had scheduled an early meeting that sounded too important to be put off.

When Thompson entered O'Hara's office, he found Bill Cross also waiting. Forgoing the usual welcome-back pleasantries, the company president stated bluntly, "You have a real problem. The trustees want you to leave. But there might be a way for you to stay."

Having convened the board meeting, O'Hara had already begun to equivocate. Without even bothering to inquire what the problem was, since he immediately divined its nature, Thompson asked what solution O'Hara had in mind.

"We could create a board of editors," O'Hara replied, "which you would be a member of but not have veto power."

"That would be ridiculous," Thompson answered.

With a contemptuous laugh, Bill Cross shook his head and said, "You had to say that."

"Of course, I had to say that," Thompson said. "Partly because I'm me. But why do they want to get rid of me?"

"They're unhappy with the tone of the *Digest,*" Cross went on. "It's not the magazine Wally would have wanted. Cole and Rockefeller don't think you understand the meaning of the *Reader's Digest.*"

The three men then got into a limousine and rode in gloomy silence down to the RDA's offices in the Pan Am Building. Seated around a table, waiting for them, were trustees Rockefeller and Helm, trustee emeritus Al Cole, and corporate counsel Barnabas McHenry.

During the meeting, Thompson was informed that the magazine had become shrill, negative, and overly critical of the Reagan administration. He was also told the magazine had lost its "consciousness of things religious and of the positive things of life." A dearth of art-of-living articles was also cited, as well as a plethora of "monster" stories—most notoriously, the April 1983 piece about a baby without a face.

The trustees went on to cite three political articles they objected to. The first of these was a July 1983 piece by roving editor Jim Miller attacking the administration's gutting of the Environmental Protection Agency. "When industry's foxes were hired to guard the national chicken coop, no one—least of all the President—should have been surprised at what followed," read the opening line. Miller's enemies in the Washington bureau considered that article his final outrage and were determined to get rid of him once and for all.

Another Thompson heresy was a piece by Irwin Ross in the same issue criticizing political action committees and calling for election-spending limits. Ross's article cited the United Auto Workers' PAC as an example of undue influence but did not mention corporate PACs. If it had, Ross might also have pointed to the RDA's own PAC, organized in 1978, which in 1979–80 gave a total of $39,550 to seventy-five Republican and five Democratic candidates, including Senator Steven D. Symms, Republican from Idaho. In 1981–82 the RDA gave PAC money only to Republicans—most of them advocates of cutting taxes.

However, the PAC article had been held over at least once and was accompanied by a boxed sidebar, carrying Symms's byline, defending PACs. Though hardly a liberal piece, it was radical by *Digest* standards.

"It was very gutsy of the editor to sponsor the PAC article," said one liberal Digester. "That was one of the things that was very special about Ed Thompson. He was a conservative Republican. But he could also accept honest stories about Republican shenanigans that the D.C. office could not."

A third controversial article, in the April issue soon to appear on newsstands, was by Carl T. Rowan, a *Digest* roving editor for eighteen years. Titled "Mr. President, This Isn't Russia," the article was critical of Reagan's Directive 84, which proposed to put a gag on government employees with access to sensitive information, and to censor future memoirs. Rowan condemned the proposed use of lie-detector tests, secrecy oaths, and censorship for life as a threat to "the very freedoms it seeks to keep secure. [The directive] should be completely withdrawn—for good."

Rowan was himself a former deputy assistant secretary of state and director of the USIA—impeccable *Digest* credentials in any other set of circumstances. Writing of the Freedom of Information Act, which gave scholars, journalists, and others limited access to government files, Rowan criticized the Reagan administration for "acting as though it wants to return to the excessive secrecy that allowed massive abuses and violations of the law by the FBI, CIA and other agencies during the 1960's and early 1970's." Curiously, Rowan's article had been edited not by "liberal" Ed Thompson but by conservative Ken Gilmore, who was also responsible for the provocative title.

All of those articles, as well as a forthcoming two-part excerpt from a book titled *Reasonable Doubt,* on the assassination of John F. Kennedy—already touted in a coming-attractions box—deeply offended the overwhelming majority in the Washington bureau. Ironically, the book was written by none other than Washington bureau staff writer Henry Hurt and had been sponsored by Tony Oursler, who had spent nearly one million dollars of *RD* money chasing down yet another conspiracy theory. Among other things, Hurt was highly critical of the FBI, which he accused of having deliberately misled the Warren Commission. Gilmore was so upset by the scheduled appearance of the book that he and Oursler virtually stopped speaking to each other.

Nevertheless, Thompson knew that it was pointless even to contest whatever severance package was offered, and he resigned himself to accepting whatever the board gave him—an estimated $1.6 million. All during the proceedings he was in a state of profound shock, aggravated by the turista. His self-defense amounted to a shrug of the shoulders. Thompson asked only that he be allowed to edit the two issues then in preproduction. The request was denied.

Told that Gilmore had been selected to succeed him, Thompson then requested that he be permitted to inform Gilmore personally. Having nothing to lose, since Gilmore already knew, the board agreed. Later, when Thompson reached his former executive editor in China, where he was ostensibly researching an article, he thought Gilmore sounded oddly unsurprised and undismayed. Only Michael Randolph, editor of the British edition, and Paris bureau chief Dimi Panitza—both of whom Thompson also called—expressed outrage and had to be talked out of taking the first plane over to Pleasantville to mount a counterattack.

A press release issued by the *Digest* stated simply that editor in chief Edward T. Thompson had been "asked to take early retirement," and cited his "philosophical differences" with Lila Acheson Wallace. But the bitter Thompson told *U.S.A. Today* he thought he had always been in step with the magazine's "not Pollyannaish, but positive, perspective," and made it clear he had been fired.

Thompson did speak graciously of the man who had betrayed him, Kenneth O. Gilmore. Noting they had worked together for twenty-four years, Thompson told the reporter, "We know each other as well as two married folk, and I will do what I can to make the transition as smooth as possible," adding that he had already received two job offers.

The next day, Thompson and O'Hara met again, and Thompson repeated his warning: "Jack, I know you're next."

"Yes," O'Hara replied. "I know. But I thought I could protect you and this whole thing would pass over."

But Thompson did not believe his former friend, who he felt had deceived him. Eighteen months earlier, at an office party, Thompson had been approached by Grune and McLoughlin, through an intermediary, and asked whether he would join them in getting rid of O'Hara. Thompson turned them down. During his recent trip to Mexico, however, he had changed his mind in light of the RDA's plunging profits and a growing conviction that O'Hara, who displayed increasingly bizarre behavior, "had a screw loose." The final irony was that the impatient ex–editor in chief had procrastinated too long.

For a brief time Thompson thought there was a small chance that he could be reinstated. He felt that the trustees owed it to DeWitt Wallace and the magazine to prove that the *Digest* had been remiss in providing its readers with a sufficient quantity of art-of-living stories. But that combative sentiment soon passed.

Officially, the board of trustees was powerless to fire Thompson. Though that was a mere corporate technicality, the board of directors was convened that Friday to carry out the trustees' will. Once again, O'Hara, Cross, and McHenry gathered together, this time along with publisher George Grune, Tom Esencourt, and Dick McLoughlin, to formalize the firing. (Always the last to know, McLoughlin had phoned Thompson the previous evening, curious to know why the directors were meeting on such short notice. Thompson replied, "I'm not supposed to tell you this, but you're firing me.") After a dismal lunch with his wife that afternoon, Thompson assembled his staff in the hallway.

For months the corridors had been thick with the rumors of intrigue, but nobody quite knew what was going on—not until the very end. After the announcement, which left many in tears, Thompson went home, followed by most members of his staff. Everybody was drinking and crying. Former *Campus Courier* editor Ric Cox pursued Thompson around the house, pestering him with questions about what happened, who said what, and who did what next. Finally, in exasperation, mild-mannered Roy Herbert grabbed Cox, shoved him against the wall, and sputtered impotently, "If I hear one more fucking word out of you . . . fucking . . . I'm gonna fuck . . ."

The *Washington Post* called Thompson's firing a "masthead massacre" and quoted the wily Gilmore as saying, "When I came to work this morning [March 27] I was editor-in-chief." Gilmore also praised Thompson as "a fantastic editor" and added, "I don't see any basic changes in editorial direction. . . . I have no philosophy beyond what makes a great *Reader's Digest* story. And what evolves over a period of time will be determined by how I react from day to day and story to story."

Questioned about his own plans, Thompson said they were uncertain. "What is the past tense of 'we'?" asked the man who was now out in the cold all alone.

—

WITH the struggle on the editorial side finally resolved, Cross as new director of administration saw that it was time to address the long-festering divisions on the business side. Cole was of the same mind. Peering into his crystal ball, he decided he liked George Grune the best.

"George is strong," Cole said. "He ought to be the fellow to run that place." As for Dick McLoughlin, "I don't think Dick has the strength and mentality to do the job." Also Cole was aware that McLoughlin was not "one-two-three" with Grune.

Cross and O'Hara and their wives were the best of friends. Yet when it came to business, both knew they had to make cold-blooded decisions regardless of personal consequences. Cross agreed with Grune and McLoughlin that O'Hara had to be relieved of his position. The three of them went down to New York to visit board member Donald Platten and told him that a change was in order. There was no vote, just a mutual agreement. Later Cross also talked to Rockefeller, who concurred.

A strange event had made O'Hara's ouster all but inevitable. Weeks earlier the *Digest*'s international advertising representatives had met in Lisbon. Grune and McLoughlin, both directors of the company and former advertising salesmen themselves, showed up and found Vice-President Jeff Brown standing at the door, barring their way. In a misguided effort to contain the growing power of his two chief rivals, O'Hara had given instructions that they were not to be admitted to a meeting that, in his view, they had no business attending in the first place.

As soon as Grune and McLoughlin got home, they discussed the matter with Cross, telling the CFO they were fed up with that kind of behavior. But when Esencourt, head of international product marketing, got back to Pleasantville, the first thing he asked Cross was "Can you imagine those two people trying to get into the meeting?"

"Well, you're coming at it from a different side than I am," Cross replied. "I think it was disgraceful keeping them out."

When O'Hara got home, he confronted Cross: "I understand you think it was disgraceful keeping those people out."

"Yes, humiliating to them," Cross replied, "and stupid on your part."

O'Hara dropped the subject. But Grune would not let it drop.

Cross wondered whether O'Hara's troubles stemmed from the time he stopped drinking. Up to that point he had been an excellent businessman and manager. But after becoming president, he gave up alcohol and suddenly had no escape valve for all the tension and pressure that came with his new position. Ultimately, fearful that he might be the target of a terrorist hit squad, O'Hara had ensconced himself in the corporate version of a concrete bunker. In Cross's opinion he had become a "wild man. You couldn't deal with him. He'd be pleasant for a half hour, then explode."

But O'Hara was still an executor of Lila's will, which called for him to control 50 percent of the voting stock, now that Thompson had surrendered his claim to that role, upon her death. If he was to be removed without a struggle, it had to be done quickly because Lila was failing fast.

On Friday, May 4, the triumvirate of Grune, McLoughlin, and Cross was appointed to high office, though the public announcement was not made until the following Monday morning. Grune was now chairman and chief executive officer, McLoughlin became vice-chairman, and Cross was made chief operating officer. At 10:00 A.M. on May 7, 1984, a stunned staff learned that, following so soon after the departure of Ed Thompson, Jack O'Hara had retired and a new executive group was now in charge.

While Digesters were still reeling from that news, a voice came over the seldom used loudspeaker at 10:10: "It is with deep regret that we must inform you that Lila Acheson Wallace passed away this morning." Only minutes earlier, at 9:48 A.M., she had died quietly, at the age of ninety-five. Grune, McLoughlin, Rockefeller, Platten, and Cross had managed to get rid of O'Hara literally in the nick of time.

A subsequent memo distributed among employees was signed by Kenneth O. Gilmore and George V. Grune. It asked that, instead of flowers, money be sent to Boscobel Restoration, her "favorite project." The memo also reassuringly explained, "Under the terms of her will, [all the shares of the voting stock] will pass to the DeWitt and Lila Wallace Trust. Through this trust agreement, the Wallaces have ensured The Reader's Digest Association, Inc., will continue to be a private company."

The passing of Lila Acheson Wallace, philanthropist, was front-page news in the *New York Times*—which had relegated to a back page the obituary of her husband, who had merely founded the most widely circulated magazine in the world. At the time of her death, Lila was the richest woman in the United States. During her lifetime she had given away a minimum of $60 million, and her net worth was at least $250 million—two and a half times the size of the estate left by Henry Luce. The company she and her husband chose to give to charity was worth billions.

The next day, May 10, the *Times* ran a brief editorial on Lila Acheson Wallace titled "Uncondensed." It recapitulated her philanthropy and suggested that "her most wonderful benefaction may be a gallery that offers an unhurried and uncondensed glimpse of ancient Egypt." It continued, "Together with the Temple of Dendur, the Met's Egyptological holdings are among the richest and surely the most visible outside the lands of the Pharaohs. A gracious but determined woman, Mrs. Wallace saw to it that her gifts went to innovative projects, ranging from the floral displays in the museum's entrance hall to the splendid World of Birds building at the Bronx Zoo."

The memorial service for Lila was held on May 25, 1984, at High Winds and attended by a small group of high-ranking Digesters and their spouses. Norman Vincent Peale again gave the tribute, and a choral group performed "America the Beautiful" and "Abide with Me." In Chappaqua, flags were flown at half-mast. In his eulogy, Peale remarked:

"On this day, when Lila has taken her way to the higher country, all nature is aflame with beauty because she walked in beauty. She could have become the greatest women's rights leader of her time, but . . . she lost herself in Wally and he lost himself in her and they formed the most unique marital partnership in the history of the United States."

Later McHenry added her ashes to those of Wally in the rose garden.

VI

THE MACHINE

[1984–]

27

The Hidden Hand

IN THE EARLY SEVENTIES, when George V. Grune was in circulation promotion, there was a standard joke about the RDA's go-for-broke supersalesman, the man sent into the breach when every other tactic failed—that he never had any idea what was going on. After a meeting to coordinate a big promotional campaign, operations people like Ralph Rink would wait for Grune to say, "So what was decided? What were they talking about?" And they would answer, "Don't worry, George. It's all taken care of."

After Grune became president, Rink and a few others asked themselves, "How did *that* happen?" They decided that the board had installed him because he was tractable and would do what he was told—since obviously, in their view, he did not have any ideas of his own.

On several occasions Ed Thompson had made a similar complaint to Jack O'Hara when they were running the company. Thompson thought O'Hara was letting Grune get away with reports to the board of directors that were "stupid," insofar as they all invariably had the same theme. Each quarter the ever optimistic Grune reported that Condensed Books had just set a new record, with more single sales and greater gross revenues than ever before.

"Jack, maybe no one is snowed," Thompson protested more than once, "but you let him appear very successful when, in fact, he's losing ground. His profits are going down because of inflation." Thompson's point was that, though gross income was higher, net income was actually lower, owing to soaring production and other overhead costs paid for with a weakened dollar.

But O'Hara did not rein him in, and Grune continued to play to the board. The strategy worked. His infectious enthusiasm earned him the favor of the directors, as though they believed, with true art-of-living confidence, that not just the editorial but the business side needed only a little incurable optimism to triumph over all the obstacles lying in the way of greater profit.

Appearances to the contrary, though, Grune was no pawn and knew exactly what was going on. One thing he understood was that the RDA was a mail-order business. Under O'Hara, even within the constraints imposed by DeWitt Wallace, the company had tried to diversify into non-mail-order fields, including Source, *Families,* and the manufacture of pleasure boats and German comic books. In that sense O'Hara was only the terminus of a continuum begun by the aging Al Cole, with his door-to-door Victrolas, and perpetuated by Hobe Lewis.

The greatest challenge facing Grune was to streamline the marketing operation into a lean, profit-hungry machine. That also meant finding a new source of profit, since the domestic markets for the *Digest,* Condensed Books, and General Books were already saturated. Grune's master plan was to return the RDA to an all-mail-order business, or at least to exploit fully the 100 million-name global mailing list as the highest priority, by creating new domestic markets interrelated with the *RD* and Condensed Books and by expanding those on the international front.

Another headache for Grune was Barnabas McHenry, who still had a hammerlock on the RDA's vast philanthropic program, for which the company was getting relatively little credit. Millions were being handed out by RDA-associated foundations whose munificence generated virtually no goodwill or publicity for the company, because nobody knew what fund names like High Winds or Lakeview referred to. Other millions being given in the name of DeWitt Wallace and Lila Acheson Wallace were also a poor investment, strictly from a PR point of view. Wally and Lila had so successfully guarded their privacy that in death, as in life, hardly anyone outside of New York knew who they were.

Another major problem revolved around the company's voting stock, all 10,000 shares of it controlled by the proxy members of the Wallace Trust. In order to avoid substantial excise taxes, the trust had to sell 50 percent of the voting stock to the public by the year 2000—though if there was any way around that rule, the RDA's officers and board were determined to find it. Nine of the cash-hungry charities that were among the RDA's new proprietors owned no voting stock, all of which was inherited—5,000 shares apiece—by the DeWitt Wallace Foundation and the L.A.W. Foundation.

Compounding the problem was an IRS requirement that the company raise a $20 million dividend payout to the charities, or else face the possibility of selling itself to the highest bidder.

Further complicating matters was Grune's often fractious relationship with his two chief lieutenants, Dick McLoughlin and Bill Cross. As publisher of the *Digest,* the former had earned Al Cole's contempt as an incompetent who failed to promote the magazine properly on the newsstands. Many other Digesters shared the view that McLoughlin's two chief assets were his cutthroat ambition and Boy Scout good looks.

Cross was just the opposite. An aptly named, choleric man, the quintessential dark-suited, unapproachable chief operating officer, he—unlike Grune—had no talent for mixing in public, let alone for public speaking. Though his bad mood was partly explained by the mess the RDA was in, Cross also suffered from serious health problems. Ever the skeptic, he doubted, too, whether the company could find a way around IRS regulations and remain forever private.

Apart from differences in style and temperament, Cross and Grune had a fundamental disagreement about the substance of the company's future. The major point of contention concerned acquisitions. Grune wanted the company to embark on a series of purchases of other magazines that would exploit the *Digest*'s over-fifty, primarily female market. Those new magazines, in turn, would extend the markets for Condensed Books, General Books, and Music & Records.

Cross held that the RDA was not a good magazine operator and never had been. Despite Wally's lifelong love affair with the *Digest,* and his indifference toward the company's other divisions, the fact remained that the RDA's main profit maker was Condensed Books, followed by Music & Records, with the magazine now a distant third. The *Digest*'s incomparable name recognition and reputation for honesty and dependability helped lure consumers into the book clubs. In Cross's view, the system was simply not capable of handling more than one magazine.

Instead, the new chief operating officer (COO) wanted to eliminate waste, cut costs drastically, and leverage profits while at the same time remaining faithful to the spirit and letter of the trust. As a measure of his determination, Cross eventually reduced the RDA's worldwide staff of nearly 10,000 by more than 20 percent, to about 7,400. Other cost-cutting measures included the elimination of subsidized bus service and of free Thanksgiving turkeys for employees.

New vice-chairman Dick McLoughlin served mainly to generate support for Grune's ideas among the troops and protect his flank. But as former director of magazine operations, he also had his own ideas about what kind of magazines the RDA ought to be publishing, and did not always see eye to eye with the CEO. As former publisher of *Families,* he had also demonstrated an affinity for start-ups—far riskier and more expensive propositions than the acquisitions that Grune was now eager to pursue.

Editor in chief Ken Gilmore posed no threat to Grune's authority. With the passing of DeWitt and Lila Wallace, the primacy of the editorial over the business side had come to an end. Gilmore was tractable by nature and had no choice but to play second banana anyway. Nor was broad editorial policy any longer the editor in chief's sole preserve. Wally's wishes to the contrary, the Reader's Digest Association was hell-bent on becoming a communications giant like Time Inc.; among other things that meant, at least in Pleasantville, that the CEO served as final editorial arbiter and spokesman.

Behind Grune stood Laurance Rockefeller, whose deft hidden hand was discernible in the restructuring of both the RDA and its philanthropies. He and the other trustees wasted no time in turning the RDA into the exact opposite of what its founder wanted it to be—into a company that put profit firmly first. It was a logical, necessary, and inevitable decision if the RDA was to regain its marketing momentum. A business sublimely indifferent to the bottom line was possible only within the context of private ownership.

As both chief architect and "cheerleader"—the term was Rockefeller's—for the all-new sixty-three-year-old company, Grune quickly made a reputation as an upbeat promoter of himself and his product in the Lee Iacocca mold. Not only was he adept at generating enthusiasm among the troops, but he was also not above picking up a scrap of litter as he walked down the corridors of power.

Among the CEO's first acts was to order the doors of the two conference rooms to be kept open at all times when not in use—to demystify them, make them seem not the exclusive sanctums of the elite but simply the rooms, containing tables, chairs, and a few price-less masterpieces, where the leaders of the company met to make decisions.

As before, however, the composition of the board was kept a murky secret, leading the media to speculate about who really held the keys to the Pleasantville kingdom. There appeared to be no guideline stating that, for example, the editor in chief or, for that matter, the head of the RDA was an ex officio member of the trust. A company spokesman even wondered whether the composition of the board might have to wait until Lila's will was decided by probate.

The same unidentified spokesman also downplayed the significance of the Wallace Trust, stating that the RDA board of directors wielded the real power, even though on paper the board of trustees was the higher body. Either that spokesman was greatly misinformed or he was reading Grune's mind—to abolish the trust, half of which was drawn from within the company, as the RDA's collective guiding spirit and replace it with a board of directors drawn mainly from the outside.

When Grune took power, the board of directors consisted of the four members of the executive committee—Grune, Cross, McLough-lin, Gilmore—plus Thomas Esencourt, director of international prod-uct marketing; Barnabas McHenry, corporate counsel; and Norman Racusin, director of international administration. The board also in-cluded three outside directors: Laurance Rockefeller; Donald Platten, chairman of the executive committee of Chemical Bank; and Theo-dore Brophy, chairman of the GTE Corporation. But Esencourt was quickly transferred to Europe and removed from the board on his first stop out of the company. O'Hara's ally Racusin also left the company within months, though his retirement had been announced the previ-ous year. Only Cross survived from the pre-1984 top hierarchy.

Cross and Rockefeller, the two remaining trustees, working with Grune, were now obliged to name four trustees within the coming months. Cole had relinquished his trusteeship in 1982 when he turned eighty-seven, though he continued to serve as a trustee emeritus. Chemical Bank chairman Harold Helm had also been obliged to resign upon the death of Lila Acheson Wallace. (By a provision of her will, all trustees over eighty were automatically dropped.) That state of affairs left Rockefeller, seventy-four, not only as sole outside trustee but as power broker. Rockefeller himself was allowed to stay a trustee, ac-cording to another provision of the will, until he was seventy-nine. A majority vote by the remaining trustees was necessary to elect new ones. This situation allowed Grune, who had Rockefeller's unqualified support, momentarily to work from the outside, through the board of trustees, rather than fight from within, on the board of directors. Moreover, after the trust was successfully abolished, Rockefeller could stay on for as long as he and Grune chose.

In the event, those named to the board of trustees were either allies of Rockefeller and Grune (Platten and Brophy) or easy to manipulate (Gilmore). Grune, of course, was also named, so the board was once again, if only for a time, composed of three directors from the outside and three from within. Conspicuously absent from the board was Grune's sidekick Dick McLoughlin. Odd man out because he disagreed so strongly with the RDA's new expansionist philosophy was Bill Cross.

———

ALL of the mysterious goings-on in Pleasantville in recent months did not escape the attention of the press. The *Economist* reported that the intrigue was "worthy of the court of the Medicis." A front-page story in the *New York Times* included Grune's sinister-sounding disclaimer: "It was coincidental that Lila died shortly after [O'Hara's] resignation." It had, of course, been anything but. Thompson admitted to being "grossly unhappy and angry," yet still considered the *RD* a "great source of good." Gilmore dissembled: "As far as I am concerned, I didn't have any major differences with Ed Thompson." *Time, Newsweek,* and most other national publications joined in trying to find out what exactly was going on in Pleasantville, where nothing ever happened.

In a sympathetic evaluation of Thompson's editorial tenure, the *Columbia Journalism Review* claimed that the *Digest* was still publishing just as many "superbly crafted tearjerkers" as it had ten years earlier—though admittedly the occasional negative piece was popping up. A February 1984 article titled "Making Ends Meet" reported that 15 percent of all Americans lived below the poverty line; a May 1984 article about the nation's homeless said not very optimistically that "solutions for their plight are not easily found." But both pieces, according to the *CJR,* adhered to the familiar *Digest* line that government not be looked to for solutions. Another recent article that had arguably negative or at least anti-big-business overtones was one proposing that people cut up their credit cards as a way of staying out of debt.

Moreover, said the *CJR,* rumors of the demise of conservatism in Pleasantville had been grossly exaggerated. Under Thompson the *Digest* had continued to maintain its traditional political stance with such articles as "an uncritical insider's account of the United States–led invasion of Grenada." And, as usual, the KGB's nefarious activities and terrorism remained staples of the scare-'em-good editorial diet.

The last word, though, on Thompson's editorial performance was provided by *RD* readers in the "kick reports" for January through July 1984. Prepared by the editorial correspondence department and distributed among top editors, the monthly kick (complaint) reports summarized reader letters to the editor, as well as phone calls, and also included compliments to the magazine. Most complaints were about excessive advertising. But Ed Thompson's swan song, the April issue, garnered an unusually high number of compliments, seventy-seven in all, about the cover art. In the art-of-living category, nine people sent in their own home remedies for curing the common cold in response to "The Common Cold: Still Champ," including one subscriber who advocated spending ten to fifteen seconds in a tear-gas chamber.

"Mr. President, This Isn't Russia," the article that so incensed the Washington bureau, garnered twelve commendations and forty-seven complaints, including fifteen cancellations. Some found the piece too liberal, others too boring, and still others too political, while a few readers thought the FOIA, cited by Rowan, was good only for "spies and criminals." Almost twice that number complained about all the advertisements in the May issue, especially those for condoms (another recent breakthrough) and liquor, and thirty-nine complained about an RDA book titled *Into the Unknown,* on the paranormal and occult, because of its satanic associations.

Gilmore's first issue, in July, earned several general compliments about the *Digest*'s return to old-fashioned American values—a rather curious coincidence, considering that the issue was virtually the same as the one preceding it. Another twenty-one readers wrote in to express sympathy at the death of Lila, who had been memorialized in the *Digest* in an unsigned two-page obituary written by John Allen. But four readers were offended by the word "damn" in an item in "Laughter, the Best Medicine."

WHILE the titanic battles involving Thompson, O'Hara, Grune, and the board of trustees were being waged on the first floor of RDA headquarters, another momentous power struggle was taking place upstairs in Condensed Books. On the morning of March 20, 1984, the day after the editor in chief of the *Reader's Digest* was deposed, international CB editor Noel Rae went to the office of editor in chief Joe Hotchkiss. The affable, white-haired Hotchkiss was a generic Digester, virtually indistinguishable from a dozen others, while the forty-something Rae—high-strung, British born, and sharp-tongued—possessed a distinctly different personality and résumé.

Rae assumed that the purpose of the meeting was to discuss routine matters. On entering the room, though, he thought Hotchkiss seemed flushed and agitated. As soon as Rae closed the door, the editor in chief told his longtime associate—responsible for running the thirteen editions of Condensed Books around the world—that this was the unhappiest day of his working life. But now he had no choice. After eighteen years of working with the company, Rae was fired. Surely, Hotchkiss added, the news came as no surprise. But Rae was stunned—taken as unawares as Ed Thompson had been the day before—and he asked for an explanation.

Hotchkiss referred to a meeting two weeks earlier attended by Rae, Hotchkiss, and John Zinsser, the executive editor and Hotchkiss's heir apparent, and also by Barbara Morgan, now managing editor of CB and Zinsser's own heir apparent when he retired within three and a half years. The subject of that meeting was the training of visiting editors from abroad, and in particular the role to be played by Eleanor Hard Lake, who was seventy-eight years old and had been with the department for three decades. After retiring as managing editor, Lake remained a consultant and a key player in the training program.

At the meeting Zinsser and Morgan declared that it was time for Mrs. Lake to go, adding that the quality of her work had declined. Rae disagreed with both judgments, saying the quality of her work remained excellent. However, he offered to reduce the time she spent training, in order to make room for a younger person's career advancement. The session ended inconclusively when Hotchkiss left to keep another appointment. Hotchkiss now said Rae's conduct at that meeting had been unacceptable. The CB editor in chief had come to realize that the differences between Zinsser and Morgan on the one hand and Rae on the other were "irreconcilable." On hearing the news, Rae cleaned out his desk and quickly departed.

What Rae's firing really amounted to was the removal of the chief obstacle from the career path of Barbara Morgan. Her original mentor, Jack Beaudouin, had remained in office until he took early retirement in November 1982. He had not planned to retire so early, but in the meantime Joe Hotchkiss had also taken an avuncular interest in Morgan's advancement. Until Morgan came along, he had shown little interest in succeeding Beaudouin as editor in chief and also talked from time to time about retiring.

But then Beaudouin, an alcoholic, started drinking again. Concerned, Hotchkiss decided to pay a visit to Norman Racusin, then director of corporate affairs, who like O'Hara also worried about security and occupied a double office in the back, with a private corridor, so that no one could rush in and kidnap him. After the two men conferred, Racusin summoned Beaudouin. When he left Racusin's office, the editor in chief of Condensed Books found he had just elected to take early retirement.

Rae considered Hotchkiss, the new editor in chief, a friend, and the two men occasionally visited each other socially. But Rae also viewed Hotchkiss as another sentimental alcoholic who over the years had promoted the careers of a succession of protégés, most of them women. No sex was involved. Hotchkiss had a daughter who had once dived into a swimming pool, broken her neck, and become a quadriplegic; and Rae now theorized that the CB editor was lavishing attention on Morgan as a kind of surrogate daughter. As soon as Hotchkiss became editor in chief, his routine cordiality toward Rae changed abruptly to pronounced antagonism.

An even greater worry, so far as Rae was concerned, was the international department, which had long been his exclusive domain. But when Hotchkiss succeeded Beaudouin, Zinsser was named the new executive editor, and now Rae's and Zinsser's paths crossed again.

The two men were not unalike. Also fluent in several languages, and an opera lover who sometimes judged contests for the Metropolitan Opera, the urbane, extrovert Zinsser was perhaps McHenry's only remaining RDA rival in the exclusive, sophisticated world of the New York arts. Zinsser had also been CB's first international editor, then fled Pleasantville to succeed Ken Wilson as both the magazine's and the book club's liaison with New York publishers, with offices in the Pan Am Building.

Rae had made substantial changes in the foreign operations in the intervening twelve years, encouraging the use of local books by foreign editions and delegating the work of condensing to the sponsoring office. To ensure that the books were edited in accordance with proper procedures, a long succession of editors were brought to Pleasantville for training, much of which was handled by Mrs. Lake.

Rae enjoyed excellent working relations with virtually all of the international editors, many of whom were hired on his recommendation. Beaudouin had found it difficult to accept both the decentralization and the gradual downplaying of American-oriented editorial content, but he was pragmatic enough to recognize that the policy of localization was an important factor in the growing success of the international editions. Though figures were kept secret, the international CB division was recognized as one of the RDA's largest profit makers.

Rae was not thrilled by the prospect of Zinsser's return to Pleasantville. During his absence and Rae's growing independence, differences in personal styles had been accentuated. In particular, Rae feared that Zinsser would begin to inaugurate some of his own ideas in the international field, which had long been Rae's sole domain.

Thus in the weeks following Beaudouin's resignation, but before Hotchkiss assumed his new office, Rae negotiated to preserve the modus operandi he had established—specifically, a job description and the title of executive editor (international). During those discussions Rae also pressed to know who Zinsser's successor was to be. Many in the department assumed that Hotchkiss intended to advance the candidacy of his protégée Barbara Morgan. But Rae, a skeptic, thought she was manifestly lacking in qualifications and dismissed the idea out of hand.

At the same time, though, he harbored no expectations of becoming editor himself. The position required spending considerable time on the American edition, which Rae would not have found congenial and for which he did not feel properly qualified in any case. Rather, he hoped special-projects editor Herbert Lieberman would be designated the heir apparent.

But Hotchkiss suggested that the matter was not in his hands. Rae asked if, on Hotchkiss's retirement, the heads of the international and the U.S. divisions could be put on an equal footing—a not unreasonable request, since the number of books originated abroad exceeded the number produced by the domestic edition. Also, the number of editors reporting to Rae exceeded the number of editors on the do-

mestic edition, while foreign sales exceeded domestic. Hotchkiss did
not say yes or no.

Rae did come away with one concession from the meeting, however. He asked if being promoted to executive editor meant that he
was moving pari passu with the other executive editors, and Hotchkiss
replied with "an unequivocal yes." It was to be their last amicable
conversation.

Soon afterward Hotchkiss summoned Rae to his office and began to
scold him for a variety of misdeeds, including behaving badly at a
dinner party in Sydney, when Rae got carried away and told a well-
known commercial author how to write his books.

Hotchkiss further accused Rae of undermining morale by telling
people that as executive editor he was on the same footing as Zinsser
and Lieberman. Rae reminded him of his agreement that there was pari
passu equality among the three. From Hotchkiss's embarrassed manner, Rae deduced that his supervisor had not known what the Latin
term meant and so dropped the subject.

In February 1983 Rae was once again summoned to Hotchkiss's
office, this time for having berated his secretary in a loud and bullying
manner in front of other people. Rae insisted the accusation was completely untrue. Hotchkiss also complained that Rae ordered the three
full-time editors, one editorial consultant, one secretary, and two clerical members of his staff to have nothing to do with the staff of the
domestic edition. Rae replied that the accusation was not only untrue
but absurd. Again he asked Hotchkiss who his accusers were, but
Hotchkiss only said it was "someone no longer on the staff."

On subsequent occasions Hotchkiss accused Rae of disparaging the
work of American editors, of "radiating hostility," and of "running
down Jack Beaudouin." The only thing Rae could think of regarding
the latter was a meeting he had had in Mexico City in 1983 during
discussions about reviving Condensed Books in that country. The
managing director asked about Beaudouin. Speaking confidentially,
Rae revealed that the CB head, who had a long history of sporadic
alcoholism, was drinking again. Word soon got back to Pleasantville
that Rae was bad-mouthing the editor in chief. Rae was summoned to
meet with a member of senior management, who assured him that
Beaudouin's problems were being dealt with "sensitively and compas-
sionately" and that spreading rumors was not helping.

Rae tried to explain that he mentioned the drinking only in a precautionary way because Beaudouin was planning to visit Mexico soon, but he gathered that the executive did not believe his account of events. The episode continued to crop up now and again, and eventually even Beaudouin himself complained to Rae about it. Then Hotchkiss himself confided to Racusin about Beaudouin's drinking—a meeting that led to the editor in chief's early retirement.

In July 1983 Rae was given a revised job description, which took away some of the authority given to him by Hotchkiss the previous November—notably, that he could approve or reject books on his own authority. The most significant clause was the final one, which declared that, in the absence of Hotchkiss or his deputy Zinsser, the "delegated authority" was Morgan. That seemed to confirm the rumor that she was to be designated Zinsser's successor, effectively eliminating the possibility of Zinsser's naming his own.

Zinsser later told Rae that he did not like having Morgan foisted on him either but that both would just have to accept the situation. Worse, Rae also realized that Zinsser intended to leave much of the running of the U.S. edition to Morgan and to spend more time on international matters.

In an exchange of memos, however, Zinsser assured Rae that he did not intend to cut back on the number of books originated abroad, and agreed that his duties and responsibilities were to be those set forth in November 1982 rather than in the revised and reduced description of July 1983. Zinsser's proposals for change seemed reasonable enough to Rae, who thought things were looking up.

One area where Zinsser had not proposed any changes was the training program for visiting editors. To help Mrs. Lake, CB had hired a former college professor with the intention of handing over to him the day-to-day management of the program once he became more experienced. Hotchkiss had agreed to that arrangement but asked that Morgan, the managing editor, coordinate the training. Thus it was that Rae requested a meeting to clarify who was responsible for what. In the absence of Hotchkiss, who was away on a business trip, the meeting included Zinsser, Morgan, the ex-professor, and Rae and took place in February 1984.

With Morgan concurring, Zinsser said it was time for Mrs. Lake to go. Rae objected. Zinsser said Mrs. Lake could continue to do reading and book reports, but he and Morgan wanted her off training. Rae asked that a decision be withheld until Hotchkiss returned. When

Hotchkiss got back, Rae made his case, pointing out that a recent trainee volunteered that he had learned much from her. Hotchkiss agreed to think matters over. In March the meeting was reconvened with Hotchkiss in attendance. It was at that meeting that Hotchkiss made the decision to fire Rae.

Later that year Hotchkiss retired, and Zinsser took over as editor in chief. To no one's surprise, Morgan was named executive editor. Rae, meanwhile, attempted to take his revenge by starting up a condensed-book club of his own.

━━

ALL during this time Pleasantville was awash with rumors—of stock splits and equivalency units being handed out on a grand scale to a select few. Special bonuses and fourteen-karat golden parachutes were also being paid out to top executives. Others were given golden muzzles. As a result observers wondered what Barnabas McHenry's next move would be. They noted that it had taken two years to settle Wally's estate. Since the future of the company was now at stake, a protracted legal and power struggle seemed to loom.

One of McHenry's moves, soon after Lila's death and the ouster of O'Hara, was to fire his two top associates. Both Margorie Normand and David Otis Fuller were lawyers with ten years of experience in Pleasantville. McHenry farmed out much of the legal work to outside firms, but his own department consisted of only three full-time attorneys, including himself. Fuller was the deputy in charge of litigation. As such he also had overall responsibility for giving legal approval to each issue, except in those instances where he had to consult with McHenry himself.

One Friday in August 1984 McHenry invited Fuller to lunch and informed him, "You're leaving today." Stunned, Fuller asked why he was being let go, without ever having received a reprimand. McHenry explained that Bill Cross had lost confidence in him. Only a week before, Fuller had favorably concluded a case for the *Digest* and won McHenry's congratulations.

As the two lawyers with the longest tenure, Fuller and Normand were at the high end of the pay scale. Sacrificing them might have been one way for McHenry to placate Cross in his Sherman-like march through every department in the company. But with no experienced associates to take his place, McHenry perhaps hoped to heighten the perception of his indispensability. Fuller, for one, thought that was the only logical explanation.

In the spring of 1985 McHenry hired a young woman named Arlene Schuler, who had previously worked for him part-time, as executive director of the RDA's funds. It was only through Schuler, whose position required her to serve as liaison with Grune, that the CEO found out how the foundations were spending their money. Rockefeller, apparently, had been in no rush to keep Grune apprised of that aspect of the RDA.

Four months later Schuler left the company, and McHenry resigned as house counsel to succeed his former assistant as executive director—a lowly clerical title in foundation nomenclature—and not chairman as he had hoped. In June 1986, after only six months on the job, McHenry resigned from that position as well. Grune had won another round.

———

IN DECEMBER 1983 the RDA had given up trying to establish a Greek edition and stopped circulating its Asian edition in the Philippines, where its 120,000 copies represented the company's largest Asian regional market. A year and a half later, the RDA also phased out its Spanish edition after thirty-two years and admitted that it had not been properly promoted, even though the circulation stood at 400,000. In its place other editions of *Selecciones* were to be distributed.

The RDA also sold its 80 percent interest in *Asiaweek,* an English-language news magazine based in Hong Kong, to Time Inc. and consolidated its Danish, Swedish, and Norwegian editions. But the biggest problem, and what was to become both the company's most monumental loss and its most difficult exit, lay in Japan—at the very time Grune was making a concerted effort to expand the RDA's international market under a new corporate motto, "Plan globally and act locally."

In the summer of 1984 the circulation of the Japanese *RD* stood at 550,000, while CB sales were a steady 500,000—though both of those figures were markedly down from the days when the magazine had enjoyed a circulation of well over a million. Partly, the explanation for the drop lay in Pleasantville's editorial policies, which still dictated a predominantly American content for international editions of both the magazine and the condensed books. Though Japan's fascination with American culture continued unabated, the country's spectacular economic success had also given it a new sense of national identity and pride—one not fully reflected in the Japanese edition of the *Reader's Digest*.

As a result the company had been losing money for six years. To compound matters, it was also plagued by serious labor disputes. Disadvantageous currency rates were another complication. But when the Reader's Digest of Japan (RDJ) announced that it was going to shut down operations altogether and leave the country by the end of 1986, the Japanese media played up the closing as a major story.

At the heart of the dispute, so far as the unions were concerned, was an unwritten Japanese law requiring management to discuss any drastic moves with employees. But the RDJ had no intention of negotiating. Its cost-cutting program had failed, and labor laws made it difficult to dismiss employees. To the Japanese such an attitude amounted to betrayal. Nevertheless, all nonunion employees agreed to take a lump-sum retirement payment. Union employees rejected the package.

For its part the RDJ was fearful the union might try to occupy its offices and even take some executives hostage. Like O'Hara's fear of an attempt on his life, the company's attitude was not entirely ground-less. In Japan unions had a constitutional right to organize and "act" collectively, and that right had been interpreted in the courts as including taking executives as hostages. In addition, the unions and their members were immune from any criminal and civil penalties that arose through legitimate action.

The RDJ also thought the union might have a hidden political agenda. The company's pay scale and benefits were far superior to those provided by most Japanese publishers, and that complicated the present problem. The RDJ claimed, too, that it had reliable information that the union president was a card-carrying Communist. The U.S. embassy likewise viewed the union as a "far-left" organization intent on carrying out a Marxist-Leninist campaign to tar all foreign firms in Japan as anti-union lawbreakers.

On January 31, 1986, the RDJ ceased operations. That did not deter the union, whose members for years continued to show up for work at the Palaceside Building. Not until early 1992 did the two sides finally settle on terms.

———

IN THE summer of 1985 the new high command of the once secretive RDA opened its windows wider to the public with a one-million-dollar corporate advertising campaign, the first in its history. The joint themes of the campaign were a celebration of the business acumen of the RDA executive leadership and the influence of the magazine throughout the world and particularly in the halls of Congress. Grune also hosted the RDA's first-ever reception for the local Westchester business community to unveil its new, state-of-the-art data-processing center, saying the company had finally decided to "lift the shades so people can look inside."

But some observers thought that, Grune's denials to the contrary, the concerted effort to raise the public profile of the RDA on the local, national, and international fronts was really part of a program to lay the groundwork to take the company public. Grune repeatedly denied any such intention.

Like Wally, the CEO also continued to devote himself energetically to building esprit de corps, scribbling congratulatory notes to editors, cafeteria workers, security guards, salesmen. He also made a point of frequently eating lunch in the cafeteria, sitting with whoever happened to be there.

In January 1986, to the applause of advertising agencies and media analysts, Grune reduced the circulation of the *RD* by 1.5 million from its 17.75 million rate base in order to eliminate unprofitable subscriptions. The move signified that the *Digest* was abdicating its title of largest-circulation magazine, since it had once again overtaken *TV Guide,* whose circulation stood at 17.17 million. At the root of the problem was a steady decline in newsstand revenues—on average about 600,000 lost sales per year over the past six years, which meant the *Digest* had to bring in an equivalent 600,000 incrementally to maintain the rate base. Those particular subscriptions were very expensive to obtain. In an increasingly crowded field, other mass-circulation magazines, including *Playboy, Family Circle,* and *Time,* had also taken steps to reduce their rate bases and respond to advertisers' concerns, in some cases by adopting issue-by-issue guarantees.

At the same time, however, the *Reader's Digest,* the first magazine to discover an international market, still outdistanced competitors from *Time* and *Business Week* for mass-market readers and sometimes even business readers. But the *Digest* was also a victim of its own success. Since its international editions were viewed as a network of indigenous publications, many advertisers and agencies interested in global media shunned it. One London media director even doubted whether the *RD* was a genuine international medium, because each edition was "so specifically tailored to the local market." As a reflection of that thinking, the international editions had sustained a 4 percent drop in total advertising pages between 1980 and 1983.

Overall the company was now earning an annual profit of between $75 million and $110 million before taxes, on revenues of $1.4 billion. One *Digest* watcher said that the new team was applying "the iron laws of the business schools to the Wallaces' magic kingdom."

Early in 1987 Grune sold Source Telecomputing to a New York venture-capital firm for an undisclosed price. The subsidiary had at last turned a small profit on annual revenues of $14 million and had seen the number of its subscribers climb to 61,000, but it had no place in Grune's master plan to return the company to direct mail. Grune also closed the Original Print Collectors Group, which sold framed prints by mail, and unloaded an educational division that was "selling software nobody wanted," according to one executive. A third operation sold off was the Bartholomew Map Company, a Scottish subsidiary O'Hara had bought in order to have an excuse to visit his relatives back home.

In November 1987 Grune appeared on CNN's "Inside Business." The first question put to him was whether the RDA was going public. Grune said no. It was also the first question put to Grune by a *Crain's New York Business* reporter doing a story on private businesses. Grune again replied in the negative. In an employee newsletter Grune further reassured his employees that the RDA was not going public.

Despite Grune's open-door policy, a survey of RDA employees by an outside consulting company showed that 67 percent received their most useful information about the company through the grapevine, and the grapevine said the company was going public. The grapevine also had it that Grune's two closest allies, Bill Cross and Dick McLoughlin, were not long for Pleasantville, now that the CEO had consolidated his power.

The grapevine was right. Grune was ready to embark on his program of acquisitions. Like the more than two thousand Digesters whom he had forced into early retirement in the preceding twenty-four months, Cross now found himself with no choice but to follow them down the same path, though he was not yet sixty. His replacement as COO, effective the beginning of 1987, was straw man Dick McLoughlin, who also assumed the title of president. Both titles, as everyone knew, were just as meaningless as McLoughlin's other title of vice-chairman. It was only a matter of time before he, too, decided he wanted to spend more time with his family and work on his golf game.

———

AT THE INSISTENCE of Laurance Rockefeller, Barnabas McHenry's place as overseer of the Wallace funds was briefly taken by Stephen Stamas, a high-profile and highly respected member of the arts world whose mere presence, in the opinion of the RDA board, would help counteract the fallout from the messy ouster of his predecessor, which had been the subject of considerable scuttlebutt in the arts world. Previously, Stamas had served as chairman of the Exxon Foundation, the largest corporate giver in the United States. In 1981 alone he had overseen the distribution of $45 million—or more than the Rockefeller and the Carnegie foundations combined.

However, Grune had contracted the same case of hobnob fever that McHenry once had, and he had no intention of allowing a mere outsider to enjoy all the social perks, much less the power, that derived from the RDA's vast wealth. Though an overseer at Harvard and president of the New York Philharmonic, Stamas was given the lesser title of president of the Wallace funds while Grune became chairman.

Undeterred, Stamas set about trying to make his mark. One of his first priorities was to try to persuade Grune to take the company public. The RDA was under considerable pressure to meet its annual payouts to the nine outside supporting organizations, and it could not meet those payouts simply on the basis of dividends. Soon after Stamas's arrival the company faced a serious payout crisis. Yet the new foundation president could never figure out what exactly was going on—namely, that Grune and the trustees did not want to take the company public, at least as that procedure was understood at the time, until the public offering could be positioned in such a way that each of them was a primary beneficiary. Just how to do that, however, remained for the moment a mystery.

The situation worsened in late 1986 after Cross resigned. Stamas demanded that the RDA hire a high-powered CFO to straighten out what he perceived as the company's financial paralysis. Once again Grune resisted. Bringing in an outsider meant bringing in someone who was not malleable. Instead, RDA veteran Vernon Thomas, who had reported to Cross as CFO, was kept on for the time being.

Five months after he arrived, Stamas—as much of an outsider as ever—quietly resigned. "He had been under the misapprehension," as Cross drily noted, "that he might actually have something to do with running the funds." His place was taken by Chris DeVita, another Grune loyalist who willingly accepted the title of executive director. DeVita had formerly been McHenry's secretary. She had gone to law school at his urging, but after gaining her degree she grew disaffected with her former boss and switched her allegiance to the new CEO.

As chairman of the funds, Grune now planned to exploit RDA charity to full PR advantage. At the same time he also appropriated the foundation's season pass to the glitzy world of art and society that McHenry had formerly reserved for himself.

In March 1987 McHenry's masterpiece, the $26 million Lila Acheson Wallace Wing of Twentieth-Century Art of the Metropolitan Museum of Art—$11 million ultimately given in Lila's name, plus an endowment to cover half the operating expense—was opened to the public. The architectural highlight of the four-story building, which featured twenty-two galleries on three levels comprising 40,000 square feet of exhibition space, was an indoor sculpture court covered by a sloping glass skylight. On display were paintings, sculpture, works on paper, industrial designs, and decorative arts from the Met's twentieth-century collection. Representing the RDA at the gala opening night was, of course, not McHenry, whom everybody knew, but George Grune, whom nobody knew. On the other hand, everybody assumed that Lila Acheson Wallace was the one really responsible for the new wing.

"[Mrs. Wallace's] vision, though, did not hit you in the eye," said *Wall Street Journal* critic Manuela Hoelterhoff. "The checks bought a barn of a wing for a collection as spotty as a Dalmatian and not half as beautiful."

Money was to blame, Hoelterhoff fumed. "Money from people like Mrs. Wallace and her advisers, who think space is better spent showing a Julian Schnabel painting covered with broken plates than a remarkable collection of perfect Meissen porcelain." But Lila had probably never even heard of Julian Schnabel and would doubtless have preferred Meissen porcelain to anything by Jackson Pollock.

Two years earlier, moreover, a Rockefeller-inspired anomaly called the DeWitt Wallace Decorative Arts Gallery had opened in Colonial Williamsburg, displaying eight thousand American and English antiques. Wally had no more interest in antiques than Lila did in abstract and postmodern painting. But the McHenry-Rockefeller team had given $14 million of the $17 million cost—outraging, in the process, Al Cole and other RDA executives—and the money had come out of the funds established by Wally. Everything was all topsy-turvy. Two very private philanthropists were being publicly remembered by monuments to things they had had no interest in while alive. Then, of course, there was the Sloan-Kettering Memorial Hospital, which was now one of the eleven new owners of the RDA. Neither of the Wallaces had ever showed much interest in that hospital either. But Laurance Rockefeller was its honorary chairman, meaning chief fund-raiser, and that was that.

28

Semper Fido

THE *ATMOSPHERE* of poisonous mistrust in the editorial ranks, in the aftermath of Ed Thompson's firing, in March 1984, was nowhere better illustrated than in a curious incident at the Victoria and Albert Museum, in London, on the day after the debacle. International book editor Jeremy Leggatt was in London, on his way back to the States after having trained editors in Milan in the art of cutting books. Finding himself with a few free hours, he decided to visit the museum. By sheer coincidence he bumped into Nathan Adams, the Washington bureau staffer who had worked so assiduously undercover to overthrow the editor in chief—going so far, the previous January, as to boast that Thompson was only a few months away from his own private Waterloo. Like Gilmore, Adams wanted to be as far from the heat as possible.

When he ran into Leggatt, an opinionated troublemaker and presumed liberal ally of Thompson, Adams became very paranoid, not even wishing to be seen in his company. Leggatt told him he was being ludicrous. Obviously, there were no Pleasantville spies strolling about in the heart of London. After he calmed down, Adams told Leggatt how Schulz, Barron, and all the rest had been working behind the scenes for months and months to get rid of Thompson. Now that he was gone, Adams suddenly realized, it made no difference what people like Leggatt thought.

Though Thompson was gone, his ghost was not; it continued to haunt the man who now sat at his desk. One night, soon after being named editor in chief, Ken Gilmore called Connie McGowan, one of Thompson's most intimate friends and a trusted aide, whose responsibilities included planning the company's worldwide editorial conferences. Racked by guilt, Gilmore spent nearly an hour trying to convince McGowan—now *his* assistant—that he had nothing to do with his predecessor's downfall and had been taken completely by surprise.

In the months that followed, Gilmore repeated the pattern, insisting to Thompson loyalists that he was only an innocent bystander and not the Brutus of Pleasantville. To a considerable extent the strategy worked. Thompson himself took Gilmore at his word, and so did many others. Yet rumors persisted that Gilmore's hand had also been on the knife that stabbed Ed Thompson in the back.

In the fall of 1985 the fourth worldwide editorial conference was held in Colonial Williamsburg. The gathering turned out to be a complete disaster, partly because of Gilmore's strange behavior. Recently, he had been walking more slowly, almost shuffling, and finding it harder to concentrate. Some people wondered if he had Parkinson's disease. As it turned out, they had guessed correctly. But Gilmore was determined to keep his disability secret. Not even a life-threatening illness was going to drive him from the office he had craved so desperately.

Secretly, McGowan despised Gilmore for the obsequiousness he brought to the position of editor in chief—which seemed all the starker in contrast to Thompson's aggressive style. But Gilmore was no boat rocker. Also, he loved the perks—hopping on the company plane, for example, just as Thompson was criticized for doing so often—and the millions in stocks and bonuses the post-Wallace RDA management was awarding to itself in compensation.

Under Gilmore the editorial content of the *RD* was, to borrow a well-worn quotable quote, déjà vu all over again. Familiar stock-in-trades were the near-monthly revelations of KGB terror and deception and relentless criticisms of big government, which also carried their own brand of inspiration—to keep patriotic vigilance high and liberal Democrats out of office. The formula was as potent as ever. More than a million reader-voters mailed in a postage-paid response card in 1985 asking Congress to "Halt the Deficit."

Mostly, though, there was the art of living—uplifting sermonettes from Norman Vincent Peale nestling with tales once again proving that no obstacle was insurmountable for anyone with enough self-confidence and an indomitable will. Gilmore's own triumphant experience was perfect proof.

Articles on sex and diet also regained their former pride of place.

Portly John Allen once opined that the secret of the *Digest*'s success was diet—that even one article a month on how to lose weight was not too much. Harry Harper thought the same thing could be said about sex. Gilmore covered his bets by publishing at least one and often two articles on either topic per issue. Under the new editor in chief, the *Digest* was almost becoming a caricature of itself, with none of the eccentric and almost uncategorizable selections that had been a hall-mark of Wally's editorship, or even anything similar to Hobe Lewis's passionate Nixonism. Banished forever were the let-the-chips-fall-where-they-may investigative stories initiated by Gilmore's predecessor Ed Thompson. Editorial content had become mere merchandise.

What investigative journalism the *RD* did undertake was directed at the usual suspects. "Murder of a Polish Priest" in December 1985 implicated the Polish government in the 1984 slaying of a Solidarity activist, while yet another story questioned the value of the Synthetic Fuels Corporation, which sought to displace oil and gas as America's primary sources of energy with fuels drawn from non-fossil-based, nonnuclear sources. But in the former the KGB was yet again the villain, while the latter could only please the big automobile manufac-turers and major oil companies who were important *Digest* advertisers.

Not surprisingly, the Washington bureau was also given a freer hand than ever before. Gilmore's heart had always been in D.C. to begin with. Now that he had won the office envisioned by Chuck Stevenson decades before, the new editor in chief embarked on a strategy to extend the bureau's right-wing editorial domination over every depart-ment and feature in the magazine.

Among Gilmore's first significant acts toward that end was to ap-point Ken Tomlinson, Voice of America head and former bureau star, as a managing editor and coequal of Jeremy Dole, Peter Canning, and Mary Louise Allin. Tomlinson's return to the *Digest* neatly coincided with Thompson's departure. In fact, the very week that he had been fired, Thompson had a meeting scheduled with Bill Schulz, head of the D.C. office, in which he intended to name Tomlinson head of the Washington bureau and bring Schulz up to Pleasantville. But the rum-pled, gray-maned Schulz, who once boasted he had managed to avoid all communication with Hobe Lewis during the Vietnam and Water-gate years, was too outspoken for the new leadership. Moreover, he had made it known that he did not want to transfer unless he had a real shot at the top.

Tomlinson's appointment was widely interpreted as more than just an act of simple favoritism. It was also seen as an expression of the collective will of the trustees, CEO George Grune, and Gilmore himself concerning the matter of editorial succession. Health and politics were among the primary considerations. Even though Gilmore had scarcely taken office, his physical condition was already of some concern to the Pleasantville management.

Moreover, it was typical of Grune's long-term approach to all aspects of corporate planning to take early steps to ensure that the next changing of the editorial guard was not accompanied by the turmoil and upheaval that marked both Thompson's and Gilmore's ascent to power.

Finally, Rockefeller, an ardent admirer of Nixon, and other members of the staunchly Republican board of trustees had no intention of anointing another wild-card conservative to the top editorial position. Tomlinson was a known and proven quantity, a Reagan administration insider with an unimpeachable right-wing pedigree.

The nominal leader of the defeated conservative faction in Pleasantville was executive editor Tony Oursler, who occupied the peculiar position of being a general without troops. Many of the higher-ranking editors were either Thompson loyalists or fellow travelers—Dole, Canning, David Mintner, Dan O'Keefe—who eschewed both Oursler's high Toryism and the bureau's right-wing zeal.

Though not operating as a united loyal opposition, they continued, by dint of a shared sensibility, to exercise a powerful and generally cohesive influence over the magazine's editorial content. Yet that influence was being eroded, month by month, as Gilmore consolidated his power with the help of Tomlinson and the Washington bureau.

A protégé of Schulz, the thirty-eight-year-old Tomlinson traveled with the far-right *Human Events* crowd and was now in the position Gilmore had been in a score of years earlier—that of the boy wonder who might some day grow up to be editor in chief. A former reporter for the *Richmond Times-Dispatch* in his native Virginia, the prolific Tomlinson had written more than fifty articles for the magazine over a fifteen-year career and was also the coauthor of *P.O.W.,* a history of American prisoners in Vietnam. His second wife, Rebecca, was a former congressional staff member.

Tomlinson was a "real survivor," according to Chris Kirby, a New York researcher who had worked with the Washington office. But Kirby was distinctly unimpressed with the man, regarding him as "a lightweight, self-dubbed wild character" with "a false sense of flair." In his desk drawer Tomlinson kept a bottle of Jim Beam; he was fond of saying that the two most important things in life were whiskey and country-and-western music.

Dole, though he got along well enough with Thompson and had been selected as his successor in the event of sudden death, had never been a great admirer of the former editor in chief. But now, with Gilmore in charge, managing editor Dole was shunted off the main route to the top by being named to succeed the retiring Alain de Lyrot as executive editor of *RD*'s international editions.

Canning found himself facing similar problems. Though highly regarded as an editor, he was widely perceived to be a poor manager, in part because Gilmore curtailed his authority and made sure no articles too suggestive of liberalism got into the magazine.

Oursler, twice passed over for the position of editor in chief, particularly resented the appointment of the much younger Tomlinson as a managing editor and obvious chief rival for the editorial throne. In sublimated schoolboy fashion, however, they coped for a time by playing out their mutual hostility in a series of practical jokes.

None was more disgruntled over Tomlinson's appointment than his old mentor Bill Schulz, head of the Washington office. Though cynical about the *Digest*'s grind-it-out conservatism, he kept an autographed photograph of Joe McCarthy in his home and claimed that the Wisconsin senator was a very misunderstood man. Once at dinner with a group of staffers, all were discussing what epoch of history they would have preferred to have lived in. Some looked back to the Renaissance or ancient Greece. But Schulz replied wistfully, "The fifties, where I grew up. That's what I would like."

Under Schulz's command the Washington bureau continued to devote itself primarily to ghosting articles by congressmen and other political officials. On the average three articles per issue now originated in Washington—a sign of its burgeoning influence and independence.

Like Oursler, Schulz still considered himself young enough, and possessing the proper political bona fides, to succeed Gilmore if his health forced him from office sooner rather than later. Moreover, the new editor in chief was displaying little talent for administration, editorial morale continued to plummet, and there was a sense among younger editors in particular that Gilmore lacked any sort of editorial vision. Despite the abundance of art-of-living items and the standard right-of-center rhetoric, the result, month after month, seemed bland.

Back in the good old days, Schulz and his protégé Tomlinson had been known as Pudge and Fido. When Fido got appointed head of the Voice of America, Pudge was tickled. His scenario was that Fido would eventually return to take over the bureau while Pudge trudged up to Pleasantville to be editor in chief. Fido fancied otherwise. His idea was to move into the big house in Pleasantville and let Pudge keep the doghouse in Washington all to himself. As a result, Pudge and Fido, who used to be such bosom buddies, became estranged because the protégé had become the boss.

Tomlinson had only recently returned to Pleasantville when he was invited to a black-tie dinner party in New York in honor of Lady Bird Johnson and actress Helen Hayes. Gilmore's wife was unable to attend, so he asked Connie McGowan to sit in for her. At one point during the dinner, Tomlinson leaned over and said to his companion, "Boy, things are a real mess."

McGowan agreed, saying, "Yes, there's too much work for Ken to handle. I hope you can take some of his burden."

"Gonna do the best I can," he replied. "But no one gets close to Ken."

Later, at a meeting on Cape Cod of international editors, Tomlinson demonstrated his priorities by spending much of his time listening to country music on his Walkman and displaying in general a lack of interest in international problems and procedures.

Despite Gilmore's low-key editorial style, the *Digest* was soon back on the front pages of the world's newspapers, albeit inadvertently. Early in May 1985 President Reagan announced plans to visit the U.S. air base in Bitburg, West Germany. Controversy erupted when it was revealed that the president's itinerary included not only a memorial service at the site of the Bergen-Belsen concentration camp, where 50,000 Nazi victims were buried in mass graves, but also a wreath-laying ceremony in a cemetery where 2,000 German soldiers were interred, including officers of the Waffen SS. As it was impossible to back out of the latter without offending his host, German chancellor Helmut Kohl, Reagan elected to defuse the crisis by giving a talk afterward at the air base on the theme of reconciliation.

In his prepared speech the *RD*'s First Reader wrote in an anecdote, offering it as an example of how hope "could sometimes be glimpsed in the darkest days of the war." Longtime readers of the *Digest* might have remembered the famous tale of a woman and her son who lived in a cottage in the Hürtgen Forest, on the German–Belgian border, in the waning hours of World War II. Three lost, frostbitten American soldiers, one badly wounded, knocked on the door.

"Even though sheltering the enemy was punishable by death," said Reagan, "she took them in and made them a supper with some of her last food." While they were eating, there was another knock. Four German soldiers were at the door. "There will be no shooting here," the woman told the soldiers, inviting them in. One of the Germans tended to the wounded American. All seven soldiers slept in the cottage overnight and in the morning went their separate ways.

"The boys reconciled briefly in the midst of war," Reagan concluded. "Surely, we allies in peacetime should honor the reconciliation of the last 40 years."

As the world soon learned, the story had first appeared in the January 1973 issue of the *RD,* billed as a Christmas parable, and its author was Fritz Vincken, the woman's son, by then a baker living in Honolulu. The Hürtgen Forest at the end of 1944 was the scene of some of the worst fighting of Germany's Ardennes offensive, known as the Battle of the Bulge, which opened with a surprise attack on the Allies on December 16 with a rapid advance to the Belgian–German border.

Ultimately, Germany was forced to retreat, leaving behind 100,000 dead, wounded, or captured, while the Allies sustained 81,000 casualties. Of that number, 77,000 were American, the heaviest U.S. battle toll in history, a fact the *Digest* story failed to mention. The savagery of the fighting was illustrated by an incident on the second day of the offensive when Waffen SS soldiers gunned down 86 American prisoners of war in Malmédy, Belgium, which the Christmas tale of reconciliation also glossed over.

Managing editor Tomlinson confirmed to the news media that the White House had inquired about the authenticity of the story the previous weekend. When attempts by the media to reach Vincken in Honolulu proved unsuccessful, Tomlinson related how, back in the early seventies, senior researcher Ursula Naccache had tracked the mother, Elisabeth Vincken, to Aachen, West Germany. According to Tomlinson, Mrs. Vincken gave substantially the same account as her son without having read her son's version. "We're convinced, without a doubt, that the story is true," he said.

In fact, the research team had gone to heroic lengths to verify the story, but Tomlinson's version of events was complete fiction. In 1972 James Finan, editor of first-person stories, asked the Paris bureau to check the story out. Naccache, fluent in both German and French, and considered the bureau's crack researcher, was assigned to the case. Vincken had assured Finan that his parents still lived in Essen, earning their living as bakers. But Naccache had no luck tracking the couple down by phone and decided that Finan had misheard, because nobody in Essen would live in a forest cottage anyway, but those in Aachen (a sound-alike name to an American ear) might.

She did locate a Mrs. Vincken in Aachen, but the woman was too deaf to talk on the phone. So Naccache went to visit her personally. However, the woman was by now very old and her memory failing. She could not recall the incident. The researcher had no other choice but to find the cottage in the Hürtgen Forest. Crossing and recrossing into Belgium, she was arrested by border guards for trespassing on government property. She never did find the cottage. But Naccache, who had helped Cornelius Ryan with his war books, decided that a lot of strange things happened in war. Ergo, the story must be true. "If somebody had made this one up," Naccache reasoned, "they would have tried to make it seem more spectacular."

In any case, Grune was thrilled by all the attention. The day after the story appeared in the *New York Times,* he—and not, significantly, Gilmore—sent out a memo to all department heads, editors in chief, and managing directors around the world, noting that Reagan had cited the *Digest* on his recent trip to Germany and that the article's message, as strong now as when first published, was "reconciliation." He went on to say, "The president's use of our story is further—and continuing—proof that our editors—world-wide—are committed to what DeWitt Wallace demanded of his articles: 'lasting interest.' " While Reagan's homey telling of the anecdote proved no such thing, it did confirm once again that the president, like J. Edgar Hoover, counted the *Reader's Digest* as his favorite magazine.

IN MID-SEPTEMBER 1984 a Soviet journalist who had spent the previous year in England showed up unexpectedly at a news conference in Moscow and claimed he had been abducted by British agents while attending the Venice Film Festival. During his stay in England, Oleg

Bitov had earned a reputation as an anti-Soviet commentator for the *Sunday Telegraph,* in London, but for more than a month he had been missing. His reappearance was also front-page news in the *New York Times* and other papers.

During his dramatic news conference, Bitov declared that he had simply waited until he had won the confidence of his purported captors and then bought an airplane ticket and flew home. The journalist also accused the British of having forced him to undergo drug treatment and grueling questioning. Finally, he was offered "a well-paid job in the gallery of mud-slinging anti-Sovieteers." Seven weeks later a statement was issued to the British press in his name protesting the treatment of Soviet intellectuals.

Skeptical British and American intelligence officials and journalists who had worked with Bitov on the *Telegraph* were convinced, however, that he had defected voluntarily and returned to the USSR merely to be with his wife and teenage daughter. Some even speculated that Bitov had been induced to "defect" only after threats had been made against his family.

A month after his news conference, Bitov was back in the headlines when a Russian émigré writer and friend of Bitov insisted he had been forcibly returned to the USSR because the Soviets feared he would give evidence to Italian officials investigating the attempt on the life of Pope John Paul II. The lie to that theory was given by year's end when Bitov returned to his job on the *Literaturnaya Gazeta.*

Whether Oleg Bitov was a genuine defector who elected to repatriate and risk the consequences or a KGB plant was never ascertained. Indisputably, though, two senior editors of the *Reader's Digest* were once again assigned to be his handlers in the media—John Barron and John ("Dimi") Panitza, the former in the United States and the latter in Europe. On March 11, 1985, the BBC interviewed the erstwhile Soviet defector about his interlude in the West. Bitov wrote in *Literaturnaya Gazeta,* as quoted by the BBC:

"Panitza called on me in London and the minute he arrived, he asked whether I knew the Bulgarian capital well. I answered that I knew it pretty well. And the street adjoining the monument to the Tsar-Liberator? I recalled it. And the most attractive building in that street? Panitza remarked: 'Were it not for the Communists, that house would be mine.' "

The house was also part of *Digest* lore. In the last year of World War

II, editor Harry Harper—on leave as a war correspondent—was informed that a ranking member of the Bulgarian aristocracy and a fervent anti-Communist wished to defect. Harper received directions to the house but, upon entering, found it abandoned. Wandering through the rooms, he eventually discovered the fourteen-year-old Panitza crouching in a corner on the top story. After completing his education at *RD* expense, Panitza was hired by the magazine's Paris bureau as a researcher and later became its head.

The so-called plot to kill the pope originated in Langley, Bitov claimed, "and John Dimitri Panitza, a former Bulgarian and now U.S. citizen living in Paris, was instrumental in bringing it into the world. His official post is European editor of the U.S. magazine *Reader's Digest.* Claire Sterling works for the *Reader's Digest* as a roving correspondent based in Rome and is consequently subordinate to the European editor, John Panitza. But whereas he has two masters, she has three: *Reader's Digest,* the CIA and Mossad."

Another outspoken critic of the *RD*'s cozy relationship with the CIA was Manuel Buendia, whose daily muckraking column "Private Network" appeared in *Excelsior,* Mexico City's leading newspaper, and was syndicated in more than two hundred other papers. Among Buendia's frequent targets: official corruption, drug trafficking, U.S. intelligence activities in Mexico. The latter eventually furnished enough material to be collected in book form, *La CIA en México,* published in 1983.

Among Buendia's CIA writings was a series on the relationship between *Selecciones* and an American writer named Dr. Daniel James, whose articles appeared frequently in the Spanish-language edition of the *RD* but seldom in the U.S. edition. According to Buendia, "in the last 20 years, Daniel James has only written what he has been ordered to by the CIA." James lived in Mexico from 1956 to 1978 and received both his bachelor's and doctoral degrees from Pacific Western University, largely on the basis of books he wrote during his journalism career, including the 1954 *Red Design for America: Guatemalan Prelude.* James also held the mostly honorary position of managing editor of the *New Leader,* a Cold War liberal publication with ties to the CIA not unlike those of the *RD* itself.

Buendia further identified Antonio Rodriguez Villar, director of *Selecciones* in Mexico City, as a CIA agent. A charter member of Harry Morgan's World Press Institute, Villar had also served as press spokesman for the Argentine federal police during the junta's "dirty war," during which twenty thousand people allegedly disappeared. Buendia claimed that the CIA, "a longtime friend of *Selecciones,* [had] taken over its Latin American editions, through individuals such as Rodriguez Villar."

On May 30, 1984, after leaving his office, Buendia was shot four times in the back at point-blank range in a parking lot. The Mexican Federal Security Directorate, charged with the investigation into the murder, later destroyed most of Buendia's files. Five years later José Antonio Zorrilla Pérez, former head of the directorate, was arrested in connection with the killing following a seven-hour siege of his hideout in Mexico City. Prosecutors said the murder of Buendia was drug related.

James later showed up in Washington, D.C., where *Excelsior* found him ensconced in a think tank called the Mexico–United States Institute. The newspaper charged that James was a CIA agent during his years in Mexico and MUSI part of a conspiracy to destabilize the Institutional Revolutionary Party (PRI), Mexico's ruling party. The story led to a cancellation of a two-day conference by the Dallas Council on World Affairs and aroused the interest of the *Dallas Morning News.*

James, who had admitted to the *New York Times* in 1977 that he had ties to the CIA, now repeatedly refused to discuss his background with the Dallas paper or even to state his age. But the *News* discovered that James's doctorate in Latin American studies and his bachelor's degree were obtained by mail order and that MUSI was funded by wealthy Dallas conservatives. Though an unknown to the Dallas community, according to the paper, James was well known in Mexico, where he was considered a "longtime meddler in Mexican affairs," while MUSI was suspected to be a "front for the Central Intelligence Agency and right-wing Mexicans intent on undermining the PRI." James now strenuously denied any connection with the CIA.

———

In October 1986 thirty-year-veteran John Allen, another member of the Thompson generation, took early retirement and went to work for his father-in-law as director of the Foundation for Christian Living, in Peale's hometown of Pawling, just north of Pleasantville. Only the previous December, Allen had been named executive director of the

RD Foundation. Under the publicity-conscious regime of George Grune, even Allen's former sinecure as PR director had not proved a safe haven.

Allen's departure more or less coincided with a fast and furious masthead boogie going on at the top, much of it occasioned by Gilmore's failing health and the need to consolidate Tomlinson's position as his heir. Oursler managed to hold his own for a time and was named deputy editor in chief, while Tomlinson moved up to the post of executive editor and the *Digest*'s ranking female editor, Mary Louise Allin, elected to retire.

What ultimately cleared the political air was money, which, as McHenry once observed, could solve any problem, though in this instance it was the company's stinginess that neatly accounted for the departure of its four most ideologically isolated editors—Oursler, executive editor Jeremy Dole, managing editor Peter Canning, and senior staff editor Dan O'Keefe. In the wake of Cross's global cost cutting and Grune's rebuilding program, the price of company stock—accumulated at bargain rates mostly through stock-option plans—stood at a record high.

When the gang of four decided to sell their stock, they also gave management just the pretext it was looking for to solidify the magazine's right-wing homogeneity. The RDA repurchased the stock, then informed them that the sale of stock by an employee was tantamount to resignation. Though stunned, Oursler and his colleagues demanded they at least be given severance. Grune and Gilmore refused. Oursler prudently decided that the time had come to make his exit. But for a time Dole, Canning, and O'Keefe hung on, like survivors in shark-infested waters.

After the latter three finally followed Oursler out of Pleasantville, they filed suit against the RDA to collect severance pay and damages. Oursler, however, though equally bitter at feeling betrayed by the company both he and his father had served for so long, found it emotionally impossible to join in the suit. Also, as the one with the longest tenure, and an old Wally favorite, he owned far more stock than any of the others.

At the same time that Thompson-tinged editors were being driven into the cold, numerous other contributors and roving editors, many of them despised by the Washington bureau, saw their assignments drying up. There ensued a waiting game between management and

rovers over who would make the first move. Gilmore wanted Lewis/
Thompson-era roving editors—Joseph Blank, John Hubbell, and Jim
Miller in particular—to resign in disgust and accept a much modified
pension package. For their part, the go-no-more-a-roving rovers
hoped management would offer them a favorable severance package
just to get rid of them. The result was a standoff, though a few were
eventually able to collect a pension.

Regardless, roving editors had become an endangered species because they were a luxury the cost-conscious Grune thought the company could no longer justify maintaining. Most earned a salary in the
$60,000 range for their part-time contributions, plus expenses, as well
as $3,000 or $4,000 per article and medical benefits.

Not long after the departure of Oursler, Bill Schulz in Washington
and Dimi Panitza in Paris were invited to relocate to Pleasantville.
Both declined. Though an admirer and friend of Ed Thompson,
Panitza also managed to get along with Gilmore, who helped obtain
for him a promotion to managing editor. In Paris, though, he had his
independence. What Tomlinson and Grune really hoped was that the
independent-minded Bulgarian ex-aristocrat would cash in his shares
and retire a rich man. Grune also considered the Paris office too
expensive and wanted to close it down.

For his part, Schulz likewise wished to retain his independence by
continuing to run the bureau and had no intention of going up to
Pleasantville and suffering the humiliation of taking orders from Fido.
Like Panitza, he had been promoted to managing editor, a mostly
honorary position, while a new crew of assistant managing editors now
served as issue editors.

The housecleaning extended to the foreign editions. In July 1987
RD editions in England and Asia got new editors in chief, Russell
Twisk replacing Michael Randolph in London. New editors were also
named for the Asian, Australian, Italian, South African, Norwegian,
Swedish, Danish, French, and Canadian editions, while new managing
editors were appointed in Finland and Germany, sites of two of the
RDA's most prosperous subsidiaries.

In October 1988 the *Digest* was back in the news with another
"debate in print," similar to the one pioneered by Thompson between
the Republican incumbent, Gerald R. Ford, and his Democratic challenger, Jimmy Carter. This time the candidates were Vice-President
George Bush and Michael Dukakis, governor of Massachusetts. In a

lackluster contest the debate managed to stir up considerable interest in the national press. Bush declared in the debate—published a month before the candidates' televised exchange—that he opposed tax increases, while Dukakis admitted they were a last resort.

Bush came out in favor of the death penalty, school prayer, and aid to the Nicaraguan Contras, and Dukakis opposed all three. Once again, by fashioning the debate around Republican issues, the nation's largest magazine was sending a familiar message to Middle America— candidate Bush was one of them while the Democratic contender was an eastern liberal.

The article was later featured as a center-spread advertisement in the *New York Times*—the *RD*'s first-ever two-page self-promotion in the newspaper of record. Full-page and occasionally double-spread celebrations of weightier *Digest* stories—and never art-of-living pieces, the magazine's bread-and-butter—ultimately became a monthly feature in the advertising pages of the *Times* and other major newspapers.

Newsweek called the Bush-Dukakis debate, titled "Quest for the Presidency: The Candidates' Debate," the "single most influential magazine article of the year," while the *New Republic* dubbed it the most important 1988 election-year story. The *Washington Post* quoted a top Bush campaign official who credited the story with "creating a firestorm at the grassroots" of America.

There was never any doubt, of course, where the *Digest*'s own sympathies lay. The same month that the debate in print was published, twenty-two editors from *Digest* editions worldwide assembled at the White House to interview the future president. It was not only yet another example of the Americo-centricism of the *Digest* but a clear indication that it intended to remain the unofficial house organ of the Republican party. The interview was published simultaneously in January 1989 in all thirty-nine foreign editions. A similar interview was conducted soon afterward with British prime minister—and stalwart Reaganite—Margaret Thatcher, though this time the interviewers consisted only of Gilmore, Twisk, and right-wing journalist-historian Paul Johnson. The two-part retrospective of the prime minister's ten years in office likewise ran simultaneously in all editions.

The following summer, at an editorial conference of six editors at Seabrook Island, off the South Carolina coast, Gilmore told his key aides, "It may sound corny, but people love this magazine. They laugh with us, they cry with us and they identify with us because *Reader's*

Digest is America. Far beyond any other publication, it reflects the heart and the soul, the goodness and the guts, the true nature of this nation. It is an American institution, and if we ever lose this priceless asset we are finished."

Meanwhile, largely because of Tomlinson's influence, the *Digest* was stocking up with a new editorial staff drawn mainly from other right-wing media. Art-of-living themes got a big boost with the addition of yet another roving editor, John Pekkanen, one of the best health writers in the country. At the same time, roving editor Carl T. Rowan, the author of "This Isn't Russia, Mr. President," which landed Ed Thompson in such hot water, decided to retire.

———

IN THE FALL of 1986 the *Digest* published "Congress Is Crippling the CIA," by Rowland Evans and Robert Novak, two nationally syndicated conservative columnists who were also *RD* roving editors. The pair cited an alleged security breach by Patrick J. Leahy, Democratic senator from Vermont and a member of the Senate Intelligence Committee, who a year earlier had said on television that the United States had intercepted the phone calls of Egyptian president Mubarak in connection with the hijacking of the Italian cruise ship *Achille Lauro* in 1985 by Palestinian terrorists. Mubarak told the media that the hijackers had left Egypt, but U.S. intelligence knew otherwise.

Not so coincidentally, the article appeared just before Vermont voters went to the polls. Though Leahy was reelected, he later concluded that Evans and Novak had cited the alleged security leak in such a way that it could have come only from CIA chief William J. Casey.

In trademark *Digest* apocalyptese, Evans and Novak also declared that if World War III had broken out in the late seventies or early eighties, the United States might have lost. The blame for that perilous state of affairs they put squarely on government bureaucracy. Cuts by the Defense Department, according to the two columnists (who contested published accounts that some of their articles were ghostwritten), had made it possible for spies to avoid a rigorous five-year check and thus betray America's strategic defenses.

A spectacular case in point was provided a few months later in an excerpt from John Barron's latest book, *Breaking the Ring,* a compelling, as-told-by-the-FBI adventure yarn about the bureau's capture in 1985 of master spy John A. Walker, Jr. As a navy warrant officer, Walker had the job of repairing encoding devices called cipher machines. In need of quick cash, he simply walked into the Russian embassy in Washington, D.C., and began providing the KGB with documents revealing navy strategy on the use of nuclear missiles, battle plans, U.S. vulnerabilities, and other secrets that allowed the Soviets "to achieve surprise and tactical advantage in combat."

Walker had also enlisted his son, brother, and best friend Jerry Whitworth in his treasonable activities. The spy cell went undetected for so long, according to Barron, mainly because the financially strapped FBI could not afford to conduct a more rigorous five-year check on the errant officer. During Walker's trial in San Francisco, Barron served as a prosecution witness. He also testified at the trials of rogue FBI agent Richard Miller and Walker's associate Jerry Whitworth and at the court-martial of marine Clayton Lonetree, who claimed he had read Barron's book to learn more about the KGB.

FBI officials maintained that Barron was used as an expert witness because, as a writer not officially connected with the bureau, he did not have to worry about inadvertently revealing any secrets while on the stand. Testifying under oath at the Whitworth trial, however, Barron admitted he had security clearance, which he implied gave him access to satellite photography. So sensitive was overhead photography, according to Barron, that "we can see the color of a man's beard"—a detail which, if true, was not generally known.

Barron also testified he had not been compensated for his services to the FBI, but had received a great deal of bureau assistance, which translated into commercial success for his books. As a result *Breaking the Ring* was considered by some bureau observers to be the definitive account of Walker's capture.

Unlike his two KGB books, *Breaking the Ring* attracted considerable media attention, including favorable reviews in the *Wall Street Journal* and the *New York Times Book Review,* which noted that, while unfailingly sympathetic to the FBI, it did not gloss over the bureau's several missed opportunities.

The same year his book on Walker was published, Barron was handed yet another opportunity to lambaste government bureaucracy and defend America's intelligence and security agencies, when it was revealed that construction on the new U.S. embassy in Moscow had to be abandoned because it was riddled with bugging devices. In his June

1987 piece "Our New Moscow Embassy—Bungled and Bugged," Barron charged that foreign-service officers had no business administering vast, worldwide construction programs and that, in particular, the State Department should be stripped of all responsibility for overseas construction. Rather, according to Barron, the job should be done by the Army Corps of Engineers and the Navy Seabees, who were experienced in "building in adverse environments."

What Barron did not reveal was that the Army Corps of Engineers had, in fact, supplied four primary engineers to assist the Moscow project. Furthermore, Navy Seabees had also provided security construction support to detect any introduction of clandestine devices or other security penetration. Nor did Barron mention successful construction projects in Saudi Arabia, Malaysia, and Pakistan, recently completed under adverse conditions. All that information had been made available to him before he wrote the article.

One reader who needed no convincing that Barron's attack on government bureaucracy was right on the money was President Reagan, who that very month appointed RDA senior counselor Melvin Laird to a four-person study group to investigate what the United States should do as a result of the Kremlin's massive bugging of the planned U.S. embassy.

—

In August 1987, on schedule, John Zinsser retired as CB editor in chief, and his place was taken by Barbara J. Morgan, exactly as her mentors Jack Beaudouin and Joe Hotchkiss had hoped. For the most part, Zinsser had served as a caretaker, somewhat like his counterpart Ken Gilmore at the magazine, but with considerably more independence and flair. One reason Zinsser did not have to worry was that he owned more company stock than George Grune. Never afraid to speak his mind, Zinsser had gone so far as to express to Grune his reservations about the choice of Tomlinson as Gilmore's heir apparent, and about other Grune appointments as well. Though Zinsser regarded Gilmore as a "wimp," he heartily endorsed Morgan as his successor—publicly, at any rate. Privately, he had his doubts.

Zinsser's departure came at a decisive moment for the division as a whole, when it faced the most formidable new competition in its history. Morgan, by now transformed into the consummate professional, despite the misgivings of her erstwhile rival and colleague Noel

Rae, was inheriting an office filled with challenges perhaps greater than any of her predecessors had known. She was more than equal to the task.

Rae, meanwhile, had failed in his effort to start up his own rival condensed-book club, called the Select Reader, though the coup de grace was delivered not by the RDA but by Time Warner, which coincidentally had just begun its own condensed-book club, Time Life Book Digest. Amazingly enough, even though the *Reader's Digest* had to fend off numerous competitors almost from the beginning, it had taken the publishing world nearly forty years to realize there was even more money to be made in condensing a handful of best-sellers into a single volume to be sold by direct mail.

Time Life Book Digest differed from Condensed Books in that condensed nonfiction played a more prominent role in its editorial mix. Otherwise the volumes bore a remarkable similarity. Book Digest also undersold CB by one dollar, $11.95 versus $12.98. Furthermore, Time Warner's huge mailing list was able to draw not only on its own home-marketing resources but also on that of its mammoth subsidiary the Book-of-the-Month Club, acquired in 1977, which was of proven durability and effectiveness.

For the time being, however, CB stuck to its tried-and-true formula, which stressed family reading—no explicit sex or unnecessary violence. Even so, changing times and the threat of unprecedented competition did encourage CB to do books in 1987 it would not have done ten years earlier. Though all CB titles still had to uphold family standards and values, not every book had to have a happy ending any longer. One such departure was *Kafir Boy,* a nonfiction book about growing up black in South Africa.

The biggest challenge facing Morgan and her staff—who numbered more than a hundred and included six scouts working in New York with publishers and agents, reviewing upward of 3,500 books a year—was to determine how to expand CB's share of an already saturated domestic market, either through a new product line or by reaching different segments of the reading public. By now the club had published more than 700 books, with the average annual number of copies sold reaching the 10 million mark both in the United States and in Canada, Britain, Western Europe, Australia, and other global markets. Still another 80,000 readers subscribed to the large-type edition.

The most obvious market for expansion lay with the international editions, Morgan's original hunting grounds. CBIE was now published in thirteen editions, in ten languages, in seventeen countries. Despite some liberalization, however, editorial control was still strongly centralized in Pleasantville, which provided most of the publishable material by circulating reports on CB volume contents to all international offices. In addition, Pleasantville operated a pool program that condensed English-language books for translation and use in international editions. Since not every book published in the United States appealed to non-American readers, the international division also provided a list of "separate use" books that foreign editions were permitted to use. All this was in fulfillment of Grune's corporate mandate—"Plan globally and act locally"—though too much local independence was as suspect as ever.

However, Grune and Morgan had good reason for not wanting to tamper with success. As it approached its fortieth birthday, Condensed Books remained the largest and most successful book club in history. A typical U.S. volume sold nearly two million copies. The CB book club also enjoyed another distinction. Not one of its selections had ever been read by the man whose fiat brought it into being, DeWitt Wallace.

29

No Business like CEO Business

IN THE SPRING of 1985 *Penthouse* publisher Bob Guccione bid $5.5 million for High Winds and its surrounding 105 acres. The Gooch, as he was known, wanted a place where he and his "pets" could relax on the weekends, and the secluded, sumptuous grounds suited his tastes to an X. Besides, like Lila, he was a big-time art collector; and, like DeWitt, a magazine publisher and fellow member of the *Forbes* 400.

Real-estate prices that year were at an all-time high in Westchester County, and the Reader's Digest Association could afford to bide its time and be picky about who would be accorded the privilege of buying the home of its founders—who, of course, had not wanted it sold at all but made into a visitors' center. But that was then. This was now.

The RDA not only turned Guccione down but rudely told him to get lost. A year later High Winds was sold to industrialist Nelson Peltz, who had built his immense fortune with the help of junk-bond king Michael Milken. The $6 million price, a Westchester County record, was a droplet in the bucket for Peltz, who later cleared a profit of $520 million when he sold his share of Triangle Industries, a manufacturer of jukeboxes. Among the first things Peltz and his wife, Claudia, did when they moved in was tear up the rose garden, where McHenry had strewn the ashes of Wally and Lila, to install a playground for their children.

The sale of High Winds was symbolic of the new RDA and its near-obsession with profit—a perhaps understandable attitude, given that the company had operated for so long at such a capitalistic disadvantage, and also given the intense pressures that Grune and his associates now faced to feed the eleven nonprofit organizations that were the company's new proprietors.

But there was another motive, and that was to thwart a hostile takeover bid by some other company. If the trustees were to turn down a direct offer, a raider might complain to the New York attorney general that management was entrenched and the stock undervalued. A precedent for such a scenario was a 1984 ruling by that office forcing the Altman Foundation, which owned the B. Altman department store, to sell its retail division and invest in assets with a better immediate return for beneficiaries.

But Grune and Rockefeller, who personified the brave new mood at the RDA, were still determined to find a way not only to reduce the company's vulnerability but also to keep it private. In early 1986 the RDA chairman had lunch with Time Inc. president and CEO Richard Munro, who complained about his advertising problems. An ex–advertising salesman, Grune knew that while Munro was worrying about declining revenues, a book called *The Fanciest Dive,* by Christopher Byron, had just been published; it gave a behind-the-scenes account of what happened when Time Inc. launched and then killed *TV-Cable Week,* a costly and embarrassing failure.

"No one has written a book like that about us," Grune later told his managers. "And I'm determined that no one ever will. Our results are too good—and our teamwork between divisions too strong—to ever let that kind of episode happen at *Reader's Digest.*"

Yet something very similar had been predicted by former COO Bill Cross when he resigned—that Grune's master strategy to launch not just one but four magazines, in order to invent new markets for the *Digest*'s primarily over-fifty, female readership, was a recipe for disaster.

So intent was Grune on motivating his troops that in 1987 he hired a songwriter to compose a company anthem called "I Can Make a Difference." At Christmas, cassettes and sheet music were distributed to employees so that they could listen to it at home. The theme was that the *Reader's Digest* was nothing less than the greatest force for good in the entire world. Echoing *RD* philosophy, the lyrics declared that the magazine left the life of no reader untouched, and even suggested that recipients of junk mail underwent a quasi-religious experience (the sweepstakes allowed the hopes of joyful winners to "survive").

In 1988 the last vestige of the Wallaces' presence in Pleasantville was abolished when Lila Acheson Wallace's ornate office was dismantled and partitioned into smaller offices for editors. For years it had served as the RDA's unofficial shrine. Oursler saw the change as "a symbol of the dispossession of the *Digest*'s origins by current management. An institution that loses a sense of its origins may find that its destiny deteriorates."

As for any memorial to DeWitt Wallace, employees and visitors were directed to a basement area not far from the company store where his portrait hung on the wall. Even his memory had been condensed almost to the point of obliteration. The company's annual reports also ceased to make even a nominal mention of the RDA's cofounders.

On September 19, 1989, Al Cole died after a brief illness at his home in Greenwich, Connecticut, at the age of ninety-two. The RDA's fiercest competitor had managed to live to be one year older than Wally. Eighteen days later, Ralph Henderson passed away in a Mount Kisco hospital. Henderson was ninety. (In his last years, after his wife, Clifford, died, the cleanest-cut octogenarian in Pleasantville had become infatuated with a self-styled Russian princess—much to the dismay and delight of old-time Digesters.)

With their passing, the last of the original pillars of the house of Wallace were gone. The longevity of Cole, Henderson, Wally, and Lila was striking. All had lived into their nineties, with Lila surpassing everyone in the sheer accumulation of years. If they shared an epitaph, it was perhaps the prescription for good health and a long life rendered by Rear Admiral Cary T. Grayson, personal physician of President Woodrow Wilson, as quoted in volume 1, number 1, of the *Reader's Digest*: "Eight hours for work, eight hours for sleep, eight hours for play, and all to God." They might have cheated a little on those rules, but not much, and Wally least of all.

IN DECEMBER *1986* the RDA made its first domestic magazine acquisition with the purchase of *Travel-Holiday* for an undisclosed amount in cash. A well-established travel magazine with a circulation of 778,000, *Travel-Holiday* also possessed just the sort of *Digest*-like demographics the company was looking for: a readership that was 60 percent female and over the age of fifty, with an average household income of $42,000.

The acquisition spree continued in the fall of 1987 when the RDA bought a 50 percent stake in Dorling Kindersley, a global packager of reference and self-help books, with annual revenues of $16.8 million. Dorling had previously created such popular titles for the RDA as *Success with House Plants, The Good Housekeeping Illustrated Cookbook, The American Medical Association Family Medical Guide,* and *Quest for the Past.* Later the RDA also purchased Joshua Morris Publishing, a children's book publisher, for an undisclosed price. Quality School Products likewise bought out a competitor, TV Guide School Plan.

Grune's second magazine acquisition, in early 1988, was the *Family Handyman,* obtained from Maxwell Communications for an estimated $30 million—a relatively high twelve times cash flow—followed by *50 Plus* from Whitney Communications. The circulation of the *Family Handyman* was 1.2 million; that of *50 Plus* was 500,000. Despite the low numbers for the latter, Grune wanted a vehicle to reach the 61.6 million Americans who were over fifty, or one in three adults. That same target audience also accounted for about half the nation's discretionary income, about $132 billion.

Among Grune's first moves was to change the magazine's title to the non-age-specific *New Choices for the Best Years* because research showed no one liked to be categorized as "over 50." The editorial was also given an upbeat *RD* tone—articles on second careers, travel, and the joys of being fully involved in life replaced those on how to handle depression.

Yet, from the beginning, the new magazine unit—all editorial operations were relocated in the Manhattan office—was plagued by mounting losses. In fiscal 1988 it posted a $14 million deficit. Meanwhile, the magazines were also being test-marketed in Europe. Each launch in each country was exorbitantly expensive. At the same time, the operating profit of the *RD* also slipped in fiscal 1989, as did those of the book divisions and home entertainment.

Despite its huge circulation the *RD* no longer ranked in the top ten in advertising pages, trailing *TV Guide, Business Week, People, Vogue,* and *Modern Bride,* among others. And though the magazine had regained its circulation lead over *TV Guide,* both were dwarfed by a relatively new player on the scene, *Modern Maturity,* published by the American Association of Retired Persons, which claimed 50 million subscribers.

Cross's gloomy view that the RDA had never been an efficient publisher of magazines was seemingly being borne out again. Overall the company was averaging an unimpressive profit margin of only 6 percent, compared with 9 percent at McGraw-Hill and 10 percent at Gannett.

In the fall of 1989 Grune appointed Thomas M. Kenney, an investment banker, as president of the newly formed Magazine Publishing Group (MPG), which was now set to acquire a fourth member, *American Health*—thus "completing" the circle of special-interest topics geared to the *RD*'s geriatric readership: travel, the art of postretirement living, home repair, health. An ex-marine, like Grune, Kenney had some magazine experience—he had edited the *Okinawa Marine* during his Vietnam tour. Each of the four publishers of the magazines reported to Kenney, who in theory reported to COO Dick McLoughlin. In fact, Kenney reported to Grune, who many thought had already begun to groom an heir.

But the push into specialty magazines was to prove even costlier. In 1989 the MPG sustained yet another huge deficit—this time a $17 million operating loss on revenues of $47.3 million. Competitors also thought Grune was slow to fix problems. Numerous travel magazines had cropped up in the late eighties, for example—all giving *Travel-Holiday* severe competition. Yet he had taken three years to revamp the magazine's stodgy design.

As always, the book and home entertainment groups remained the company's powerhouses, but even there the competition was heating up. Grune's abiding problem was still to find new growth areas. One belated but potentially lucrative response was Today's Best Nonfiction, the RDA's answer to the Time Warner condensed-book club, which unlike CB favored nonfiction. TBN volumes, published five times a year, featured up to five condensed selections of current nonfiction and reached customers six months after the publication of the original hardcover but well before the paperback edition. By RDA standards, though, the numbers were small, with an initial print run of "only" 250,000.

A far more profitable and, indeed, thriving operation was the International Book Publishing Group, whose goal was to publish two books a year that could be sold around the world. Formerly known as General Books, it had marked its twenty-fifth anniversary in 1988 and since its founding had enjoyed total sales of a Bible-rivaling 334 million books. Major markets were the United States, the United Kingdom, Australia, France, Germany, and Italy, which meant that each book had to have universal appeal without requiring extensive and expensive local adaptations. Favorite categories continued to be health and nature, scenic wonders, strange and amazing facts, world history, and self-help. Odd facts about the animal world, the Solar System, or the human body were also dependable sellers.

Borne aloft by the book divisions, which accounted for 53 percent of the company's revenues, Grune next ventured into European acquisitions and start-ups, especially in the area of personal finance—not an area where the *RD*'s reputation was strongest. The merging of markets into the European Economic Community was only a few years away, and the moment to expand seemed opportune. In early 1990 the RDA purchased Britain's *Money* magazine and renamed it *Moneywise.* Around the same time, the company launched its first new magazine in ten years with *Budgets Famille,* a French monthly aimed at affluent thirty- to forty-five-year-old readers. Somebody computed wrong again, however, and the magazine lasted only about a year.

Plans were also made to start up editions of the *Digest* in Hungary and, once again, in Russia, bringing the figures on the *RD* tote board up to forty-one editions in sixteen languages. Ironically, with the disintegration of the Soviet Union in the *glasnost* era, eastern Europe and the former USSR—the *Digest*'s sworn enemy for a half century—loomed as just the sort of virgin market Grune had been praying for. No sooner had the Berlin Wall come down than West German Digesters entered East Berlin in vans to give away tens of thousands of copies of *Das Beste* and collect names for the data bank.

Long-term strategy also included the launching of several new product lines, including home videos, Great Biographies, World's Best Reading, and the AMA Home Medical Library. All of those products, originated in the United States, were exported to the international companies.

———

IN 1990 the RDA reached not so much a crossroads as a point of no return with its transformation into a public company, though in a very limited sense, through a public stock offering. Not only was the offering intended to raise $50 million for the charities that owned the RDA, but it forced the company to open its books. Financial details filed with the Securities and Exchange Commission indicated that the Reader's Digest Association was worth at least $3 billion, though some analysts thought the figure was much too low, because the voting stock was far more valuable than the nonvoting stock on which the figures were based. Grune personally owned a portfolio of company stock worth $5.9 million. During his five-year tenure, counting bonuses and incentives, he had earned a total of $13 million.

Just before the company went public, however, Pleasantville was rocked by the resignation of longtime Grune ally Martha Farquhar, RDA general counsel and the company's highest-ranking female employee. Farquhar, in fact, was the intermediary for Grune and McLoughlin who had once approached Ed Thompson to see whether he would join them in an attempt to overthrow O'Hara. To close friends, though, she would confide only that there were some hoops through which she would not jump.

A few months later, to nobody's surprise, McLoughlin also announced his resignation, at age sixty-two. His titles of president and COO were assumed by Grune for an indefinite period.

Following those two resignations the RDA's chief financial officer, Vernon Thomas, also announced his decision to leave the company. Grune later claimed that McLoughlin's and Thomas's resignations, like so many others at the RDA, were "health-related" and coincidental and that Farquhar resigned because she was unwilling to accept a change in job responsibility. Many insiders assumed that Grune simply wanted a general counsel with a bigger profile and more clout now that the company was going public. Farquhar, by contrast, was a home-grown product.

The emergence of the long-secretive Reader's Digest Association into the public eye occasioned considerable analysis, speculation, and second-guessing in the media. In a review of Grune's first five years, *Business Week* noted that the new CEO had increased revenues by 40 percent, to $1.8 billion, and driven net income from $21 million to $152 million, a sevenfold gain. But there was still some question whether he could foster real growth, even after surging profits and fat cutting. Much of what Grune accomplished had been begun by Bill Cross and was simply the result of putting the company into the high gear it should have been in years earlier.

On the downside, operating profits fell in 1989 from $213 million to $207 million. Moreover, as *Business Week* observed, the company continued to be staggered by a puzzling number of departures—losing, in eight months alone, its president, chief financial officer, and general counsel. The year before, departing executives had included the director of corporate planning and development.

The public also learned, as a result of the stock offering, that the various funds established and formerly overseen by Wally had since been consolidated and renamed the DeWitt Wallace Reader's Digest Fund, while those initiated by Lila were rechristened the Lila Acheson Wallace Reader's Digest Fund. Between them the two funds now controlled 100 percent of all RDA voting stock. With the consolidation of the funds, and the public offering, the Wallace Trust was dissolved. Some of its trustees, such as Laurance S. Rockefeller, became trustees of the new funds. With the abolition of the trust, Rockefeller was no longer obliged to step down at seventy-nine. In fact, in 1990 he turned eighty.

In the offering, the DeWitt Wallace Reader's Digest Fund—the largest RDA shareholder, with 17.7 million shares—sold 5.9 million shares of its nonvoting stock. The second-largest shareholder, the Lila Acheson Wallace Reader's Digest Fund, tendered 4.6 million of its 11.4 million shares. Similarly, the fund for the Metropolitan Museum of Art, which owned 11.7 million shares, sold off 2.5 million shares, and the other proprietary charities did likewise.

But the linchpin of the public offering, and of the company's very future, was the disposition of the voting stock. In order to meet IRS requirements and divest themselves of a combined 50 percent of their voting stock by the year 2000, the DeWitt Wallace and Lila Acheson Wallace Reader's Digest Funds had arranged to sell 20 percent of voting stock to an employee pension fund. Ultimately, in other words, only 30 percent of the voting stock would fall into public hands. The other 70 percent would remain under the control of the two funds and the pension program, all of which were overseen by Grune and the funds' trustees—thus ensuring that the RDA, though public, also stayed forever private. The RDA's highly paid legal advisers had finally found the loophole they had been searching for.

At a meeting of senior managers in the fall of 1990, following the successful stock offering, Grune delivered an optimistic "State of the Business" address, noting that RDA stock had not been severely affected by the recessionary climate. The RDA global organization now comprised a network of sixteen companies in more than fifty cities worldwide. Among the international editions, the United Kingdom *RD*—with a circulation of 1,600,000—was by far the largest outside the United States. It was followed by the English-language Canadian edition (1,306,000), German and Austrian (1,250,000), French (1,035,-000), Italian (750,000), Mexican (670,000), and Australian (450,000).

Meanwhile, Condensed Books had marginally increased its sales to 21 million copies, for revenues of $311 million worldwide. In fiscal 1990, music generated revenues of $240 million on 5 million cassettes sold worldwide, while the sale of home videos was approaching the 800,000 mark. To promote its products, the RDA was offering an industry-leading $10.25 million in sweepstakes prize money annual, with a grand prize of $5 million.

By now Gordon Grossman's gimmick had proved so popular that direct-mail sweepstakes were enjoying something of a golden age, with more than three thousand imitators nationally and untold thousands more locally, even though the average return was now less than 5 percent. The RDA, on the other hand, had succeeded in increasing its rate of return from 57 percent in 1987 to an astounding 70 percent in 1989. Since nearly every American household with a known address received the offer, the odds of winning the grand prize were a minute 1 in 197,100,000. Even so, the RDA had given away almost $57 million, to more than 1.7 million Americans, since originating the sweepstakes in 1962.

Grune's optimistic message notwithstanding, profits continued to decline 7.5 percent despite a 9.5 percent jump in revenues. Advertising revenues remained flat. As previously, analysts worried that the company faced a very serious, basic, and disturbing problem—that the Reader's Digest Association, for all Grune's energetic and optimistic international search to find new markets at home and abroad, had reached its full growth potential.

In the fall of 1991, after another series of executive shuffles and departures, the RDA got a new president and chief operating officer in the person of James P. Schadt, who had previously held similar positions at London-based Cadbury-Schweppes, one of the world's largest beverage and confectionery manufacturers. Schadt's résumé also included stints at Pepsico and Procter & Gamble. By now any resemblance between the aggressive global marketing of the RDA editorial product and the service-oriented vocation of publishing that DeWitt Wallace had sought to bequeath to his successors was purely coincidental.

———

ONE DAY in July 1990 Ken Gilmore summoned his editorial staff to make an announcement. As they stood jammed in the corridors, he informed them he was suffering from Parkinson's disease and that executive editor Ken Tomlinson was assuming the title of deputy editor in chief. "I cannot carry as full a workload as the editor in chief role requires," Gilmore admitted, but he did not specify whether he was thinking of retiring or when.

At the end of the year, though, to no one's surprise, Gilmore did finally retire, and his place was taken by Tomlinson. Editorially, the new year was marked by the blessed uneventfulness that Grune and Rockefeller wanted for the magazine, after decades of raucous internal upheaval and controversy, though its strong right-wing bias was still evident in article after article. Under Gilmore the *Digest* had been given a three-piece suit to wear and told to act more respectably. For the first time in its history, the world's most widely read magazine had succeeded in becoming merely innocuous. It made no difference who succeeded Gilmore. The editorship had become an interchangeable part of the corporate machinery.

Demographically speaking, more than one-third of the *Digest*'s readers were now over sixty-five, meaning that a significant portion of its subscriber list overlapped with that of *Modern Maturity*. The most often checked occupation category among readers was "Not Employed" (28.2 percent). The biggest readership bulge was among women over fifty-five.

In March 1992, a month after its seventieth anniversary, the *Digest* attempted to move beyond Middle America by apportioning 4.1 million households on its lists with an aggregate income of $50,000 and up. Those households now received not the regular edition of the magazine but the editorially identical *Reader's Digest* Power Plus edition, whose advertising pages sold at a boutique rate of $95,000 per page, compared with $131,000 for the flagship edition. This latest blue-chip *Digest* could boast more than twice the affluent readership of *Time* and marked yet another attempt by Grune and company to ferret out a lucrative new market to boost flat advertising revenues.

But the idea was not new. Back in 1970 whiz kid Gordon Grossman had thought that one up, too, calling his million-circulation high-class *Digest* Demo 1. When advertisers failed to take the bait, he closed it down a year later.

———

SHORTLY before George Grune delivered his "State of the Business" address, Ben Cheever, a dyspeptic ex-Digester and son of novelist John Cheever, had decided to give one of his own. The forum he chose, appropriately enough, was the *Digest*'s oldest antagonist, the *Nation*. There were "bad days in Pleasantville," claimed Cheever, who had once worked as a book editor for the *Digest*. Moreover, he was then wrapping up his first novel, a roman à clef about a certain magazine called the *American Reader*. Cheever's prime proof that things were bad was that employees no longer received a Thanksgiving turkey.

A friend of Canning, Dole, and O'Keefe, whose suit against the company was still pending, Cheever admitted that the RDA's brand of nineteenth-century paternalism could not continue indefinitely. What makes the loss of the turkeys so interesting, he wrote, is that "it comes at a time when the top executives of this same company are being treated with the sort of generosity that might have made Andrew Carnegie blush. And Carnegie sold steel. A big part of what these people market is an idea of right and wrong."

Cheever then waxed nostalgic for the benefit of the *Nation*'s left-wing readership on how delightful and civil a man Wally had been, even though some of his views were reactionary, and how generous he and Lila had been as philanthropists, and also how the *Digest* had once been not just a place to work but "something to believe in."

Cheever further conceded that what was going on in Pleasantville in the way of cutbacks was "harmless when compared with big corporate shuffles like the one at RJR Nabisco. But the *Digest* is a publishing company. People read the magazine. These people vote. They raise families. . . . Now the men at the top are businessmen, who see the magazine as just another product."

Two weeks later, though, the *Nation*'s own acerbic media critic, Alexander Cockburn, laid into Cheever in a column called "Hello History, Get Me Rewrite." Railing against what he perceived as a tendency in the media "to rehab freestanding swine as 'populists,' rough-hewn but kindly," Cockburn would only admit that Cheever had justly painted the present regime in Pleasantville in appropriately harsh terms—as "a bunch of unfeeling money-grubbers, too concerned with lining their own pockets even to give out free turkeys to their own employees."

But he refused to go along with Cheever's sappy revisionist portrayal of Wally as "a generous, 'tolerant' old boy." Asked Cockburn, "Is this what 'the end of the cold war' means? That we have to call DeWitt Wallace tolerant? . . . Like most people who give out occasional free turkeys, Wallace was an autocrat entirely intolerant of dissent." Though Cheever "whistles up the old standard about a great man who 'believed in the American dream,' " Cockburn remembered that Wally's dream was "nicely represented by his heroes, Richard Nixon and J. Edgar Hoover, and his nightmare was the prospect of Martin Luther King's march on Washington in 1963."

Amid all the upheaval and change, though, some things in Pleasant-ville did remain the same. Not long after the RDA became a public company, two employees decided to have some fun, following the lead of the *Digest*'s founder, and have sex on one of the regal conference tables that Grune had opened to public view as a democratic gesture. Unfortunately for them, security guards were watching on hidden cameras and the two were fired.

30

The *Digest*
Condensed

ONE DAY, soon after he arrived in Paris to help establish the international editions of the Reader's Digest Association in postwar Europe, Paul Thompson asked Paul Palmer what he thought the future of the company was—in whose hands Wally, already approaching sixty, intended to entrust the RDA? Palmer replied, "In my opinion, DeWitt Wallace couldn't care less what happens to the *Digest* after he's gone."

Thompson himself later came to agree that the perpetuation of the *Digest,* along guidelines Wally had established, was never one of his highest priorities.

But the Wally both men were working side by side with back in the midforties was the pragmatic editor who lived in a world rich with deadlines, assignments, great events, the rush to make the *Digest* a household name around the world. He was also a man passionately immersed in his own private, very male Disneyland populated with such attractions as poker parties, beautiful women, perfect martinis, Ping-Pong, blue humor, old cars, monoplanes, and travel.

By the midsixties, however, another Wally had begun to emerge—a man who was also better than his former self, better than the obdurate reactionary that was his editorial persona, a man evincing a genuine streak of nobility and largeness of spirit.

From the very beginning, of course, the two great driving forces of DeWitt Wallace's existence were to have fun and help mankind. In an odd way those two converged; the perennial schoolboy and the unorthodox servant of mankind were the Janus-faced profiles of the same individual. The *Digest* was the convenient instrument for both passions—for Lila as well as Wally—in equal and extraordinary mea-

618

sure. But neither was a fool. Both knew that, like every other institution founded by man or God, the *Digest* would change after they were gone, just as it began to change while they were still alive.

From a *Digest*-like, commonsensical point of view, the logical solution to the problem of the company's future was simply to bequeath the RDA to Lila's beloved niece Judy and her husband, Fred Thompson, protégé of Al Cole and a man almost universally admired in the far-flung kingdom of Pleasantville. Fred Thompson was not only a brilliant businessman but something of a saint—one of those rare specimens of corporate America, a man without enemies. The Wallaces were also fond of the Thompsons' two sons, whose education they paid for, so in the even longer term a family dynasty seemed guaranteed. Furthermore, if Wally wanted an assurance that the company would not be sold after his death, Fred Thompson would have kept his word as nothing less than a sacred trust. Wally knew that.

But then, as happens from time to time, in *Digest* tearjerkers and in real life alike, tragedy struck. Sometime in 1965 Wally's penchant for fun—his Achilles' heel—became the occasion for, if not his downfall, then the unequivocal and nonnegotiable rejection of that arrangement by Lila, the aggrieved wife.

To atone for his infidelity—the one infidelity above all others that Lila would not tolerate—Wally gave her the power to decide the fate of the company. Though she had no alternative to propose, she banished the heir apparent and his wife from the kingdom. The fatalistic culmination of events, the cataclysmic denouement, had an almost Shakespearean cast, and for a long while thereafter Wally endured a Lear-like existence in his gilded wilderness. He became estranged from his oldest and staunchest business ally, Al Cole, and later from the two men he treated almost like his son and godson—Hobe Lewis and Harry Morgan, respectively. James Wood, Wally's closest friend at the time, thought Wally always seemed inexplicably lonely.

Lila, too, discovered that she had been betrayed by the two men outside her marriage whose company, over the long term, she most enjoyed and on whom she most depended—Harry Wilcox and Bill Kennedy. The man who served her best, despite his opportunistic altruism and their intermittent estrangement, was Harry Morgan.

In 1972, when DeWitt Wallace was already eighty-three, his banker Harold Helm finally presumed to ask about the future of the RDA, and Wally still had no permanent solution to his plight. All he knew was that he wanted to keep the company private—to keep it within the larger Pleasantville family if not his own smaller one. Presumably, the RDA had already been left to charity, with Barnabas McHenry as sole executor. What Wally most feared was a corporate machinery that would exist merely to churn out profit. By giving the company away, he made sure that no matter how profit-oriented the RDA became, those profits would always be ultimately in the service of mankind.

When Helm and Rockefeller were named the first two outside trustees, their word, and not Fred Thompson's, became the promise Wally had been looking for that the RDA would always remain in private hands. But when Al Cole later asked to peruse the will and discover its specific provisions, McHenry refused. Though Cole eventually did succeed in getting Ed Thompson and Jack O'Hara appointed coexecutors, the company's longtime business manager was never permitted to see the numerous and complicated codicils to the will of Lila Acheson Wallace, who had inherited her husband's share of the company and whose will determined the final disposition of the RDA.

Ultimately, Cole and others came to suspect, with good reason, that the hidden hand of Laurance S. Rockefeller had successfully executed a game of philanthropic three-card monte, while Lila was in her dotage, and installed some of his own favorite charities among the Wallaces' stepchildren. But it remains true that, out of defeat and tragedy, DeWitt Wallace had fashioned not only triumph but redemption.

On the other hand, outwardly at any rate, Wally seems to have been considerably less concerned about the continuation of his editorial legacy along immutable lines, and that is perhaps what Paul Palmer guessed and Paul Thompson ultimately concluded. Both men were wrong, however. Sooner or later, Wally came to realize that, though the editorial formula of the *Digest* had always evolved organically, its essence had finally crystallized to a point where it could never be changed without being destroyed.

In other words, by the time DeWitt Wallace withdrew from active participation in the company, the *Digest* had become a unique mass-market magazine in which the interchangeability of editors was a strength, not a weakness. It was a formula magazine that almost any team of editors picked at random could duplicate. That was not always true, but Wally ultimately succeeded in making it so. Just as he himself was more complex than the often simplistic publication he edited, so the essential editorial formula of the *Digest* was and remains, in its very simplicity, impervious to the creative tinkerings of its individual editors.

Perhaps also, in some dim and intuitive way, Cole suspected that by injecting true investigative reporting, complexity, and diversity of opinion into the magazine, Ed Thompson was threatening that essence, that in the long run—regardless of how little or how much art-of-living material the magazine was running—the *Digest* was in danger of becoming something beyond the reach of Everyman.

Today, with its mass-market sensibility firmly restored, the Reader's Digest Association depends for its very existence on a form of legalized gambling called the sweepstakes. This is the new cornerstone and bedrock of the RDA empire, and without it the *Digest* and all of its affiliates would be nothing. The sweepstakes has replaced the intrinsic editorial worth of the magazine as the source of the *Digest*'s primary appeal to subscribers. Like television, the medium it most closely resembles, the *RD* and its related marketing operations not only cater to but are governed by the mass market that is both its audience and its tyrant.

Though the *Digest* must publish pabulum or perish, and though it will continue to be scorned as inconsequential or worse by media watchers and scholars, it remains a more potent political and cultural force within the electorate, not only in Middle America but in almost every democratic country where it now publishes, than any other publication in the world.

WHAT else, then, remains to be said that might aspire to enduring significance and lasting interest? Perhaps only this: that, despite its length, this has been a portrait painted in the broadest strokes. A dozen chapters, the lives of hundreds of Digesters, a thousand anecdotes remain untold.

Most of all, though, its author is aware that the central figure in this group portrait still sits in his big wing chair, half hidden in the shadows, smiling enigmatically, glimpsed but not fully fathomed. In death, as in life, DeWitt Wallace has remained the most uncelebrated of prominent people, the most famous unknown man of his time. Despite the vast presence of his magazine around the world, Wallace himself, like the *Digest,* continues to be almost unanimously excluded from the collective memory of cultural historians, biographers, memoirists, pundits, chroniclers of the rich and famous, media columnists; condensed into near-total oblivion as much through his passionate quest for privacy as through a conventional wisdom that has limited the club of publishing giants to William Randolph Hearst, Henry R. Luce, and other self-promoting legends in their own time. Wally would have enjoyed, even relished, his posthumous lack of renown, but one small exception to the rule would have pleased him greatly, and for that he owed thanks primarily to Barnabas McHenry.

In April 1983 the periodicals room of the New York Public Library was rechristened the DeWitt Wallace Periodicals Room and re-opened to the public following a lavish $20 million restoration. It was there that the *Reader's Digest* had begun in earnest—in the ornately paneled beaux-arts room with its huge arched windows and marble doorways, its crowds of students, noontime browsers, the homeless seeking a few hours of inspiration, entertainment, or respite just as they had sixty-one years earlier when the staff occasionally mistook the diligent borrower of magazines as one of the room's eccentrics.

Today, as the Reader's Digest Association approaches its seventy-fifth anniversary, in 1997, it has evolved into a global company generating more than two billion dollars in annual revenues. It can and ought to be, and obviously is, doing whatever it feels necessary to ensure its own survival and growth. But as it marches into the twenty-first century, it also marches into the anonymity of a high-profile communications giant even as it recedes from the unsung individualism, genius, idealism, and breathtaking liberality of its founders.

Acknowledgments

AN AUTHOR'S ACKNOWLEDGMENTS page is the ultimate act of editorial condensation, and also his or her greatest challenge: how to boil down into a few, embarrassingly inadequate words the sincere gratitude he or she feels for the countless number of large and small favors, the hand-holding and encouragement, the tireless readings, the stern criticism, the helpful advice, and all the other things that very early on disabuse any author of the notion that this is "his" or "her" book. Though the imperfections and shortcomings of *TWTK* are obviously my responsibility, I gladly not only acknowledge but celebrate the fact that whatever virtues it possesses are the work of many hands.

Above all, this book would not have been possible without the inspired vision and steady guidance of my brilliant editor and good friend Mary Cunnane, who first proposed the idea to me in the spring of 1989. At every stage, from inception to final revision, she has played an indispensable role. Her uncompromisingly high standards have served as a beacon, tonic, lash, impossible dream, and a few other mixed metaphors as well. Similarly, my agent Thomas C. Wallace has supplied me at various critical junctures with much needed encouragement, perceptive criticism, and enthusiasm, and I am in his debt far more than he knows.

At a level too deep for words, I could not even have begun to write this book without the love and support of my wife, Pat. The day will come, "dear bride," when we, too, will sit "in the cool of the even in front of a café in Heaven." My four children—Mary, John, James, and Margaret—have also variously applied artificial inspiration to Dad when his muse temporarily disappeared behind a cloud. Last and no doubt least, but still treasured companions during the long hours, months, and years of writing, were our cats Pierre, who now sleeps beneath an azalea, and Sonya.

Also my deepest thanks to the following, each of whom has been not only of invaluable help but a pleasure to rely on: Elizabeth Lockwood, Lisa Miller, and John E. Taylor of the National Archives; Marvin Pelacz of the Department of Labor Statistics; Jack Grossman and Eugenia Radunsky for their help in translating from the Russian; Angus MacKenzie of the FOIA Project for his assistance with Freedom of Information Act procedures and transcripts; Frank Chmidling, an affable Kansan who has lent me assorted issues of the *Reader's Digest* from his complete collection; Paul Chang for his extraordinary help with WordPerfect, modems, and other post-typewriter mysteries, including the loan of his own printer when mine had a nervous breakdown; the Reverend John Sheppard, minister of the Presbyterian Church of Pleasantville; Brian Thomas for his instructive reading of the material on the Central Intelligence Agency; Daniel Brandt for his invaluable Namebase, and for other research help; Ralph McGehee of CIAbase; Robert M. Gavin, Jr., president of Macalester College; Harry M. Drake, former archivist of the Macalester College Library, and his successor, Eunice Weisensel, for their hospitality and unstinting cooperation; W. Barnabas McHenry, executor the estates of DeWitt and Lila Acheson Wallace, for permission to reprint from their correspondence and journals; Dave Emory of Archives on Radio; Eve Pell of the Center for Investigative Reporting; Laurence Moore of Ramparts Press; Steve Rendall and Jeff Cohen of Fairness and Accuracy in Reporting; CIA media expert Fred Landis; Pleasantville historians Carsten Johnson and James Lyall; Harriet Rabb of the Columbia University School of Law; Jack Tanzer, formerly of the Knoedler Gallery; free-lance writer and art specialist Bill Sherman; Professor Ronald Grele of the Columbia University Department of Journalism; Mark Weitzman of the Simon Wiesenthal Center; Jerry Baumgarten of the Anti-Defamation League; Richard Olson of the World Council of Churches; Dr. Lewis Weeks of the Louisville Presbyterian Theological Seminary; Larry B. Dendy of the University of Georgia; Frank Schworer for his dispatches from Frankfurt and the annual *Maifest;* Gray Williams, Doris Konig, Jack Mulligan, John Bainbridge, John Davis, Joseph H. Cooper, Ralph Ginzburg, Al Silverman, Richard Philp, Anne Perkins, John Carmichael, Naomi Schneider, Marie Berzins; and the wonderful librarians and clerical staff—unsung heroes all—at the New York Public Library main branch, newspaper annex on West Forty-third Street, and my own local branch in Jackson Heights, Queens.

I am also indebted to Otto Sonntag for a ruthless, instructive, and altogether splendid job of copyediting; Caroline Crawford for innumerable favors; Ruth Mandel for her heroic assistance in obtaining photographs for reproduction in this book; and Linda Puckette for heroically transcribing one too many interviews.

To my friends and fellow writers Susan Bakos and Mark Lasswell, a special thanks for the encouraging words, noon-hour solidarity and all-around sympathy and support; to Irv Muchnick, cheering from the bleachers in Berkeley; and to Harlan Ellison, for that "advance" of $50 that he has probably forgotten all about, but I have not.

Notes

A NUMBER of people whom I interviewed in the course of researching this book simply felt too vulnerable, for professional reasons, to be listed by name. Yet they took the risk of talking to me because they wanted the true story of the *Reader's Digest* to be told. I thank them for their trust in me and for their courage. Especially among the old guard of Pleasantville and surrounding counties, the cult of DeWitt Wallace remains strong, and a significant number of former Digesters—even those dismissed by the company—refused point-blank to see me. Not a few other interviews turned out to be pointless encounters, perhaps occasioned by mere curiosity about the interloper. The Reader's Digest Association itself provided only limited cooperation. My requests for interviews with current or former top executives and high-ranking editors, with the exception of Chairman George V. Grune, were denied.

Yet many other Digesters, some of whose careers dated to the magazine's very earliest days, were extraordinarily forthcoming. Some of those interviews lasted for many hours and over two or three days, and remain among my most pleasant memories of the time spent researching this book. In particular I wish to express my deepest thanks to John Allen, Genevieve Beck, Joseph Blank, Norma Canfield, Peggy Winston Cole, H. Barclay ("Buck") Cornell, Ric Cox, William J. Cross, Gordon Davies, Marshall Davis, Urith Dillon, Willard Espy, David Otis Fuller, Gordon Grossman, Gordon Hard, April Herbert, Roy Herbert, Wilhelmina Neil, Walter J. Hunt, Bernice Hunter, Betty Johnson, Chris Kirby, Mary Kirby, Virginia Lawton, Bruce Lee, Ruth Lee, Edie Lewis, Hobart Durkin Lewis, Dorothy Little, Doris Lund, Teresa ("Mickey") Lynch, Connie McGowan, William Barnabas

McHenry, Ida de Mary, Jim Miller, Harry Morgan, Gertrude Murphy, John A. O'Hara, Bob Parker, Anthony Paul, Noel Rae, Kent Rhodes, Ralph Rink, Beth Day Romulo, Marjorie Grant Scribner, Dorrie Schreiner, Samuel A. Schreiner, Jr., Jim Shuman, Susan Smith, Roland Strand, Edward T. Thompson, Nancy Cale Thompson, Paul W. Thompson, Susie Jacobson Thompson, Richard Waters, Kenneth Wilson, John Wulp, John S. Zinsser, Jr., and Jeanne Zipp.

The collective memory of these named and unnamed Digesters forms the warp and woof of this book. Though meager in quantity and not always reliable, the published literature on the *Digest* also proved occasionally useful: in particular, *James Wallace of Macalester,* by James Kagin (Garden City, N.Y.: Doubleday, 1957); *Wallace-Bruce and Closely Related Families,* written and compiled by James Wallace (Northfield, Minn.: Mohn, 1930); *Little Wonder; or, The Reader's Digest and How It Grew,* by John Bainbridge (New York: Reynal & Hitchcock, 1945); *Of Lasting Interest: The Story of the Reader's Digest,* by James Playsted Wood (Garden City, N.Y.: Doubleday, 1958; rev. ed. 1967); *The Condensed World of the Reader's Digest,* by Samuel A. Schreiner, Jr. (New York: Stein and Day, 1977); and *The Solid Gold Mailbox,* by Walter H. Weintz (New York: John Wiley, 1987). James Playsted Wood also completed a biography of DeWitt Wallace that was never published. A copy of his manuscript and his numerous collateral notes reside in the Macalester College Library. Similarly, I have enjoyed exclusive access to the unpublished biography and collateral notes of DeWitt Wallace written by his friend and former *Digest* senior editor Charles W. Ferguson. *The Magazine in America, 1741–1990,* by John Tebbel and Mary Ellen Zuckerman (New York: Oxford University Press, 1991), has also been a valuable resource.

The numerals in the left-hand column below refer to page numbers in the book. Abbreviations used in the notes are as follows:

BW	=	*Business Week*
CJR	=	*Columbia Journalism Review*
GWN	=	*Gannett Westchester Newspapers*
NYT	=	*New York Times*
RD	=	*Reader's Digest*
TNY	=	*The New Yorker*
TNR	=	*The New Republic*
WSJ	=	*Wall Street Journal*
WP	=	*Washington Post*

Chapter 1: A Man of Few Words

Books: Dr. Frank Crane, *Four Minute Essays* (New York: Wm. H. Wise, n.d.); Jan Cohn, *Creating America: George Horace Lorimer and the Saturday Evening Post* (Pittsburgh: University of Pittsburgh Press, 1989); Joseph C. Furnas, *Great Times: An Informal Social History of the United States, 1914–1929* (New York: Putnam, 1974); William E. Lass, *Minnesota: A History* (New York: W. W. Norton, 1983); 1988 and 1991 *Mission Yearbook* (New York: Presbyterian Church [U.S.A.]); Martin E. Marty, *Pilgrims in Their Own Land: 500 Years of Religion in America* (Boston: Little, Brown, 1984); Samuel Eliot Morison and Henry Steele Commager, *The Growth of the American Republic*, 2 vols. (New York: Oxford University Press, 1962); John Tebbel, *The American Magazine: A Compact History* (New York: Hawthorn, n.d.); George Brown Tindall, *America: A Narrative History* (New York: W. W. Norton, 1988); Francis L. Wellman, *The Art of Cross-Examination* (New York: Macmillan, 1903; Collier Books ed., 1962). **Articles:** "The Reader's Digest," *Fortune,* Nov. 1936; "The Common Touch," *Time,* Dec. 10, 1951; "Those Good Old Days Were Simple Old Days," *Town Life Patent Trader,* March 2, 1983; "Reader's Digest Man," *Minneapolis Sunday Tribune,* March 24 and 31, 1946; Charles Ferguson, "Unforgettable DeWitt Wallace," *RD,* Feb. 1987; Michael Massing, "The Reader's Digest: How an Article of Enduring Significance Is Condensed in Permanent Booklet Form," *Media Peopel [sic],* Jan. 1979. **Correspondence:** Barclay Acheson, Lila Bell Acheson, Conrad Davis, Albert H. Harmon, Horace C. Klein, Edith C. Miller, Fidelia Auten Pine, DeWitt Wallace, Hattie Wallace, Dr. James Wallace, Janet Davis Wallace, John Wallace, R. B. Wallace. **Booklets:** *RD,* sample issue of Jan. 1920 (St. Paul, Minn., 1920); *Getting the Most Out of Farming: A Selected List of Publications, of Value to the Farmer and Farmer's Wife, Available for Free Distribution by the Government and State Experiment Stations,* prepared by DeWitt Wallace (St. Paul, Minn.: Webb, 1917). **Interviews:** Beck, Cornell, Dillon, Hunter, Ruth Lee, Lynch, de Mary, Neil, Scribner. **Other:** Notes and journals of DeWitt Wallace; academic records of DeWitt Wallace, Macalester College; *A Brief History of the Presbyterian Church, Pleasantville, N.Y., 1880–1967* (self-published pamphlet, n.d.); Manitoba Family Services, Office of Vital Statistics; Dakota Government Center, West Hastings, Minn.; Hennepin County Government Center, Minneapolis; County of Allegheny, Pittsburgh; Records and Archives Center, Westchester County; New York City marriage license records, New York Public Library, main branch; New York State Department of Health, Office of Vital Records, Empire State Plaza, Albany.

28. *Ever the enthusiast:* Letter of C. Greenway, General Superintendent, Oliver Iron Mining Company, to DeWitt Wallace, March 17, 1909.
34. *In a book-length family history: Wallace-Bruce and Related Families,* p. 140.
35. *In February:* Letter from Mary D. Baker, Secretary-Treasurer, Baker Land and Title Co., to DeWitt Wallace, Feb. 15, 1915.
39. *A few days later:* "Luck with Him: DeWitt Wallace, Former Macalester Athlete, Tells of Narrow Escapes in the Trenches," *St. Paul Pioneer Press,* Feb. 9, 1919.

39. *The adjutant general:* Letter from P. C. Harriss to James Wallace, Feb. 12, 1919.

40. *At first he was:* John M. Liddall, editor of the *American Magazine,* wrote DeWitt on Aug. 5, 1919, saying, "It will be possible to give you permission [to use articles]," but cautioning, "It will be necessary for you to write me and obtain permission for everything you condense and reprint as occasionally we do not possess more than the first serial rights."

42. *Shorter articles:* Complicated articles like those on the collapse of the American railways, as Charles A. and Mary R. Beard noted in *America at Midpassage* (New York: Macmillan, 1939), pp. 740–41, "could be summarized and disposed of presumably in a few 'crystal clear' paragraphs for readers who had but ten minutes to spare." *Time* magazine tried to introduce analysis in order to differentiate it from the *New York Times* and most other papers. The *New Yorker* prospectus also claimed that it would be interpretative rather than stenographic. Of the three the *RD* was the most successful in establishing an upbeat, easy-to-read style completely dissimilar from what had gone before. See James L. Baughman, *Henry R. Luce and the Rise of the American News Media* (Boston: Twayne, 1987), pp. 28–29.

43. *After being rebuffed:* A persistent but never verified rumor in the *Digest*'s early days was that DeWitt traveled by motorcycle to Hearst's castle in San Simeon, California, to intercede personally with the publisher and that he was again rebuffed.

46. *Eventually, he and Lila:* Apparently, DeWitt moved into the apartment while Lila remained for the time being in Pleasantville. Buck Cornell (see p. 58) remembered as a teenager eavesdropping on the two when Wally came to visit.

47. *In 1921 Greenwich Village:* Susan Edmiston and Linda D. Cirino, *Literary New York: A History and Guide* (Boston: Houghton Mifflin, 1976), chap. 2.

48. *On October 15, 1921:* The marriage certificate issued by the Presbyterian church in Pleasantville—an unofficial document lacking a church seal and serving mainly as a memento of the occasion—lists Barclay Acheson as officiating minister, with the Reverend Lester H. Bent, the pastor of the Presbyterian church, also in attendance. In all, twenty-three guests were present. Wally's nephew and, later, private secretary Gordon Davies, the son of Wally's older sister Helen, seems to remember they were married in New York previously, in which case the Pleasantville ceremony may have been merely for show. However, no record of a civil wedding in New York between 1919 and 1929 can be found.

50. *In the article:* So passionately did Wally believe in Wiggam's hokum that he reprinted "Can We Have a Beautiful Race?" in Sept. 1926.

Chapter 2: The Presbyters of Pleasantville

Books: James Thurber, *The Years with Ross* (New York: Grosset & Dunlap, 1957); James Playsted Wood, *Magazines in the United States,* 3d ed. (New York: Ronald Press, 1971). **Articles:** "Picking World's Best Writing and Making It Pay," *Newsweek,* June 6, 1936; "The Reader's Digest," *Fortune,* Nov. 1936. **Correspondence:** Albert L. Cole, Louise Edgar, J. C. Furnas, Albert L. Furth, Arthur E. Griffiths, Ralph Henderson, J. Fred Henry, Eric Hodgins, Harold Lynch, DeWitt Wallace, Dr. James Wallace, Lila Acheson Wallace. **Interviews:** Beck, Cornell, Dillon, Ruth Lee, Lynch, de Mary, Neil, Romulo, Scribner. **Other:** Notes and memorandums of DeWitt Wallace; draft of *Fortune* article by Albert L. Furth with editings by DeWitt Wallace.

67. *Wally was not content:* "For years the *Reader's Digest* ran first in the 'hate parade' of physicians in this country because of the publication's propensity to ballyhoo a new treatment or procedure before the medical profession at large was even aware of it or before the 'discovery' had been properly evaluated. Paul de Kruif, the famous and talented science writer, was a frequent author of such articles." Dr. Louis Lasagna, *The Doctors' Dilemmas* (New York: Harper & Brothers, 1962), pp. 206–7).

67. *The agent reported:* Letter of Jan. 11, 1928 [or possibly 1927 or 1929].

71. *But on the whole:* Most Digesters, particularly in the early years, were of the erroneous belief that in his correspondence and conversation the scholarly Dr. Wallace was routinely critical of his famous son's middle-brow magazine. Though that was not the case, the elder Wallace did devote nearly three fulsome pages of his history of the Wallace-Bruce families to firstborn son and Rhodes scholar Benjamin Wallace, and condensed DeWitt's entry to half a page. Even in such a brief space, Dr. Wallace managed to get three facts wrong, claiming that DeWitt conceived of the magazine while "in France," that it began publication in 1921, and that its name was the *Readers' Digest.*

72. *A publisher's representative:* Letter of April 1, 1929.

84. *His inattention:* A dozen years later, on Dec. 23, 1948, DeWitt and Lila were driving along a slippery road in Westchester and collided with another car. Though DeWitt was unhurt, Lila was injured and taken to a local hospital, where a spokesman refused to reveal the extent of her injuries. Details were also hushed up in Pleasantville, and Lila probably spent her birthday, Christmas Day, in bed. See *NYT,* Dec. 24, 1948.

87. *Controversy, sensationalism:* In Feb. 1936 the RD announced that it was awarding five $1,000 prizes for the best nonfiction articles by authors unpublished in a national magazine. More than 18,000 entries poured in. Not waiting until the contest was over, an exuberant Wally in June published "Modern Miracle," by New York free-lance writer Polly White, a story about a young woman with a "port wine" birthmark on her face who ran a lucrative business marketing a face plaster she had invented to hide the disfigurement. White had discovered the Einsteinian secret of the perfect *Digest* story: success $=$ tragedy^2.

87. *Immediate and tangible proof:* Though a latter-day RDA video characterizes High Winds as being "Tudor," the consensus among impartial observers is that the house's architectural style is Norman.

Chapter 3: Even the Petunias

Correspondence: Barclay Acheson, Charles Ferguson, Charles May, Rose May, Kenneth W. Payne, Theodore Roosevelt, Benjamin Wallace, DeWitt Wallace, Hattie Wallace, Lila Acheson Wallace, Robert Wallace. **Interviews:** Beck, Dillon, Bruce

Lee, Ruth Lee, Lund, Lynch, Neil, Romulo, Dorrie Schreiner, Samuel A. Schreiner, Scribner, Wilson. **Other:** Undated and unsigned memorandums documenting High Winds costs to June 30, 1936, March 15, 1937, and June 30, 1938; notes, telegrams, memorandums, and airman's certificate of DeWitt Wallace; travel itinerary for Mr. and Mrs. DeWitt Wallace prepared by the American Express Travel Department, Jan. 28, 1931; Sleepy Hollow Country Club scorecard, Sept. 4, 1934; *RD* attendance records; list of DeWitt Wallace's charitable donations for 1936.

93. *Among his other visitors:* Justin Kaplan, *Lincoln Steffens* (New York: Simon & Schuster, 1974), p. 325.

100. *Neighbors soon began:* DeWitt and Lila apparently still owed money to architect Charles May, who died before the house was completed. May's widow, Rose, wrote Wally on Dec. 10, 1937, in some perplexity, saying she had read in the local Pleasantville paper that the house had cost hundreds of thousands of dollars, yet her husband's books showed a deficit. Rose May then consulted her lawyer, who was unable to straighten out the matter. "In the meantime," she went on to say, "people had been remarking to me that Charles must have made a wonderful settlement on us because he had built such a costly house for you." After talking first to Harry Wilcox and then to treasurer Roy Abbott, and getting nowhere, Mrs. May wrote directly to Wally—and not to Lila, who had overseen construction of the house. Presumably, the account was settled to the satisfaction of both parties.

100. *The* Digest*'s fun-loving editor:* In a bill of sale dated Sept. 20, 1938, the Fairchild Aircraft Corporation of Hagerstown, Maryland, sold to the Reader's Digest Association for "$1.00 and other things of value" its 24K model, popularly known as the Argus.

100. *But he had lent:* Wally once told Urith Dillon, "The worst mistake I ever made was to take five thousand dollars from Barclay."

101. *Apart from paying the pensions:* Two of the professors were A. W. Anderson and D. Kingery, both of the Department of Philosophy (letter from Anderson and Kingery to DeWitt Wallace, Feb. 24, 1937).

Chapter 4: The Editing Factory

Books: John Patrick Diggins, *The Proud Decades: America in War and Peace, 1941–1960* (New York: W. W. Norton, 1988); Arnold Forster and Benjamin R. Epstein, *Danger on the Right* (New York: Random House, 1964); John Gunther, *Inside U.S.A.* (New York: Harper and Brothers, 1947); Eugene Lyons, *Our Secret Allies: The Peoples of Russia* (New York: Duell, Sloan and Pearce, 1954); William L. White, *Report on the Germans* (New York: Harcourt, Brace, 1947). **Articles:** "Dashiell Speaks to Librarians," *Pleasantville Journal,* n.d. [1938]; "World's Largest," *BW,* Jan. 4, 1941; Charles W. Ferguson, "Give the Public What It Wants," *Publishers Weekly,* Jan. 3, 1937; idem, "Educating the Emotions," *Bulletin of the American Library Association,* Aug. 1937; James Howard Lewis, "The Reader's Digest—Publishing Phenomenon," *Magazine World,* Dec. 1944; "Digest's Growing Pains," *Newsweek,* Oct. 19, 1942; "Digest in the Doghouse," *Newsweek,* Feb. 21, 1944; "Press Notes," *Newsweek,* March 13, 1944;

"The Cole Story (Condensed): Nineteen Million People Are Only a Beginning," *Printers' Ink,* Nov. 29, 1957. **Correspondence:** Barclay Acheson, Jack Beaudouin, Albert L. Cole, A. J. Cronin, Robert Disraeli, John W. Frost, Corinne Johnson, D. B. Lawrence, Charles A. Lindbergh, Paul Palmer, Maurice T. Ragsdale, Henry Morton Robinson, Marc A. Rose, W. L. Smith, Ida M. Tarbell, DeWitt Wallace, Alexander Woollcott. **Interviews:** Beck, Cole, Dillon, Espy, Edie Lewis, Hard, Roy Herbert, Hobart Durkin Lewis, Lynch, Romulo, Samuel A. Schreiner, Scribner, Wilson. **Other:** Notes, telegrams, and memorandums of Albert L. Cole, Ralph Henderson, Kenneth W. Payne, DeWitt Wallace, Lila Acheson Wallace, Paul Palmer; *RD* attendance records; reading-preference poll conducted by the Union Pacific System (n.d.); "Remarks in Memory of Paul Palmer," delivered on July 12, 1983 by Michael Palmer; "Profit-Sharing Bonus Trust" of the Reader's Digest Association, Inc. with DeWitt Wallace, Lila Bell Wallace and Roy Campbell Abbott as trustees, April 2, 1945.

108. *As a measure of his esteem:* Cole later arranged for the sale of *Popular Science* to the Times-Mirror Corporation for $18 million; his share of the profits was $1.5 million.

114. *As the* Digest *continued to evolve:* Wally was also fascinated by unusual methods of collecting bad debts while keeping a customer's credit rating and goodwill intact. The challenge was to collect a debt without losing a friend. He decided that women made better bill collectors than men. Thus the initials of the collection department evolved into "Carolyn Davis," whose wholesome good looks and warm smile grew familiar to millions of slow-paying readers. Every decade Carolyn received an art-department makeover to keep up with changing fashions and hairstyles.

116. *Lindbergh was also:* Harold Nicolson, *Diaries and Letters* (London: Collins, 1980), pp. 102, 126.

118. *One of the most famous:* Richard M. Ketchum, *The Borrowed Years, 1938–1941: America on the Way to War* (New York: Random House, 1989), p. 109.

119. *Not long afterward:* In 1943 a columnist for the *Daily Worker* named Sender Garlin wrote a digest-sized booklet titled *The Truth about Reader's Digest,* which sold for ten cents (New York: Forum Publishers). Garlin's thesis was that the *RD*'s glorification of Spain's Franco, its role in popularizing the anti-Semitic notions of Charles and Anne Morrow Lindbergh, and its serialization of Krebs (whom the U.S. Board of Immigration appeals board on Nov. 11, 1942, declared to be "an agent of Nazi Germany") was all very suspicious. By implication, the *Digest* itself, like Krebs, was working for the Gestapo. In fact, though, the real common denominator in all three instances, and in hundreds of others besides, was Wally's resolute anticommunism. Just as he had been among the first twenty-five youths in St. Paul to enlist in the army after America's entry into World War I, so was he among the very first Americans to serve in the trenches of the Cold War. In fact, he helped to dig them.

120. *Ultimately, George Seldes: In Fact,* Nov. 16, 1942.

124. . . . *collected his wives' recipes: The Conspirators' Cookbook* (New York: Knopf, 1967).

125. *Eugene Lyons served:* Lyons had been a disenchanted wire-service correspondent in Moscow. Under his editorship the *Mercury* became professionally anti-Com-

munist. His 1937 *Assignment in Utopia,* a blistering attack on Stalinist Russia, was the first of the "god that failed" genre popular in the early Cold War years. Spivak later sold the *Mercury* to become owner and chief interrogator of "Meet the Press," which he originated.

The *Mercury* "ultimately fell into the hands of an extreme right-wing Texan hate group." The *North American Review* survived until 1936, "when it was bought by an agent of the Japanese government as an American front." Similarly, *Scribner's* ended its distinguished career as a propaganda organ of the German-American Bund. See John Tebbell, *The Media in America* (New York: Crowell, 1974), p. 230.

131. *Author of the piece:* Kiplinger and Wally became friends after the former wrote the RD publisher on Oct. 28, 1936, following the appearance of the *Fortune* article. "I suppose you must be pretty much flooded, annoyed, and embarrassed," Kiplinger declared, adding that it had done nothing to increase his own admiration for Wally, because "it was already plenty big." Kiplinger went on to list the many qualities the two men had in common: no advertising in either of their publications, an aversion to publicity, too many imitators, a passion for brevity, profit sharing with employees, and a partner wife.

131. *Yet war correspondent Ben Hecht:* Haskel Lookstein, *Were We Our Brothers' Keepers? The Public Response of American Jews to the Holocaust, 1938–1944* (Bridgeport, Conn.: Hartmore House, 1985), pp. 113, 192; Ben Hecht, *A Child of the Century* (New York: Donald I. Fine, 1985), p. 550.

134. *The result was:* Max Eastman, *Love and Revolution: My Journey through an Epoch* (New York: Random House, 1964), pp. 637, 641–43.

134. *American socialism had been:* Eastman's relentless attacks on communism in the pages of the *Digest* finally provoked *TNR* treasurer Daniel Mebane to write a letter, on Oct. 27, 1944, in which he bitterly castigated not only the ex-renegade but indirectly the *RD:*

> "The worst thing about Communism," somebody said, "is that it produces ex-Communists." Being a specialist in humor, you will get the joke, but will you see the ominous and tragic side? Communist and socialist renegades are becoming a major menace in this country. Heavily financed by reactionaries controlling all but a fraction of the press, you fellows are no mere soap boxers. You are the principal agents for the anti-democratic forces. Men like yourself, J. B. Matthews, [Eugene] Lyons, . . . by playing Judas, have acquired immense influence for evil. At long last I am beginning to get an insight into the testimony of the Moscow trials. We couldn't believe in such treachery in 1936—nor did we think anything like it could happen to minds trained in America. But now it is tragically apparent that, just as anti-Semitism and fascism in America can assume the same shapes as in Europe, so in the backwash of the social revolution there appear similar renegades, traitors and informers whose services are for sale to the enemy.

136. *Miller later traveled: Time,* Dec. 10, 1951.

137. *In its ongoing campaign:* The one-day cure, proposed in the Sept. 1942 issue, and in

a follow-up article some months later, consisted of an artificially induced fever combined with a mixture of arsenic and bismuth.

In 1945 de Kruif published *The Male Hormone* (New York: Harcourt, Brace), and Wally was given top billing in the acknowledgments for having made the book possible. The project grew out of an *RD* article titled "Can Man's Prime Be Prolonged?" De Kruif's solution: twenty or thirty milligrams of methyl testosterone a day by injection—"borrowed manhood," in the author's phrase. Whether Wally himself followed his writer's advice is not known, though a persuasive case that he did could perhaps be made on the basis of the circumstantial evidence.

Chapter 5: More Ribaldry Than Boccaccio

Interviews: Allen, Dillon, Espy, Edie Lewis, Hobart Durkin Lewis, Scribner, Wilson. **Other:** Parody issue of the Jan. 1940 *RD;* notes and memorandums of Ralph Henderson, Dorothy Hinitt, DeWitt Wallace, Ralph Henderson, Edward T. Thompson.

142. . . . *the* Digest*'s humor policy:* The jurist's challenge probably occurred ca. 1944, when *Esquire*'s second-class mailing privileges were revoked; in 1946 the ban was lifted by the U.S. Supreme Court.

142. *As* Time *magazine later observed:* Time, Feb. 2, 1962.

142. . . . *more animal stories:* In vol. 1, no. 1, the *Digest* had run an article entitled "Watch Your Dog and Be Wise!" and one on the wonders of the firefly's abdomen, said to secrete a "peculiar substance" capable of producing light. It was the beginning of the magazine's lifelong love affair with the animal kingdom, second only to its singing the praises of women and sex, and almost no issue went by without some tribute to dogs, cats, parrots, snails, moles, turkeys, alligators, whales, or wolves. Even the rat was in due course honored, in "Rats," by Henry Morton Robinson, which ran with the blurb "Man's enemy is also his teacher."

Chapter 6: As Thirsty Men Turn to a Fountain

Correspondence: Barclay Acheson, Winston Churchill, Albert L. Cole, Henry C. Link, Marvin Lowes, Pierre de Noyer. **Interviews:** Hobart Durkin Lewis, Rhodes, Paul W. Thompson. **Other:** Notes and memorandums of Barclay Acheson, Adrian Berwick, Eduardo Cárdenas, Albert L. Cole, Ralph Henderson, Hobart Durkin Lewis, DeWitt Wallace; unpublished memoir of Paul W. Thompson, "The Story of 216 Boulevard St. Germain (with a note on Rue Scribe)." **Remarks:** Successful FOIA requests to the State Department, Department of the Army, and other government agencies resulted in several thousand pages' worth of documents relating to the *RD* being turned over to the author. Most concerned the *RD*'s overseas activities and were relatively routine in nature.

155. *The editorial director:* See below, p. 473.

156. *The Santiago legation:* Cable of Jan. 24, 1942.

157. *An address based:* Included with a letter dated May 12, 1942, from Al Cole to Philip W. Bonsal of the U.S. State Department.

157. *In return:* "Memorandum with Supporting Documents," prepared under the direction of Al Cole and submitted to Michael J. McDermott, Division of Current Information, Department of State, Jan. 13, 1944.

158. *Cole figured:* Cable to Barclay Acheson from Cairo, May 24, 1943.

158. *One Arabic editor:* Quoted in a telegram from Consul General Pinkerton in Jerusalem to the secretary of state, Jan. 13, 1944.

158. *. . . that country's so-called literates:* Brief of Sept. 5, 1944, from the American legation in Cairo to the State Department.

158. *Despite its limited audience:* The Arabic edition was not under the control of the Office of War Information: letter of June 23, 1943, from John S. Badeau, Chief, Near East Region, OWI, to W. L. Risley, Jr., Office of Printing and Publishing Administration, War Production Board, Washington, D.C.

159. *In the meantime:* A member of the board of directors of *Det Bästa* was Count Folke Bernadotte, the Swedish internationalist later assassinated by Jewish extremists while serving as a UN mediator in Palestine. Barclay Acheson and Israeli ambassador Abba Eban were among those who later established the Bernadotte Memorial Foundation to promote international peace and goodwill in his honor. See *NYT,* Jan. 14, 1951.

159. *The* New York Times: Dec. 8. See also Dec. 12, 13, 14, and 15, 1943.

159. *Guffey pointed:* In his "In New York" column in the *Daily Mirror,* April 10, 1944, Walter Winchell alluded to a Mrs. Helen Richards of Washington, D.C.:

> Her groom is a Colonel in the Office of Strategic Services. She is listed in a mag masthead as a "roving editor" though she is said to have never written a word under her name. She also is alleged to have helped Senator Butler write that article on U.S. expenditures in S. America . . . [Winchell's ellipsis] Big entertainer at the Capitol, pal of reactionaries and appeasers, and worries many people because her husband is so important to the army intelligence.

The reference was to Helen Hughes Richards, whose name mysteriously appeared on the masthead in Nov. 1942 as a roving editor, though she never wrote anything under her own byline.

160. *Wally himself was sensitive:* Letter of A. Walter Kramer, a private citizen, to Secretary of State Cordell Hull, dated Feb. 24, 1943. Kramer was disturbed that the State Department was delivering the *RD* in diplomatic pouches.

162. *In November 1943:* Telegram from the American legation in Stockholm, Oct. 27, 1943, to the secretary of state.

162. *Spain threatened:* Telegram in paraphrase dated Oct. 9, 1945, from the American consul in Barcelona to the U.S. secretary of state.

163. *Despite the* Digest's *hostile attitude:* Letter of Jan. 5, 1945, to Thomas S. Acheson, who passed the letter on to the American consul in Winnipeg, who forwarded a long excerpt to the secretary of state under the caution "Strictly Confidential."

163. *When the two McEvoys: Schreiner, The Condensed World of the Reader's Digest,* chap. 12.

170. *By 1947 the combined circulation:* Confidential memo from Marvin Lowes to William T. Stone of the U.S. State Department dated Jan. 27, 1948.

171. *Late in 1947:* Letter of Dec. 10, 1947, to C. Tyler Wood, deputy to the assistant secretary of state for economic affairs.

172. *Thompson learned:* Presumably, de la Chassaigne's duties during the Nazi occupation brought him into contact with the infamous Klaus Barbie, who was chiefly responsible for the deportation of Jews from Lyons. A preliminary search of the records of the Simon Wiesenthal Center, in New York, which maintains files on thousands of war criminals, failed to turn up any information on de la Chassaigne. However, no comprehensive list of Nazi officials and collaborators involved in the deportation of the Jews yet exists.

Chapter 7: Baseball Z and Other Diversions

Books: Fulton Oursler, Sr., *Behold This Dreamer!* (New York: Macauley, 1924). **Correspondence:** Pearl S. Buck, Albert L. Cole, Norman Cousins, Virginia Flory Cremeans, Grace Naismith, Ralph Henderson, Eleanor Roosevelt, Theodore Roosevelt, Irving Salkow, DeWitt Wallace, Robert Wallace, duke and duchess of Windsor. **Interviews:** Davies, Dillon, Espy, Edie Lewis, Hobart Durkin Lewis, Lund, Romulo, Scribner. **Other:** Notes, memorandums, and telegrams of DeWitt Wallace; Christmas Greeting List 1940 of DeWitt Wallace; *RD* attendance records; assorted issues of the *Digesters,* an occasional RDA office publication "Published Once in a While by All of Us for All of Us"; transcriptions of assorted *RD* office skits, lyrics, parodies, poetry, and other nonofficial materials; "rough continuity" script for home movie on High Winds.

182. *Lowell Thomas:* Letter of Aug. 10, 1938.

182. *Wally had quickly signed up:* Like many another celebrity who enjoyed *RD* largess but seemed somewhat embarrassed to mention the fact in public, apart from the need to parade a byline every so often, Thomas omitted any mention of his close friendship with the Wallaces in his autobiography, *Good Evening, Everybody.*

In July 1938 Al Cole and Wally protested—with apparent success—the efforts of Irving Salkow of Associated Artists, in Los Angeles, to produce a radio show to be called "Reader's Digest of the Air." Salkow claimed to have already secured permission from Hearst publications, *Scribner's, Newsweek,* and other magazines.

In May 1944 the *Digest* also became the first sponsor of radio's highly esteemed public forum "Town Meeting of the Air," which for its first ten years had broadcast without a sponsor. Cost of the thirty-nine-week sponsorship was an estimated $700,000. A May 29, 1944, *Newsweek* item noted, "The contract . . . still leaves the all-important choice of subjects and speakers with the program's moderator, George V. Denny Jr., and Town Hall, Inc."

183. *Though Wally's correspondents:* One of his least likely pen pals was poet Dame Edith Sitwell, whom he probably met on one of his trips abroad. In an undated

Christmas message, Sitwell sent Wally a postcard of her brother Osbert's eleventh-century home in Florence and copies of two of her poems, "The Two Kings" and "At Cockcrow."

186. *With America's entry:* NYT, Nov. 22, 1940.

186. *One afternoon while chatting:* John Bainbridge, "Little Magazine: I—Wally," *New Yorker,* Nov. 17, 1945, p. 33. When asked whether he had been constrained by legal reasons from including any material on the *Digest* in his five-part series, Bainbridge replied to the author on March 16, 1990, that he had omitted nothing. "The RD is not a place that breeds scandal or much in the way of irregular behavior, and though their professional conduct is often entertaining (unintentionally), it is not unprintable."

Chapter 8: The Talk of the Town

Books: Eric F. Goldman, *The Crucial Decade and After: America, 1945–1960* (New York: Knopf, 1975); Charles Higham, *American Swastika* (Garden City, N.Y.: Doubleday, 1985); Thurber, *The Years with Ross.* **Articles:** "The 'New Yorker' Rebels," *Commonweal,* Feb. 25, 1944; John Bainbridge, "Little Magazine," *New Yorker,* in five parts: "I—Wally" (Nov. 17, 1945), "II—Birth of an Aristocrat" (Nov. 24, 1945), "III—Plant You Now, Dig You Later" (Dec. 1, 1945), "IV—Chappaqua, U.S.A." (Dec. 8, 1945), "V—Dr. Wallace's Magic Formula" (Dec. 15, 1945); "Now 'Reader's Digest' Can't Use 'New Republic' Pieces," *PM,* March 2, 1944; "Un-*Digest*-ed," *Time,* Feb. 21, 1944; "Digest in the Doghouse," *Newsweek,* Feb. 21, 1944; "Let's Make a Deal," *Avenue,* Feb. 1991; Walter Goodman, "Hard to Digest," *Harper's,* June 1982; "Wendy Reves," *Dallas Morning News,* April 28, 1985. **Correspondence:** Bruce Bliven, Dwight D. Eisenhower, Anne Morrow Lindbergh, Henry C. Link, Ik Shuman, Robert A. Taft. **Interviews:** Allen, Cole, Davies, Dillon, Espy, Roy Herbert, Hunt, Hobart Durkin Lewis, Morgan, Rhodes, Shuman, Paul W. Thompson, Wilson. **Other:** Notes and memorandums of DeWitt Wallace; *What Is the Reader's Digest?* (pamphlet) (Pleasantville: Reader's Digest Association, 1952); "The RD Follies of 1948, Written, Acted, and Produced by the Editorial Staff."

192. *Also it was always pointed out:* In 1936 the once loftily literary *Scribner's* underwent a middlebrow reformatting, to no avail. Three years later it was purchased by the *Commentator,* renamed *Scribner's Commentator,* and launched as a right-wing propaganda vehicle.

192. *Wally had also tried to kidnap:* Scott Elledge, *E. B. White: A Biography* (New York: W. W. Norton, 1984), pp. 212, 239.

193. *Ross's diatribe:* NYT, Feb. 12, 1944.

196. *On January 17, 1944:* Fleischmann did add a conciliatory final paragraph: "[Ik] Shuman told me more than once of the informal and pleasant nature of his negotiations with you." In later years, when relations between the two magazines were somewhat mended, Wally endowed a scholarship in Fleischmann's name at Macalester College.

197. *Bruce Bliven:* Letter of Feb. 29, 1944.

198. *But any likelihood:* "The Reader's Digest," *TNR* March 6, 1944.

199. *A more thoughtful reason:* "Block That Trend," *America,* Feb. 26, 1944.

199. *By far, though:* Founded in 1940 by Ralph Ingersoll, former managing editor of the *New Yorker,* PM tried to break out of the newspaper stereotype but succeeded in being only "kooky," in the opinion of I. F. Stone, who worked in the paper's Washington bureau. Financing for the paper came from department-store magnate Marshall Field.

200. *What he heard:* Four-page letter from Norman Cousins to DeWitt Wallace, Feb. 18, 1944.

203. *Pravda attacked White: NYT,* Dec. 10, 1944.

204. *Halfway through the publication:* "Dig You Later," *Time,* Dec. 10, 1945.

205. *Saying he thought:* Telegram dated Dec. 18 [1945].

205. *Bennett A. Cerf:* Letter of Dec. 14, 1945.

206. *Wallace was also present:* Letter of Nov. 26, 1948, from Bradley to Wallace.

206. *Just the month before:* Barbara Branden, *The Passion of Ayn Rand* (Garden City, N.Y.: Doubleday, 1986), p. 163.

209. *Eventually, he forgot:* So did Wally. But between Nov. 1945 and May 1946, a total of five articles and book excerpts appeared in the *Digest* urging the United States to move toward world government.

209. *Far more typical:* Early in the Cold War the *Digest* also became perhaps the first major American publication to offer its readers a glimpse of the Soviet gulag when it excerpted KGB defector Victor Kravchenko's *I Chose Freedom* in two consecutive issues in 1946. "I know from extensive personal observation," he wrote, "that most of the war industry used slave contingents and that in dozens of plants such coerced labor was the principal or sole reliance." A frequent witness before congressional committees, Kravchenko was among the first in a long line of Soviet defectors to write for the *RD.*

210. *Another Cold War favorite:* Bullitt also proposed in the pages of the *RD* that the United States bomb strategic locations in China and support an attack by Chiang Kai-shek on the mainland of China.

210. *The answer was that:* A Jan. 1947 article, "The Arabs Live There Too," proposed that Jews give up all claims to Palestine.

210. *Wally also published:* Close was a neighbor in nearby Valhalla and publisher of a booklet titled *The Anti-Defamation League and Its Use in the World Communist Offensive.* Its thesis was that the ADL "was largely instrumental in the rise and continual growth of communism in [the United States] and that Jews participated prominently in the Russian Revolution." A. Forster, *A Measure of Freedom* (Garden City, N.Y.: Doubleday, 1950), p. 57. On Aug. 28, 1940, Close wrote Wally, who had just purchased two articles, thanking him for payment and his "generous and appreciative note" and remarking, "All I can say is, that as a veteran and hardened worker in the journalistic field, I find my breath taken away, and my mind exclaiming: 'Can these things be!' The biggest story of all, some day when you permit it, will be the story of D.W. and journalism."

Wally's admiration for Henry Ford, Sr., also continued unabated, even though he had been embroiled in controversy for publishing *The International Jew:*

The World's Problem and for accepting an award from Nazi Germany. Other articles besides the original homage in the first issue included "Ford Discusses Human Flivvers," "What Is Ford Doing Now?," "What Is Ford Going to Do?," "Why Doesn't Ford Quit?," "Are Gandhi and Ford on the Same Road?," and "Mr. Ford Doesn't Care."

210. *Jew-baiters in attendance:* Forster and Epstein, *Danger on the Right,* pp. 35, 116, 168, 179, 198; A. Forster, *A Measure of Freedom,* pp. 72–73.

210. *As for blacks:* Pleasantville's benevolent attitude toward blacks—liberal in view of the racist hatred prevalent in much of white America at the time—was perhaps best summed up in a March 1932 article that declared:

> As every child needs a loving parent, so every Negro under our civilization needs a white man as his guardian angel—his master, not in the imperious sense, but in the patriarchal one. . . . While the Negro in the South, as I know him, is a happy man, as human happiness goes, I hardly know a more tragic and pathetic figure than the Negro in the North. . . . In the South the Negro is more relaxed and natural; and there he indulges his racial tendency to take life easily. . . . He enjoys to live, and he lives to enjoy. . . . He is not really comfortable in Western civilization.

"A Negro Looks at the South" in Jan. 1939 optimistically noted that blacks were encouraged because in the first half of the preceding year "not a single lynching was recorded in the United States."

210. *And, as usual:* Though the "cross-examination" technique was not half so vigorous as previously, there were still exceptions. Among the most notable was the *RD*'s condensation of former vice-president Henry A. Wallace's postwar *60 Million Jobs,* which pleaded for farm supports, an increased minimum wage, extended Social Security and health insurance, housing and hospital-construction programs, TVA-like river developments, and a federal full-employment program. Other articles around this time praised reforms of the British Labour party, including government planning.

211. *The* Digest *was also becoming:* In the thirties the RDA established the Educational Book Division to exploit the company's proven ability to sell reprints to schools. Around the same time that the *Digest* was attacking Kinsey, the school division decided to do a series of books on sex education. Barclay Acheson arranged to have his mistress, who had no writing experience, hired as the staff writer of the series. After she was informed by the series editor that the sex-education course would contain no explicit language or drawings, and that a reprint of Margaret Culkin Banning's 1937 piece "The Case for Chastity" would serve as the cornerstone of the series, she resigned. The series came to nothing.

211. *When the Rockefeller Institute:*

> Some of the statements from these people were so vague as to constitute little more than a high-minded defense of virtue and antimaterialism. It was an obvious piece of trickery, and the *Digest* followed it three months later with another symposium on the same subject, composed of letters from readers

who had read the first symposium, thus getting additional usage from the idea. ... As a pretense of impartiality, the symposium included statements supporting Kinsey from a woman in North Carolina, and from Kinsey's friend Philip Wylie, whose *Generation of Vipers* must have already stamped him as immoral in the eyes of many *Digest* readers. These were two out of thirteen. The first "symposium" had been a 100 percent attack.

Wardell B. Pomeroy, *Dr. Kinsey and the Institute for Sex Research* (New York: Harper & Row, 1972), p. 302.

211. *Later High recovered: NYT,* April 19 and 22, 1950.

212. *In its tribute:* The article was written by associate editor William Miller and researched by Ruth Brine. Miller and his wife visited the Wallaces at High Winds prior to the story's publication and were presented with a Japanese doll to give to their children at Christmas. In a thank-you note dated December 10, Miller effused, "My wife, who, like the distaff side of the Wallace team, is a shrewder judge of character in a moment than I am in a week, remarked after our pleasant chat at your home: 'There are two genuinely *good* people. There isn't a mean streak in either of them, and nothing false.' I thought that, as usual, her judgment was eminently sound."

As with the *Fortune* article in 1936, Wally did not want any mention made of the fact that Lila had been previously engaged. In a Dec. 3 note to the Wallaces, researcher Brine revealed that the information was not considered off the record, since "three other people told us" about the engagement, adding, "I suppose there will be other things too that you would much rather we hadn't used, but as I was told today, that's journalism."

Chapter 9: Hyacinths for Thy Soul

Books: Michael R. Beschloss, *Kennedy & Roosevelt: The Uneasy Alliance* (New York: Harper & Row, 1980); Kenneth Davis, *Two Bit Culture: The Paperbacking of America* (Boston: Houghton Mifflin, 1984); Otto Friedrich, *Decline and Fall: The Saturday Evening Post* (New York: Harper & Row, 1970); Robert V. Hudson, *Mass Media* (New York: Garland, 1987); Walter H. Weintz, *The Solid Gold Mailbox;* Julian L. Watkins, *The Best Advertisements from Reader's Digest, 1955–1961 (And the Qualities That Made Them Effective)* (New York: Random House, 1962). **Articles:** John W. Garberson, "A Limited Number of Advertising Pages" and "By the Way, Al," *Association for Education in Journalism,* 1972. **Correspondence:** Fred D. Thompson. **Interviews:** Allen, Cole, Dillon, Espy, Grossman, Roy Herbert, Hunt, Hobart Durkin Lewis, O'Hara, Rhodes, Scribner, Paul W. Thompson, Wilson. **Other:** Notes and memorandums of Albert L. Cole, DeWitt Wallace; "Questions Most Frequently Asked about the Decision to Take Advertising in USRD" (1955 memorandum distributed to *RD* employees).

214. *For many members:* On April 3, 1950, a *Digest* messenger carrying $5,000 in cash and $35,000 in checks was shot and killed on company grounds by four men

lying in ambush. After a series of stays and appeals, three of the men were executed in Sing Sing prison, in nearby Ossining, New York, on July 9, 1955. See *NYT,* Oct. 1, 1952, June 16, July 9, 1953, Jan. 5, April 1, June 5, Aug. 13, Nov. 9, 1954, July 10, Dec. 3, 1955. Fulton Oursler, Sr., later pasted together an assortment of newspaper clippings and trial transcripts relating to the case under the title *The Reader's Digest Murder: A Tragedy in Parole* (New York: Farrar, Straus and Young, 1952).

225. *One thing the ratings:* The lowest EQ ever recorded for a Condensed Book selection was *The Leopard,* by Giuseppe di Lampedusa, a rare highbrow offering published in 1960 that garnered a miserable score of 6.

229. *"Dear Reader":* Whether by design or inadvertently, the copywriters managed both to get the poet's nationality wrong and to misquote his lines. The quotation derives from James Terry White's "Not by Bread Alone: After Hippocrates":

> If thou of fortune be bereft
> And in thy store there be but left
> Two loaves, sell one and with the dole
> Buy hyacinths to feed thy soul.

232. *At this point: TNY,* Feb. 8, 1958.

235. *In the ensuing uproar: Advertising Age,* Aug. 2, 1943.

237. *For thirty-two years:* Two years after its decision to accept advertising, the *Digest* raised its newsstand price anyway.

239. *In July 1955: NYT,* June 27, 1955.

239. *The only adverse: NYT,* July 18, 1957.

240. *Among those who wrote:* Letter of May 2, 1955. Wally's hostility toward the Kennedy family was common knowledge in Pleasantville, though no record survives of the reasons behind his antipathy. The two men shared an intense dislike for Roosevelt and were America Firsters. The *Digest* also profiled the U.S. ambassador to Britain. Yet Kennedy, who brought Roosevelt's New Deal to Wall Street, was a Democrat and a Catholic who had once wanted the presidency for himself, and that was probably sufficient cause for Wally to detest everything he stood for.

Chapter 10: Tucking America into Bed at Night

Books: Edwin R. Bayley, *Joe McCarthy and the Press* (Madison: University of Wisconsin Press, 1981); Cedric Belfrage, *The American Inquisition, 1945–1960* (New York: Thunder's Mouth Press, 1989); Kai Bird, *The Chairman: John J. McCloy: The Making of the American Establishment* (New York: Simon & Schuster, 1992); G. William Domhoff, *The Bohemian Grove and Other Retreats: A Study in Ruling-Class Cohesiveness* (New York: Harper & Row, 1974); Curt Gentry, *J. Edgar Hoover: The Man and His Secrets* (New York: W. W. Norton, 1991); David Halberstam, *The Powers That Be* (New York: Knopf, 1979); Aaron Levenstein, *Escape to Freedom* (Westport, Conn.: Greenwood Press, 1983); James Michener, *The World Is My Home: A Memoir* (New York: Random House, 1992); Douglas T. Miller and Marion Nowak, *The Fifties: The Way We Really*

Were (Garden City, N.Y.: Doubleday, 1977); Robert P. Newman, *Owen Lattimore and the "Loss" of China* (Berkeley: University of California Press, 1992); Norman Vincent Peale, *The Power of Positive Thinking,* 35th anniversary ed. (New York: Prentice-Hall, 1987); Thomas C. Reeves, *The Life & Times of Joe McCarthy* (New York: Stein and Day, 1982); Natalie Robins, *Alien Ink: The FBI's War on Freedom of Expression* (New York: William Morrow, 1992); Joan Shelley Rubin, *The Making of Middlebrow Culture* (Chapel Hill: University of North Carolina Press, 1992); W. A. Swanberg, *Luce and His Empire* (New York: Scribner's, 1972); Athan G. Theoharis and John Stuart Cox, *The Boss: J. Edgar Hoover and the Great American Inquisition* (Philadelphia: Temple University Press, 1988). **Articles:** Dr. Theodore Kamholtz, "Is Laughter the Best Medicine?" *Journal of the American Medical Association,* Aug. 9, 1965; "U.S. Challenges the Soviet in Battle for Men's Minds," *NYT,* Dec. 1, 1951. **Correspondence:** A. J. Cronin, Dwight D. Eisenhower, Samuel Goldwyn, Herbert Hoover, Charles and Anne Morrow Lindbergh, John D. Rockefeller, Jr., Billy Rose, Francis Cardinal Spellman, Walter Winchell. **Interviews:** Allen, Davies, Hard, Roy Herbert, Hunt, Bruce Lee, Edie Lewis, Hobart Durkin Lewis, Rhodes, Paul W. Thompson, Waters, Wilson. **Other:** "Regarding Westbrook Pegler's Attack," "Statement by Donald Robinson, Author of 'Mr. Brown vs. Generalissimo Stalin,'" in the Sept. 1952 *RD,* and a list of "Reader's Digest Articles in Past 10 Years Exposing the Menace of Communism," dated Nov. 17, 1952; notes and memorandums of Charles W. Ferguson, DeWitt Wallace. **Remarks:** As a result of an FOIA request to the FBI for its files on DeWitt Wallace, all but three pages were turned over to the author.

243. *Michener came to the Guest House:* Over lunch Lewis told Michener, "People who pride themselves on their education don't read it, but the *Reader's Digest* is not for them. It's for busy people who don't have lots of books and access to education. The *Digest* is written for everyone, from the non–high school educated person to someone with a Ph.D., but by and large it is for Middle America." See John P. Hayes, *James A. Michener: A Biography* (New York: Bobbs-Merrill, 1984), p. 97 and passim.

245. While Others Sleep: Though the SAC was formed in 1946 as part of the U.S. Army Air Force charged with deploying the nuclear arsenal, the American public in the midfifties was generally ignorant of its striking power. Lewis told Michener there was "a great book" to be written about the command centering on its "eternal vigilance" and "rattlesnake reputation," and he outlined the piece and book thus:

> Esprit de corps is probably the essence of it and that must come from leadership.... Perhaps this is the story of [General] Curt LeMay and his boys.... As you will learn, SAC never sleeps.... The dedication of officers and men to the job is undoubtedly impressive and it might be well to find out how the flight crews live, and where, what hours of duty, what their wives and kids know about their daily missions, how they come and go, how the practice alerts keep them poised.... I don't need to say that we count on having plenty of human interest and drama and anecdotes.

Michener visited SAC posts in different parts of the world and learned as much as security would permit, interviewing pilots, crew members, and General

LeMay; riding in a B-47 bomber; and talking with SAC wives and families. See Hayes, *James A. Michener,* pp. 138–39.

245. *When it became apparent:* The *RD*'s standard payment was $2,500 per article, but Michener received $3,500 to $5,000. Shrewdly, he also refused to sign an exclusivity clause with the magazine, on the advice of his agent, Helen Strauss, of the William Morris Agency, who was later able to negotiate article fees ranging from $10,000 to $30,000. In one month alone during 1965, the *RD* paid Michener $85,000. See Hayes, *James A. Michener,* pp. 112–13.

247. *In issue after issue:* Somewhat lamely, the U.S. Communist party attempted to return the favor, though the minuscule circulation and political clout of the *Daily Worker* were no match for those of the *RD.* Even attempts at *Digest*-like "plants" in other media fell flat, at least where smears of the *RD* were concerned. In its issue of March 7, 1949, the *C.I.O. News* joined the chorus of those accusing the magazine of fascist proclivities, adding that the recent Feb. issue made "itself the vehicle for No Vacancies, an anti–rent control tirade by Bertrand de Jouvenel, once described in the New York Herald Tribune as the 'French Goebbels.' "

The *WSJ,* on its editorial page of April 22, 1949, noted in an item titled "Coincidence Department" that the March 2 issue of the *Daily Worker* had used identical language to condemn the article. "Since the C.I.O. states that it has purged its headquarters of Communists," the *WSJ* went on to say, "we set this down as merely a coincidence, or parallelism in thought between the Communists and the independent thinkers in the C.I.O."

247. *A regular theme:* Hoover's byline appeared frequently in the *Digest,* which was his favorite publication. See Ralph de Toledano, *J. Edgar Hoover: The Man and His Time* (New Rochelle, N.Y.: Arlington House, 1973), p. 30. But he was not above dissembling in the pages of America's most trusted periodical. In "The Enemy's Masterpiece of Espionage" (April 1946), Hoover claimed that, in 1941, FBI scientists had unraveled the secret of German microdot photography. In fact, the technology was revealed to FBI undercover agents in Bermuda. See Thomas B. Allen and Norman Polmar, *Merchants of Treason: America's Secrets for Sale* (New York: Delacorte Press, 1988), pp. 129–30.

247. (*Hoover's articles:* One of the FBI director's favorites was Fulton Oursler, who wrote, among other pieces, "Why I No Longer Fear the FBI" for ACLU head Morris Ernst, which appeared in the issue of Dec. 1950. Some time after Oursler's death, Wally wrote FBI press agent Louis B. Nichols, saying, "It troubles me that since Fulton's death Mr. Hoover no longer writes for the Digest. You remember those stirring pieces, I'm sure." He went on to propose an article on union racketeering to be written by Lester Velie. Though the FBI declined, since it deemed racketeering a local and not a federal problem, more Hoover-ghosted articles soon followed.

In an appendix to *The Age of Surveillance* (New York: Random House, 1980), Frank Donner provides a list of Hoover's published writings covering the last three decades of his life. Among magazines, *U.S. News & World Report* led the pack with twenty-five, followed by the *American Magazine* with eighteen. Hoover's favorite publication placed third, with just over a dozen. Donner's conclusion: "No government official has ever communicated to a national audience in such volume as J. Edgar Hoover."

Nichols, who had a creative hand in many of those magazine pieces, resigned in 1957, after suffering two nervous breakdowns and a heart attack, to take a lucrative job in the private sector. "Like any other top executive who abandoned ship against the director's express wishes, Nichols, after leaving the FBI, was tapped, bugged, burgled, and tailed." See Gentry, *J. Edgar Hoover,* p. 451.

248. *Along with* Time:

> Hanson Baldwin, military correspondent of the *New York Times,* has to go outside his own journal to tell the public (through the *Reader's Digest* of August [1943]) that there had been "Too Much Wishful Thinking About China"—the title of his article. "Missionaries, war relief drives, able ambassadors and the movies have oversold us," he wrote. China "is not—in our sense—winning battles, but losing them." Her great contribution lay in holding down 15–22 Japanese divisions but "She has no real army as we understand the term" and her communiques were "almost worthless." Drawing on his connections in the War Department, he described all the inadequacies of health, training, equipment and defensive spirit in words Stilwell might have used himself, but Baldwin came to different conclusions. Neither the Hump nor the Road, he wrote, could supply enough for a major campaign in China . . . .

> Barbara Tuchman, *Sand against the Wind: Stilwell and the American Experience in China, 1911–1945* (New York: Macmillan, 1971), p. 386. Tuchman described Judd as Chiang Kai-shek's "most devout supporter" (p. 189).

248. *Back in the midforties:* The article in question, "The Fate of the World Is at Stake in China" (June 1945), was coauthored by roving editor Max Eastman and J. B. Powell, former editor of *China Weekly Review.* Claiming that Lattimore was "perhaps the most subtle evangelist" of the "erroneous conception" that Russia was a democracy, the authors went on to contend, "Mr. Lattimore appraised the net result of the Moscow Trials and the blood-purge by which Stalin secured his dictatorship in 1936–39 as 'a triumph for democracy.' He now urges our government, in a book called *Solution in Asia,* to accept cheerfully the spread of 'the Soviet form of democracy' in Central Asia." According to Robert P. Newman, *Owen Lattimore and the "Loss" of China,* p. 132, the article was a "cheap shot" that thoroughly distorted Lattimore's views on the subject. In *The Last Romantic: A Life of Max Eastman* (New York: Oxford University Press, 1978), biographer William L. O'Neill dubbed the *Digest* article "the worst Eastman ever put his name to," adding, "Max was losing touch with reality" (p. 227). Roving editor Bill White later persuaded the *Digest* not to excerpt Lattimore's *Solution in Asia* (Newman, *Lattimore,* p. 186). Almost certainly, the move to excerpt the book was made by book-excerpt editor Ralph Henderson, a liberal Democrat who had grown up in Asia, and the decision not to excerpt by Wally.

In April 1951 the *RD* again attacked Lattimore, in a June book excerpt by Elinor Lipper entitled "Eleven Years in Soviet Prison Camps." Material attacking Lattimore had been added to the American translation of Lipper's book by her American publisher, Henry Regnery, without the author's knowledge, and it was that material which appeared in the magazine. In her polemic, Lipper chastised Lattimore and former vice-president Henry A. Wallace for being willing dupes of their Soviet hosts, during a tour the two men had jointly made of Siberia in 1944, by not recognizing and condemning slave-labor camps for what they were. Arriving in the United States in 1951 on a book tour, Lipper acknowledged in an interview with the FBI that she knew nothing about Lattimore and was even unaware that he had accompanied Wallace, who in fact never saw any such camps. See Newman, *Lattimore,* pp. 222–23.

248. *After the article appeared:* NYT, Feb. 27 and 28, March 6, May 14, 1952. In Aug. 1957, after the State Department dropped its long-standing ban against newsmen's traveling to Communist China, the *Digest* became one of twenty-four "news organizations" given permission by Secretary of State Allen Dulles to send a reporter to China for a period of up to seven months (*NYT,* Aug. 23 and 24, 1957).

248. *Now under oath:* Richard M. Fried, *Nightmare in Red* (New York: Oxford University Press, 1990), pp. 126–27.

249. *Though Budenz was unable:* After McCarthy charged that Lattimore was head of "the espionage ring in the State Department," a special Senate subcommittee was convened under the chair of Senator Millard Tydings, a conservative Democrat from Maryland. Though McCarthy never succeeded in exposing a single Communist in government, he did intervene in the 1950 Maryland elections and help defeat Tydings, whom he branded on trumped-up charges as pro-Communist.

251. *As a monthly:* NYT, Dec. 8, 1950; *Time,* Dec. 18, 1950.

252. *The American way of life:* The trust that the American public put in the *Digest*—champion of the little people, battler against big government, defender of individual liberties, guardian of public morals, promoter of positive thinking—was amusingly typified at the funeral of the wife of maverick Missouri congressman O. K. Armstrong. A former journalist, Armstrong enjoyed writing articles for the *Digest* like "The Funniest Football Game Ever Played," about the time Georgia Tech defeated Cumberland in 1916 by a score of 220 to 0. Some mourners at the wake of Mrs. Armstrong thought it even funnier to find the deceased holding a copy of the *RD* in her hands.

252. *Peale preached a gospel:* He had also once served as chairman of the Committee for Constitutional Government, in which capacity he "exploited his ministerial position to disperse extreme political and economic theories. In 1944, for instance, he boosted . . . a book which tried to establish parallels between Franklin Roosevelt and Adolf Hitler. . . . Roosevelt's references to 'freedom from want' and 'freedom from fear' were compared with excerpts from some of Hitler's pieces." Ralph Lord Roy, *Apostles of Discord: A Study of Organized Bigotry and Disruption on the Fringes of Protestantism* (Boston: Beacon Press, 1953), p. 233.

253. *There were plenty of enemies:* The *RD* was the defendant in two suits that received national attention during this time. Preston Tucker, inventor of the rear-engine Tucker automobile, brought suit against the magazine—one of Detroit's most ardent champions—for libel after his corporation went bankrupt. Tucker claimed in his suit that a Sept. 1949 article by roving editor Lester Velie had

destroyed public confidence in the automobile at a critical time. Tucker also sued *Collier's* magazine, where the article—no doubt a plant—had previously appeared. The suit was dismissed on a technicality. See *NYT,* March 9, Aug. 10, 1950, Feb. 27, 1952.

Another plant, this time in the Sept. 1950 issue of *True Detective* magazine and reprinted the following month in the *RD,* gave an account of alleged Alabama prison and Pardon and Parole Board irregularities during the years 1947–50, when James E. Folsom was governor of the state. Author of the piece, "Devil's Island U.S.A.," was New York writer W. W. Ward, with information provided by Birmingham reporter Hugh Sparrow. Folsom and three aides sued the Dell Publishing Company, publisher of *True Detective,* and the *Digest* for libel. The suit was later settled out of court. See *NYT,* Dec. 5, 1952, Nov. 28, 1956.

254. . . . *getting the most out of sex:* Though explicit language remained taboo, the blatant use of double entendres was enough to raise *Time*'s eyebrow. In a March 10, 1958, press piece captioned "Pollyanna Unbound," the newsweekly noted that a certain magazine in Pleasantville was advertising yet another generic bedtime primer that offered "penetrating guidance" to anxious husbands and wives with "secret worries." The newspaper ads ran under the heading "What the Sex Manuals Don't Tell You."

254. *Around this time:* Cited by *NYT* April 1, 1981.

255. *The magazine also showed sympathy:* George Kennan, future ambassador to Moscow, was an ignored foreign-affairs analyst before his famous article "The Sources of Soviet Conduct"—signed only by "X"—appeared in the July 1947 issue of *Foreign Affairs,* edited by Hamilton Fish Armstrong. Though Kennan was quickly unmasked by Arthur Krock of the *New York Times,* commentator Walter Lippmann termed the article's publication "an event announcing that the State Department had made up its mind" on a policy. Kennan had also given that new policy a name: containment. Both the *RD* and *Life* reprinted long excerpts from the X article, though identifying Kennan as the author. See Walter Isaacson and Evan Thomas, *The Wise Men: Six Friends and the World They Made* (New York: Simon & Schuster, 1986), pp. 441–42.

255. *And after the Atomic:* Though later an ardent champion of nuclear energy, the *Digest* initially portrayed the atomic bomb in characteristically apocalyptic terms. A 1941 article asked whether experiments on uranium might start a chain reaction that would unravel the whole planet. In 1947 an article described how an atomic bomb would shower a city with a "mist of death." That article, along with the U.S. atom tests on the island of Bikini in 1946, were widely credited with helping to publicize the peril of radiation. See Spencer R. Weart, *Nuclear Fear: A History of Images* (Cambridge: Harvard University Press, 1988), pp. 80, 185.

256. *As the fifties turned:* In 1957 the *Digest* arranged for novelist John Dos Passos—another renegade liberal who found a conservative berth in Pleasantville—to visit Brasilia, then being carved out of the Amazon wilderness. That trip was the impetus for *Brazil on the Move* (1963), a collection of travel essays. Meanwhile, Dos Passos was already involved in a lengthy *RD* project based on findings of the Senate Committee on Improper Activities in the Labor and Management

Fields, headed by John McClellan, Democratic senator from Arkansas (aka the McClellan committee). Rank-and-file union members had written some one hundred thousand letters to the committee, protesting the way their unions were being operated. Dos Passos examined the letters, talked to McClellan, and traveled into the field in the winter and spring of 1958, talking to railroad workers, musicians, machinists. In Sept. 1958 the *Digest* published his findings, one of which was that workers wanted voluntary unions and right-to-work laws "with teeth in them." See Virginia Spencer Carr, *Dos Passos: A Life* (Garden City: N.Y.: Doubleday, 1984), pp. 514–15.

256. . . . *an almost monthly theme:* The biggest *Digest*-instigated brouhaha in this regard was its blistering attack on food waste in the armed forces. Kansas newspaperman William L. White, who in late 1944 had launched one of the first and fiercest salvos of the Cold War in the pages of the *RD* with his two-part "Report on the Russians," leaked the findings of a special executive commission investigating military waste. In "Ridiculous Waste in the Armed Services" (April 1955), White claimed that navy sailors were "now eating beef, cheese and bacon sliced in 1948." Yet the navy currently luxuriated "in large stocks of apples, carrots and catsup" and continued to stock up on supplies. Secretary of the Navy Charles S. Thomas, whose request to see a copy of the report had previously been turned down, angrily denied the charges. Louisiana Democrat F. Edward Hebert, chairman of a House Armed Services subcommittee, maintained that the commission had "fed" the information to the *RD.* The *Digest* itself refused to comment on how it had obtained the material. See *NYT,* April 6, 7, 13, and 14, 1955.

The executive commission was chaired by former president Herbert Hoover and was popularly known as the Hoover Commission. Wally and Hoover continued to maintain their warm personal friendship; only the previous year the *RD* publisher had accepted the latter's invitation to spend a week at Bohemian Grove, the ultra-exclusive, semisecret Republican businessmen's retreat in California (letter from Hoover to Wallace dated April 26, 1954, and DW's reply of May 5, 1954).

257. *Later that year:* NYT, Aug. 1, 1966. Others on the guest list included Elliott V. Bell, editor of *BW;* Dr. Harold Dodds, president of Princeton University; and John Hay Whitney, senior partner of J. H. Whitney and Company.

257. *Taking note of the article:* NYT, Jan. 8, 1956.

258. *A measure of the esteem: Look,* Oct. 4, 1955.

259. *Later, White arranged:* John H. Johnson, *Succeeding against the Odds* (New York: Warner Books, 1989), pp. 123, 170.

262. . . . *it was frequently denounced: L'Unita,* Milan's Communist party newspaper, greeted the appearance of *Selezione* by characterizing it as "cultural chewing gum" published under "the care of the active officials of the United States Information Service" (*L'Unita,* Oct. 2, 1948).

263. *Paris was the hub:* By decree of the president of the French republic dated Oct. 12, 1953, Wally was named Chevalier in the National Order of the Legion of Honor in acknowledgment of his "great talent as a newspaperman and editor" (letter of Nov. 30, 1953, from Henri Bonnet, French ambassador to the United States, to DeWitt Wallace).

Chapter 11: "—And Sudden Death"

Books: Thomas C. Reeves, *A Question of Character: A Life of John F. Kennedy* (New York: Free Press, 1991). **Correspondence:** Barclay Acheson, Bertha Lee, Judy Acheson Thompson, Jeffrey Thompson, **Interviews:** Davies, Dillon, Hunt, Bruce Lee, Morgan, Rhodes, Romulo, Dorrie Schreiner, Samuel A. Schreiner, Paul W. Thompson, Wilson, Zinsser. **Other:** Notes, memorandums, and speeches of Albert L. Cole, DeWitt Wallace, Lila Acheson Wallace, Harry Wilcox.

272. *Already the magazine:* However, the Canadian government, as well as many Canadian magazines, took a dim view of the *RD*'s seeming omnipresence in the country. In 1956 the government levied a 20 percent tax on all advertising revenues of U.S. magazines circulating in the country as special Canadian editions, whether printed there or abroad, in French or in English. The government claimed that such so-called Canadian editions were practically identical to the U.S. editions, yet enjoyed tax privileges that gave them an unfair competitive advantage over genuinely Canadian publications. The *RD* and *Time,* having the two largest circulations (1,000,000 and 220,000, respectively), were hit the hardest. *Time* paid up—a half million dollars a year—while the *Digest* refused to pay and argued in court that the tax was discriminatory. In 1958 the tax was repealed and the *RD* dropped its suit, yet the acrimony and legal sparring continued for years. Finally, in 1964, an accommodation was reached between the government and both the *Digest* and *Time* that permitted them—to the exclusion of all other foreign magazines—to continue to deduct advertising expenditures from corporate income tax. See *NYT,* March 21 and 23, April 3, May 14, Aug. 31, Sept. 13, 1956, April 23, 1957, June 19, 1958, Oct. 24, 1959, Nov. 2, 1960, June 19, 1961, Feb. 21, 1964, April 27, 1965, Oct. 23, 1974, Jan. 24 and 26, March 21, April 19, Sept. 30, 1975, Feb. 4, 26, and 27, 1976. The *RD* also encountered serious nationalist resentment on the part of Brazilian legislators. See *NYT,* Jan. 8 and 25, Feb. 21, 1966.

276. *Later the RDA: NYT,* July 22, 1961.

276. *The first episode:* NYT, Jan. 28, 1955. By year's end another reviewer was using such terms as "dreary" and "uninspired" to describe the program's dramatization of the 1925 Scopes trial, pitting William Jennings Bryan against Clarence Darrow
(*NYT,* Dec. 6, 1955).

In 1961 the *RD* briefly joined forces with the ultraconservative Freedoms Foundation of Valley Forge, Pennsylvania, which had bestowed its Freedom Medal on Wally (and later on Harry Morgan; see chapter 16), to produce a television program called "All America Wants to Know." A panel show distributed through syndication and also broadcast over radio, "All America" ran into trouble with its very first program when the air force tried to suppress an interview with General Curtis E. LeMay, air force chief of staff, on the readiness of the Strategic Air Command. Panelists included Senator Barry Goldwater, Republican of Arizona, Senator Thomas J. Dodd, Democrat of Connecticut, reporters, and aviation experts. An air force spokesman later said the show had been approved with "a couple of modifications." See *NYT,* July 23, 1961.

276. *Around this time: NYT,* Aug. 1 and 2, 1956.

277. *Not long thereafter: RD,* March 1960. See also *NYT,* Feb. 19 and 23, 1960.

277. *In May 1962: NYT,* May 21, 1962.

280. *The only serious setback: NYT,* July 22, 1960.

280. *("Remember the 26th of July!":* On July 26, 1953, Castro had unsuccessfully attacked an army post. Two years later, after being released from prison, he went to Mexico City and organized the July 26 revolutionary movement.

280. *Only the year before: NYT,* April 19, 1959. An intrepid journalist who went to Hungary in 1956 to cover the revolution for the *Digest,* working alongside James Michener, Chapelle had been seized by a Communist border patrol and put in solitary confinement for almost two months. She gained her freedom only after the regime sought to quell world opinion. A few years later Chapelle died tragically when she stepped on a land mine while covering another war for the *Digest,* the one in Vietnam.

281. *The Digest's growth:* "Drops in Profits Beset Magazines," *NYT,* June 21, 1961.

281. *The biggest news: NYT,* June 21, July 11 and 12, 1961.

285. *In 1944 John Hersey:* John H. Davis, *The Kennedys: Dynasty and Disaster, 1848–1983* (New York: McGraw-Hill, *New York,* 1984), pp. 95–97, 127, 146.

286. *(All three reprints:* Nigel Hamilton, *JFK: Reckless Youth* (New York: Random House, 1992), pp. 652–53, 755.

288. *Typical was: RD,* March 1963.

288. *Prior to their publication:* Letter of April 20, 1962. *NYT,* March 29, 1962.

288. *Replied Wally:* Letter of April 27, 1962.

290. *But the* RD*'s response:* "Are We Poisoning Ourselves with Pesticides?," *RD,* Dec. 1982.

291. *The latter spent months:* On May 26, 1962, the Kennedy administration, perhaps annoyed by the *Digest's* unremitting criticism, also requested a name check from the FBI on DeWitt Wallace. Hoover replied to Kenneth O'Donnell, special assistant to the president, that the bureau's files contained "no pertinent information" on the *RD* publisher, adding in a PS, "The bureau has had considerable cordial correspondence with Wallace and our relations have been excellent."

291. *During the three and a half years:* David S. Scheim, *Contract on America: The Mafia Murders of John and Robert Kennedy* (Silver Springs, Md.: Argyle Press, 1988), pp. 78, 215.

Chapter 12: An Unpleasantness in Pleasantville

Correspondence: Fuoss, Bill Hard, Hibbs, Hobart Durkin Lewis, Norman Vincent Peale, DeWitt Wallace. **Interviews:** Allen, Cole, Cross, Hard, Hobart Durkin Lewis, O'Hara, Rhodes, Edward T. Thompson, Paul W. Thompson, Waters. **Other:** Notes and memorandums of Hobart Durkin Lewis, Paul Thompson, DeWitt Wallace, Lila Acheson Wallace.

299. *Wally used such occasions:* His benevolence toward his employees also took the form, in 1964, of a profit-sharing plan for the RDA's 1,500 U.S. employees. Anyone over twenty-five with three years' experience was eligible. See *NYT,* Feb. 3, March 3, 1964. The following year 2,000 employees received a 15 percent bonus (*NYT,* Dec. 31, 1965). The Wallaces' largess, once limited to favored employees, was now becoming institutionalized.

300. *While Wally traveled:* In 1965 the Justice Department brought suit against Select Magazines (formerly S-M News and now jointly owned by the RDA, Time Inc., the McCall Corporation, the Popular Science Publishing Company, and Meredith Publishing) and the Curtis Circulation Company (distributors of *Esquire, Look, TNY,* and the *Ladies' Home Journal,* among others). The suit charged the nation's two largest magazine distributors with coercing newsstand dealers to ensure preferential display of their publications on retail-store racks. Curtis and Select had combined to create a jointly owned subsidiary, National Magazine Service, which distributed one-third of all magazines, children's books, and paperbacks sold in the United States. The complaint charged the two distributors and their subsidiary with violating section 1 of the Sherman Act, which forbade combinations in restraint of trade, and the antimerger section of the Clayton Act. See *NYT,* June 10, 1965. NMS was later dissolved, and Time Inc. eventually established its own distribution network.

301. *In 1962 an even more fundamental:* Friedrich, *Decline and Fall,* pp. 17, 232.

303. *Other Post staffers: NYT,* Nov. 15, 1962, July 21, 1964.

305. *The appointment of Lewis: Time*'s winged chariot of Jan. 1, 1965, cleverly noted the changing of the guard with a press item titled "Foster Parent for the Digest." Observing that the *RD* had been the Wallaces' "only baby" for forty-two years, the newsweekly went on to describe Lewis as "the predicted and the predictable choice . . . [who is], say some of his colleagues, one of the best story editors in the business." See also *NYT,* Dec. 31, 1965.

308. *But in the end:* . . . The retirement policy was announced on July 10, 1967, in a joint memorandum to all Digesters cosigned by Hobe Lewis and Paul Thompson.

308. *When Thompson returned to work:* The appointment of the new business manager was buried in an inch-high story in the Jan. 3, 1966, issue of the *NYT.*

309. *Later he joined: NYT,* Dec. 13, 1979.

Chapter 13: The Sun Prince

Books: Jerry W. Sanders, *Peddlers of Crisis: The Committee on the Present Danger and the Politics of Containment* (Boston: South End Press, 1983). **Articles:** "Reader's Digest Marks 45th Year," *NYT,* July 26, 1967. **Interviews:** Cole, Cross, Hard, Roy Herbert, Hunt, Bruce Lee, Edie Lewis, Hobart Durkin Lewis, O'Hara, Rhodes, Edward T. Thompson, Paul W. Thompson, Wilson, Zinsser. **Other:** 1967 BBC documentary tape on *RD*'s forty-fifth anniversary.

319. *Occasionally, a hoax: NYT,* Nov. 15, 16, and 29, 1953.

322. *Wally himself was eventually: Journal of the American Medical Association,* July 12, 1958.

323. *By the midsixties: NYT,* May 21, 1962, June 11, 1964, Oct. 22 and 24, Nov. 3, 1966.

323. *The results this time: NYT,* Oct. 22, Nov. 3, 1966.

323. *The beleaguered but: NYT,* Oct. 24, 1966.

324. *At the time:* Part of Wally's strategy to give up smoking seems to have been to publish enough articles in the one publication he believed in, above all others, on the perils of Demon Tobacco, much as a dipsomaniacal preacher might rail against drink by citing Scripture during his sober moments. According to an undated internal, five-page memorandum headed "R.D. Articles on Cigarettes and Smoking," the *Digest* published seventy-six articles (including reprints) attacking cigarettes from 1924 through 1981, the year of his death. Not until his midseventies did he succeed in breaking the habit.

325. *According to the liberal: Changing Times,* June 1964.

330. *He went on:* Armstrong was convicted of income-tax evasion by a U.S. district court in Springfield, Missouri, and fined $1,500 when his returns for 1946–49 reported his income as $12,000 when he in fact earned $27,974. See Warren Boroson, "The Pleasantville Monster," *Fact,* March–April 1966, p. 5.

According to the *Journal of the National Education Association* of Sept. 1946, Armstrong had also been connected with "a prewar 'Red hunt' that had harassed Omaha teachers without ever finding evidence that any of them were Communists."

Chapter 14: One Bright Light amid the Encircling Gloom

Books: Stephen E. Ambrose, *Nixon: The Education of a Politician, 1913–1962* (New York: Simon & Schuster, 1987); idem, *Nixon: The Triumph of a Politician, 1962–1972* (New York: Simon & Schuster, 1989); Morton Mintz and Jerry S. Cohen, *America, Inc.: Who Owns and Operates the United States* (New York: Dial, 1971); Morton Mintz, *Power, Inc.: Public and Private Rulers and How to Make Them Accountable* (New York: Viking, 1976); Robert Stein, *Media Power: Who Is Shaping Your Picture of the World?* (Boston: Houghton Mifflin, 1972). **Interviews:** Hard, Roy Herbert, Hunt, Bruce Lee, Hobart Durkin Lewis, O'Hara, Rhodes, Shuman, Edward T. Thompson, Paul W. Thompson, Waters, Wilson.

334. *One evening:* Fulton Oursler, "My Dinner with Groucho," *Esquire,* June 1989.

336. *. . . and the abrasive Hitesman:* In May 1973 the ambitious Hitesman succeeded Hobe Lewis as president and also took on the position of chief operating officer, while Lewis became chairman. At that point, cochairman DeWitt and Lila Acheson Wallace assumed the title "directors" (since the term "founders" might have implied they were already dead) and ceased to have even the semblance of an active role in the company. Before the year was out, however, Hitesman was gone, and the office of president remained vacant.

337. *After talking things over: NYT,* June 15, Sept. 8, 1972.

337. Newsweek *paid a visit:* June 18, 1973.

339. *Together she, Waters: NYT,* March 18, 1973.

340. *To an interviewer: NYT,* March 28, 1975.

340. *Oursler was summoned home:* But still Lewis did not give up entirely. Turning to public television, he and Strauss arranged for the RDA to produce "James Michener's World," a series of visual essays on Hawaii, Iberia, the South Pacific, and Israel. *NYT* reviewer John J. O'Connor dismissed the series opener on the Holy Land as an example of how to portray a country in "nonthreatening depth" (*NYT,* June 21, 1977).

342. *Typical of the blind alleys: NYT,* March 21, 1966.

342. *Even further afield: NYT,* Sept. 26, 1967.

342. *Another remunerative area: NYT,* April 24, 1973.

343. *In 1966, however: NYT,* Nov. 20, 1965, Dec. 9, 1966.

344. *Over the objections: NYT,* June 2, 1968.

345. *Meanwhile, the* Digest: *NYT,* July 10, Dec. 8, 1968, May 6, 1973.

345. *Despite its breakneck: NYT,* July 19, 1952, Dec. 19, 1954, Nov. 8, 1955, May 24, 1957, March 31, 1961, Oct. 27, 1963, June 30, 1964, March 17, 1975, June 5, 1973, April 24, 1978, etc.

345. *In January 1967: NYT,* Jan. 10, 13, and 15, 1967.

348. *Among the items he clipped:* Julie Nixon Eisenhower, *Pat Nixon: The Untold Story* (New York: Simon & Schuster, 1986), pp. 82–83.

348. *By the time the* Digest *published:* Roger Morris, *Richard Milhous Nixon: The Rise of an American Politician* (New York: Henry Holt, 1990), pp. 131, 750. "I Say He's a Wonderful Guy" was "as told to" Joe Alex Morris.

348. *In August 1964: NYT,* July 27, 1964.

349. *Articles on welfare reform:* "What Has Happened to America," *RD,* Oct. 1967; *NYT,* Sept. 27, 1967.

350. *Not only did it sponsor:* The *Digest* also offered an early preview of Nixon's China policy. In a 1967 article in *Foreign Affairs,* the candidate wrote, "Taking the long view, we simply cannot afford to leave China forever outside the family of nations, there to nurture its fantasies, cherish its hates and threaten its neighbors." Nixon then asked Hobe Lewis to condense and print the piece in the *RD.* See William Safire, *Before the Fall: An Inside View of the Pre-Watergate White House* (New York: Da Capo Press, 1975), p. 368.

351. *On the night of Nixon's crucial:* Julie Nixon Eisenhower, *The Untold Story,* p. 240.

351. *More significantly:* Herbert G. Klein, *Making It Perfectly Clear* (Garden City, N.Y.: Doubleday, 1980), pp. 198, 280–81.

Chapter 15: Campus Comedy

Books: William Manchester, *The Glory and the Dream: A Narrative History of America, 1932–1972* (Boston: Little, Brown, 1974); Harris Wofford, *Of Kennedys & Kings: Making Sense of the Sixties* (New York: Farrar, Straus, Giroux, 1980). **Articles:** Kenneth Gross, "The Most Unforgettable Place I Ever Worked," *Newsday,* Feb. 28, 1970; "black council at issue; cc challenges j board," *Mac Weekly,* April 24, 1970.

Correspondence: Albert L. Cole, Paul H. Davis, John M. Dozier, John Driscoll, DeWitt Wallace. **Interviews:** Allen, Cole, Cox, Cross, April Herbert, Roy Herbert, Hunt, Chris Kirby, McHenry, Morgan, Rhodes, Edward T. Thompson, Paul W. Thompson, Wilson, Wulp. **Other:** Notes and memorandums of Paul H. Davis, DeWitt Wallace.

353. *The slow, uphill struggle:* Of all of white America's mainstream defenders of the status quo, none was more intransigent and vociferous in its opposition to the civil-rights movement than the *RD*—which in earlier decades, despite the patronizing tone of its articles on the subject, and a fondness for Negro dialect jokes, had encouraged equal opportunity and rights for blacks. Typical sixties fare emanating from the big plantation house in Pleasantville: a Sept. 1962 article noting white fears of casual Negro attitudes about sex; a June 1964 defense of de facto segregation; a March 1965 piece citing statistics showing that Negroes reproduced more offspring than whites did; an April 1965 feature claiming that Negro activists were "too anxious"; and Uncle Tom's last gasp— an Oct. 1965 piece by former heavyweight boxing champion Joe Louis reassuring the white folk that he knew his place and how to behave himself, and suggesting that other Negroes do likewise.

354. *The* Digest's *Washington office:* "How the Reds Make a Riot," *RD,* Jan. 1965.

355. *Introduced in 1961: Minneapolis Star,* Oct. 18, 1961. "Points to Ponder" appeared in 1955, while in 1962 "News from the World of Medicine" was added. Another new department, "All in a Day's Work," made its debut in 1973.

355. *The* Digest's *publicity apparatus:* Address by Robert Devine, former deputy general manager of Reader's Digest International Editions and director of public relations, at the Fifteenth Annual Education-Industry Conference on Public Relations, at the University of Georgia, Athens, Oct. 24, 1968, under the auspices of the school of journalism.

356. *Just when everything: NYT,* March 17, 1966, April 14, May 2, 1967.

361. *It was obvious:* The bureau had also confidentially supplied the *Digest*—for "background" purposes only—with the secret tapes it had made of Martin Luther King.

364. *The tumult culminated:* Ironically, in the midst of all this chaos, Macalester was also host to the most prominent visiting professor in its history—thanks, once again, to Wallace largess. In 1967 the *RD* publisher gave Macalester a matching grant of $250,000 to endow the Hubert H. Humphrey Professorship of International Affairs. After the Democratic vice-president and Wally's fellow Minnesotan lost the 1968 election, he divided his teaching time between Macalester and the University of Minnesota. Wally also paid for Humphrey's country home outside St. Paul and a chauffeur-driven limousine. Though an unflinching Nixon supporter, Wally had also contributed generously to Humphrey's presidential campaign out of state pride. See *WP,* Feb. 9, 1969; *NYT,* July 25, 1968. There was also a Democratic footnote to the story. Macalester's most prominent alumna was Joan Mondale, a 1952 graduate and wife of Vice-President Walter Mondale, who in 1979 delivered the commencement address. See *NYT,* May 29, 1979.

367. *Meanwhile, in early May: St. Paul Pioneer Press,* May 10, 1970.

367. *That summer Michener:* RD senior editor Andrew Jones served as Michener's assistant (Hayes, *James A. Michener,* pp. 201–9).
369. *Only with the beginning: Minneapolis Tribune,* Sept. 10, 1976.

Chapter 16: Wally's Monster

Correspondence: Albert L. Cole, Davies, Sterling Fisher, W. P. Headden, Morgan, DeWitt Wallace. **Interviews:** Allen, Cox, Cross, Dillon, McHenry, Morgan, Paul, Edward T. Thompson, Paul W. Thompson, Waters.

371. *President Eisenhower: NYT,* Feb. 5, July 10, Sept. 26, Oct. 5 and 22, 1957, May 18, June 10, 1958, Nov. 9, 1961, Aug. 28, 1963, etc.
371. *At the invitation: NYT,* Oct. 20, 1960.
380. *At the end of the FJI's: NYT,* Aug. 14, 1962. See also *NYT,* Sept. 12, 1961, Nov. 17, 1962, Dec. 27, 1964, Jan. 2, 1977.

Chapter 17: Where There Is Beauty, There Is No Crime

Books: *Selections from the Reader's Digest Collection,* introd. by John Rewald (Pleasant-ville: Reader's Digest Association, 1985); *The Foundation Directory,* 12th ed. (New York: Foundation Center, 1989); Agnes de Mille, *Portrait Gallery* (Boston: Houghton Mifflin, 1990); idem, *The Life and Work of Martha Graham* (New York: Random House, 1991). **Articles:** "Bronx Zoo Birds Get a Palace," *NYT,* Feb. 9, 1967; "New Bronx Zoo Building a Rara Avis," *NYT,* June 14, 1972; "Portrait of a Great Patron," *NYT,* May 12, 1977; "Friends Recall the Wallaces' Generosity," *GWN,* May 9, 1984; "Abu Simbel Journal," *NYT,* Dec. 15, 1990; "Genius in Full Flower," *New York Daily News,* Nov. 19, 1991; also *NYT,* May 28, 1960, May 22 and 27, Oct. 1, 1961, March 13, May 16, 1965, March 6 and 27, Sept. 9, 1966, Feb. 9, Dec. 8, 1967, July 24, Aug. 28, Dec. 27, 1968, May 24, June 17, 1972, April 17, Sept. 24, Oct. 21, 1974, June 4, Nov. 19 and 29, 1976, Jan. 15, 1990. **Correspondence:** Allen, Albert L. Cole, William J. Cross, C. R. Devine, Charles W. Ferguson, Henry G. Fischer, Thomas P. F. Hoving, Charles Kline, DeWitt Wallace, Lila Acheson Wallace. **Interviews:** Allen, Cole, Cross, Davies, Hard, Roy Herbert, Hunt, Chris Kirby, Hobart Durkin Lewis, Little, McHenry, Miller, Morgan, O'Hara, Rhodes, Edward T. Thompson, Paul W. Thompson, Waters, Wilson, Wulp, Zinsser. **Other:** Annual reports and tax returns of the Lakeview Fund, L.A.W. Fund, High Winds Fund, Reader's Digest Foundation, De-Witt Wallace Fund; notes and memorandums of Albert L. Cole, C. R. Devine, Paul W. Thompson, DeWitt Wallace, Lila Acheson Wallace, Richard Waters.

Chapter 18: Drowning in a Sea of Pabulum

Articles: "He Edited on His Feet," *Volusia,* Jan. 16, 1983; "After 36 Years at Condensed Books, Zinsser Looks Back—and Forward," *Publishers Weekly,* Aug. 14, 1987.
Correspondence: DeWitt Wallace. **Interviews:** Allen, Cox, Hard, Roy Herbert, Hunt, Chris Kirby, Hobart Durkin Lewis, Miller, O'Hara, Parker, Rae, Samuel A. Schreiner, Strand, Edward T. Thompson, Wilson, Wulp, Zinsser. **Other:** Notes and memorandums of Robert Cousins, George V. Grune, Barnabas McHenry, John A. O'Hara, DeWitt Wallace, Lila Acheson Wallace.

400. *One facile young editor:* Schreiner, *The Condensed World of the Reader's Digest,* pp. 52–53.
404. *But Lukas contemptuously:* "Life in These United States," *[More],* June 1971.
405. *Full of self-righteous indignation:* "The Reader's Digest Supplement," Jan. 2, 1972.
406. *In January 1975: NYT,* Jan. 9, March 14, 1975; *BW,* March 24, 1975.
406. *The biggest advertorial: NYT,* Feb. 3, 1976.
408. *Among his more successful projects: Volusia,* Jan. 16, 1983.
413. *Later Lee published: NYT,* Jan. 8, 1978.
414. *The following year:* In 1979 McGraw-Hill published spy master Kermit Roosevelt's *Countercoup: The Struggle for Control of Iran,* one of the titles it had purchased from the Reader's Digest Press. Soon after publication it was obliged to recall all 7,000 printed copies and issue a corrected version when British Petroleum objected to the description of its alleged role in the coup. See *NYT,* Nov. 10, 1979.

Chapter 19: I Am Joe's Headache

Correspondence: Ben Hibbs, Ann Landers, James A. McCracken, Grace Naismith, Robert O'Brien, Daniel O'Keefe, Leland Stowe. **Interviews:** Allen, Canfield, Cole, Cox, Cross, Davies, Hard, Roy Herbert, Hunt, Johnson, Chris Kirby, Bruce Lee, Hobart Durkin Lewis, Lund, Miller, Morgan, O'Hara, Parker, Rae, Rhodes, Samuel A. Schreiner, Strand, Edward T. Thompson, Waters, Wilson, Wulp, Zinsser. **Other:** Notes and memorandums of DeWitt Wallace; White House transcript of *RD* fiftieth-anniversary celebration, Jan. 28, 1972.

417. *The series:* The Joe series was among the *RD's* more lucrative reprint offerings. Overall it sold more than 7,960,530 individual reprints as of May 22, 1985. Winner by a large margin was "I Am Joe's Lung" (862,083).
419. *. . . . Eisenhower's ghostwriter:* In his retirement, Eisenhower became little more than a hack mouthpiece for the *RD's* right-wing political views. In April 1966 he came out in favor of prison for draft-card burners (*NYT,* March 23, 1966). That was followed by a proposal to limit the terms of Supreme Court justices (*NYT,* Dec. 27, 1966). A year later, in the Jan. 1967 issue, he urged that all elected officials, "particularly members of Congress, be required to make public an

annual, certified accounting of their financial affairs—all income and all hold-ings." The measure was strongly opposed by Senate Republican leader Everett McKinley Dirksen of Illinois (*NYT*, Dec. 26, 1967). On March 27, 1968, Eisen-hower made the front page of the *Times* with a harsh attack in the April issue on peace candidates in the presidential elections, as well as militant peace groups, which he accused of near-treason. In his last ghosted hurrah for Pleasantville, in the May 1968 issue, he asked for cadres of ten "law-abiding, hard-working" inhabitants of America's slums be assigned to each active policeman to help prevent and quell riots.

426. *After a particularly forceful article:* Wally's last known comment on abortion, an old passion, characteristically enough took humorous form. In 1975 he asked advice columnist Ann Landers to put down in writing a joke she had told him about the Jewish position on abortion. On July 14 she replied, "When someone asked Ann Landers to explain the Jewish position on abortion, she said, with a perfectly straight face, but an impish look in her eye—'The fetus is not viable until it becomes a doctor or a lawyer.' "

   Wally forwarded the letter to editor in chief Hobe Lewis with the notation "For your amusement. Far-fetched, but clever?" Lewis replied, "And true, no doubt!"

430. *On January 28: NYT,* Jan. 29, 1972.
431. *A few days after: NYT,* Feb. 1, 1972.

Chapter 20: Indigestion

Books: Carl Bernstein and Bob Woodward, *All the President's Men* (New York: Simon & Schuster, 1974); Michael Myerson, *Watergate: Crime in the Suites* (New York: Inter-national Publishers, 1973); Laurence Shroup, *The Imperial Brain Trust: The Council on Foreign Relations and United States Foreign Policy* (New York: Monthly Review Press, 1977); S. Weissman, *Big Brother and the Holding Company: The World behind Watergate* (Palo Alto, Calif.: Ramparts Press, 1974); Theodore H. White, *Breach of Faith: The Fall of Richard Nixon* (New York: Atheneum/Reader's Digest Press, 1975). **Correspon-dence:** DeWitt Wallace, Lila Acheson Wallace. **Interviews:** Allen, Blank, Cox, Cross, Davies, Davis, Hard, April Herbert, Roy Herbert, Hunt, Johnson, Chris Kirby, Mary Kirby, Bruce Lee, Virginia Lawton, Bruce Lee, Edie Lewis, Hobart Durkin Lewis, Lund, McGowan, McHenry, Miller, Morgan, Murphy, O'Hara, Parker, Paul, Rae, Rhodes, Samuel A. Schreiner, Strand, Edward T. Thompson, Nancy Cale Thompson, Susie Jacobson Thompson, Waters, Wilson, Zinsser.

434. *Rockefeller relented: NYT,* July 13, 1973.
441. *The bank and the Dade County: NYT,* Dec. 6, 1973.
442. *In December 1973: NYT,* Dec. 12, 1973, Feb. 1, 1974.
442. *In 1972 they had legally: NYT,* Nov. 3 and 4, 1972, Sept. 29, 1973, Nov. 4, 1974.
443. *In mid-November: NYT,* Nov. 15, 1976.
446. *Then he walked out:* Lewis and Wally were later reconciled. The former chairman presented his old boss with a blue flag displaying a white Pegasus in the center.

Chapter 21: The Fab Four

Interviews: Allen, Blank, Canfield, Cole, Cox, Cross, Hard, April Herbert, Roy Herbert, Hunt, Johnson, Chris Kirby, Mary Kirby, Lawton, Bruce Lee, McGowan, Morgan, Murphy, O'Hara, Paul, Raw, Dorrie Schreiner, Samuel A. Schreiner, Shuman, Edward T. Thompson, Nancy Cale Thompson, Susie Jacobson Thompson, Wilson, Zinsser. **Other:** Notes and memorandums of Betty Johnston, Edward T. Thompson, DeWitt Wallace.

450. *The only newsworthy item: NYT,* Sept. 20, 1976. In Feb. 1983 the *Digest* published an article carrying the joint bylines of the two former presidents in which they claimed that the occupation of the West Bank and Gaza Strip by the Israeli government was "the major obstacle to any moderate, Arab initiatives" for peace in the Middle East (*NYT,* Jan. 28, 1983). First reader Ronald Reagan publicly agreed with the article (*NYT,* Jan. 14, 1983).

457. *Subsequently, the president's widow: NYT,* June 26, 1977.

457. *His personal physician: NYT,* June 27, 1977. See also *NYT,* June 28 and 29, 1977.

457. *The use of filler material:* Though some foreign editions had their own filler programs, all such material was processed through the Pleasantville office. In 1978 the U.S. edition itself used only fifty-four items, which had originated in twelve different international editions.

457. *By far, though: NYT,* March 10, 1978, March 20, 1979.

The March 1976 issue of the *RD* carried the single most expensive print advertisement in publishing history—a 48-page behemoth reaching "only" 7,275,000 subscribers. A guide to bicentennial celebrations and paid for by the Bicentennial Commission of Pennsylvania, the advertisement cost $1.28 million. Previous titleholders, recorded in the *Guinness Book of Records,* were a 40-page, $950,000 insert from Uniroyal and a 36-page, $877,000 insert from Ford, both of which also ran in the *Digest* (*NYT,* Feb. 19, Nov. 9, 1976).

Chapter 22: Cold War Hothouse

Books: Philip Agee, *Inside the Company: CIA Diary* (New York: Stonewall, 1975); idem, *Dirty Work: The CIA in Western Europe* (New York: Dorset Press, 1978); John Barron, *KGB: The Secret Work of Soviet Secret Agents* (New York: E. P. Dutton/Reader's Digest Press, 1974); *The Bulgarian Connection: Verbatim Report from the International Meeting of Journalists Held in Sofia on February 7, 1985* (Sofia: Sofia Press, 1985); James Bamford, *The Puzzle Palace: A Report on America's Most Secret Agency* (Boston: Houghton Mifflin, 1982); Sidney Blumenthal, *The Rise of the Counter-Establishment: From Conservative Ideology to Political Power* (New York: Times Books, 1986); Raymond Bonner, *Waltzing with a Dictator: The Marcoses and the Making of American Policy* (New York: Times Books, 1987); Howard Bray, *The Pillars of the 'Post': The Making of a News Empire in Washington* (New York: W. W. Norton, 1980); Ronald I. Brownstein and N. Easton, *Reagan's Ruling Class: Portraits of the President's Top 100 Officials* (Washington, D.C.: Presidential Accountability Group, 1982); William E. Burrows, *Deep Black: Space Espionage and National Security* (New York: Random House, 1986); Bertram Cross, *Friendly Fascism: The New Face of Power in America* (New York: M. Evans, 1989); Donner, *The Age of Surveillance;* Edward Jay Epstein, *Deception: The Invisible War between the KGB and the CIA* (New York: Simon & Schuster, 1989); idem, *Legend: The Secret World of Lee Harvey Oswald* (New York: McGraw-Hill, 1978); Ernest B. Ferguson, *Hard Right: The Rise of Jesse Helms* (New York: W. W. Norton, 1986); Larry Gurwin, *The Calvi Affair* (London: Macmillan, 1983); Paul Henze, *The Plot to Kill the Pope* (New York: Scribner's, 1983); Seymour Hersh, *The Price of Power* (New York: Summit Books, 1983); Warren Hinckle and William Turner, *The Fish Is Red: The Story of the Secret War against Castro* (New York: Harper & Row, 1981); Vladislav Krasnov, *Soviet Defectors: The KGB Wanted List* (Stanford: Hoover Institution Press, 1985); Martin A. Lee and Norman Solomon, *Unreliable Sources: A Guide to Detecting Bias in News Media* (New York: Carol Publishing Group, 1990); Julius Mader, *Who's Who in the CIA* (Berlin: Militärverlag der Deutschen Demokratischen Republik, 1968); Tom Mangold, *Cold Warrior: James Jesus Angleton: The CIA's Master Spy Hunter* (New York: Simon & Schuster, 1991); Victor Marchetti, *The CIA and the Cult of Intelligence* (New York: Knopf, 1974); Vitali Petrusenko, *A Dangerous Game: CIA and the Mass Media* (Prague: Interpress, 1977); S. Steven Powell, *Covert Cadre: Inside the Institute for Policy Studies* (New York: Jameson Books, 1987); John Ranelagh, *The Agency* (New York: Simon & Schuster, 1986); Beth Day Romulo, *Inside the Palace: The Rise and Fall of Ferdinand & Imelda Marcos* (New York: Putnam, 1987); Scheim, *Contract on America;* Claire Sterling, *The Secret War of International Terrorism* (New York: Holt, Rinehart and Winston/Reader's Digest Press, 1981); Christopher Simpson, *Blowback: America's Recruitment of Nazis and Its Effects on the Cold War* (New York: Weidenfeld & Nicolson, 1988); James L. Tyson, *Target America: The Influence of Communist Propaganda on U.S. Media* (Chicago: Regnery Gateway, 1981); David Wise, *Molehunt: The Secret Search for Traitors That Shattered the CIA* (New York: Random House, 1992). **Articles:** Seymour Hersh, "The Angleton Story," *NYT Magazine,* July 25, 1978; Brock Brower, "Spying's Dirty Little Secret," *Money,* July 1987; Edward Jay Epstein, "The Spy Who Came in to Be Sold," *TNR,* July 15–22, 1985; Fred Landis, "The CIA and the Reader's Digest," *Covert Action Information Bulletin,* Winter 1988; Michael Ledeen, "The Bulgarian Connection and the Media," *Commentary,* June 1983; Rudy Maxa, "Spy Wars," *Playboy,* Sept. 1987; Milton Mayer, "Professor from Pleasantville," *Progressive,* Nov. 1982; Conor Cruise O'Brien, "The Roots of Terrorism," *TNR,* July 25, 1981; Anthony Paul, "The Soviets' Afghan Quagmire," *World Press Review,* July 1980; Edward Teller, "On Facts and Hopes," *Bulletin of Atomic Scientists,* April 1983; Joseph Sobran, "Poisoning Trust," *National Review,* July 8, 1983; Kathleen Tyman, "The Seeds of a New Journalism," *Washington Times,* June 20, 1984; Michael Wines, "Cold-War Riddle: A Most Unusual Spy," *NYT,* Jan. 23, 1990; "The Great Superpower Spy War: KGB vs. CIA," *U.S. News & World Report,* Oct. 29, 1984. See also, passim, *Lobster: A Who's Who of the British Secret State, CovertAction Information Bulletin (CAIB), CounterSpy.* **Interviews:** Allen, Cox, Gordon Hard, Roy Herbert, Hunt, Chris Kirby, Bruce Lee, Edie Lewis, Hobart Durkin Lewis, McGowan, Morgan, Rhodes, Paul, Samuel A. Schreiner, Edward T. Thompson, Paul W. Thompson, Waters. **Other:** CIAbase, Namebase; *Reader's Digest Association* v. *Federal Bureau of Investigation, Central Intelligence Agency, United States Department of Justice* (civil action file 79 Civ. 4812), U.S. District Court, Southern District of New York; "Fred Landis Digests *Selecciones,* " Paper Tiger Television, n.d.; Dave Emory/Nip Tuck Archive Tapes, "Who Shot the Pope?," pts. 1–5. **Remarks:** An FOIA request to the CIA for its files on DeWitt Wallace and on the *RD* was denied, as was an appeal.

471. *In October 1977:* "CIA and the Media: How America's Most Powerful News Media Worked Hand in Glove with the Central Intelligence Agency and Why the Church Committee Covered It Up," *Rolling Stone,* Oct. 20, 1977.

473. *Besides Terence Harmon:* After World War II the *RD* was also seriously involved in negotiations to hire Archie Roosevelt as an editor of its Arabic edition. A cousin of Franklin Delano and a prominent member of the American intelligence community, Roosevelt chose the newly founded CIA instead. See Archie Roosevelt, *For Lust of Knowing: Memoirs of an Intelligence Officer* (Boston: Little, Brown, 1988), pp. 203, 231.

473. *. . . notably Dennis McEvoy:* Schreiner, *The Condensed World of the Reader's Digest,* pp. 183–84.

473. *. . . . André Visson:* Landis, "The CIA and the Reader's Digest," *CovertAction Information Bulletin,* Winter 1988, p. 42.

474. *In 1975 journalist Edward Hughes: NYT,* Aug. 3, 1975.

474. *But two journalists: NYT,* March 27, 1976.

475. *The* New York Times: Sept. 12 and 13, Oct. 7, Dec. 25, 26, 27, and 28, 1977.

476. *Among Barron's early articles . . .* " While on the *Star* Barron had covered the Senate investigation into President Johnson's influence-peddling aide Bobby Baker, who routinely bought favors from politicians with bribes and call girls. Among the most vocal of Baker's critics was Senator John J. Williams of Delaware. When opponents of Williams began circulating a story credited to Baker's private secretary Carole Tyler that Williams had been seen in a roadside diner with a young lady, Barron responded with an *RD* article defending Williams against the charge ("She was my granddaughter," Williams claimed). Since potential witnesses against Baker were fearful of being similarly smeared, the article was given national play in the press. See *NYT,* Aug. 25, 1965.

476. *The information had been leaked:* Interview with Anthony Paul.

476. *The* New York Times*: . . . NYT,* Dec. 25, 1977.

477. *In June 1979: NYT,* June 27, 1979.

478. *An exception: NYT,* April 15, 1976.

479. *On each of the appointed days:* Interview with Anthony Paul.

481. *In a postmortem: Harper's,* June 1982.

483. *The* New York Times *implied:* Feb. 27, 1982.

483. *The* Nation *responded:* March 13, 1982.

484. *While Ford was still: NYT,* March 9, 10, and 23, 1977. Laster also succeeded Helen Strauss as agent for James Michener.

485. *Ford's former press secretary: NYT,* May 25, 1977.

485. *Winthrop Knowlton: NYT,* April 4, May 24, 1979. See also *NYT,* Jan. 28, 1982.

486. *The case, tried in U.S. district court:* NYT, Jan. 25 and 28, 1982, Feb. 18, 1983.

486. *In February 1983:* NYT, Feb. 18, 1983; *Time* Feb. 28, 1983.

486. *In an editorial protesting:* July 9–16, 1983.

486. *In another editorial:* March 5, 1983.

486. *In November: Newsweek,* Nov. 28, 1983.

486. *In May 1985:* NYT, May 21, 1985. See also NYT, May 30, 1984.

489. *Epstein then contacted:* Epstein, *Deception,* pp. 18–20.

489. *Unknown to Epstein:* Epstein, *Legend,* prologue, passim; Epstein, *Deception,* p. 294. After he was released from prison by the CIA, Nosenko was hired by the RD as a "counterintelligence consultant" (Epstein, *Deception,* p. 62).

490. *After ridiculing Shevchenko's:* Epstein, "The Spy Who Came in to Be Sold," *TNR,* July 15–22, 1985.

490. *. . . its trial run in a 1983 book:* NYT, April 14, 1983. In a letter to the editor of *TNR,* cited by Epstein, Barron later protested he did not know that Levchenko was in the control of the CIA.

491. *In an arrangement:* Barron later protested he was unaware that Levchenko was under CIA control. But as Epstein pointed out, "the fact remains that Levchenko did deliver CIA secrets to Barron (including the identity and recruitment of three CIA clandestine agents) when he was under CIA parole. This means that Levchenko could have been arbitrarily deported, without any redress, if he made a wrong move, or otherwise displeased the CIA. He then very possibly might have faced a Soviet firing squad."

491. *Barron, for whatever reason:* Epstein, "The Spy Who Came in to Be Sold."

491. *That same year: Atlanta Journal,* June 5, 1983.

492. *In a subsequent book-length account:* Claire Sterling, *The Time of the Assassins: Anatomy of an Investigation* (New York: Holt, Rinehart and Winston, 1983).

493. *At first Sterling's article:* NYT, Aug. 17, 1982. Sterling was quoted as saying she had spent not nine but four months investigating the shooting. In its statement, the Soviet Union declared, "The absurdity and unfoundedness of this claim are obvious." See NYT, Aug. 19, 1982.

493. *On December 16:* "Cross in the Cross Hairs," NYT, Dec. 16, 1982.

493. *Two days later:* "The Assassin's Trail of Blood," NYT, Dec. 18, 1982.

493. *Six weeks later:* NYT, Jan. 27, 1983.

494. *Ed Thompson later wrote:* NYT, Feb. 7, 1983.

Chapter 23: God Is My Copublisher

Books: *The Reader's Digest Bible: Condensed from the Revised Standard Version of Old and New Testaments,* ed. Bruce M. Metzger (Pleasantville: Reader's Digest Association, 1982); John S. Saloma, *Ominous Politics: The New Conservative Labyrinth* (New York: Hill & Wang, 1984). **Articles:** Joseph H. Cooper, "Election Commission, Editorial Campaigns Are Not Your Province," NYT, Feb. 15, 1981; William Griffin, "Condensing the Bible," *Publishers Weekly,* May 21, 1982; "Article Denounced," *Christian Century,* Aug. 18–25, 1982; "Ecumenical Agencies under Attack," *Christian Century,* Sept. 1–8,

1982; "Reader's Digest Attacks World Church Council," *Christianity Today,* Sept. 3, 1982; "Streamlined Bible Begets a Storm," *U.S. News & World Report,* Oct. 4, 1982; Paul Albrecht, "Ecumenical Illiteracy in the 'Reader's Digest,' " *Christian Century,* Nov. 24, 1982; Robert McAfee Brown, "Laughter in Pleasantville: A Fable," *Christian Century,* Feb. 2–9, 1983. **Interviews:** Hard, Edward T. Thompson, Zinsser. **Other:** "Response to Reader's Digest Article, 'Karl Marx or Jesus Christ,' August 1982," official response of World Council of Churches, n.d.

497. *In a brief item: NYT,* Jan. 5, 1979.

497. *The* Times *even weighed in:* "The Bible, in Brief," Sept. 19, 1981. A favorable second editorial, "So Saith the Lord, Briefly," appeared on Sept. 29, 1982, following the book's publication.

497. *In a humorless letter: NYT,* Oct. 6, 1981.

499. *In September 1982: NYT,* Sept. 22, 1982.

499. Newsweek*'s religion editor:* Oct. 4, 1982. See also *NYT,* Nov. 29, 1981.

501. *Barron's story:* Theodore H. White, *America in Search of Itself* (New York: Harper & Row, 1982), pp. 276–77; Davis, *The Kennedys,* pp. 581, 590–91, 597; Max Lerner, *Ted and the Kennedy Legend: A Study in Character and Destiny* (New York: St. Martin's Press, 1980), pp. 111–12. See also *NYT,* June 16 and 19, 1980, Feb. 15, 16, and 24, March 20, July 14, 1981; *Time,* Feb. 23, 1981.

501. *Among the six unmarried women:* Including Catherine Powell ("beautiful and a Democrat," in the words of a colleague), a Washington-based *Digest* researcher who refused to help prepare the hatchet job.

505. *. . . West had administered:* Alan W. Scheflin and Edward M. Opton, *The Mind Manipulators* (New York and London: Paddington Press, 1978), p. 149.

507. *To add insult:* The Scientology-RD feud flared up again in Oct. 1991 when the magazine reprinted a *Time* cover story on the organization that had been published the previous May. This time, though, Scientology sued the *Digest* not in the United States but in France, where the reprint had appeared in *Sélection* and where libel laws tended to be less favorable to the media. See *New York,* Feb. 3, 1992.

In another suit involving the *Digest* and a controversial, cultlike organization, the California State Supreme Court ruled on Nov. 20, 1984, for the first time, that journalists could sometimes withhold confidential sources and unpublished information supplied by such sources. The ruling grew out of a libel action by Synanon, a drug-rehabilitation group, and its founder Charles E. Dederich. In July 1982 the *Digest* had published an article by David MacDonald describing how two reporters for the *Point Reyes Light,* a California newspaper, had won a Pulitzer Prize for their series of articles critical of Synanon. Dederich had contended that three sentences in the *RD* article were defamatory. The libel suit was thrown out of court. See *NYT,* Nov. 21, 1984.

507. *In the November elections:* Politicians in Texas demanded that, if the reports were accurate, the FBI expose the movement's leaders as "godless aggressors." Neither the CIA nor the FBI would allege that Soviet agents manipulated the nuclear-freeze movement. See Ronnie Dugger, *On Reagan: The Man and His Presidency* (New York: McGraw-Hill, 1983), pp. 281–84.

509. *On December 6:* Kitty Kelley, *Nancy Reagan: The Unauthorized Biography* (New York: Simon & Schuster, 1991), p. 413.

509. *The next year Reagan: WP,* Sept. 3, 1982; "Dyspepsia Time," *National Review,* Oct. 29, 1982.

512. *It was a simple:* But one with a suspiciously unpious curiosity in the preternatural. Articles on the Bermuda triangle, UFO's, and other "unexplained mysteries" were common fare. The *Digest's* excerpt of Ruth Montgomery's *A Gift of Prophecy* on so-called seer Jeane Dixon catapulted the book into best-sellerdom and transformed Dixon, a New Jersey realtor, into an international celebrity. Complaints from the *RD's* fundamentalist readers about the magazine's longtime fascination with the occult were numerous.

In 1977 a group called the Committee for the Scientific Investigation of Claims of the Paranormal, whose members included scientists, philosophers, and others concerned about the rising tide of uncritical belief in astrology and parapsychology, excoriated the *Digest* for presenting paranormal subjects as if they were scientifically credible. Milbourne Christopher, a magician and member of the committee, noted that some two hundred people were known to have killed themselves as a result of believing an unfavorable horoscope, palm reading, or other alleged forecast of the future. Another member, James Randi, cited thousands of dollars spent by sick people who flew to the Philippines to undergo "psychic surgery." See *NYT,* Aug. 10, 1977. The magazine's resident expert on magic was senior editor Dan O'Keefe, author of *Stolen Lightning: The Social Theory of Magic* (New York: Continuum, 1982), a work of consummate scholarship, encyclopedic range, and zero readability.

513. *Back in 1971: RD,* Oct. and Nov. 1971.

514. Newsweek: Feb. 7, 1983.

514. *. . . columnist Colman McCarthy: WP,* Feb. 27, 1983.

514. *Not much was known:* Kathleen Schultz, "An Analysis of the Christian Left in the United States," *Monthly Review,* July–Aug. 1984.

Chapter 24: You Will Receive $1.75 Million

Correspondence: Mary Louise Allin, DeWitt Wallace. **Interviews:** Cole, Cross, Davies, Fuller, Grossman, Hunt, Mary Kirby, Edie Lewis, Hobart Durkin Lewis, Little, Lund, McGowan, McHenry, Morgan, Murphy, O'Hara, Romulo, Samuel A. Schreiner, Smith, Edward T. Thompson. **Articles:** Nat Hentoff columns in the *Village Voice* for Nov. 7 and 14, 1982. **Other:** Notes and memorandums of DeWitt Wallace, Lila Acheson Wallace.

519. *The contest between: NYT,* July 12, 1975.

521. *The highest-ranking woman:* In Oct. 1968 Wally the benevolent headmaster of the People's University circulated a memo asking his younger editors to tell him what they did over the summer vacation. Allin, then an associate editor, responded with a handwritten parody of a child's essay written in block letters titled "How I Spent My Summer Vacation." It can also be read as an unwitting

parody of Digestese and a chilling example of female submission to Pleasantville patriarchalism. The essay recounted Allin's visit to Block Island, Rhode Island, with her "mommy and daddy." Every afternoon, she wrote, "we went down to see the people and other animals get off the boat. One day it rained and we all stayed inside and argued. Then it was time to leave." A delighted Wally scribbled back, "This is a great improvement over your messy lesson last week. . . . Perhaps the switching I had to administer then explains the differences."

525. *On November 5:* The next day the *Times* also ran an editorial applauding the settlement.
526. *Another lawsuit: NYT,* March 24, 1977.
526. *The chances of winning: NYT,* Feb. 1, 1981.
526. *As of February 1977: NYT,* Feb. 6, 1977.
527. *Despite the ubiquity: NYT,* July 4, 1980; *WP,* July 8, 1980.
527. *The RDA then took: WP,* Jan. 19, 1982.
527. *In October 1983: Federal Register,* Oct. 25, 1983; *WP,* Oct. 26, 1983.

Chapter 25: The Men Who Would Be King

Correspondence: Cuyler MacRae. **Interviews:** Allen, Cole, Davies, Fuller, Grossman, Hard, Roy Herbert, Hunt, Chris Kirby, Mary Kirby, Lawton, Bruce Lee, Hobart Durkin Lewis, Little, McHenry, Miller, Morgan, O'Hara, Paul, Rhodes, Samuel A. Schreiner, Strand, Edward T. Thompson, Susie Jacobson Thompson, Paul W. Thompson, Waters, Wilson, Zinsser.

534. *Employees also continued:* In Dec. 1968 Wally resurrected his old idea of a four-day week. Against the strenuous objections of business manager Paul Thompson, he decreed that henceforth the company's employees, now numbering 2,800, were to have every Friday off in May. See *NYT,* Dec. 2, 1968.
535. *. . . with the exception:* "Reader's Digest: Modernizing the Beat of a Different Drummer," *BW,* March 5, 1979.
537. *Added to all that: NYT,* March 15, 1968.
537. *In January 1980: NYT,* Jan. 14, 1980.
538. *Soon after the RDA: NYT,* June 4, Sept. 24, 1980.
538. *After getting the go-ahead: NYT,* April 17, Sept. 5, Nov. 14, 1980, May 22, 1981; *Writer's Digest,* Dec. 1980.
539. *Twenty-one months: NYT,* April 28, 1982.
539. *While* Families *was being launched: NYT,* Sept. 25, 1980, April 14, 1981.
540. *. . . and in March 1983: NYT,* March 22, 1983.

Chapter 26: The Final Condensation

Books: Henry Hurt, *Reasonable Doubt: An Investigation into the Assassination of John F. Kennedy* (New York: Holt, Rinehart and Winston, 1985); *From: the President: Richard Nixon's Secret Files,* ed. Bruce Oudes (New York: Harper & Row, 1989). **Articles:** "The Reader's Digest Story," *Buffalo News,* March 26, 1983. **Correspondence:** Edward T. Thompson. **Interviews:** Allen, Cox, Cross, Davies, Fuller, Hard, Roy Herbert, Hunt, Johnson, Chris Kirby, Mary Kirby, Doris Konig, Little, McGowan, McHenry, Morgan, O'Hara, Paul, Dorrie Schreiner, Samuel A. Schreiner, Strand, Edward T. Thompson, Susie Jacobson Thompson, Wilson, Zinsser. **Other:** Notes and memorandums of Kenneth O. Gilmore, George V. Grune, John A. O'Hara, Fulton Oursler, Jr., Edward T. Thompson; eulogies of DeWitt Wallace and Lila Acheson Wallace delivered by Norman Vincent Peale.

542. *O'Hara's paranoia:* A chill also ran through Pleasantville in the spring of 1980 when retired senior editor Eleanor Prouty, sixty-seven, was raped and strangled and her invalid husband severely beaten. Two teenagers from nearby Lincoln Hall, a correctional institution, were later charged with the killing. Prouty had hired them on a work-release program, and they mistakenly believed she kept large amounts of cash in the house. See *NYT,* May 26, 27, and 28, June 6, July 8, 9, and 16, Aug. 8 and 24, 1980.

542. *. . . and a bomb: NYT,* May 30, 1982.

544. *The following year:* Wally grew almost completely deaf and lost most of his sight in his last years and probably also suffered from incipient Alzheimer's, to judge from anecdotal evidence—including loss of "present memory." Friends took him four times to see the musical *Evita* because he could never remember having seen it.

545. *In the* New York Times: April 1, 1981. See also *WP,* April 1, 1981.

547. *. . . Wally had once facetiously proposed: Time,* April 13, 1981.

547. *A week after Wally's death: NYT,* April 5, 1981.

547. *As usual, though:* George Seldes, "DeWitt Wallace—The Story Money Couldn't Buy," *Nation,* May 23, 1981.

551. *In the grand Wallace tradition: NYT,* April 14, 1982.

553. *All this time: Patent Trader,* Jan. 13, 1984.

553. *Only recently: NYT,* Jan. 12, 1983.

556. *In descending order:* In *Iacocca: An Autobiography* (New York: Bantam, 1984), ghosted by *RD* roving editor Robert Novak, Chrysler chairman Lee Iacocca admitted he looked up the list of words in "Enrich Your Word Power" in every issue (p. 16).

560. *But the bitter Thompson: U.S.A. Today,* March 27, 1984. The press-release version of Thompson's "resignation" was announced in the May 26, 1984, issue of the *NYT,* and the next day in the *WP.* But as word of all the turmoil in Pleasantville spread, some of the news stories began to dig deeper: "At Reader's Digest, a Fight over Philosophy," *NYT,* June 1, 1984; Roy Rowan, "Intrigue behind the Ivy at Reader's Digest," *Fortune,* June 25, 1984; Miriam Lacob, "Reader's Digest: Who's in Charge?," *CJR,* July–Aug. 1984; "Editor's Dyspepsia," *Economist,* July 2, 1984; *Advertising Age,* Dec. 3, 1984.

563. *On Friday, May 4: NYT,* May 9, 1984; *GWN,* May 10, 1984.

563. *Only minutes earlier:* The official cause of death was cardiac arrhythmia resulting from atherosclerotic heart disease. Lila's date of birth was incorrectly stated on the death certificate as Dec. 25, 1887; she was in fact born on Christmas Day of the following year.

563. *The passing of Lila: NYT,* May 9, 1984. See also Nancy Q. Keefe, "Lila Wallace: A Most Ironic Character," *GWN,* May 1, 1984.

Chapter 27: The Hidden Hand

Articles: Lee Smith, "The Unsentimental Corporate Giver," *Fortune,* Sept. 1981; Geoffrey Thompson, "What's Ahead for Reader's Digest?," *GWN,* May 13, 1984; Geoffrey Thompson, "Reader's Digest: A Whole New Story," *GWN,* July 7, 1985; Edwin McDowell, "Why the Digest, Finally, Wants to Make Money," *NYT,* Feb. 9, 1986. **Interviews:** Allen, Canfield, Cross, George V. Grune, Hunt, Johnson, Lawton, Little, McGowan, McHenry, Morgan, O'Hara, Rink, Strand, Edward T. Thompson, Susie Jacobson Thompson, Wilson, Zinsser. **Other:** Notes and memorandums of John M. Allen, George V. Grune, Walter B. Mahony, Jr.

568. *Another headache:* Many veteran Digesters were concerned that McHenry was going through the files of DeWitt and Lila Wallace, destroying some pages and sending the rest to Macalester College. In a confidential memo dated Dec. 11, 1984, to Condensed Books head John S. Zinsser, public affairs assistant Irmgard Monsees grumbled, "WBMcH has decreed that we send him all the DW archives. . . . He promised to have someone go through them for 'historical interest' stating that such stuff would not be destroyed. However, experience has proven otherwise. . . . I can't help but feel that an untold story will be forever lost. . . . I feel very strongly that the DW archives should remain with the parent company forever—Amen!"

Former executive editor Bun Mahony also met with Ken Gilmore on a Sunday afternoon at company headquarters and demanded to know by what authority (a clause in either DeWitt or Lila's will? a vote of the trustees?) McHenry was disposing of the papers to Macalester; and how a deadline of Jan. 7, 1985, for delivery of Wally's papers was justified.

Dorothy Little, Lila's former personal secretary, took it upon herself to destroy virtually all of Lila's files and correspondence, deeming them "purely personal." Whether and what parts of DeWitt Wallace's files were destroyed by McHenry—who no doubt was likewise acting solely in his former employer's best interests—cannot be ascertained. Ultimately, the remnants of Wally's papers—a jumble of notes, letters, office memorandums—were tossed into several cartons, which were then posted to Macalester College Library. There the boxes were shelved away, uncataloged and half forgotten by a college seemingly uncertain whether it wanted the honor of being the repository of the papers of its greatest benefactor.

569. *Nine of the cash-hungry charities:* The shares of nonvoting common stock owned by RDA stockholders were broken down as follows, according to the 1990 prospectus the RDA offered to the public:

NAME	NO. OF SHARES	% OF CLASS
DeWitt Wallace Reader's Digest Fund	17,785,040	18.19
Lila Wallace Reader's Digest Fund	11,444,960	11.70
Metropolitan Museum of Art	11,768,480	11.42
Lincoln Center	11,000,000	11.25
Macalester College	10,270,000	10.50
Community Funds	10,110,000	10.34
Hudson Highlands	9,500,000	9.72
Colonial Williamsburg	5,000,000	5.11
New York Zoologicial Society	5,000,000	5.11
Sloan-Kettering Cancer Center	4,000,000	4.09
Jenkins & Co., Nominee for Macalester College	360,000	—

580. *A year and a half later:* NYT, Sept. 5, 1984. Publication ceased with the June 1985 issue.

580. *The RDA also sold:* NYT, Sept. 17, 1985.

581. *But when the Reader's Digest:* NYT, Dec. 26, 1985.

581. *At the heart of the dispute:* Memorandum from the American embassy in Tokyo to the secretary of state, April 1989.

581. *The RDJ claimed, too:* Memorandum from the American embassy in Tokyo to the secretary of state, Jan. 1986.

581. *That did not deter:* Sunday Telegraph (London), March 25, 1990. To eke out a subsistence living, Japanese Digesters busied themselves publishing a monthly newssheet and selling through direct mail such un-*Digest*-like items as noodles, toys, and fireworks.

581. *In the summer of 1985:* NYT, June 26, 1985.

582. *Grune also hosted:* GWN, Dec. 17, 1985.

582. *In January 1986:* NYT, Sept. 10, 1985; Folio, Nov. 1985.

582. *One London media director:* Kevin Cote, " 'Digest' Wrestles with Local Image," *Advertising Age,* Dec. 3, 1984.

583. *Like the more than:* WSJ, Aug. 18, 1986.

585. *His place was taken:* Under the extraordinarily energetic and far-sighted leadership of DeVita (later promoted to president), and with the obvious blessing of Grune and the board, the rechristened Lila Acheson Wallace Reader's Digest Fund emerged in 1992 as the leading funder for the arts in the United States, surpassing both the Andrew W. Mellon Foundation and the Pew Charitable Trusts, with grants amounting to $32 million in fiscal year 1991 (*NYT,* April 2, 1992). The fund's generosity was matched by a conspicuous absence of both conservative ideology and clannish beau monde provincialism.

585. *"[Mrs. Wallace's] vision:* WSJ, March 17, 1987.

Chapter 28: *Semper* Fido

Books and articles: See the bibliography for chapter 22. See also Carl T. Rowan, *Breaking Barriers: A Memoir* (Boston: Little, Brown, 1991); Kenneth Y. Tomlinson, "VOA Needs a Real American Accent," *WSJ,* March 28, 1988; Mitch Broder, "Did You Hear the One . . . ," *GWN,* March 5, 1990; John Summa, "Reader's Digest Condenses Africa: A Continent Reduced to Right-Wing Clichés," *Extra!* July–Aug. 1991; "Magazine Personality and Publishing Power: Interview with Kenneth O. Gilmore," *Media Management Monograph,* Aug. 1986. **Interviews:** Allen, Blank, Cox, Cross, Hard, Roy Herbert, Hunt, Johnson, Chris Kirby, Mary Kirby, Lawton, Hobart Durkin Lewis, McGowan, Morgan, Murphy, Parker, Paul, Rae, Samuel A. Schreiner, Strand, Edward T. Thompson, Wilson, Zinsser. **Other:** Notes and memorandums of George V. Grune, Bruce S. Trachtenberg.

588. *The formula:* The *Digest*'s primal xenophobia was also as virulent as ever. In June 1985 the magazine published "America's Refugee Mess," by Jane Hamilton-Merritt, a "consultant"—a term broad enough to include part-time outside free-lance writers—to the U.S. coordinator for refugee affairs with the Department of State. A freewheeling attack on the bureaucratization and policies of the American refugee program, particularly in Southeast Asia, the article outraged not only many in the refugee field but also eight U.S. senators, including Ohio Democrat John Glenn and Oregon's two Republican senators, Mark Hatfield and Bob Packwood. Soon after the article appeared, the eight cosigned a letter to President Reagan demanding that, as a result of the article, he relieve Ambassador Eugene Douglas of his duties as U.S. coordinator for refugee affairs. While allowing that there was room for improvement in the U.S. resettlement program, they characterized the *Digest* article as an "assassination of the refugee program . . . prepared by an individual on the payroll of the Coordinator's office." The article itself was decried as a "smear of the integrity, motivation, and patriotism of tens of thousands of Americans who have worked with or within the voluntary agencies . . . and [is] thoroughly shameful." In conclusion, the senators suggested that Reagan "relieve Ambassador Douglas of his official duties before his wrecking ball swings wildly again at the very programs [Reagan was] admirably committed to maintain." Douglas, who had already been making plans to leave office, resigned soon afterward.

588. *. . . uplifting sermonettes:* The *Digest* was also still prone to occasional church bashing. With the Wallaces now dead, it turned its holier-than-thou wrath on the Presbyterian church itself, accusing its leadership in the Dec. 1990 issue of being "out of step" with its congregations because it had embraced religious and political liberalism. Disgruntled author John S. Tompkins, an elder of the Madison Avenue Presbyterian Church, in Manhattan, claimed people were "fed up" with such liberal tendencies as the elimination of militaristic or sexist hymns, challenges to U.S. military policies, and the substitution of "social, economic and political action for the real business of religion" (*sic*).

592. *In his prepared speech:* NYT, May 5, 6, and 7, 1985.
595. *His reappearance:* NYT, Sept. 19, 1984.
595. *A month after:* NYT, Oct. 13, Nov. 22, 1984.
595. *Bitov wrote:* Transcript of BBC broadcast, March 11, 1985.
596. *The latter eventually furnished:* (Mexico City: Ediciones Océano, 1983).
597. *Five years later:* NYT, June 15, 1989.
597. *The newspaper charged: Excelsior,* Oct. 12, 1987.
597. *The story led: Dallas Morning News,* Nov. 19, 1987.
597. *James, who had admitted:* NYT, Dec. 25, 1977.
601. *The pair cited:* Bob Woodward, *Veil: The Secret Wars of the CIA, 1981–1987* (New York: Simon & Schuster, 1987), p. 487.
602. *During Walker's trial:* In *Breaking the Ring* (Boston: Houghton Mifflin, 1987), pp. 138ff., Barron described how KGB security officer, and later defector, Vitaly Yurchenko regularly met with FBI agents in Washington, D.C., from 1975 to 1980 at a restaurant called Danker's, on E Street. An "unofficial spokesman for the FBI," Barron himself often sat in on those friendly chats. See Allen and Polmar, *Merchants of Treason,* p. 76.
602. *He also testified:* "[Barron] played an important role in the FBI effort to publicize the official story about John Walter. . . . Barron was so much a part of the prosecution team at the Whitworth trial that Assistant U.S. Attorney William Farmer asked that Barron be allowed to sit with the team during the trial. The judge turned down the request." Allen and Polmar, *Merchants of Treason,* p. 234.
603. *What Barron did not reveal:* Letter of J. Edward Fox, assistant secretary, Legislative and Intergovernmental Affairs, U.S. Department of State, dated Sept. 2, 1987, to Senator Dennis DeConcini, Democrat of Arizona.

Chapter 29: No Business like CEO Business

Book: Ben Cheever, *The Plagiarist* (New York: Atheneum, 1992). **Articles:** Chuck Reece, "Reader's Digest Is Out to Acquire . . . Pleasantly," *Adweek,* July 22, 1985; Scott Donaton, "Reader's Digest Jumps on Fast Track," *Advertising Age,* Oct. 9, 1989; Patrick M. Reilly, "Reader's Digest Breaks 67-Year Silence," *WSJ,* Dec. 20, 1989; Mark Land, "Reader's Digest," *GWN,* April 22, 1990; "The Man Who Rewrote Reader's Digest," *BW,* June 4, 1990; Randall Rothenberg, "Junk Mail's Top Dogs, *NYT Magazine,* Aug. 5, 1990; "Pulp Profits," *Economist,* Oct. 20, 1990. **Interviews:** Cross, George V. Grune, O'Hara, Edward T. Thompson, Zinsser.

607. *But there was another:* "A Tempting Target," *Forbes,* April 18, 1988.
608. *In December 1986:* NYT, Dec. 19, 1986.
609. *Despite its huge circulation: WSJ,* March 26, 1989. On the other hand, with 50.3 million readers, the *RD* boasted an advertising market second in size only to that of Bill Cosby's television show, the perennial prime-time front-runner in the late 1980s.
610. *One belated: WSJ,* Sept. 7, 1989.
611. *Financial details: Washington Times,* Dec. 12, 20, 1989.

612. *In a review: BW,* June 4, 1990.

614. *By now, Gordon Grossman's gimmick:* "The Sweepstakes Binge," *Newsweek,* Jan. 23, 1984.

615. *In March 1992: NYT,* Sept. 2, 1991.

615. *When advertisers failed: NYT,* July 25, 1972.

615. *The forum he chose: Nation,* May 7, 1990.

616. *What makes the loss:* Grune's compensation in 1990 was $1,965,000.

616. *Two weeks later: Nation,* May 21, 1990.

Chapter 30: The *Digest* Condensed

Interviews: Davies, McHenry, Morgan, O'Hara, Edward T. Thompson, Paul W. Thompson, Wilson.

622. *In April 1983: NYT,* April 6, 1983. In Oct. 1992 the DeWitt Wallace Reader's Digest Foundation donated $40 million to thousands of school libraries in twenty-five cities around the United States—the largest such bequest ever. *NYT,* Oct. 26, 1992.

Who's Who in Pleasantville

[Condensed Version]

Barclay Acheson Brother of Lila Acheson Wallace; ordained Presbyterian minister who later became the first head of the RDA's international division.

John Allen Senior editor and son-in-law of Norman Vincent Peale.

John Barron Roving editor in the Washington bureau with close ties to the FBI and CIA.

Jack Beaudouin Second editor in chief of Condensed Books, succeeding Ralph Henderson.

Albert Leslie Cole The *Digest*'s fourth business manager and the man most responsible, after DeWitt Wallace, for building the RDA empire.

William J. Cross Chief financial officer, later director of administration and finance, and an RDA trustee.

Charles Ferguson Senior editor hired in 1934 who later became DeWitt Wallace's biographer and closest friend.

Victoria ("Victo") Ferguson Wife of Charles Ferguson and mistress of DeWitt Wallace.

Kenneth O. Gilmore Second Washington bureau head, who later became the *Digest*'s fourth editor in chief, succeeding Ed Thompson.

Arthur Griffiths The RDA's third business manager.

Gordon Grossman An RDA marketing strategist and the man who invented the publisher's sweepstakes.

George V. Grune Chairman and CEO of the RDA as of May 1984.

Harold Helm Former Chemical Bank executive and one of the RDA's first two outside trustees.

Ralph Henderson The *Digest*'s first employee, briefly its first business manager, and later founder of Condensed Books.

Joseph Hotchkiss Third editor in chief of Condensed Books, succeeding Jack Beaudouin.

William Kennedy Interior decorator who flourished in New York ca. 1970s and oversaw initial restoration of Boscobel.

Bruce Lee First publisher of the Reader's Digest Press.

Hobart ("Hobe") Durkin Lewis The *Digest*'s second editor in chief, succeeding DeWitt Wallace; also the RDA's first president and CEO.

Harold Lynch The RDA's second business manager, later reassigned to editorial.

Walter B. ("Bun") Mahony Longtime managing and later executive editor of the *Digest*.

W. Barnabas ("Barney") McHenry Corporate counsel of the RDA and also executor of the estate of Lila Acheson Wallace.

Richard F. McLoughlin Former publisher of the *Digest* who in May 1984 became vice-chairman of the RDA.

Barbara Morgan* Fifth editor in chief of Condensed Books, succeeding Zinsser.

Harry Morgan* Protégé of DeWitt Wallace, founder of Ambassadors for Friendship and World Press Institute.

Lucy Notestein Cousin of DeWitt Wallace on his mother's side who began the *RD*'s first excerpt department in Cleveland.

John A. ("Jack") O'Hara British-born RDA marketing executive, later its president.

Fulton ("Tony") Oursler, Jr. Son of Fulton Oursler, Sr., noted Catholic convert and *Digest* contributor; rose to rank of executive editor and briefly served as deputy editor in chief.

Paul Palmer Longtime political adviser to DeWitt Wallace and *Digest* executive editor.

Noel Rae Editor of international division of Condensed Books.

Kenneth Payne The *Digest*'s first managing editor, later its first executive editor.

Kent Rhodes The RDA's longtime head of production, later its chairman.

Laurance S. Rockefeller Conservationist and philanthropist; one of the RDA's first two outside directors.

William Schulz Third head of Washington bureau, succeeding Gilmore; later promoted to managing editor.

Claire Sterling Rome-based roving editor specializing in terrorism.

Charles ("Chuck") Stevenson First head of Washington bureau.

Edward T. Thompson* Editor in chief, 1976–84.

Frederick Thompson* Protégé of Al Cole who married Judy Thompson in 1939.

Julia ("Judy") Thompson Daughter of Barclay Acheson, favorite niece of Lila Acheson Wallace, and wife of Fred Thompson.

Paul Thompson* Former brigadier general who became the first head of the RDA's European operations with headquarters in Paris; brought to Pleasantville to succeed Barclay Acheson, later succeeded Al Cole as business manager.

Kenneth O. Tomlinson Fifth editor in chief of the *RD,* succeeding Gilmore.

DeWitt Wallace Founder of the *Reader's Digest.*

Dr. James Wallace Presbyterian lay preacher, professor of Greek, and father of DeWitt Wallace.

Janet Davis Wallace Mother of DeWitt Wallace.

Miriam Davis Wallace Sister of Janet Wallace, second wife of Dr. James Wallace, and stepmother of DeWitt Wallace.

Lila Acheson Wallace Cofounder of the *Reader's Digest,* wife of DeWitt Wallace, and philanthropist.

Richard Waters Treasurer of the RDA.

Walter Weintz Director of circulation.

Harry Wilcox Manager of RDA buildings and grounds and confidant of Lila Acheson Wallace.

Kenneth Wilson Liaison with New York Publishers for both the *RD* and Condensed Books.

John Wulp Condensed Books editor and the first RDA employee to resign over a matter of conscience.

John S. Zinsser, Jr. First international editor of Condensed Books, later its editor in chief.

---

*None of the three RDA executives named Thompson are related; nor are Barbara Morgan and Harry Morgan related.

Index